SIMON & SCHUSTER MEGA CROSSWORD PUZZLE BOOK

Series 1

300 never-before-published crosswords

Edited by John M. Samson

A Fireside Book
Published by Simon & Schuster
New York   London   Toronto   Sydney

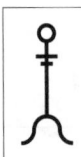

FIRESIDE
A Division of Simon & Schuster, Inc.
1230 Avenue of the Americas
New York, NY 10020

First Fireside trade paperback edition February 2008

FIRESIDE and colophon are registered trademarks of Simon & Schuster, Inc.

For information about special discounts for bulk purchases, please contact Simon & Schuster Special Sales at 1-800-456-6798 or business@simonandschuster.com.

Designed by Sam Bellotto Jr.

Manufactured in the United States of America

10 9 8 7 6 5 4

ISBN-13: 978-1-4165-5700-5
ISBN-10:   1-4165-5700-8

COMPLETE ANSWERS WILL BE FOUND AT THE BACK.

FOREWORD

In 1924 Simon & Schuster published its first title, *The Cross Word Puzzle Book*. Not only was it the then-new publisher's first release, it was the first collection of crossword puzzles ever printed.

The popularity of the *Cross Word Puzzle Book* quickly brought the start of the longest-running crossword series in publishing history. In 1989, solvers told us that there simply weren't enough puzzles! Obligingly, we increased the Series to six books annually and have done so since—until now.

In 2008, with *Simon & Schuster Mega Crossword Puzzle Book 1*, we are once again increasing our yearly output of original crosswords—from 300 puzzles annually to 900—a triple play of wordplay! Each *Simon & Schuster Super Mega Crossword Puzzle Book* will have 300 never-before-published crosswords . . . including 100 Sunday-size challengers constructed by leading cruciverbalists, enigmatists, and wordsmiths. Solvers can now look forward to a new Mega-sized Crossword Book every January, June, and October.

Within these pages expect to encounter Americana themes, educational themes, trivia themes, pop-culture themes, punny themes, race-against-the-clock themes, and even (excuse the oxymoron) unthemed themes. And of course expect lots of straightforward and directly misleading clues. Clues of all shapes, sizes, disposition, and humor . . . especially humor.

The Margaret Award winners are CENTERPIECE by Harvey Estes and MIXED BREEDS by Fred Piscop.

JOHN M. SAMSON

1 WORDS   by John M. Samson

"Words are alive. Cut them and they bleed." — Ralph Waldo Emerson

ACROSS

1 Yahoo
5 Light lunch
10 Takanohana's sport
14 Italian princely family
15 Brazil seaport
16 Unit of matter
17 Incision
18 Betelgeuse locale
19 Pelée effluent
20 **"Words are what hold ___": Stuart Chase**
23 Farm addr.
24 "A Man and a Woman" composer
25 Tejano singing star
28 Where 49ers hit paydirt
33 Fugard's "A Lesson from ___ "
34 Author Deighton
35 "___ e Leandro": Mancinelli opera
36 **"Words are ___ on.": Henry Ward Beecher**
41 "___, Mine": G. Harrison book
42 "Star Trek" escape craft
43 Violin-family members
44 Separate
47 Mug
48 Thun's river
49 Sony rival
50 **"Words are the only things ___": William Hazlitt**
59 Saint Peter's Church locale
60 Sri Lankan language
61 Japanese shrine center
62 Bates in "Duet for One"
63 "Kazaam" star
64 Excursion
65 Wilson of "La Femme Nikita"
66 Lets off steam
67 Splinter group

DOWN

1 Catfish Row resident
2 Scandinavian capital
3 Auditory
4 AARP members
5 Nova ___
6 Condor nest
7 Milk from la vache
8 King of early comics
9 Like some earrings
10 Unratified treaty of 1979
11 Sevier Lake locale
12 Dislocate
13 Sharif in "Hidalgo"
21 John ___ Steinbeck
22 Cockney's noggin
25 Flavorful
26 Perfume resin
27 Best Met seats
28 Woodland clearing
29 Kricfalusi's dog
30 Lurches
31 Benedict XVI's cape
32 "Definitely not!"
37 Jim Croce hit
38 Torrid
39 More frigid
40 Climb-downs
45 Chain
46 End of an Irish lullaby
47 Hillocks
50 Augusta hazard
51 Green cavity
52 Amo, amas, ___
53 Capital of Yemen
54 ATF employees
55 Italian car
56 Golf trophy
57 Rev. Camden of "7th Heaven"
58 Engrossed

2 TERMITES   by Linda Finnerty
White ants (termites) are not really ants; cockroaches are their relatives.

ACROSS

1 Banned orchard spray
5 Class distinction
10 "The Wizard of Oz" star
14 Granary
15 Essential oil
16 Superior's inferior?
17 Truck adjunct
18 "Rachel, Rachel" star
20 Slumgullion
21 Harvest goddess
22 March of ___
23 Flu-ridden
25 Land down under?
28 Made a comeback
32 Blackout
33 Early hrs.
36 Go up
37 "Measure of ___": Aiken
39 Mild cheese
40 Art ___
41 Flair
42 Proboscis
43 Living legend
44 Curtain color
45 Enter Eton
46 Giant of a Giant
47 "Cool!"
48 Wise
50 Rare bear
52 Nervous spasm
53 Rely on
56 Self-image
58 Had the answer
62 "Welcome to Sarajevo" star
65 Life of Riley
66 Undercover agent
67 Sierra ___
68 Low-fat
69 Site of Vulcan's forge
70 Vespa
71 High-five

DOWN

1 Uraeus figures
2 Merry melody
3 Hyacinth cousin
4 1919 Peace Nobelist
5 Coax
6 Surmounting
7 Hoard
8 Tawny
9 Eet's Kellogg's pal
10 Al of Grandpa Munster fame
11 "My Name Is ___": Saroyan
12 Retain
13 Cranberry and cherry
19 Paradise
24 Fabrication
26 Early calculator
27 Clammy
28 Philco 90 "cathedral"
29 At attention
30 Lacy loop
31 Emulated Mumble
33 Dote on
34 "Max Dugan Returns" star
35 Silvery fish
38 Scratch up
39 These coins don't jingle
41 Sharp
45 Center front
47 Teri in "Oh, God!"
49 Reconciled
50 Anorak
51 "The Hen and the Fox" fabulist
53 December 31st word
54 "Come again?"
55 Rate
57 "Long Time ___": Dixie Chicks
59 Pinkie part
60 "¿Como ___ usted?"
61 Blubber
63 Majestic tree
64 The lion in summer

3 GILT-RIDDEN by Don Law
The color of 52 Across is international orange.

ACROSS

1 Bloke
5 Salt-I concern
10 Composer Stravinsky
14 Pasternak heroine
15 Synagogue scroll
16 They lead to mi
17 Wang Lung's wife
18 "To ___ own self . . .": Shak.
19 "Judge Dredd" villainess
20 Fairy-tale housebreaker
22 Dump problem
23 Vaulted arch
24 Sarcophagus
26 "Uncle Tom's Cabin" villain
29 Be a bookworm
31 Loser to JFK
34 Wolfpack member
35 "For ___": Beatles
36 Three, at times
37 Cartoonist's transparency
38 Theater-in-the-___
39 "Crossfire" network
40 Suffix for drunk
41 "On Beyond Zebra" author
42 Alan in "Little Miss Sunshine"
44 ___ Jeanne d'Arc
45 Archer in "Fatal Attraction"
46 Swank
47 Cambridgeshire river
49 Joie de vivre
50 Prefix for normal
52 Bridge in "A View to a Kill"
58 Blame
59 Emerged
60 "Holy moly!"
61 "Ask Me" singer
62 Fyn Islanders
63 Viking letter
64 Scott Turow book
65 Former Penn State coach
66 Hayes of "Will & Grace"

DOWN

1 Congest
2 Lunar ring
3 Kazakhstan sea
4 Eve, in Greek mythology
5 Churchill's successor
6 Long row ___
7 Roberts in "Heaven's Prisoners"
8 Plummeted
9 Stephen King novel
10 "Hands down" is one
11 Fort Knox slackers?
12 Bologna bear
13 Admiral type
21 "___ no respect!": Dangerfield
25 Rhapsodic poem
26 "Star Wars" director
27 Film reviewer Roger
28 "24-karat is the best," e.g.?
29 Motivate
30 Big times
32 Skimpy skirts
33 Jackass
35 Gerund
38 Turncoat
41 ___ Marino
42 Composer Hovhaness
43 New York or Texas team
46 "Fawlty Towers" star
48 Atelier sight
49 Henry Ford's son
50 Somewhat, in music
51 By and by
53 "The Plague" setting
54 Like Rapunzel's hair
55 Malaria symptom
56 Blue Nile source
57 Land west of Nod

4 BORN ON THE FOURTH OF JULY   by Tim Wagner
According to the Four Cohans, George M. was also born on the Fourth of July.

ACROSS

1 Ashen
5 Tippler
10 Coffeehouse
14 Warts and all
15 ___ barrel
16 Flirt unsubtly
17 El Paso college
18 Card of fortune
19 Anthracite
20 Jazz legend born on July 4th
23 Smarmy
24 Concert ending
25 Noble partner
28 Fireplace filler
30 Chicago hrs.
33 Phillips of "Star Trek: Voyager"
34 Evening in Bologna
35 Osso ___ (veal dish)
36 Advice columnist born on July 4th
39 Diane in "Hollywoodland"
40 Jousting wear
41 Ding-___
42 Summer in Provençe
43 Lingers
44 Small bays
45 Cadge
46 Rival of Seles
47 President born on July 4th
54 Krung Thep citizen
55 Strikeout ace Ryan
56 Spur
57 Two in a row?
58 Take the honey and run
59 South Pacific dance
60 Small bills
61 Postal machine
62 Disney World transport

DOWN

1 Painter Gauguin
2 Regarding
3 Stead
4 007's field
5 Sums
6 Pistil part
7 Salon wave
8 Piccadilly Circus statue
9 "Separate Tables" playwright
10 Après-ski beverage
11 Balanchine ballet
12 Standard
13 Conger
21 College near Albany
22 Shot givers
25 Handy's "___ Street Blues"
26 Facing the mound
27 Cologne river
28 Jeans
29 Viva voce
30 Chemistry Nobelist: 1911
31 Chanel No. 5, e.g.
32 Cookout tool
34 Metal waste
35 Fiesta brava
37 Pictured
38 Trite
43 Ivanov of ballet
44 Pressman?
45 Happiness
46 Freak out
47 "Rumble in the Bronx" star
48 Swiss river
49 Cap'n Andy's daughter
50 Coagulate
51 Somber
52 Red-orange apple
53 Smorgasbord cheese
54 As well

5 DEAR JOHN by John M. Samson
This theme is not about letters—although 50 Across certainly was.

ACROSS

1 Lat. gender
5 Orally
10 All-purpose trucks
14 Olive in a Caesar salad?
15 Finnish ski-jumper Nykäanen
16 What a transept crosses
17 Ollie's partner
18 Machu Picchu residents
19 Electric sword
20 John with a distinctive signature
22 John with a school namesake
24 Bastille Day season
25 Future fish
26 Put an end to
30 Hiking snack
34 Cats
35 In advance
37 Groan getter
38 Sleeping
39 "___ and Ivory" (1982 song)
40 Jargon
41 Cameroon language
42 American dogwood
43 Goodly
44 Field of dreams?
46 Put up a tower
48 Lucky Charms grain
49 Bolt a torpedo
50 John who won a Pulitzer Prize for Fiction
54 John with a society namesake
58 Not his
59 Checks
61 Marquis in "Quills"
62 Coward's confession
63 Asinine
64 Blind god
65 Disbursement
66 Funnel-shaped
67 Snail-mail salutation

DOWN

1 Concert pit
2 Lady Bird Johnson's middle name
3 Connery in "Thunderball"
4 Stamped stamps
5 Liturgical vestments
6 Long and lean
7 Bulletin Board letters
8 Zion National Park state
9 Confusion
10 Not on the level
11 Sarong cloth
12 Anon companion
13 Coconut, e.g.
21 Mayberry drunk
23 MapQuest line
26 John who was President
27 Bill Clinton's nickname
28 "___ Indolence": Keats
29 Convent wear
30 31 Down, e.g.
31 MoMA exhibit
32 Pounce
33 Fed the kitty
36 Tiller's tool
39 Abstruse
40 Leafless plants
42 Norwegian saint
43 Coveted role
45 "It ___ get any better than this!"
47 Like some glass bottles
50 Smart
51 2004 Jet Li film
52 Mauve Decade et al.
53 Washoe County seat
54 Youngest Brontë sister
55 Adriatic resort
56 Garlic quality
57 Agent Youngfellow's boss
60 Bannen in "Waking Ned Divine"

6

1-2-3 by Jean Peterson
43 Down is best known for "The Scream."

ACROSS

1 La Salle and Stutz
5 On behalf of
8 Feline musical
12 U.S. Open winner Dutra
13 Biblical mount
15 "East of Eden" character
16 Art ___
17 Yoga squat
18 Stationer's shade
19 ONE
22 Door glass
23 MTA stop
24 Least plentiful
27 Lead a ___ life
31 "Movie Home Companion" author
32 "___, a female deer . . ."
34 Henley essential
35 TWO
39 Wizened
40 Cato's year
41 Inkling
42 Merit
45 House, for one
46 "Zip-a-___-Doo-Dah"
47 Moroccan garment
48 THREE
56 Tibetan monk
57 Stephen King-ish
58 Wings
59 Seaweed extract
60 Honeybunch
61 Holler
62 Schmo
63 "Brat Farrar" author
64 Düsseldorf duck

6 Evangelist Roberts
7 Santoni in "Dirty Harry"
8 Kind of salad
9 Sacramento arena
10 Rent
11 Comfy
13 Spook
14 Wailing spirit
20 Bob Marley was one
21 Greek vowel
24 Replace a lawn
25 White poplar
26 Clarinet and oboe
27 James in "Wholly Moses"
28 Like a good cake
29 "___ Win": Haas
30 Clothesline alternative
32 One of the Brontës
33 Cozy room
36 Vacillated
37 Zeno follower
38 Hopping competition
43 Painter Munch
44 Singer Des'___
45 Thompson of track
47 Fleecy
48 Schedule
49 Wrath
50 Netman Camporese
51 Red veggie
52 Dies ___ (Latin hymn)
53 "The Good Earth" heroine
54 Poet Whitman
55 Take-out order

DOWN

1 Musical postscript
2 Baldwin in "The Departed"
3 Not low-cal
4 Prowlers
5 "All That Jazz" director

WOODSTOCK '69*   by John M. Samson

The original festival was not held in Woodstock, but in Wallkill—40 miles away.

ACROSS

1 Theme
6 Sixth President
11 Elly May Clampett's dad
14 Rodeo rope
15 Homophone of carrot
16 Geneva-based UN org.
17 He sang "Amazing Grace"*
19 60 sec.
20 Notable times
21 Prohibitionist Carry
23 Big leagues
27 Conductor Zubin
28 Norwegian monarch
29 Expand upon
32 Regale
33 Crazy bone
34 Golden Globe, e.g.
36 Flanders of "The Simpsons"
39 Earth
40 Advice columnist Trump
41 "Spamalot" creator Eric
42 Aliens
43 Bergen dummy
44 Hershiser of baseball
45 Baez who sang "We Shall Overcome"*
47 Canard
49 Smoke glass
50 Assassin of 1865
52 Muscular disorder
54 Allure
56 Where it's at
58 Cartoon frame
59 He performed "Raga Manj Kmahaj"*
65 Word form of "mouth"
66 Battery terminal
67 Knock off
68 Bert Bobbsey's twin
69 More modern
70 Loathes

DOWN

1 Refrain syllable
2 Anthem contraction
3 Chum
4 Skater Midori
5 Piston or Pacer
6 Court records
7 Dit partners
8 Abbr. at Heathrow
9 Chicken chow ___
10 Irate
11 He sang "Purple Haze"*
12 "Silas Marner" author
13 Ritchie Valens hit
18 "Superman II" villainess
22 Hanoi holiday
23 Shiner
24 Apportion
25 She sang "Piece of My Heart"*
26 Ellipsoidal
30 Pianist Brubeck
31 Sleepy or Sneezy
32 Painter Angelico
35 "Me, Myself ___": Vitamin C
37 Kate Nelligan film
38 "Brave New World" caste
40 Motorist's stopover
41 Whit
43 Desiccated
46 Suffix for Capri
48 Avon spa
50 IHOP side
51 Met life?
53 Tutor
55 "Penny ___": Beatles
56 45's A or B
57 Czech river
60 Pledge
61 3-R's org.
62 "Night Secrets" author Martin
63 Enzyme suffix
64 Legal thing

WOODSTOCK '94* by John M. Samson
Woodstock '94 took place in Saugerties, New York, about 10 miles from Woodstock.

ACROSS

1 Tenterhook
5 Aristocratic
10 Laugh-track cue
14 Blanchett in "The Aviator"
15 Center Shaquille
16 Site of a 1943 Russian victory
17 Composer Khachaturian
18 Oscar de la ___
19 Acts human
20 They sang "Dream On"*
22 Type of tactics
23 Long in "Big Momma's House"
24 Army address
25 Fruity quaff
28 Record blemish
31 False front
35 Uncle ___ Rice
37 John Phillips was one
39 Clove hitch
40 Alan in "The Aviator"
41 "Counter-Strike" player
42 "The Love Object" author O'Brien
43 RAF Harrier, e.g.
44 Olive genus
45 Gather in
46 Down-and-dirty
48 Gunfight command
51 ___ Anne de Bellevue
52 PBS funder
53 It often follows an ad
55 Hot compress
58 They sang "One"*
64 Skye writing
65 Tooth
66 Half court game?
67 Cry
68 Quidditch must
69 One in a full house
70 Snakebite cures
71 "Sealed With ___": Gary Lewis
72 Catwoman Selina

DOWN

1 T. Roosevelt Award org.
2 Lake of Thun river
3 ___-TASS news agency
4 Bright yellow
5 Well-adjusted
6 "Dedicated to the ___ Love": Shirelles
7 Rounded
8 Carpenter's strip
9 Guido's pinnacle
10 He sang "You Are So Beautiful"*
11 Bank of America founder Monnette
12 Deborah in "The Sun-downers"
13 Besides
21 Close relative
22 Balneotherapy spot
24 A way away
25 Lower in esteem
26 Atlanta-based airline
27 Home of the Ewoks
29 October birthstone
30 Emulated Clyde Beatty
32 El Misti locale
33 "Goodbye, Mr. Chips" star
34 Warehouse
36 They sang "Shoop"*
38 Anjou
41 Spanish painter
47 Giggle half
49 Bells and whistles
50 Wheaton in "Stand By Me"
54 Jack in "King King"
55 Bar-tacks
56 Charlie Brown's kite catcher
57 Chat-room visitor, e.g.
58 Robin Williams role
59 "The Time Machine" race
60 Santa Fe Trail stop
61 "Now ___ me down . . ."
62 Showalter in "Fargo"
63 General's gofer
65 Wharton degree

9 WOODSTOCK 1999*   by John M. Samson
This 1999 concert was held in Rome, New York, about 156 miles from Woodstock.

ACROSS
1 Jazz group
6 Lager ingredient
10 Exactly, time-wise
14 Sidestep
15 Stage actress Menken
16 "Miami Vice" cop
17 "Natural High" singer Haggard
18 It's "given" at birth
19 Savvy about
20 Canal to Oneida Lake
21 They sang "Show Me What You Got"*
23 "Fear and Loathing in ___ Vegas" (1998)
24 Socials
25 Honshu shrine center
26 Oceans
28 Virgin Airlines founder
32 They sang "Torn" and 5 Down*
34 Intoxicating
36 Skedaddle
37 Table d'___
38 Does a laundry job
39 "Monopoly" expense
40 Fork lift?
41 Puget Sound, for one
42 Job extras
43 Emancipation
45 Ragtime pianist Big ___ Little
46 Siamese sound
47 Spiral
49 Ton's 2000
52 He sang "Cold Sweat"*
56 Fitzgerald's forte
57 ___ Bator
58 Swiss river
59 Sacher cake
60 Bring in a tarpon
61 Redgrave in "Shine"
62 "___ Oe" ("Blue Hawaii" song)
63 Longings
64 Meadows
65 She sang "Down So Long"*

DOWN
1 Ship of the desert
2 "You've got me ___ barrel"
3 Alanis who sang "So Pure"*
4 Spleen
5 See 32 Across
6 Suffix for Beatle
7 "Watership Down" novelist
8 Light object?
9 Hitchcock's "Psycho" successor
10 Chilled to the bone
11 Rocky's pet turtle
12 When Romeo meets Juliet
13 Beep
21 Muppet Zealand
22 "Really, old chap?"
24 Golfer Purdy
27 The Phantom's creator Falk
28 Square sheet of cotton
29 She sang "If It Makes You Happy"*
30 Babe's comment
31 They hang from rims
32 Animated Isaac Hayes role
33 Laugh boisterously
34 Ian of Bilbo Baggins fame
35 Homophone for heir
38 The Simpsons' cat
39 "What ees it, man?" source
41 Roman calendar day
42 Lulu
44 Writes a final draft
45 High fashion
47 Rene's "Lethal Weapon 4" role
48 Buck of "Hee Haw"
50 Lave
51 Baseball stat
52 Onyx month
53 Wings
54 "The Magic Mountain" novelist
55 "Little Rock" singer Collin
56 "O ___ Mio"
59 Mahal in "Sounder"

"NUTS!"   by Norman S. Wizer
A special thank-you to Gen. Anthony McAuliffe and Mr. Peanut.

ACROSS

1 Above it all
5 Nylon netting
10 Show of hands
14 Mezzanine area
15 South African corral
16 Styptic pencil
17 NUT
20 Terrific bargain
21 Emit
22 Edwin Drood's fiancée
25 Come into view
26 NUT
33 Speed (up)
34 "___ the torpedoes!": Farragut
35 Haarlem bloom
36 Phone abbr.
38 Part of MGM
41 "Brave New World" sedative
42 Peppershrike
44 "Nuts" director
46 Avant-garde
47 NUT
51 J. Maguire et al.
52 Caffeine nut
53 Two-handled jar
56 Word from the waitress
60 NUT
63 "Temple of Dullness" composer
64 Heavenly whale
65 Spillane's "___ Jury"
66 Horse of a certain color
67 Snail trail
68 Honeybunch

DOWN

1 Wear for the Masses
2 Bender
3 Girl-watch
4 Loud firecracker
5 Win for Rocky Balboa
6 Simba's grandmother
7 "M" director
8 Barrio resident
9 Hendecagon number
10 Mistlike
11 King Harald's dad
12 Sward
13 CPR expert
18 Sun screen
19 Be moved
23 Con
24 "When My Baby Smiles ___"
26 Validate
27 "The Volga Boatmen" painter
28 Explicit
29 Prefix for mural
30 Replay mode
31 Simba's friend
32 Garden tool
37 Occur again
39 Hazard
40 One of the Ringling Bros.
43 Zero
45 Like some bathrooms
48 Zeno's followers
49 Its flag shows a Magen David
50 Not rehearsed
53 Field: Comb. form
54 Sassy bird
55 Opposed
57 Balanchine jump
58 Job safety org.
59 River near Nieuwpoort
60 Otoscope view
61 Goo on a shoe
62 Sugar suffix

11 1947 by Karen Motyka
"Who Framed Roger Rabbit" was set in the year 1947.

ACROSS

1 Proboscis
5 Albert in "The Unforgiven"
10 Karma
14 Make eyes at
15 "Get ___ of this!"
16 Pedestal occupant
17 Kind of history
18 She turned men into swine
19 Mysterious loch
20 1947 World Series champs
23 Scrabble 3-pointer
24 Lex Luthor's friend
25 Dirty
29 Unbroken
33 Thespian
34 Browse the Web
37 Papuan port
38 1947 George Gershwin song
42 Militarize
43 Drying oven
44 Uranus moon
45 Wise Greek
48 Capitivity
49 Has
51 Poivre partner
52 1947 film comedy
59 "What's My Line?" panelist
60 Chameleon
61 Fountain treat
62 Maple seeds
63 By and by
64 Trevelyan in "GoldenEye"
65 Commanded
66 Talks like Sylvester
67 Painter Magritte

DOWN

1 Twelve sharp
2 Mother Goose villain
3 Shredded dish
4 Congerlike
5 Sacrosanct
6 Two peas in a pod
7 Colorful parrot
8 Mitchum-Russell film
9 Empathize
10 "This was their ___ hour": Churchill
11 "Zip-___-Doo-Dah"
12 Mix lightly
13 South African golfer
21 "Fidelio" is one
22 Relative
25 The Archfiend
26 Tawny pigment
27 "National Enquirer" couples
28 Sampras shot
30 Reynolds of baseball
31 Jim Palmer's nickname
32 Dabbling ducks
34 Reggae forerunner
35 "Network" network
36 Fink
39 City SE of Ottawa
40 Comedienne Poundstone
41 Bruin great
46 Chewy confection
47 Take out a mortgage
48 Postpones
50 Six-Day War arena
51 Carry
52 Rochon in "Waiting to Exhale"
53 Grandson of Cain
54 Daycare charges
55 Autocrat
56 Cavity
57 Tree of Knowledge locale
58 Futurity
59 Taxi

12 STRIPES by Linda Finnerty

Another clue for 25 Across could be "Legendary Nintendo princess."

ACROSS

1 Fit for duty
5 "Wild Hogs" director Becker
9 Magna ___
14 Provender
15 Elbe tributary
16 Tatum in "Little Darlings"
17 Kirghizian range
18 Obie winner
19 Marsh of whodunits
20 Striped officials
22 Reluctant
23 Celebratory verse
24 Nutmeg skin
25 Striped herbivore
29 Sudden terror
31 Medicare org.
34 Blue-pencils
36 1912 Peace Nobelist
37 Flesh and blood
38 Falls behind
39 Salad days
41 4th-and-long call
42 Peter out
43 Adventure-filled tale
44 Mr. Jinks' color
46 Key below Z
47 Puccini songs
49 Signed a contract
50 Leg bender
51 Conductor Pekka Salonen
53 Bats an eye
56 Flagg's striped pointer
61 Peep show
62 Global area
63 Peace Nobelist Myrdal
64 Pontifical cape
65 Canasta term
66 Like VMI now
67 Postprandial candies
68 Juice bar drinks
69 "Catch!"

DOWN

1 Place of worship?
2 Oak trunk
3 Lallygag
4 Uma in "Be Cool"
5 Exhausted (with "out")
6 In the arms of Morpheus
7 Where grass roots
8 Give it a whirl
9 Striped yard bird
10 Della Reese TV role
11 "To the ___, march!"
12 Mai ___ (rum cocktails)
13 Sunblock additive
21 Fork locale
22 Operatic style
24 Soon
25 Mrs. F. Scott Fitzgerald
26 Latter-day letter
27 Engender
28 Clinic employees
30 Pepsi Center, e.g.
31 Striped animal
32 Brown
33 Started a kitty
35 Rubbernecks
40 HOMES subdivision
41 Chimp genus
43 Striped team
45 Iranian currency
48 Doddering
50 Prepared to say the rosary
52 A ton
53 Ichabod's rival
54 Country singer White
55 Persian Gulf land
56 Like hand-me-downs
57 A pop
58 Astringent fruit
59 Say for sure
60 Put together
62 "I ___ lineman for the county . . ."

13 WET SET   by Michele Sayer
The original name of 11 Down is Leslie Sebastian Charles.

ACROSS

1 Garland's 1939 costar
5 Chopin's paramour
9 QM2 room
14 Russian range
15 Athens locale
16 Like a cat burglar
17 Blucas in "The Alamo"
18 Smidgen
19 Model material
20 Dagwood Bumstead portrayer
23 Land map
24 Sitcom steed
25 The hunted
27 Wheedle
30 "Manon" highlight
32 Yoko at the 2006 Olympics
35 PING products
36 Hepburn's love
37 Use a mower
38 "On the ___": Kerouac
39 "Dead ___ Society" (1989)
40 Muralist José María
41 Doer's word
42 Seine tributary
43 "Harvey" playwright
44 Drop a pop-up
45 Celtic New-Age singer
46 It's yours for a while
47 Memo starter
49 "The King and I" star
50 Carry on
52 1973 NASCAR Rookie of the Year
58 Hill nymph
60 Saddle with
61 Nice notion
62 Like Windsor wives?
63 Take a bath
64 Austrian article
65 ___-partout
66 Word of assent
67 Tennis ranking

DOWN

1 Prayer wheel user
2 Like Hermes' sandals
3 "My Funny Valentine" lyricist
4 Old Dominion capital
5 Evening shindig
6 Get ___ of (contact)
7 Naldi of silent movies
8 Walker of football
9 "Hi-De-Ho Man" Calloway
10 Slack-jawed
11 "Loverboy" singer
12 Visitor to Rick's Place
13 Tidy
21 Google listings
22 Long movies
26 Stingaree
27 Medea's aunt
28 Like the pounding surf
29 "Can we talk?" comedienne
30 Detroit's Joe Louis ___
31 Give it three stars
33 "Scrubs" extra
34 Aquatic mammal
36 Conservative Brit
39 Twelve just men
40 Sanford markers
42 Debussy subject
43 Cortland center
46 Dutch city
48 Closes in
49 Rogue
50 Rollick
51 Side by side?
53 Raines in "The Suspect"
54 Linguist Chomsky
55 Jon Arbuckle's pet
56 Hawaiian honker
57 Act
59 Color eggs

14 KING AUTHOR by John M. Samson

There are three "dwarf" planets in our Solar System: Ceres, Eris, and 5 Down.

ACROSS

1 Kind of golf
5 Acme
9 Regales
14 St. Louis landmark
15 Taylor in "Rudy"
16 Prevent
17 Jordanian queen
18 Salt Lake City team
19 Bello in "Thank You For Smoking"
20 Naysayer
21 J Dilla album
23 Monopoly token
25 Capp and Capone
26 Valletta locale
29 Givey
32 Eccentric wheel
35 Circumvents
37 Drumstick
38 Emperor's Cup sport
39 Mountain pool
40 Radical
42 Elvis ___ Presley
43 Fork finger
44 Sugar snap
45 Give in
47 High note
48 Brings up
50 Shelf
51 Spoil
52 Quiet
54 Treat for Fido
59 Catfight
63 Advisory
64 Sign a lease
65 Walesa of Warsaw
66 Significance
67 Arab potentate
68 Kauai's neighbor
69 Phosphate, e.g.
70 "The ___-Motion": Little Eva
71 Uno plus dos

DOWN

1 Scully of "The X-Files"
2 Mangle
3 Ayr resident
4 Fury that went into a fury
5 Dwarf planet
6 Any one of two
7 Not windward
8 Letter sealer
9 "We Are ___": Sister Sledge
10 "Dewey" who played in Fenway
11 Hatcher of "Desperate Housewives"
12 Activist Brockovich
13 Prenuptial party
22 Airbus home
24 Taken
26 Film finish
27 Be of value to
28 Blackmore heroine
30 Mensa locale
31 Suffix for cloth
32 Healed
33 With many
34 Three-card game
36 Five-star
38 "To be known as the 'Witch City' will forever be ___"
41 Sward
46 Pipe bend
48 Agassi rival
49 Picturesque
51 David in "Hearts in Atlantis"
53 Chevy van
54 Underpinning
55 Tavern tipples
56 Chap
57 Pitcher Hershiser
58 "Bleak House" character
60 A fruitwood
61 Advil target
62 And so

15 KNIGHTS OF THE ROUND TABLE* by John M. Samson

Answers to clues* were all members of the one and only Algonquin Round Table.

ACROSS

1 "Paradise Lost" figure
5 Magic Johnson, once
10 Scooted
14 "The Living Daylights" actress
15 Chip away at
16 Baltic port
17 Huff
18 Surrounded by
19 Cumming in "Spy Kids"
20 Hart's "Once in a Lifetime" collaborator*
23 Unconscious
24 Jeans label
25 Incline
28 Most marvelous
33 Have a hunch
34 Spick-and-span
35 D-Day transport
36 "Idiot's Delight" playwright*
40 Bungle
41 Becomes compost
42 Bicker
43 "Rocky Balboa" star
46 Jon in "Hot Shots!"
47 Still
48 Ursula Andress film
49 "Brevity is the soul of lingerie" source*
56 Gilpin of "Frasier"
57 LCM chair designer
58 Comply
60 Scented powder
61 Prepares potatoes
62 Beehive State city
63 Juice drinks
64 "Tribute" playwright
65 "Shark Tale" dragon fish

DOWN

1 15-second spots
2 "Drat!"
3 Anne Nichols hero
4 John P. Marquand sleuth
5 Federation
6 Camelot helmet
7 Crackpot
8 Author Ferber
9 Govern
10 "Who ___ Roger Rabbit" (1988)
11 McCann of country music
12 "Boxiana" author
13 Pale
21 Pollster Elmo
22 Marsh
25 Good loser
26 Gwyneth Paltrow's sign
27 Ketel ___ vodka
28 Legionnaire Beau
29 Bowl shouts
30 Funeral oration
31 Scrub
32 Destroyer of sandcastles
33 Azurite and tinstone
34 EATS sign
37 Hambletonian hopefuls
38 Less available
39 Bent
44 Mercer's words
45 Bloom in "The Producers"
46 Square-dance step
48 Velocity
49 Lifeless
50 Heraldic border
51 Exodus plague
52 Village People hit
53 ___ & the Gang
54 Spanish river
55 Highlands dance
56 School gp.
59 Soprano Sumac

16 "BAH, HUMBUG!" by Tim Wagner

"Fum, Fum, Fum!" would be another example of 45 Across.

ACROSS

1 Sugar amts.
5 Watson in "The Boxer"
10 Detroit arena
14 ___-kiri
15 Gymnast with a theme
16 Part of U.S.M.A.
17 Welsh John
18 Canadian ice star
19 Award for "Art"
20 Bridge maker
22 Releases
24 Dana in "The Sting"
25 Crazy bones
26 1962 Mr. Magoo role
32 Arm of the Amazon
33 Singer Adams
34 Battleship colour
35 V-shaped fortification
36 Cancún coin
40 Concerned comment
41 1980 Super Bowl team
45 What "Patapan" is
48 Book keeper
49 Alkaline compound
50 Lining fabric
53 Crested
55 "___ pinch of salt"
56 Pergola
58 Go off the deep end
59 Participating
60 Thelma in "Thelma & Louise"
61 Feminine ending
62 Fires
63 Like scones
64 Moselle feeder

DOWN

1 Peter Benchley novel
2 End of a palindrome
3 Santa's sledder
4 1966 Wimbledon winner
5 Seth begat him at 105
6 K ___
7 Couch topics
8 Stead
9 Salt's spinining
10 L.L. Bean mailing
11 She plays Gabrielle
12 Ace, for one
13 Best-selling magazine
21 Limerick loc.
23 Judah Ben-___
27 Japanese sandals
28 Super Tuesday word
29 Build a better barrier
30 ___ Zagora, Bulgaria
31 Stocking stuffers
36 New Jersey city
37 Spiny anteater
38 "Stars Shine Down" author
39 Joan of Arc liberated it
41 Plagued pharoah
42 Journalist Huffington
43 1990 Super Bowl MVP
44 Eurostar car
46 Possibilities
47 Long Beach loc.
51 "Otello" baritone
52 Side by side?
53 Indian bread
54 Qum locale
57 Plunk down

17 PARK PLACE by Jean Peterson

The park at 21-A covers 4,210 acres; the park at 4-D only an acre and a half!

ACROSS

1 Dietary supplement
5 Tanks
9 "M*A*S*H" character
14 Gad
15 Lake Michigan neighbor
16 Peace goddess
17 Over again
18 "New Jack Hustler" rapper
19 Concert piano
20 Not even one
21 Griffith Park locale
23 "___ on a Grecian Urn"
25 Explorer Johnson
26 Hallowed
29 Cow bell?
31 Ribbed fabric
35 Like a sieve
36 Gentlemen:
37 Novelist Bellow
38 Vase
39 Catbird's color
40 Brownies' org.
41 In original condition
43 Chewable antacid
44 Brilliance
46 Fleshy fruit
47 U2 record label
48 Goddess with an owl
49 Suffix for expert
51 Small whale
52 Forest Park locale
58 Pen
62 Educe
63 Shower-gel additive
64 Seaweed
65 It runs in a taxi
66 Chattanooga loc.
67 Effrontery
68 Mad as a hornet
69 Miami team
70 Singles

DOWN

1 Where Farsi is spoken
2 "Five Women" author Jaffe
3 "Your turn," radioed
4 Gramercy Park locale
5 Shrouded
6 Sacramento arena
7 Father's Day gifts
8 Bristle
9 1973 "Battle of the Sexes" loser
10 Overdue payment
11 "Let's Make a ___"
12 Poet Bradstreet
13 1981 Beatty/Keaton film
22 Grafton's "N Is for ___"
24 10th Iranian month
26 Period of decline
27 Alpine abode
28 Tropical flower
29 Tropical Park locale
30 Kitchen scraps
32 Colonel's insignia
33 South Korean port
34 Buenos Aires river
36 Where the living ain't easy
39 Danielle of romance
42 Bauble
44 Hot time in Provence
45 Lincoln Park locale
48 Green light
50 Cordwood measure
52 Turnpike traveler
53 State decisively
54 Minute amount
55 Curse
56 1997 Peter Fonda role
57 Scots island
59 Wang Lung's wife
60 Give the glad eye
61 Sidekicks

18 NASHVILLE CATS   by Don Law
11 Down was only 13 years old when "Blue" became platinum.

ACROSS

1 Horse relative
6 Peter I, for one
10 Utah ski spot
14 Tickle
15 Fortunate one
16 Repast
17 Ella Phant's friend Soupy
18 Ghostbuster Spenler
19 Cotton unit
20 "Cowboy in Me" singer
22 Stockade ___
23 City on the Danube
24 Ripped
25 Ukase
29 Come up short
31 Ewe's mate
34 Rub the wrong way
35 Nurtured
37 Ugandan exile
38 Western farewell
40 Squiffed
41 Cowell of "American Idol"
43 Sign on a door
44 Slow, to Mehta
47 Simply
48 Know-how
49 Bell sound
50 Prejudiced
52 Cobbler's product
54 Fiver
55 Dazzling effect
57 "Free" singer
63 Fortress ditch
64 City of the Seven Hills
65 Ambiances
66 Elephant's fear
67 Birthplace of Bahaism
68 Andean ruminant
69 Refuges
70 Remain unsettled
71 Abated

DOWN

1 Trial balloon
2 Kirghiz range
3 Beach in SE Florida
4 "Star" couple
5 Salvage
6 Unit of heat
7 Heroic account
8 Concede
9 Stimpy's sidekick
10 Fossilized sap
11 "Blue" singer
12 Locker-room powder
13 Helm position
21 "Galveston" singer Campbell
22 Pleats
24 Office neckwear
25 Noh, for one
26 Large duck
27 "Killin' Time" singer
28 1904 car
29 Wife of Odin
30 Sparkling wine
32 Be smitten with
33 Booby-trapped
36 Prussian cavalryman
39 Wooden shoe
42 1996 BT album
45 Pinpoint
46 Last write-up
51 Respire
53 Partner of Hall
54 Addict
55 Spice Girls member
56 Coconut fiber
57 Warning at Doral
58 "___ for All Seasons" (1966)
59 South Pacific dance
60 Cleopatra's maid
61 Fabric for a Dior gown
62 Start off
64 Home-run swing

ACROSS

1 SEC team, for short
5 Mexican agave
10 Flower holder
14 ___ Bator, Mongolia
15 Super stars
16 Young Saarinen
17 "Hopalong Cassidy" star
18 Trap
19 Two-winged fly
20 **With HOTEL: $2000 property**
22 Pick up on
23 In a snit
24 Lake of Brienz river
25 Less than -est
26 **St. Charles Place neighbor**
28 Baylor rival
31 Detain
34 Lady Penelope Devereux
36 Lusitania's call
37 "___ go down . . .": Masefield
39 Minor-league org.
40 Monopoly cards
42 Quakers founder
43 Did penance
46 Soothsayer
47 Promissory note
48 The Highwayman's love
49 Parabola
51 Pique
53 The Almighty
57 Mansfield in "Too Hot to Handle"
59 **With HOTEL: $1500 property**
61 Rhine duck
62 Free-for-all
63 Bedouin
64 Go off the deep end
65 Prettify
66 Enameled metalware
67 Printed matter
68 Pomegranate features
69 Inclusive abbr.

DOWN

1 Forrest Gump's friend
2 Crazy as ___
3 Guatemalan native
4 They're almost human
5 Responses
6 One-celled entity
7 Track lap
8 Merry prank
9 Shoe width
10 "Against the Wind" singer
11 **With HOTEL: $950 property**
12 Historic periods
13 Jot
21 Congo red, e.g.
22 Nonalcoholic bar
24 Feel strange
26 Rock concert attire
27 Winglike petals
29 Depeche ___
30 Country in a Beatles song
31 Stereo
32 "Typee" sequel
33 **Neighbor of 20-A & 59-A**
35 Anderson's "Night Over ___"
38 Put aside a motion
41 Increase
44 Titleist holder
45 Shades in
50 D.C. VIP
52 Bungling
53 Belief
54 The Hanged Man, e.g.
55 Elizabeth Ashley's birthplace
56 "He's a ___" (1962 hit)
57 Josh
58 Bancroft heard in "Antz"
59 Dumas ___
60 Helm position
62 AWOL apprehenders

20 ITALIAN MASTERS by Norman S. Wizer
Juan Gris, Jean Cocteau, and Pablo Picasso all sat for portraits by 28 Down.

ACROSS

1 PC character set
6 Gift from the barber
10 Religious painting
14 Mont of the Savoy Alps
15 Tale spinner
16 California wine valley
17 "Coronation of the Virgin" painter
19 Allen of radio days
20 "You got it!"
21 Gumby's material
22 Tea company founded in 1892
24 Sparkle
25 High-ranking state off.
26 "My Name Is Earl" county
29 First State
32 Gladstone's alma mater
33 Noted cosmetician
34 Teutonic lang.
35 Jerks make them
37 Sawmill product
38 Fury
40 Darth Vader, as a boy
41 Signore, e.g.
43 Compiégne river
44 Local
46 Sent packing
48 Ominous look
49 Short-order man
50 Frying pan
52 "___ of Eden" (1955)
53 Viper
56 Kirghizian range
57 "St. George and the Dragon" painter
60 "SNL" alumna Nora
61 Marooned
62 Like a scone
63 Friend of François
64 River near Dunkirk
65 Cherry, e.g.

DOWN

1 Mrs. Bradford of "Eight Is Enough"
2 Gin berry
3 They pussyfoot around
4 QB misfire: Abbr.
5 Winter stalactite
6 Do a spring thing
7 Slick
8 Jazz pianist Waldron
9 Stiff hair
10 Receipts
11 "Fortune Teller" painter
12 Gazette page
13 Nothing
18 Hatfields, for one
23 Guam capital
24 Red Skelton's first wife
25 Place for a flower box
26 Composer Franck
27 Wear a hair shirt
28 "Girl in Pink Blouse" painter
29 Humorous
30 Shortstop under Durocher
31 Messed up
33 Where two become one
36 Vermont ski resort
39 Cozy corner
42 In a torpid manner
45 Jimmy Hatlo's little girl
46 Not too bad
47 Souped-up wheels
49 Humor
50 Thompson in "The Entertainer"
51 "Clue" professor
52 Feminine suffix
53 W Aleutian island
54 Stride
55 Johnnycake
58 Hawaiian hawks
59 Otoscope view

ACROSS

1 Menu fish
5 Lots and lots
10 Kind of bake
14 White of Nashville
15 Insertion mark
16 Midway attraction
17 Waxed cheese
18 Delta Center, e.g.
19 Salenko of soccer
20 "My Left Foot" Oscar winner
23 Aberdeen denial
24 K–O links
25 Escalator alternative
28 Minstrel
30 Award for an RAF ace
33 Where to head 'em off
34 Intended
35 Kanga's kid
36 "The Goodbye Girl" Oscar winner
40 Guido's high note
41 Nautical imperative
42 Advance
43 Kreskin's forte
44 Hebrew letter
45 Star wear
47 Nine-digit ref.
48 Outwrestle
49 "The Silence of the Lambs" Oscar winner
57 Twosome
58 Reduce
59 Moose order: Abbr.
60 Killer whale
61 Ticket, on the streets
62 Anent
63 Profound
64 Centers the pigskin
65 Handle

DOWN

1 Coaster
2 "If I Only ___ Brain"
3 Irish wool sweater
4 Lessen
5 The Balance
6 Christmas ___
7 A code we live by
8 Turn down
9 "Cliff-hanger" star
10 Apex
11 Taylor of "Six Feet Under"
12 Citrus coolers
13 Ryan in "Courage Under Fire"
21 Pitcher part
22 Exhausted
25 Wild time
26 Tux
27 Tin Pan Alley org.
28 Car or chair
29 Elwes in "Liar Liar"
30 Pagan priest
31 "Cabaret" director
32 Michelangelo masterpiece
34 III x DXVII
37 Embarrass
38 "The Cannonball Run" star
39 "Peanuts" character
45 Trivia category
46 Hop partner
47 Subway support
49 Bern river
50 Riviera resort
51 "-ness" word
52 Blue Triangle grp.
53 Mound
54 Mother Goose editor Opie
55 Average
56 Neverland pirate
57 Group of whales

22 **BEST ACTRESS** by Jean Peterson
"Be yourself. The world worships the original." — 20 Across

ACROSS

1 Zinger
5 Garner
10 Scrabble piece
14 Insect wings
15 Prophetic card
16 Ruffle
17 Rapunzel's claim to fame
18 Miss USA crown
19 Article
20 "Anastasia" Oscar winner
23 Start of MGM's motto
24 Spock and Seuss: Abbr.
25 Cappuccino
29 Whodunit game
31 Omaha Beach craft
34 Stir up
35 Minimal
36 Ending for Brooklyn
37 "Butterfield 8" Oscar winner
41 Author
42 Objection
43 Gusto
44 Unit of work
45 River of Turkey
46 Teachings
48 "The Last ___ Left": MacDonald
49 Wide shoe width
50 "Dead Man Walking" Oscar winner
57 Ballerina Osipenko
58 Hibiscus, for one
59 Oscar winner Arkin
61 Overcharge
62 Emulate Romeo and Juliet
63 Paraguay tea
64 Shah Jahan's tomb site
65 Storms
66 Chilly powder

DOWN

1 Ebenezer's first word?
2 Kirghizian range
3 Somerset Maugham story
4 "Lulu" composer
5 Dandy's concern
6 Upstairs girls
7 Bahrain native
8 Miffed
9 Carmichael classic
10 Prunes
11 Scintilla
12 Mechanic's ___
13 Stately tree
21 "Norma ___" (1979)
22 Scacchi in "Shattered"
25 ___ suzette
26 Merchant ship
27 Spree
28 Moroccan city
29 Sky whale
30 Cowardly Lion actor
31 City in N France
32 Ermine
33 Sea swallows
35 "Champagne Tony" of golf
38 City in Turkey
39 "The Big Chill" star
40 Yearn
46 Joshes
47 Poetic dusk
48 Honshu port
49 Burst out
50 Move through mud
51 Suffix for gland
52 Ward in "Double Jeopardy"
53 In a while
54 Aswan and Hoover
55 Wang Lung's wife
56 Western alliance
57 Mad ___ hatter
60 Just-released

23 BEST PICTURE   by Jean Peterson
51 Across was the winner of 10 Academy Awards.

ACROSS

1 Clutch
5 Libya neighbor
9 Microsoft magazine
14 Jafar's parrot
15 Places
16 Big Poison of baseball
17 Short pencil
18 Anhydrous
19 Mites
20 Oscar-winning film of 1965
23 Liter's 1000: Abbr.
24 Hospital staffer
25 Giant step
28 Ovine sound
30 "God's Little ___" (1958)
34 Raccoon's cousin
35 Latakia, today
37 1/1000 of a yen
38 Oscar-winning film of 1954
41 Palindromic tribe
42 Persian rulers
43 Car contract
44 Ping-___
46 European vetch
47 Persian Gulf vessel
48 Catcher Karkovice
50 Comic Philips
51 Oscar-winning film of 1939
60 "The Little Mermaid" mermaid
61 Jeanie's was light brown
62 Jordanian royal
63 Glossy fabric
64 Elbow–wrist link
65 Wellington's alma mater
66 Winter precip
67 Envisioned
68 Royal in "Johnny Guitar"

DOWN

1 Heart
2 Early-blooming
3 Chills and fever
4 "Howdy Doody" host
5 Contract detail
6 Triceratops feature
7 DNA, for one
8 Prank
9 Quagmire
10 Hiatus
11 Mallard genus
12 Hatcher in "Tomorrow Never Dies"
13 Montross of the NBA
21 Hits from "Your Hit Parade"
22 Panache
25 Exclusive for Drudge
26 Kemo Sabe's friend
27 Boca ___
28 Old wives' tales
29 God of war
31 Kick the bucket
32 Washer cycle
33 Keyboard key
35 Moselle tributary
36 Blazing
39 "___ Grow Too Old to Dream"
40 Famous
45 "Bonanza" star
47 Iran capital
49 Baby hooter
51 Fissures
52 Doctorate prequel
53 Supreme Court number
54 Thence
55 Hearty companion
56 Fork feature
57 Scintilla
58 Lunchtime
59 First Bond film

OLD GLORY   by Karen Motyka
A good one to unfurl on June 14.

ACROSS

1 "Madcap Maxie" of boxing
5 King Lear's daughter
10 Wolfish look
14 Friend in need
15 Fragrance
16 Writer Wiesel
17 Concourse
18 Melancholy
19 Helper
20 Novel set in the year 10,991
21 Contribute
22 Hit the roof
24 Carnival show
26 Mean and nasty
27 Soprano Vaness
30 More recent
32 Dr. Schlessinger
33 Turkish general
34 Brainstorm
38 Wagnerian songs
39 Former Serbian capital
40 Honor ___ thieves
41 Outback reading
42 Make the effort
43 Catherine de Médicis, e.g.
44 Ford collectible
47 Former SAG president
48 North in "Breakout"
51 Brazilian dance
54 Sing like a bird
55 Socko sign
56 Southpaw's paw
60 "East of Eden" director Kazan
61 Granny, often
63 Make Darjeeling
64 Guinness in "The Lavender Hill Mob"
65 Puff up
66 Sweet tangelo
67 "Live at Red Rock" musician
68 ___ Salaam
69 Lose a layer

DOWN

1 Troubador
2 Moises of baseball
3 Joie de vivre
4 RED
5 Big Bird's teddy
6 Diminish by friction
7 WHITE
8 I love: Latin
9 Like AAA widths
10 BLUE
11 Top of the heap
12 Downy duck
13 Like Ichabod Crane
23 Subsist
25 "Oi, vai!"
27 Steamer
28 Solothurn's river
29 Undoing
31 No sweat
33 Go to pot?
35 Rub out
36 Feminine suffix
37 Antiquing device
40 Kuwaiti
45 Harness driver Cameron
46 Like tournament stars
48 Blood, ___ & Tears
49 Berry in "Executive Decision"
50 Cleveland Indians
52 Sierra spur
53 Folkways
57 Therefore
58 Knock down
59 Dweeb
62 Océano wave

ACROSS

1 Room at a posada
5 Kiddy carrier
9 Oodles
14 Wide-mouthed pitcher
15 Elevation
16 Allocate
17 Bryan of Bon Jovi
18 "Queens Logic" star
19 Act the coquette
20 **"Love is a . . ."** (**Louisa May Alcott**)
23 City near Utrecht
24 Nashville great Foley
25 Take-home scrap
26 Sorrowful
27 Place
29 Roofing goo
32 Low man on the ___ pole
35 Vaccines
36 Collette in "Shaft"
37 **"Love is . . ."** (**Maureen Duffy**)
40 Leafy green vegetable
41 Top Untouchable
42 Spectacle
43 Pei's wing
44 Specks
45 Danny's "L.A. Confidential" role
46 Double-fault
47 Go (for)
48 Yao's org.
51 **"Love is the . . ."** (**Samuel Johnson**)
57 Grayish
58 Head
59 Red tide organism
60 Treasure-hoarding dwarf
61 One with frosting finesse
62 "A Day Without ___": Enya
63 In conclusion?
64 French 101 verb
65 Free-throw scores

DOWN

1 Water grass
2 Prize
3 Flood defense
4 Code type
5 Poked around
6 Het up
7 Polo grounds?
8 Choice list
9 Thurber's genre
10 Chin feature
11 Jai tail
12 Medicate
13 Ending for team
21 Lady's love
22 Sum up
26 Like the Kalahari
27 Children's Dr.
28 Cleopatra's maid
29 Vacation option
30 Sister of Emily and Charlotte
31 Catch a shuttle
32 Filming segment
33 Aussie gem
34 William, who missed his son
35 Proofreading term
36 Garter snake's lunch
38 Huge, poetically
39 Drop a line
44 Had a buzz on
45 Walk of life
46 Tomato swelling
47 Badger relative
48 Lloyd in "Lady in the Lake"
49 ". . . just like ___ and Bacall": Higgins
50 King and Jackson
51 Cut-ups
52 "But as it ___, it ain't": Carroll
53 Chopine
54 Anthony's radio partner
55 Almanac item
56 Doc Holliday's card game

26 "ARF!" by Michele Sayer
Never let it be said 33 Down leads a dog's life!

ACROSS

1 Kiss
5 Gibber-jabber
10 Gummi Bears' foe
14 Squad
15 Mature
16 Terrain
17 Hoarfrost
18 Bodements
19 Observes
20 George and Marion Kirby's Neil
22 Trend
23 Gunpowder holder
24 Diner dish
25 Cambodia's neighbor
27 Fancy marble
28 Comical caveman
31 Niatross, e.g.
34 Terrier type
36 GI hangout
37 Residue
38 Elizabeth II's pet pooch
39 Catch a few z's
40 FL–ME road
41 Photo finish
42 Chaplain
44 Rally yell
45 Um relatives
46 Racetrack fence
48 Well-trodden
50 Splits
54 Baggy
56 The Jetsons' Astro
59 Small salmon
60 Ark groupings
61 "Darn it!"
62 Border on
63 Dreary
64 Six picas
65 Generation of the '60s
66 Quesadilla go-with
67 Washington nine

DOWN

1 Break
2 Splice
3 Nala's mate
4 Belfry locale
5 Quickly
6 "Green Mansions" girl
7 Mime
8 Keep bar
9 Lowest commissioned off.
10 Malt dryers
11 The Simpsons' Santa's Little Helper
12 Falter
13 Life of Riley
21 Have a belly laugh
22 Like lumber
24 Mata ___
26 Dundee denizens
27 Auburn mascot
29 Gravelly ridges
30 Vatican VIP
31 Henry VIII's sixth
32 "The Thin Man" dog
33 Paris Hilton's Tinkerbell
35 MoMA contents
38 Witty one
41 Unassuming
42 Painter Mondrian
43 Genie's master
47 Mount McKinley locale
49 Bakula of "Star Trek: Enterprise"
51 Bulgarian city
52 Make into law
53 Pecksniff and Thomas
54 Blackguard
55 Earring site
56 Big party
57 Cambodian currency
58 Important times
60 Charlie Rose's network

27 "MEOW!"* by Michele Sayer
Asterisked clues relate to the title.

ACROSS

1. "A Chorus Line" producer
5. Alex Haley book
10. Emperor's kin
14. Peeve
15. Calypso's father
16. Slugger Sandberg
17. Somalian supermodel
18. Cordwood measure
19. Utah ski resort
20. Down East omnivore*
22. "Cry Me a ___"
23. Rough Riders' city
24. Leonine locks
25. Cartoonist Lazarus
27. "This is the life!"
28. Ship pronoun
31. Eldrick Woods*
34. Tales
36. Cross-shaped
37. Crew competitor
38. Building wing
39. Be off
40. Bordeaux buddy
41. Ancient Peruvian
42. George Jetson's son
44. Brood mare
45. Ultimate degree
46. Hammett terrier
48. Provides a "Jeopardy" answer
50. "Born in ___" (1987)
54. Soupy ___
56. Like the yeti*
59. One of the Twelve
60. Go by bike
61. Crossword diagram
62. Saharan
63. Oxidize
64. ___ of the above
65. Delivery trucks
66. More talented
67. John in "Spy Hard"

DOWN

1. Super
2. Shoot for
3. Tress
4. Nom de plume
5. Varlet
6. Cartoonist Soglow
7. Bread spread
8. Mountain lake
9. San Francisco–L.A. dir.
10. Orient Express, e.g.
11. He's had a Rocky career*
12. Pay to play
13. Posterior
21. Pitcher
22. Shea shouts
24. Douglas denizen*
26. Kelly in "Cocktail"
27. The Spectrum, for one
29. Big sandwich
30. Macabre
31. Warty hopper
32. "___ Rock": Simon & Garfunkel
33. Hellcat*
35. Literary fragments
38. Crawling colonists
41. Signs a contract
42. Wrap-up abbr.
43. Garfield's favorite dish
47. Blacktop preserver
49. Feeder filler
51. Innsbruck locale
52. "Moonlight Gambler" singer
53. El Misti locale
54. Slovak, e.g.
55. Glow
56. Trumpeter Alpert
57. Pedestal figure
58. Forced
60. Shell-game item

28 ZODIAC CIRCLE by Eva Finney
The mascot of 4 Down is T.C.

ACROSS

1. Signed voucher
5. Darrin Stephens was one
10. See eye to eye
14. Incautious
15. Did a jeté
16. PayPal founder Musk
17. Archer in "Fatal Attraction"
18. MGM mascot
20. Crossed swords
22. Windows XP successor
23. Wits
24. Do checkout work
26. Baldwin/Kidman film
29. Ex-Beatle Sutcliffe
30. "Into ___ life . . ."
34. Editorialize
35. One of a Latin trio
36. Bikini half
37. Checks
38. Apothegm
39. Excitements
40. Standoffish
41. Churn up
42. Weightlifting lift
43. Trepidation
45. Animation unit
46. Full of holes
47. Diamond Head locale
49. Ginger on "Gilligan's Island"
50. Carioca's cousin
53. Julie in "10"
57. In ___ (up in the air)
61. Soccer star Dumitrescu
62. ___ majesty
63. Chaparral members
64. Radius adjunct
65. Jerusalem's Mosque of ___
66. "Gladiator" director
67. Laid eyes on

DOWN

1. Crosspatch
2. Mandlikova of tennis
3. "As it ___, it ain't": Carroll
4. Kirby Puckett played for them
5. Maintain
6. Monopoly cards
7. Shanghai's Jin ___ Tower
8. Liable
9. Imprecise ordinal
10. Mr. Jinks, for one
11. Beaver State motto word
12. Gaffer
13. Resort NNW of Siracusa
19. Green in "Casino Royale"
21. Corset feature
24. Proscenium
25. Baby-faced
26. Floral ___
27. At a good clip
28. Qaddafi's country
29. Like Verne Troyer
31. "American Idol" judge
32. Mostar resident
33. Reckless
35. Parting word
38. Place de l'Étoile sight
39. Hit from "Hair"
42. Hourglass sight
44. Mosstrooper
46. Crème de la crème
48. Remote battery
49. Be silent, musically
50. Normandy battle site of 1944
51. "Excuse me"
52. City near Phoenix
54. Covergirl Macpherson
55. Sommelier's domain
56. Madonna's ex
58. OCS grads
59. Slo-pitch path
60. Friend of Morpheus

29 THIS AND THAT   by Tim Wagner
The nickname of 31 Down is "Digger."

ACROSS

1 Orkney Islands settler
5 Nashville sound?
10 Flushing Meadow stadium
14 Home of the Starzz
15 Signe in "The Black Bird"
16 It's hit on the head
17 Jot
18 Buddy in "Born to Dance"
19 Lowdown
20 Credit
22 Positive
24 "Cabaret" song (with "Mein")
25 Put on notice
26 Deceptive one
33 Zhivago's inspiration
34 Words with "Disturb!"
35 "___ I": Crosby hit
36 Helen Thomas' org.
37 Gulf of Aqaba port
38 Like the Edsel in 1957
39 Convalesce
41 "Who ___ Be Now?": Men At Work
42 Place for a pie
43 Where a bassoon plays grandfather
46 "The Silencers" hero
47 "So ___ to you, Fuzzy-Wuzzy": Kipling
48 John Keats verse
51 Soccer position
54 Terry's possessive?
55 Orchestral group
57 Language of India
58 Gross in "A Midnight Clear"
59 Betelgeuse locale
60 "If ___ the Circus": Seuss
61 Hunch
62 Medicated
63 Hoggett in "Babe"

DOWN

1 Catamount
2 "How sweet ___!": Gleason
3 Banned Salinger novel (with "The")
4 Carmelites founder
5 James Cagney/Bette Davis comedy
6 ". . . gimble in the ___": Carroll
7 Jenny may be one
8 60 billion equal a min.
9 1937 Pulitzer Prize winner
10 "Peer Gynt" dance
11 2005 NBA Finals winner
12 LP designation
13 Carolina campus
21 Manhattan metro
23 Out-and-outer
26 Like Santa
27 "Charmaine" composer
28 Michael in "Light of Day"
29 "___ Out" (Kevin Kline film)
30 "I ___ Bad, and That Ain't Good"
31 "The Life of Riley" undertaker
32 Muppet pianist
40 Kind of fishing
42 Honey
44 P.O. dept.
45 Aforetime
48 Chulalongkorn, for one
49 Bunch
50 Indy driver Palmroth
51 Wild plum
52 Bronco booter
53 Viking letter
56 "___ for Lawless": Grafton

30 ANAGRAMS   by Norman S. Wizer
The American Airlines Center ("The Hangar") is the home of 6 Down.

ACROSS

1 Lavender
6 Unspecified number
10 He crosses the line
14 Vacation island
15 Race for Harmonious
16 Biblical weed
17 AUSTRALIAN celebration?
19 "A Bug's Life" princess
20 Hurricane heading
21 Eaglet's home
22 Enters
24 Poker bullets
25 Gathers
26 Emerge
29 Dial "M" for this
30 Catty comments
31 Depressed
32 Arabic robe
35 Golfer Aoki
36 Carries on
37 Paraffin-coated wheel
38 Enzyme suffix
39 Mira's constellation
40 Grover's Veep
41 Hit the road
43 Anaheim team
44 Satirized
46 Bathgate of hockey
47 "Howards End" actress
48 Compact
49 Botanist Gray
52 Hussein's third wife
53 Crustacean hiding in the CRISPBREAD?
56 Approaching
57 Einstein's article
58 Siouan language
59 Electronics giant
60 "You ___ Me": Cooke
61 Christened

DOWN

1 Zap with light
2 Armenia's neighbor
3 Renaissance instrument
4 Monkey in "Aladdin"
5 Venezuelan capital
6 Dallas hockey team
7 City near Les Halles
8 Miss Piggy, self-referentially
9 Display cases
10 Carving
11 CASTLE CARD game?
12 Ava's ex
13 Not worth a hill of ___
18 Kind of do-well
23 Countercurrent
24 Flying start?
25 Takes in
26 Samoan port
27 Kitty
28 REPARATION for a Roman magistrate?
29 Downhiller's bump
31 Espoused
33 Jezebel's god
34 "The Old Devils" author
36 Transposes
37 Nervous
39 Bistro
40 Fireplace piece
42 International service org.
43 Green Gables girl
44 Looks over
45 Prehistoric: Comb. form
46 Lent a hand
48 Neighbor of Ont.
49 "My Name Is ___": Saroyan
50 Aromatic herb
51 Not up
54 Round chart
55 Johnny Reb's org.

1	2	3	4	5		6	7	8	9		10	11	12	13
14						15					16			
17					18						19			
20				21					22	23				
			24					25						
26	27	28					29							
30					31						32	33	34	
35				36						37				
38				39					40					
		41	42					43						
44	45					46								
47					48					49	50	51		
52			53	54				55						
56			57				58							
59			60				61							

31 CYBER COMEDY   by Don Law
A good one to solve at your workstation.

ACROSS

1 Munch
5 "The Sting" director
9 "Peace on earth, good-will ___!"
14 Solothurn's river
15 Skater Kulik
16 Mother's kin
17 Fast-talking
18 Bartlett
19 ___ cotta
20 Fraternal org.
21 Tiger Woods tee shot?
23 What Liz said twice to Richard
25 Unit of absorbed energy
26 Place for a Peke?
29 Coliseum sign
31 Seniors' org.
35 Heavenly ram
36 Read a bar code
37 Giuseppe's god
38 A quarter has two
39 Keel
40 Weasel relative
41 Mexican bruin
42 Flu symptom
43 Mike Mussina's nickname
44 Tear violently
46 Apply lightly
47 Resulted in
48 Merino mama
50 ___ in Harold
51 Google's revenue?
56 Per
60 Nose type
61 "The murmur of ___ . . .": Dickinson
62 Trick
63 Restaurateur of song
64 Stadium section
65 In the thick of
66 Trails
67 Wimbledon units
68 Jutlander

DOWN

1 "Ghost Rider" star
2 Avery Fisher ___
3 Composer Satie
4 Cellars and attics, e.g.?
5 Sage Francis' music
6 Jejunum neighbors
7 Pinocchio, often
8 Fat
9 Colorful fish
10 C New York lake
11 "Home Alone" burglar
12 Peut-___ (perhaps)
13 Pedagogic org.
22 Pilotless plane
24 John ___ Passos
26 Drudgery
27 Derive
28 Spike for K-2
29 Third-stringer
30 Wrath
32 "Ta-ta, Toledo"
33 Hair tint
34 Nudged
36 Chronicle
39 German spa
40 Hole in the wall?
43 Bleat
45 Disengage
47 Kirstie Alley series
49 Sommelier's stock
51 Cap'n Andy's daughter
52 Discharge
53 Long-running musical
54 NY stage award
55 "___ the Applegates" (1991)
57 "Lonely Hearts" heroine
58 Invent
59 Jekyll's alter ego
60 Coolio's music

BIRDS OF A FEATHER by Linda Finnerty
The name of the restaurant at 63 Across is an acronym.

ACROSS

1 Vapor
5 Eskers
9 Wacky
14 Susan in "Beauty and the Beast"
15 Split
16 Greeting from Maui
17 Join forces
18 Mother of Romulus
19 Scarecrow stuffing
20 "Thomas and Beulah" poet
22 Chris of Coldplay
23 Bengal ender
24 Cuba libre ingredient
25 Wine server
29 Point
30 Compos mentis
34 Quickly
35 Like R.L. Stine stories
37 Journal
38 "I Think I Love You" singers
41 Afore
42 With bed or home
43 News summary
44 Exercise aid
46 Nanny has three
47 Purposeful
48 Dodge trucks
50 Compass point
51 Leach and Williams
54 College member
59 Woke
60 Golden Fleece carrier
61 New Mexican house
62 Drawing room
63 Emeril's Big Easy restaurant
64 Norse war god
65 Seedling
66 Astounded
67 Pioneer 10's org.

DOWN

1 Phobia
2 Wrinkly tangelo
3 Brewer's grain
4 "Amarantine" singer
5 Indolent
6 Work a puzzle
7 Racer Luyendyk
8 Cell component
9 Of the proboscis
10 Extremists
11 Legal wrong
12 Siamese
13 Show boredom
21 Postpones
22 Theme
24 Pitted
25 Superhero wear
26 In pieces
27 Peep show
28 Take measures
29 "Le Foyer de la Danse" painter
31 She met Humpty Dumpty
32 "Ryan Express" of baseball
33 Land of pyramids
35 Heavenly places
36 Part of ERA
39 Details
40 Confronted
45 Hoosegow
47 Foray
49 Concerning
50 Boston College mascot
51 Gravelly voice
52 Verbal
53 Cowboy tie
54 Singer Sheryl
55 "Bird" Parker, for one
56 Zilch
57 Sale stipulation
58 Turner in "Cass Timberlane"
60 Literary fragments

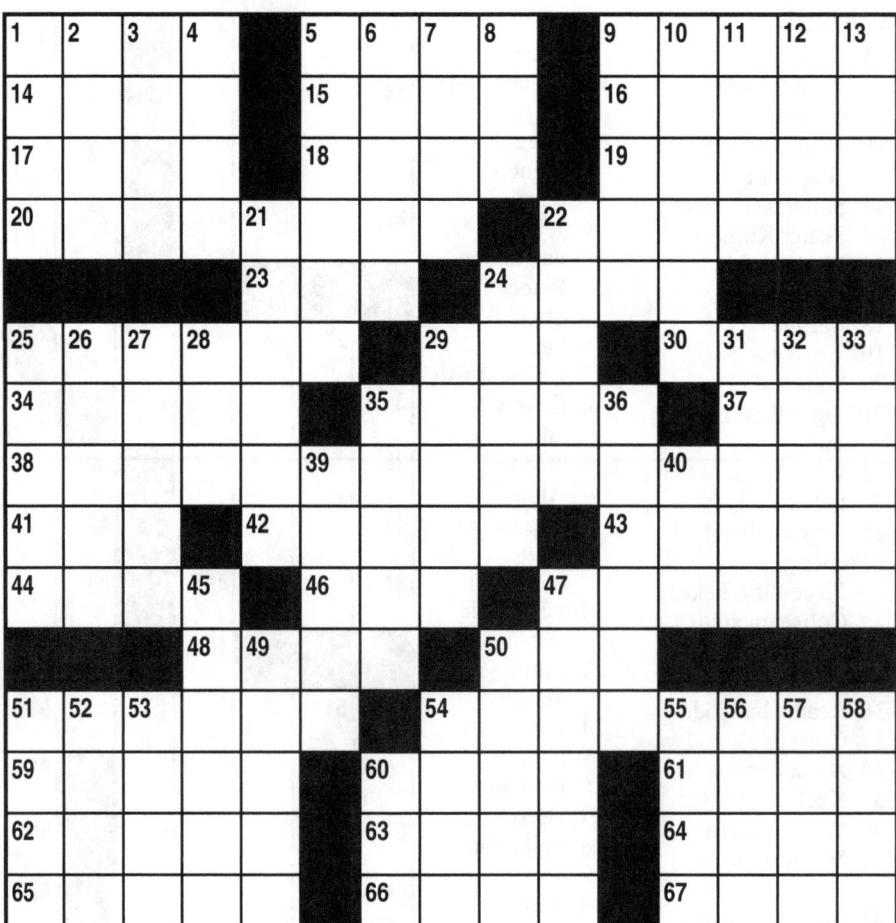

33 COLORBLIND by Danny Touse
Dichromats have a definite solving advantage here.

ACROSS

1 Pooh's 100 ___ Wood
5 Windjammers
10 Say the rosary
14 Jogger's gait
15 Smoking, for one
16 "Pandora's Box" painter Magritte
17 Single ___ Scotch
18 Bout site
19 Muesli ingredients
20 Sad-looking lettuce?
23 Hebrew letter
24 Anger
25 Nobelist Pinter
29 Failure
31 Israeli airport
34 Mimicry
35 "Octopussy" director
36 Pueblo Indian
37 It's played at lawn parties?
40 Feels lousy
41 Longest Swiss river
42 Coeur d'___, Idaho
43 "Treasure Island" auth.
44 Hayseed
45 Wasn't greedy
46 Racket
47 Kingston Trio hit
48 Cowardly explorer?
55 "___ the Roof": Taylor
56 Supermarket reading material
57 Pianist Feinberg
59 Hereditary unit
60 Jupiter moon
61 Owlish, in a sense
62 Hilton ___ Island
63 Wound-up
64 "Forget it!"

DOWN

1 Citi convenience
2 Crosspatch
3 Croissant
4 Famous last words
5 Removed a Vandyke
6 Seraglio
7 "___ to differ!"
8 Deck wood
9 Outposts
10 Poke around
11 Like McCoy
12 Toss in a chip
13 Short answer
21 Playwright Williams
22 A Dada founder
25 Viking of comics
26 When croci bloom
27 Lurches
28 Magnetite and malachite
29 Distress signal
30 ___ majesty
31 Nonmedalist
32 Think
33 Cut up
35 Take hurriedly
36 Hawaiian dance
38 Half-finger glove
39 Taj of Atlantic City
44 Rocker Ocasek
45 Stone markers
46 Spent an evening at Lutèce
47 "Wayne's World" star
48 Rapier
49 Gossip maven Barrett
50 Healthy
51 Israel's first UN delegate
52 Croquet area
53 Mixed bag
54 Mud dauber
55 "Yuck!"
58 Bo Derek, ___ Collins

34 HIGH CARDS   by Kayen Motyka

37 Across is a popular drink in the Conch Republic.

ACROSS

1 Square column
5 Writer Dahl
10 Recital site
14 Cobb in "12 Angry Men"
15 Provide
16 Suffix for million
17 JACK
20 Wiesbaden, e.g.
21 Rhine tributary
22 Gung-ho
23 ANA members
24 Highland negative
25 QUEEN
34 City near Venice
35 Bank (on)
36 Grassland
37 Key ___ martini
38 Bygone
39 Domino or Waller
40 Reckless goddess
41 Go bonkers
42 Word form of "mother"
43 KING
47 Short road
48 Otto I, for one: Abbr.
49 Racket
52 Cupid
54 "Maple Leaf ___": Joplin
57 ACE
60 "A Loss of Roses" playwright
61 "Dead Ringers" star
62 In a muddle
63 Kind of beer
64 "The Divine Comedy" poet
65 Flog

DOWN

1 Isère's source
2 Low high tide
3 Honduran port
4 Steely Dan album
5 Replaced a player
6 Ripsnorter
7 "___, a female deer . . ."
8 Scandinavian horn
9 Kim in "Mission to Mars"
10 "Messiah" composer
11 Deputy
12 Scientologist Hubbard
13 Pre-Easter period
18 Skater Kerrigan
19 Verbal
23 Glassmaker Lalique
25 Fond ___, WI
26 First Lady in 1901
27 Indy official
28 Tehran man
29 Human herbivore
30 Emulate Gable and Lombard
31 Israeli seaport
32 Prefix for active
33 Arafat
39 Fortune's wheel
41 Olympian no-no
42 Razorbill auk
44 Press agent?
45 Hospital imperative
46 In the saddle
49 ___ the air (uncertain)
50 Johnnycake
51 Baltic port
52 Prolific author
53 Blanc, for one
54 Subterfuge
55 Territory
56 Punkie
58 Painter Angelico
59 Scandal sheet

35 FLAGS OF THE WORLD   by Eva Finney
"Home of the red, white, and blue" could mean France, Panama, or Netherlands.

ACROSS

1 Cast-of-thousands film
5 Rockefeller Center statue
10 Explorer Tasman
14 Russo in "Major League"
15 Brook fish
16 "I Don't Want To Wait" singer
17 Garonne tributary
18 Aquarium fish
19 "Ring of Fire" singer
20 Its flag has a golden olive branch
22 Its flag has a red star within a red crescent
24 ___ de jambe (ballet movement)
25 Stray
26 Its flag is red and white
29 Brainy
31 Its flag is green, white, and red
32 Boom
33 Smeltery dross
37 Casino area
38 Denoted
39 Overthrow first
40 Parrot
42 "Gone ___-Finnigan"
43 Madonna-and-child work
45 Former Argentine president
47 Its flag is red with a white crescent and star
48 Friendly ghost
51 Pressing
52 Its flag is blue, black, and white
54 Its flag is blue with a red/white cross
58 "Brilliant ___" (1997)
59 Spend ___ (1985 Derby winner)
61 Purim's month
62 Adams in "Lover Come Back"
63 Verse romance
64 How the Graces are usually portrayed
65 What willows do
66 Puccini opera
67 Pushing up daisies

DOWN

1 "Asian Princess Suite" artist
2 Fleshy fruit
3 Crucifix letters
4 Delacorte Theater's park
5 Show up
6 Walk
7 His wife looked back
8 Pervasive character
9 Sturdy
10 Underscores
11 Two-by-four
12 Borden bovine
13 "The Land of Smiles" composer
21 Israeli animator Oren
23 Long-jawed fish
26 Meerschaum
27 Ear-relevant
28 Wooden strip
29 Its flag has the pillars of Hercules on it
30 "Buddenbrooks" novelist
32 Utah's flower
34 Onion relative
35 Commedia dell'___
36 Weimaraner's color
38 Conjugality
41 Anti
43 Simple partner
44 Its flag is green, white, and orange
46 Chaucer's twilight
47 ___-tape parade
48 Walk of Fame name
49 Stage whisper
50 Tankard
51 Pronouncements
53 In the hay
55 In unison, musically
56 Zippo
57 Stowe novel
60 REL's opponent

ACROSS

1 Sidewalk eateries
6 Tiff
10 Abhorrence
14 Tickle
15 Perry's creator
16 Algerian port
17 Model Evangelista
18 Eternal City
19 Experienced
20 Private eye
21 **Where Bob was "Painless" Peter Potter**
24 Abominable creature
26 Author LeShan
27 Scholars
29 Captain Hook's alma mater
31 ICU workers
34 Windy City hub
35 1902 Derby winner ___-Dale
36 Seeing stars
37 "Clair de ___"
38 Defendant's story
39 Cover a dice bet
40 Knack
41 "Awake and Sing" playwright
42 Bum
43 Cape
44 Freshwater fish
45 "I Love Paris" composer
46 Novelist Clancy
47 Melville book
48 **Where Bob was John Kidley**
54 "Luck ___ Lady"
57 Bronson's "House of Wax" role
58 Gradient
59 Southern accent
61 Fox's home
62 Mental image
63 Estuary
64 Audrey Hepburn's birth name
65 Minstrel poet
66 Capital near Giza

DOWN

1 Gael
2 "I cannot tell ___"
3 **Where Bob was Arthur Tyler**
4 Schedule abbr.
5 "Frasier" setting
6 Like the Gobi
7 Buttress
8 Mrs. Alfred Hitchcock
9 "Fun With Dick and Jane" star
10 Jack Nicholson film
11 Territory
12 Bath powder
13 German duck
22 With nibs or nobs
23 Novelist O'Brien
25 Home of the Corrs
27 Big bear
28 Lt. under Kirk
29 Crème de la crème
30 Filing helps
31 **Where Bob was Harold Gridley**
32 Prod
33 Beefer
35 Scots name
38 Tracy/Hepburn film
39 Betting game
41 Aroma
42 Laughable
45 Polynesian dish
46 ___ firma
48 Bluish green
49 "Yikes!"
50 Null
51 Verdi opera
52 River near Dunkirk
53 Extinct
55 Wide-mouthed pitcher
56 Voice above tenor
60 Genetic acid

37 COMEDY DUOS   by Tim Wagner
"A laugh is a smile that bursts." — Mary H. Waldrip

ACROSS

1 Time to give up?
5 Gooseneck ___
9 Clean with friction
14 ___ fixe
15 "Desperate Housewives" character
16 Diamond home
17 Arabian gulf
18 Last word in the Bible
19 Sharpened
20 "Sailor Beware" stars
23 Feral shelter
24 Coffeepot
25 Arrest
29 White-tailed eagle
31 Second sight
34 Win by ___
35 Baldwin in "The Edge"
36 Pooch of puzzles
37 Canadian comedy duo
40 Roberts in "Rude Awakening"
41 Dele opposite
42 "Superman" star
43 Hedaya in "Wise Guys"
44 Landing
45 One-sided
46 Bounder
47 LeMay's WW2 outfit
48 "Sons of the Desert" stars
56 Ingraham of talk radio
57 Sleep like ___
58 Florentine farewell
59 Started a line
60 Mi preceders
61 "___ on Entebbe" (1977)
62 Swap
63 Venison
64 Lanchester in "Die Laughing"

DOWN

1 Neeson in "Kingdom of Heaven"
2 Norse epic
3 ___-do-well
4 Pavilion
5 Horseshoe score
6 Space seller
7 Demeanor
8 Hang fire
9 Bailiwick
10 Clarabell, for one
11 Punjab princess
12 Salt Lake City team
13 Murphy namesake
21 "Do ___ to eat a peach?": Eliot
22 Brown-bag contents
25 Crowed
26 "From the Terrace" author
27 NBA hanger
28 Case in "Route 66"
29 Church official
30 Breather
31 "Ginger Pye" author
32 Carlton or Canyon
33 Whittled down
35 Stud fee
36 On the briny
38 Digression
39 "The Lazarus Man" star
44 Halloween event in Greenwich Village
45 Harass
46 Sugar-___ ham
47 Late-night buzz
48 Hibernation site
49 Special quality
50 "Whispering Smith" star
51 Sunburn soother
52 Ranch unit
53 Iranian coin
54 Toastmaster's spot
55 "Return of the Jedi" sage
56 D-Day craft

"IT'S ELEMENTAL"   by Michele Sayer
71 Across won an Oscar for his role in that film.

ACROSS

1 Thailand king
5 Mrs. Gorbachev
10 "Gee, Officer Krupke!" singers
14 Sixth Hebrew month
15 "As You Like It" forest
16 Indigo source
17 Confront
18 Kelly who voiced Nala
19 Arizona city
20 Edgar Allan Poe tale
22 Stone in "Bobby"
24 West end of L.A.
25 Ten-percenter
26 Hunter near the Bull
30 Adequate
34 Dealey Plaza site
36 Sea monster
37 The Mauve Decade et al.
41 "Heroides" poet
42 Endangered gazelle
44 Cut some slack
45 Marine hazard
46 Cologne article
47 "___ Right Moves" (1983)
49 On cloud nine
52 Potok's Lev
53 Employee request
56 Meal starter
58 "Micki + Maude" star
60 Jalopy
65 Reunion member
66 ". . . ___ of skimble-skamble stuff": Shak.
68 Galley slaves
69 Whetstone, e.g.
70 Esther in "Rosewood"
71 Arkin in "Little Miss Sunshine"
72 First word in a Noel poem
73 TV bunch
74 Tennis great Lacoste

DOWN

1 Oceans
2 Wife of Esau
3 Postman's defense
4 Code type
5 Sly person?
6 Stimulate
7 Beatnik's "Got it!"
8 Spanish-1 verb
9 Mallard genus
10 Tonto portrayer
11 Toughen
12 Meerkat in "The Lion King"
13 Incline
21 Crazy bone
23 Witch
26 Musk, for one
27 4-star review
28 "Would ___ to you?"
29 Constitution's nickname
31 Hullabaloo
32 Malachite, e.g.
33 Abdul-Jabbar's alma mater
35 Emmy winner Thompson
38 Early-blooming
39 U.S. Open stadium
40 Sibyl
43 Lout
48 Sol followers
50 Cariou in "Lady in White"
51 Ivanka's father
53 Bank of Paris
54 One-way sign
55 Ivanka's mother
57 Tin Pan or Kirstie
59 Beau Brummell's concern
60 Ward in "Rainbow Drive"
61 Lot's city of refuge
62 Graziano ring rival
63 Azerbaijan's neighbor
64 Crossword serf
67 Palme ___ (Cannes award)

39 KING IN HIDING   by Linda Finnerty
The king is hiding in the grid circles below.

ACROSS

1 Hydroxyl compound
5 Refuge
10 Give the villain his due
14 Dull, as a party
15 Skip over
16 "The Black Stallion" hero
17 The McCoys, for one
18 Feudal vassal
19 ___ avis
20 #1 hit of 1958
23 Minnesota twins?
24 "Green Grow the ___"
25 Straighten
29 Combine
31 Central
32 They play for pay
33 Motorist's org.
36 #1 hit of 1969
40 Netherlands city
41 Slews
42 Clarinetist Shaw
43 Pistol-packing
45 Vaquero's rope
46 Match
49 Auth. submissions
51 #1 hit of 1956
58 "As much ___ my dukedom": Shak.
59 Wichita newspaper
60 Bangkokian
61 Kinsmen
62 Lland animal?
63 Pool cover
64 Once, once
65 Played the siren
66 Temple team

DOWN

1 Emulate Jongkind
2 Lion King's queen
3 Poet Khayyám
4 Float a loan
5 Oscar winner Mirren
6 Pseudonym
7 Competed
8 Advantage
9 "___ to say . . ."
10 Fugard's master
11 Mexican fruit
12 Icy mountaineering hazard
13 Leafs through
21 Painter Estienne
22 Take the cake
25 Basilica end
26 Like Hawaiian shirts
27 Steppat in "Madeleine"
28 Mountain pass
29 Mope
30 Curmudgeon
32 Mound
33 Stage org.
34 Miner's way in
35 Clueless
37 "Wichita Lineman" singer
38 Bittern's milieu
39 Incense
43 Slap the cuffs on
44 Path to nowhere
46 Full moon, e.g.
47 Odin's clique
48 Blank-verse feet
49 Scandinavian port
50 Irish dagger
52 Chest rattle
53 "Zounds!"
54 Kruger in "Treasure Island"
55 Melt
56 Banjoist Scruggs
57 Manlis in "Dick Tracy"

OXYMORONS by Norman S. Wizer
The clue at 36 Down is also an oxymoron.

ACROSS

1 Sharks or Dolphins
5 Moor's god
10 Pavilion
14 Word form for "high"
15 Dinero
16 Indy driver Luyendyk
17 Like Betty with a makeover?
19 ___ colada
20 Seaweed-wrapped delicacy
21 Fabric ___
23 Friday, Pepper et al.
26 Three-___ sloth
27 Peter Pan's mystery
30 Tucks away
32 Renew the lease of
35 Set within a set
37 Cutlery
39 MC
40 Peck's ___ boy
42 Waistcoat
43 Conductor's cry
46 Pacific wind
49 Type of basin
50 Detective Wolfe
51 Surcharge
52 Cap-and-gowner
54 Attentive
56 Food of the gods
60 Edmonton puckster
64 Krung Thep citizen
65 Colonial workplace?
68 Fit ___ tied
69 Manifesto
70 Baffin Bay hazard
71 Letters on a Stealth
72 Whoop-___
73 Polio vaccine developer

DOWN

1 G.I. lullaby
2 Raw-silk color
3 Olympian hawk
4 Closet eaters?
5 Composer Beach
6 Piniella of baseball
7 Nautical diaries
8 Divvy up
9 Muckraking tool
10 Recorded "Regis and Kelly"?
11 Land of poets
12 Niblick's number
13 Spree
18 Tammany Hall symbol
22 Superboy, e.g.
24 Confucian truth
25 Broadway memento
27 Indonesia locale
28 Culpability
29 "Don Carlos" princess
31 Salmon eggs
33 Turn inside out
34 AC-motor inventor
36 Sweet sorrow?
38 Charon's river
41 Whitetail
44 Casino game
45 Threw light on the subject
47 Mme. of Mexico
48 "I'm Sitting on ___ the World"
53 Part of LED
55 Quarrels
56 Aleutian island
57 Ohm reciprocals
58 Rum cake
59 Between
61 Kedrova in "Zorba the Greek"
62 Environmental sci.
63 Smoke
66 "The Name of the Rose" author
67 Buffalo-hunting tribe

41 HAVING A BRAWL   by John M. Samson
The theme below is synonymous with "brawl."

ACROSS

1 "Buffalo ___"
5 Where Yazd is
9 Kind of light show
14 Scorpio birthstone
15 He sang "For Mama"
16 Emulate Pericles
17 Mother of Artemis
18 Most quoted author
19 Lipstick shade
20 TV show about a liberated wife?
23 LEM monitor
24 ___ carte
25 Think out loud
29 Settled in
33 Stunning defeat
34 Atlantic City game
37 Gardner in "Show Boat"
38 Get the "Louie, Louie" group out of jail?
42 Bart Simpson's age
43 Court cry
44 Revise
45 Source
48 Red-blooded
49 Finalize
50 Luncheon closer
53 Poker-table rule for dealers?
61 Daytime TV host Tony
62 Eskers
63 Wings
64 Computer chip giant
65 Jaunty
66 It has a Lincoln center
67 Otis in "Wild Orchid"
68 Alternative
69 High schooler

DOWN

1 Ryder Cup sport
2 Parrot
3 Like George Apley
4 Sour plum
5 The Donald's first wife
6 Storms
7 Waikiki welcome
8 Hawaiian honker
9 Place
10 Olfactory stimuli
11 Madras dress
12 And others
13 Swear by
21 Static
22 Papal cape
25 "We're ___ see the wizard . . ."
26 Kitchen knife
27 Ancient Celtic tribe
28 Born as
30 Domesticates
31 Happening
32 Beau Brummell
34 Crucial
35 Squeeze by
36 Serbian city
39 Japanese car
40 Greek physician
41 SWC team
46 Codger
47 Breathe
50 Ford flop
51 Peter and Ivan
52 German cake
53 S&L insurer
54 Frog genus
55 ___ 'acte (intermission)
56 "Forget it!"
57 Mad
58 Nobelist Wiesel
59 Troglodyte's home
60 Sharp

42 PIED PIPER by Linda Finnerty
A recent visit to Hamelin inspired this theme.

ACROSS

1 Primary person
5 Libya neighbor
9 Antic
14 Nevada resort
15 Nathan in "Mouse Hunt"
16 Love to bits
17 Famous last words
18 Narodnaya's mountains
19 Clive in "Frankenstein"
20 Envisaged
21 Sherlock Holmes actor
23 Russian news agency
25 Sneaker width
26 Tin Pan Alley org.
29 "___ Smile": Hall & Oates
32 Humane org.
36 Alley scores
38 Purge
39 McKellen in "Scandal"
40 Venetian evening
41 Recurrent pattern
43 Leading man
44 Down a sub
45 Suffix for eight
46 Relaxed
48 Links hazard
50 Table insert
52 Oceanic ray
53 It lights up Venus
55 End of a terse challenge
57 "Kid" Ory hit
62 Swards
66 Charlton Heston film
67 Skater Kulik
68 Flog
69 "What's in ___?": Shak.
70 They're tied to newlywed cars
71 Narcissus spurned her
72 ___ Day weekend
73 "I said, but just to be ___ . . .": Dickinson

74 Start for stat

DOWN

1 Hermes' half-brother
2 Heidi's aunt
3 Dealer's request
4 Noah's landfall
5 Black suit
6 Dog
7 Teal genus
8 Salami seller
9 Hiding place
10 Pueblo bricks
11 Equestrian sport
12 Jason Walton's sister
13 Surrealist Magritte
22 Captain
24 Simian
26 Great trait
27 Harpoon
28 ___ blanche
30 Houston's Summit
31 Brim
33 Michelangelo sculpture
34 Insertion mark
35 Battery terminus
37 "___ by Starlight"
42 ___-haw
43 Subterranean bar
47 Three dots, in Morse
49 Baffin Islander
51 Catty
54 Part of BPOE
56 Lessee's holding
57 Kind of ticket
58 Radius neighbor
59 Strikebreaker
60 Isinglass
61 Spill the beans
63 Apiece
64 Flushing Meadow stadium
65 "Amscray!"

ACROSS

1 Claudia ___ Taylor Johnson
5 Luau, e.g.
10 Mild oath
14 "I Kid You Not!" author
15 Printing hand
16 Abate
17 Exclude
18 Bitter-___ (diehard)
19 Mouthful
20 1965 Beach Boys hit
22 Badger State capital
24 Sped
25 Beckett drama
26 Taking the booby prize
28 Make ___ of it
29 Jack, in cribbage
32 "Message received"
35 Cameleer, e.g.
37 Freshwater fish
38 Miami Heat home
39 Knightly quality
40 "Take On Me" group
41 "Citizen Kane" studio
42 Niatross, e.g.
43 "Battling Bella" activist
45 Answer Trebek
46 Census info
47 It's given to a new arrival
49 Qatar ruler
51 Did dockwork
54 Iris rings
57 Tasty steak
59 Sabre handle
60 Engaged
62 "Dies ___"
63 Use a trier
64 38 Across, for one
65 Biblical wall word
66 Tub contents
67 Breckin in "Rat Race"
68 Paradise lost

DOWN

1 N.T. book
2 Truman's birthplace
3 Siberian forest
4 Particular
5 W.C. in "Poppy"
6 Danube tributary
7 Expand upon
8 Appear to be
9 Nolan Ryan was one
10 Account entry
11 Nicolas Cage/Holly Hunter film
12 In re
13 Middle schooler
21 Caboose locale
23 Kind of prize
27 Vestige
28 Dress up
30 "Magnum, P.I." setting
31 Vaunt
32 ___ avis
33 Sturdy trees
34 "Black Iris" painter
36 O'Neill sea play
39 "Where Was I?" panelist
42 Bucket
43 "Amo, ___, I love a lass": O'Keeffe
44 Story hour
48 Affirmed rival
50 Epigraph
52 Misjudged
53 Keaton in "Marvin's Room"
54 Epiphany phrase
55 Banister
56 Hibernia
57 Aloha State bird
58 Hammer head
61 Marina Del ___

44 MIXED-UP GUYS   by Michele Sayer

5 Down was born Maria del Rosario Pilar Martinez Molina Baeza de Rasten.

ACROSS

1 Little of "The Wire"
5 Cable channel
10 Bisection
14 Large hall
15 Intoxicating
16 ". . . oh, oh, oh what ___!"
17 Mellows out Johnnie Walker
18 Plant cover?
19 ___ many words
20 DIEHARD'S SURF CRY
23 Egg ___ yung
24 Kalahari stopovers
25 Puccini heroine
29 "Last Supper" home
33 Cornell's home
35 Peace in Russia
36 Egyptian skink
40 BEST ELEVEN GRIPS
43 It springs eternal
44 Digit
45 Williams of tennis
46 Walkway
48 Green reptile
49 Redress
53 Literary collection
55 FED OVAL SHAD FISH
63 Demeanor
64 Tread the boards
65 Length × width
66 Heche of "Men in Trees"
67 Lent a hand
68 Speed
69 East Rutherford team
70 Peter and Ivan
71 Padua neighbor

DOWN

1 Line of eskers
2 Epiphany trio
3 Stage actor Clunes
4 Skin eruption
5 "Cuchi-Cuchi" girl
6 Once in a great while
7 Shelled out
8 Hebrew month
9 Big Apple Big Board
10 Israeli port
11 "___ Dei"
12 Director Hallström
13 Dental product
21 "I've Just Seen ___": Beatles
22 Thither
25 Mrs. Addams, to Gomez
26 Kruger in "Murder, My Sweet"
27 Name for a herd dog
28 Troll's home
30 Urge forward
31 Twice XXVI
32 Nephew of Poseidon
34 Con
36 ___ Kadabra (The Flash foe)
37 Insect repellent
38 James Bond foe
39 Japanese gelatin
41 ABBA hit
42 On the up and up
46 Apply a rider
47 Feast for "Messiah"
49 Clio contender
50 Summer home of Andrew Wyeth
51 Happening
52 Dressed to the ___
54 Demands
56 Police pressure
57 Suzy in "Twister"
58 Scotch friend
59 Despise
60 Magnetite and malachite
61 Trick
62 Subway token

45 MIXED-UP GALS by Michele Sayer
Bono thinks she's the greatest! (See 31 Down)

ACROSS

1 Killer exam
5 Elroy Jetson's dog
10 2006 Disney/Pixar film
14 Basilica end
15 Backhoe bucket
16 Grace ender
17 "Now I've ___ everything!"
18 "Jefferson in Paris" star
19 University of Nevada site
20 CHEROKEE HALL ART
23 Ubiquitous verb
24 Jackie ___ Haley
25 "Get ___ of this!"
29 1957 Cy Young winner
33 Orléans is its capital
35 Pale potable
36 Bath and Baden
40 VILLAINESS WAS MA
43 "My Home Town" singer
44 Raggedy Andy's friend
45 Captain Flint, for one
46 Clean the slate
48 Lends an ear
49 Tragedian
53 Piece for a hood
55 ARTIER BRASSBAND
63 Drama award
64 Knight mare?
65 Away from the wind
66 Aswan and Hoover
67 Succinct
68 Object of worship
69 Other
70 Off-kilter
71 Northern European

DOWN

1 Blowout
2 Fencer's foil
3 With the fleet
4 Landlord's due
5 Ed of "Studio 60"
6 Multitude
7 Fare
8 Newspaper section
9 Org. for Libya
10 Ballerina Fracci
11 Bahrain bigwig
12 Kidney-related
13 Uvular noise
21 Hell
22 Barbie's beau
25 Thomas ___ Edison
26 Temporary grant
27 Hog "hello"
28 Side by side?
30 Some queens, formerly
31 Bono's wife
32 Join in
34 Overlord
36 Beget
37 Prefix for legal
38 Cupid
39 JFK boomers, once
41 Memorabilia
42 "Just Between Friends" star
46 Misreckon
47 Way out
49 Domicile
50 Conspiracy
51 Decorates the tree
52 Like sumo wrestlers
54 Mosquito genus
56 "After the Thin Man" dog
57 It winds up on watches
58 Garr in "Tootsie"
59 Articulated
60 "Everyone Says I Love You" star
61 Elton John's "In ___"
62 Mark for omission

FLOWER GIRLS   by Jean Peterson
55 Across was first seen in the 1937 cartoon "Porky's Romance."

ACROSS

1 Escalator part
5 Nag
10 Sixth-day creation
14 Hem length
15 Faux pas
16 Large hall
17 Stage direction
18 Dorothy, to Em
19 Old Thailand
20 Edith Ann's alter ego
22 Ab ___ (absent)
23 Tokyo Big Board: Abbr.
24 Mineral
25 Dot on a map
27 "TV Guide" abbr.
28 Jack salmon
30 "___ for Deadbeat": Grafton
33 Golfer Pavin
36 Witchy meeting
37 Party game
38 Heckelphone kin
39 Gentled
40 Off-white
41 Cocteau's "___ Enfants Terribles"
42 Playwright Shaffer
43 Hillbilly
44 Cyclops feature
45 New York City river
46 French negative
47 Kenneth in "Young Frankenstein"
49 Semi
50 Thonon-les-Bains, e.g.
53 Blackleg
55 Warner Bros. character
59 Mystique
60 Cape worn by Pius V
61 Its finger is fickle
62 Sand
63 Furry swimmer
64 Eisenberg of Nog fame
65 "What is most like ___ in May?": Carroll
66 Demands
67 Flat fee

DOWN

1 Silvery fish
2 De Palma dispatches
3 Philip Nolan, e.g.
4 "___ the fool!": Mr. T
5 Lady of Spain
6 Infraction
7 Pitcher Hershiser
8 Places
9 Soaked
10 Resource
11 Disney character
12 "Ah, me!"
13 Rosalind Russell role
21 Belch in "Twelfth Night"
26 Conductor Marin
27 Caddie's handout
28 "Deep Impact" threat
29 CB word
31 Concerning
32 Faust sold his
33 Drummer Cozy
34 Toe the line
35 "The Dick Van Dyke Show" actress
36 Old Deuteronomy's musical
39 About 5 milliliters
40 Years on end
42 Part of RPM
43 Hall-of-Famer Berra
46 NFL team, for short
48 Decrease
49 Like legal paper
50 Fifth tire
51 Mountaineer's spike
52 Maxwell Smart, e.g.
53 Grand narrative
54 Hydrant locale
56 Art Deco name of fame
57 "Valley of the Dolls" star
58 Light-years away

47 A+ by Michele Sayer
Excellent clues and wordplay.

ACROSS

1 Rounds
5 Ninth MLB commissioner
10 Detente
14 British chap
15 Antonio Banderas film
16 ___ Hashanah
17 Presque Isle's lake
18 "Air Music" composer
19 Modicum
20 Notify an Olympian about a Joel hit?
23 Ending for Louis
24 Chaney in "The Monster"
25 "La Pucelle d'Orleans"
28 First Biblical book
32 Formed a sphere
33 Practice in the ring
35 Play about Capote
36 Equine trainer with a low, rough voice?
40 Who the CIA reports to
41 Quarterback Lomax
42 Woody vine
43 Shore
46 Winter DPW truck
47 F. ___ Bailey
48 Some volleyball hits
49 Skybox VIP?
57 Old maid, for one
58 Skyscraper support
59 NE Nevada city
60 "Where's Daddy" playwright
61 "No problemo!"
62 "___ Love": Beatles
63 Aviation pioneer Sikorsky
64 "The Merrymakers" painter
65 It's strictly taboo

DOWN

1 Help a perp
2 Scant
3 Flexible armor
4 Youngman joke
5 Pacific
6 Portuguese city
7 Modena money
8 White-flowering shrub
9 Casino clientele
10 Three in one
11 Cowboy Gibson
12 Cold duck's kin
13 One of the five W's
21 Four-H Club "H"
22 Suffix for ball
25 "Weeping Women" painter
26 Irregularly edged
27 Banana fiber
28 Author Sheehy
29 Ma's cello is one
30 Bedard in "Pocahontas"
31 More certain
33 ___ 'Pea of "Popeye"
34 Sorority letter
37 Indigenes
38 Beetle Bailey's buddy
39 Doc Brown's dog
44 Maddux pitch
45 Front finisher
46 Homily
48 "The Maltese Falcon" sleuth
49 Early third-century date
50 Put up a picture
51 Golden Fleece carrier
52 Blind as ___
53 Branta sandwicensis
54 "Men in Trees" setting
55 Comparable
56 Kissing disease

48 MELTDOWNS   by Eva Finney
The first word in the poem at 15 Across is "wrath."

ACROSS

1 Litmus reddener
5 Destiny
10 Pakistani language
14 Pigeonhole
15 Poem of 16,000 lines
16 Daybreak
17 Treble ___
18 Gray in "La Parisienne"
19 No-___ mutual fund
20 John Steinbeck work
22 Cha-cha cousin
23 Canary or teal
24 Hellenic T
25 Like a wasp nest
28 In a precarious situation
32 Demilitarize
33 Break down
36 "___ Blue?"
37 Stones
38 Got wind of
39 Blowout
40 Native suffix
41 Aunt Em's husband
42 Relentless attack
43 Reykjavik resident
45 Safari member
46 Prime ___
47 Gussy up
49 Speed gun
52 Summertime treat
56 Norwegian king
57 Highest Alpine peak
58 With who or whom
59 Use a bolter
60 Slow, musically
61 Homophone of urn
62 Millinery
63 Bus fare
64 Blackthorn fruit

DOWN

1 Sacramento arena
2 Young whale
3 Newsbreak
4 Graffiti artists
5 Generously responsive
6 "King of the Hill" beer brand
7 Equestrian
8 Street name
9 Ohio Northern U. site
10 It's found in Köln
11 Latitude
12 Dun-colored
13 Loosen
21 Comic Crosby
22 Umpteen
24 Frog relative
25 Learner
26 Singer Baker
27 Eucharist holder
29 Czech coin
30 Public-relations concern
31 Saltpeter
33 Cozy room
34 Vase handle
35 Lament
38 Trumpeter Alpert
39 They have showers
41 Beneficiary
42 Have the look of
44 Bar orders
45 Hill of Boston
47 Shenanigan
48 French annuity
49 ___ Hashanah
50 Suffix for Saturn
51 Balmy
52 "Pinocchio" goldfish
53 Track shape
54 Dr. in "Sleeper"
55 Homophone of urn
57 PBJ alternative

49 TOUCHDOWNS by Don Law

34-D was given the Skytrax Best Airport of the Year Award in 2006.

ACROSS

1 Refuge for strays
5 Scuffle
10 Black, to bards
14 Show concern
15 "Without a Clue" star
16 Confront
17 Psyche's lover
18 Braeden's "Titanic" role
19 Belarussian, e.g.
20 City served by Louis Armstrong
22 Sicilian volcano
23 Dakota dwelling
24 Large tangelo
26 Powers that be
27 Shoot the breeze
29 Moonstruck
32 Syrian president
35 Pool adjunct
36 Mouths
37 Briny deep
38 Remove an imperial
39 Palavering palomino
40 Motel
41 Horrify
42 Candy man
43 Sink down
44 Fuss and feathers
45 Tarnish
46 Adjoin
48 Egg on
52 Masking ___
54 City served by Bob Hope
58 Taj Mahal machine
59 Brotherly love
60 "___ Worry, Be Happy"
61 Rhine tributary
62 "When pigs fly!"
63 Bacchanal cry
64 Kampuchean coin
65 Feats of derring-do
66 Like the Gobi

DOWN

1 Patchouli, e.g.
2 Cole Porter song
3 "Cinderella Man" star
4 Like "The Fox and the Grapes"
5 Libra
6 Instance
7 Poet Dove
8 By and by
9 Coax
10 Ford fiasco
11 City served by Thurgood Marshall
12 North African port
13 St. Petersburg river
21 Tear in two
25 It merged into Verizon
27 Mild cigar
28 Drones drone here
30 God worshiped in Athens
31 Miami county
32 "Lucky Jim" author
33 Yemen capital
34 City served by Changi
35 Planking fish
38 Prestwick Airport locale
39 Ruehl in "Frasier"
41 Early Beatle Sutcliffe
42 Buzzed
45 El Paso team
47 Chewable leaf
49 "___ Lucy"
50 Kind of sax
51 Coco's colleague
52 Potentate
53 Kirghizian range
55 Curved molding
56 Salvage
57 Mocked

50 POLYNESIAN PARADISE   by Michele Sayer
A recent vacation to the Big Island inspired this theme.

ACROSS

1 Jean in "Arsenic and Old Lace"
6 French mushroom
10 Annie Oakley
14 John Lennon, by birth
15 John of "Men in Trees"
16 Monumental
17 Food-bearing tree of Hawaii
19 It flows past Pisa
20 Potent ending
21 Followers of Jackson
22 Gilbert of fashion
24 Ernst's movement
25 Songwriter Greenwich
26 Dick Grayson alias
29 Pepe le Moko's hangout
33 Copy editors' list
35 World's largest volcano
39 Fabric joint
40 LeVar Burton TV classic
42 Rhine tributary
43 Kapiolani Park locale
45 Tasmanian capital
47 Frisco team
49 Lotharios
50 Showy blooms
53 Jan. or Feb., e.g.
55 Phylicia of "Cosby"
57 Morales of "Vanished"
58 Ben Affleck, by birth
61 Room opener
62 Colorful Hawaiian attire
65 Hawaiian banana plant
66 Hawaiian goose
67 West Indian magic
68 Attention
69 Letter sealer
70 In vain

DOWN

1 ___ Longa
2 Flower bed
3 "One clover, and ___ . . .": Dickinson
4 It can be rolled over

5 Jubilant
6 Carson role
7 Tall birds
8 Luau dish
9 Spanish pronoun
10 2001 Josh Hartnett film
11 Showery month
12 Mount in Exodus
13 Tea biscuit
18 It's all the craze
23 Cain in "Lois & Clark"
24 Oahu landmark
26 Hebrew letter
27 Nabisco cookie
28 Healthy muffin
30 ___-propre (self-esteem)
31 Was a jurist
32 Blueberry, for one
34 ___ for one's money
36 Where poi is popular
37 River to the Elbe
38 Song and dance
41 Fronton cheer
44 Dr. Cuddy of "House"
46 "Only the Lonely" singer
48 Cummerbunds
50 "Midnight Blue" singer Lou
51 Smallest Hawaiian island
52 "Rudy" star
54 Meadow bleat
56 Like some basements
57 Twelfth of never?
58 Homophone of Lou
59 Elizabethan and Victorian
60 Will-___-wisp
63 Muumuu accessory
64 Cinemax brother

51 HOLLYWOOD LEGEND by Peggy O'Shea
A salute to two-time Academy Award winner Bette Davis.

ACROSS

1 Street in NYC's Chinatown
5 French WW2 battle site
9 Flash
12 Edible fish
13 Artemis' blood
14 100m race
15 Scrabble piece
16 Lerner's partner
17 Mrs. Charles Laughton
18 Abbadon
19 Eye
20 Fall pile
22 Reverse
25 "Lust for Life" author
26 South Carolina river
29 Tralee citizens
31 Raise the spirits
32 Harem rooms
33 Mezzo Borodina
37 Count's counterpart
38 Vertical
39 Busy time at Wendy's
40 Duke coach Krzyzewski
41 Delicate
42 High-end fiddle
43 "El Amor Brujo" composer
45 Society Islands island
46 Statesman Thurmond
49 Come forth
51 Nathan Lane film
53 Summer along the Seine
54 Kiara's den mother
58 Best review
59 Bits for a salad
61 "And while ___ the subject . . ."
62 Dice toss
63 Light-colored
64 Northern diver
65 ___ diem
66 Bream and Fernandez
67 "Aphrodite" sculptor

DOWN

1 Former woolly bear
2 Aunt Bee's charge
3 Lanky
4 Where Bette was Regina Giddens
5 Marker
6 Where Bette was Joan Winfield
7 Blue or "Moo!"
8 Cy Young winner Hershiser
9 Volley
10 City WSW of Lünen
11 Chevy in "Three Amigos!"
13 "___ a Parade": Arlen
14 Where Bette was Marie Van Schuyler
21 Start of spring?
23 Miss-named
24 Trueheart's love
26 Give the impression
27 Half a Miami sport
28 Drugbuster
30 Professional suffix
32 Papal cape
34 Actress Singer
35 Hircine ruminant
36 "The King ___" (1956)
38 Blueprint extension
42 Get droopy
44 "What ___ to do?"
45 Fashion
46 Flog
47 Hint
48 Jefferson or Madison
50 Stiff collars
52 Subsides
55 Love, to Juanita
56 Despoil
57 British royal
60 Mel Tormé's fourth wife

52 THE DISTRICT   by Don Law
4 Down is also the locale of the Ronald Reagan Building.

ACROSS

1 Marty McFly's enemy
5 D.C. subway
10 Steeve
14 Plaintiff
15 Ibuprofen targets
16 Robert of "The Sopranos"
17 Coconut, e.g.
18 Ontario river
19 Japan's first capital
20 "Mad About You" star
22 Zeniths
23 Mrs. Gorbachev
24 Mass. statesman Edward
25 "The Departed" won four
28 Auctioned security
30 Prowl about
31 Era of 1913–21
35 "Sugar Lips" trumpeter
36 Feverish
37 Luke Skywalker's wife
38 Jay & The ___
41 Paul of "Lonesome Dove"
42 "___ deal?"
43 Confuse
44 Michael Reagan's father
47 Gaucho's turf
49 Arrange in a row
50 First Family member in 1980
54 Rhames in "RFK"
55 Labrador color
56 Part of the Louisiana Purchase
57 Stuntman Knievel
58 Mushroom caps
59 City near Ta'izz
60 ___ majesté
61 Pitcher Hammaker
62 Feudal bigwig

DOWN

1 43rd President
2 "Aha"
3 Have a hunch
4 Ariel Rios Building locale
5 "Small World" singer
6 Off-whites
7 The Washington Monument locale
8 "Seasons of Love" musical
9 East, in Berlin
10 Site of King's "I Have a Dream" speech
11 Willow relative
12 Shortstop Jeter
13 Take off a disc
21 British stoolie
22 Guthrie in "Roadside Prophets"
24 "___ for Burglar": Grafton
25 Job conditions org.
26 Fat-free milk
27 Dry tobacco
29 Counter offers?
31 "___ Women Want" (2000)
32 Metrical foot
33 Brackish Asian lake
34 Peter's "Six Feet Under" role
39 Cay
40 England's FBI
41 Moon goddess
43 First Lady in 1963
44 Student of Fauré
45 One of Swee'pea's guardians
46 Dressed to the ___
48 School for a jeune homme
50 Made a touchdown
51 Hustle and bustle
52 It holds water
53 Fan dancer Sally
55 Theatrical degree

53 ETONIANS by Linda Finnerty
10 Down's most famous spy was also an Etonian.

ACROSS

1 "Pygmalion" playwright
5 "Baywatch" actress Gena
10 Water-depth measure
14 I, in Ithaca
15 Sardonic remark
16 Pathetic
17 Pack of pennies
18 Like Thor Heyerdahl
19 Serbian river
20 Pal of hop and jump
21 Elway's target
22 Meddle with
24 They're heavily armed
27 Itemizes
28 Ambush
31 Munitions city
33 Fudd in "The Unruly Hare"
34 Gotham endings
35 Where eagles don't fly
39 Varnish base
40 17th Chief Justice of the U.S.
43 La Méditerranée, e.g.
44 Gunfight command
46 Existed
47 Overhead
49 "Mother-___": Ernie K-Doe
51 Dexterous
52 Flagstone stone
55 Environment
57 Etonian poet Edmund (1606–87)
59 Prefix for trust
60 ___ fide (not genuine)
64 Old hag who beat Thor
65 Yosemite photographer Adams
67 Sierra Club founder John
68 Lamb's nom de plume
69 ___ Perilous
70 Heaven on earth
71 Come down hard
72 Gabby in "The Plainsman"
73 Reel thing

DOWN

1 Letter opener
2 Etonian Barrie pirate
3 "Volsunga Saga" king
4 Etonian Prime Minister (1721–42)
5 XC, in Roman numerals
6 Down East college town
7 Etonian Sayers sleuth
8 Some Seles serves
9 Russian denial
10 Etonian author of spy novels
11 Clanton foes
12 Formicary resident
13 Eye drops
23 Grogshop fare
25 Former KISS drummer Eric
26 River to the Rhone
28 Join metal to metal
29 EPA-banned spray
30 Yankee Stadium song
32 2005 Prince hit
34 Letter-shaped bar
36 Herman Melville tale
37 1990 PGA Player of the Year
38 Dwell on
41 Night game fancier
42 "Justine" novelist
45 Etonian Prince of Wales
48 Etonian dandy Beau
50 Before marriage
51 Target areas?
52 Saccharine
53 Berry in "The Program"
54 Holden Caulfield's brother
56 Faithful
58 Sumac effect
61 Honda competitor
62 Jennifer of Kes fame
63 "Rule, Britannia!" composer
66 Long in "Boiler Room"

54 CLOSE ENCOUNTERS by Jean Peterson
Glenn received a Tony for the portrayal in 20 Across.

ACROSS

1 "Porgy and ___"
5 Meek
9 Sherlockian actor Jeremy
14 Toyota sedan
15 Mine approach
16 À la King
17 John Boy's sister
18 Civil disobedience
19 Tough guys
20 Where Glenn was Norma Desmond
23 Sturgeon product
24 Shinto shrine center
25 Cesar in "Ocean's Eleven"
29 Fragrant herb
31 Darling
34 Composer Montemezzi
35 Beach blanket?
36 Jazz-session highlight
37 Where Glenn was Alex Forrest
40 Light haircut
41 Limit
42 Jessica in "King Kong"
43 Baltimore newspaper
44 Beauregard Burnside's wife
45 Rosalynn Smith ___
46 "Poppycock!"
47 Droning beetle
48 Where Glenn was Linda Spector
57 Michael in "Batman Begins"
58 ___-addressed
59 Omnium-gatherum
60 Greenwood's "Oklahoma!" role
61 Westminster gallery
62 Diminutive
63 "The Merrymakers" painter
64 Aquila's appendages
65 Tortilla con carne

DOWN

1 Apiary residents
2 Hosiery shade
3 Leg bone
4 "The ___ of Katie Elder" (1965)
5 Skinny drawing?
6 Reader company
7 "The Farm" painter Joan
8 Rebuke to an assassin
9 Command
10 He told a "Canterbury" tale
11 Bulgarian river
12 Echelon
13 Minister to
21 Documentarian Morris
22 Ronstadt or Wertheimer
25 Rock fissures
26 Harbor on Ishikari Bay
27 Nice morning
28 Jack of westerns
29 Film finish
30 In the matter of
31 Purport
32 Funeral oration
33 Copier cartridge
35 Dam up
36 White dwarf or red giant
38 Stradivari's mentor
39 Bow in "Call Her Savage"
44 Futuristic
45 Mocha, for one
46 Radick of "Ally McBeal"
47 "Luann" character
48 Writes "Happy Birthday"
49 Beer ingredient
50 63,360 inches
51 Dog that starred with Loy and Powell
52 Pond duck
53 Early GM director
54 Mother of Romulus
55 Hayes of "The Mod Squad"
56 Duncan's toy

55 FAMOUS FLORENTINES   by John Hynes
7 Down was a patron of Michelangelo and 4 Down.

ACROSS
1 Vituperate
5 Great grade
10 Somewhat
14 Oklahoma native
15 Ford Field team
16 Nursery word
17 Kissing disease
18 José ___ Olazabal
19 Metallica's guitars
20 Mount Corno's chain
22 Celestial ram
23 Luann's love
24 Estevez in "Men at Work"
25 "300" setting
28 Woody Allen title character
30 Countless mass
31 "The Greatest Generation" author
35 Opening soccer score
36 Stevens of "Pink Shoe Laces" fame
37 Mouse cousin
38 "Boiler Room" star
40 Interdict
41 "___ With a View": Forster
42 Detective Lupin
43 Lee in "Cat Ballou"
46 Result in
48 Figure skater Lutz
49 Robert Louis Stevenson's birthplace
53 "Buddenbrooks" novelist
54 Andrew Lloyd Webber musical
55 "Bye now"
56 ___-a-brac
57 Legal
58 Bellagio's lake
59 Sci-fi magazine of 1978–95
60 Trombone part
61 Author Dinesen

DOWN
1 Pear-shaped tomato
2 Looking down from
3 Actress Skye
4 Florentine Renaissance man
5 Gulch in "The Wizard of Oz"
6 Schroeder's instrument
7 Florentine Renaissance patron
8 Joined, along the Seine
9 Fed. check senders
10 Florentine explorer
11 Kiss-me-Nicholas herb
12 John Hancock Tower architect
13 "Torrismondo" poet
21 Ska guitarist Albert
22 "The Kite Runner" hero
24 North Sea feeder
25 Street blade
26 Georgian seaport
27 Nog player Eisenberg
29 Pianist Gilels
31 ". . . farewell ___ sweet a guest": Shak.
32 Elite beef
33 Colmes of radio
34 Are no longer
36 Richmond of "Van Wilder"
39 Showy June flower
40 Thrash
42 Congenitally attached
43 Cha-cha cousin
44 Civilian's reveille
45 1998 De Niro film
47 Lustrous
49 Vile
50 Rafter rival
51 Vasco da ___
52 Golf goof
54 Scrabble 1-pointers

56 SHOW TUNES by Cindy Lather
Judy Collins received a Grammy for her recording of 4 Down.

ACROSS

1 Woofer's range
5 Stair post
10 Spicy Sichuan sauce
14 Seagirt land
15 Coeur d'___, Idaho
16 Customer
17 Mortgage security
18 Appropriated
19 Ponzi scheme
20 Alan in "The Carpetbaggers"
21 "Lord, is ___?": Matt. 26:22
22 Indolent
24 Dress
27 Wasn't quite oneself?
28 Wall bracket
31 Dry, as Italian wine
33 Persephone's husband
34 Brown or Louise
35 Print preference
39 Liquid asset
40 Bobby Goldsboro hit
41 Kite catcher
42 Stud stake
43 Protective trench
44 Forward
45 Congeals
47 Provocateurs
48 "Nobody Does It Better" singer Simon
51 Jungle doctor
53 Melodic passage
55 It's worn under a chasuble
56 Cuzco Indian
60 "Inspector Gadget" villain
61 Accelerator, for one
63 "Tell me more!"
64 Bristol loc.
65 Gush
66 Put an end to
67 Real followers
68 Bullied
69 Ethnic cuisine

DOWN

1 "Show Boat" song
2 East of the Urals
3 Iditarod racer
4 "A Little Night Music" song
5 Aboriginal
6 Perk up
7 "The King and I" song
8 Compass point
9 Voice of Crimson Chin
10 "The Phantom of the Opera" song (with "The")
11 Tie alternative
12 Hire out
13 Ready for battle
23 'Twixt tic and toe
25 E-7, for one
26 Belief
28 Stray's friend
29 MacGregor, for one
30 Beat the incumbent
32 Low island
34 "Key Largo" gang member
36 Opera conductor Daniel
37 In a glass by itself
38 Turner and Mack
40 Wellness gp.
44 Izmir honorific
46 Fleur-de-___
47 Sauntered
48 Prickly plants
49 Van Gogh painted here
50 Joyful
52 Winged
54 Oily acronym
57 Beery in "Beau Geste"
58 Bubbly beverage
59 Dissenter
62 Bellini's "Giovanni ___"

57 HIGH TEA   by Norman S. Wizer
A good one to solve while having a cuppa.

ACROSS

1 Visa color
5 Corpsman
10 Elbow
14 Mayberry moppet
15 Kind of football
16 Tax
17 Potato-cabbage dish
20 Upshot
21 UPS delivery
22 Epsom ___
26 SOS response
27 Treat for Wallace
33 ___ Baltimore cake
34 Greek salad ingredient
35 Part of TWA
37 Saybrook College resident
38 Middlesex middles
40 EPA-banned spray
41 The brainy bunch
43 Chowder type
44 Fill up
45 Spit-roasted dinner entrée
48 Heart ward: Abbr.
49 "The Little Colonel" of baseball
50 Early calculator
53 "___ Italiano": R. Clooney
57 Scone topping
62 Fabric ending
63 Large sea duck
64 Key
65 Macy's department
66 Place for a cast
67 French site of Norman ruins

DOWN

1 Mongolian desert
2 ASCAP award
3 Ad-___ (wings it)
4 "La Mer" composer
5 W.C.'s "chickadee"
6 Timeline span
7 Vixen's home
8 Pachelbel's "Canon ___"
9 Algiers quarter
10 Despoil
11 "The Third Man" director
12 West Wing office
13 Flood prevention
18 Rachel's sister
19 Silences
23 "That's ___": Sinatra
24 Bunker
25 Satisfied property litigant
27 One of the Studebaker brothers
28 Nurse Adams of "ER"
29 "Ab Fab" character
30 Wine bottle
31 Begin's peace partner
32 Put an ___ (cease)
36 Chevy pickup
38 Mexican resort
39 Plus-size model
42 Aids
44 Common fatty acid
46 Blasphemes
47 Gyrene's org.
50 Economist Smith
51 ___ noire
52 Stratford river
54 Badlands rise
55 Christian in "Batman Begins"
56 Telltale sign
58 Best-seller
59 Rhoda Morgenstern's mom
60 "Andy Capp" cartoonist Smythe
61 Long leader?

MEN OF PEACE   by Pat McCarthy

"Peace is the only battle worth waging." — Albert Camus

ACROSS

1 Hanna-Barbera frame
4 1978 Peace Nobelist
9 It works according to scale
12 U.S. Open winner Dutra
14 Smidgeon
15 Nigerian writer Soyinka
16 Kerry locale
17 Swiss alp
18 Cager Birdsong
19 "Topper" dog
20 Lionized actor?
21 Numbers game
22 Rubén Blades' music
24 The Auld ___
25 Puget Sound port
28 1974 Peace Nobelist
33 "Love & Pride" singer Davis
34 "The Avengers" heroine
35 "The Good Earth" heroine
36 Defensive wall
37 One more time
38 Chill-factor factor
39 Draft-eligible
40 Cooking fat
41 Up and about
42 Burt in "Deliverance"
44 Tricker pitch
45 Like Moselle
46 1983 Liam Neeson film
48 Riverine mammal
51 Almost shut
52 Blemish
56 Anima
57 Flat busted
58 Melange
59 Psychologist Hollingworth
60 Fjord
61 El ___
62 Columbus campus
63 Peace Nobelist Roosevelt
64 "Master Melvin" of baseball

DOWN

1 "Fargo" director
2 Peace Nobelist Wiesel
3 Modena money
4 Designer McCartney
5 Met songs
6 1961 Peace Nobelist
7 Maple genus
8 Thrice: Comb. form
9 1946 Peace Nobelist
10 Got grounded?
11 Cuban coin
13 1993 Peace Nobelist
15 1919 Peace Nobelist
21 Arced throw
23 Physician's org.
24 Radar sweep
25 Small drum
26 Coeur d'___
27 "I Don't Wanna Cry" singer
29 Betwixt
30 Epic of 24 books
31 Thanks, in Bonn
32 Orson Scott Card cycle
34 "By gar!"
37 Supporter
41 Kit and caboodle
43 Bear of a Bruin
44 Pledge
47 Did a croupier's job
48 Nobel Peace Prize site
49 Frostbite targets
50 Moira Shearer's wear
51 "Rosamond" composer
53 A daughter of Zeus
54 "___ No Woman": Four Tops
55 Back the varsity
57 Drill insert

59 COMIC STRIPS by Tim Wagner
Lee Falk (3-D) was also the creator of Mandrake the Magician.

ACROSS

1 Pied Piper's pack
5 Gulag
9 Comic strip orphan
14 Turkish commander
15 Melville book
16 Idle
17 Piqued
18 ___-footed (fleet)
19 Fairy chasers
20 Siestas
21 Russ Myers comic strip
23 Overhead lighting
25 "___ out!"
26 Ullman in "Ready to Wear"
28 "Mein ___" ("Cabaret" song)
30 Droll person
33 Flips one's lid?
34 Spanish cats
35 Personal-ad abbr.
36 Grasshopper's fabled opposite
37 It goes with tea
38 San Diego attraction
39 "___ to Pieces": Cline
40 Cultural center of Italy
41 Boeing product
43 Yvonne or Yvette
44 Suffix for cell
45 First Estate
46 Antique
47 Knight chaser
48 Winsor McCay comic strip
54 Iditarod Trail terminus
57 Strad's sister
58 "For pity's sake!"
59 "Make the most ___"
60 Mickey Mantle's number
61 Regal address
62 "Sounder" director
63 Mixes it up
64 Harold of the comics
65 Suffix with chick

DOWN

1 Drizzle
2 One-time Mogul capital
3 Lee Falk comic strip
4 George Baker comic strip
5 Buckaroo
6 Arabic commander
7 Like early vinyl records
8 Walt Kelly comic strip
9 Bumstead's boss
10 TV studio sign
11 Mrs. Chester A. Arthur
12 Harriet Beecher Stowe book
13 "___ Miracle": Manilow
22 Comedian Cohen
24 Article in "Paris Match"
26 "Up" singer Shania
27 "Only You" singer
28 "I Can't Drive 55" singer Sammy
29 Harrow's cricket foe
30 Parker and Hart comic strip
31 For ___ (cheap)
32 Schmaltzy
34 Big bash
37 "The Happy Prince" author
40 Moon of old comics
41 Mideast org.
42 "Fidelio" heroine
45 Elect
46 Fun-loving mammal
48 Colleen
49 "___ a man who wasn't there . . ."
50 Kipling's "Rikki-tikki-___"
51 Cartoonist who lampooned Tweed
52 Nobelist Wiesel
53 Black Beauty's mom
55 Tiny parasite
56 Feminine suffix

60 SIR MICK AND COMPANY by John M. Samson
Lines from Rolling Stones songs lead to their titles.

ACROSS

1 Tiger Hall-of-Famer
5 Raconteur's repertoire
10 Mail drop
14 Love personified
15 Not together
16 Wilson or Rose
17 NBC late-night host
18 "Gloria" singer Branigan
19 Dog in "Song of the Thin Man"
20 Anne Murray hit
22 "The ___ of Red Chief": O. Henry
24 Pedagogues' org.
25 Gels
27 Clergyman's abode
30 Breaks
35 Right and left
37 Sault ___ Marie Canals
38 Courtney Love's band
39 Super Bowl prize
40 Word of farewell
42 OK city
43 Endoscopic focuses
44 Google search area
45 Spanish specie
47 "CHiPs" star
49 Big Bertha's birthplace
50 Beatles film
52 Romanian vehicle
53 Tiger type
57 Flo's cartoon hubby
62 Suit to ___
63 Ran in place
65 Benson of The Four Tops
66 Horse color
67 Lamblike
68 Emmy winner Kudrow
69 Advance payment
70 Frisco pro
71 "___ Prudence": Beatles

DOWN

1 Ripkin Jr. and Sr.
2 Augury
3 "Time" 2005 Person of the Year
4 **"Gold Coast slave ship . . ."**
5 Shire in "New York Stories"
6 On ___ with (equal)
7 Canonical hour
8 Bobble a grounder
9 **"You make a grown man cry . . ."**
10 About nine inches
11 Fruit finisher
12 Sgt. Snorkel's dog
13 Capitals, for one
21 "___ there, done that"
23 DEA head Hutchinson
26 Spanish direction
27 Chemist Curie
28 Seed cases
29 Work for nine
31 **"I'm so hot for her . . ."**
32 Whets
33 Best of the best
34 Coupe alternative
36 **"Tell me if she laughs or cries . . ."**
37 ___ tight (wait)
41 Trade
46 Out of this world
48 Sherlock's shout
51 "Brazil" star
52 Totalizer
53 Vamp of Hollywood
54 Orwell's alma mater
55 "Super!"
56 Singer Pitney
58 Brazil NBA star
59 Anne Nichols' Levy
60 Tuscany city
61 Bottom-heavy fruit
64 506 on the Appian Way

61 SPOOKY NIGHT by Cindy Lather
Put on your fright wig and start solving.

ACROSS

1 Figure heads?
5 Halloween costume
10 Mars, Greek version
14 Gordon in "Rosemary's Baby"
15 Marc Anthony's "___ Ayer"
16 Camembert source
17 Camp addition
18 "The bombs bursting ___ . . ."
19 Pre-euro coin
20 Halloween costumes
22 "Good Night, and Good Luck" star
24 Chef Lagasse
25 Incorrect
26 Halloween TV viewing (with "The")
33 Mausoleum
36 Straw bundle
37 Perón and Gabor
38 Birthplace of The Boss
39 Unusual
40 It warms up Brie
41 Colorado State team
43 Unreal experience
45 Habituated one
46 Halloween costume
49 Caesar's 98
50 Christmas stealer
54 Halloween costume
58 Halloween costume
59 Plenty
60 Work shift
62 Last words
63 Hal's "A Space Odyssey" nemesis
64 Jungle vine
65 Overflowing
66 Who or whom ender
67 "Father Murphy" actor
68 RFK nine, for short

DOWN

1 "Cinderella Man" star
2 Jewish feast day
3 Tête-___
4 ___ soup (Southern dish)
5 "Suddenly Susan" star
6 Silverstone items
7 Explorer Johnson
8 Auricular
9 Voice of the Grinch
10 1984 Martin/Tomlin film
11 Death Valley rarity
12 Leprechauns' land
13 Match an ante
21 Shrouded
23 Son–gun links
27 "Young Man with ___" (1950)
28 Ancient Persians
29 1978 Peace Nobelist
30 "Summer Magic" star
31 Fashionable, in some circles
32 Belgian river
33 Bailiwick
34 Glacial mounds
35 Remembered one
42 Brandy glass
43 Yvonne of "The Munsters"
44 "You've Got Mail" star
45 Mythical creature
47 Jimmy's "Vertigo" costar
48 "The Boys from Brazil" author Levin
51 Aida's native land
52 Montgomery in "The Misfits"
53 Despises
54 Slosh
55 Regal Norse name
56 Aphrodite's realm
57 Labourite Kinnock
58 Copenhagener
61 West end of Vegas

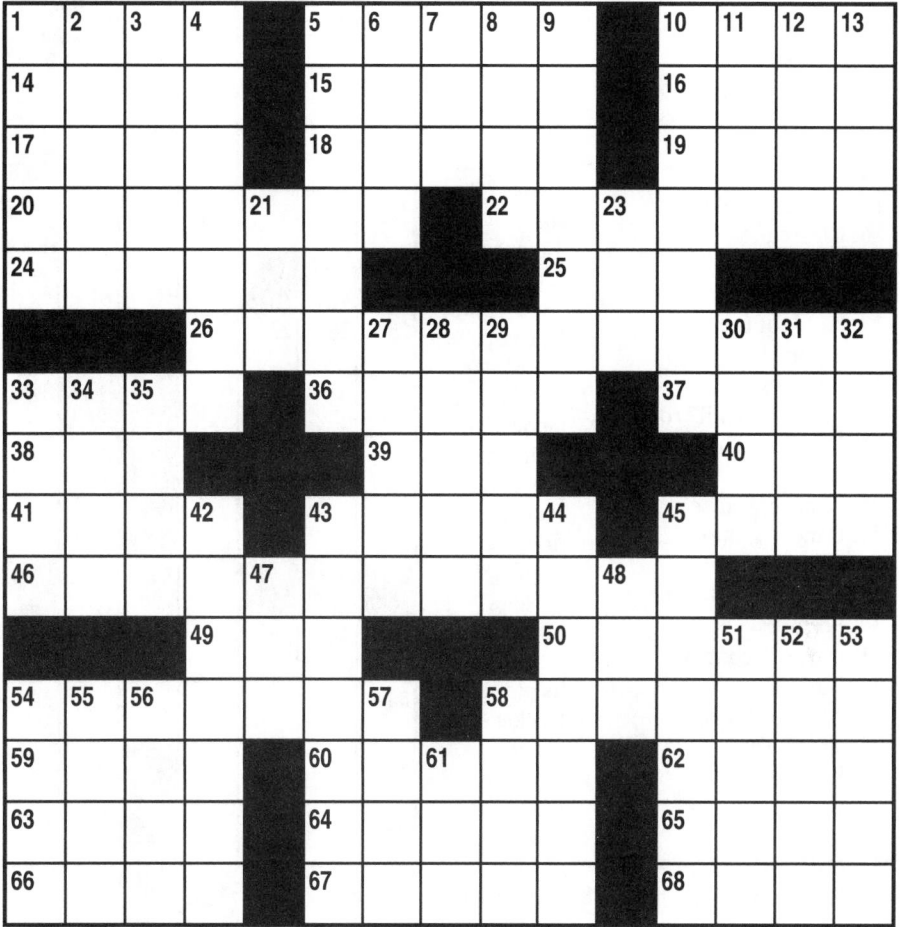

62 STAR TREK STARS   by John M. Samson
"I am not Spock." — Leonard Nimoy

ACROSS

1 Trades
6 ___ adjudicata
9 Server of Duff beer
12 Florid
14 Before
15 Battles royal
16 Cleared
17 Long in "Big Momma's House"
18 Killer of Castor
19 Trapped
20 Increase
22 "The Sea Gull" role
24 Jean Paul Getty et al.
25 "Dance, Dance, Dance" group
28 Fontaine issuance
29 Onassis or Meyers
30 Fortune
31 Bird sacred to Tut
33 Little bit
37 "Amber Waves" singer Tori
38 It happens
39 Luau dress
40 Exited
41 Callao's country
42 Passing yardage, e.g.
43 Crossword worm
45 Writer Tolkien
47 Offended
48 Rodeo workers
51 Russian lake
53 Connect anew
55 Round Table head
59 Ending for cell
60 McKern or Genn
61 Fitness guru Austin
62 Cartoonist Caniff
63 Yalie
64 Like some crackers
65 Dijon dance
66 Gaseous sound
67 Jumper

DOWN

1 Steve Douglas had three
2 St. Paul's Cathedral architect
3 Architectural pier
4 "Star Trek: Nemesis" star
5 Take the tiller
6 "Star Trek: Deep Space Nine" star
7 Discordia's Greek counterpart
8 Maine lure
9 Palindromic title
10 Emulate Pericles
11 Museum Folkwang locale
13 Rocker Van Halen
15 "Star Trek" star
21 Hydroplane support
23 Wet behind the ears
25 Talon
26 Cronyn in "Lifeboat"
27 Revered object
32 Inter
34 South African Nobelist
35 Vizquel of baseball
36 Mongrel
38 Readings in church
44 TLC specialists
46 Turns some pages
48 Mouse's find
49 George Sand novel
50 "___ the nerve!"
52 Deadly sin
54 Vermiform food
56 Whitewash
57 Puts to work
58 Johnny Bench's team

63 AMERICAN AUTHORS   by Jean Peterson
The first names of 7-D & 10-D are James and Newton.

ACROSS

1 Memory unit
5 "American Buffalo" playwright
10 "The ___ Day": George Strait
14 "___ to Perdition" (2002)
15 "Do ___ to eat a peach?": Eliot
16 Wine prefix
17 Wide-eyed
18 "Tender Mercies" heroine
19 Algerian port
20 Forbid
22 "Gulliver's Travels" is one
24 ___ Puffs cereal
26 Joy
27 "An American Dream" author
30 "The Verdict" director
32 "Roots" actor
33 Suffix for Saturn
34 Pequod captain
38 Opera box
39 Shade of blue
40 One-in-a-million
41 San Francisco transport
42 "___ kleine Nachtmusik"
43 Buckeye city
44 Curved
46 Capital of Somme
47 Entertain
50 "Hello Mary Lou" singer
52 U.S. Ambassador to the UN (2005–06)
54 Avoided a pink slip?
58 Poet Bradstreet
59 "Lazy ___ Molly": Chubby Checker
61 Oceanic heave
62 Rip
63 Renaissance instruments
64 Scott Turow book
65 Observes
66 Ferber and O'Brien
67 Hawaiian goose

DOWN

1 Pitt in "Babel"
2 Bear or Berra
3 New Mexican art colony
4 "Spoon River Anthology" author
5 The Divine Miss M
6 Tijuana ta-ta
7 "Key Largo" playwright
8 "___ tu": Verdi aria
9 Giveaway shirts
10 "Penrod" author
11 Spooky
12 Springe
13 Skin conditioner
21 Evil smile
23 Cable award
25 "Mother Goose ___": Ravel
27 Fountain treat
28 Ancient lyre
29 "Young Frankenstein" heroine
31 Whitman in "One Fine Day"
33 "___ Nation" (1988)
35 "Pravda" playwright
36 Johnny Bravo's city
37 Blue and Cross
39 NYSE overseer
43 Mine, in Cannes
45 Classic car
46 Size up
47 Ease off
48 Wherewithal
49 Forearm bones
51 "The Pearl Fishers" heroine
53 2006 Olympic mascot
55 1982 Broadway musical
56 Novelist Phillpotts
57 Take-out sign
60 Ceiling

64 RAT PACKERS by John Hines
The original Rat Pack had Humphrey Bogart as its leader.

ACROSS
1 Blues singer Mahal
4 Like Heidi
9 Boris Godunov, e.g.
13 Langston Hughes poem
15 "Over the Rainbow" ending
16 "She's Leaving ___": Beatles
17 Coffeehouse reader
18 Williams of "Happy Days"
19 "Night" author Wiesel
20 1996 Leslie Nielsen film
22 "Ocean's Eleven" star
24 Telephone inventor
25 Howard Hughes' airlines
26 Rat Pack member MacLaine
29 Second American in space
33 Disarray
34 Earth, in sci-fi stories
36 Elephant's-ear
37 Suffix for sheep
38 "Stained Glass" composer
39 Efface
40 General ___ chicken
42 "___ of One's Own": Woolf
44 Thompson in "Wit"
45 Cleveland airport
47 "When Harry Met Sally . . ." star
49 Hoosier St.
50 Starring role
51 1970 Dean Martin film
55 Palace of Las Vegas
58 Basketball
59 Irish premier De Valera
61 Bacchanal cry
62 Bancroft in "The Graduate"
63 Song from "Rent"
64 "Green Mansions" girl
65 Brown U. mascot
66 Playground sight
67 Sun Yat-___

DOWN
1 Lagniappes
2 At the apex
3 "Ocean's Eleven" star
4 "A Study in ___": Doyle
5 Tinker Bell's holding
6 Electees
7 Converti-plane
8 "Ocean's Eleven" star
9 "___ and the Furious" (2001)
10 Fly alone
11 Prince of Arabia
12 Clarinet, e.g.
14 The rest
21 Whole nine yards
23 "What Price Glory?" setting
26 Bessie of blues
27 "___ Fine": Chiffons
28 Chiliad's 1000
29 "Forrest Gump" author
30 "Ocean's Eleven" star
31 Suffix for pan
32 Capone rival Bugs
35 Greek P
41 Gilligan's friend
42 "Thoroughly Modern Millie" star
43 Sporty Spice
44 Puzzler's need
46 She saved Odysseus
48 "Well, I'll be!"
51 Daggoo's captain
52 Skye in "Moonglow"
53 Ellen ___ Barkin
54 Shadow
55 Frigophobiac's fear
56 "Lady in Cement" sleuth
57 Irish "John"
60 Year in Henry III's reign

65 NYC by Peggy O'Shea

4-D was named one of the Seven Wonders of the Modern World.

ACROSS

1 Rob in "St. Elmo's Fire"
5 McNabb aerial
9 Pharmacy stock
14 Saroyan protagonist
15 "Dream Girl" sculptor
16 Ishmael's half-brother
17 Sharp bark
18 Wizard center Thomas
19 Schumann study
20 Sun: Comb. form
21 "Three's Company" star
23 "Even Stevens" sister
24 L. Berkman's alma mater
26 Gallery
28 John who plays Q
31 A real stand-up guy?
33 Phar Lap, for one
34 Elder penguin in "Happy Feet"
35 Kind of sleep
39 Pontificate
40 Terrarium creature
41 Source of some fliers
42 Animal-rights org.
43 Thumbelina almost married one
44 "Kiss From ___": Seal
45 Alvarado in "The Babe"
47 Rena Inoue, for one
48 See 3 Down
51 Chewable leaf
53 Mysterious Fleming agent
54 Wright in "The Little Foxes"
56 Early days
60 Eloise's home
62 Formerly, of old
63 Short-stemmed succulent
64 Irate
65 What it ends with?
66 Sideline shouts
67 Step
68 Redgrave in "Spider"
69 Nautical speed

DOWN

1 Potato-chip brand
2 Creme-filled cookie
3 NYSE home (with 48-A)
4 Art Deco building of Fifth Avenue
5 Met tenor Jan
6 Chef on "The Sopranos"
7 Gift from France in 1886
8 Dispatched
9 One of the Curies
10 Ego ending
11 Julianne in "The Hours"
12 Packed a mule
13 Panorama
22 A pop
25 Understanding words
27 Belvedere Castle locale
28 Hew
29 Traditional knowledge
30 Quod ___ faciendum
32 Final check
34 Broadway luminary
36 Get growing
37 Highlands language
38 Painter Jan van der ___
41 Nihonshu
43 Dab
46 Record over
47 ___ Island Ferry
48 NYU group
49 Realty sign
50 Roundup rope
52 Germany's Pittsburgh
55 True
57 Alda or Arkin
58 Greenwich Village neighbor
59 New York Regents, e.g.
61 Swiss lake

66 JAZZ GREATS by Linda Finnerty
4 Down first achieved fame as a trumpeter.

ACROSS

1 Lake larger than Huron
5 Archetype
10 Former British Airways jet
13 Tryout tape
14 Lamblike
15 Whaler's adverb
16 Omar's "father"
17 Irene in "Me, Myself & Irene"
18 Sharpen
19 "Naughty" operetta heroine
21 Gets out a knot
23 They take their time
25 Jazz pianist Marsalis
26 "Take the ___": Ellington
29 Elusive Handford character
31 James Bond actor
32 Batman actor
33 Inches away
37 Soft cheese
38 Legionnaire Beau
39 Lund in "Casablanca"
40 Boys, to men
41 Shea shouts
42 Wise lawgiver
43 Country singer Clark
45 Little mouse?
46 First Super Bowl MVP
49 "Undisputed" star
51 "True ___": Lauper
53 Prince's awards
57 Viking war god
58 Made a choice
60 Ibsen Festival city
61 Singer k.d.
62 "___ in the place, except . . ."
63 Patricia of "Cookie's Fortune"
64 Gallein, e.g.
65 They provide inheritance
66 Bellagio game

DOWN

1 Man not born of woman
2 Singer McEntire
3 Cupid
4 "Heebie Jeebies" scatter
5 "Jelly Roll" of jazz
6 1980 Olympic track star
7 "Queen of the Blues"
8 Rome-Tivoli dir.
9 Onion relative
10 Sea school
11 Scottish singer Thom
12 Keyless lock
15 Bop pioneer
20 Fashion designer Saab
22 Jimbo's friend on "South Park"
24 Deices a road
26 "Rag Mop" brothers
27 "Don't Tell Me What ___": Tillis
28 Imitation morocco
30 Grant in "Plaza Suite"
32 Chicago team
34 Scat queen Fitzgerald
35 Ancient instrument
36 Diatribe
38 Rottweiler warning
42 Arrest
44 Boot one
45 Black suit
46 Reprimand
47 "Who's on First?" catcher
48 Flare-bottomed skirt
50 "Green Acres" cow
52 Ditty
54 "So that's it"
55 Joie de vivre
56 Duet for one?
59 "The Bells" poet

67

AMERICAN THEATER by Jean Peterson
A classic Humphrey Bogart movie is based on 44 Across.

ACROSS

1 Fashionable
5 According to Hoyle
10 Maggie Sheffield's nanny
14 "Oxford Blues" heroine
15 In harmony
16 Location of some Swiss banks
17 Cuckoopint
18 Edward Albee play
20 Raipur wrap
21 The other woman
22 "___ a Letter to My Love" (1981)
23 Like Heidi Klum
25 Business agent
27 Dugout equipment
28 Edward Albee play
33 Room mate
36 Staying power
37 Knoll
38 Having the wherewithal
39 Mum
40 "Madam, I'm ___"
41 Gaylord Ravenal's love
42 Kon-Tiki worshiper
43 Unlocks
44 Maxwell Anderson play
46 Russian Blue or Havana Brown
47 Name separator
48 Seconds have these
52 Shoptalk
56 Sleep phase
57 Emu relative
58 Donald L. Coburn play
61 Taste
62 Michelle's mother
63 Hormel product
64 In the know
65 Beginning of time?
66 James Bond, for one
67 Exceptional item

DOWN

1 Oafish
2 Hourly
3 Get tough
4 Tennessee Williams play
5 Dither
6 Old number?
7 Attendee
8 Successful pols
9 Darjeeling export
10 Goldfish swallowing et al.
11 "Boom Boom Room" playwright
12 "Star Trek" actor Eisenberg
13 Word to the queue
19 Beats at the buzzer
24 Pater
25 Aqua ___
26 Needle point?
28 Plaster work
29 Neil Simon play
30 Lieutenant
31 Schematize
32 Tall trees
33 John Ashley target
34 Double-reed woodwind
35 Colleague
36 Jessica in "Frances"
39 Monster truck "monster"
43 Lummox
45 Protest marcher
46 Dam material
48 Succubus
49 Kind of letter
50 Ready to snap
51 "When I Need You" lyricist
52 Unpaid tellers
53 Flow: Comb. form
54 Pathogen
55 S-shaped molding
56 Le Mans event
59 Carmelo Anthony's org.
60 Suppress

ACROSS

1 QB George
5 Moles
10 Susiana
14 Mixed bag
15 "Network" director
16 Legends
17 "Sleeping Murder" sleuth
19 French cathedral city
20 "A Chorus Line" number
21 Devotees
22 "___ Stand By"
24 Away from aweather
25 "The Thin Man" sleuth
26 Inviolate
29 Like caramels
30 It's as good as a mile
31 Biggers sleuth
32 Muslim judge
36 Small hawk
37 Cocteau's "___ Enfants Terribles"
38 ___ Bator
39 Garden snake locale?
40 Main church area
41 English model Beverly
42 Brown corundum
44 Arguello of boxing
45 "The Long Goodbye" sleuth
48 Oat husk
49 Loves, in the Louvre
50 Agapemone, e.g.
51 Computer key
54 Caper
55 "I, the Jury" sleuth
58 Kyrgyzstan range
59 Mother of Idas
60 Like some straits
61 Knoxville loc.
62 Not as old
63 Like molasses in January

DOWN

1 Olympic skater Starbuck
2 Vigor
3 Topflight
4 Word in a sentry's question
5 On the docket
6 Reduce to mush
7 Holy terrors
8 Sargasso Sea denizen
9 Physicist Hawking
10 "Cat of Many Tails" sleuth
11 Unswerving
12 "Mighty Lak' ___"
13 First Egyptian king
18 Dr. McCabe on "Medical Investigation"
23 Matlock's purview
24 "813" master thief
25 See 29 Down
26 Tempura aperitif
27 Surrounded by
28 Instance
29 "Fletch" star (with 25-D)
31 Journalist Boothe Luce
33 "Fatal Attraction" psycho
34 "Galatea" artist
35 Spanish model Sastre
40 Clark Kent, e.g.
41 Buenos Aires river
43 Hungarian painter Than
44 Zodiac figure
45 Tennis star Safin
46 Soap plant
47 "Rosemary's Baby" director Polanksi
48 Clothier Geoffrey
50 Wood chisel
51 Jannings in "Quo Vadis"
52 Sleuth Wolfe
53 Teenage sleuth Nancy
56 Fury
57 OR workers

69 "ERIN GO BRAGH!"   by Danny Touse
Wear green when you solve this one.

ACROSS

1 Melodramatic cry
5 Friend of Vera Charles
9 Goodyear's home
14 Geoffrey in "Munich"
15 Islands off Galway
16 Yellowish-brown
17 Internet's ___ Vista
18 "You Don't Own Me" singer
19 "___ Thief" (1965)
20 Drink for stout-hearted men?
22 Carroll O'Connor role
23 Ted Williams' number
24 Stirrup, for one
25 Not quite
28 Irish friendship ring
32 Eight bells
33 Where the world is flat
35 Edward Norton's alma mater
36 Sushi fish
37 Saw print
38 Sen fraction
39 Raison d'___
41 Hooded jacket
43 Seat in court
44 Symbol of Eire
46 Cut, in a sense
48 Wriggly
49 Flynn Boyle of films
50 Place for a bronco
53 Edward Lear poem
57 Ryan in "Barry Lyndon"
58 Emmy winner Ward
59 Wife of James Joyce
60 Sam in "Jurassic Park"
61 "The Circus Fire" author
62 Pitcher of puzzles
63 "Grease" heroine
64 Covenant
65 Two-master

DOWN

1 Limp as ___
2 "Oh Me Oh My" singer
3 Italian wine commune
4 Ireland's longest river
5 Orchid color
6 Got up
7 Love of Venus
8 Helm heading
9 Teem
10 Irish-American President
11 Basketball coach Pitino
12 Double curve
13 Proximal
21 Grafton's "___ for Noose"
22 Roaring Twenties wear
24 Poker-faced
25 Deal prerequisites
26 Reluctant
27 Kelly who voiced Nala
28 Gable of moviedom
29 City W of Zurich
30 Glitter
31 Thus
34 Spencer in "Tortilla Flat"
40 ___ Isle
41 John Zogby specialty
42 Uncompromising
43 Castle near Cork
45 Certainly
47 Dander
49 Lavender
50 Pros and ___
51 Draft status
52 Pull back
53 Olin in "Mystery Men"
54 "Field of Dreams" setting
55 Shell team
56 Malden in "On the Waterfront"
58 Conciliatory gift

70 " 'TIS THE SEASON"   by Cindy Lather
4 Down also appeared in a 1954 seasonal classic.

ACROSS

1 Tragic king
5 Rake over the coals
10 "Bewitched" director Ephron
14 Voice from a loft
15 Tati's "Mon ___" (1958)
16 Orenburg's river
17 Exchange ___ (tie the knot)
18 "Borstal Boy" author
19 Domestic
20 North Carolina river
22 "Star Trek: Voyager" hologram
24 Swordfish relative
26 Council town of Italy
27 "The Maltese Falcon" star
30 Grinch's disguise
32 Startle
33 Conductor Klemperer
34 Crowd
38 Put trust in
39 Jazz trumpeter Ziggy
40 Sky box?
41 Spa powder
42 Tel Aviv transport
43 Authorized
44 Falana and Albright
46 Announce
47 Flatten
50 Reconnoiters
52 Outlook Express rival
54 Give play-by-play
58 Opposed, to Elly May
59 Soft cap
61 Joe Hardy's girl
62 Closeout
63 Show feelings
64 Sound from Harpo
65 Long basket
66 Sorrow
67 "China Roses" singer

DOWN

1 Of the flock
2 Valencian footwear city
3 Astride
4 "Suzy Snowflake" singer
5 Humorist Benchley
6 Ryan in "What's Up Doc?"
7 Charles Dickens classic
8 Hearst kidnapping gp.
9 Watch
10 Tchaikovsky ballet
11 Spout off
12 Happy Feet's friend
13 On one's toes
21 Growing business
23 Giant outfielder
25 Of birth
27 Homer and Marge's son
28 Latin olive
29 Nerve
31 Eatery section
33 Spicy stews
35 Latvian capital
36 Ubiquitous abbr.
37 Dyer's rocket
39 Bioelectric fish
43 Apollo's mother
45 "Catch-22" pilot
46 One in a stand
47 Luau, e.g.
48 Hoosier statesman
49 "Swan Lake" villainess
51 "It takes ___ know one!"
53 Retired for the night
55 Meridian hour
56 Sate
57 "Do I dare to ___ peach?": Eliot
60 Philips of "UHF"

71 DIVAS   by John Hynes
Could Mick Jagger or Warren Beatty be the vain one in 20-A?

ACROSS

1 "___ unto my feet": Psalms 119:105
6 Jack in "The Way West"
10 Dalmatian name
14 City near Joplin
15 Phonograph record
16 ___ passu (side by side)
17 Harrisburg suburb
18 First blank on a check
19 Felt sorrow for
20 "You're So Vain" singer
22 Macpherson in "Sirens"
23 Sneaker width
24 TV's "___-Team"
26 Rhea's planet
30 Calliope's sister
32 Epitome of ease
35 Claude of "Lobo"
36 Seaboard
37 Poor reception?
38 Prong
39 Quick pass from Manning
40 Biblical country
41 "This ___ fine mess . . ."
42 Threefold
43 Crow
44 Body-shop fig.
45 Current measure
46 Oscar winner Matlin
47 Informed about
49 Jackson of "Men in Trees"
50 Louisiana vegetable
52 "Us" singer
59 Car mar
60 Music halls
61 Three-striper
62 Till fill
63 Teen fave
64 Lilliputian
65 Golfer Sabbatini
66 Electronics giant
67 Sierra Club patron Adams

DOWN

1 McCowen in "Gangs of New York"
2 Superboy's girlfriend
3 Love, in Madrid
4 Shopping complex
5 Devotions
6 Monsoon of "Ab Fab"
7 Neeson in "Ethan Frome"
8 In the matter of
9 "Queen of Country" Reba
10 Indulgent spell
11 "My Love Is For Real" singer
12 City founded by Ivan IV
13 It rises and falls
21 B. Boxer, for one
25 Clod-breaker
26 Les Six composer
27 "Sealed With ___": Gary Lewis
28 "Private Dancer" singer
29 That's one for François
30 War dance accompaniment
31 Data's brother
33 Famed frontiersman
34 "Positivism" pioneer
36 Rip
39 Composer Couperin
40 Listener's loan
42 Ark limit
43 Redgrave in "Camelot"
46 Sadie Hawkins Day catches
48 "Absolutely Fabulous" heroine
49 Onion roll
50 Annoying smell
51 1–90 numbers game
53 Taro root
54 "Topaz" author Uris
55 "Greenback Dollar" expletive
56 Pension rollovers
57 Fix, visually
58 Actress Carter

72 THE DUKE by Effie Pelifian
John Wayne received a Best Actor Oscar for the role of 14-D.

ACROSS
1 Misfield
4 Afterward
9 What this isn't?
13 Coequal
15 Poet's inspiration
16 Beau ideal
17 Logical beginning
18 Marner of Raveloe
19 Logan of Broadway
20 Gargantuan
22 Rockies' raptors
24 Postcard-pretty
26 Orchard nightmare
27 Olive Oyl's sister
30 "Simpatico" star
32 Medieval hard hat?
33 French city
34 Jeremy Brett's alma mater
38 Berth place
39 Christine of "Jack & Bobby"
40 "Fat chance!"
41 Baldwin of "Elizabethtown"
42 Simians
43 Li'l Dogpatch denizen
44 Pastiches
46 Rivera mural
47 Dramatize
50 Long sword
52 Portugal's cultural hub
54 Ballerina
58 Words to a backstabber
59 Wrestling giant
61 Pinehurst sand
62 "___ Lap" (1983)
63 Serbian tennis star
64 Hypotenuse, for example
65 Sea swallow
66 Aviary sound
67 Diocese

DOWN
1 Momentous
2 Emend entirely
3 Move unsteadily
4 Len of "Seinfeld"
5 Suffix for sect
6 1944 John Wayne and Ella Raines film
7 Grand Central abbr.
8 Stage mom in "Gypsy"
9 1968 John Wayne and David Janssen film
10 "Anybody home?"
11 French arena city
12 Clink glasses
14 "True Grit" protagonist
21 Fellow from Fife
23 Astern
25 Super Bowl XLI winners
27 Matador's cloak
28 Nutmeg appendage
29 A foe of Pan
31 Le Havre law
33 Flavor
35 Plenty
36 Oil cartel
37 "Gambit" sleuth
39 Medieval lyric poem
43 Thebes deity
45 "Seinfeld" uncle
46 Best
47 Lay dormant
48 Give on Sunday
49 "Swinging On ___": 1944 hit
51 1929 Porter hit
53 He published "Vogue"
55 "Redemption" author
56 "The Sweetest Gift" singer
57 Sword with a bell
60 Neoteric

73 PAINTERS by John Hynes

John Leguizamo portrays 7 Down in the film "Moulin Rouge!"

ACROSS

1 Bard
5 Pakistan instrument
10 Studio effect
14 Hold dear
15 Pay the penalty
16 Siberian river
17 Mine access
18 Frighten
19 2003 Spacey role
20 Horsehide
22 "Fur" director Shainberg
24 Measure out
26 Like noble gases
27 Hens' pens
30 Knight's thigh protector
32 Shocked
34 Wimbledon unit
35 Enterprise level
39 Seat of the Inca Empire
40 Fred Astaire's sister
42 Epochal
43 Yukon river
44 A thousand thou
45 Attentive
47 Echo
50 Butter the Butterball
51 Tangled
54 Altaic language group
56 Lilt
58 Broad-minded
62 Cremona craft
63 Wrists
65 Gabon president Bongo
66 Mouse target
67 "___ a Million" (1956 hit)
68 Bulwer-Lytton heroine
69 Supermodels, e.g.
70 City in the "heel" of Italy
71 Radiotherapy beam

DOWN

1 Meat-loaf serving
2 Song finale
3 Broadtail genus
4 "Three Graces" painter
5 Camp David Accords figure
6 Slanted type
7 "At the Moulin Rouge" painter
8 Fay in "King Kong"
9 Soaks flax
10 "The Massacre at Chios" painter
11 Hanker after
12 Czech coin
13 Scented
21 Spiny-finned fish
23 Sit back?
25 Violinist Gow
27 Honest Abe's creator
28 S-curve
29 Czech river
31 Part of the procedure
33 Pack tightly
36 Greek Bellona
37 Carrie Chapman ___
38 "Legend of the Nile" artist
41 Lose a spare tire
46 Award for "Pterodactyls"
48 Bracket shape
49 Line around the globe
51 Thumb-twiddle
52 Feydeau play
53 "Loot" playwright
55 Kevin in "De-Lovely"
57 Earth sci.
59 Son of Venus
60 Visitor in "Deep Space 9"
61 Triple-pipped card
64 Brittany burro

74 ANTIHEROES   by Richard Drumm
Identify the novel with its antihero (clued in caps).

ACROSS

1 "Le Freak" genre
6 Arab mother
10 Three-spot
14 Epitome
15 Shortly
16 Chinese calendar animal
17 "Giant" ranch
18 Yawn
19 Sicilian spa
20 After-shower powder
21 "The Last ___ I Saw Paris"
22 Athirst
23 Therefore
25 ___ gratia artis
26 PTA member
29 Summarized
34 Advisory
35 "Corydon" essayist
36 Art Deco designer
37 Collette in "Little Miss Sunshine"
38 Sped
39 German valley
40 Snow-goose genus
41 Algerian port
42 Ashley Wilkes' sister
43 Mayflower
45 Viewpoint
46 Easter entrée
47 Kishke
49 Make merry
52 Author Harte
53 High-priced spread
57 Sharif in "Hidalgo"
58 Gaze
59 Hawk nest
60 Unctuous
61 Kirghizian range
62 Angling basket
63 Gratis
64 Docile
65 Romanov rulers

DOWN

1 Hoover target?
2 Impression
3 "Kiss From a Rose" singer
4 HOLDEN CAULFIELD (with "The")
5 Bunyan biographer Winslow
6 Copperfield's forte
7 STEPHEN ROJACK
8 "Clue" murder weapon
9 Tampa-Lakeland direction
10 NAMELESS NARRATOR
11 Buzzed
12 Coastal eagle
13 One Earth orbit
21 High explosive
22 MLB stat
24 Tolkien forest giant
25 Got a hole-in-one
26 Stop-smoking aid
27 Island greeting
28 Rejuvenate
30 Heaven on earth
31 Prissy one
32 System of morals
33 Rid of rodents
35 Teri in "Young Frankenstein"
38 Chat area
42 Doctrine
44 Hotspur's slayer
45 "What Is ___?": Tolstoy
48 Out of this world
49 Mouth part
50 Qatar ruler
51 Dale
52 Composer Bartók
54 Field
55 Floor
56 Stork's supper
58 Bit of butter
59 "Ile" has one

75 NO THREES by John M. Samson
An unthemed challenge devoid of three-letter words.

ACROSS

1 Karl Malden TV series
5 Hillside
10 Explosive sound
14 Delicious discard
15 Russian river
16 Drag
17 Look the other way
18 St. Theresa's town
19 Auxiliary
20 Elbert Hubbard essay (with "A")
23 Madrid crowd
24 Soccer org.
25 MIT units of length
28 Go downhill
32 "Look Homeward, Angel" author
33 Clubs
34 Wal-Mart rival
35 Endor furballs
36 1981 Tom Cruise film
37 Martinet's trait
39 Sporty Chevy, for short
40 Not a friend of Flicka
41 Kurt of Nirvana
42 Chinese weight
43 Legatee
44 Stadium giveaways
51 Square mileage stat
52 "Lost in Yonkers" aunt
53 It's driven
54 "Phooey!"
55 2 Down, for one
56 Sushi fish
57 Something ___
58 "Lest we lose our ___": Browning
59 Skittish

DOWN

1 Cheat
2 Cager Bryant
3 Nephew of Poseidon
4 Singles
5 They took the Overland route
6 "Somebody ___ me . . ."
7 Newspaper notice
8 Shirt styles
9 Rainbow runner's genus
10 "Villette" novelist
11 Secular
12 Porsche rival
13 Guilty, for one
21 "Vissi d' ___": Puccini
22 "Even ___ speak . . ."
25 Swagger
26 Very, musically
27 Senior
28 Anserine
29 Charro's rope
30 Start of a 30-day mo.
31 Museum Folkwang site
33 Wave crest?
35 Weaken
38 "Batman Theme" composer Hefti
39 Vacuum
41 "Snow Falling on ___" (1999)
43 "Jump" group Van ___
44 Show
45 Buccal
46 Plays red
47 Sommer in "A Shot in the Dark"
48 Acclaim
49 Woo of "Ally McBeal"
50 Overwhelm, as by humor

The hub of 43 Across is Denver International.

ACROSS

1 Broadband, for short
4 Mecca pilgrim
9 Southern nuts
15 Double agent Penkovsky
17 Splice
18 Water weed
19 SHORT
22 Popeye's pick-me-up
23 Squeals
24 Seventh in a series
25 Big Bertha's birthplace
26 Open a crack
28 "___ Fall in Love Again": Anne Murray
30 "Ionisation" composer
33 Zhou En-lai's successor
34 SHORT 'N' SWEET
42 Ballad ending
43 United Airlines airline
44 Bait the hook
45 Bubalus quarlesi
46 ___ bifida
48 Baroque, for one
50 Paquin and Pavlova
51 Sgt. Snorkel's dog
52 "All gone!"
53 Sticky stuff
55 Wednesday's cousin
56 "SWEET 'N' SHORT" (1991)
60 Agent 99's friend
61 Gentlemen of Mazatlán
62 Electric dart gun
65 Toyota subcompact
67 Ras al-Khaimah leader
71 Solicit
72 100m race
74 Italian rice dish
76 SWEET
80 Climbing perch
81 Luft or Doone
82 Relative of -trix
83 Concern
84 It has 114 suras
85 1946 Alan Ladd film

DOWN

1 Divine water
2 Early birthday greetings?
3 Brand of denim shorts
4 Org. that investigated Alger Hiss
5 Looped cross
6 Burn out
7 Bible bk.
8 Mural beginning
9 Smart-alecky
10 Paradise
11 Alpine pass
12 Word of farewell
13 Termitaria
14 Took a place
16 League of Nations site
20 Matching card game
21 Dinghy adjunct
26 PR time
27 Medusa
29 Ichiro Suzuki's native land
31 Tommy Chong's daughter
32 To the ___ the earth
33 Tiller's tool
34 Chapala coins
35 Word form of "thin"
36 Verdi aria
37 Brynner of films
38 A Greek islander
39 Wedding celeb.
40 Raccoon's cousin
41 "A ___ of Honey"
47 "Who did it?" reply
49 Craggy hill
50 It's out under a limb
52 Kiss of peace
54 "Wheel of Fortune" purchase
57 Construction worker
58 Major suit?
59 Absorb gradually
62 Turkic language
63 In sync
64 "Here's mud in your eye!"
65 Heading of 112.5°
66 White Cliffs of Dover, e.g.
68 Cultural prefix
69 Stiff collars
70 Bowlines
73 Altar locale
74 Bullfrog genus
75 Baha'i birthplace
77 "TV Guide" abbr.
78 With yoo or boo
79 Infamous Aqua Teen in Boston?

77 SENSES CENSUS by Jay Sullivan
39 Down is an interesting factoid.

ACROSS

1 Tourist guides
5 Like flamingo feet
11 Small dams
16 No longer engaged
17 Relaxed
18 Spoke at length
19 It stands for something
20 Humble abode
21 You can't do it all by yourself
22 Not up on things
24 Place side by side
25 Isherwood's "The Berlin ___"
26 Put out
28 Done, to Donne
29 Kokomo loc.
30 Daisy's cousin
32 Puts two and two together
33 Social class
36 For rent
37 Do one's part
38 Bean town?
39 Not fooled by
40 Unpaid bills
44 Picnic cooler
45 Within eyeshot
47 Small whale
48 "Time will tell"
50 Hung a right
51 Take the lead
52 Umpire's call
53 Attention-getters
55 Jesper Parnevik, for one
56 Safari camp
58 Walks wearily
59 Be on the run
60 One of the little people
61 Round home
62 "You suppose?"
66 Err
68 One way to get the word
71 Titleholder
72 Photoelectric cell, e.g.
73 Went a-courting?
74 Inheritance, of sorts
75 Slots jackpot
76 It's on the house
77 "Gypsy" composer
78 Goes with the flow
79 Piece of wedding cake

DOWN

1 Cretan labyrinth builder
2 Break point
3 Charon orbits it
4 Lady of Spain
5 Three sheets to the wind
6 Group psychology
7 Gentleman caller
8 French bench
9 Art lover
10 Bengals mascot Who ___
11 Like many presents
12 Dodge City marshal
13 Refined
14 Got up
15 Bad looks
23 Ticket price
24 Basketball center
27 Grinding stones
30 Start to freeze?
31 Maneuvered through muck
32 Serve well done
33 Grizzly weapon
34 West Wing worker
35 Is suspect
36 Opens
37 Boxer's warning
39 Number of time zones in China
41 Casting requirement
42 Hit the books
43 "Your highness!"
45 Left end?
46 Sewer lines
49 Rebel leader
51 Golf clubs?
54 Quick-tempered one
55 Hide
56 Muddles
57 Like some sweaters?
58 Get-up-and-go
59 Pickup-game team
61 Handle with care
62 Fly catcher
63 Hawaiian island
64 Screening device
65 Curiouser and curiouser
67 "___ there, done that . . ."
69 Celtic New-Age singer
70 Wringing wet
72 Marienbad, notably

ACROSS

1 Fancy dos
8 Den chief
13 Int.-bearers
16 Bellhops run them
17 Shopping area
18 Mare's morsel
19 **Start of a poetic query**
21 Tin or iron container?
22 Tetley competitor
23 Soviet auto
24 Enthusiastic
25 Utah's Hatch
27 **Query: Part II**
31 Crossword pens
34 USPS assignments
36 Historic Spanish river
37 **Query: Part III**
41 Newfoundland and Labrador
42 ___ May Clampett
43 Mason's org.
46 Takes charge of
47 Sniffles causes
49 Spelunkers' destinations
51 HRE pt.
52 Not worth debating
53 Queen of mystery
54 **Query: Part IV**
59 Malt oven
60 Campus drillers
61 "Let's leave ___ that"
62 **Query: Part V**
66 ___ und Drang
68 1,000-kilometer chain
69 Suffix for Campbell
71 Grave
75 Sergio Garcia's org.
76 **End of query**
80 Moo goo gai ___
81 Surround tightly
82 Convenience
83 Roll-call call
84 Strong glue
85 Andromeda's spouse

DOWN

1 Fastened with stitches
2 ". . . ___ that teacheth, on teaching": Rom. 12:7
3 Gripes of wrath
4 Deteriorate
5 Key word
6 "Nixon" or "The Truman Show" star
7 Compass heading
8 Hightailed it
9 Golf-shoe stud
10 Parquetry wood
11 Mossad weapon
12 Bermuda brown
13 Murmured
14 Provoked, perhaps
15 Memo taker
20 "Haystacks" artist
24 Speed measure
26 Technical Inst. based in Carmel, IN
28 Cocktail-party wear
29 Pierre Omidyar's company
30 Miss
31 Source of 2 Down
32 Like some legal proceedings
33 Cut-rate, slangily
35 "Gimme ___": Rolling Stones
38 Transportation ntwk.
39 Later years, poetically
40 Attack
44 "You can observe a lot by watching" source
45 Till now
47 Terra ___
48 "I'm impressed!"
49 Cavs, on the board
50 "Bucketfoot" who batted .392 in 1927
52 Jibe

53 "I beg your pardon"
55 Dozes
56 Crow sound
57 "I don't want ___ the world on fire"
58 43-A member
62 One of the Yokums
63 Pond buildup
64 Popular toothpaste in Turkey
65 Clorox mold remover
67 Oarsman
70 In good order
72 Mold-ripened cheese
73 Words of accusation
74 "Wide Sargasso Sea" author
76 Itsy-bitsy
77 Sitter's handful
78 Wall St. action
79 W.J. Clinton's church

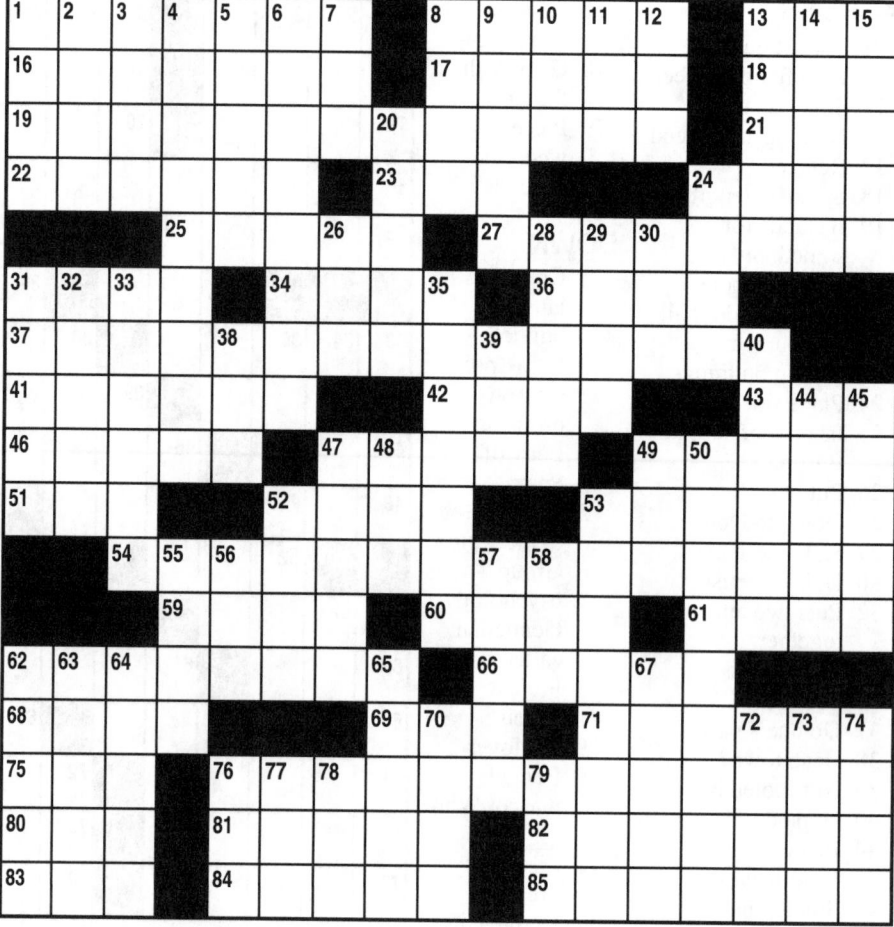

79

COMMERCIALISM   by Norma Steinberg
"Tom Terrific" (11-D) was a cartoon on the "Captain Kangaroo" TV show.

ACROSS

1 "So last year!"
6 Asparagus stalk
11 Flugelhornist Mangione
16 Force
17 "Anybody home?"
18 Happy Feet's friend
19 Gullible
20 Edward James in "Selena"
21 More than enough
22 Sen. H. Reid's state
23 Weathercock
24 Ms. Midler
25 Speaker's podium?
30 Without a stitch
31 Elevs.
32 Have a go at
33 Tuck away
36 Get all teary
37 "Understand?"
38 "Beat it, Fluffy!"
40 With reference to
41 Like a concert in the park
43 CIA gathering
44 Castilian copywriter?
48 Exodus plague
49 NFL Hall-of-Famer Lance
50 FNMA part
51 Diversify
53 River of South America
54 ___ Mahal
57 Bandleader Severinsen
58 Muscle spasm
59 Suffix for federal
60 Florentine waterway
61 Chief Counsel?
66 Derinds
68 Final
69 Quark's younger sib
70 Classic rock piece
71 Danger
73 Sorta
76 Super Tuesday word
77 Dilfer or Lott
78 Succinct
79 Oceanic fluctuations
80 Conn
81 Favorite of Queen Bess

DOWN

1 Brooch
2 Sawbones gp.
3 Washer cycle
4 Serious
5 Ecole student
6 "___ 'nuff!"
7 Ischium locale
8 Violinist Mischa
9 On the side of
10 Stone with hiero-glyphics
11 Appleton of "Tom Terrific"
12 Veronica of "Hill Street Blues"
13 Immeasur-able amount
14 Alan "The Horse" Ameche was one
15 Leg joint
25 Jackson 5 #1 song
26 ___ es Salaam
27 Patina
28 Shorthand, for short
29 Expertise
34 ___ of expertise
35 Business card abbr.
37 They'll get you in hot water
38 Inane
39 Avian stomach
40 Move forward slowly
41 Augury
42 At a distance
43 A fan of
44 As well
45 Threw out
46 Inspector in "The Daughters of Cain"
47 Fire sign
48 Flagpole-sitting was one
51 X – III
52 Regards as fact
54 Quakes
55 Raggedy Andy's friend
56 Scribble
58 Some are plasma
59 Regal fur
60 Hacienda bricks
62 Scrape a windshield
63 Put forth effort
64 "... after they've seen ___"
65 Chewing nails
66 Rhymester
67 "That's ___ need to know!"
72 USPS item
74 Take advantage of
75 Panhandle handle

BIRDWATCHING   by Fran & Lou Sabin
Audubon Society members will like this one.

ACROSS

1 Hem in
6 "The Sound of Music" family
11 Today, in Tijuana
16 Without exception
17 Watch 7 Down, perhaps
18 Rope fiber
19 Yodeler's heaven
20 Regarding bees
21 Caduceus coiler
22 Piano piece
23 Inches off
24 Swamp pests
25 **Cyanocitta cristata**
28 It's to be taken home
29 Yang's partner
30 Warm-water game fish
35 Driving hazard
38 Garfield's foil
42 Merit badge, e.g.
43 Celebes beast
44 Pas de deux windup
45 **Turdus migratorius**
50 Rainbow
51 Wahine's specialty
52 "You're ___ friend!"
53 Williams and Kluszewski
54 To the left, boatwise
56 ___ v. Ferguson (1896 decision)
57 Match ender, at times
58 Disclose, poetically
60 **Columbina passerina**
69 Colombian's capital
70 Bigotry
71 ___ the coop: escaped
73 Sister of Calliope
74 See 49 Down
75 "C'est ___!"
76 Mary of "The Maltese Falcon"

77 Loose
78 Work on a speech
79 Tick carriers
80 Medicated
81 Ice cube grabbers

DOWN

1 ___ noire
2 Patti LuPone role
3 Vaccine
4 Wear down
5 Polk's predecessor
6 Semi-conscious state
7 Some TV fare
8 ___ flu
9 Ama's find
10 Quill, perhaps
11 Designate
12 Pilgrim at Ajodhya
13 Orange type
14 Croupier, often
15 Nut-brown quaffs
24 Rum cocktail
26 Overnight stop, often
27 "___ the Tiger": Survivor
30 Like a silent partner
31 Mindful
32 In a heartbeat
33 NBA tactic
34 Offbeat
36 Harry S. Truman's birthplace
37 Chem. suffix
38 Palette paint
39 Lavishes love
40 Ned Rorem opus
41 Confederate general Jubal
46 Mambolike dance
47 Nepalese coin
48 UN agency

49 Chick
55 1982 Jessica Lange film
56 Zip
57 Equity members
59 Victimized (with "on")
60 Code name
61 Colorful marble
62 Whirlybird blade
63 Horned beast
64 Observes Yom Kippur
65 "Eroica" key
66 San Antonio shrine
67 Wicca get-together
68 NBA great, Patrick
69 Wampum unit
72 Beatty and Buntline
74 Hoot Gibson's horse

81 "GATHER YE ROSEBUDS . . ." by Arlan and Linda Bushman
Evan Esar first found fame with his "Comic Dictionary" published in 1943.

ACROSS

1 Mistake
6 Dwight's opponent
11 Not in order
16 Drab color?
17 Drink heartily
18 Jeeves, for example
19 **Start of an Evan Esar quip**
21 Modern therapy agent
22 Inn name
23 Positions
25 Robust energy
26 Cold reliever
27 Nov. election day
28 "Finding Neverland" star
29 Dwell on
30 Those in control
32 Fictional Jane
33 Spanish bear
34 Pendragon counselor
36 Hairnet
37 **Part 2 of quip**
41 Belt
42 Elliptical
43 **Part 3 of quip**
51 B.D. and Anna May of films
52 Rockette?
53 Brown league
55 Roll topper, perhaps
56 Pieces of candy
58 Hubbub
59 Frayed
60 Otologists explore them
61 Washes out
63 Fabergé creation
64 1998 NL MVP
65 Nursery ensemble
67 Conductor Leinsdorf
69 **End of quip**
72 Jug band instrument
73 Ian Fleming villain
74 Kind of figure
75 Refine rocks
76 Bothered
77 Rental sign

DOWN

1 Chaney of horror films
2 Stout building?
3 Rotates atop
4 Willowy
5 Spine-tingling
6 Greenish blue
7 Obligation
8 Thai's neighbor
9 Well-to-do
10 Less certain
11 Gardner and Fabian
12 Sully
13 Faith Hill song
14 Some weekend athletes
15 Chisholm Trail worry
20 Handheld gadget, briefly
24 Road wrinkle
26 Ins. choice
27 Kind of bed
28 Alaska national park
30 Image maker
31 ___ Miss
34 Customs
35 Argus extras?
36 Do to do
38 Insider talk
39 Fails miserably
40 Daredevil name
43 Fortnight
44 3-D image
45 Put new life into
46 Collapsible lid
47 Polanski film
48 "When Will ___ Loved": Ronstadt
49 Certain flight stabilizer
50 Fingerprint, perhaps
54 C. bits
56 ___ Speedwagon
57 Locale in a Cheech Marin film title
58 Begins
61 High seed's perk, at times
62 Minimum
64 Chance
65 Annika Sorenstam's org.
66 Very much
68 Mountain pass
70 Sooner than
71 NBA game buy

82 GRASS ROOTS by Richard Silvestri
The quip below was spoken by Arj Baker in "The Marijuana-Logues."

ACROSS

1 Paul Anka chart-topper
6 Moving about
11 The poop
16 Romeo and Juliet, e.g.
17 "Mule Train" singer
18 Spud spot
19 **Start of a quip**
22 Bucolic
23 Goddess of peace
24 ORD info
25 Stand up to
27 Stars and Bars defender
30 Vitality
33 Influential people
36 World Wildlife Fund symbol
38 Sign of resistance?
40 Skirt shaper
41 Assert before proving
42 Make a selection
43 REM event
45 No-fly zone enforcer?
46 **Middle of quip**
48 Practical person
51 Rainer in "The Good Earth"
52 Elton's john
55 Chocoholic, for one
56 Boston or Chicago
57 Kansas City pro
59 Formation fliers
60 You may have a hand in it
62 Little dog
63 Blow up, in photog.
64 Soho subway
65 Hopper load
67 President of Syria
70 Comedy bits
75 **End of quip**
79 "Gunga Din" setting
80 Counting everyone
81 Cardiac chambers
82 Devoutness
83 At cockcrow
84 Cries out for

DOWN

1 Tap trouble
2 Buffalo Bill's birth state
3 Word of woe
4 Rainy-day provision
5 Take ___ (try)
6 Aquatic plant
7 Satirist Mort
8 Barrio uncle
9 Country place
10 Pieces of the past
11 Small flute
12 Middle East gulf
13 Zinfandel alternative
14 Tue. plus two
15 One full of high spirits
20 Land south of the Caspian
21 Pique condition?
25 Define
26 Homer Simpson's father
28 Head start, perhaps
29 Max of the ring
30 Gnu home in San Diego
31 Gremlin
32 Monarch catcher
34 Deal maker
35 Tub or tub toy
36 One on the field
37 Meter preceder
39 Abby's offering
41 They have a point
44 Tympanist's time-out
45 Lose traction
46 Elm City collegians
47 Cousin-german's mother
48 Storm
49 Churchill's successor
50 Miss in "Guys and Dolls"
52 Soap ingredient
53 Furniture wood
54 Opry adjective
56 Chest protector
58 Work
60 Inedible "pastry"
61 Observe carefully
64 Kind of cross
66 Aired in syndication
68 Incision
69 Command to Spot
70 50 Down, for one
71 Friend in strife
72 Concerning
73 Indigestion cause
74 Grazing grounds
75 Marcel Marceau character
76 Cycle starter
77 Airline to Tokyo
78 Feather bed?

83 SUCCESS STORY by Jim Page
David O. Selznick commissioned 49-A and thought it to be "wretched."

ACROSS

1 Robert in "1941"
6 Atkins Diet no-nos
11 Embarrass
16 Arctic bear
17 Tony winner Denis in "Assassins"
18 "___ Millions": O'Neill
19 Emmy-winning Susan Lucci role
20 Kind of laser
21 Zoo sounds
22 **Start of a report taken from 49-A**
24 Beach color?
25 Elected superior
26 Actress MacRae
27 Triple Crown trio
29 Concorde wing
30 **More of report**
33 Pitt in "Babel"
37 Mournful sound
38 "Barney Miller" actor
39 Of old Norse poems
41 "Dumb" girl
44 Backsides
49 **RKO Pictures audition (Jan. 1933)**
52 Put off
53 Lighten up
54 False front
55 Sign a contract
57 Cyclotron bit
59 Forehead
60 **More of report**
66 Black, in poetry
67 Rental paper
68 Magazine publisher
74 Court tie
76 Tax paid quarterly: Abbr.
77 **End of report**
78 "The West Wing" creator Sorkin
79 Bargain-basement
81 Nile perch genus
82 Hot corner at Shea
83 John Denver album
84 Combat zone
85 Squiggles
86 Urges on
87 Homeless mutt

DOWN

1 Glasses
2 Synagogue scripture
3 Sixties dress style
4 Peyote and saguaro
5 African village
6 Oft-checked item
7 River in W Germany
8 Unkempt
9 Bring up
10 Barracudas
11 U.S. bike-racing org.
12 Monkey bread tree
13 Oil-rich region
14 Dead Sea discovery
15 Oversaw a reception
23 "Dream a Little Dream of Me" singer
27 Nucleic acid sugar
28 Aspen area
31 Golden vein
32 Cy of Cooperstown
33 Lacy lingerie items
34 Burst forth
35 Kitty chip
36 Soap for telemarketers?
40 Honda passenger car
42 Elvis Presley's label
43 Garlicky gas
45 Evidence of admission
46 Next in line
47 Canadian gas
48 Étouffée, e.g.
50 Kidney artery
51 Antidiscrimination org.
56 Patella
58 Goldman on "Family Guy"
60 Composed
61 West Indies charms
62 Muslim beauties
63 Concert extra
64 Vixen's stablemate
65 Star: Comb. form
69 Marner of Raveloe
70 Crank up
71 Verbalize
72 Tennis pro Dementieva
73 Iterate
75 Pulls the plug on
77 Nairobi Trio members
80 Lend a hand

84 "ARE NOT!" by Norma Steinberg
The answer to 31 Down is not San Diego.

ACROSS
1 Indo-European
5 Svelte
9 Oedipus' realm
15 Volkswagen subsidiary
16 Greek hell
18 Newspaperman Greeley
19 ASAP in the OR
20 Put on a pedestal
21 No can do
22 Strapping novelist?
25 Naughty
26 Comportment
27 Tappan ___ Bridge
28 Yale students
29 Bowling challenges
32 Store fat
34 Uproar
35 Blueprints
36 Curve
37 Fairy tale's second word
38 McNally's partner
39 Math course, for short
40 Snarl
43 "___ so it goes"
44 Yardbird food?
47 Lillie in "Thoroughly Modern Millie"
48 Queen's guard
50 Sheep farm mamas
51 Chèvre source
52 Down mood
53 "Results may ___"
54 Cache
55 Name on an elevator
56 SpongeBob's pet snail
57 Disturbed by events
58 German Valley
59 Poult parent
60 Achievement
61 Suffix for Campbell
62 Saturn production problem?
68 In the ___ (planned)
70 Double-jointed
71 Tiger's growl?
72 ___ del Fuego
73 Tied
74 Yekaterinburg's range
75 Director Soderbergh
76 Miami's county
77 Nightingale's night light

DOWN
1 Pinafore tie
2 Stringed instrument
3 Alan Arkin's son
4 Milk fortifier
5 Embarrasses
6 Burdened
7 Role model
8 Mr. Griffin
9 Prince Valiant's kingdom
10 Sharpen
11 Period in history
12 Novel full of run-on sentences?
13 Dessert cart passenger?
14 Burpee products
17 Took
23 Flea eggs
24 Permit
28 Prince William's alma mater
29 Atomizer
30 Craft
31 Charger country?
32 Ego
33 Indistinct
34 Hot tubs
36 Prohibit
37 Southwestern Indians
39 Bop over the head
41 Furlough
42 Devoured
44 Fires
45 Amiss
46 A-Major, e.g.
49 Noted naturalist
51 ___ Dead
53 Willful defacer of property
54 Chiang Mai citizen
55 Costume
56 Mil. rank
57 Break away from
58 Street fights
59 Traditional Navajo home
60 Put in numerical order
62 About
63 "By gar!"
64 Pay-stub abbr.
65 Krank in "Skipping Christmas"
66 Stuff
67 Puppy's cry
69 Robbins of Baskin-Robbins

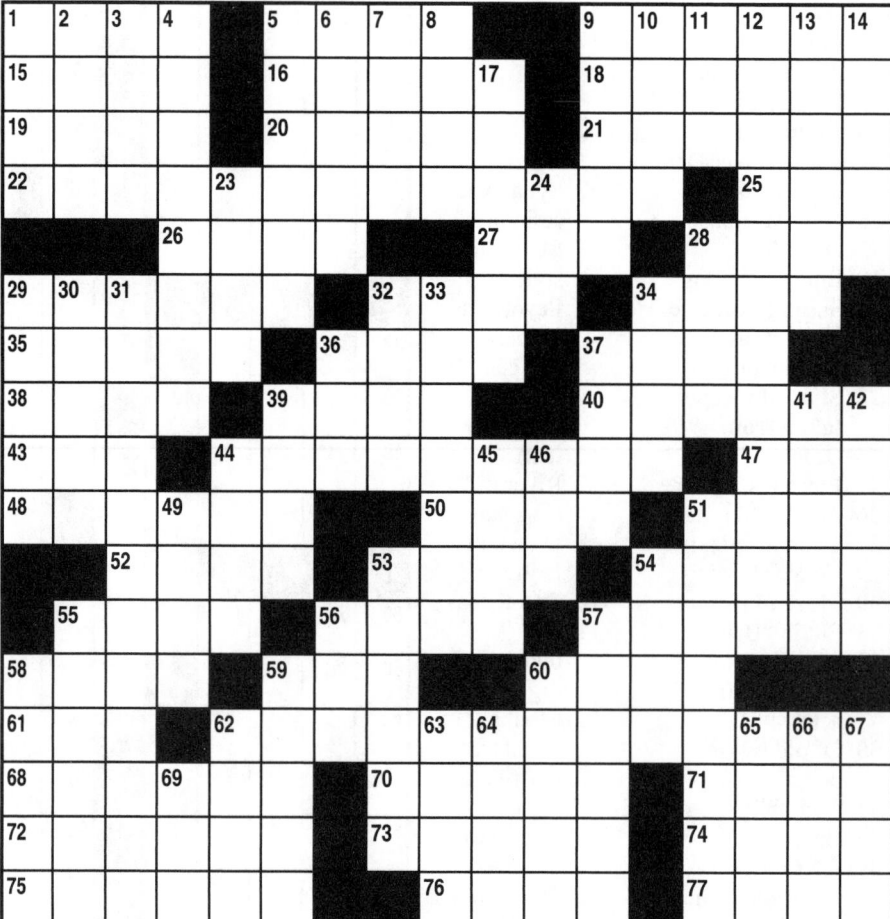

85 FLICK PICKS by Patrick Jordan
"These are a few of my favorite . . ."

ACROSS

1 Tuesday, to Toulouse
6 Gary in "Under Siege"
11 Area within a chancel
16 Mork or ALF
17 Joint below the fibia
18 Yogi in 14 World Series
19 "My Favorite Martian" star
21 Powerless to move
22 Critic/screenwriter James
23 Past deadline
24 Went ballistic
26 Nice ___ (prude)
28 Country or miracle follower
29 Egg cells
30 Done dozing
33 Sun language
34 Capital of the Tang dynasty
35 "My Favorite Blonde" star
39 Cod-liver product
40 Fierce anger
41 Central
42 Emulate a masseur
45 Termini of basilicas
47 Mental miasmas
51 Novice newsie
53 Grocery-store receipt word
55 ___ de Cologne
56 "My Favorite Season" star
61 Grand Prix driver Stirling
62 Tiara twinklers
63 Yellowstone spouter
64 Not rarely, in rhyme
65 35th-anniversary stone
66 Subside
68 Palate cleansers
70 Screw groove
71 Tadpole food
75 "Precisely, Percy!"
76 "My Favorite Year" star
79 Anesthetized
80 Bluto bugs her
81 Borneo ape

82 Shangri-las
83 Ready to drop
84 Home state of the Dixie Chicks

DOWN

1 Goya's naked subject
2 "Shake ___!" ("Get moving!")
3 Copiously supplied (with)
4 Air-raid warden's concern
5 Mich. neighbor
6 Lacking novelty
7 Cohesion
8 ___-Ball (carnival game)
9 Pipe bend
10 Rabbinical seminary
11 Stomach
12 Horne of Broadway's "Jamaica"
13 Girl Scouts emblem
14 Bus-station announcement
15 Wickerwork material
20 Completely original
25 Smoke-detector signal
27 "The Deep" menace
28 Sugarcane cutter
30 How the undisciplined run
31 Frequent Seattle forecast
32 Await the green light
33 Skypad Apartments family
34 Member of a fast-food combo
36 Keogh alternative
37 Kindergarten break
38 Relieve (of)
43 Vaudeville segments

44 "Why didn't I think of that?"
46 Downcast
48 Bolt-action god?
49 Roof overhang
50 Litigant
52 Sired, in Scripture
54 Smoothly, to Mehta
56 Help to establish
57 On both sides of
58 Jupiter feature
59 Volleyball need
60 Sty or stye, e.g.
61 Where an imam preaches
65 Shouts from a tough audience
66 Anacin alternative
67 Like some daydreamers
69 Bingo call
70 Use a swizzle
72 Urge gently
73 Bone beside the radius
74 Memory units
77 New Haven student
78 Day-care enrollee

86 AGE GROUPS   by James Arthur
42-A composed the film score for "The Good, the Bad, and the Ugly."

ACROSS

1 Not many
5 Good times
10 Ideologue
16 Ranee's wrap
17 Dirty film, at times
18 Stand on one's own two feet?
19 "Kiss of the Spider Woman" author
20 Ninth baseball commissioner
21 Fine point
22 Modern gangsta rap's genre?
25 Have something
26 Really big shoe
27 '05 Super Bowl champs
31 Mother Goose's dog of comics
34 Centerfolds?
38 Sports-column entry
39 Palindromic diarist
40 Source of cones
41 Beehive State athlete
42 Film composer Morricone
45 Be on the bottom
46 High blood pressure, e.g.?
53 Grade-school trio
54 High ground
55 Keanu in "The Matrix"
56 Composer Rimsky-Korsakov
60 Not 'neath
61 Say so
62 Play area for children
65 "Gypsy" composer
66 "May I have your attention"
67 Get outta Dodge
68 Have something
69 Where to keep a pet carnivore?
75 In the vicinity of
79 The way of the world
80 Cutting remark
82 Melodic
83 You must remember this
84 Mixed bag
85 Playful pet
86 Mating place
87 Yahoo! cofounder

DOWN

1 Death on the Nile source?
2 Butterfly with eyespots
3 View from Cleveland
4 Nomad pads
5 Near the bottom
6 First name in fashion
7 Have an eye for figures
8 Did serious harm to
9 Made the transition
10 Pueblo people
11 Big picture
12 Short result
13 Rebel leader
14 Stable particle
15 Rugby score
23 Net support
24 Starter starter
27 Page of music
28 Cabinet dept.
29 Spot for a Sunday driver?
30 Abbreviated course
31 Surfeit
32 "American Pastoral" author
33 Catch phrase?
34 Yao of the NBA
35 More intimate
36 Former Disney honcho
37 ___ fixe (table d'hôte)
39 Like brain activity
43 Number of Disney Dalmatians
44 "Beware ___ "
47 Union man
48 Woody offshoot
49 "A Death in the Family" author
50 Turn green?
51 "Smells like ___ Spirit": Nirvana
52 Those were the days
56 Secret gov't. letters
57 Prussian pronoun
58 "Evita" narrator
59 Puerto Rico, por ejemplo
61 "Way to go!"
63 Washington address
64 Lacking principle
65 Cul-de-___
68 Fragrant compound
69 Knocker's reply
70 Coward of note
71 Necrology
72 Jazz singer Simone
73 Big do
74 Where the Shannon flows
75 Don't bet on it
76 It sounds like 77 Down
77 Every breath you take
78 Take the gold
81 Wetland

87 UNEQUAL EQUALS   by Thomas W. Schier
"Dúlaman" would be one of those songs alluded to in 57 Across.

ACROSS

1 Supports
6 Guppy or grouper
10 Medicinal amount
16 Get the most out of
17 Pigmented eye part
18 De-creased?
19 **Start of a quip**
22 Sub stratum?
23 "Back in the ___":
Beatles
24 Courtroom fig.
25 Diving duck
26 Abrupt transition
29 Salary limits
31 In the time left
32 Prophetic sign
33 "Alas"
34 Cleo's means to an
end
37 **More of quip**
40 Hand out
homework
43 Bearers of good
moos
44 Two-D extent
45 CBS founder
William
46 Walking papers?
48 Hampshires' homes
49 Idle of "Monty
Python"
50 Working-class
member
51 Siberian plain
52 **More of quip**
56 Your, of yore
57 Its found in Celtic
Woman songs
58 One taking off?
59 Five-star general
Arnold
62 Plow puller
63 Bear in the air
64 Not great, not
terrible
65 ___ spell (relax)
68 Pie perch
70 C&W artist
Yoakam
72 **End of quip**
76 Embryonic sac
77 Yves Saint
Laurent's birthplace
78 Caseharden
79 Disheveled

80 Trap stuff
81 Son of
Snuffy Smith

DOWN

1 Excessively
proper
2 Handle
differently?
3 Wholesale
store
4 "Stop yer
joshin'!"
5 Be,
apparently
6 Hare hair
7 It's creepy
8 Put together
9 Cries of glee
10 Miniature
re-creations
11 Boston Bruin
great
12 High-protein
beans
13 Premed sci.
14 Chivalrous
chap
15 River vortex
20 Getty or
Rockefeller
21 Abstains
from
27 International org.
begun in 1958
28 Red army member?
30 Unit-cost word
32 Bacchanalian blast
33 "My name's
Friday—I'm ___ "
34 Anchor position
35 Submissive group
36 "Oats, ___, beans
and barley . . ."
37 Minuet or mazurka
38 Hockey infraction
39 Like Baby Bear's
porridge
40 "Don't be ___ "
("Don't bug me")
41 Strange on "Men in
Trees"
42 Offensively vile
46 Like pressure
waves
47 Cut off

48 Paint-can directive
50 Expression
51 Main squeeze
53 Woods' "launching
pad"
54 Limbo obstacle
55 Good times
59 Fruit of the brown
hickory
60 Taking liberty
61 Rowling hero
62 Implied
63 Excessive
64 Tuscany city
65 Practice on canvas
66 Rombauer of
cookbook fame
67 Zip
69 Sayer and Tolstoy
71 Mandamus or
mittimus
73 Worn ___ frazzle
74 Solo in space
75 Wrap up

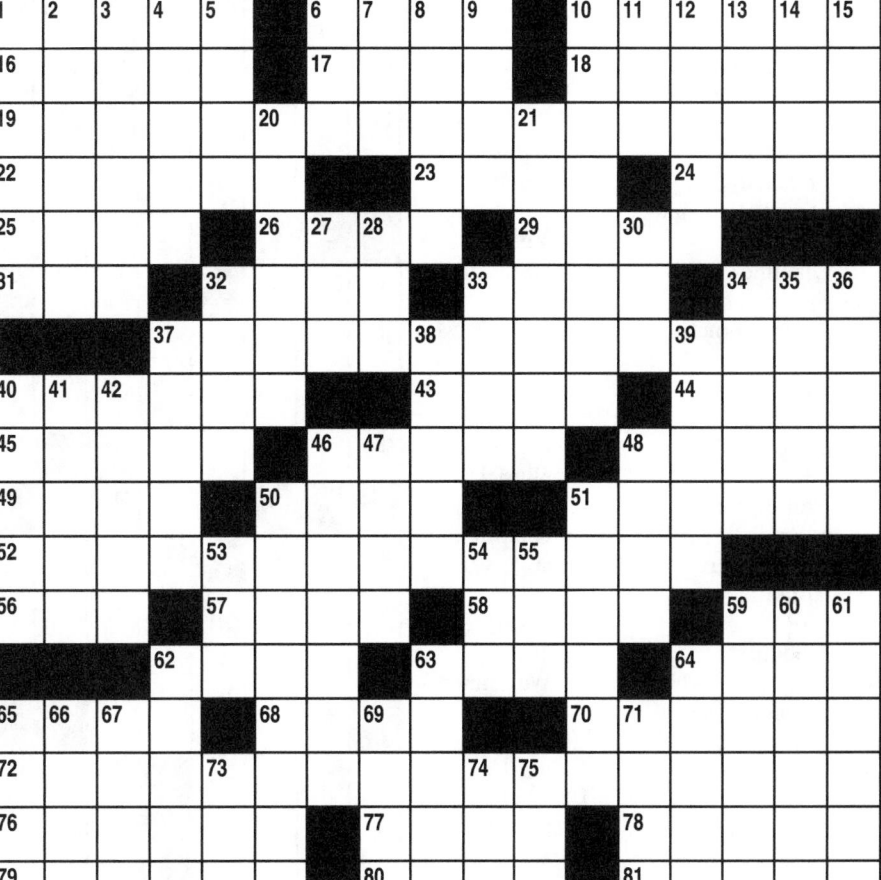

88 IN-FAMOUS by Leonard Williams
Bruce Lee played the role of 21 Across on television.

ACROSS

1 Food Network stars
6 "The Sound of Music" song
12 Diminutive Jedi
16 Founder of a French dynasty
17 Stranded in winter
18 Utah town
19 Onetime Olds
20 Sports palaces
21 Green Hornet's driver
22 Opened on Broadway
24 Terre ___
26 NBA Hall-of-Famer, naturally?
30 ___ Schwarz
33 Août time
34 Poet
35 Mapquest suggestion: Abbr.
36 Nonbelieving Cuban leader?
40 Make a hem
41 Oklahoma town
42 Violent unrest
43 Brontë character
45 UPS rival
47 Eff follower
49 Quite a complication
53 Spheres
56 Sandler of "Little Nicky"
59 Algerian seaport
60 Spring mo.
63 Humorist fond of private jokes?
66 Intentionally mislead
67 Ma of classical music
68 ___-cone
69 Pal in the 'hood
70 Christmas poet in a foul mood?
75 Johanna Spyri classic
76 Mixologist
80 Film ___
81 Abstains
84 French river
85 Part of TAE
86 Pass by
87 Grab hold of
88 Hive residents
89 Intuited
90 Welcome sights in the desert

DOWN

1 USSR, in the USSR
2 Jeanie's was light brown
3 Fencer's weapon
4 Famous physicist
5 Soiled
6 Gladstone's archrival
7 White pawns, e.g.
8 "Peg Woffington" novelist
9 Byrnes of old TV
10 Ovid's 1002
11 Like the White Rabbit
12 "Li'l Abner" clan
13 Bryan and Cicero, e.g.
14 Nixon-Kissinger policy
15 Part of a Latin conjugation
23 Cross the threshold
25 Passions
27 Atlanta superstation
28 More than dislike
29 Splendor in the grass?
30 Feudal estate
31 Poet Sexton
32 "The Wizard ___": Parker and Hart
37 Logical prefix?
38 Load the dice
39 Mr. T show
44 Plenty, in old verse
46 Scanned luggage
48 www.yale.___
50 Many a Yemeni
51 Klinger on "M*A*S*H"
52 Disjoin
54 Platitudes
55 Eye problem
57 Mixed-bag
58 City north of Bismarck
60 "The Greatest"
61 Type of camera
62 Catch a punt
64 Long time
65 Shaver brand
71 Old money of Italy
72 Recipe measures: Abbr.
73 Parsonage
74 Cookbook author Prudhomme
77 Lunes y martes
78 Celtic tongue
79 Ribbed fabrics
80 Thieve or catch a thief
82 Mano-a-mano cheer
83 Suffix with Tyrol

89 "I'M OUT!" by Victor Fleming
A bad case of Hold'em fold'em inspired this title.

ACROSS

1 Noted pie makers
5 Juror disqualifier
9 "That call infuriated me!"
16 Clue
17 Ruler unit
18 Range
19 Stowe villain's offspring?
21 Oats container
22 Holy war
23 London underwriters
25 Is for many?
26 Result of too much will power?
30 Eel trap
33 Artlessness
35 Pale
36 Zinger
38 C. Icahn manuever
39 Greeting for a Parisian pal
42 Still-hunt
44 Taste
46 Took a wrong turn, say
47 Dual-lane highway experience?
50 Beltway passer?
52 Status ___
53 Contort
56 Like flamenco dancing
57 Oaf
59 Gym site
60 Since
61 Pre-email transmissions
65 Reduce the fare?
66 How old you look to yourselves?
70 Prefix for light
72 Palenque pals
73 Comparatively stubborn
77 Mascot at 79 Down
80 Like many regrettable photos?
82 Dip
83 Columnist Bombeck
84 Govt. cultural org.
85 Poked, as a horse
86 No longer work
87 Tube alternative

DOWN

1 Catchall: Abbr.
2 Septic tank problem
3 Ordering aid
4 Quesadilla accompaniment
5 "So what!"
6 As to
7 Its count may be 1 or 11
8 Put on the back burner
9 Earlier
10 Wild daisy
11 Angled pieces?
12 Didst possess
13 Having five sharps
14 Fed. benefit source
15 Line part: Abbr.
20 Procure
24 "___ bygones be bygones"
26 Roundish
27 Road competition
28 Hardly risqué
29 Woman with legendary patience
30 "This Old House" address
31 Meal source
32 Covert passage cover
34 "A Doll's House" playwright
37 TNT product
39 Network launched on 8/1/81
40 It may be left on a copier: Abbr.
41 Fran Drescher role
43 Vandeweghe of the NBA
45 "Now!"
46 Red Cloud, for one
48 Ocasek of The Cars
49 Has one's way
50 Dress down (with "out")
51 VFW member
54 Zenith rival
55 Bodybuilder's target
58 Has unwanted gains
61 Got good wood on
62 Psyche part
63 Not as great
64 Cashless transaction
67 One making an assessment
68 Sydney who's into stars
69 Dentist's directive
71 PUZZLE SUBTITLE
73 Begged-for money
74 Land in a Beatles tune
75 Royal figure of sci-fi
76 Food wrapped in red
77 Badly, at first
78 Foul caller
79 Doak Walker's alma mater
81 ". . . ended, ___ it begun": Dickinson

90 FRUIT BASKET by Fran & Lou Sabin
We'll give you a hint: "banana" is not one of the fruits.

ACROSS

1 Leo's locks
5 "The Institute" of Israel
11 Blood component
16 "American ___"
17 Receiving guests
18 Aaron Copland ballet
19 Robert de ___
20 Mouse
21 Sister of Terpsichore
22 FRUIT
25 Krupp Steelworks city
26 Meadow
27 Flaxen fabric
28 Tutor's end
30 Go with
31 FRUIT
42 Wee stream
43 Goes ape
44 St. Petersburg river
45 "This room's ___!"
46 "Seascape" playwright
47 Painted again
48 Short-billed rail
49 Boy or Girl follower
50 Demential
51 FRUIT
54 "Blast off!" preceder
55 Moreover
56 Unyielding
59 River to the Rhine
61 Products of 22 Across
66 FRUIT
70 Be ready for
71 "Knock ___!"
72 Definite rejection
73 Joke's payoff
74 "The Odds Against Me" author
75 "___ us a child . . ."
76 Nine: Comb. form
77 Memorable Mother
78 Shepherdess Bo

DOWN

1 Reduce to snippets
2 "Gotta go!"
3 Test standards
4 Skip town
5 Pennant holder
6 Shakespearean murderer
7 British county
8 Actress Braga
9 "I hope so!"
10 "Jurassic Park" star
11 Advance screening
12 GPS forerunner
13 "___ With Judy" (1948)
14 Attack
15 6 Down, for one
23 Glues together
24 Cassini and Maskaev
29 Musically high
30 Blade of yore
31 Understanding
32 Tabloid topic
33 Diciembre follower
34 1942 Preakness winner
35 Hull's lowest deck
36 Afghani's capital
37 "Can ___ Witness": Gaye
38 Upturned
39 Corpsman
40 Spanish province
41 "Unsafe at Any Speed" author
46 High point
47 Further emend
49 Grand Prix champion Ayrton

50 Warming agent
52 Country singer Lynn
53 Maxim's staff
56 Attach a patch
57 Lionel in "Murder by Death"
58 "Slate" is one
59 Talaat Sadat's uncle
60 Love to pieces
62 Centerfold
63 Oxygen with an odor
64 Al ___ (pasta order)
65 Nosy sort
66 Location of 1 Across
67 Unsalvageable
68 Noun suffix
69 Concept

91 "CELEBRATION" by Nancy Salomon
Nancy thanks Kool & the Gang for the title.

ACROSS

1 Test for gold
6 1983 Mr. T flick
11 Snail-mail item
16 Colorful aquarium fish
17 Bucky Beaver's toothpaste
18 Staff addition
19 Celebrate like a cardiologist?
21 Script direction
22 I love Latin?
23 Bub
24 Book-jacket briefs
26 Mouth-burning candies
27 Turn tail
28 Webzine
30 Celebrate like an escape artist?
32 Pvt.'s boss
34 Out beyond the buoys
36 Rowboat rower
37 Celebrate like a graffiti artist?
44 Sonic sounds
46 Incurred, as debts
47 Fly like an eagle
48 Cummerbund cousin
49 Guiding genius
52 Lucy's costar
54 Dream Team team
55 Custom
57 Twist out of shape
59 Far from tan
61 Celebrate like an exhibitionist?
65 Scratch and dent
66 Sooner State native
67 Chew the fat
69 Celebrate like a survivalist?
74 Rubik of cube fame
76 Mooch
78 Jannings in "The Blue Angel"
79 Eve's grandson
81 Nervous twitch
82 Rich rock
83 Earth Day month
85 Celebrate like a suit?
88 Reeves in "The Matrix"
89 Grenoble's department
90 Mercury and Saturn
91 Glass ingredient
92 Sellers of movies
93 Tearing up

DOWN

1 Even, at Sawgrass
2 Nobelist poet Heaney
3 Limburger asset?
4 Sotheby's stock
5 Self-congratulatory cry
6 Like Matchbox cars
7 Number-cruncher
8 Atkins diet no-no
9 Madcap
10 Marshy backwater
11 H. Rider Haggard adventure
12 Small-time gamblers
13 Threepio's buddy
14 Swim competitions
15 By itself
20 Purim villain
25 Bends down
29 "Don't be absurd!"
31 Court TV topic
33 Highlander's hat
35 "Eureka!"
38 Distinctive doctrine
39 Run over
40 Calendar col.
41 Circus laborers
42 Marco Polo's heading
43 Sturdy cart
44 Try to strike
45 Orchestral "tuning fork"
50 Peter Lorre's "Casablanca" role
51 Inits. in comedy
53 Wall St. debut
56 History book feature
58 P, on fraternity row
60 8 in a date: Abbr.
62 Red sushi fish
63 Winter wind
64 Bottled spirit
68 Freshwater cod
69 Security issue
70 JFK Library designer
71 Like yellow fever
72 Square
73 Savoir-faire
75 Philosopher of "razor" fame
77 Fraught with complications
80 Scratch a dele
84 Unilever soap brand
86 Due follower
87 George Sand's "Elle et ___"

"MARK MY WORD"   by Richard Silvestri
38 Down made his mark hitting homers for the Reds in a cutaway jersey.

ACROSS

1 It's all there is
6 Child, in combinations
10 Polish off a theorem
15 In the loop
16 Fax forerunner
17 Was nuts about
18 Radio, TV, etc.
19 Occupied
20 Slack off
21 Above-the-line punctuation mark?
24 Dawn deity
27 Men in white hats
28 Betrayer
29 "The Open Window" author
31 Room for relaxing
32 "___ Old Black Magic"
34 Court return
37 Went around
39 Destroyed by degrees
41 Regular guy
42 Tune from your teens
45 Mexican munchie
46 Very long punctuation mark?
50 Word on an invitation
51 Put a stop to
52 Butt end
53 Singer of 4 Down
55 To the point
59 Some magazine pages
60 Moo child?
62 Bit of resistance
63 Red army?
64 Polo Grounds star
65 Book after Acts
68 Rook
69 Third punctuation mark?
74 Terpsichore's sister
75 In pieces
76 Capacitance unit
80 Compare
81 Knave of Hearts' booty
82 Shade of blue
83 Looks like a letch
84 Theater gp.
85 Pick up an option

DOWN

1 Kiltie's cap
2 Be in the hole
3 Little bit
4 "Elsa's Dream," e.g.
5 Spot check?
6 Distinctive flag
7 Get away from
8 Have done with
9 Plow pullers
10 Appease
11 Assembly-line worker
12 Not quite circular
13 Presidential no
14 Tree of Life locale
16 Arranged in rows
22 Relinquish
23 Rubbed the wrong way
24 Slalom track
25 Symbol of sturdiness
26 Conquers the 90-meter hill
30 Press agent?
33 1968 hit musical
34 Grinding together
35 Imprint firmly
36 Overly
38 Kluszewski of baseball
40 Mississippi River source
42 Roulette bet
43 Cleaning solution
44 Memphis, to Mumble
46 Place for an ornament
47 Author Adler
48 Organic compound
49 Rock's Steely ___
50 Civil war monogram
54 Deeds
55 Makes the Top 40
56 Old Dodge
57 Sloppy digs
58 Uncommon sense?
61 Wok
62 Puzo novel
64 Beaver's kin
66 Eyeball-bending designs
67 Up to now
69 Take effect
70 Buffalo's county
71 Do fall work
72 Pro follower
73 State of befuddlement
77 Shutout spoiler
78 Exist
79 Drops in the grass

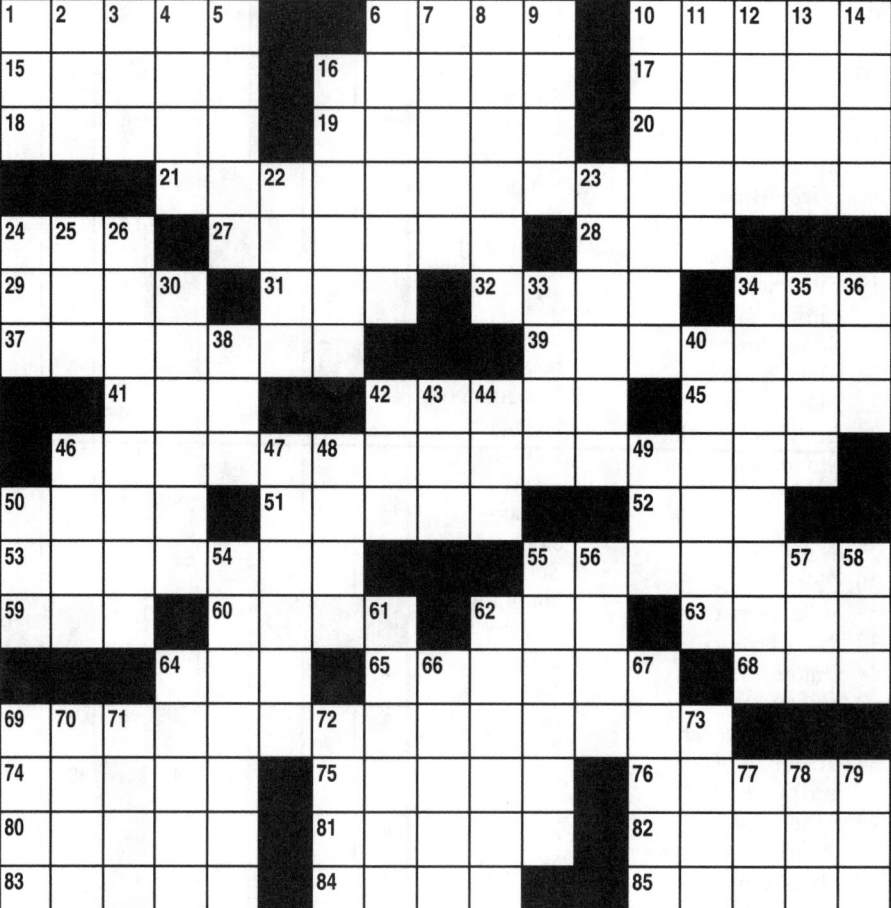

SERIOUS WORK   by Bruce Venzke
The funny lady below was a regular on the "Dean Martin Celebrity Roasts."

ACROSS

1 Crony
4 Skating champion Midori
7 Meddle
10 Swabs not meant for decks
15 Indian elephant
17 Mauna ___
18 Enemy in "The Enemy Below"
19 **Phyllis Diller quip: Part 1**
22 Redgrave and Swann
23 Act of faith?
24 Puppet ending
25 Test mineralogically
27 Red Planet saloon?
31 **Quip: Part 2**
34 Not suitable
37 Jungle swinger
38 Pint in a pub
39 **Quip: Part 3**
43 Famed television chef
46 Saw through?
47 Vast, poetically
48 Level-headed one?
50 Intravenous injection
54 Miss. chocolate dessert
56 Issue
58 **Quip: Part 4**
62 Course standard
63 Cousin of a puffin
64 French film award
65 **Quip: Part 5**
68 Toss
71 Red noes
73 Scholarship money
74 Emmy winner Falco
76 "Round up the ___ suspects"
80 **Quip: Part 6**
85 Popular tannery?
86 St. Pat's land
87 Spiffing (up)
88 They may be drawn
89 Glad-to-be?
90 Cambridge-shire town
91 French possessive

DOWN

1 Ratchet part
2 Grayish
3 Bank claim
4 "Yes"
5 One of the Cratchits
6 Seat of Marion County, FL
7 Fund-raising letter, e.g.
8 Frolic
9 "I'm thrilled!"
10 Mysterious
11 They give some vacationers a lift
12 T-bill, essentially
13 "April Love" singer Boone
14 Porky's place
16 Year's record
20 Excite
21 "Bulworth" star
26 Span. titles
27 Tower of faith
28 Prohibit
29 Quick
30 ___ adjudicata
31 Wan
32 Colmes of TV
33 Portuguese painter Paula
35 Sunburn cream
36 Send packing
40 Keep guessing
41 Southern Arizona city
42 Nod neighbor
44 Considerable force
45 Censor's target
49 Is indisposed
51 Intently interested
52 Four Corners state
53 Marginally sufficient
55 Go one way or the other
57 No happy face
58 Wee bit
59 Decorator's concern
60 Just make, with "out"
61 Banks in Cooperstown
66 Well-built
67 "How I Spent My Summer Vacation," maybe
69 Make very dry
70 Venice's Bridge of ___
72 "Fiddler" matchmaker
74 Light brown
75 Colored
77 Ton, for one
78 Teen woe
79 Longevity at the box office
80 Dwindle
81 "Cry ___ River"
82 Attack a sub?
83 Point of a pen
84 Up to, for short

94 SHANKS' MARE RIDERS   by Victor Fleming
Something's afoot below!

ACROSS

1 Paparazzi prey
6 Granville who played Nancy Drew
12 USN rank
16 "Would you like to see ___?"
17 Without a key
18 "___ Cookie Blues": Lonnie Mack
19 Johnnie Walker
21 Act as lookout
22 Poetic night
23 Rote of the '50s Giants
24 Chest muscle
25 One third a 1970 film
26 "___ and weep!"
28 Hopscotch spaces
30 Namath, once
31 Jimmie Walker's catchword
34 Take after
36 Curriculum follower
39 Little shavers
40 Certain cap source
41 Needing an analgesic
42 Muscular fitness
43 "West Side Story" duet number
46 Darned spot
47 "Chicago" star Richard
48 Incompletely
49 Percolation solution
50 Like gridlocked traffic
52 "That'd be fine"
53 Brit. lexicons
54 Gravitate (toward)
55 Come across as
56 Not on the edge
57 Shoots
59 Clint Walker title role
61 Certain seekers
62 Dinner course
64 Tower rentals?
68 DC nine
70 Morse code click
71 Actress Lee
73 Secret employer, maybe
74 What "there oughta be"
75 Doak Walker's team

78 Cash in Capua
79 Actually
80 Cousins of ospreys
81 Like duck soup
82 Wanders
83 Travis of country music

DOWN

1 One involved with a cover-up?
2 Show host
3 Harry Helmsley's wife
4 Suffix with absorb
5 OSU fan
6 Wail
7 Prince's "Sign ___ Times"
8 Top-ranked
9 Here and there
10 "___ to your leader"
11 One of the King Sisters
12 Balmacaan
13 Jerry Jeff Walker song
14 Green tractors
15 Take turns
20 Song sung in pews
27 WW2 turning point
28 Fur
29 Bakery goodie
32 Prayer opening
33 Place for a comb
35 ___ polloi
36 Vintners' vessels
37 Cathedral item
38 Junior Walker's back-up
40 Rain or shine preceder
42 High school subject?
43 "Careless Hands" singer
44 Park of London
45 Audition
47 Tumbler on a mat?
48 Chop ___

51 "Radio Song" group
52 Start a garden
53 Ready to serve
55 Break into bits
56 Asthma reliever
57 Windup
58 Bologna's place, but not salami
59 Gore, to Boies (in 2000)
60 U. of Arkansas coach Houston
63 ___ Ababa
65 Home of the Huskies
66 In a queue (with "up")
67 Cat in "Homeward Bound"
69 Vacillate
71 Red or pink
72 One-eighties
76 D. Tutu's land
77 Lyricist of puzzles

95 QUIT QUIP   by Richard Silvestri
Stick a "long i" into the answer at 73 Across.

ACROSS

1 Having style
7 Fats Domino's "Whole ___ Loving"
12 Fusion material
16 Regarding this point
17 Suspect's out
18 Timber wolf
19 **Start of an ex-smoker's statement**
22 More wise
23 Colorado or Ohio
24 New-car option
25 School founded by Henry VI
26 Copier chemical
27 Source of malt
28 Chaney in "Oliver Twist"
29 Little dents
30 Put down
31 "___ Erma's Cope Book"
32 Large terrier
36 Moisten the meat
39 Ancient prophet
42 Blazed trails
43 Permission to enter
45 Hill denizen
46 Thingamajig
49 Brady Bill opponent
50 After-dinner drink
53 Twist of fate
54 Peridot, for one
57 Man is one
59 Data's evil twin
60 Decrees
62 R&B's ___ Hill
65 Call again?
68 Conscience-stricken
69 "It's ___ real!"
70 End of a Garbo line
71 Young haddock
72 Pesto ingredient
73 **End of statement**
76 "Zip-___-Doo-Dah"
77 Military assault
78 Corvo, Pico et al.
79 Pay attention
80 Passion
81 Stupid mistakes

DOWN

1 Sculpting tool
2 Smooth and connected, musically
3 Region of NE Spain
4 Winning roll
5 Occupational suffix
6 Part of WYSIWYG
7 Decisive defeat
8 Canapé toppers
9 Comerica Park cat
10 Vail machine
11 Bring up publicly
12 Modified
13 Wreck beyond repair
14 Broad at the beam
15 Saunter
20 Without delay
21 Fill with happiness
26 ___ lizzie
27 Yawning
29 Union jack?
30 Nothing
31 Scarfed down
32 Official proceedings
33 Designer Gucci
34 Mean companion
35 Water whirl
36 Report of a shooting?
37 One of the back forty
38 Ponzi scheme, e.g.
40 Fury
41 Gloucester's cape
44 Beat the goalie
47 Painting medium
48 Assayer's concern
51 I, to Claudius
52 "How Does a Poem Mean?" author
55 Oblique
56 "My Cousin Vinny" Oscar winner
58 Swine confines
60 1976 Horse of the Year
61 One with pressing matters?
62 Wish for
63 "This Is Spinal Tap" director
64 Hedger's word
65 Hindu honcho
66 Steer clear of
67 "Long time ___"
68 Timetable, for short
69 Stick on the track
71 Work at a gravy job?
72 Dumb guy
74 Secret govt. group
75 Fleet member

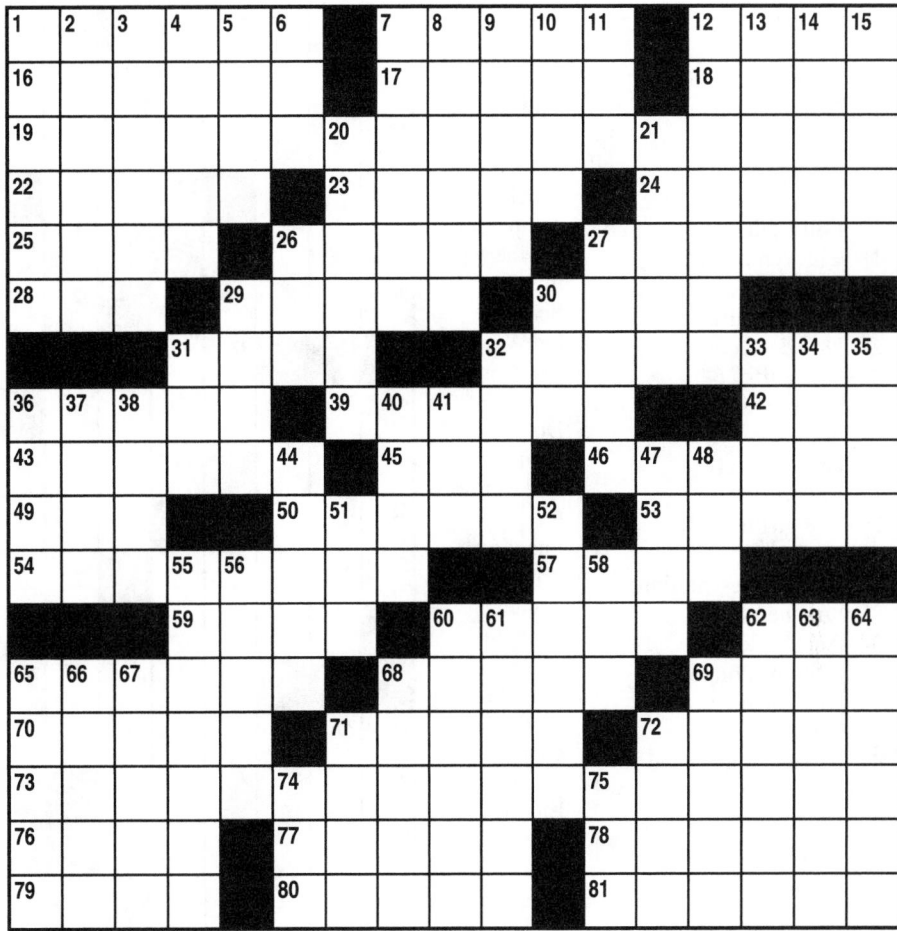

96 VITAMIN SUPPLEMENTS   by James Arthur
The answer to 29 Across is not April (Dancer).

ACROSS

1 They're entitled
6 Support financially
10 Growing places
15 Never were, perhaps
16 "Got it!"
17 Full-scale
18 Chicken coop group?
20 Rough house
21 Duo date
22 Had a life
23 Extensive screen writing?
25 On the level
27 Lay low
29 The girl from uncle?
30 Encore presentation
32 "As we speak . . ."
34 Acknowledge
37 Pluto or Pongo
39 Dr Pepper Museum home
41 Greeted and seated
43 Not intended
47 Drug unit
49 Midori on ice
50 Tenor's top note?
52 Dallas apartment?
55 Rook takes rook, briefly
56 Does something knotty
58 Christopher Robin's father
59 You'll get a rise out of it
62 Means of support
64 It's a racket
65 University of Chicago
67 No alternative
69 Got a handle on
73 Napoleonic force
75 Had a beef?
77 Gene sites
78 Second-rate social event?
82 Round figure
84 Tic-tac-toe figures
85 Slicker
86 Runner's munchy?
89 Dr. Isley, a/k/a Poison Ivy
90 Vaulted arch
91 Certain sari wearer
92 Knee-high to a grasshopper
93 Affirmative actions
94 More than sore

DOWN

1 Cloak companion?
2 Hit the big time
3 Scanty
4 One whose job is on the line
5 Do a slow burn
6 Makes room for
7 Function
8 "Hud" Oscar winner
9 Rum, to some
10 Swindles
11 Oakland's county
12 Ellen ___ Barkin
13 La Scala music director (1986–2005)
14 Short-runway plane
17 "Luck and Pluck" author
19 Patient reply
24 Capital of Cyprus
26 Bare-naked ladies
28 Average guy?
31 Biblical matchmaker
33 Gum glob
35 Volunteer's response
36 Tennessee gridder
38 Pesky pest
40 Inner ear?
42 Step on a scale
43 "Atlanta Trilogy" playwright
44 Turned down
45 Jazz vocalist Carmen
46 Major minor league
48 "Omigosh!"
51 Chance introduction?
53 Key of Mahler's Third Sym.
54 This is a test
57 Sushi sauce
60 Springer
61 Muckraker Ida (1857–1944)
63 Royal pain, for a princess
66 Shady spot
68 Gets excited
70 It's heard in the herd
71 Copycat
72 Mickey Mouse operation
74 Brand or John
76 Be off
78 Daddy-o
79 Jedi portrayer Neeson
80 ___ mater
81 Kids' construction set
83 Theda in "Cleopatra"
87 Homer Simpson's neighbor
88 Darken during the day

ACROSS

1 Destiny
6 In ___ (untouched)
10 Buster of Flash Gordon serials
16 Like some columns
17 Distributed afield
18 Throw off schedule
19 He played 79-A in 1947
21 Of the ankle
22 NFL line positions
23 Canceled
25 Veteran's quality
26 Spotted
29 Young socialite
31 It's pulled out for a rain delay
33 ___ plaid
34 Quality beef cut
37 Circus attire
39 Cracklings in the lungs
40 Halpert on "The Office"
42 Old brand of toothpaste
43 Punching tools
44 Dynamite inventor
46 Hatfield in "Here Come the Brides"
49 ___ chi
50 He played 79-A in 1935
52 Strong acid
53 Rink rat, at times
55 First name of Tarzan's creator
56 Undercover?
57 Food from heaven
59 "___ who?"
60 Epigram
61 Give an assessment of
64 Grandes dames
66 Internet column
67 Is off one's feed
69 Escape route
70 Tolkien creature
71 Used a Singer
73 Insulation material
75 Rhodolite, e.g.
77 Chalking location
79 S.S. Van Dine sleuth
84 "What's My Line?" panelist Francis
85 Wagnerian article

86 1978 Broadway revue
87 "The Desperate Hours" star on Broadway
88 Baseball stats
89 Williamson in "Excalibur"

DOWN

1 Rondo maker
2 IM provider
3 Genetic letters
4 Coin source
5 Gives the okay
6 Abbr. on an old Asian map
7 Tiniest bit
8 Fence-building game
9 Open up
10 Ill. clock setting
11 Harvest
12 Self-important
13 He played 79-A in 1930
14 Slanted
15 Pompeo and Greene
20 Microsoft customer
24 German crowd?
26 Nursery-rhyme couple
27 Antilles tribe
28 He played 79-A in 1933
30 Old Boston theatre
32 Pallet wood
35 Julio or Agosto
36 Gideons' gift
38 Home of Sam McCloud
41 Blends gradually
44 C.S. Lewis land
45 Sledded at top speed
47 NHLers
48 Charles, to Elizabeth II

50 Clinton's Energy Secretary
51 Buzz-making toy
54 Aimed at
56 ___ Arbor
58 Like
60 Settle the score
61 Ozzie Myers' downfall
62 Lung membranes
63 Ladder carrier, perhaps
65 Balkan car of yore
68 Title of respect in India
72 Sup
74 Van size
76 Hawaiian whale-watching locale
78 Scribe
80 Guitar man Paul
81 Katie Couric's old home
82 AFL's partner
83 Slippery swimmer

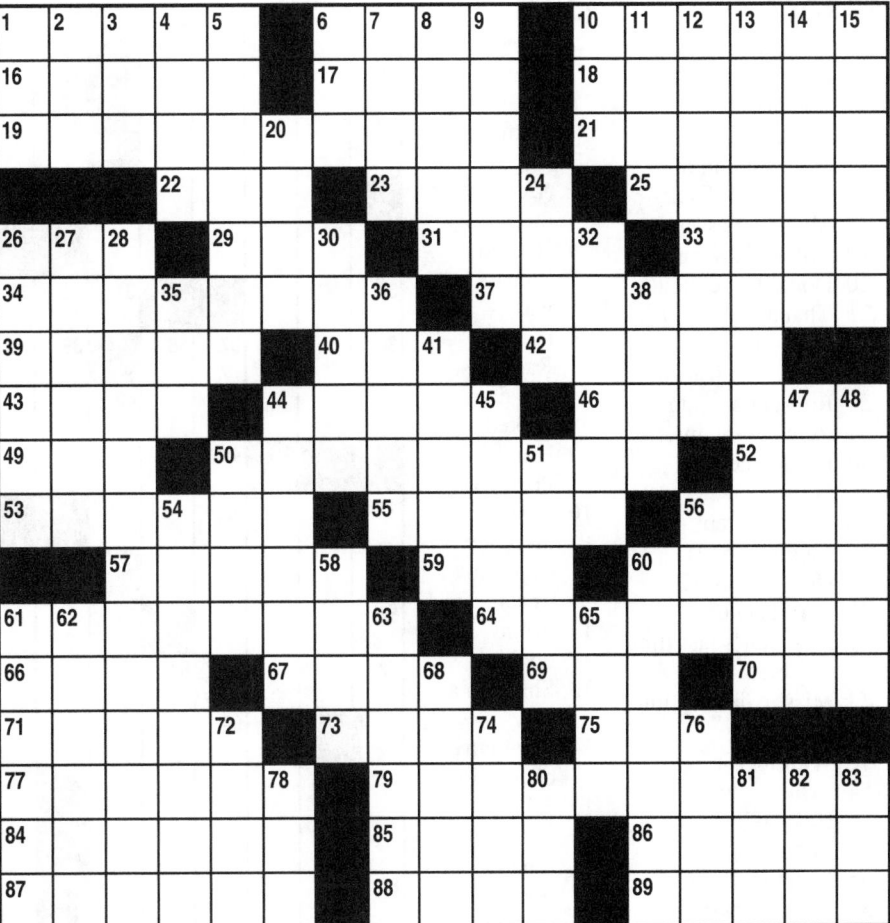

98 SIZES   by Robert Zimmerman
Bob says he thought of this theme while watching "Little Big Man."

ACROSS

1 Cook's cutter
6 Larger-than-life
10 Canvassed
16 Close call
17 Witherspoon in "The Bank Dick"
18 Melodic passage
19 Colorful swimmer
20 Donald's nephew
21 Channel changer
22 Hash-slinger
25 Dynamics lead-in
26 Roll-call responses
27 Remove the interior
30 UK lexicon
31 On and on
35 Musical step
36 English ponds
39 Not A, B, or C
40 Island state?
41 Bachelor's last fling
43 ___ bleu
44 Missile description
47 Candy nut
50 With fervor
54 "The ___ of Heaven": Thompson
55 Venetian Polo
57 Painful spasm
58 Denomination
59 Dub in vocals
61 Long, long time
62 Sash for Cio-Cio-San
63 "You ___ seen nothin' yet"
64 Opens, in a way
67 Getting on in years
72 "Malefactors of great ___ ": T. Roosevelt
74 Israel's Barak
75 Chamber-music groups
77 Aerie youngster
78 Ward of "54"
79 Park in CA or NJ
80 Pavement grippers
81 Tailor's line
82 Inched along

DOWN

1 Summer time
2 Polar platform
3 Ex ___ (from the throne)
4 Boo-boo
5 Prepare for war
6 Parrot
7 Rain cats and dogs
8 Ticked off
9 Hot Porsche?
10 Doorstep discovery
11 Lunchbox treats
12 Prom booking
13 Shine, in a way
14 Superlative conclusion
15 John of police reports
23 Sock part
24 Guffaw
25 Turkeys
28 Cancel a keyboard mistake
29 Adolescent
32 Singer Amos
33 Question for Brutus
34 Versifiers
35 Flail
37 Beethoven overture
38 Pay out
40 Synonym compiler
42 Tot up
43 King's channel
45 Sexy
46 Elvis ___ Presley
47 Mr. Moto's "I see!"
48 Leopold's codefendant
49 Glue

51 Part of a lobbyist's job
52 Way out?
53 Yearnings
55 Skirt or bus type
56 Propensity
59 Broadway luminaries
60 Director's call
63 Joined the game
65 Plea of innocence
66 Carved out an Empire?
68 Jar
69 Quaker pronoun
70 Hoop of the '50s
71 Dutch cheese
72 Streisand album
73 Knack for music
76 Turf

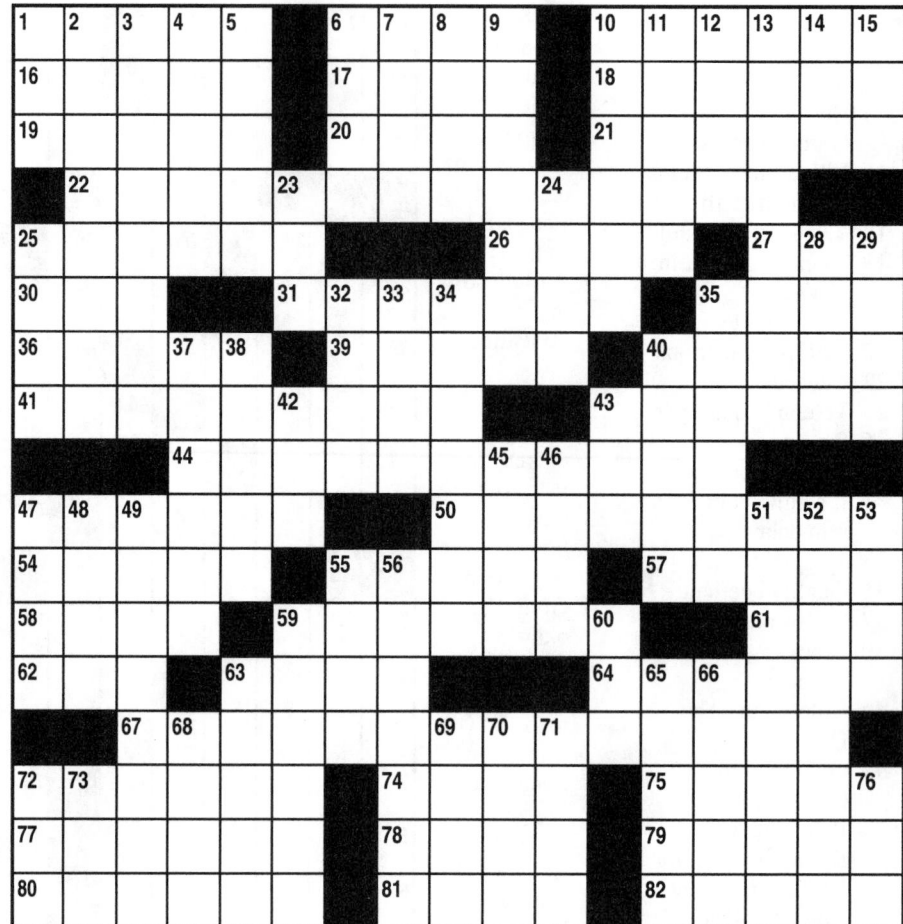

99 FREE OF CHARGE by Jay Sullivan

48 Down received the Academy Award for Best Picture of 1958.

ACROSS

1 Homer Simpson's beer
5 California range
11 Kathy in "Titanic"
16 Gumbo veggie
17 Run off
18 Visibly awed
19 The Old Sod
20 Home of the Niners
21 Share with
22 Warmed the bench
23 Scene?
25 Capone cohort
27 Lo-cal
28 Steelworker?
32 Leg bones
38 Shore thing
39 Ceiling
40 "The Russia House" author
41 "Tamu-Tamu" composer
44 Much the same
45 Girl reporter?
49 High clouds
50 Griffith in "Body Double"
51 Joan Girardi's hometown
53 Leach of hockey
54 Gung-ho
58 Sycophant
59 Lipitor expiration date?
62 Caesar's cohort
64 Spaceship Earth locale
65 Swiss nunnery?
73 Before, of yore
74 Rust, e.g.
75 Overage
76 Winged deity
77 It sucks
78 Famous list words
79 Refuse to
80 Take the wheel
81 "For shame!"
82 Seeing things

DOWN

1 Fails to
2 Kiev locale
3 Corn cake
4 Bat the breeze?
5 Muslim mystic
6 With respect to
7 Clapton or Close
8 Retail
9 Spring back
10 In flight
11 Arthur in "Arthur"
12 Flu symptom
13 Takeoff sound
14 Large-scale
15 On the way
23 Flagstick
24 Champagne head
26 Soldier or solder material
29 Hebrew "A"
30 Lower limits
31 "What have ___ to deserve this?"
33 Start of Caesar's boast
34 Indonesian island
35 Bit of eye makeup?
36 Places of refuge
37 Go with
40 European finch
41 Where Zeus grew up
42 Programming language
43 Glittery headpiece
45 Cause for alarm
46 Semicircles
47 Hit the books hard
48 Vincente Minnelli film
49 Small island
52 Pyramid builder
54 Mont Blanc, e.g.
55 King's deputy abroad
56 Start of an opinion
57 Can't stand
59 Hightails it
60 Pacific Coast evergreen
61 Web site
63 "Maids a-milking" group
65 Plenty
66 Leave the scene
67 Lake Albert's river
68 Border line
69 Take a turn
70 It can come as a shock
71 Connecticut collegians
72 Peace Garden St.
76 It sounds like you

100 BURIED TREASURE by Victor Fleming
Think pirates, and a map, perhaps.

ACROSS

1 USO customers
4 Spattered
12 Offer destructive criticism
16 Brief item from a register
17 They have sharp blades
18 It has a dull blade
19 Letters on a tongue?
20 **Regarding the buried treasure:** ___
22 Magician's utterance
24 Not be accurate
25 Marley of reggae
26 Novelist Susan
29 Mrs. Potts, for one
33 **The ___ . . .**
36 Realtors' asset
39 Clod choppers
40 Gets sere
42 Most supremely good
45 Tax return ID
46 The race to get Dad a gift often results in ___
47 "Hold on!"
48 "Honor Thy Father" author
50 Erase, in a way
51 "Help!" et al.
54 Housed, as 1 Across
56 Every couple of years
58 Arduous journeys
59 Mystery writer Josephine
60 **. . . has an ___ . . .**
65 They're watched a lot by babysitters?
66 Heart's place, for some
67 Dominating, in a way
70 Coin of Hanoi
73 Negatives of Nairn
74 **. . . in fact, ___!**
80 "80" computer of old
81 Kin of -trix

82 Testers of ore
83 Gator extender
84 Get edged out
85 Becomes edgy
86 Kicker?

DOWN

1 Fatty oil
2 Ed Norton's fridge
3 Breastbones
4 Govt. stipend
5 Polling amt.
6 Shoot a light gun
7 DH, e.g.
8 Athens rival
9 Brothers and sons
10 '60s Tarzan
11 Summer hrs.
12 Suit
13 "Lipstick on ___" (2006 Torie Clarke book)
14 Hang ___ Index
15 Lamarr in "Samson and Delilah"
21 Molecule formed by lightning
23 "___, Topeka and . . ."
27 Make amends
28 Some singing groups
30 La Guardia info
31 Puts on or puts on follower
32 Like some non sequiturs
34 IV sites
35 Memphis setting
36 Choral work
37 Oscar winner Rainer
38 Knight mare
41 Fuller Brush reps
42 Harbor suspicions
43 Lint collector

44 May 8, 1945
49 ___ halide
52 Do roadwork
53 Open an envelope
54 Appliance meas.
55 Grp. that gets a pay cut?
57 Kim in "Vertigo"
61 Las Vegas casino
62 Outdo in
63 Go to extremes
64 Renter
65 Ruth's number
67 Skating maneuver
68 String after K
69 Partner of pots
71 ". . . so long ___ both shall live"
72 Unlocks, in poetry
75 Lost a lap
76 "Prufrock" auth.
77 QVC rival
78 Tulsa college
79 1/6 fl. oz.

101 CRONE JEWELS by Harvey Estes

The school's nickname at 46 Down was shortened in 2004.

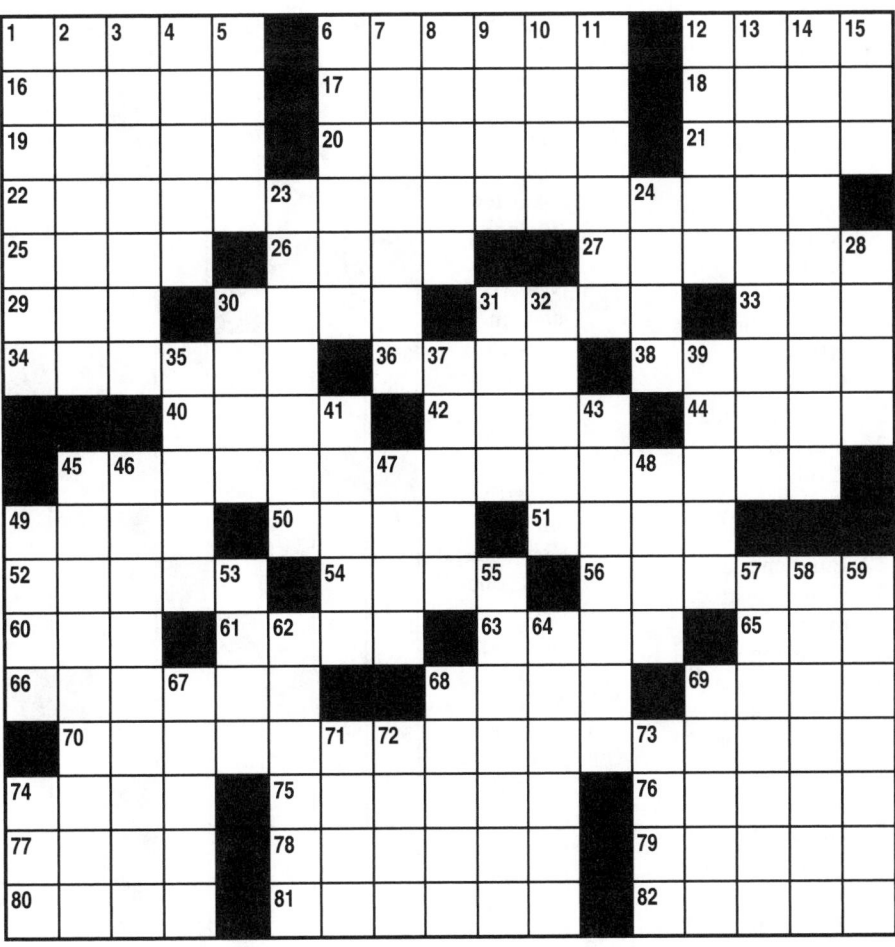

ACROSS

1 Phony
6 Means of entry
12 2006 Emerald Bowl team
16 Say "nothin'," say
17 Start of two Henry Miller titles
18 Get ready
19 First name in TV talk
20 Stir
21 "Nothing ___!" (duck soup)
22 Bend the bartender's ear while elbow-bending?
25 Spatter guards
26 Ambulance personnel
27 Old Roman magistrate
29 Rep. Hutchinson
30 Role for Liz
31 Very, in Vichy
33 Not to
34 Desert rat
36 Pianist Peter
38 Blue hue
40 Bit to split
42 Buster Brown's dog
44 Drawing place?
45 Grating Gene Pitney remaster?
49 Political district
50 Matching
51 Hoosier Bayh
52 Green lights
54 Painter Chagall
56 Texas city in "Friday Night Lights"
60 Knowledge
61 Hassle
63 "Exodus" author
65 Go one better
66 Some scouts
68 Sunburn result
69 Dream-home amenity
70 Unoriginal Cole Porter cover?
74 Counselor's employer
75 Some appliances
76 Uta of the screen
77 Sailing the Pacific
78 Christmas, in the Vatican
79 Like krypton
80 Auto pioneer Karl
81 Angles from the stern
82 Flip

DOWN

1 Diner's tie-on
2 Order in the court
3 Unit of pressure
4 Ideal locations
5 Painter Magritte
6 Like half a season's games
7 Crunchy salad ingredient
8 Colorado brewery
9 Omar of "ER"
10 Rural structure
11 Like the Yangtze River dolphin
12 "The Jungle" novelist Sinclair
13 Character lines
14 Unhurried
15 Meet
23 Canary and daffodil
24 "Mahogany" star
28 Veg out
30 Quote as a reference
31 The Dixie Chicks, e.g.
32 Herd stray
35 Toss back and forth
37 Anesthesia of old
39 Bale binder
41 Heat setting?
43 French chef's shout
45 Walk
46 2003 NCAA hoop champs
47 Counterfeiters' nemesis
48 Places to crash
49 Responded to the alarm
53 Job detail, briefly
55 Off-the-rack item?
57 Howard brothers' stage name
58 Cornhusker rivals
59 Galore
62 Not on the level
64 A peanut-butter cup
67 Two-mile-high capital
68 Type of colony
69 Try this first
71 "ER" actor Epps
72 Cold war defense assn.
73 Hellenic XXX
74 It's often hailed

102

"MAY DIVORCE BE WITH YOU!" by Richard Silvestri
"It's a Barnum and Bailey world . . ."

ACROSS

1 Teaching assignment
6 Strike down
11 Yellow fruit
16 Rashness
17 June in "Love Nest"
18 Hellenic marketplace
19 "___ in the Dark" (1964)
20 Love to bits
21 Drag participant
22 **Start of a quip**
25 Erotic
26 Buck's mate
27 Poke
30 Ethyl ending
31 Common street name
33 Reducing resort
36 Futile
39 Slight coloration
40 Wharton Sch. course
41 Vocal passage
42 Punch ingredient?
43 Chambers of the heart
44 **Middle of quip**
47 Prince of Darkness
49 Bulb bloom
50 Feeling no stress
53 Rink jump
54 St. Andrews warning
55 Ranted and raved
56 Tie the knot
57 Pseudoesthetic
58 Noshed
59 Down in the dumps
60 Hellenic vowel
61 Escorts
64 **End of quip**
72 Kitchen appliance
73 "Silas Marner" author
74 Make a case
75 "What the Butler Saw" playwright
76 Parsonage
77 Sip slowly
78 Lowly workers
79 Prepared for printing
80 Get together

DOWN

1 "Rugrats" character
2 Wield the whip
3 New York stadium
4 Uses a warehouse
5 Attack
6 Medicine men
7 Butterfly, for one
8 Key material
9 Alas., once
10 "I'll speak a prophesy ___ go": Shak.
11 Governor's prerogative
12 Banded quartz
13 Somewhat, in music
14 Province
15 Put on notice
23 Makes sure of
24 Make a long story short
27 Project
28 Pompeii fallout
29 Yelled at
31 Erroll Garner tune
32 Against
33 Gets loud
34 Luau fare
35 Collection of anecdotes
37 Not express
38 Pull down
39 Ring quest
40 Engine-starting spray
42 Oberon, for one
43 Kind of sax
45 Soak up
46 Dormant
47 Dust maker
48 Borden's weapon
51 View from the bridge?
52 Teacher's deg.
54 Where pledges are taken
55 Was frugal
57 2004 Olympics site
58 Songlike
60 Encourage
61 Teetering place
62 Burkina Faso's neighbor
63 Liquid medication
64 Harvest
65 Bernese Alps river
66 Biblical preposition
67 Sphere starter
68 Verve
69 City on the Jumna
70 Galoot
71 Links litter

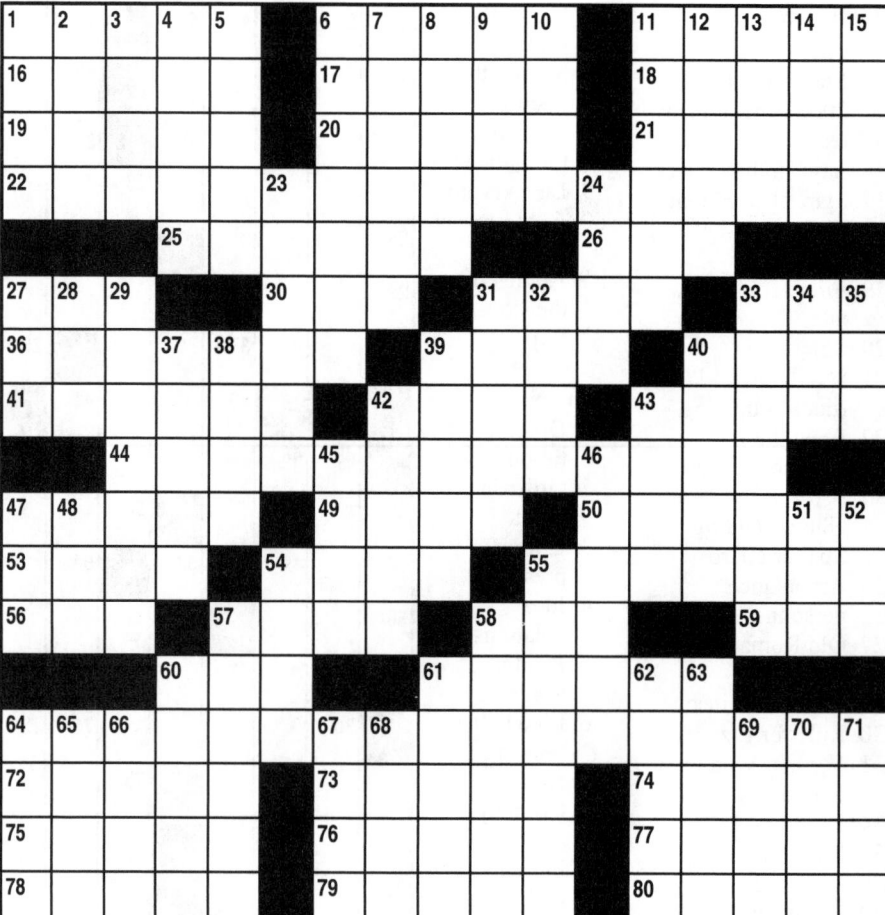

103 "DON'T GET BURNED!" by Joel D. Lafargue
The quip below is a good example of "clean" bathroom humor.

ACROSS

1 Virginia senator
5 Busted
10 Jean Harlow's nickname
14 Blue Bonnet et al.
16 Skip the ceremony
17 Lew in "Young Dr. Kildare"
18 Odorous
19 Diamond side
20 Put words to paper
21 **Start of a quip**
24 Manche capital
25 Seedy pet?
26 Heat-shield locale
30 Silly
34 "Respect" singer Franklin
35 Before now
37 "___ lose our Edens": Browning
38 Weight-loss target
39 Unaffected
42 Patriotic org.
43 Sandpiper relative
46 Secondary
47 Puffball seed
49 **Middle of quip**
52 Edges
53 This may swing
54 Kitchen tie-ons
57 Bwy. letters
60 O.K. place for a gunfight?
64 Street talk
65 Cugat's ex
67 Complaint
68 Father of Cush
69 Spock's arms
71 Irritate
72 **End of quip**
77 Empower
78 Clay workers
79 "Bikini Beach" heroine
80 Duck à l'orange, e.g.

DOWN

1 Cashmere
2 She wrestled Thor
3 Steakhouse complaint?
4 Feverwort
5 Nonstick surface
6 Half a handball game
7 Turtle in Wonderland
8 Dueler's blade
9 Break off
10 Detours, maybe
11 Lined up
12 ___ noire
13 Flanders river
15 Do sutures
17 For a time
22 "Doonesbury" reverend
23 Pitchman's partner
26 Takes a snooze
27 Black Bears' college town
28 Commence
29 Part of EIK
30 "Une Matinée" painter
31 "___ me!" ("My treat!")
32 Village green
33 Epitaph opener
36 ___-ho
40 "Cornflake Girl" singer Tori
41 Cuckoopint genus
44 Amigo of Guevara
45 Southfork family
47 Be a Paul Pry
48 Sky pilot
50 QM2 letters
51 Charles Dutton sitcom
54 Cinder
55 Went up against, competitively
56 Impala in "Cars"
57 Alan Ladd classic
58 Skin ailment
59 Two-toned snacks
61 Idolize
62 Loath
63 Nemesis of Clark and Lois
65 Santiago is its capital
66 One ___ other
69 Tillie's titular mate
70 Figure on a Boston Common boat
73 Salt Lake City athlete
74 Remove what's unwanted
75 Likely (to)
76 Thrice, in the pharmacy

104 WINGING IT   by Norma Steinberg
Our test solvers loved all these puns—especially 62 Across!

ACROSS
1 And so
5 "Leave as is"
9 White-sale items
15 Meat-and-potatoes dish
16 Closes in on
18 Arrow poison
19 Surface size
20 When prompted
21 Lewis and Clark destination
22 Liberal bird?
25 ___ Gatos
26 They're worth waiting for?
27 Leprechaun
28 Toon Le Pew
29 Conscientious cricket
32 Pinion's pal
34 WW2 servicewomen
35 To date
36 National ___
37 Rutherford B. Hayes' state
38 "A ___ home is his castle"
39 Comic Carvey
40 Navigates
43 Sheepcote sound
44 Dueling bird?
47 Spigot
48 Cod congregation
50 Refuse to recognize
51 Yearn
52 Abeyance
53 Programmer's output
54 Horse blanket
55 Partner of now
56 Footed vases
57 New York wing
58 Qt. or ft.
59 Felipe's gold
60 Terse
61 Branch of math
62 What Hooters oozes?
68 Nerve cell
70 Early Brit
71 Director Kazan
72 Blessed event?
73 Ointment
74 Dodge that was "all" that?
75 Worked for
76 Lecher's expression
77 Reminds over and over

DOWN
1 "Take ___!"
2 "Murmuring Judges" playwright
3 Consumer
4 Shacks
5 Brown dog
6 Bivouac shelters
7 Per capita
8 Pop-quiz answer
9 Make fun of
10 "The Big Chill" star
11 Prior to
12 Rockies crag?
13 Soldiers
14 Intuit
17 Blue-ribbon
23 Hint of color
24 Tundra wanderer
28 Bucket
29 Parts of windows
30 Shorthand inventor Pitman
31 Farm bird?
32 Ashcroft's predecessor
33 Maroon
34 Pinwheel's sound
36 ___ es Salaam
37 House of Nashville
39 Last name in computers?
41 Pierre's aunt
42 Piece of asparagus
44 Pit
45 Bunks
46 Trois divided by trois
49 Couple's pronoun
51 Where Raphael is buried
53 Throngs
54 Fashion designer Jacobs
55 Treasure State capital
56 Website
57 Steering mechanism
58 Cleric's home
59 Held the deed on
60 Dirk Pitt's creator Cussler
62 Exudate
63 Spoken
64 Reign
65 "Brokeback Mountain" wife
66 Super Bowl prize
67 "___ oui!"
69 Stimpy's friend

105

JUMBLES by Fran & Lou Sabin

Harold Hill (47-A) is the hero of "The Music Man."

ACROSS

1 Elizabethan home?
7 Tournedos meat
12 "___ off!"
16 Rough ridges
17 Chevy van
18 Carmela on "The Sopranos"
19 Sounds from stalled goats?
21 Yemen port
22 iPod downloads
23 Grub
24 Ward off
25 Chubby love child
26 Military issue
27 Marksman, at one point
29 Word of warning
30 Matchmaker at work?
34 Normal behavior
35 Nincompoops
36 Dawn Chong in "Goodbye America"
37 Clothes basket
41 "Death of a Saleman" son
43 Kind of bit or byte
44 Oscar or Edgar, e.g.
45 Business trainee
46 Explorer Amundsen
47 Harold Hill's "hometown"
48 Hotel employees
49 Rock hunter's collection
50 Smiley face smile
51 Kind of race or war
52 Explode
53 Harsh critic of halfway houses?
57 Party people
61 Fred Astaire had it
62 Like haunted houses
63 Tenant's rental
64 Clear sky
66 Lose it
67 Prefontaine of track
68 Express anger
69 Whitman's Sampler sampler?
72 Legal matter
73 Let up
74 Peter in "Venus"
75 Stand in the woods?
76 Junkyard dog
77 Marshall and Singleton

DOWN

1 Clobbered
2 Maestro Toscanini
3 Be inclined?
4 Ideally
5 Disney collectibles
6 Malt finish
7 Genoa export
8 Feared fly
9 Greek letters
10 Tate display
11 Puts on the deck
12 Happy hunting grounds
13 Herpeto-phobia?
14 Stadium level
15 Wowed
20 "Back in the U.S.A." singer
24 "London Fields" author
26 Lightyears away
27 Suit yourself!
28 Questionable
31 Slangy turndowns
32 Birdie's better
33 Turns some pages
34 Join
37 "___ the Horrible"
38 Mindful
39 Aquamarine amulet?
40 Attempt to open
41 Israel port city
42 Write a P.S.
43 Sound from the pasture
45 Marathoner's meal
46 Agent
48 Rumple (up)
49 Like "Dawn of the Dead"
51 Chamonix lift
52 Bad boys in "COPS"
54 Siren calls?
55 Governing group
56 Focus of a house-warming party?
57 Stages
58 Two thousand pounds
59 Bouncing around
60 Cubic meters
64 Romain de Tirtoff
65 Cat's-paw
66 Place in 55 Down
67 Fill to bursting
69 Computer key
70 Hitter's stat
71 Spinner

QUEEN OF CRIME by Kelly Clark
Don't be thinking Ellery here.

ACROSS

1 Voice of Tweety
6 Pinch pennies
11 Frets
16 True-blue
17 Start of a counting game
18 Forbidden
19 End of ___
20 "The Fugitive" singer Haggard
21 Fab Four road
22 Mustachioed sleuth of fiction
25 ___ Inn
26 Like tedious chores
31 Harborbound, in winter
35 Acting the copycat
37 Leisure
38 How Mrs. Mallowan was known after 1971
40 Cunning
42 Moran of "Happy Days"
43 Attenborough's title
44 Cease
45 Is ___ (probably will)
47 Attempts
49 Bitter
54 Layer
56 Blue soap pad
57 Auxiliary
58 Ireland, affectionately
62 Spinster sleuth of fiction
65 Tide type
66 Gia in "The Guns of Navarone"
68 In dreamland
69 With composure
71 Boston Common, for one
73 Sentiment of 22, 38, and 62 Across
79 Erie, for one
83 Caesar's land
84 Jack in "The Great Dictator"
85 Solo
86 Moor
87 Ivy League sch.
88 What the Knave of Hearts stole
89 Slalom curves
90 Assignments

DOWN

1 Dullsville
2 Like a certain Ranger
3 "Yesterday," to Pedro
4 Pusher pursuer
5 Model Schiffer
6 City southeast of Omsk
7 Perserveres
8 Geisha's box
9 Citizen's army
10 Use a keyhole
11 Hidalgo, e.g.
12 Keyboard key
13 Tide type
14 Misery
15 Tofu base
23 Kent's Smallville friend
24 Loft instrument
27 Harden
28 Lout
29 2000 NCAA hoop champs
30 Sushi choice
31 "Little grey cells" product
32 Quibble (at)
33 Give out
34 Fender-bender result
36 Like some verbs
39 Org.
41 Letters on a cereal box
44 Latin-101 verb
46 "So that's your game!"
48 "The Little Corporal"
50 ___ Maria von Weber
51 Ready to pick
52 Run in neutral
53 Profound
55 1959 Ford model
58 Add-___ (extras)
59 Common Korean name
60 Ward, to Beaver
61 Vichy, for one
62 Future lettermen
63 "Grand old name" of song
64 Invites to dinner
67 Dress
70 Shower squares
72 Far East nannies
74 Big times
75 Andalusian appetizer
76 Squeaks out
77 Curling team or surface
78 Urges
79 Witch's pet
80 In the manner of
81 Negative conjunction
82 Social insect

107 "CAN WE TALK?" by Maggie Davidson
The grid diagram below is an example of top-bottom symmetry.

ACROSS

1 Oscar adjective
5 Split suits
12 Kind of transit
16 ___ 'acte
17 The same
18 Brute leader?
19 One short of a quartet
20 **Start of a Laurence J. Peter quote**
22 Alfonso of baseball
24 Preeminent
25 **Quote: Part II**
29 Youngest Manning brother
30 Mar. honoree
31 Guitarist Kottke
32 Inundations
34 Comfort-giver
37 Parisian pop
38 Wearisome uniformity
43 Have an impact on
46 **Quote: Part III**
47 **Quote: Part IV**
48 Lets the air out of
50 Miss Randall of Sunnybrook Farm
54 Uncouth onlooker
56 Excoriation
58 Blank area
63 3M pt.
64 Football coaching family
66 **Quote: Part V**
70 Position for Norman
71 Common numbers?
72 "Don't buck me on this!"
74 X-ray dose units
75 **End of quote**
79 Old waste allowance
80 Having some merit
81 ". . . baked in ___"
82 Short criteria
83 "Move over!"
84 ___ rea (criminal intent)

DOWN

1 "___ Wedding" (1990)
2 Implant deeply
3 Arouse
4 Three-person team
5 Victor in "Hush . . . Hush, Sweet Charlotte"
6 One way to go downhill
7 Joke around
8 "___ woodchuck could chuck . . ."
9 Eggy drink
10 "___ my case"
11 2005 Pitt/Jolie roles
12 Cry like a baby
13 Trade topics
14 Thieves
15 Frankie Carle's "___ Serenade"
21 Leak through
23 Doodlebug prey
26 Confederate
27 Idyllic setting
28 Places
33 Pongid
34 Works in a mailroom
35 Beginning
36 Glowing bit
38 On the warpath
39 Ketel ___ vodka
40 Hot check letters
41 Night stalker
42 Café brew
44 Where Samuel Adams gets drunk
45 Driving directions abbr.
49 Cooke, Shepard, and Nunn
50 82 Across
51 Premier ___ (First Growth)
52 Steam organ
53 "Henry and June" role
55 D.C. United's stadium
57 Some flies
58 Pig patter
59 Certain '60s paintings
60 Remained
61 Freewheels
62 June hrs. in Orono
64 "Hmm . . ."
65 "Tallyho" setting
67 "The best is ___ come!"
68 Grayish
69 Triangular sign
73 River Kwai locale
76 Chemical ending
77 ___ in Quebec
78 "Where Nero?"

108

The clue from 16 Across came from Disney's "The Little Mermaid."

ACROSS

1 Jeweled wear
6 Acquire from the animal shelter
11 Gerald Ford's birthplace
16 Friend of Flounder and Sebastian
17 "Yes ___!" ("You betcha!")
18 Venetian way
19 Chutzpah
20 Watusi weapon
21 Discharge
22 **Word and start of its definition**
25 Fly like Road Runner?
27 Great Plains tribe
28 Lawrence-to-K.C. dir.
29 Sulky
31 Mazda model
35 Snake eyes
38 **Definition: Part 2**
42 Sitcom veteran Charlotte
43 Ultrasound determination
44 Like some spoiled wines
45 "___ Shandy": Sterne
50 Unchanging nature
52 Ed Norton's neighbor
53 Itinerary preposition
55 Oriole legend Ripken
56 **Definition: Part 3**
63 ". . . dead ___ his prime" (Milton's "Lycidas")
64 Sacred poem
65 Skylit court
66 "___ matter of fact . . ."
68 Cyclotron particle
70 Clutch components
71 **Definition: Part 4**
78 Reserved
79 Gained prominence
80 ___-3 fatty acid
83 Way more than necessary
84 Established fact
85 Eye surgery tool
86 Has "legs"
87 Gardener's packetful
88 Get-go

DOWN

1 West Palm shade
2 Sorehead's display
3 Everglades transport
4 Overhauls
5 Eldest Baldwin brother
6 Beauty or brains, say
7 Wizard's gift to the Scarecrow
8 Cookie brand since 1912
9 Fruit with a core
10 "Trillion" prefix
11 "Loverboy" singer
12 Microwave vacuum tube
13 Over again
14 Discuss, with "out"
15 Midrange chorister
23 Street rod
24 Carnivore's craving
25 Turn sharply
26 Day or square follower
30 Off-color
32 Successful candidates
33 Poker bullets
34 Milton Berle's longtime sponsor
36 "What ___ you thinking?!"
37 Acorn droppers
39 Lifts laboriously
40 South American wildcat
41 Bad, at first?
45 III, in modern Rome
46 All-night dance party
47 Robert of "The Sopranos"
48 Command to a search party
49 Easily cleaved mineral
51 1948 Peggy Lee chart-topper
54 Turner Field loc.
57 Render infertile
58 Poor marksman's comment
59 Morgan in "Bruce Almighty"
60 Liger's mother
61 O, in a billet-doux
62 Mickey Mouse's monogram?
67 Bank fixtures
69 Unseals
71 Israel's first king
72 Karate expert's board-breaking bone
73 Silent bidding signals
74 Unlikely derby winners
75 Lake fed by the Cuyahoga
76 Practiced basketry
77 Game on a 300-yard field
81 Beaver Cleaver expletive
82 Superior skill

109 "SAY IT EITHER WAY" by Richard Silvestri
Paul Newman voiced the character at 58 Down.

ACROSS

1 Complains constantly
6 Tinseltown trophy
11 Nimble
16 Atka native
17 BP brand
18 Quarrel
19 Posturepedic company
20 Shaggy jacket?
22 Star of "The Little Colonel"
24 Where to get down
25 Utah's state flower
26 Leave length, often
28 Sea bird
30 Yellow jacket
33 It's measured in MB
35 Old geezer
37 Fall bloomer
39 Base-clearing blast
41 Neck warmer
46 Rose to the occasion?
47 "A Doll's House" heroine
48 Bern's river
49 Things to get over
50 Key
51 ___ deaf ear to (ignore)
52 Inclusive abbr.
53 Particular
54 Toss out
55 Do-over button
57 Unbroken
59 Former capital of Japan
60 Open a bit
62 Jersey, e.g.
64 Proof annotation
65 Outline
69 AOL founder
71 Professional opening
72 Radio reply
77 Takes an oath
81 Supply steam?
84 Meat mold
85 "A Lesson from ___"
86 Type type
87 Low man at La Scala
88 Blair House
89 Tore
90 Like sherry

DOWN

1 Angler's action
2 Safe from the storm
3 Twenty quires
4 Flabby folks?
5 Do a do
6 Lunkhead
7 Self-satisfied
8 Required curriculum
9 Piece of land
10 Rogers and Clark
11 Contemporary art
12 "Tonight Show" invitee
13 Draw conclusions
14 Loyal subject
15 Make a U turn?
21 Auto dealer's takeback
23 Balance center
27 The old college cry
29 JFK posting
30 Leakage preventer
31 Clever
32 Leaf openings
34 Komodo dragon's lizard family
35 Earthenware
36 Kind of testimony
38 Short thoroughfares?
40 Tryst locale
42 Pert piece of playground equipment?
43 Snowman nose
44 Baroque
45 ___ Dome scandal
50 Traveler's OK
51 Sound of reproach
56 Toe preceder
58 Hudson in "Cars"
61 Peer group
63 Used to be
65 Horrify
66 São ___, Brazil
67 Slip
68 Gave a glowing review
70 Infirmary supply
73 More than
74 Big bash
75 Grist for DeMille?
76 Surf sound
78 Church recess
79 #1 hit for Herb Alpert
80 St. Andrews resident
82 Ogee shape
83 Roulette bet

110 MATURATION POINT by Ed Burnside

Zidane received a 15-D for head-butting in the 2006 World Cup final.

ACROSS

1 Letting in bugs
5 Cautionary verb
11 Concrete support
16 Cortland center
17 Blues singer Ma
18 Cast out
19 **Start of a quip**
21 Flattened
22 Kind of mail
23 Laugh-track user
25 Certain belief system
29 Employee move
30 "Poppycock!"
33 **Quip: Part II**
38 Progeny
39 Causes to stop
40 Shebat follower
41 10 Downing St. residents
42 Deck protector
43 Kennedy or Murrow
45 Mainstream
47 **Quip: Part III**
50 Like J. Lieberman in 2006
51 Former NBC anchor
54 "___ the news today . . .": Beatles
56 Harbor problem
59 Fit to be tried
60 Of no definite term
63 Close
64 **Quip: Part IV**
67 Orange Bowl stats
68 "Ally McBeal" lawyer
69 Carvey and Delany
70 Cosa ___
72 Elbow
76 Examine
79 **End of quip**
83 Show place
84 Weather influencer
85 Dexterity front
86 Ford products, for short
87 Close and Ford
88 Sack out

DOWN

1 Woolf's "Between the ___"
2 W.C.
3 BART's "A"
4 Domiciled
5 It may be strapless
6 Cochlea locale
7 Michelle of golf
8 Army members
9 Gives back one's job
10 Pilot's hurdle
11 Put on another top
12 It rhymes with cram
13 Industry, informally
14 India pale ___
15 Soccer card color
20 Robt. at Gettysburg
24 Almost touching
26 "Help ___ hand"
27 Wander off
28 Chef Batali
30 Say goodbye
31 Way, way off
32 Oater group
33 Medicinal amt.
34 Fringe
35 Answers
36 Not ersatz
37 Croquet site
42 Resort
44 "The butler ___ it!"
46 Cleared
48 Sole pattern
49 Salon coloring
51 Cellar, in ads
52 Bust
53 Patricia O'Conner's "___ I!"
55 Annex: Abbr.
57 Caliber, e.g.
58 Ode preposition
61 Inseam site
62 Dim-sum selection
63 Coffee request
65 Big name in coverage
66 Positive principle
70 "Traffic" cop
71 First-rate
73 Noggin
74 Oodles
75 Touch up
76 Buck passer
77 Cow or sow
78 Base address
80 Relations
81 Rustic stopover
82 Turndowns

111 SPECIAL DELIVERY   by Jim Page
If it's any consolation, the med student at 76-A was a first-year one.

ACROSS

1 Flimflams
5 Butte's brother
9 Puts down in writing?
15 Mind
16 OPEC member
17 Clique
18 **Start of a question for med students**
20 Rough draft
21 "Rad!"
22 Old World area
24 Vista click-on
25 1998 Julia Roberts film
28 Alla ___ (cut time)
31 **More of question**
36 Hi-___ monitor
39 Diarist Anais
40 Seeger bid her "goodnight"
41 "Drop ___ line!"
42 Intestinal inflammation
44 "I ___" (Turner autobiography)
45 Minnow or Orca
46 Ford of the '70s
47 Hooked undergarment
48 Film noir, e.g.
49 Hawaiian wahoos
50 Spicy cuisine
52 More pushy
54 Part of FYI
55 Cliburn's instrument
56 ___ pro nobis
57 T. Brady bunch
58 **End of question**
62 "___ a Grecian Urn"
63 Blocks
66 One hour before one
69 Ming thing
71 Alpine ridge
73 Gallery event
76 **Med student's answer**
79 One calling it quits
80 It may be gray
81 Some are cream
82 "Easy, dude!"
83 Antarctic explorer
84 Where Kilroy was?

DOWN

1 Joe McCarthy's counsel
2 Philharmonic instruments
3 Unfamiliar with
4 Pony player's strategy
5 Low sound?
6 It'll never fly
7 Stromboli sausage
8 Common bonds
9 ___ Diamond Phillips
10 Telecom giant
11 Faith
12 Funnyman Idle
13 Great White in "Shark Tale"
14 "Has Anybody ___ My Gal?"
17 Rough up
19 ___ bed (hit the sack)
23 Hispania, today
26 Cato's 1502
27 Has in hand
29 "Giant" author Ferber
30 Honking skein
32 Sulfuric acid
33 "It's being taken care of"
34 Closed in on
35 Fast breakers
36 Scam
37 "Three Weeks" novelist Glyn
38 León lady
43 "___ Howdy Doody time . . ."
45 "Promised Land" heroine
47 High-potassium fruit
48 Pontiac Phoenix successor
50 Whitewall
51 Home of Dartmouth
52 Prayer start
53 The Auld Sod
55 Foot: Comb. form
59 Oft-removed tissue
60 Hypothesis
61 Six-winged angel
64 Even the score again
65 Beefer
66 Meth confiscator
67 Lunchbox cookie
68 Miranda in "The Lord of the Rings"
70 Mariner's mop
72 Being, to Brutus
74 Onassis or Meyers
75 Pig tail?
77 Riviera sight
78 Michael Jackson album

ACROSS

1 Shuck peas
6 Tap choice
10 Tail
16 Tiptop place to live
17 Basque for "merry"
18 Zeus abductee
19 Elizabeth Taylor film (with "The")
22 Before
23 Excels
24 Map
25 Short otolaryngologist?
26 Boggy area
27 Time out of mind
28 Hook's #1
29 James Stewart film (with "The")
35 Experience
36 Shipping unit
37 Pappy Yokum's grandson
38 Atlas feature
40 "___ alive!"
41 Doctor of sci-fi fame
42 Tailward
45 Where dogs come clean?
47 Master Splinter's adversary
49 49 endings
50 Killarney loc.
51 Edgar Award honoree?
52 Hotel accommodation
53 Painter Lippo Lippi
54 Stalked one
56 Far from forward
57 Ali MacGraw/Richard Benjamin film
61 Dunce cap
62 Eats like a pig
63 Duran Duran album
64 Just right
65 Giant great Barber
67 Avatar of Vishnu
69 Beret's cousin
72 James Stewart film (with "The")
76 Handheld device
77 Prurient glance
78 Famed painter of water lilies
79 Combat sites
80 When your team bats first
81 "Witness" group

DOWN

1 Markdown
2 Get word of
3 Highlands tongue
4 Put a match to
5 Dear John, e.g.
6 Summer place
7 Fronton cheers
8 Medieval lyric poem
9 Dump (with "of")
10 Bar-tacks
11 Cadence counters
12 Altar in the sky
13 Bucks
14 Speaks up
15 Fritter away
20 Architectural column
21 She's in a family way?
26 ___ mignon
27 Would-be newts
28 Mystery writer Grafton
29 Man of La Mancha
30 Chiapas currency
31 Stereotypic
32 "Dagnab it!", e.g.
33 Bert in "Ship Ahoy"
34 Reeds in pits
35 Flute's cousin
39 Classic car
41 Deal's partner
42 "See ya!"
43 Treats royally
44 Long haul
46 Classy equine
47 Stand-up
48 Disney classic
51 Vic Tanny's pride
53 One to fight
54 Garçon has one
55 Myanmar, once
57 Minnesota native
58 One way to buy
59 Symbol of oppression
60 Unwholesome effluvium
61 "Platinum Blonde" director
65 See 42 Down
66 Fateful time
67 Mrs. DeVito
68 Like a breezeway
69 Grammy winner Braxton
70 Hawkish son of Zeus
71 Jackalope, for one
73 Chaney in "False Faces"
74 Sunday seating
75 Male turkey

"BEGONE!" by Victor Fleming and Bonnie Gentry
26 Down was an All-Star pitcher for the Oakland A's.

ACROSS

1 Cereal addition
8 Watery dirt
11 Fence material?
15 Indict for
17 Fed on
18 Black comedy
19 One who refuses to leave a project?
21 Worth thinking over
22 Caesar's closer
23 In that case
24 Weird and then some
25 Sunset Boulevard, for one?
30 It may go up in smoke
33 Ending like "-like"
34 Antique auto
35 Candler of Coke fame
36 Key contraction?
37 Local pol
39 No takers?
43 Is for several?
44 Mr. of mysteries
45 1945 conference site
47 Jai follower
51 Fleur-de-___
54 Phone tone for a key call?
57 Darrin's TV wife
61 Philologist's ref.
62 Pulitzer-winning Akins
63 Ref. volume
64 JFK watchdog
65 "Funny Girl" star
68 Where suits are also dudes?
71 Attach a nametag
72 University of Latvia's city
73 Unwanted word from a dentist
77 Dynamic start
78 Music for successful groups?
82 React to seeing red
83 Place to pasture
84 "Fish Magic" artist
85 Sailing ropes
86 USPS delivery
87 Field worker

DOWN

1 "A ___ to Live": O'Hara
2 Fünf und drei
3 "Law & Order: SVU" star
4 Surgical stitch
5 Suffix for 30 Down
6 Mr. Anderson in "The Matrix"
7 Diatonic scale tone
8 Popeye's pal
9 Tongs, e.g.
10 Austrian article
11 Vietnam's ___ Tho
12 Like Polk's presidency
13 Across the pond
14 Puts the finger on a Brother?
16 Islamic declaration
20 Impostor
24 Limonite's pigment
26 "Blue Moon" of baseball
27 Kind of rug or code
28 Irish port
29 Meat stamp
30 Oasis tree
31 Aoki of the links
32 Treaty
37 Letter letters
38 Stationer's unit
40 Source of caffeine
41 Supergirl's birth name
42 Judge in Samuel
46 Where Xanthippe shopped
48 Pookie in "The Sterile Cuckoo"
49 Directly
50 Picked out of a lineup
52 For laughs
53 Errors, e.g.
55 Driver's ed student, often
56 Lyrical
57 Overlook
58 Kind of attack
59 4-time U.S. Open winner
60 Kitchen wear
65 Utah lily
66 March
67 Hard-drive needs?
69 Hens' pens
70 Parish priest
74 Joad family's home st.
75 Hammer part
76 Dele killer
78 Evil
79 Literary monogram
80 Parisian way
81 According to

114 "I'VE PUT AN END TO THINGS!" by Jay Sullivan
. . . some things, not all!

ACROSS

1 Center of Florida
6 Spot of tea
11 Periodontist's concerns
15 Neo in "The Matrix"
16 Pola's silent-screen rival
17 Without letup
19 Kids' stuff
20 Orange coats
21 Firefighter Red
22 "I was framed," e.g.?
25 Verdi opera set in Cyprus
27 Ruin a shutout
28 Says "Who?"
29 Conversation fillers
30 His job is on the line
32 Bit of wd. play
33 Conks out
34 Eye piece
36 Have something
38 Strike count
40 You be the judge
41 Letter from camp?
45 In with
46 Green span
47 Nick in "Cape Fear"
52 Age of anxiety?
57 Got fed up
60 Before, of yore
61 Garden party
62 Kitchen addition?
63 Priggish people
65 Bumblers
68 Smiley's smile
70 Daytime darkening
71 Chichen Itza, say
72 Macbeth and Banquo
74 Factotums
76 Nervy?
79 Wishful words
80 Chicago planetarium
81 Karate shops
84 They cover all the bases
85 Early Roman dictator
86 Son of Cain
87 Birds do it
88 On edge
89 Joaquin's "Walk the Line" costar

DOWN

1 Ticker-tape letters?
2 Podded plant
3 Farm worker from Oaxaca
4 Center of Florida
5 Bit of a shoving match
6 "The Bell of ___": Longfellow
7 Street weapons
8 Roman tragedian
9 Throws in
10 Former Ferrari rival
11 The joke's on him
12 Like a zombie
13 Is serious
14 Mini ha-ha
18 Not at all casual
23 Ping thing
24 More than half of Israel
25 Medium's medium
26 Guitar sound
31 On the dark side
35 Go to the devil
37 Light air
39 Rare bird (except in crosswords)
42 No Mr. Nice Guy
43 Small whale
44 Goalie's goal
48 Groundbreaking discovery
49 Cast of four, in Vegas
50 Demolish
51 Chicago expressway
53 Jagged-edged
54 Ocean liner
55 NASA spacewalk
56 Concealed
57 Like the Cowardly Lion
58 Mention briefly
59 Quintessence
64 Takes potshots
66 Hot dip
67 Flicks pix
69 Not so hot
73 Get the lead out?
75 In concert
77 Chest protector
78 Thank God
82 Lt. academy
83 Third party

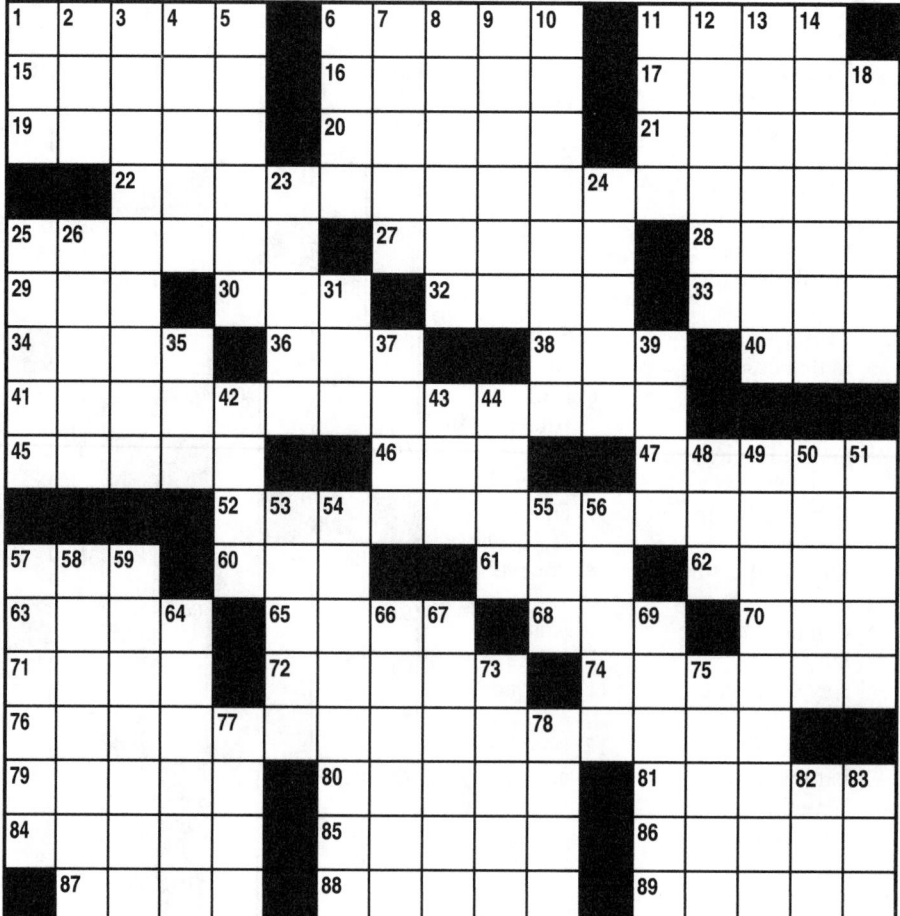

115 HIDDEN BUNNIES by Lucille Sloan
"They're not exactly in a hat, but . . ."

ACROSS

1 Caribbean island
6 Domestic
10 Place in a psych ward
16 Jots
17 Business leader?
18 Pungent cheese
19 Twelve places?
21 Like the Antarctic seal
22 Look for
23 Prevails
25 Julia's "A Bug's Life" role
26 Banquet
28 Camping gp.
29 Signed voucher
30 Civilian army
33 Where Regulus is
34 Roofing material
35 2002 Charles Aznavour film
36 Pessimist, often
38 Get a handle on?
39 Book end?
40 "Old what's-___-name"
41 Upper-left key
44 Penn, e.g.
45 Govt. mortgage appraisal
48 Roxy Music's Brian
49 Musket attachment?
50 Start of a German farewell
51 Unprocessed
52 Sitcom interruption
53 Bad actor
56 Stick like glue
58 Part of a drum kit
60 "___ I Kissed You": Everly Brothers
61 Gratifies
62 Shepard or King
63 ___ Jeanne d'Arc
64 Don't exist
65 "Me neither!"
66 Orbiter of 7/10/62
68 Matching
72 Toyota minivan
74 DON'T DO THIS WHILE SOLVING?
76 Lift-giver
77 Important periods
78 Con's cover
79 Kind of basketball pass
80 Where Kellogg is "K"
81 Dallas suburb

DOWN

1 Troubles
2 Philandering sort
3 Alternative magazine
4 Blow up in one's face
5 Elastic wood
6 Tomei of "In the Bedroom"
7 Deal maker
8 Nest eggs
9 Not follow
10 2005 tariff eliminator DR-___
11 Buckeyes' school
12 Cana event
13 "Dancing in the Street" singer
14 "Ha! ha!"
15 As yet
20 Be ready for
24 GI entertainment
27 Capt.'s prediction
30 Preacher's abode
31 Plenty sore
32 National anthem of Spain
33 Gridiron toss
34 Pt. of CBS
36 ___ Tamid (synagogue lamp)
37 Something to come up for
39 War of 1812 pirate
42 Trap
43 Some are made of bars
45 ___ accompli
46 Play a kazoo
47 Helping sort
52 "We're done here"
54 Encountered
55 Ratings name
56 Heads-up
57 Cubs' home
58 NPR host Liane
59 Philippines province
61 Give kudos to
63 "All the King's Men" protagonist
64 Book with routes
67 With a spring in one's step
69 Sills delivery
70 Cruel
71 Flying "A" rival
73 "The Matrix Reloaded" hero
75 General Arnold

116

53 Across won her first Wimbledon Championship at the age of 15.

ACROSS

1 Stuffed deli dish
6 About .035 ounces
10 Start to eat
15 Postulate
16 Signal light
17 Gay of crosswords
18 **Start of a quip**
21 Disapproval
22 Old hat
23 Rose–rose link
24 Shell game?
26 Nitwit
29 Pitney's "___ Without Pity"
32 Be contingent
35 Raconteur's repertoire
37 Words of wisdom
39 Gaucho's weapon
40 Big name in brushes
41 Top of some dials
42 Put things right
44 Rowling's Madam Pince
45 **Middle of quip**
51 Sinewy
52 "What Price Glory?" director Walsh
53 Five-time Wimbledon winner
54 Of the near past
57 Bullion units
58 Ride
60 On the edge of
61 Traveler's problem
63 Marvel superheroes
64 Alley target
65 Big bag
66 Still
68 Teapot part
71 Femme fatale
75 **End of quip**
80 Opposite of neo
81 Little Lord Fauntleroy
82 "Dirty Dancing" director Ardolino
83 Essence of roses
84 Village
85 Buy more "Time"

DOWN

1 "Camptown Races" syllable
2 Short suit?
3 Plenteous
4 In dew time?
5 Make ___ (be sloppy)
6 Jubilation
7 Did a 10K
8 Finesse
9 Put one's cards on the table
10 Bankruptcy factor
11 Memo words
12 "The Chimpanzees of Gombe" author
13 Kind
14 Dundee denial
16 2006 Nicole Kidman film
19 Campus area
20 Swerve, at sea
24 Whoop it up
25 Genetic material
27 "Dick and Jane" verb
28 Lat., formerly
29 Prepare for takeoff
30 Valhalla VIP
31 Stand in line
33 Key material
34 Atari's first game
35 Uproar
36 Lament for "poor Yorick"
38 Making lighter
40 Haus wife
43 Suit material
44 Deca- times two
46 Western author Wister
47 Father of Tiger Woods
48 Dutch export
49 Socks
50 Tree of Life locale
54 Grammy category
55 Cantab's rival
56 Give professional advice
57 Take the odds
59 Like Arctic winters
61 Wrote quickly
62 Peer of literature
65 252-gallon cask
67 Novocain precursor
69 Defense statement
70 Glade target
71 Queue before Q
72 B'nai B'rith org.
73 Related
74 Soccer legend
75 GAO employee
76 Feedbag tidbit
77 Back
78 Like defective mdse.
79 Evergreen tree

117 ROADIES by Fred Piscop
George W. Bush and John Kerry were both 53-Down members.

ACROSS

1 Achieve stardom
7 Break off
12 Company with a bulldog logo
16 Basilisk cousin
17 Weather, to bards
18 Present time
19 "Fat Actress" star
21 ___ Canaria island
22 Key on a keypad
23 "Inside the Third Reich" author
24 Inn instrument
25 Diva Lehmann
27 George Harrison played one
29 Graf's love match
32 Sundance's gal
36 Amigo
37 Litter little ones
40 ". . . card, ___ card"
41 Do some groundskeeping
42 Bindlestiff
45 Journalist Hamill
47 Travolta musical
49 Tennis great with a great tennis name
52 Furrow filler
54 Radius neighbor
55 Trickles down
58 So last year
59 Boom preceder?
61 Ogden Nash priest
63 Kingston inst.
64 "Hollywoodland" star
67 Withstand stress
70 "Well, ___!"
71 Not shy
73 Home of golf's Blue Monster
76 One of the Bee Gees
78 Preserves, in a way
82 "Ben-Hur," e.g.
83 1988 Super-G gold medalist
85 ___ Valley (Reagan Library site)
86 Rude awakener
87 Mass. governor (2003–07)
88 Quick-witted
89 Takes a hit in share price
90 Short gridiron kick

DOWN

1 Lapel item
2 Opposed to, in dialect
3 Cobain or Russell
4 Spots for charts
5 Emcee lines
6 Clavell's "___-Pan"
7 Suffix with moon
8 "Allure" competitor
9 Most foul
10 Retiree's title
11 Marina Del ___
12 Temptations classic
13 Kirlian photography image
14 Kiltie's group
15 Casino attraction
20 Garage-work fig.
24 Scroll material
26 Tout's offering
28 "The Rain in Spain" is one
29 EIK spot
30 Long-jawed swimmer
31 Bay Area city
32 Winwood in "The Misfits"
33 Tiger Woods, in 1995
34 Trig fig.
35 Flock member
38 "Pull ___ chair!"
39 Silver-exporting land
43 "Spy vs. Spy" magazine
44 Market before building
46 Sight from Taormina
48 Poet's preposition
50 George Foreman product
51 Web-video gear
52 Hut material
53 Skull & Bones member
56 Boston landmark, for short
57 Don't chug
60 Audrey Hepburn title role
62 FOX competitor
65 Yeast is rich in it
66 Paul Wolfowitz, for one
68 Penn. home of Larry Holmes
69 Bells and whistles
71 Hampton's instrument
72 "Double Fantasy" singer
73 Carrel item
74 Ronny Howard role
75 Icy coating
77 Basenjis rarely do this
79 Filmmaker Riefenstahl
80 What the hot-headed golfer was?
81 Lid woe
83 L.A. hrs.
84 Good news at the B.O.

118 HALF FULL   by Victor Fleming
"It takes both rain and sunshine to make a rainbow."

ACROSS

1 Hold forth
6 Kind of girl party
12 Rotating parts
16 Hemmed in
17 Ethically indifferent
18 Lots
19 **Start of a definition**
21 Noodle product
22 Wins out over
23 Berlin article
24 Catch on to
25 Computer suffix
26 **Definition: Part II**
28 Sign of a hit
31 Boaz's wife
33 Joint ownership word
34 Editor Talese
35 **Definition: Part III**
38 Duel-purpose blade
40 Cel material
41 Mouthful in a lea
42 Tinseltown terrier
46 Tori Amos song
47 **Definition: Part IV**
48 Mr. Big
50 "The Godfather" composer Rota
51 Half a bray
52 Payday, vis-à-vis Zero
53 Milky liquid
56 **Definition: Part V**
57 Spain's "Beethoven of the Guitar"
60 Boston catch
61 Mincemeat ingredient
62 Nest-egg acct.
63 **Definition: Part VI**
66 "___ for Lawless": Grafton
69 Vocalist Gormé
70 Windy City–Motor City dir.
71 Notwithstanding
75 Fair-hiring watchdog
76 **Definition: Part VII**
78 Nosedive
79 ___ needed
80 Career soldier
81 Doe and dam
82 Lyric poems
83 "Family Ties" mother

DOWN

1 Bk. after Amos
2 Conductor Leibowitz
3 Since
4 Home on the range
5 James and Place
6 Dawber and Shriver
7 Bordeaux buddy
8 Novelist Conrad
9 Shaw of swing
10 Major artery
11 L. Gehrig's disease
12 Stone marker
13 When Sol rises
14 Brandy Norwood role
15 Fasten in a way
20 Say over
24 Blood and guts
26 Wore away
27 Nautilus, e.g.
28 Beau
29 Christina in "Monster"
30 Glyceride found in fat
32 Hawaiian strings
36 Maj.'s superior
37 Bad, in Bordeaux
38 File a complaint
39 Reached the amount of
41 Ally of Fidel
43 Book genre
44 Joint ownership word
45 Blood distributor
47 Joe who sang "Skinny Legs and All"
48 Wastes no time
49 Giant legend
51 Fly low
52 Family-tree word
54 Fluish feeling
55 Tip for a ballerina?
56 Coach
57 Cookies, candy, etc.
58 "I'd forgotten about that!"
59 Fixed
61 ___ tomatoes
64 Shaving mishaps
65 Calendario page
67 Basketry fiber
68 Go bad
71 Temperance advocates
72 A bit doubtful
73 Neckwear
74 Basic French verb
76 "The Wasteland" auth.
77 Lego inventor Christiansen

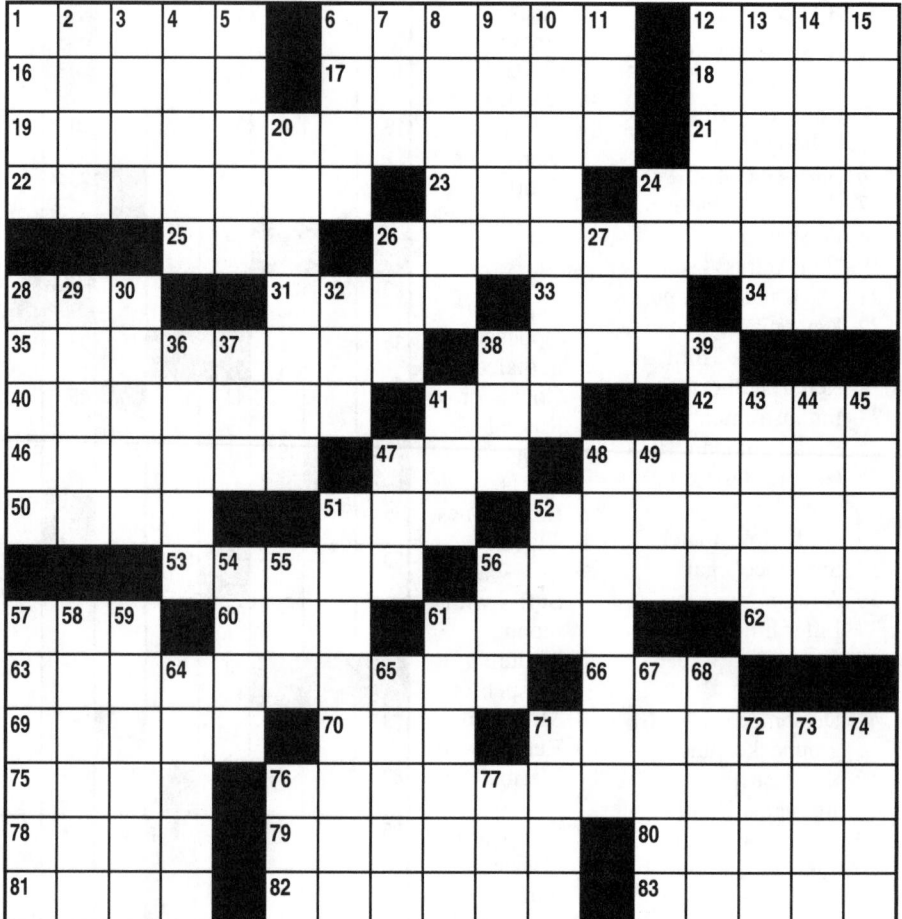

119 GRIDIRON GROANERS by Robert Zimmerman
A good one to solve on Super Sunday morning.

ACROSS

1 Mellows out?
7 Remote control?
13 Summertime
16 "Pronto!"
17 Jubilant
18 Poetic contraction
19 NFC Pro Bowl lineman?
21 Gibraltar denizen
22 Clothed
23 Cicatrix
24 Singer Arie
26 Website visit
27 Stevie Wonder's "___ Duke"
28 Wedding dance
31 New York–Washington, D.C., e.g.
35 Confuse
36 Glen Jacobs' ring name
37 Newts
39 Draftable
42 Toyota pickup
45 Make corrections
46 Huxley's "___ Hay"
47 "Miss Peach" lad
48 Resentful receiver?
51 Age
52 Slow, for Humperdinck
54 Punctilio
55 Idolized
57 Kind of lamp
58 Kind of e-mail filter
59 Declare openly
60 Tin Pan Alley org.
62 Uniformity
66 Really pleased
69 They go on for yrs.
70 Lender's receipt
72 Hussar's weapon
73 Thunderhead
75 Cuckoos
76 Hot Springs, for one
77 Dolphin-hunting lineman?
82 Crescent
83 Buttress
84 More repugnant
85 Asian ox

86 Makes a mess of things (with "up")
87 They go with leaps

DOWN

1 House dressing?
2 Font option
3 Chip material
4 Geraint's love
5 E-9, for one
6 .01 yen
7 Pull-away binder
8 Picasso's first wife
9 Gene Tierney title role
10 Stage actress Hagen
11 It's full of eau
12 Flowed in a circle
13 Exhausted lineman?
14 Photo tint
15 Pick up the tab
20 Digression
25 Synthetic fiber patented 1937
27 Sharm al-Sheikh locale
29 Caribou order
30 Mormon inits.
32 Original "King Kong" studio
33 "First Blood" hero
34 Cashes in
38 The CIA, so-called
40 Meath locale
41 Educational inst.
42 Cultivate
43 L × W
44 Painted runner?
45 "Tell Mama" singer James
46 Enlarge the house
49 Melanie Griffith's mom
50 Church features

53 Decorator's asset
56 Pay with plastic
58 Convened, as a tribunal
59 In the midst of
61 Two, in a Cadillac XLR-V
63 Restitution
64 Hit home
65 Besmirched
66 Emerson's "Compensation"
67 "State of the Union" director
68 Small salmon
71 Employers, of a sort
74 Bannister's distance
75 Sacco-Vanzetti case org.
78 NASDAQ newbie
79 Moo ___ pork
80 Rustbucket
81 "Give it ___"

120 WORLDLY HUMOR by Thomas W. Schier
75 Down appears on the Connecticut quarter.

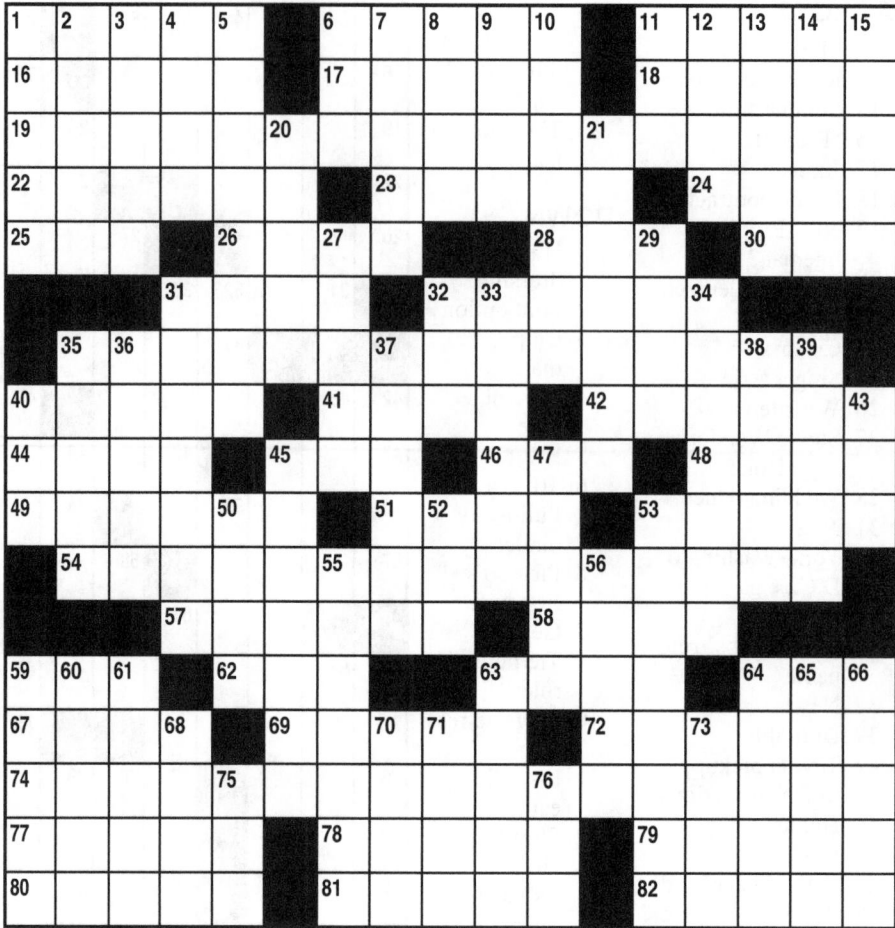

ACROSS

1 Novi Sad natives
6 Laughing
11 Passport stamps
16 Doggie reward
17 Deity of the Koran
18 Put on the books
19 **Start of a Flannery O'Connor quote**
22 Toxic atmosphere
23 Fourth Republic coin
24 To ___ (perfectly)
25 Get-up-and-go
26 Chocolate-syrup brand
28 Roth arrangement
30 Roush of Cooperstown
31 Snopes of Faulkner books
32 Rescinds
35 **More of quote**
40 Impertinent ones
41 ___ on the back
42 Loud musical passages
44 Sitting on
45 Whiz-bang
46 Bit of hope
48 Hangover at home
49 Kinetic art form
51 Pull up to the bar
53 Daniel's "Sonnets to ___"
54 **More of quote**
57 "Total patient" philosophy
58 Cook's smidgen
59 Traffic ___
62 Weep convulsively
63 Feudal underling
64 Fancy home amenity
67 Prized mount
69 Rich meal
72 Fast freshwater fish
74 **End of quote**
77 Ventrical outlet
78 Furnace brand
79 Kitchen bulb
80 Not do openly
81 All meshed up?
82 Affront-filled fete

DOWN

1 Get snow off boots
2 Keebler's head elf
3 Catch up to again
4 Loading dock slots
5 Enticement
6 Uncurved, as test scores
7 Start of a Bennett classic
8 Apple application, once
9 Japan's first capital
10 Tim Daly TV series
11 Churchillian gesture
12 Worshiper at Pachacamac
13 Make veal scaloppini
14 Like Ted Turner, notably
15 Silver, e.g.
20 Eberhard ___
21 Untidy
27 Lock up
29 Moreover
31 Fancy-pants
32 It's near Miss.
33 Acid from saltpeter
34 Harsh cry
35 Being pulled
36 Mournful mother of myth
37 Times to remember
38 Chateaubriand novel
39 Author Shute
40 Houston, for one
43 Great White hunter's milieu
45 Strip
47 Cellpart
50 Buscaglia and Tolstoy
52 Don't commit
53 Unfortunate regard
55 Like some monks
56 Day of la semaine
59 Hombre's homes
60 Bellatrix's constellation
61 Man with a mission
63 Double's doing
64 Narrow furrow
65 Guadalajara green
66 Looks ___ everything
68 Software protype
70 Wistful words
71 Congressman's prize
73 Gambling haven
75 Connecticut's "Charter" tree
76 House denial

121 HAPPY HOUR HUMOR by Jim Page
"You're not drunk if you can lie on the floor without holding on." — Dean Martin

ACROSS

1 Toothpicked sandwiches
5 Bollywood dresses
10 Payable now
15 From the hip
16 "Peanuts" character
17 ___ in sight
18 Knobby
19 Talked and talked
20 ___ dancer (RR worker of old)
21 **Pub sign: Part 1**
23 Like poltergeist
24 PC key
25 Luck, good or bad
26 180° from Westen
28 "Jeopardy!" host before Alex
30 Half of MIV
31 Part of UNICEF
33 Art brush material
36 "Inside Report" columnist Robert
38 "I'd hate to break up ___"
40 Pianist in "Mad Love"
41 Compass point
42 Impress clearly
44 Fish hawks
46 **Pub sign: Part 2**
49 Twinkie maker
52 "Pearl Harbor" hero
53 Islands off New Guinea
56 Mexican Oscar
57 Security problem
59 Elkins of whodunits
61 Sweater type
63 Sweater sizes: Abbr.
65 "___ As Directed"
67 K2's NYSE symbol
68 "Free ___ Bird": Beatles
69 Tiebreaking pds.
70 PBS benefactor
71 "Maids a-milking" group
74 **Pub sign: Part 3**
78 Roll cloud
79 Shannon Airport's county
80 Remove more squeaks
81 They have their pride
82 Slanted surface
83 Bodybuilder Vic
84 Shoot-'em-up band
85 Salad green
86 Surfboard fin

DOWN

1 One of two hockey-rink markings
2 Happy-hour offering
3 Dana perfume
4 Parthia's ancient neighbor
5 Understudy's study
6 "Nerts"
7 Madras monarch
8 Hematite, e.g.
9 ___ Anselmo, CA
10 "Summer Brave" playwright
11 Parasail
12 Possible to contradict
13 Coat below
14 Dreyer's ice-cream partner
15 Out of favor
22 Casey Stengel once managed them
23 Takeoff guesstimate: Abbr.
27 Enhance
29 Gumshoes
32 Like an antimacassar
34 Sec. class?
35 Unpaid debt
37 Checked for accuracy
39 He-Man's sister
43 Silicon Valley autos
45 B-2 bomber
47 Port opener
48 Churchill Downs filly race
49 Grub Street resident
50 Handel's "Esther" is one
51 Hot Sicilian winds
54 When the second Ali-Liston fight ended
55 Blind
58 Empowering one
60 Catalogues
62 Hood's heater
64 Trendy mushrooms
66 With time to spare
72 Wine casks
73 Being, in Caesar's day
75 Icicle anchor
76 Start of a Cockney toast
77 News source
78 Snowy peak
79 "Hockey Night in Canada" producer

In 1984 28-A was the first woman athlete to appear on a Wheaties box.

ACROSS

1 "Because ___ so!"
6 Unhappy with
13 Where to catch a Magic act
16 Harry Coombes' cat
17 Poets Amy and Robert
18 Malleus locale
19 Stroll to discuss opinion pieces?
21 Health supplement chain
22 Rest stop?
23 School near Astor Place
24 Golfer Isao
25 Like an Inverness iota
26 Last name in fashion
28 Gymnast on a Wheaties box
30 Cloakroom conference?
34 Valium maker
37 Kazan of movies
38 Cell messenger
39 Moor of tragedy
42 Numerical prefix
44 Numerical prefix
47 Appearing duly licensed?
51 A-line border
52 Crème–crème connection
53 Beg urgently
54 Vivacity
57 ___ Zone (big name in parts)
59 Present-day hero?
60 Space for blitzing or bearing off?
65 Become whole again
66 Nurture
67 South American Mrs.
70 Period pieces?
71 Option at Hertz
74 Certain measuring device
77 "Ladders to Fire" writer
78 Sport of kings?
80 Bumstead nickname
81 Manet and Monet
82 Relay hardware
83 Bass in a barrel
84 Promised one
85 Nodded

DOWN

1 Inventory listees
2 Lot's lost city
3 Author Loos
4 "Sock ___ me!"
5 Word with barn or storm
6 Demonstration of excellence
7 Virginia city
8 32 Down mascot
9 Basted
10 Make laugh a lot
11 Magnetism
12 "Naughty, naughty!"
13 Collective bargaining
14 Trust
15 Like Jabbar's sky hook
20 One way to get out of Dodge
24 Envelope abbr.
27 One on the move?
29 Chariot add-on
30 "ER" doctor
31 Remained fast
32 Houston campus
33 Prefix with linear
34 Hebrew "beginning"
35 Oklahoma tribe
36 Trifling sum
40 It goes to pot?
41 1916 Chaplin silent
43 Bread-line locale?
45 Existed, in the Bible
46 Just a thought
48 Down
49 ___ facto
50 Deception
55 Squeaks (out)
56 2007 Southern Hills event
58 City on the Susquehanna
60 Vaccaro in "Midnight Cowboy"
61 Wave catcher
62 "An Inconvenient Truth" figure
63 Salad veggie
64 "Straight up ___ the rocks?"
67 Condition
68 Swab over
69 "___ you ashamed?"
72 Low mil. ranks
73 Twice tres
75 Classic British sportscars
76 Alike, to André
78 Big pod
79 Carpal tunnel syndrome, e.g., briefly

123 MEANS TO AN END by Jordan P. Conway

The Fearsome Foursome at (65-D) were L.A. Rams defensemen in the 1960s.

ACROSS

1 SRO show
6 Kid-lit pachyderm
11 Bogart sleuth
16 Necktie party group
17 Dress with a flare
18 Fax forerunner
19 Means of getting a spear carrier?
21 Rack filler
22 Make public
23 Stay-at-home ___
24 Avian sources of red meat
26 L.A. necessity
27 Cigar store purchase
29 Means of getting a piano?
32 Gucci rival
34 '60s tripper
35 "Men in Trees" working girl
38 Timbuktu's land
40 "The Hours" star
44 Inter ___
45 Objects of "dumb" jokes
48 Polar pioneer
49 Race part
50 Means of getting an expo?
52 Fam. tree listing
53 Java allure
55 Far from flustered
56 ___-Soviet relations
57 Coif protectors, of sorts
59 Monopoly stack
60 In fighting trim
61 Attack, puppy-style
64 Words to live by
66 Means of getting a loo?
70 Printing proofs
74 Rock-___ (jukebox brand)
75 Sea dust, in diners
76 In vitro cells
77 Abbr. in car ads
78 Fertilizer compound
81 Means of getting a stiff drink?
84 EGBDF part

85 Sacked out
86 Master of the double-take
87 Marsh plant
88 Long-eared equines
89 Places to roost

DOWN

1 Fisherman's tool
2 Classic soft drink
3 Kansas motto word
4 Former map inits.
5 Soccer shot
6 Sonneteer
7 Publican's offering
8 One waiting around
9 Cracker type
10 Get back into pitch
11 Urban grid: Abbr.
12 Get-up-and-go
13 Trixie's TV pal
14 Joltless joe
15 Put out
20 Durango "dang!"
25 Home of Sioux Falls: Abbr.
28 Film-rating org.
29 In profusion
30 Utter nonsense
31 Dark alter ego
33 "The Burning Giraffe" et al.
35 Waldorf ___
36 The last 76-Down made
37 Vicissitude
39 Emcee's job
41 Mme. Tussaud
42 Site of a big event
43 Parachute fabric
46 Soak to the bone
47 Not so dotty
50 Dickens dastard
51 Have coming

54 Jazz flutist Herbie
56 Schmaltz
58 1974 Sutherland/Gould comedy
62 Maine national park
63 Sharp grippers
65 Fearsome Foursome member (with 66-D)
66 See 65 Down
67 Source of oil
68 Couldn't stomach
69 Concert mementos
71 Needs a bath badly
72 Bibliography abbr.
73 "Land ___ alive!"
76 Discontinued GM line
79 Work unit
80 Bar stock
82 Contest of sorts
83 Have, to Burns

ACROSS

1 Jet who wore #12
7 Final Bible bk.
11 Members of the flock
16 Long river in Chile
17 Biblical wedding site
18 Where the fat lady sings
19 Neighborhood Watch volunteer?
21 Bach's score, essentially
22 Pry
23 They bear down
24 Like some parking meters?
30 Early mall
31 Winter time in Halifax
32 Aka, in commerce
33 He's cool
36 Dunkirk evacuee's destination
37 Volunteer's response
38 Merger announcement
39 Office party
40 Flip-flop
43 Nae sayer
44 Not Marcel Marceau?
47 Mushroom
49 Put on a happy face
50 Blades of yore
53 One of us
54 Order to go
55 Make up
56 Treat like a dog
57 EarthLink rival
58 Crash site
61 "Sun Valley Serenade" skater
62 Detergent targets?
65 Bring out
69 Biscotti flavoring
70 Genetic triplet
71 Rind?
77 Rumpus
78 Tricolor color
79 He had a good laugh
80 Not at full power
81 IRS info.
82 Endorser

DOWN

1 "ER" site
2 Every breath you take
3 "Who me?" in Paris
4 SDI weapon
5 Casual Friday option
6 "Why is that?"
7 What this answer isn't
8 Prove successful
9 Afternoon hour
10 Tesla namesake
11 James T. Farrell's Studs
12 Like two peas in ___
13 Parcel (out)
14 Remus relation?
15 Lip or cheek
20 Christie or Karenina
23 Preserve, in a way
24 Root-beer label
25 "___ a Woman": Charles
26 Heeds marching orders
27 Heretofore
28 Bank job?
29 Phising catch?
33 Tour guides
34 Hustle and bustle
35 Day-care charge
37 What would Descartes think?
40 Mogadishu resident
41 In a row
42 It's got the Blues
43 Makes a big hit
45 Take places
46 Sun Valley site
47 Swindle
48 Marine preschoolers
51 Tight end?
52 Gets the picture
54 Lake Huron bay
58 Writers
59 Parting words
60 Jr., to Sr.
63 Goes postal
64 Bergamot and Bartlett
65 Remembrance of things past
66 Daffy duck
67 Role model
68 Small salmon
71 Wgt. watcher's loss
72 Luau chow
73 Hang loose
74 Pour thing?
75 Rebel leader
76 Be off

EDUCATIONAL PROCESS   by Chase McFarland
The answer to 40 Across is not ground round.

ACROSS

1 Dana of "MacGyver"
6 Type styles: Abbr.
11 Looking down
16 "A light he was to ___ but himself": Frost
17 Recipe phrase
18 Fat
19 "Tootsie" Oscar winner
20 Coeur d'___
21 "Poor Richard's Almanack" tidbit
22 **Start of a Laurence J. Peter quip**
25 Close a zip-lock
26 Benefit
27 Not esta or esa
28 Assay
29 Mrs. Addams, to Gomez
32 Stringency
34 2007 Oakmont Country Club event
36 Org. of crackers
37 Routing org.
40 Chuck alternative
43 "Star Trek III" director
45 Pitch card
47 **More of quip**
51 Battery brand
52 It often has a top but no bottom
53 Curse
54 Pother
55 Kind of whoop
58 Some early computers
60 Links legend Walter
62 Tiny bit
63 Kick out
66 Sculptor Nadelman
69 No good and more
71 Solidarity cofounder
73 **End of quip**
77 Jerry Marcus comic strip
78 Less inept
79 "___ at the office"
80 Implodes, maybe
81 Gaucho's turf
82 Unconventional
83 Radiate
84 Attach a patch
85 All possible

DOWN

1 Join
2 Bum
3 Twitty of Nashville
4 L.A. slugger
5 Orders more take-out?
6 1970s "Vogue" discovery
7 Knight fight
8 Button's leaps
9 Straight
10 Enter at an exit, maybe
11 NFL guard Faneca
12 Try to buy
13 Hanging dazzlement
14 Enthusiasm
15 Diuretic target
23 Whopper toppers
24 Partner of rules, slangily
30 Barbecue accessory
31 Virile one
33 Vow
34 Pyle's org.
35 Largest Finnish company
37 Distinctive quality
38 Final word
39 Altar area
40 End notes
41 Tinged
42 Cartoon mate of Janis
44 Busybody
46 Yanks' opposition
48 Tall Corn State
49 Photo finish
50 Like a fixed fight
56 They make up eons
57 Leaks
59 Visualize
60 Didn't ignore
61 Hardly clumsy
63 "Stop acting up!"
64 Letter-closing phrase
65 To wit
66 Argentine province ___ Ríos
67 "I speak for the trees" speaker
68 Axiom developer
70 Show that featured Arnie Becker
72 Win Rockefeller's title
74 Where Ford gets an "F"
75 Game of chance
76 It's sometimes cast

126 ANIMAL CRACKERS by Fran & Lou Sabin
Put on a black tie while solving 78 Across.

ACROSS

1 Clemson logos
5 Lets up
11 Sherman and Abrams
16 Land rush unit
17 Secret doctrine
18 "Mefistofele" role
19 Escaping Tweedy's farm, e.g.?
21 A Barrymore
22 Disagreeable
23 Semana segment
25 City on the Oka
26 Retired "bird"
27 Mistreated bird?
33 Ecdysiast wear
34 Eras and eras
35 Big as all get-out
38 Tiny bit
39 2004 running mate
43 Store sign
44 Nairobi native
46 Mine yield
47 Played for a fool
48 Collector's collection, perhaps
49 Limited seating?
51 "___ Love": Beatles
52 Cartoon dog
53 Inherited property
55 Heavenly peacock
56 Like the Walk of Fame
60 Kuwait biggie
61 Lollapalooza
62 Diamond decision
63 Sat on eggs
65 Fan of knights?
69 Omelet option
72 Chill factor?
73 "Playboy" founder, familiarly
74 Valuable viola
76 Hair jobs
78 "Zoo Story" sequel?
83 Notorious Peron
84 Richards in "Jurassic Park"
85 Mattress support
86 Extend (a subscription)
87 Abutting
88 Chrysler engine

DOWN

1 War-ending deals
2 Unguent's target
3 Band site
4 Offshoot group
5 Suit topper
6 Black out
7 Kindergarten song start
8 "The way" of puzzles
9 Remains on the loose
10 Flavorful
11 Kick-off support
12 Penn State campus site
13 India's first P.M.
14 Pants parts
15 Maison room
20 Sedgwick in "The Closer"
24 Like Dom Perignon, 1890
28 Japanese metropolis
29 Put into speech
30 Mays, Ott, Hubbell et al.
31 Delilah in "Samson and Delilah" (1950)
32 Classroom assignment?
33 Revolve around
35 Working time
36 Surprise conclusion
37 Davis in "The Fly"
39 Diseased leaf growth
40 Like the Appian Way
41 Cruising gear
42 Mexicali man
45 Southwestern poplars
50 Hidden
51 Big Apple seller?
54 Swabbies
57 Leopard spot
58 Wish otherwise
59 Draw with acid

63 In the past
64 "L'___, c'est moi": Louis XIV
65 Man-___ (misandrist)
66 Pointed arch
67 Take "downtown"
68 She-Ra's brother
69 Berry in "Losing Isaiah"
70 Peppard series (with "The")
71 El ___ (Peru volcano)
75 1970 Sutherland film
77 Hand or band follower
79 "No way!"
80 McPhee of "American Idol" fame
81 Middle Earth creature
82 Ming of the NBA

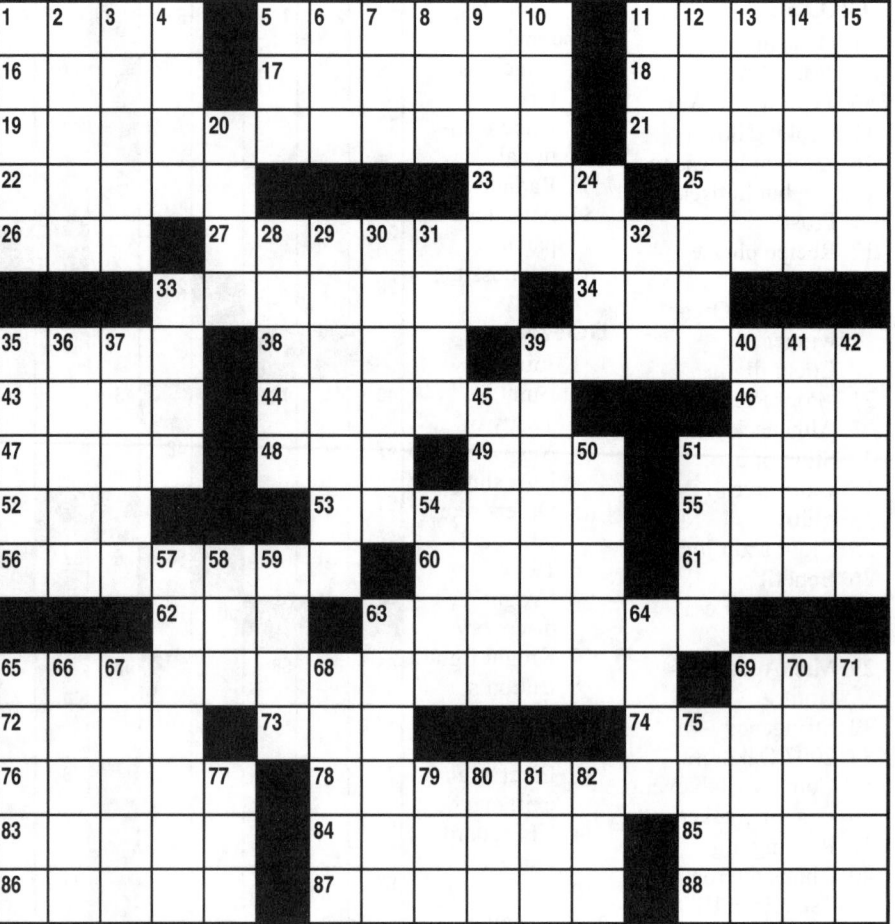

127 SUPERHEROES   by Peggy O'Shea
The real name of 47 Down is James Howlett.

ACROSS

1 Warren females
5 Noble mounts
11 Sherlock's violin
16 Invitation letters
17 Small rug
18 Recurring melody
19 Kirghizian range
20 "Measure for Measure" nobleman
21 Move a fern
22 Lasso of Truth wielder
24 United Airlines hub
25 Russian violinist (1891–1967)
26 Isolated
28 Soft ice-cream server, e.g.
31 U.
32 Ants
34 Lettuce cultivar
35 Supergirl's birth name
39 How acronyms appear
40 Todd of "Lizzie McGuire"
43 Welcome ___
44 High times
45 Battery type
46 Be in a holding pattern
48 Kara ___ desert
49 Bursts out
51 1966 U.S. Open winner (tennis)
52 Footfall
54 Sobriety org.
55 Sermons
57 "Toy Story" pig
59 Change over
60 Circumvented
64 Lenya in "The Appointment"
65 Makes money
66 Black Beauty's passenger
71 Aristocracy
72 Homeless girl
73 Little bit
74 Lacy loop
75 "New World Symphony" key
76 Undiluted
77 Comes across as
78 Secret MPAA group
79 Peterson in "North Country"

DOWN

1 Gunslinger's command
2 Where the Storting meets
3 Novelist Hunter
4 Peter Parker alias
5 Bees, at times
6 Old pots and pans
7 Have ___ one's face
8 K–6
9 Bartolomé ___ Casas
10 Steve Austin's nickname
11 Amble along
12 Bruce Banner's alias
13 Fix car brakes
14 Love, in Livorno
15 Outmoded
23 Geometric curve
27 "___ fan tutte": Mozart
28 "Neon Leon" of boxing
29 Prevail
30 "Antony ___ from the field": Shak.
33 Flotilla members
34 Skirmish
36 Charlotte ___, Virgin Islands
37 Vituperative one
38 Corroborate
41 "Don't just sit there!"
42 Corrode
45 Connecticut citizen
47 One of The X-Men
50 Shropshire lads?
51 Comical brothers
53 Skull Cave resident
56 Gabrielle on "Xena: Warrior Princess"
58 Cash and charm
60 Road Runner noises
61 Skull & Bones member
62 "The Fly" star
63 Emmy category
64 Hanover river
67 Radiate
68 Christmas
69 All-inclusive abbr.
70 Larenz in "The Postman"

WORLD DANCES   by Linda Finnerty
Debutantes should have a ball with 45 Down.

ACROSS

1 In a way
6 22, for one
11 Mediterranean country
16 "Paradise Lost" angel
17 Oahu yoo-hoo
18 Regional
19 Magisterial
20 Shoe size
21 Vista pictures
22 Andalusian Gypsy dance
24 Folk dance of Portugal
26 Big name in faucets
27 John Irving's Piggy
28 Lightweight topsail
32 Borgnine and Bloch
36 Cliquish
38 Winged deity
39 Peanut's subfamily
40 Roughen up
41 Nobelist Canetti
43 Porter's "Anything ___"
44 ___-nez
45 Cliff rocks
46 "I do" pledge this
47 Army division
48 Freeload
49 "I'm Outta Here" singer
50 West end of L.A.
51 "Mares eat ___ and . . ."
52 "Sleeping With ___" (1991)
54 "Only U" singer
56 Plant lice
57 AC-motor inventor Nikola
59 In ___ (undisturbed)
60 Hawaiian dance
63 Celtic dance
68 Childish retort
69 How many view Leno
71 Miss America's crown
72 "Daktari" tongue
73 Schiller's "___ Joy"
74 Paul of "Lonesome Dove"
75 Transmogrify
76 Barcelona babes
77 Remove all traces

DOWN

1 Hang ten
2 City founded by Ivan IV
3 Baltic capital
4 USA, in Ryder Cup play
5 Renaissance dance
6 Voids
7 What March may come in like
8 Whole bunch
9 Food Network stars
10 Cuban dances
11 Winless horses
12 Video-game center
13 Watergate prosecutor Jaworski
14 NASA Gemini drink
15 Additionally
23 "Honest to Pete!"
25 Peter and a Wolfe
28 Shoulder blade
29 White elephants, e.g.
30 Waterproof coat?
31 Put on the books
33 Canoodled
34 Links appointment
35 Square-dance steps
37 Grinders
38 Number of octagon angles
42 Lancelot du ___
43 Siegfried's steed
45 Royal dance of France
46 Disco dance
48 Crispin apple
49 Dr. Phil's b'day
51 "___ Photo" (2002)
53 Fauxhawk and Mohawk
55 Herb Alpert's "___ of Honey"
58 "Biography" network
59 Dos y cinco
60 Czech composer of "Matka"
61 Orenburg's river
62 Penitential season
64 Word form of "sacred"
65 Publication for MDs
66 "Antony and Cleopatra" role
67 Money from ticket sales
70 Fed Chairman Bernanke

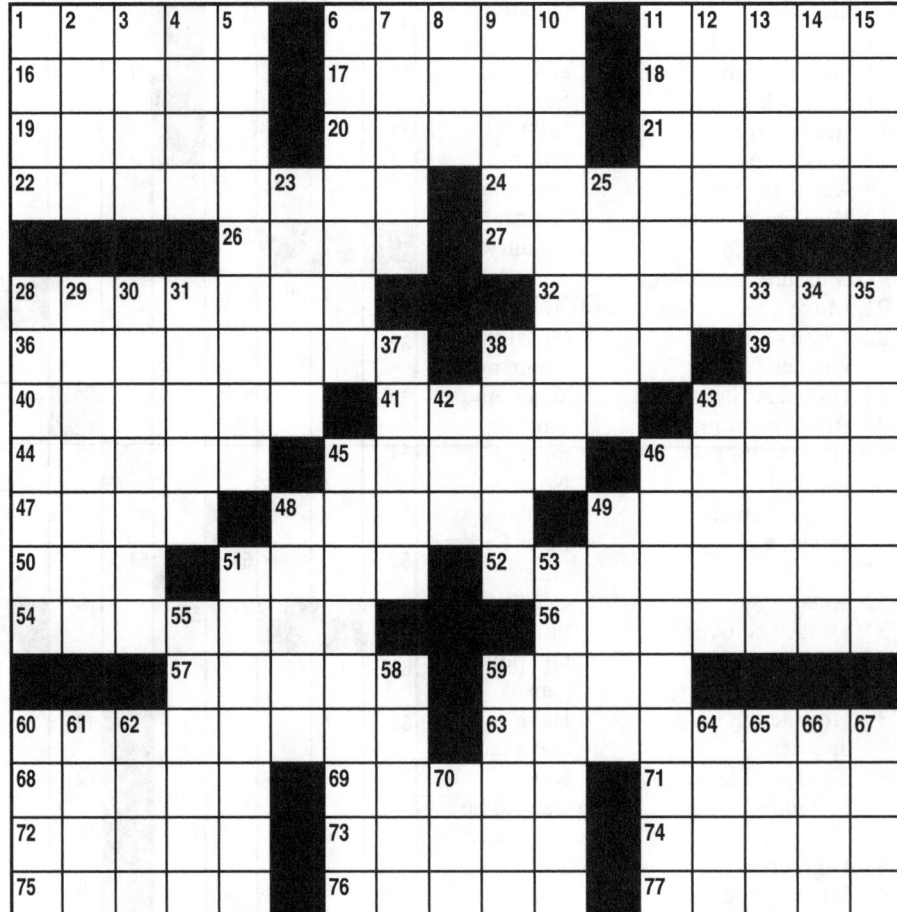

129 "YESTERDAY" ONCE MORE   by Jean Peterson
Lines from Beatles songs lead to their titles.

ACROSS

1 ___ Kringle
5 Zero in "The Producers"
11 Delicacies
16 "There's a Kind of ___" (1967 hit)
17 Camden Yards mascot
18 Gloria Stivic's mom
19 Apt
20 Shellback
21 Offset print, briefly
22 Dirigible part
23 **"Here come old flattop . . ."**
25 Wholly
27 Aver
28 There's one in two
31 Garlic ___
33 Societal customs
36 Large-eyed primate
38 ". . . in ___ called Honah Lee"
43 Given to mimicry
44 Pancake pile
45 Sexy Beatles girl
46 A great deal
47 Magazine for an exec
48 Madrid lady
49 An enemy of Sparta
51 Web-footed mammal
53 Gore Vidal book
54 Guinness brew
55 Mortify
56 Auspices
57 Croupier's tool
59 In a way
61 Sentimental song
65 Heaps
69 **"All the lonely people . . ."**
75 Puebla pot
76 Through
77 "Wayne's World" town
78 "Morning, ___ & Night": Sheldon
79 Grazing land
80 Like point-de-gaze designs
81 Big Apple's finest
82 Total
83 Doctrines
84 Citrus coolers

DOWN

1 Drab color
2 Sierra of baseball
3 Map dot
4 **"When I saw her yesterday . . ."**
5 St. Basil's Cathedral site
6 Double Delight cookie
7 Burma's 1939 neighbor
8 Heavy reading
9 City of S Israel
10 Carson's successor
11 Dulcimer cousins
12 Mine approaches
13 Parishioner pledge
14 Wild blue yonder
15 Like Verne Troyer
24 Friday, in the office?
26 Reggae pioneer Peter
29 Holland couple
30 **"And in my hour of darkness . . ."**
31 Happy outcome
32 Okla. neighbor
33 "Last of the Red Hot ___"
34 Some MoMA designs
35 Richard Starkey
37 Ecuador city
39 **"Sunday morning creeping like a nun . . ."**
40 Really fancy
41 Sturdy chiffon
42 Smith and Jones
50 "Beautiful ___": Madonna
51 Iowa's state tree
52 P, at the Parthenon
53 Sleuth played by Lorre
58 Hurly-burly
60 Kansas City nine
61 Bedtime story trio
62 Muhammad's god
63 Sierra ___
64 Jessica in "Big Fish"
66 Harold in "Why Worry?"
67 One way to unionize
68 Las Vegas implosion of 1996
70 Rapids transit
71 Bylaw
72 On-board job?
73 Impale
74 Ally Sheedy's "Pack"

130 BASEBALL NUMBERS by John Hynes
Most of these uniform numbers have been retired.

ACROSS

1 Shell game
5 Yankees' #7
11 Suffix for Dixie
15 Weightlifter Nott
16 Crayon artist
17 Priest of the East
18 Islamic chieftain
19 Like Penn State's logo
20 Teal genus
21 Deferential
22 Munched
23 Yankees' #3
25 Orioles' #22
27 Shangri-la
28 Cymbals sound
31 Window part
33 Chad language
36 Miller's salesman
38 City in NW India
43 King thing
44 Ty Cobb's home
45 Herman's Hermits lead
46 Prefix for freeze
47 Tax deduction
48 Stats for S. Koufax
49 Yankees' #8
51 Jennifer's "Ab Fab" role
53 Pirates' #14
54 Fender-bender cause
55 Arafat
56 Trident trio
57 Keep in step
59 Squash rebound
61 Peaceful
65 Legislates
69 Pirates' #21
72 Salamander
74 World Series loser
75 On a flattop
76 Brandy cocktail
78 Twig-breaking wind
79 Virna in "Arabella"
80 River in an Enya song
81 "I am a villain; yet ___": Shak.
82 Prepare to shower
83 Provoke

84 Glacial ridges

DOWN

1 Roy Campanella's 2006 honor
2 "Along ___ spider . . ."
3 Prospero freed him
4 Cardinals' #25
5 French champagne
6 Shampoo additive
7 Sine qua ___
8 Former NYC paper
9 Headey in "300"
10 Antarctic volcano
11 Mild cigar
12 "The mouse ___ the clock . . ."
13 Noted violin maker
14 Lt. Yar on "Star Trek: TNG"
16 Bow in "It"
24 Hawke in "Lord of War"
26 PayPal founder Musk
29 Tape speed
30 European vacation
31 Infernal
32 Boulogne burro
33 Union foes
34 Synthetic fiber
35 ___ Dame
37 Yankees' #9
39 Yankees' #5
40 Dummy
41 From mom
42 Staff breaks
50 Make up for
51 Spud sprout
52 Supernal altar

53 Waist-length jacket
58 Robby in "One on One"
60 So old it's back in
61 Savalas shaved his
62 Miss Marley of rhyme
63 Dodgers' #1
64 Cyberspace message
66 Carry ___ to Newcastle
67 Shire in "Deadfall"
68 Beefer
70 One in an 18-wheeler
71 Emulate Max Perkins
72 Sci. branch
73 See eye to eye
77 Treebeard is one

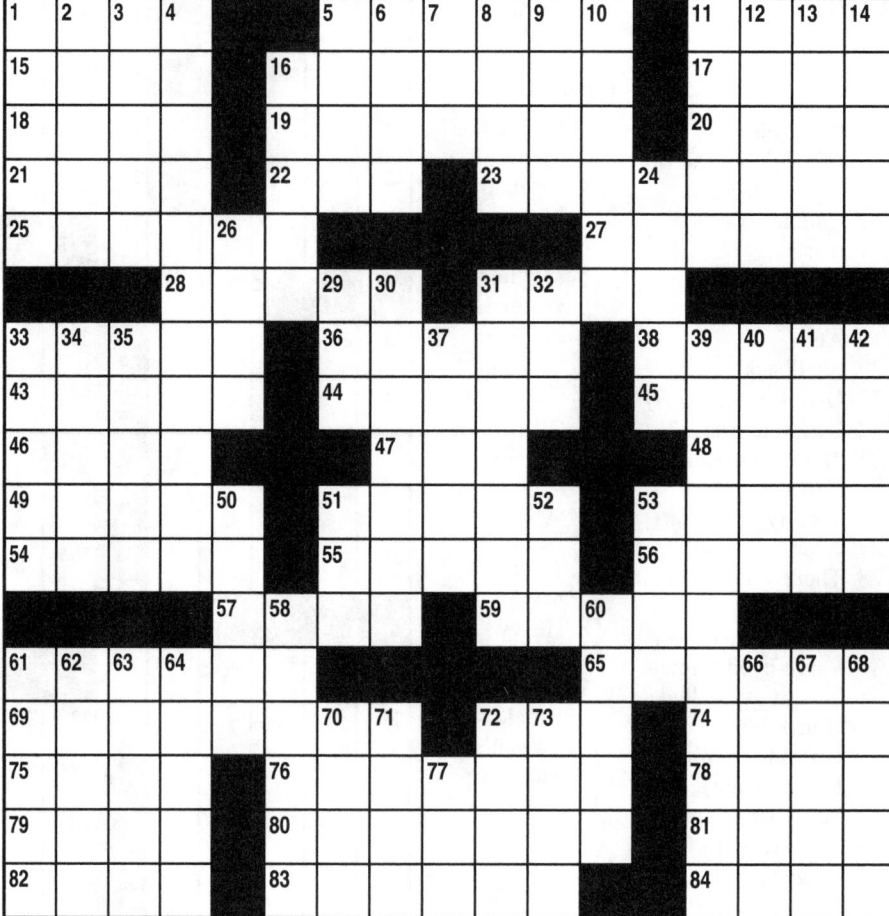

131 PALMER METHOD by John M. Samson
Every caddie should be required to solve this one.

ACROSS

1 "___ Vinci Code" (2006)
6 Chevy SUV
11 Stewed
16 Medieval instrument
17 On one's toes
18 12:50
19 **Start of an Arnold Palmer quote**
22 Mescal
23 Medical test
24 Frazzled
27 Present time
29 Short reply
30 **More of quote**
33 IRS review
34 Like limes
35 Butterfly with eyespots
38 Apple core
41 Manuscript mark
42 Jackie of Uncle Fester fame
43 Philip in "China Sky"
44 **More of quote**
49 Met contralto Podles
50 All tied
51 Ellen ___ Barkin
52 Chaney in "The Black Bird"
53 Gets one's feet wet
55 ___ Olay
56 Game console of the '80s
57 **More of quote**
59 "It just came to me!"
62 MLB VIPs
63 E German secret police
64 Delhi Zoroastrian
66 Riviera resort
70 **End of quote**
76 Twist partner in a Beatles song
77 "Ice Maiden" of tennis
78 Pseudo-convertibles
79 "St. Louis Blues" composer
80 Judi in "Casino Royale"
81 "Common ___": Paine

DOWN

1 Stumble
2 Little laugh
3 Auction site
4 "Hopelessly ___ You" ("Grease" song)
5 Turn to vinegar
6 Do needlework
7 Ring king with a sting
8 With it
9 Lunch leftover
10 Ordinal suffix
11 Simple song
12 Spreadsheet lines
13 City on the Barge Canal
14 Lloyd in "Airport"
15 Oasts
20 Gas prefix
21 Evangeline, for one
25 BMX protective gear company
26 Minister's assistant
27 Invasion of 1961
28 "Invincible" Hindu goddess
30 Tarboosh feature
31 Intermezzo follower
32 Culkin in "The Cider House Rules"
36 Soybean products
37 Letters after C. Schumer's name
38 A cooking oil
39 Wunderkind
40 Like walking on thin ice
45 Gardens of London
46 The gospel
47 "Four questions" dinner
48 Come from
54 "I Am ___ Spock": Nimoy
55 In a way
58 Brocaded fabric
59 Gorillalike
60 ___-yoga
61 Firebug's offense
62 Like title roles
65 Desert Storm missile
67 ". . . and shalt bear ___": Gen. 16
68 Fleshy mushrooms
69 Soho steed
71 Monitor type
72 Twelfth Night, for one
73 Cub Scout group
74 Sun's path
75 To the ___ degree

132 FLORAL BOUQUET by Michele Sayer
"Lady's-earrings" would be another clue for 20 Across.

ACROSS

1 Tennessee's blue flower
5 Extremist
12 Now partner
16 Gas-grill rock
17 Gourmand
18 Drago in "Rocky IV"
19 Epps of "House"
20 Hanging-basket flower
21 Grass of greens
22 "The Fountainhead" author
23 Consumption
24 Arcadian god
25 "Summer Brave" playwright
26 October bloomers
28 Season for lilies
30 Reunion member
33 Bric-___
35 News groups
38 City in Turkey
40 Latin dance
44 Shaq or Ryan
45 Stiff
46 Song of Solomon
47 A Benedictine
48 Woolen cap
49 Cuba libre ingredient
50 Flash
53 General Mills cereal
55 Rivera of stage musicals
57 Macho dude
58 Rugged ridge
59 Chinese tea
60 "Sugaring Off" painter
62 Word form of "nine"
64 Mother of Dionysus
67 Lady's slipper, e.g.
71 Lod Airport carrier
72 "Silly Ho" group
75 Abner's radio partner
77 New Rochelle school
78 Gateway rival
79 Fragrant flower

81 Four-term Georgia senator
82 Negative one
83 Polecat geranium
84 Enterprise's voyage
85 Project Galileo org.
86 "Here We Are" singer
87 Bring on board

DOWN

1 Flower goddess
2 Tibetan gurus
3 ___-garde
4 Corsage flower
5 Pass on
6 Bird of Paradise constellation
7 Chancy cubes
8 Potsdam pronoun
9 Molar tip
10 "Samson et Dalila" highlight
11 Not as plump
12 State flower of Hawaii
13 Milestone
14 Purview
15 Keyboard word
27 Capital of Iran
29 NRTA parent
31 Bentley, e.g.
32 Film cutters
33 Draw a cartoon
34 Defective
35 One is named after Mars
36 Become used to
37 Acid-washed fabric
39 Banded stone
41 Ruth's record breaker
42 Belushi's "Animal House" role
43 Jordanian city

51 Alabama's flower
52 Organic compound
53 Microphone inv.
54 Lesser of "Seinfeld"
55 "Bang Bang" singer
56 Fragrant flower
61 Avoid a trial
63 ___ feat (superior deed)
64 300 for the road
65 Skater Valova
66 Fountain treats
68 Muslim maid of paradise
69 Spiritual
70 "Thanks, Ludwig!"
73 Meadow lands
74 Inclination
75 Sit around
76 Bill the Goat's school
80 Hwy.

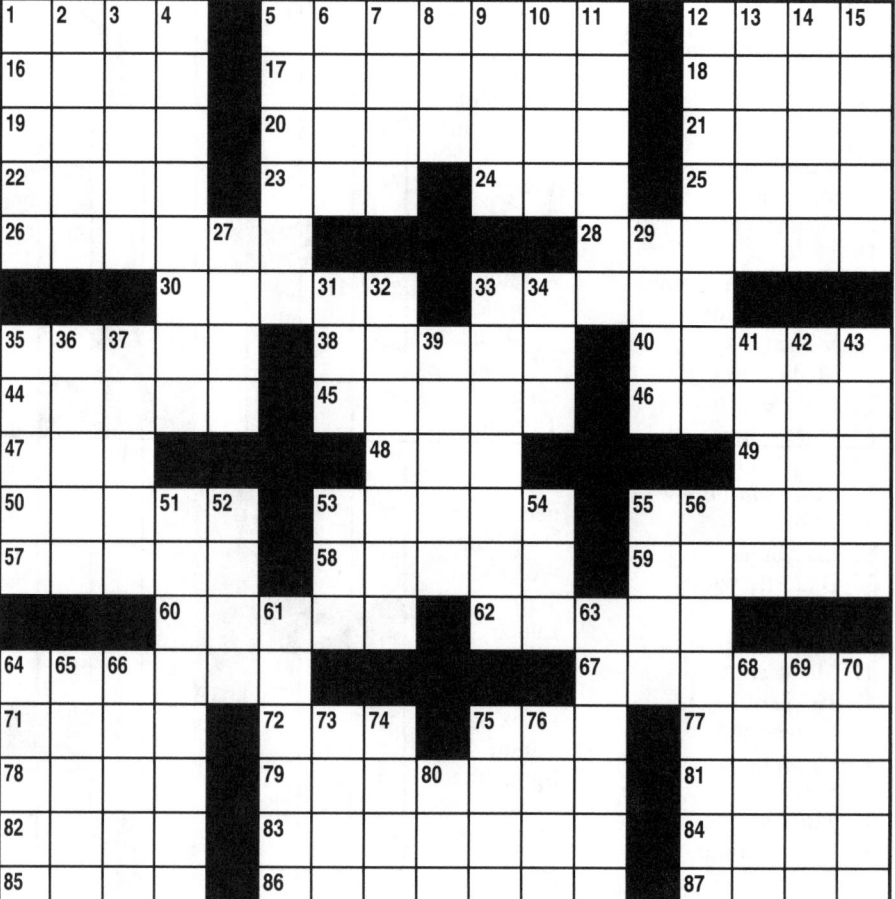

TV LANDERS   by Pat McCarthy
How many of these TV Land denizens can you remember?

ACROSS

1 Wired blades
6 Goober Pyle's cousin
11 Tibetan capital
16 Deck with a Queen of Wands
17 Entertain
18 Trough type
19 Auburn tint
20 Beaver Cleaver's teacher
22 "Try ___ might . . ."
23 Refusenik's refusal
25 Portray
26 Kathie Lee Gifford, ___ Epstein
27 Heckles
29 "Soap" family
31 Lola, to Maude
32 He was Jethro Bodine
33 "It's My Party" singer
34 ABC's "Men in ___"
35 Dr. Hartley's wife
37 "___ Help Lovin' Dat Man"
38 Cellist Jacqueline du ___
39 Peeve
40 Sprightly
41 Matt Dillon's deputy
45 Ted Danson sitcom (1996–97)
46 Rob Petrie's boss
48 "Deep Space Nine" changeling
49 Comedy trio
51 Arctic birds
52 Go off the deep end
53 Hopalong's pal
54 Shirley played by Megan Follows
55 Rap out
56 Change a bill
59 Mark of Dracula
60 Creditor's claim
61 "Put the blame on" her
62 "Fame" star
63 "Wings" brothers

66 Darth Vader, as a boy
67 ___ Altos
68 Radar's unit
69 XXVI x II
70 She chased Dobie Gillis
74 Syrian president
76 Taurus neighbor
77 "Kung Fu" hero
78 Avignon river
79 Herman of Herman's Hermits
80 Foppish footwear
81 Taboos

DOWN

1 Phillips of "Star Trek: Voyager"
2 Bel ___ cheese
3 Fort Baxter sergeant
4 Many millennia
5 Helen Roper's husband
6 Fun partner
7 Drop
8 Greek letters
9 Superman's letter
10 Empathize
11 Fast time
12 Owned
13 One of Monopoly's 17
14 Placid
15 Resources
21 Good hole card
24 Suffix for saw
28 NASCAR legend Earnhardt
29 Sunshine Cab Co. driver
30 Gumby creator Clokey

31 Apollo's half brother
33 Senator on Discovery
34 "South Park" creator Parker
35 Goddess of discord
36 Julep ingredient
37 Tax specialists
38 Doctorates
40 Skeleton racer
41 Torte
42 Jeannie's master
43 Sweet-milk cheese
44 Hogtie
46 Like cognac
47 Viking letter
50 Moselle tributary
52 Chiang Kai-___
54 Broadcast
55 Ellery Queen's father

56 River of 3,900 miles
57 "Saturday Night Fever" hero
58 Designer Pucci
59 Rudiments
60 Vegas airport code
62 Ratchet
63 Linc of "The Mod Squad"
64 Ex-Red Sox "Looie"
65 Ocean motions
67 "Daily Planet" reporter
68 Peak of the Alpes
71 Wilson of "The Jack Benny Show"
72 Pool length
73 Estuary
75 "___ 'nuff!"

134 CATCH A WAVE by Don Law
Oahu's wave riders should know the answer to 4 Down.

ACROSS

1 David or Pendleton
5 Muffler maker
10 Corridor
14 Singer Stewart
15 Cold-water surfing wear
17 Mother of Remus
18 Splendor
19 Carmen of "Baywatch"
20 Londoner's umbrella
21 A Great Lake
22 Thompson in "Red Dawn"
23 Adjust a skirt
24 Med. insurers
25 Brown ___ spider
27 Magnet
29 "Like" suffix
30 "¡___ favor, Señor!"
31 Troy college
32 "Suds" singer Sara
35 Sea birds
36 Utopian
40 Go for a spin
41 Horned TCU mascot
42 Belfry topper
44 "Give ___ rest!"
45 Malibu "fish"
47 Puccini's Cio-Cio-___
48 Sunflower Staters
50 "Night" author Wiesel
51 Cornucopia
52 For all to hear
53 Foray
54 Rat Pack name
55 "Awesome!"
57 "The Name of the Rose" author
58 Sadie Hawkins Day catch
59 Partial lie
63 Imply
67 Bogosian in "Ararat"
68 Collection
69 ___ de deux
70 18-wheeler
71 Madeline in "Blazing Saddles"

72 1963 hit by the Surfaris
74 Soho streetcar
75 Hide
76 "Peace Train" singer
77 Wexford locale
78 Loom reed
79 Plant swelling
80 Garden State cagers

DOWN

1 Pickled bud
2 Love, Italian style
3 Copycat
4 1963 hit by the Chantays
5 Donnybrook
6 Virginia willow
7 Award for heroism
8 Swift and Fast
9 Begat
10 When surfing is best
11 Besieged site in 1836
12 7-Up flavor
13 Slip
15 Like Timothy Dalton
16 Clyde Beatty, e.g.
26 Carrier letters
27 Home of the Queen Mary
28 Emulated Philby
30 Teacher
32 Christensen in "The Banger Sisters"
33 Life-or-death
34 Major Joppolo's post
35 Goofs
37 English derby site
38 Bedroom buzz
39 Vegetarian shark in "Shark Tale"
41 "Fun, Fun, ___": Beach Boys

42 Chimed in
43 Three, in Roma
45 Nasser's successor
46 Mishmash
49 1963 Jan & Dean hit
51 Surfs
53 Recorded over
54 Hollywood union
56 Sketches
58 Essentials
59 Assists
60 Disney mermaid
61 DeGaulle's birthplace
62 Band together
63 Room with hot rocks
64 Creepy
65 Stylish
66 "Fast ___ at Ridgemont High" (1982)
69 Sonnet
73 Abel mother

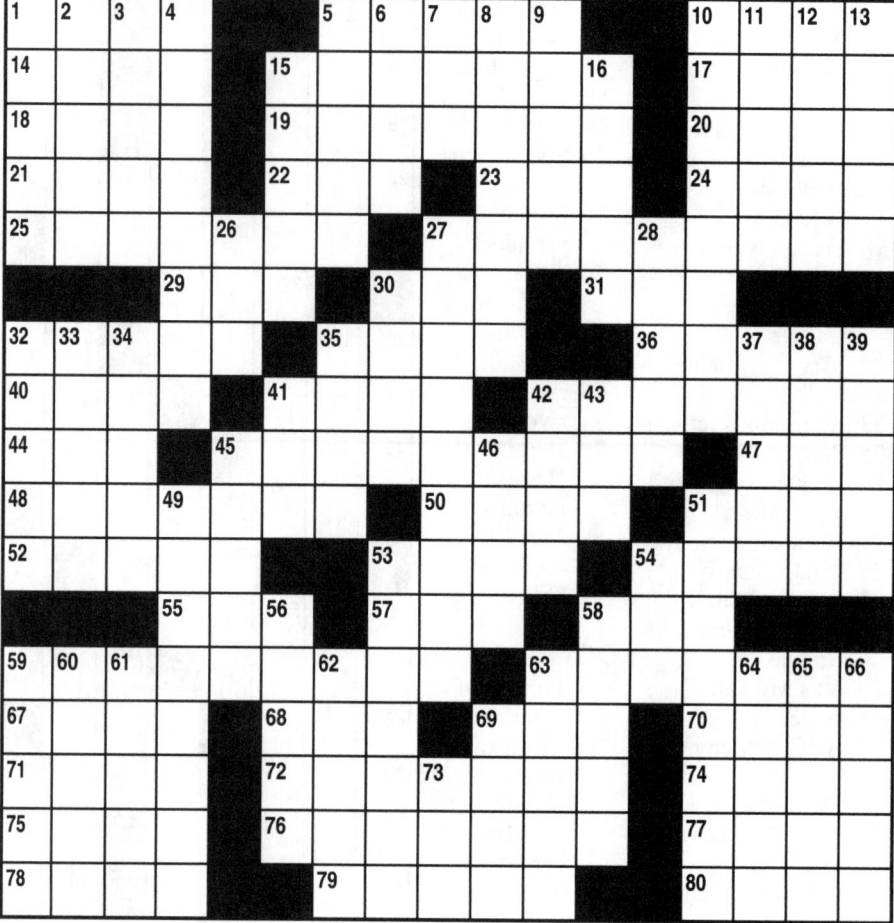

135 ROCK HALL-OF-FAMERS by Cindy Lather
The RIAA has listed 3-D as the best-selling band of all time.

ACROSS

1 "The Divine Miss M"
6 He sang with The Comets
11 Overbearing
16 "Paganini" composer
17 San Antonio landmark
18 Combine
19 Sugar Bowl, e.g.
20 "Born In The U.S.A." singer
22 Brother or sister
23 Tennis units
25 ___ Moines
26 Little louse
27 Get the point
28 TV Tarzan
29 Van Morrison's group
31 "___ and the King of Siam"
32 Taj Mahal site
34 "The Way of Love" singer
35 School group
36 Surfeits
38 Limerick writer
39 Not safe at home
40 Prow locale
41 Scant
42 "One Of Us" singer Joan
46 Dutch commune
47 "It's My Turn" singer
49 Dinghy thingy
50 Sorority members
52 Actress Rowlands
53 Genesis garden
54 Genetic letters
55 Kind of circus
56 Billiards stroke
57 Rainbow fish
60 Prompted
61 "Round and Round" group
62 Goddess of youth
63 Brinker or Conried
64 Lemon
65 She raised Cain
68 Beer
69 Prohibit
70 Western alliance
71 Married
72 "Butterfly" singer

76 Approaches
78 Stiff collars
79 Teamsters, e.g.
80 Audacity
81 Meaning
82 Herman's Hermits lead
83 Russian co-op

DOWN

1 Bill of fashion
2 Creepy
3 "Something" group
4 Beige
5 Pencil ends
6 Impulsive
7 Swiss peaks
8 Burmese gibbon
9 Record label
10 "Way Down ___ in New Orleans"
11 Smooch
12 Canadian province (abbr.)
13 Burnt pigment
14 Tankards
15 Gossips
21 Jewel
24 Guido's high note
29 "Hotel California" group
30 ___ up (agitated)
31 Female voice
33 Congeal
34 Maize
35 Sammy Sosa's former team
36 "___ a Lady": Tom Jones
37 German car
38 Sugar snaps
39 Greek peak
41 Sorvino in "Summer of Sam"
42 Charlie Chaplin's wife
43 "I Was Only Joking" singer
44 Dundee denials
45 Coastal eagle

47 Bumper car mark
48 Clarinet or oboe
51 Tried and ___
53 Scarf down
55 Amusement
56 "Beautiful Stranger" singer
57 London river
58 Empathize
59 Merle in "Wuthering Heights"
60 Mexican resort
61 Stuck in a ___
63 "So there!"
64 "Tell It To My Heart" singer
66 Brio
67 Ford flop
69 First or second
70 Elton John's "In ___"
73 Officeholders
74 Spanish year
75 Duran Duran hit
77 Suffix for rocket

136 PISCINE PUZZLER by Eva Finney
Expect a little struggle at 62 Across.

ACROSS

1 Kind of fat
6 Encompassed
12 Theatre org.
16 "___ heart!"
17 Clubber
18 Charon, to Pluto
19 Remove a CD
20 "Patriot Games" author
21 Unlike some roughs
22 Tuna relative
24 Hippocampus
26 ___ majesty (high crime)
27 Winning 1993 World Series manager
28 Dunn of "EastEnders"
31 Shank
32 Mosaic maker
36 Student aid
37 Not up yet
38 An octave higher than written
39 "Glamour" competitor
40 "It's ___ a hard day's night . . ."
41 "Million Dollar Baby" Oscar winner
42 Sgt. wannabe
43 Ferocious fish
45 Agt.'s cut
46 Because of that
48 Karate school
49 Rock's Mötley ___
50 Qatar coins
51 NYC-based bank
52 National Mall gallery
53 Bridge opening, briefly
54 Mod endings
55 Agree to
56 "No ifs, ___ buts"
58 Largest of the Near Islands
59 Source of caviar
62 Sole sister
66 Places
67 Tap
69 City NNE of Tampa
70 Literary tidbits
71 ___ and 4 (Dr Pepper hours)
72 First saint canonized by a Pope
73 "Champagne Music" man
74 "Das Kapital" editor
75 Logic

DOWN

1 Joyce Carol Oates novel
2 E Indian prince
3 "___ plaisir!"
4 Décolletage
5 Shiny fabrics
6 Roast host
7 "The Old Curiosity Shop" girl
8 Early ABC show
9 Saudi Arabia's first monarch
10 Playtime
11 Have a ___ (attempt)
12 Squid's extinct relative
13 Jordanian queen
14 Snowboard lifts
15 Daughter of Queen Elizabeth II
23 N. Mandela's land
25 Steaming brew
27 Rat-tail of the ocean
28 Foe of Spider-Man
29 Mahi-mahi
30 Tasty lake fish
31 Highway ham
33 Eel that's not an eel
34 Fire-drill participant
35 Fit throwers
37 Ethereal
38 Religious calendar
40 Streisand, in fanzines
41 Japan's highest peak
43 Be a member
44 Tent beds
47 Chanced it
49 Throw in the towel
51 Doubling up?
52 Idiotic
54 2006 Winged Foot event
55 ___-Ko-Vor (Klingon heaven)
57 Villa ___ (Italian landmark)
58 Choir group
59 Shredded salad
60 Fashion
61 Berkeley school
62 Duck or turkey
63 "Shucks!"
64 Yale team
65 Three-legged contest
68 Former AT&T rival

137 WORLD TOUR by Karen Motyka
Three cities on this tour were former Olympic hosts.

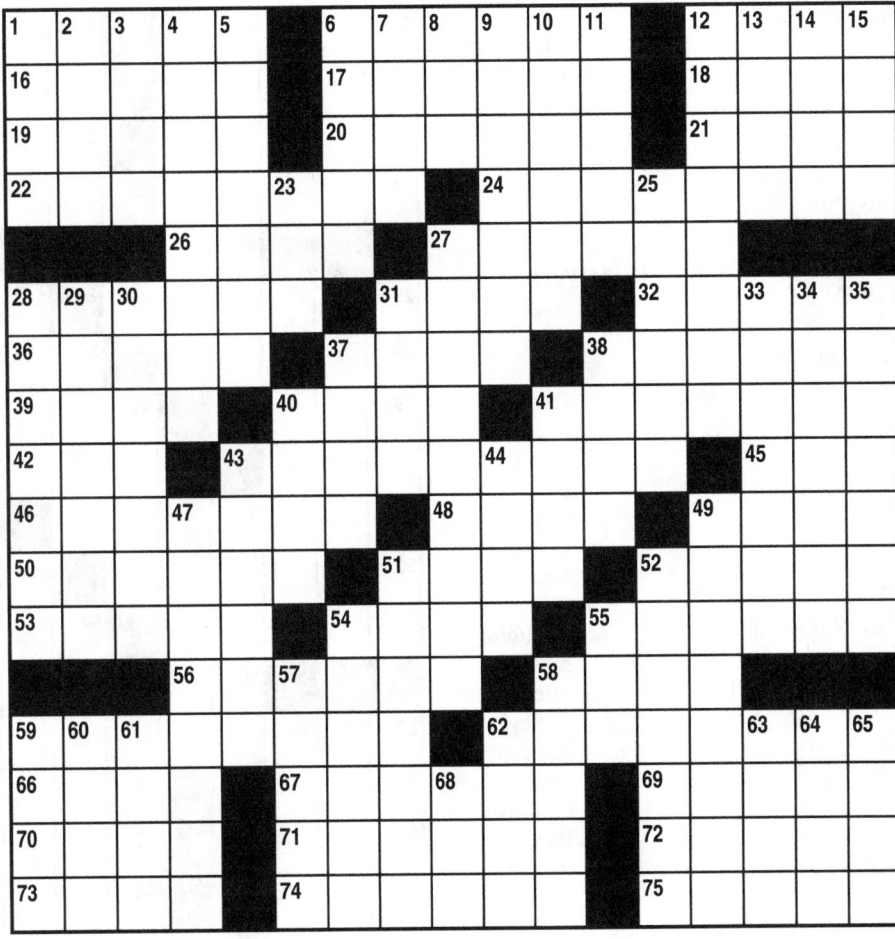

ACROSS

1 Techniques
6 "Key Largo" star
12 Colorful fish
16 Dubliners
17 Put to work
18 Windmill sail
19 Clemency
20 "___ In New York" (2000)
21 Soprano role in "Lohengrin"
22 Hagia Sophia site
24 Place des Arts locale
26 Vegetable fuel
27 Treat with heat
28 Hyphen's big brother
31 "Diary of ___ Housewife" (1970)
32 Met heavies?
36 Links measures
37 Option word
38 Find a station
39 Robert at Appomattox
40 Nuthatch food
41 "Blast it!"
42 Hearty lettuce
43 La Sagrada Familia locale
45 Cameraphone inv.
46 Experience
48 Disneyland attraction
49 Mind-bending drugs
50 South Carolina river
51 Pothers
52 Baby's woe
53 "Riders to the Sea" playwright
54 Poker pro ___ Le
55 "West Side Story" Oscar winner
56 Blow up ___
58 Miami-___ County
59 Pitti Palace locale
62 Bob Marley Museum locale
66 Authentic
67 Ben Hogan won it four times
69 Verse form
70 Major addition
71 1921 Wimbledon champion
72 Da Vinci System surgeon
73 Capsule contents
74 Easily irritated
75 Chevy pickups

DOWN

1 Rogers in "The Doors"
2 Rock group
3 Inside dope
4 Prank
5 Shrinking violet's trait
6 Lulu
7 Dairy co-op of India
8 USN rank
9 Wellesley grads
10 Scotland's largest loch
11 Jeff of the Traveling Wilburys
12 Jeep Grand Cherokee model
13 The P in VSOP
14 Italian "AP"
15 Put right
23 "Fiddlesticks!"
25 ___ rasa
27 Rijks Museum site
28 Binoculars pair
29 Former Mötley Crüe drummer Samantha
30 Brühl's Terrace locale
31 Fictional spy Leamas
33 Space Needle locale
34 Buckle up
35 "Rhinoceros" dramatist
37 Continental coin
38 Fashion
40 Savant
41 Pantheon members
43 Samuel Finley ___ Morse
44 Sphinx body
47 Masters of poetry
49 Achilles' heel
51 Nimbus
52 Old blokes
54 Alert
55 Joan Daemen, for one
57 Bolt attachments
58 Alley Oop's pet
59 Gwynne in "The Munsters"
60 A consort of Zeus
61 Filly filler
62 Boat backbone
63 "Oh, ___ in England . . .": Browning
64 Orne tributary
65 NBA team
68 Doctor's drug bk.

138 LEGENDS OF THE GAME by Tim Wagner
Legends from eight different sports are honored below.

ACROSS

1 Davis and Dourif
6 Van Halen's "___ is Love?"
12 Tim Conway character
16 Put on board
17 Out-and-out
18 Plaintive woodwind
19 À la disco
20 Headly on "Monk"
21 Sapient
22 One of two boxing legends
24 Golf legend
26 Hula instruments
27 Plenty
28 Lug
31 In great shape
32 ___ latte
36 Not worth ___ of beans
37 Sleuth Wolfe
38 Country homes
39 Bog ooze
40 Vice President in 1804
41 Least imaginary
42 Pensacola airport code
43 Hockey legend
45 NYC subway org.
46 Pee-wee Herman portrayer
48 Software-testing phase
49 Colorful display
50 Perceptive
51 Japan's largest lake
52 Slant-cut pasta
53 "What thou ___, write . . .": Rev. 1:11
54 Where Paul Klee painted
55 Maze borders
56 Remove Pb from
58 About: Abbr.
59 Baseball legend
62 Auto-racing legend
66 Take another tour
67 Tight one
69 British Columbia neighbor
70 Acastus sailed on it
71 "The Rainbow Connection" singer
72 Daisy in "The Secret Garden"
73 Pig or lion's share
74 London square
75 CSX stop

DOWN

1 Lesage's "Gil ___"
2 Newman's Own sauce rival
3 ". . . I've been working like ___": Beatles
4 Fifth Republic president
5 "Beetle Bailey" sergeant
6 Grand narratives
7 Paris air terminal
8 Uno, due, ___
9 Luke Skywalker's friend
10 Existing at birth
11 Stanches
12 Ruin
13 "Village Voice" bestowal
14 Ponselle or Parks
15 Satellite hook-up
23 Workout unit
25 Like ants
27 Basketball legend
28 Tennis legend
29 Standard Mandarin
30 Hairy
31 Marjoram, e.g.
33 Figure-skating legend
34 Pull a ___ (cozen)
35 Brideshead and Biltmore
37 Aftermath of a rough shave
38 Sail on high
40 Cast member?
41 Herb-of-grace genus
43 Improve
44 Chopped down
47 NYC's Port Authority, e.g.
49 Sauna wood
51 Save the day
52 Nestlé water brand
54 U. in Arden Hills, MN
55 Cached
57 ___ out (is on a roll)
58 Big bill
59 "Dracula" author Stoker
60 Top-Flite golf ball
61 Funny Bunny
62 Neat as ___
63 Monikers
64 This alternative
65 Opie of Mother Goose fame
68 "I ___ simple maid . . .": Shak.

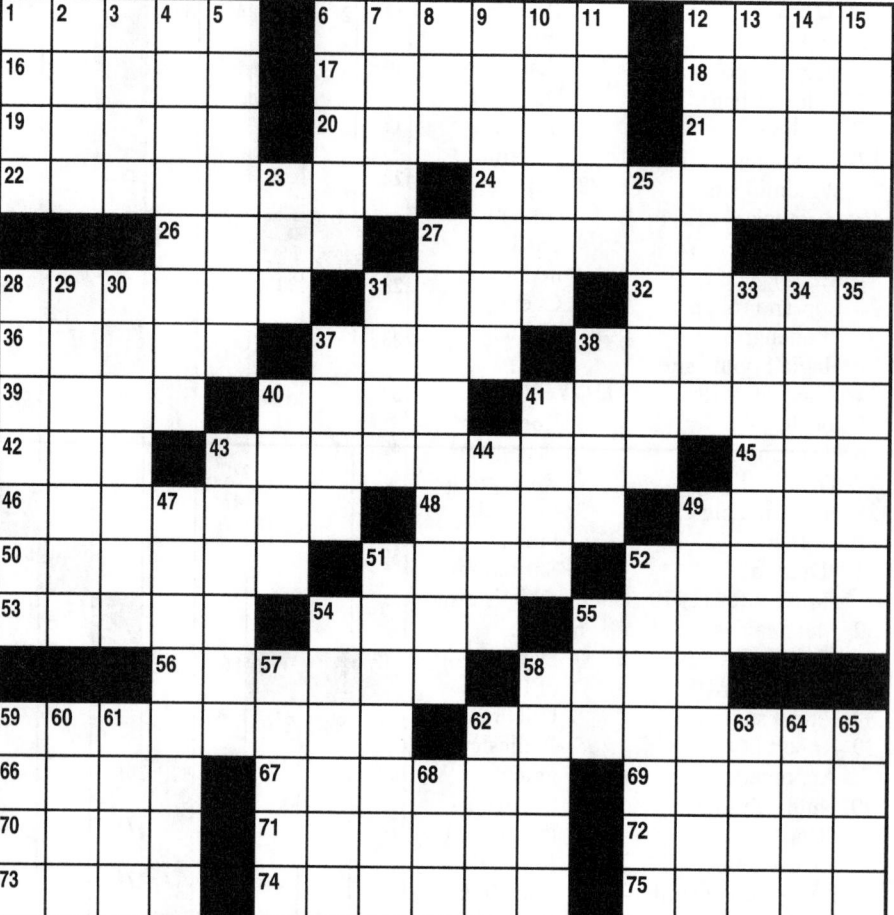

139 THAT WAS THE YEAR THAT WAS by Don Law
. . . and that year was 1988.

ACROSS

1 Defender of the Aesir
5 "___ the Wind": Seger
12 Continental breakfast item
16 "Sticks and Bones" dramatist
17 Team up again
18 ___ in one's bonnet
19 Vergil's successor
20 2003 Christina Ricci film
21 Sorority letter
22 Tank top
24 ___ capita
25 Dodge Colt's successor
26 Rubber dog toy
27 Margolyes of Harry Potter films
29 "Analyze This" director
32 Large-scale productions
34 Harry S Truman's birthplace
38 Cat-___-tails
39 "Married . . .with Children" dog
40 Fireworks finish
41 Doesn't burn
42 Indubitable
43 An Everly brother
44 Hound or horse
45 2006 AMD merger partner
46 Cathedral nook
47 Chicago soccer team
48 Honshu volcano
49 Lauren of "Men in Trees"
50 Dome shout
51 Stinger
52 Collective abbr.
53 Gave the slip to
55 Ice melter
56 Toxemia symptom
57 Succubus, e.g.
58 Porsche in "Cars"
59 Slander

60 "A Scanner ___" (2006)
62 Test-drive car
64 Uneven hairdo
67 Yes, in Tokyo
68 A hit with hit men
72 Thornfield governess
73 "___ Sunshine of the Spotless Mind" (2003)
75 Senate cover-up?
76 Take-off artist
77 Ragout
78 Toward the mouth
79 Polanski film
80 Wagnerian hero
81 Pram pusher

DOWN

1 Meadowlands gait
2 "___ Gun, Will Travel"
3 Theater award
4 1988 Super Bowl winners
5 Mueller-Stahl in "Avalon"
6 1988 election winner
7 Cousin-german's mother
8 Current administration
9 Find fault
10 Longhorns
11 Singer Gibbs
12 Best Film of 1988
13 Cor anglais
14 Mother of Artemis
15 Lanky
23 Gardener's need
27 Pinky and the Brain

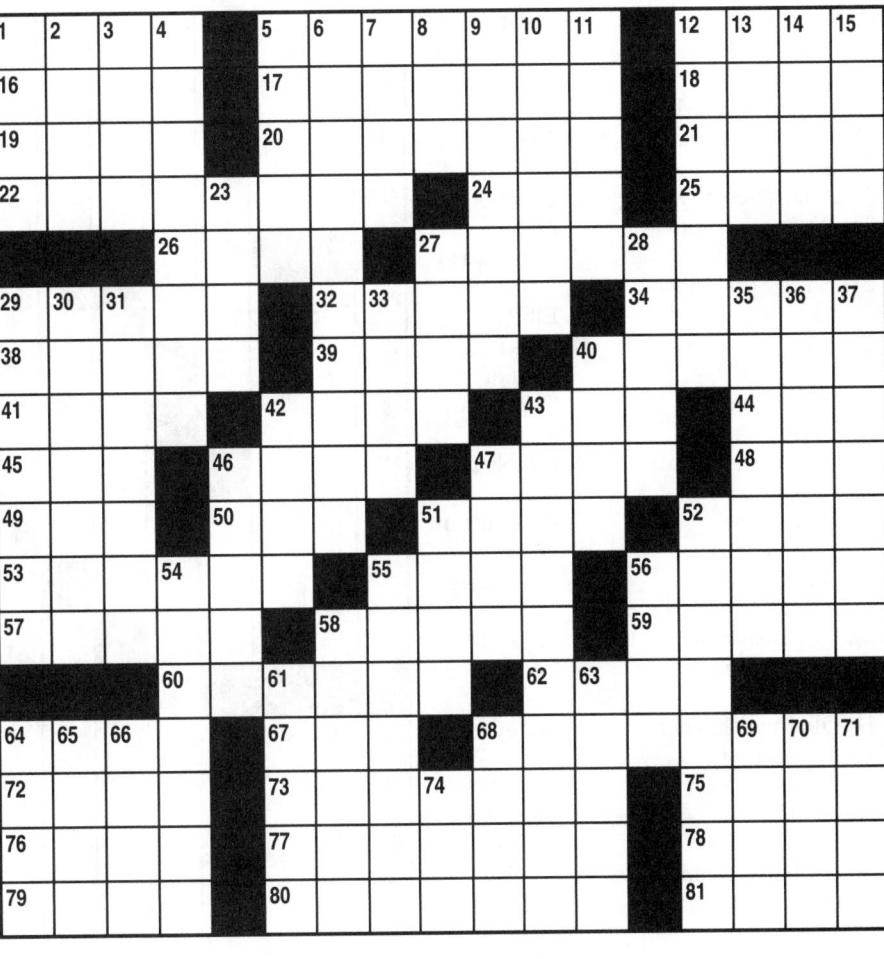

28 Dress with a flare
29 Revolved
30 "Penguin Island" author France
31 Cabaret assessment
33 Like the driven snow
35 Sea World attraction
36 1988 Sun Bowl winners
37 Accustomed
40 Sumter or McHenry
42 French WW1 plane
43 1988 Michael Jackson hit
46 Sphere of action
47 Football season
51 Tyne of "Cagney & Lacey"
52 1988 Stanley Cup winners

54 1988 World Series winners
55 Mozart's rival
56 Farmer's wife in "Babe"
58 Cool dancer?
61 Bonnie Blue's dad
63 Original first name of 51-D
64 Trousers part
65 Publicize
66 Hera's bellicose son
68 Testy state
69 Mindy's grandmother
70 Susan in "Beauty and the Beast"
71 J. Gielgud's alma mater
74 Short Line and Penn.

WEATHERED LOOK by Richard Drumm
Owen Wilson fans know the answer to 24 Down.

ACROSS

1 Blow a fuse
9 Reprieves
17 Contract adverb
18 Los Angeles suburb
19 Small fire
20 Attack verbally
21 Wave at a gypsy
22 Iowa State team
23 NYC's first subway line
24 Sri ___
25 Plush
28 Pageant put-on?
30 Raison ___
35 "___ sow, so shall ye reap"
36 Bullyboys
37 Crosier carrier
38 A little night music?
39 ___ Hashanah
40 2006 Google purchase
41 Old English letter
42 Superhero in Disney's "Sky High"
44 Heading of 11.25°
45 Air Force Academy cadets
47 Trig
48 1502 on the Appian Way
49 Charitable golf events
50 After-dinner candy
51 Sat finishers
52 Suffix for photo
53 Turbine blades
54 Limestone rock formation
55 "Sing ___ of sixpence . . ."
57 Macavity, for one
58 Bob Dylan album
62 White hare, at times
67 "Pink Elephants ___" ("Dumbo" segment)
68 Foot-dragging
69 One rash with trash
70 "Summer of Sam" director
71 49ers gave them the business
72 "Diamonds Are Forever" actress

DOWN

1 "Watch out!"
2 Superior ___ cava
3 "Able was I ___ saw Elba"
4 Gets it
5 Duff of "Lizzie McGuire"
6 Establish as law
7 Razor handle
8 Where Aida and Radames expire
9 Rapscallions
10 Comedienne Boosler
11 Corn-dog holder
12 Catalytic-converter catalyst
13 Peculiar prefix
14 Bristol loc.
15 Düsseldorf duck
16 Brazil saints
24 McQueen in "Cars"
25 "Shrek" was this
26 Four Seasons Hotel founder Sharp
27 Lagoon of Disney World
28 Pub pourings
29 Rumple (up)
31 Great finish?
32 Mountain of Disney World
33 "West Side Story" choreographer
34 "Touché!" sayer
36 "A nest of robins . . ." source
37 PT and U
40 "The Lake Isle of Innisfree" poet
42 "The Number 23" star
43 Auberjonois of Odo fame
46 "Love Story" composer
48 Brunswick dish?
50 Miss ___ (Judith Martin)
53 Check canceler
54 New Zealand conifer
56 Moselle tributary
57 Farrell in "Minority Report"
58 La Paz greeting
59 Composer Fuleihan
60 Detailed accts.
61 Punchcard info
62 Broadband letters
63 Sugar-yielding palm
64 Prefix for graph
65 Filled cookie
66 Saw

ROLE REFUSALS by Karen Motyka

Hedy Lamarr turned down the role of Ilsa in "Casablanca."

ACROSS

1 "A Chapter on Ears" essayist
5 Diana Ross song (with "It's")
11 Request of Mr. Bojangles
16 Letter-shaped beam
17 Stephen King book
18 "The Bostonians" director
19 Café card
20 Good Witch of the North
21 ___ Wences
22 Political faction
23 He turned down Wolverine in "X-Men"
25 "Bewitched" cousin
27 PC key
28 Dazzler
31 "Sesame Street" favorite
33 No and J
36 Paradigm of pokiness
39 "Crazy Cool" singer Abdul
41 Shooting sport
43 Tenor Bergonzi
44 Queen ___ lace
45 Like many a Poe tale
46 Bedouin headband cord
47 Federal procurement agcy.
48 Watermelon, e.g.
49 Like Cujo
51 "I've never ___ purple cow . . .": Burgess
53 Fin
54 Liqueur flavoring
55 Cupid's dart
56 Standouts
57 Betty Boop's scarf
58 Skimbleshanks' musical
60 NYC's Saint ___ Hotel
62 Artful
63 Meal
67 He turned down Robert Rusk in "Frenzy"
75 Maturation agent
76 Place for a crown
77 Silverstone of "Miss Match"
78 Vito Corleone, e.g.
79 Double
80 Town cars
81 List extender
82 Surrendered
83 "Old Folks at Home" river
84 Roar

DOWN

1 An arm and a leg
2 White poplar
3 Baronial domicile
4 He turned down Sam Wheat in "Ghost"
5 "Cowboy in Me" singer
6 Korean border river
7 Speaker in the Hall
8 Samovars
9 Tease
10 "Topper" dog
11 Spill the beans
12 Prevent
13 "___ Song": Ringo Starr
14 Heckle or Jeckle
15 Peter in "Dragonslayer"
24 Felon's flight
26 ___ contendere
29 AARP founder
30 Mark Messier played for them
31 Boston Tea Party ship
32 Musical A's
33 Issue
34 "The Princess Bride" director
35 Texas Longhorns
36 Jewelry beetle
37 Honshu city
38 Asian peninsula
40 1992 Indy 500 winner
42 He turned down Dr. Powell in "K-PAX"
50 Proclaimed
51 Plopped down
52 Fear and wonder
53 Pâté de ___ gras
59 "Affirmative, admiral!"
61 "We Go Together" musical
62 Battier of the NBA
64 Marble
65 Floral leaf
66 Fishing lure
67 Caesar's 2200
68 Hercules' captive maiden
69 Oaf
70 Bonnie girl
71 Skein of yarn
72 Elton John stage musical
73 "Anything ___ do?"
74 Opening hour at the bank

ACROSS

1 Like the Grim Reaper
9 Aardvark
17 Museum in Las Vegas
18 Cutting-edge product?
19 Kind of stand
20 More than you'd like
21 Banned Philip Roth book
23 Rotten Tomatoes parent
24 "The Waltons" production company
25 Mexican artist Frida
28 Asian lemur
29 NOW and WHO
33 Adam's grandson
34 "Sorry, Wrong Number" heroine
35 Olympus product
37 Suffix for Mozart
38 Lead for Rin Tin Tin
39 "Big George" of boxing
40 Four-act play by Shelley
43 Like the third-string?
44 Meander
45 Hip-hop's ___ Kim
46 Rue ___ (regret)
47 "Rubber Capital of the World"
48 Petruchio's wife
49 Court cry
50 "___ Fell": Teresa Brewer
51 Enterprise-D officer
52 They're followed
55 Tom Collins ingredient
56 It's hung by the chimney with care
63 Jib or genoa
64 Wood spirits
65 Beseech
66 Come before
67 Cheeky to the max
68 Veal fillet

DOWN

1 Feed the hogs
2 "The Pearl" protagonist
3 Hair stylist José
4 Soup pods
5 "___ bragh!"
6 Append
7 In need of Motrin
8 Frees
9 Waldorf-___
10 Campbell and Watts
11 Soap-opera time slot
12 Deadly virus
13 Italian sports car
14 M. Hulot portrayer
15 Early plot?
16 Flat payment
22 Nebraska team
25 ___ oneself (doesn't socialize)
26 Misrule
27 Person on a stamp, e.g.
28 Vermont statesman
30 Coneheads' planet
31 Mount Rushmore rock
32 "Reign Over Me" star
34 Allow to pass
35 Robert E. Howard barbarian
36 Terence Trent D'___
38 River in Poland
39 Fad
41 Pluvial hillside hazards
42 Marcia in "Honey, I Shrunk the Kids"
47 Pigged out
48 "Painter of light"
50 Fesses up
51 An embarrassment of ___
53 Poule d'___ (French horse race)
54 "___ told by an idiot . . .": Shak.
55 "The Teflon Don"
56 Cartoonist Addams
57 Type of air filter
58 Emulates Ludacris
59 "A ___ 'clock scholar . . ."
60 ___ the finish
61 Rowling Death Eater
62 Jollity

143 GRAMMY GIRLS by Eva Finney
4 Down holds the record for being the youngest Grammy winner.

ACROSS
1 "I've got ___ she's Big Foot Sal . . ."
5 Vitascope inventor
11 Mubarak's predecessor
16 Door glass
17 1998 Olympic site
18 Patsy's "Absolutely Fabulous" sidekick
19 Site of Vulcan's forge
20 Enhances
21 ___ guerre
22 Hold in
23 "Someday" singer
25 Sight or hearing
27 Native suffix
28 Het up
31 Ariose
35 Color to dye for?
37 Capt. Janeway's ship
39 Yellow Monopoly bill
41 Besieged site in 1836
42 "My word!"
43 Give goosebumps to
45 Greene's third man
46 One of Abbott's infielders
47 "The Arrangement" director Kazan
48 One of the X-Men
50 Arledge of crosswords
52 They're among the most wanted
53 Zoc, for one
54 Penn State campus site
56 Capital of Alpes-Maritimes
57 Postponed
59 Inert gas
61 Hula wear
62 Lacking the knack
65 "Honey, I'm Home" singer
72 Radio knob
74 Bide one's time
75 Blah
76 Western pyramid builder
77 Tigger's creator
78 Come on the scene
79 Ear-related
80 Champion or Trigger
81 More concentrated
82 Study aid

DOWN
1 Simon Says player
2 McFadden of "Star Trek: TNG"
3 Potts in "Crimes of Passion"
4 "How Do I Live" singer
5 Graniteware coating
6 Baby talk
7 Borodin's prince
8 Long, filmy wrap
9 Choreographer White
10 Tidbit
11 Ottawa hockey team
12 Loved to bits
13 Where FDR appears
14 E.B. White's nickname
15 ___ kwon do
24 "The Sixth Sense" boy
26 Farm structure
29 Eden name
30 Virginia's state tree
31 "Who's That Girl" singer
32 Daily and Marshall
33 Type style
34 Bright red
35 "Halo" enemy
36 Hall-of-Fame Jet
38 Lout
40 Not on the rocks
41 "Dark Angel" star
44 "Live" singer
49 Resourceful
50 1 or 66, e.g.
51 Ring site
52 Presently
55 Year in Nero's reign
58 "Ishtar" director May
60 Rogers in "42nd Street"
63 Dappled
64 Unvoiced
65 Loretta in "Whoops Apocalypse"
66 In great shape
67 Still dreaming
68 "Sounds good ___!"
69 Small songbird
70 Snobbery
71 "Bus Stop" playwright
73 Point de gaze
74 Early hrs.

144 U.S. OPEN WINNERS by John M. Samson
59 Across has won the U.S. Open four times.

ACROSS

1 Mideast majority
6 One of the Seven Sisters
12 Even-tempered
16 Eastwick clique
17 Attribute
18 Omnium-gatherum
19 Non-Polynesian, in Hawaii
20 Was inclined?
21 Kirsten Flagstad's birthplace
22 1997 U.S. Open winner
24 1986 U.S. Open winner
26 "K-i-s-s-i-n-g" place
27 Chinese noodle dish
28 Winter wear
31 Prizm and Metro
32 Jackson or Owens
36 "___ Fashioned Love Song"
37 Memory: Comb. form
38 Detroit hoopster
39 Blood pigment
40 Key of Haydn's "The Hunt"
41 Solving needs
42 Sanyo's Solar ___
43 1982 U.S. Open winner
45 Mountaineers' sch.
46 ABC, for one
48 Piles of carpets
49 Dingo's dwelling
50 Aleve alternative
51 "It's ___ out there!"
52 Tin-lead alloy
53 "He's ___ nowhere man . . .": Beatles
54 "Jimmy Crack Corn" singer
55 Popular corn chips
56 Intrusive igneous rock
58 Hence
59 1953 U.S. Open winner
62 2003 U.S. Open winner
66 "The Time Machine" slaves
67 Whistled a happy tune
69 Aerosol propellant
70 Loads
71 Actually, legally
72 Sill
73 Pure and simple
74 Is a first-stringer
75 Daughter of Strom Thurmond

DOWN

1 Feel pain
2 Sound after a score
3 Bath waters
4 Disparage
5 Scoffed at
6 Pleasant suffix?
7 Des Moines suburb
8 Tunbridge Wells, e.g.
9 It's solar heated
10 Special Forces units
11 Apply more henna
12 Composure
13 In addition
14 Pond pad
15 Ambiance
23 "Hiroshima Maiden" Obie winner
25 Suva resident
27 1993 U.S. Open winner
28 Title for Gandhi
29 Off the beam
30 1992 U.S. Open winner
31 Chew like a beaver
33 1999 U.S. Open winner
34 Mira in "Mighty Aphrodite"
35 Safeguards
37 CC × XX
38 PGA members
40 ___ about-face
41 Nickname of a Bruin legend
43 Gloria of "The Sopranos"
44 Kit Carson Museum site
47 Driver shaft material
49 1970s suits
51 "Anne of Green Gables" setting
52 Pricey tuber
54 "If ___ broke . . ."
55 British rival of "GQ"
57 Trademarked tangelos
58 Rip or red followers
59 "___ me up, Scotty!"
60 Fashion magazine
61 Jordanian queen
62 "Surely you ___"
63 Checkers side
64 Jellystone bear
65 Joint in "Sonny Boy"
68 Original "Dungeons & Dragons" co.

145 ACTORS AND THEIR ROLES   by Eva Finney
4 Down received a Best Actor Oscar for that role.

ACROSS

1 Jabba's slave dancer
5 "Shrek" princess
10 Book after John
14 Punxsutawney ___
15 Jackie in "Roseanne"
17 Booster
18 Freeway access
19 Jimmy Doolittle, e.g.
20 Gentle
21 "Bel piacere" is one
22 "For ___ a jolly good . . ."
23 "Bingo!"
24 Robert on Traveler
25 Lane in "Lois & Clark"
27 Grandpa in "Little Miss Sunshine"
29 Comparative suffix
30 Singer DiFranco
31 151, to Pliny
32 Slope
35 Deck wood
36 Grenoble river
40 Cadillac crest, e.g.
41 Trait carrier
42 Mr. Potato Head in "Toy Story"
44 Altar in the sky
45 Bob Guccione magazine
47 USMA grads
48 It's often honorable
50 Language of 51-A
51 Drogheda locale
52 Aquarium mollusk
53 "Rhyme & Reason" rapper
54 Humbert in "Lolita"
55 Flaw
57 Islanders' org.
58 ___ Plaines
59 Maverick Mitchell in "Top Gun"
63 Woodhouse in "Emma"
67 Omar's "father"
68 Q–U links
69 Water from the Seine
70 Sported
71 Title for Beethoven
72 Princess Jasmine's love
74 Earthen pot
75 Glacial mounds
76 Permissive
77 Ugly Duckling's genus
78 Elverish
79 Tenure
80 Refuse to grant

DOWN

1 Sofia in "The Color Purple"
2 Butler's belle
3 Fishing cap?
4 Frank Slade in "Scent of a Woman"
5 Cat scratch ___
6 End of an affliction
7 Italian goose
8 Singer Imbruglia
9 Love, in Maui
10 Star in "M*A*S*H"
11 Sidewalk marker
12 Maggie in "Wild Hogs"
13 Rembrandt contemporary
15 "Real Time" host Bill
16 Old French coin
26 Flying off the shelf
27 Marin Frist on "Men in Trees"
28 Linda Lavin role
30 "___ No Money": Cash
32 Shuts vehemently
33 Best Actress of 1961
34 Guam capital
35 Paul Rivers in "21 Grams"
37 Fashion designer Perry
38 Fashion trend
39 Düsseldorf neighbor
41 Chevy ___ Tracker
42 Deteriorate
43 Honshu shrine center
45 "For Whom the Bell Tolls" heroine
46 City of W Russia
49 King Arthur in "Spamalot" (2005)
51 Callahan in "Sudden Impact"
53 Jiffy
54 Spice Girl Brown
56 Country
58 Intimidate
59 Deep Nevada lake
60 Corpulent
61 Aesop's point
62 Elba and Aruba
63 Colorant
64 Florida Evans on "Good Times"
65 Textile fabric
66 Bushed
69 Ideal garden
73 Nero's 502

146 THE LAST FRONTIER by Don Law
The length of the race at 11-D is roughly 1,150 miles.

ACROSS

1 "Finding Nemo" shark
5 Alaskan fish
11 Pictograph
15 Sub ___ (secretly)
16 Slip up
17 Capitol Building roof
18 Cain's victim
19 Feared funnel
20 March 15
21 Volcanic Polynesian island
23 Trice
25 "The Boy Is ___": Monica
26 Cancún catnap
28 Alaskan ___
30 The Highwayman's love
31 Times to remember
34 Rappers, e.g.
35 Combustible sod
36 Validated
38 Church projection
39 Clean a briar
40 Kerchief
41 Naval address
42 Cat call
43 Thing to avoid
44 Maze navigator
45 Downpour
47 Presidio
48 Gov. Romney
49 Adjusts for fit
50 Play charades
51 Capt. Kirk's doctor
52 Closeout phrase
53 On one's rocker?
54 Capt. Picard's #1
55 B-complex vitamin
57 Munro's pen name
58 Iron-selection factor
61 Tom in "Sliver"
65 Jim Davis dog
66 Fill with life
69 Togo capital
70 Winslet in "Iris"
71 Change the order of
72 Serbian river
73 Syrian name
74 Native Alaskan
75 Leap ___

DOWN

1 Alaskan king ___
2 Homemade Halloween costume
3 ___-un-friendly
4 Alaskan sled dog
5 Boutique
6 Saturn sedan
7 K following
8 Wharton degree
9 Beatle songs, e.g.
10 Las Vegas luminaries
11 Alaskan sled race
12 Musical epilogue
13 Harbinger
14 Harrier home
16 Fourteen pounds
22 Ebay offers
24 Canned heat
26 Tailor's line
27 Suffix for lobby
28 "Marie Antoinette" director
29 Some are seaside
30 Kodiak Island creature
32 Parsimony
33 Ottawa puckster
34 Angel hair, e.g.
35 P&G shampoo
36 Respire, doggie-style
37 Bumppo of "The Pathfinder"
39 Hose ladders
40 Egoist, for one
42 Sparta's foe in "300"
43 Alaskan gold rush city
46 Alaskan ruminant
47 Friend of Sawyer
48 Alaska Range mount
50 "Men in Trees" entrepreneur
51 Pitcher Mussina
53 Movie makeup
54 Spectacle
56 With a dropped jaw
57 Spat
58 Japanese artist Matsumoto
59 Grandfather of Enos
60 Hayworth in "Pal Joey"
61 Cowardly Lion's creator
62 Skirt panel
63 Madame Bovary
64 Keister
67 Annoy
68 Roman "Space Odyssey" year

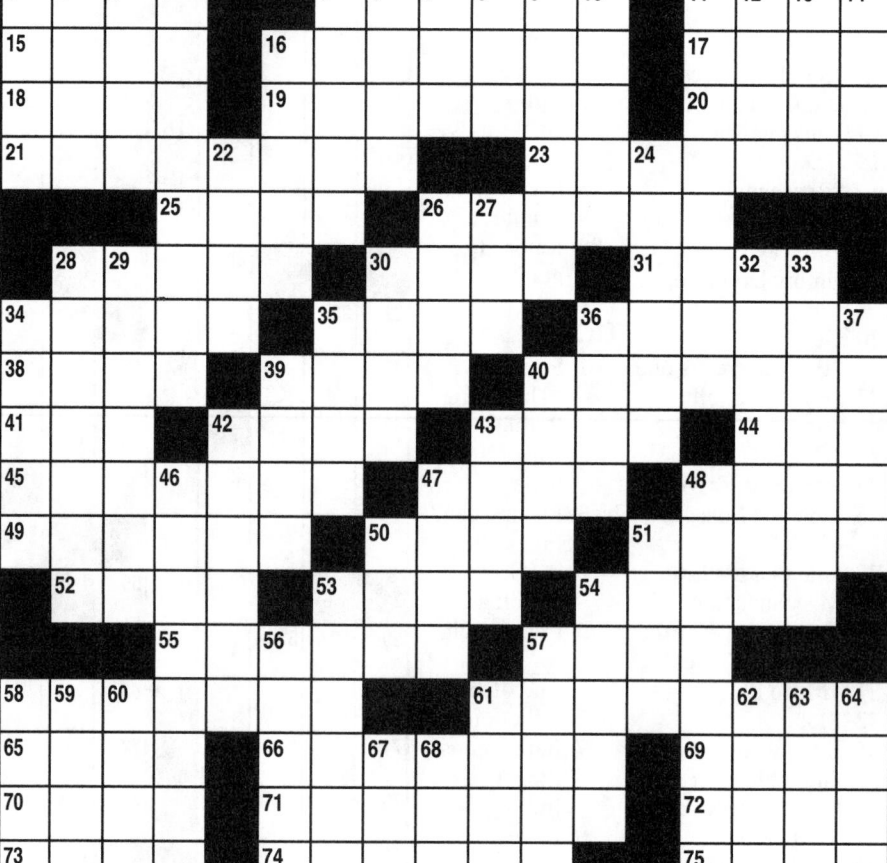

147 ALL-CENTURY TEAM by Tim Wagner
Many feel 63-A was the greatest ballplayer of all time.

ACROSS

1 Mere
6 Express shock
10 Repose
14 Bladed apple gadget
15 Hermione Granger's friend
17 Sommer in "The Winds of War"
18 "Centipede" game maker
19 Cesar in "Ocean's Eleven"
20 Ballet bend
21 All-Century Team third baseman
23 All-Century Team outfielder
25 2000 Peace Nobelist
26 Visit
27 Less friendly
30 Shoots 72 at Augusta
31 Prurient glance
34 Real Quiet sound
35 Trade center
36 "The Rose" star
38 Cup-and-saucer lamp
39 Barbarians
40 Deerstalker
41 Star quality?
42 All-Century Team outfielder
44 All-Century Team outfielder
46 Penn Station abbr.
47 Rowling's Mad-___ Moody
48 Predicament
49 2000 Super Bowl winners
50 Ray in "Cop Land"
52 Coffin cloth
53 "Rocky Horror Show" heroine
54 11th-century date
55 Minotaur's home
56 Bay State college
57 Emulate Frankenstein
59 Little john
60 All-Century Team shortstop
63 All-Century Team outfielder
68 Creator of Perry and Della
69 Bang and zoom
71 Cell-phone name
72 Punt
73 Sweet smells
74 Unlike a klutz
75 Some winged queens
76 Belt rivet
77 Meuse tributary

DOWN

1 Boom or bowsprit
2 "The Elder" of Rome
3 Horse for Lawrence
4 Italian saint
5 Whimwham
6 "Yes, yes, continue!"
7 Source of bills
8 "Tonight's the Night" singer
9 Dangers
10 Rued the day
11 Lois Lane's mother
12 Take off the cream
13 Golf shirts?
15 Senior dance
16 Parker House, e.g.
22 Percivale's title
24 1962 film remade in 1997
26 Disney/Pixar film
27 The time being
28 Opponent of K.A.O.S
29 Nero's wraths
30 Window sheet
32 Like the Presidential Suite
33 Administrations
34 Calyx component
35 Polyhymnia, e.g.
36 Auntie of Patrick Dennis
37 Crow bar
39 Georgetown cager
40 "The Sting" director
43 Put out a batter
44 Hawaii's first governor
45 1995 Wimbledon winner
48 Smog
51 Political slate
52 Roger Sherman, e.g.
53 "Satires" poet
55 Rockies milieu
56 Scandal sheet
58 Birthplace of Ceres
59 Glasgow gal
60 McEntire sitcom
61 Club for Annika
62 Intrigue
63 Dewdrop
64 Mocked incessantly
65 Mandolin relatives
66 Alice's income
67 Loathe
70 Doak Walker's alma mater

GAMES by Peggy O'Shea
48 Down was featured in the 2004 documentary "Word Wars."

ACROSS

1 Con game
5 Mulcted
10 Guitarist Atkins
14 Clef type
15 Peopled
17 Mauna Kea neighbor
18 Fish-eating bird
19 Game with dice cups
20 Jazz singer Fitzgerald
21 Reprimand
23 Laid down the law?
25 Hurry
26 Tapered off
28 Be a killjoy
30 Ill-gotten gains
31 They're mounted but not ridden
34 To any extent
35 Cola with a kick
36 Rail
38 "The Lion" of golf
39 Kind of music
40 Colt's home
41 Child-care author LeShan
42 Wood of boat decks
43 Bear lairs
44 NYC's Fifth
45 Memorial on the National Mall
47 "Ruth Benedict" biographer
48 Little detail
49 32-card game
50 Well-being
51 In short supply
52 Ravioli filling
53 Annoy
54 "To a Mouse" poet
55 Key West, for one
57 Airborne GI, for short
58 Two-deck game
61 Baltimore oriole
65 Provided excellent service
66 Board game with discs
69 Color of dolor
70 French name
71 White legume
72 Kind of sausage
73 Greek Mars
74 Hibachi remnant
75 Bed of roses

DOWN

1 Baker in "Lord of the Rings"
2 Oaf
3 It's often smashed
4 Money game
5 Martinmas, e.g.
6 Yearning
7 Utmost degree
8 Cantab's rival
9 Cactus milieu
10 Jumping game
11 Sword handle
12 Fashion monthly
13 Garter snake's lunch
15 Exxon Valdez accident
16 Merrill in "The Player"
22 Singer Sedaka
24 "___ in the Outfield" (1994)
26 Auctioneer's word
27 Like habaneros
28 Bowl
29 "City Slickers" star
30 Peek
32 Cape in S Greece
33 "Oh Very Young" singer
34 Jane Eyre's pupil
35 Crawford in "The Women"
36 Miss Moneypenny's friend
37 Fabricate
39 Hawaiian song
40 Put right
42 Rich cakes
43 Arrangement
46 Pantomime game
47 Hot sandwich
48 Tournament game
50 No-brainer card game
51 Incontestable
53 Col. Sanders' beard
54 Münchhausen's title
56 Desist
57 "For Whom the Bell Tolls" heroine
58 "___ Mia"
59 Maple genus
60 Goose of Maui
61 Take off
62 Mother of Romulus
63 Ty Cobb's 2,245
64 Hockey fake
67 Prosciutto
68 "Zorba" lyricist

149 STOP OR GO? by John M. Samson
The answer to the title can be found at 54 Across.

ACROSS

1 Bridge of Prague
8 Gondolier, e.g.
15 Concocted
17 Imagine
18 Hot wheels
19 Totaled (with "to")
20 Promise, e.g.
22 Def in "Civil Brand"
23 Curled the lip
24 Vienna, in Vienna
26 "___ is human . . ."
27 Noted whistle-blower
30 Thames tributary
31 No-nos
32 Brunch time
35 Number that means an A or a C
36 Fix a button
37 Ties the knot
38 One worshiped at Memphis
41 Apollo 13 challenge
42 Growlers
43 Previous to
44 Ill will
45 Tracks down
46 Sit-outs
47 Eyelid woe
48 Grapefruit soft drinks
49 Landing
50 Stamp in "The Collector"
53 Vacation mo.
54 STOP or GO?
59 "Naughty ___": Herbert
60 "Just because"
62 Kind of stuffing or cocktail
63 Third-class, on the Titanic
64 In any event
65 With jam or bull

DOWN

1 Apple key
2 Rhodes of "Daktari"
3 Aussie golfer Scott
4 Workout routine
5 He landed at the feet of Clay in 1964
6 James and Place
7 Chickadee food
8 B-1, for one
9 "We'll be ___ way"
10 Not dull
11 Camping wear?
12 Acarid
13 State confidently
14 Beatty in "1941"
16 Papillon, for one
17 Chair persons
21 Hit combo
24 Flannel shirts, sweaters, etc.
25 "What a perfect gift!"
26 "That is ___ . . ." ("In other words . . .")
28 Al Capp's Fleegle
29 Swiss court star
30 Old Olds
31 Darlings
32 Viscount's superiors
33 Lixivia
34 "The Highwayman" poet
36 Q–V span
37 Hits the cuspidor
39 10,000 Maniacs album
40 Aussie kestrels
45 Imply
46 What little pitchers have
48 Attacked
49 Sieves food
51 Fluid accumulation
52 Ancient lyres
53 Up ___ (stuck)
54 Papilloma
55 Lingual
56 They can't pass the bar
57 Morales in "Bad Boys"
58 Like a boxed pizza
59 B.B. King's label
61 All-Star pitcher Robb

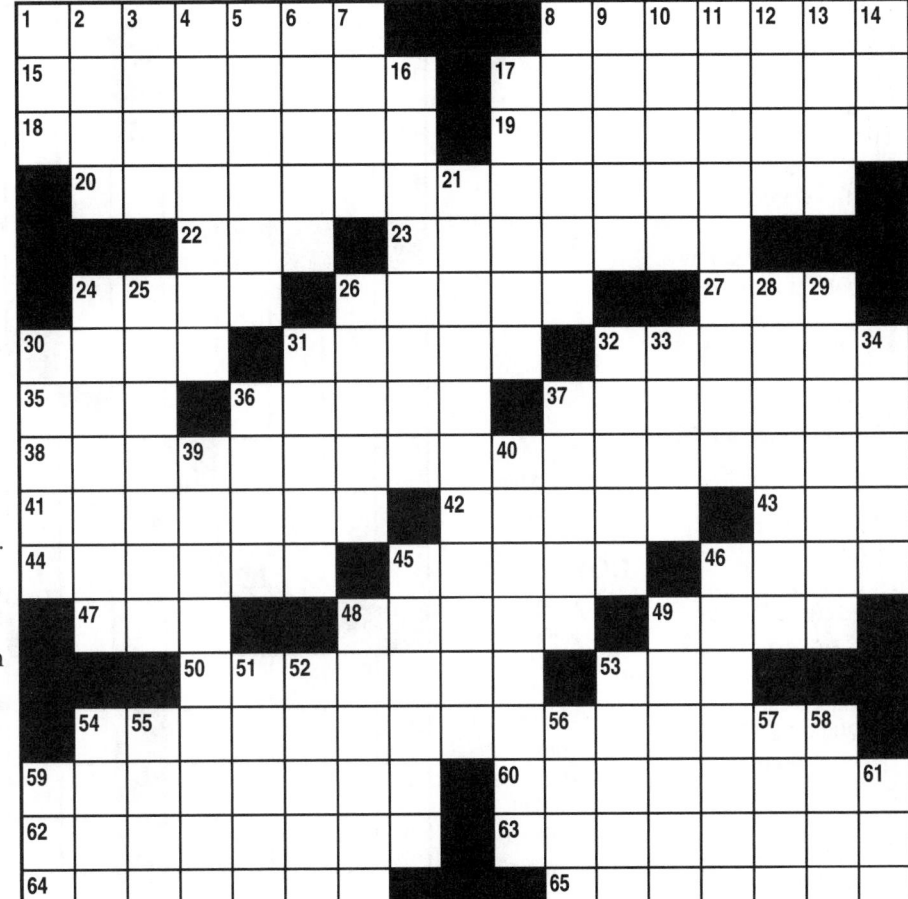

150

A salute to winners of the American Crossword Puzzle Tournament.

ACROSS

1 Pet peeves
6 Voices for Tevye and the Mikado
11 Wins in a walk
16 Key partner
17 Tap water alternative
18 What Olympians sought in Barcelona (1992)
19 "Battlestar Galactica" commander
20 Niki of Grand Prix fame
21 "___ no?"
22 2007 ACPT champion
24 Fruitless
25 Richard Wilbur, e.g.
26 Voice of Buzz Lightyear
28 2003 ACPT champion
33 Nevus
34 Pet peeves
35 "Charlie Chan at the Opera" star
37 Personal-ad abbr.
40 The right to bare arms?
41 RN's ASAP
42 Failure to yield right ___
44 Castle in Limerick
45 Hamptons homes
48 Green and Hardin
49 Moony
51 Like Death's horse
52 Pageboy, e.g.
54 Suffix for crossword
55 Covent Garden designer Jones
57 Big fan of Samuel Adams
58 Contract writer
59 2004 ACPT champion
61 1978 ACPT champion
65 IHOP opener
66 Folded
67 2000 ACPT champion
73 Like Gray areas?
74 "Cell Block" dance in "Chicago"
75 "Sleeping Beauty" fairy
76 Yemeni port dweller
77 1976 Houston Open winner Lee
78 "What the Butler Saw" playwright
79 1987 ACPT champion
80 Gild the lily
81 "Arms and the Man" heroine

DOWN

1 Goodyear gone bad
2 Macbeth, for one
3 All-inclusive abbr.
4 High-water mark
5 Chinese canines
6 Convictions
7 Studebaker or Lemmon film
8 Skirret genus
9 1977 "Time" Man of the Year
10 Lifeless
11 2005 ACPT champion (Div. B)
12 Soccer stadium cheers
13 N Iraqi city
14 Kind of poetry, ironically
15 Philosopher Kierkegaard
23 1984 Whitney Houston hit
27 Jamaican gent
28 "In the jingle ___ morning . . .": Dylan
29 Eye
30 Chuck Berry hit
31 Bosnian river
32 Just a few
36 After the bell
37 Like a maelstrom
38 2007 ACPT champion (Div. B)
39 India's "City of Palaces"
41 Pat Paulsen's party
43 ___ coin
46 Aromatic brew
47 Words on an invoice
50 2001 ACPT champion
53 Seek (a job or loan)
56 Minus expenses
57 Small-time gambler
58 Like most sunbathers
60 Block-and-tackle specialist
61 Say "@#$%!"
62 "Otello" aria
63 Paper-chase runners
64 "The BFG" author Dahl
68 Neutralize
69 Zhivago's inspiration
70 Conductor Riccardo
71 By and by
72 Visitor in "Deep Space 9"

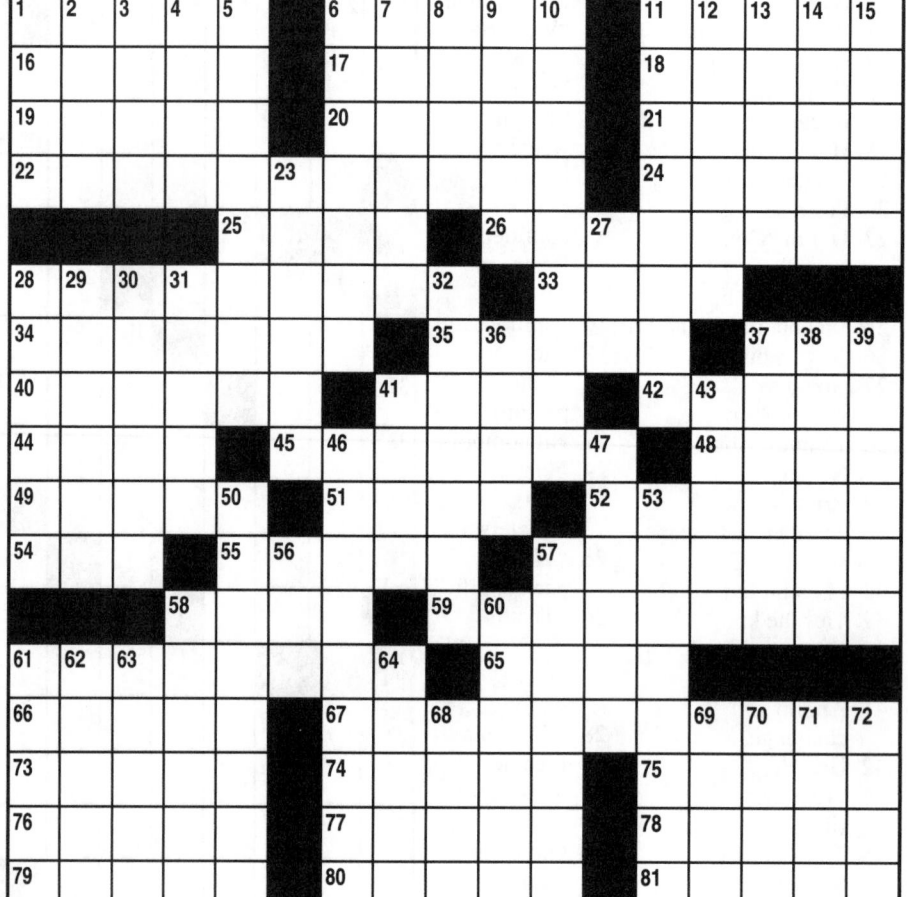

151 BAD ADVICE   by Patrick Jordan
Sometimes the best advice is no advice.

ACROSS

1 Act like a baby
5 Karate shot
9 Watch over
13 Classroom cheater's note
17 Jai ___
18 CW sitcom set in Houston
19 Conical woodwind
20 Occupy a duck blind
21 Helium, neon et al.
23 Prop in Harry Potter films
24 Tissue softener
25 Advice from Rich Little's mom?
28 Drawing medium
31 Under quarantine, perhaps
32 1984 race medalist Sebastian
33 Reynolds Wrap maker
34 "Begone, bug!"
36 Comedian's repertoire
41 Advice from Lon Chaney's mom?
44 Sharpshooters' org.
45 Mayberry's Otis, for one
46 Three-sided sails
47 Squeezed (out)
48 Seeks a 74-A from
49 Body-shop figure
52 Born partner
53 Imperfect
54 Culminating point
55 Horned pachyderm
57 Females
58 Unseen Beckett character
60 Comfortably close-fitting
61 How a daydreamer stares
65 Elizabethan expletive
66 It acquired Alfa Romeo in 1986
67 Ashcroft predecessor
68 Shaq's shoe width
69 80-A site

70 Advice from Franz Schubert's mom? (with 81-A)
74 Answer
76 Alligator's warning
77 When prompted
78 Glory or guard preceder
79 Canada's Thanksgiving d.
80 Chin-up muscle
81 See 70 Across
88 Calista Flockhart role
89 Alimony recipients
90 Liquidates gradually
94 Crop ears?
95 Lovesick exhalation
96 Terra, to Tiberius
97 Word wizard Webster
98 Garbs oneself in
99 Spend the night
100 Caustic chemicals
101 Like "Halloween" movies

DOWN

1 "Coyote Ugly" setting
2 Bit of French on a menu
3 "Low Rider" band
4 Rest upon
5 Grovel
6 "___ Rebel" (1962 hit)
7 Comply with
8 Juliet Mills soap opera
9 Locker-room snapper
10 Web site with PowerSellers
11 Tyke's taboo
12 Took away
13 Drink after drink
14 Make wrathful
15 Perfection symbol
16 Kobe, notably
22 Glint
26 On-line diary
27 Lobster and sturgeon eggs
28 Far from fashionable
29 Some choristers
30 Catbert's creator
34 "Mad TV" bit
35 Sleep til spring
36 Agents for new faces?
37 Scored 1 at Sawgrass
38 Urgency
39 Torah holders
40 Girl
42 King Telamon's warrior son
43 Adder's-tongue, for one
48 "Well said!"
50 Popular MP3 player
51 Had a gathering
52 1988 Tom Hanks fantasy
53 Successful solver's shout
56 "Gilligan's Island" abodes
57 Dumfries denizen
58 Shifting selection
59 Folkloric fiend
60 Confessional disclosures
62 Aardvark's snack
63 Advantage, colloquially
64 Go-aheads
66 Predilection
67 Udometer measure
70 Kewpie
71 Hammer-throwing god
72 Lifting device
73 Advancing slowly
75 Living coral, essentially
79 Netlike
80 Aviary occupants
81 1/220 furlong
82 Imperial, e.g.
83 ___ Bator
84 Turnoff
85 Harp star
86 "If ___ be excused . . ."
87 What the fourth little piggie had
91 Chaotic place
92 It can be plugged or tugged
93 Like shrinking violets

RETRONYMS*   by Victor Fleming
"In the beginning was the word . . ."

ACROSS

1 Desert brick
6 Tuba blast
12 Deem necessary
18 Domingo's voice
19 TV's "___ and Greg"
20 Hispanic Muppet
21 Virgule*
23 Buck topper
24 Handily (after "with")
25 In the thick of
27 Spice Girls member
28 Egyptian symbol of power
30 Declares
33 Three-stringed instrument
36 Pont-l'Évêque is made of this*
39 It goes postal*
43 "The Millionairess" actress
44 British isle
45 "All I ___ Do": Crow
46 Cry to a calf
47 Firm up the engagement
49 Smoothed, as wood
50 Part of SASE
51 Name qualifier
52 Bone dishes
53 Halloweenish
55 Singer Winans
58 What answers to clues* are
62 Delicate
63 Can opener?
65 "Baby I'm ___"
66 Goombah
68 "Ooky" cousin
69 No longer sick
71 Army food of WW2
76 "Losing My Religion" band
77 Picture puzzle
78 Prussian pronoun
79 Subdues (with "down")
80 C-130 Hercules, e.g.*
82 Unformatted file*
84 Stuffy-sounding
85 Little inn?
86 Oft-mismarked possessive

87 Be het up
89 Jacob's father-in-law
92 Hunter of fiction
95 Sew on, e.g.
98 Place to get a drink*
103 Comfort
104 Pseudo-suave wooers
105 El año's commencer
106 Below or above leader?
107 Some cameos' attributes
108 Common thing?

DOWN

1 FBI cousin
2 "In excelsis ___"
3 Subject to sanctions, maybe
4 2001 MLB Manager of the Year
5 Historical divisions
6 Unmatched, in a sense
7 Surprised gasps
8 Foolish talk
9 Tot toters
10 Schoolyard retort
11 Chemistry Nobelist Otto
12 Overseas Mrs.
13 Geologic division
14 Prize
15 It needs loading*
16 Covered couple
17 "American Pie" actress Reid
22 Pack of paper
26 Pontiac G6 predecessor
28 Punchers
29 Jeff MacNelly strip
31 ___ Cong
32 "Legally Blonde" blonde
34 "___ Kleine Nacht"
35 Gillette Blue ___

37 Listed
38 "The NeverEnding Story" writer
39 Old beaus
40 Tyke tender
41 Column choice
42 Mrs. Howell's sobriquet
48 First Family mem. of 1933
49 Shy
52 Royal Caribbean booking
54 Mama Cass
55 Happy sound
56 No faster?
57 Bulky workstation display*
59 Check out
60 Springsteen's "Born ___"
61 Watering hole?
64 Marine ___
67 Business-letter letters
70 The Sail constellation

71 Firing chamber
72 Take in a story
73 Long odds
74 Ensuing
75 Jets no longer flying
78 Exercise wear
81 Gourmet's pride
83 Skeptic's scoff
85 Mild, weatherwise
87 Criticize harshly
88 Native Nebraskan
90 Height: Comb. form
91 Benefit
93 Neck shapes
94 "Artaxerxes" composer
96 Tai ___
97 Dumb cluck?
99 Misery
100 Simpleton
101 MGM motto start
102 "The Purloined Letter" writer

ACROSS

1. Syn., to ant.
4. It may be piped in
9. Jamaican gent
14. Case study?
17. Dernier ___
18. Safe havens
19. New York island
20. Do the wrong thing
21. Site of a 1966 Beatles concert
24. Dating result
25. Break point
26. Morales of "NYPD Blue"
27. Shopping for suds
29. Luddite's tool?
33. They may be carved in stone
34. In two parts, musically
35. Do groundwork
36. Base fig.
37. Comes together
40. Geiger counter meas.
42. Show piece
44. Use UPS
47. Chop sticks?
48. Care or care for
49. Clinton and Bush, formerly
52. Photo option
53. Gold Coast, today
55. Cavalry weapon
57. Like America's most wanted
59. In an ill-bred manner
61. Hindu disciplinarians
63. State bordering Arizona
64. Sizeable number
66. Punny poet Nash
68. USGS maps
69. Center of Raleigh?
70. Casual wear
72. "Jeepers!"
74. She had a little lamb
75. Catch sight of
77. Spy novelist Deighton
78. Cooling-off period
79. IRS ID's
80. "CSI" regular George
82. Moldy cheese
85. "Othello" fellow
87. Wildly successful, in "Variety"
89. Western weapon
94. Licorice flavoring
97. Stick together
98. Handy
99. Big London attraction
100. Red blades with white crosses
104. Like Mozart's "Jupiter" Symphony
105. Nearing the hour
106. Refrain from farming?
107. End of August?
108. Kabuki kin
109. It's played at Camden Yards
110. "Don't just sit there"
111. Morse code

DOWN

1. Razor-sharp philosopher?
2. Home of "The Nude Maja"
3. Blame
4. Fountain favorite
5. Put into play
6. CBS unit
7. Take in, perhaps
8. Wilhelm et al.
9. Punt over
10. Mont Blanc, e.g.
11. Pitcher's perch
12. Spare change
13. They wish to know
14. Boy Scout's task?
15. Bandy words
16. Royal Navy non-combat branch of WW2
22. "Sorcerer's Apprentice" composer
23. Biblical miracle site
28. Floor decor
30. Doctor Zhivago
31. Disaccustoms
32. Patch up
36. Leaves in
37. Speech impediment
38. Disentombs
39. Sure thing
41. Make-or-break time
43. Secret service
45. Like some nails
46. Delights
48. Colorful cardinals
49. Those with safe jobs
50. Extra dry
51. It's a sin
54. The puck stops here
56. Border's order
58. It contains Mayo
60. Pep squad repertoire
62. "Sonic the Hedgehog" creator
65. Not to a Scot
67. It's the truth
71. "Mad Money" channel
73. Croat or Serb
76. Beasts of the East
78. Commodity contracts
79. Former Chicago Symphony maestro
81. Inflicts upon
83. Prepares to surf
84. F. Scott she's not
86. "Faust" composer
87. Polio pioneer
88. Brief bridge bid
90. Send in
91. Life-like
92. Nicholas Gage best-seller
93. Gateway button
95. Tall vessel
96. Make a dent in
101. FM selection
102. House call
103. Close one

154 INVENTIONS by Ernest Lampert
Arthur Wynne is credited with inventing the crossword puzzle in 1913.

ACROSS

1 French Morocco?
6 Fusilli's shape
12 Used an 18-wheeler
18 "Made ___"
19 Not level
20 "Yeah, right"
21 James Ritty invention
23 A Lennon sister
24 "Only U" singer
25 Israelis' ancestors
27 "Don't ___ dumb!"
30 Stephanie Kwolek invention
31 Richard Drew invention
36 Gerrymander
37 Storekeeper in "The Simpsons"
40 Unit of pressure
41 "Die Fledermaus" maid
43 To the extent that
46 Northern natives
49 Citation of 1958
51 Ready
52 Like some elements
54 King Gillette invention
57 P&G toothpaste
59 South African village
60 Warren Marrison invention
66 Legs diamonds?
70 Bert's friend
71 Home of Kia Motors
73 Watch mechanism
74 Sadie Hawkins Day cry
77 Game guru Edmond
79 Globe plotter
80 Plural ending
81 Biographer Winslow
83 George Crum invention
86 George de Mestral invention
89 Questionable service call?
90 Most
94 Wear for a bank job
99 Record listing
100 Ladislo Biro invention
103 Friend of Peppermint Patty
104 The "I" of LASIK
105 Joseph Lauder's wife
106 Lab vessel
107 Discriminating person?
108 Partner of stop

DOWN

1 Isinglass
2 Literary olios
3 Thrill
4 Fed. watchdog
5 "Magnificent" Carson role
6 The Arrow constellation
7 23rd Greek letter
8 They, to Thibaudet
9 Campus mil. group
10 Vertical, asea
11 "My Fair Lady" lyricist
12 2004 Viggo Mortensen film
13 Bellini's sleepwalker
14 Carrier with a hub at PHL
15 Fontanne's husband
16 Donegal Bay feeder
17 Odd couple?
22 Make an impression on
26 Budget alternative
28 "Is It a Crime" singer
29 Reader-opinion pages
31 Solo, in a way
32 Pension perk
33 Metal rock group
34 "Rooster Cogburn" prequel
35 Einstein's second wife
37 Tombstone loc.
38 Flamenco guitarist de Lucía
39 Patron
42 J. Pershing's command
44 Scavenge
45 Problem-solving
47 Quetzalcoatl worshiper
48 North African port
50 Albanian bread
53 EDGAR parent
55 Part of a chorus line
56 Back grounds
58 1964 Peace Nobelist: Init.
60 Cunard Line liner
61 Inclination
62 Long stretches in Spain
63 Awesome answer?
64 Prado's whip
65 Single out
67 Dinah's mother in "The Red Tent"
68 Subj. on a report card
69 Where to get off
72 Hymn part
75 Where to keep a Colt
76 "The Nazarene" novelist
78 Dines downtown
82 Mideast peninsula
84 Kind of torch on "Survivor"
85 Offers a view
86 Crew alternative
87 "Ah, Wilderness" mother
88 Malayan "person of the forest"
90 Souvlaki meat
91 "Dies ___" ("Day of Wrath")
92 Banker Monnette
93 Other than that
95 ___ Helens
96 Mass-transit org.
97 Visionary
98 Shinbone end
101 Weeks in a Julian calendar
102 Qt. halves

155 JOHNNY ONE NOTE by Bonnie L. Gentry

Bonnie borrowed her title from a "Babes in Arms" song by Rodgers and Hart.

ACROSS

1 Oakland reliever Alan
7 A Bonn vivant?: Abbr.
10 He helped topple Batista
13 Lith. and Ukr., formerly
17 Unyielding
18 Put up
20 Scallion relative
21 Ability to be on one's own
23 Gucci fragrance
24 "Waiting for the Robert ___"
25 Some Realtor's houses
26 Ken of the Merry Pranksters
27 K. Hernandez was one
29 Catch a second airing
30 2005 Eric Mabius film
32 Scout unit
34 Karate ranks
37 "Yada, yada, yada . . ."
40 Actor Lee Van___
44 Mon., on Tues.
45 Bug repellent
46 Soft ball
48 Ink for une plume
50 "American Gigolo" star
52 Radical 1960s org.
53 Ship spines
55 Battery type
57 A+ and A–
59 Irish patriot Robert
60 Put back in office
62 Trattoria offering
65 Pitchers' place
67 Schopenhauer contemporary
68 February forecast
69 Year of Chaucer's death
71 Exercise count
73 Put back in the cage
75 Site of a WW1 Allied victory
76 A little juice?
78 Bingo call
80 Last word for the defense
82 ___ Anne de Bellevue
83 Called up
86 Playboy Hugh's nickname
88 Let off steam
89 Lucky number in Napoli
93 Board game with stones
97 "Ten ___ a Dance"
98 Dürer et al.
100 It may be breaking
101 Noted Folies-Bergère designer
102 It remains under wraps
105 Glassmaking oven
106 U.S. Attorney General (1985–88)
107 Soap box?
108 Very, in Valence
109 One with drill skill: Abbr.
110 Balmoral Castle river
111 Calm, cool, and collected

DOWN

1 Big Bertha's birthplace
2 7,300-ft. Nevada peak
3 Brazilian seaport
4 Put more paper into
5 Days of yore, in days of yore
6 Watchful one
7 V-formation fliers
8 Seaside flock
9 Cincy baseballer of yore
10 Warehouse supply: Abbr.
11 Ramsey of '70s TV
12 Joseph of ice-cream fame
13 Made lustrous
14 Inanity
15 Went back
16 Absolut alternative
19 Salad leafstalk
22 Part of MPH
26 Bluesman Mo
28 Gumshoe, for short
30 Moves elsewhere
31 Jotting in a journal
33 Atlanta Braves' div.
35 MD's skull session?
36 D and C, in D.C.
37 Skating gold-medalist Karin
38 Be abuzz
39 Peppermint liqueur
41 Converted to code
42 Behold, to Brutus
43 Former FBI chief
47 Zipped along
49 "Oklahoma!" aunt
51 Omar in "Major League II"
54 Dump closure?
56 Cubist Fernand
58 Like elvers
61 French chef's fungus?
63 Nair competitor
64 Start of a famous "soliloque"
66 Yeshiva scholar
69 Méditerranée, for one
70 Less dense
72 It's often heard on Sun.
74 Unspecified degree
77 Lincoln and Kennedy
79 Oh Henry! maker
81 National Chicken mo.
84 St. Helens et al.
85 Knocked flat
87 "En garde!" sayer
90 This and that
91 Home of the brave
92 RCMP's "SWAT" unit
94 Moxie
95 Certain preadolescent
96 Lauder of lipstick
97 Druid, for one
98 Boulevard liners
99 They flew for nearly 35 years
102 Formed a union
103 Byrnes who was Kookie
104 Ample shoe width

156 BULLETS by Fran & Lou Sabin
If you don't understand the title, ask a poker player.

ACROSS

1 Noise pollution
4 Final, e.g.
8 Mind-set
12 Grapefruit League loc.
15 It may be big
17 Windblast
18 Olympics event
19 Exuded sap
20 Smug satisfaction
22 Street-level street?
24 Lovebirds in flight
25 Wharton degrees
27 Of no use
28 Put down
29 Says, slangily
30 Like most cattle
31 Ghostly
34 ___ Stanley Gardner
35 "The Old Wives' Tale" playwright
36 New Mexico ski spot
37 Pacific proposals
39 Spanish envelope abbr.
43 Between you and me
44 Ward heelers
45 Declamations
47 Cutting
48 Tabletop items
50 Pointer's indication
52 Site
54 Bernstein opus
55 Like some vacant lots
56 "Le Roi d'Ys" composer
57 Undercover agent
59 Begets
60 To whom Macbeth says "lay on"
63 Euripedes drama
64 Post-summer bloom
66 Boardwalk neighbor
67 Desire undone
68 Tommy of Broadway
70 Buckingham post
73 Tasmania's highest peak
74 Prevailing style
76 As recently as
77 Climber's goal
78 Brainiac
81 Sheep shed
82 "The Gold Bug" author
83 George Eliot's Silas
84 Johnnie Walker's friend
85 Whipped cream portions
89 Pair of pistols
91 "Beyond the Sea" star
93 Commotions
94 Brigade element
95 Wraps up
96 Tufted caracal features
97 Puck dropper
98 NBA team
99 Plane section
100 D-Day craft

DOWN

1 Yahtzee quintet
2 Kelly Clarkson became one
3 Verne submariner
4 Ornamental window work
5 Time out of mind
6 Follicle
7 Shaky vocal effect
8 Western flattops
9 "Mr. Holland's ___" (1996)
10 ". . . the ramparts"
11 Kelley of "Star Trek"
12 1889 Johnstown disaster
13 Temporary contract
14 Wrote a P.S.
16 Pomaceous fruits
19 Salt solutions
21 Be inclined
23 Paint solvent
26 Gripe
29 Mythical beauty goddesses
30 Swiss capital since 1848
31 Sitting on
32 Israel's first king
33 Nathaniel Hawthorne's brother-in-law
34 Beady-eyed fish
35 1909 North Pole visitor
37 Chef's collection
38 Allen and Friendly
40 Railbird's milieu
41 Robert Morse monodrama
42 Mr. Universe's pride
44 Trattoria fare
46 Sagging
49 Sadie Hawkins Day catch
50 Luxury-suite feature
51 Half a giggle
53 Venerable
55 Exercise (power)
56 Hog fat
57 Coal mine
58 "Skip to My ___"
59 Music holder
60 Queen of Scots
61 Much ado
62 Awesome act
65 Scuba diver's weapon
66 Whitish
69 Racial group
71 "Yeah!"
72 Up for grabs
73 Thug's threat
75 Atoll feature
77 Thames tributary
78 Imprison
79 Part of a fencer's cry
80 By the ___ God
81 Profit reducers
82 Modeling asset
84 Foul state
85 Netflix rentals
86 October stone
87 NBA team
88 Part of CBS
90 Low number in Lisle
92 "Music for Airports" composer

157 WHERE IT'S AT by Harvey Estes

The answer at 2 Down is also the title of a popular Ricky Martin song.

ACROSS

1 See 38 Across
5 Gets ready to drag
9 Seesaw sitter of rhyme
13 Village Voice award
17 Gray matter output
18 Set down
19 Miles from Hollywood
20 Minimal change
21 Totally inedible suet?
25 Obeying
26 String along
27 Kate's sitcom partner
28 Radial swing?
29 Rock
30 Amusing
31 Zenith
32 Panama procession?
34 Driving aids
36 Moo goo ___ pan
37 Drains
38 John Grisham's alma mater (with 1-A)
40 Formic acid source
41 Naive
43 Bettor place
47 Zenith rival
48 Vacation spot
49 Get by
50 Ruhr industrial center
52 Quarrel with refinement?
55 "The ___ Girls" (Leachman film)
58 Trumpet blasts
59 Band aide
63 Saw along the grain
64 Backwoods beast
66 Green Mountain State
67 Weisshorn, for one
68 Slick stuff
69 Scent of a woman
70 Lobbying group
71 Tolstoy and Sayer
73 Absolutely concerning?
78 Stock sector
79 On the ball
81 Ladies' men
82 First name in folk
83 Barrel part
84 Little one
85 Bright yellow
87 No slugger?
90 A party to
91 Man, for one
92 Firewood measure
93 Carol Burnett's alma mater
94 It is written
95 Miami-___ County
96 Canal of song
97 Kind of pressure

DOWN

1 Series opener?
2 "Makes no difference"
3 Establish boundaries
4 "On Language" columnist
5 Do a critic's job
6 Subordinate Claus
7 They're blue, in rhyme
8 "Prairie Home Companion" actress
9 Waffle expert
10 Toledo title
11 Nog player Eisenberg
12 Egypt and Syr., once
13 Leopardlike cat
14 Listen intently
15 Without saying a word
16 Novel ending
22 Request to Sajak
23 ___ Hari
24 Shot spot
29 Lights-out tune
30 Crème ___ crème
31 Petri dish gel
32 Until, in Tijuana
33 Wooden peg
35 Oliver's partner
37 Peter Maas book
39 Not a pretty picture
42 TV series set on an island
43 Charged
44 Iguodala of the NBA
45 Bit of frivolity
46 I problems
49 Brewery grain
51 Pillow covering
53 Investor's choice
54 Start of a legal conclusion
55 Asian Sea
56 Rite of passage
57 Where Lee surrendered
60 Wear a hair shirt
61 How dogs chase their tails
62 Emulate Munch
65 Break in relations
66 RSVP part
69 Support with cheers
72 Erudite one
74 "Torch Song Trilogy" hero
75 Chewy candy
76 "Diary of ___ Housewife" (1970)
77 "No fighting, please"
78 Get into shape
80 NBA stat
82 Unsettle
83 Blue funk
84 "___ small world!"
85 Hand over
86 Sentence unit
88 Lend a hand
89 Good d. in Lent

158

NOT QUITE ALL   **by Jay Sullivan**
The clue at 14 Down is right on the money.

ACROSS

1 ___ Formula 16
8 Badge of honor
13 Chips off the old flock
18 Police warning
19 "Me, too!"
20 Get tough
21 Shell Oil shell
22 Marine weather forecast?
24 Crack the whip
25 Butter containers
26 Crude craft
27 "Bosh!"
30 Christo's "Wrapped ___"
32 Sanctuary section
33 Small detail
34 "Just Like Jesse James" singer
35 Comes out of the blue?
39 Blue-gray shark
40 Lade?
43 Skywalker nickname
44 To-do list
46 Stocking stuff
47 Take the gold
48 Go with the flow
50 Nicholson's favorite NBA team
54 Stocking point
55 Sit on
58 Cabinet dept.
59 Electrons and neutrinos
61 Funny thing
62 Mocha resident
64 Band stand
65 Crude dude
66 Short and sweet
68 Black Sea port
72 Wear and tear
73 Deface with graffiti?
77 Tchaikovsky's "Marche ___"
78 Where to find a shore thing
80 Pool surface
81 One for the books
82 Little grimace
83 In an appropriate fashion

85 Cavalry weapon
86 Excepting
89 Gilbert & Sullivan titles
90 Spurs a cur
92 McCartney unnerved?
94 Flustered
98 Compère
99 Son of Vito Corleone
100 Okay
101 Considers
102 Article of faith
103 Doesn't have to

DOWN

1 Baseball VIPs
2 Rocker Ocasek
3 Time frame
4 "Please reply immedi-ately!"?
5 Paulie, to Rocky
6 Furors
7 Household solvent
8 Skillful
9 Arab follower?
10 Applies sparingly
11 Part of a Latin trio
12 Short, for short
13 Acted as a go-between
14 It's over a buck
15 Cogitate
16 Remus relation
17 Third Day creation
23 Easy strider
27 Wild cat
28 Glitch or hitch
29 Walk on the wild side
31 Go back to school
32 Lab cry
34 Monopoly position
35 Hit on the head
36 Took care of

37 Local group
38 Respighi subjects
41 Strictly female
42 Hog, wild
45 Lacey on "Cagney & Lacey"
49 Part of a resistance group
51 Peyton's little brother
52 A summer place
53 Put the pedal to the metal
55 Rain drain
56 Resembling
57 Lacking nutrition
58 From the top
60 Crossed the line, in a way
63 Latin "and others"
64 Cut loose
67 Pianissimo passage?

69 Pitching rubber
70 Wise guy
71 Say it isn't faux
73 Better halves
74 Mannerly
75 Courtroom anonym
76 Heavenly
79 It's a sign
83 "Invisible" singer Clay
84 Bluenose
85 Make quake
86 Made like
87 Like Chester Goode
88 "Fortune" founder
89 Put out
91 "Picnic" playwright
93 Less than e'er
95 Beauty mark
96 Judge Lance of L.A. law
97 Raise a stink

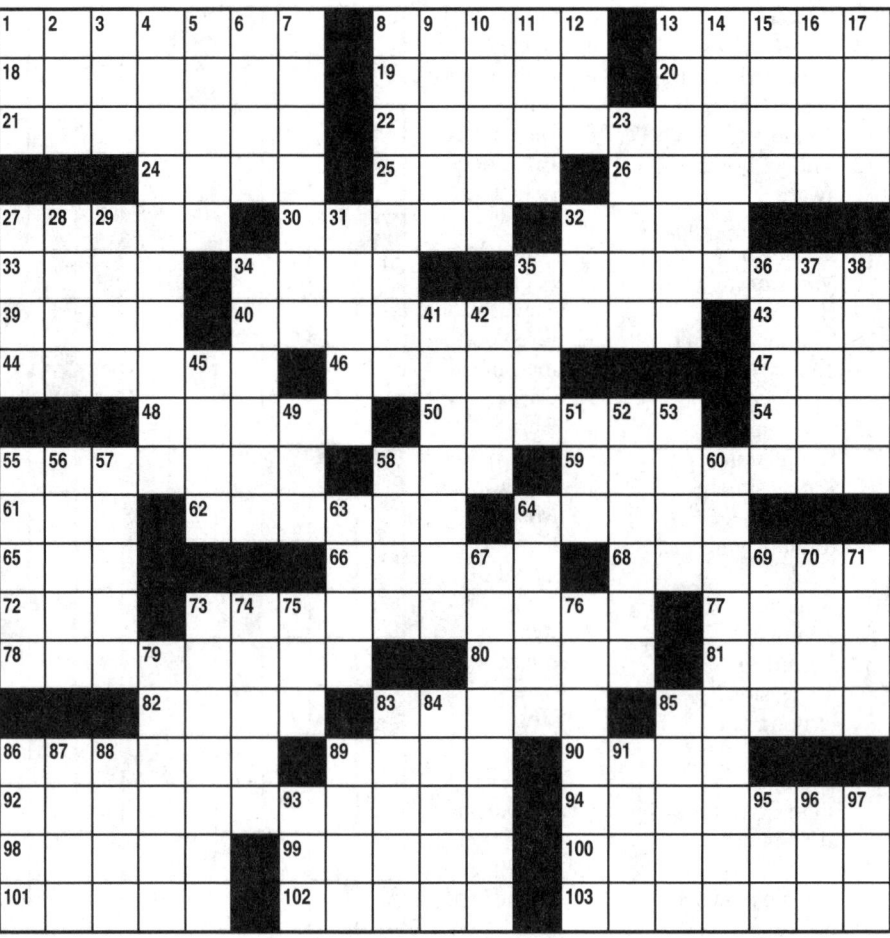

159

ACROSS

1 The Rock's are chiseled
4 Reefy
10 Cartoon explorer
14 Hearing-impaired comm.
17 Angular or pod start
18 Chemistry Nobelist Frederick
19 Hydroxyl compound
20 4, at best
21 Broth spoilers
23 Wire
25 Caesar's last day
26 Turkeys
27 Kennedy matriarch
28 Solemn event
29 Unscrewed anew
31 Harrison of "My Fair Lady"
32 Rabbit fur
33 Dada founder
34 Celtic deity
36 Held firm
38 Port on the Strait of Dover
41 Prayer books
42 Close to closed
46 Cecil B. De ___
47 Erato or Calliope
48 Give a face-lift to
50 Off-base
52 Sinewy creatures
56 He's paid his dues
61 Parks on a bus
62 Ghana money
63 Beloved senior
64 New Look designer
67 Sheer fabric
69 Dines in the eve
70 Chief Pontiac's people
74 Brook
76 Newspaper section
77 Butte's brother
78 Female cat
83 Chord type
84 Norma Desmond's love
85 Middle ground
88 Gem for a Libra
89 Happy starter?
91 ___-raspberry juice
92 Essen basin

93 Igpay atinlay, e.g.
95 Score a pitch coup
97 Beehive State tribe
98 Snooze
99 Dig big-time
100 "Hail, Caesar!"
101 Air-leak sound
102 Ruth's sultanate
103 Sorenstam's birthplace
104 Made the first move

DOWN

1 A habit, for some
2 Hennery
3 San ___ (Hearst castle site)
4 Fig. with two dashes
5 Mozart contemporary
6 Perfectly timed, dramatically
7 Buy or steal
8 Albanian coins
9 More than 24 mos.
10 Betty Ford Center, e.g.
11 Binary digits
12 Frasier, to Kelsey
13 Capp's quaff
14 Antony and Cleopatra's defeater
15 Like depth perception
16 Bemoans
22 Egyptian cobras
24 Homecoming group
27 Thing, in law
30 Abbr. after a comma
31 Popular cabinet wood source
32 Unfinished business
35 Stored fodder

36 Laura Bush's alma mater
37 Frank McCourt title
39 Part of USA
40 Taylor of "Six Feet Under"
42 Where to get shot
43 Raspberry
44 Rounds or clips
45 Commits a cradle crime?
47 Metric liquid meas.
49 Western HBO series
51 Detestable
53 Byrnes and Roush
54 Stead
55 Center's move
57 ATM mfr.
58 Price of passage
59 Opposite of aweather
60 D and E, e.g.
65 Creator of M and Q

66 Hush-hush WW2 agcy.
68 Locked in
70 Briny invertebrate
71 Mammoth traps
72 Battlefield medical processes
73 In any way
75 Comm. device
77 Gob's swab
79 It has Swiss banks
80 Hibernal
81 Befit
82 Told a whopper
84 Jamie Lee's mom
86 Graded
87 Cavern
89 Put on hold?
90 Maugham's "___ of Lambeth"
91 ___ the fat
94 Junk mail, mostly
95 Sophs. two years later
96 Lady lobster

160 THIS AND THAT   by John M. Samson
The age-old mystery at 39 Across has finally been solved.

ACROSS

1 Seersucker, e.g.
7 Jason in "The Alamo"
13 Monument Valley features
18 Sufficient
19 Melodic section
20 Cavern
21 George Bell homer
22 Saturated
23 Sculptor Noguchi
24 Chief Ouray's tribe
25 Scotties
27 Fools
29 Personal history
31 "Twister" turns
32 Square meters
33 Make it to class
35 Relief
36 Blender sound
39 Where life began
43 Widespread
44 Cowards
45 Preakness month
46 One-time salve for sprains
47 Parlor purchases
48 Behchoko aborigine
49 Catwalker's asset
50 Spaghetti ___
51 Be worthy of
52 Pulp
53 Riots
54 Wolfish
55 67.5° on the compass
56 Odysseus slew them
57 Guarded residences
58 "Für Elise" is one
60 TV picture setting
61 Munich men
62 Rapparee
63 "White ___": Janet Fitch
66 Comes around
67 Ballpark figure
71 Solicit opinions
72 Avery Island sauce
74 "Deep Space Nine" changeling
75 Elks, for one
76 Shanty singer
78 Penitent
80 Twice DIV
81 "Vampire" painter Munch
82 "Don't Fence Me In" composer
83 "___ Win": Haas
84 Pooh-poohs
85 Pooh's pal

DOWN

1 Tired of it all
2 Nashville singer Cochran
3 Spock's doc
4 Trapdoor concealer
5 "___ the picture"
6 Andrew Wyeth model
7 Fast lane
8 "Coming ___ Again": Carly Simon
9 Ocean motions
10 Curtain hardware
11 Verb suffix, in Suffolk
12 "The Rainbow ___": Kermit
13 Crow's-nest locales
14 Tangle
15 One of a flight
16 Napoleon's troops
17 "On Beyond Zebra" author
26 All in
28 A span has nine
30 Besmirch
32 Monitor blinkers
34 Date back in time
35 Girls, in a family way
36 Made presentable?
37 Miss Marple, for one
38 Touched off
39 Wader of bogs
40 Ferrera of "Ugly Betty"
41 Obedience-school students
42 Focus of a Snellen chart
44 Stylist Vidal
47 More surly
48 Breaks camp
50 Maître d'hôtel charges
51 Prefix for cultural
53 Jazz positions
54 Harold Pinter play
56 Shooting script
57 Cold-cream brand
59 Sick admission?
60 False rumors
62 Come out of one's shell?
63 "___, let us remove! ": Shak.
64 Baby bug
65 Sever ties
66 Cheekbone
68 Fran Striker's Indian
69 Like ___ in the headlights
70 Derek Jeter's manager
72 Popular DVR
73 Sioux speaker
77 General's asst.
79 Rossini count

161 THAT AND THIS by John M. Samson
67 Across was also the winter home of Thomas Edison.

ACROSS

1 Euphonium metal
6 O.J. Simpson trial attorney
13 Yoga hand gesture
18 "Fireside Chats" medium
19 Game Boy game
20 Loathe
21 Harbor on Ishikari Bay
22 Fatty
23 Polar explorer Amundsen
24 American dogwood
25 Ishtar's city
26 Trestle ___
27 Much obliged?
29 College scholarship?
31 Fol-de-___
32 PAC that's packing
33 Humperdinck hit
39 Sob-story conclusion?
45 Grandfather
46 Secret society of Naples
48 Baritone Hawkins
49 "The Princess and ___"
50 Taken for ___ (assumed)
51 "Beau Geste" novelist
52 Turkey's Gulf of ___
53 Atlanta's ___ Creek Park
54 "Seize the Time" author
55 Robert of "The Sopranos"
56 Donates
57 Suffix for song
58 Saint Philip ___
59 Bristles
60 Sobieski in "Max"
61 Like charcoal filters
63 Philo Vance's creator
65 Latin gram. category
66 Apropos
67 Where Henry Ford wintered
73 Like The Fourteen Points
79 Biting
80 Cockcrow
82 Coloratura's asset
83 Sri Lankan native
84 Barker
85 Garcia and La Douce
86 Sixties dress style
87 "Sesame Street" sponsor
88 Adjust as you must
89 Casual goodbye
90 "Aha!"
91 Canonical hour

DOWN

1 Quidditch must
2 "Midnight Cowboy" role
3 Firefighter Red
4 Danube tributary
5 Vintner's nightmare?
6 Sequin
7 Ralph Vaughan Williams cantata
8 "There's ___ of hush . . ."
9 Le Moko in "Algiers"
10 Start of a meeting proposal
11 Buddy who played in Shibe Park
12 Points scored by Chamberlain on 3/2/62
13 Bradbury's "The ___ Chronicles"
14 Lusitania sinker
15 Abu ___
16 Brother of Dido
17 "As You Like It" forest
28 Italian Alps resort
30 Profound fear
33 Greek wine
34 Let the air out
35 Girl watchers
36 ___ Armani watches
37 Mike Hammer actor Darren
38 From the heart
39 Hyundai sedans
40 NHL trophy
41 Gave the bride away, and then some
42 Kibbutznik
43 Brigitte in "Rocky IV"
44 Rochester river
47 Might, to Shakespeare
53 How the diligent work
54 Loud
56 Hayes of westerns
57 High-fives
62 Ranch house
64 Harper in "Rhoda"
67 Like Alex Forrest's attraction
68 Florida citrus city
69 Mail payment
70 Threefold
71 Mumbai money
72 Hissy fits
73 Shenanigans
74 Rhône tributary
75 Sunshine Cab driver
76 Soldier in "Cold Mountain"
77 Brotherly love
78 Terminix targets
81 1924 winner over Capablanca

162 "EN GARDE!" by Arlan and Linda Bushman
Be on your guard for some pointed puns below.

ACROSS

1 Audible
6 Cossack plain
12 Popular fund-raiser
18 Set to rest
19 Old explosive device
20 Raglan, for example
21 Chewy restaurant offering?
23 Candle material
24 Much-used pencil
25 Consumers
26 Tile design
27 Poisonous plants
29 Daily drama
31 Spree
33 Genesis twin
34 Supermarket section
36 "Young Mr. Lincoln" star
37 Dam, for one
40 1997 demand for Steve Jobs' return?
43 Swipe
44 Piquant
46 Excited
47 Maximum
49 Amneris rival
50 Toho Studios monster
52 The Last Frontier capital
54 Bleak
55 Tends the garden
56 Present
57 "Hardball" home
60 Mirage
62 Hocks
63 Razor brand
64 ___ Blanc
66 Turn sharply
67 Promise
68 Kid
69 Campus figures sign up?
74 Kvass ingredient
75 Fancy
77 Aspire to
78 Haggard pair
80 Note for a staff
81 Phuket dweller
82 Aid in remembering
86 Doubleday and Yokum
88 Quick checkout claim
91 Lawless role
92 Like most mountain roads
93 Admission impossible?
95 Stately dwellings
96 Esprit de corps
97 Less adorned
98 Young swan
99 Convinced
100 "Who's there?" reply

DOWN

1 Strident
2 Extract with a solvent
3 Snaps holder
4 Unruly mob
5 Batik need
6 Voice an opinion
7 Bivouac sight
8 Disk extension
9 Henry's last Catherine
10 Urgent
11 Dutch commune
12 Camera setting
13 Melodramatic cry
14 Italian treat
15 Chance meeting at a sub station?
16 Alligator pears
17 Bow wood
22 Summarize
26 Irish county
28 Anthem start
30 Mordor regular
32 Deeply absorbed
34 "Ballet Rehearsal" painter
35 "___ Flux" (2005)
36 Lavish party
37 Unaccompanied
38 Plait stuff
39 Chicory crop-dusting?
41 Fraught
42 Ancient letters
45 Urchin
48 Flashy parrot
50 Lorelei's river
51 Winning game line
52 Paragon
53 Spigoted item
56 Frequent
58 Heehaw
59 Wariness
61 Agree (with)
62 Supplication
64 Pack tight
65 Retreat
66 Gilligan's boat
67 Goblet part
70 Contented sighs
71 Long of Hollywood
72 Touched off
73 Take care of
76 Zippo competitor
79 Fenway attire
81 Romantic get-together
82 "A Year in Provence" author
83 Almost equals
84 Legal phrase
85 Inner circle
87 Raison d'___
89 Maria's other
90 "King Kong" actress
92 SHO subsidiary
93 German river
94 Ginza band

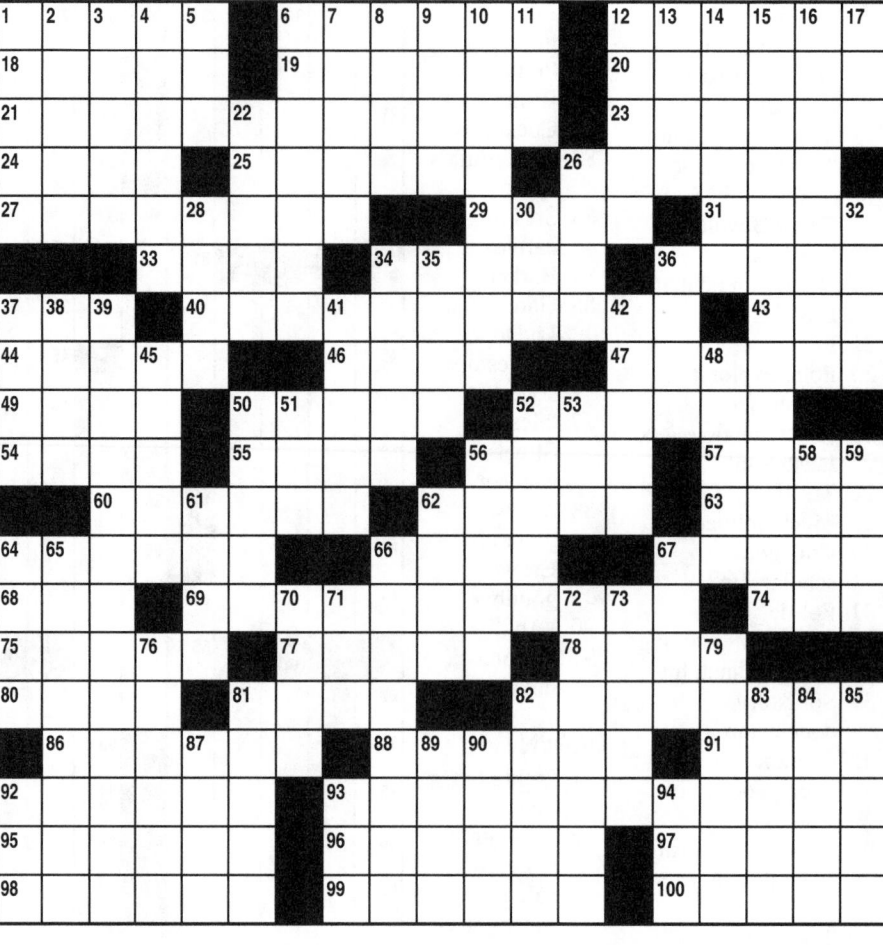

163 TOOL BOXES by Richard Silvestri
Rich dedicates this one to Bob Vila and Tim Taylor.

ACROSS

1 Put one's foot down
5 Snatch
9 RIT or MIT stat
12 The former Mrs. Cugat
17 Divine light
18 Musical McEntire
19 Duster's need
20 Suite spot
21 Bar on a car
22 Melodramatic cry
23 In the past
24 Like some pitchers
25 TV show about carpenters?
27 Stock holder
28 Banish
29 Shape up
31 Up to now
33 Taught
37 In the style of
39 Cushion adornment
44 Side by side?
45 Carpenter's home?
47 Third point at Wimbledon
49 Saratoga Springs, e.g.
51 Half of hexa
52 Himalayan sighting
53 Female in the fold
54 Vocal passages
58 Point the finger at
60 Carpenters' notices?
62 Most exposed
64 Enclosed part of an airplane
65 Shake a leg
68 Merry king
69 Corporate VIP
71 Afore
72 Crop killer
74 Group of great carpenters?
78 Idle of comedy
79 Chaste
80 Open a keg
81 Haphazard
85 Distinctive doctrine
87 Harbor city
89 Extra
93 Sculpture and such
95 Careless carpenters?

100 Telecast component
101 Coffee
102 Manitoba native
103 Marine leader?
104 Calculator button
105 Royal possessive
106 Org.
107 A deadly sin
108 Muscle injuries
109 Cartoon Chihuahua
110 Name of a Rose
111 Toy with a tail

DOWN

1 Fakery
2 Travel toward the terminal
3 She, in Seville
4 Service piece
5 Loose rock
6 Enjoy, nostalgically
7 Put down
8 City on the Rhine
9 Come to grips with
10 Call for
11 Feeling of defeat
12 Fast feline
13 Piltdown man, for one
14 Abruzzi bell town
15 Turn round and round
16 Shoppe description
26 Promising words
30 Do crew work
32 Moral
33 Call at first
34 Contrite meal
35 Roll-call response
36 Stable staple
38 Colonist of a kind
40 Russian spacecraft
41 Seeks legal redress
42 Noble name of Italy

43 Luau favor
45 "As it ___ the beginning . . ."
46 Baby rocker
48 Home of the Bulldogs
49 Convent address
50 Not neg.
55 "People Got To Be Free" group
56 Son–gun links
57 "Attack, Fido!"
59 B+ group?
60 Coat of arms
61 Always, in sonnets
62 Heavyweight champ Riddick
63 Start of a Shakespeare title
65 Bar mitzvah dance
66 Goddess of fertility
67 Make a lasting impression

68 Cleveland cager, for short
70 Polo Grounds hero
73 Like half the deck
75 French chalk users
76 New York's time
77 Make like
81 Few and far between
82 Part of LCD
83 A real Dahl
84 Bottom-of-page abbr.
86 Of great importance
88 BMI rival
89 It's undeniable
90 Mark off evenly
91 Birth of a notion
92 Politician, too often
94 Libertine
96 Polio pioneer
97 Iso kin
98 Shade of brown
99 Fill to the brim

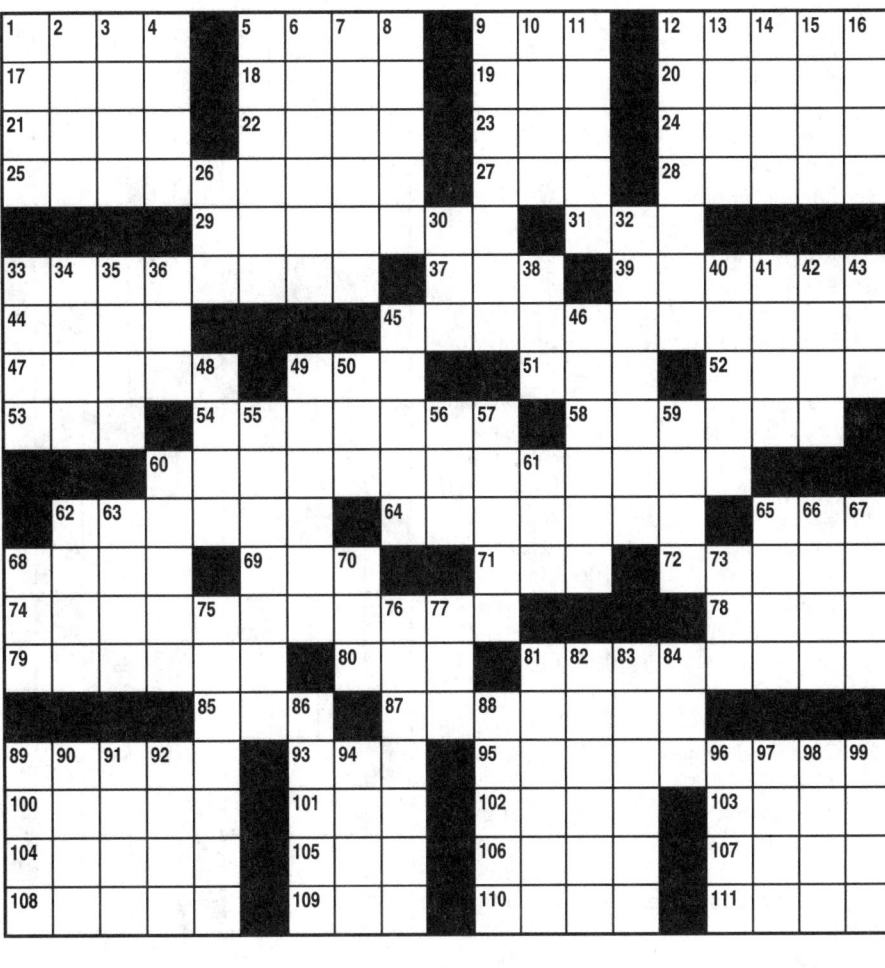

164 WILD THING by Victor Fleming
Be careful not to go against the grain here.

ACROSS

1 Queens pros
5 Simple life
10 "Tiny" singer
13 Herbal "pet"
17 Smart fellow?
18 Less believable
19 Covert WW2 agcy.
20 Rough golf swing
21 Lego line since 2005
23 Santa Anita maiden
24 In the main?
25 Gobbled down
26 Sot's syllable
27 Winter Palace occupants
29 Canisius College's conference
32 Not have a ___ stand on
34 Items from a pool
35 Major ISP
36 Miss Kitty's establishment
37 Clyde and Bentham
40 Trickster
41 Pol Hutchinson
42 Must be
43 Sked. letters
44 Electronic branches
46 Not slip off
48 Language of 94-A
49 Verdi's "___ Chorus"
52 Ginger chaser?
54 Comedienne Sykes
56 Like ___ (no piece of cake)
63 Gauchos' plain
64 Sitcom diner owner
65 "Later!"
66 Criteria: Abbr.
69 Viking 1 mission
71 Soccer org.
74 Super ___ (video game name)
75 Cry of discovery
76 Do darts
77 RB's count
79 Conductor's car
82 Slow musical passages
84 Skier Tommy
85 Wilson of The Beach Boys
86 Bundle
87 Relocate to the Big Peach
92 "I'll see you then"
94 Internet start-up?

95 Cartesian conjunctions
96 Gin flavoring
97 Self center
98 PUZZLE TITLE
100 Controversial orchard spray
101 Fish-fowl go-between
102 "All ___": Temptations
103 Lender's protection
104 D-Day craft
105 2006 Rihanna hit
106 Motown Records founder
107 Erosion

DOWN

1 Respectful address
2 Select group
3 Basic precept
4 Fear inspirer
5 Key abbr.
6 Numbered exam?
7 Sends quickly
8 "Life Goes On" role
9 Biblical vessel
10 It's down in the mouth
11 ___ Asimov Award
12 Priest's sup.
13 "No. 5" maker
14 Tries
15 Interstate pileup cause
16 Dossier letters
22 ". . . never see ___ lovely as . . .": Kilmer
27 Pseudo-convertibles
28 "Now ___ me down to sleep . . ."
30 "Dragonwyck" author Seton
31 Skater Naomi Nari ___
33 Law school newcomer
36 Refuse

37 Psychologist Piaget
38 Volcano near Paterno
39 Norah Jones' father
40 Part of an archipelago
41 MLB pitcher nicknamed "Kitty"
45 Political science, for one
47 Choreographer Tharp
48 Have trouble standing?
50 Panacea's targets
51 Diamond girl
53 Scary street
55 Brief prosecutors
57 Directory entries
58 Chew like a beaver
59 SLR part
60 "Biggest Little City"
61 Takes a gander at
62 Alleviate
66 La companions
67 Wolfe's "___ Beyond"

68 Perfectly accomplished
70 Boiling point?
72 Wrote poorly
73 Milk from la vache
76 #1 Frank Zappa song?
78 Sad ending?
80 Put into bundles
81 In the zone
83 Stunning instruments
84 Part of GMAC
85 Pinhead?
87 Myopic Quincy
88 Strong bridge opening
89 Marsh of mystery
90 Conference giveaways, often
91 Orgs.
93 Hibernators' hideaways
96 Mineo of movies
98 Oil driller's setup
99 Joseph of ice-cream fame

165 HEN PARTY by Brad Wilber
Lulu and Gale are two of the attendees below.

ACROSS

1 Protestant denom.
6 Mischief-makers
13 Veil material
18 "Julius Caesar" conspirator
19 Dan Aykroyd, by birth
20 Moon of Uranus
21 Heart of Provence
22 Words accompanying a shrug
23 Cockamamie
24 **Hen party attendee (5)**
27 "Punk'd" network
28 The Untouchables, e.g.
29 Excessive
30 "Songs of a Wayfarer" composer
33 Faction within a faith
35 They make history
40 **Hen party attendee (4)**
43 Vitellius' predecessor
44 Poor-box contents
45 High-end Toyota
46 Cartoon one-liner
49 "The Day of the Locust" narrator
50 Like a rattled rattler
52 Billie Holliday standard
53 Construction site crosspieces
55 [not my erratum]
57 Mushroom house dweller
58 1971 Woody Allen movie
60 "Arrested Development" character
62 Peaked
65 Photosynthesizing protozoan
66 Femme fatale
67 Shag rug feature
68 Garden party quaffs
69 **Hen party attendee (5)**
72 Shrew
75 Habit
76 Fiorentino and Cardellini
77 Home of the Shoshone Falls
79 Court seat
80 Keydets' college
83 **Hen party attendee (3)**
90 Garlicky condiment
92 Tea ball
93 "The Flying Finn" of track
94 Banister attachment
95 Extra minute?
96 Toto-type terrier
97 Aquarium cleaner
98 Congressional riders, e.g.
99 Ex-roomie of Sally Bowles

DOWN

1 "___ ridente" (Rossini aria)
2 Peacock blue
3 "Aha!"
4 Moves like a coackroach
5 Sundae topping
6 Sign of spring
7 Egyptian solar deity
8 Guys only
9 Suffragist Carrie Chapman ___
10 Bashful cowboy's comment
11 Bemoan
12 "It's possa-bull" dummy
13 ___ 101 tower, Taiwan
14 Coffee klatch need
15 Neeson in "Kingdom of Heaven"
16 Palm Sunday period
17 Welcome sign abbr.
25 Deborah in "Sundowners"
26 "___ Wiedersehen!"
30 Aspiring doctor's exam
31 "___ & Janis" (cartoon strip)
32 **Hen party attendee (4)**
33 Cannonball Adderley's equipment
34 Professor's asset
36 Blackhawk blade
37 **Hen party attendee (4)**
38 "Jack Straw's Castle" poet Gunn
39 Volume unit
41 "Truth" singer
42 Treasure hunter Fisher
46 "Ocean's Eleven" setting
47 Wife of 30 Across
48 Bonus
50 Work with rattan
51 Birthplace of Camus
54 Modelist's wood
56 Barbizon school painter
58 Wally Cleaver's sib
59 Quattro automaker
61 ___ Paese cheese
63 Alan in "The Aviator"
64 Boss of 28 Across
66 Cosseted
67 On time
70 Dwindle
71 Subsidize
73 Important legislation of 1944
74 Literary memorial
75 Imitated a mosquito
78 Antacid target
79 Vino alternative
80 HOV lane traffic
81 Carriage
82 Big Ten school
84 Sphere segment
85 "The doctor ___" (sign for Lucy)
86 Steamed (with "off")
87 Rainbow goddess
88 Jezebel's father-in-law
89 Tony-winning musical of 1982
91 Island chain?

166 BATTLE OF THE UNSERS   by Amy Reynaldo and Victor Fleming
Looks like the Unsers have the grid principals boxed in.

ACROSS

1 Places folks flock to
7 Be a dilettante
13 Rue Morgue murderer
18 Inspirational air?
19 Marshy tracts
20 Cold, in a negative sense
21 High-fiber Kellogg's product
23 11-time Pro Bowl player Bob
24 Big wheels for a big wheel
25 Letter-shaped beam
26 Steve of the comics
27 Black-ice disasters
30 Alpo eater's complaint
31 Palindrome and start of one
32 Smith role of 2001
33 UPN comedy (1996–2001)
35 Moore in "Deconstructing Harry"
36 Engine cylinder
39 Trig term
41 Missing a match
42 Seniors' org.
43 "East of Eden" heroine
44 Cool temperature range
46 Like Sharia, e.g.
49 Straight and tall
50 Pole, for one
52 911 respondents
53 Lubricate
54 Natural food processor?
57 Lit
59 Polaris bear
60 Hardly one who abstains
61 Streetwise
62 Barbecued fare
64 Half a 1969 Archies hit
68 Wings
69 Astrological edge
70 Do poorly
72 Granted
73 ConAgra cooking spray
74 Street-closing indicator
75 "I can live with that!"
78 Hack off
79 Its job is raising dough
81 Malay Peninsula isthmus
82 Prairie bananas
84 Cursive
86 Mystery writer Nevada
87 "Dies ___"
88 Wranglers' competition
89 Strip-mined Pennsylvania rock
94 Word with drive or power
95 Fruit, flakes, and nuts
96 Give power to
97 Guthrie and West
98 Threw snowballs at
99 Richards in "The World Is Not Enough"

DOWN

1 Thunderbird degree
2 Schubert's "The ___-King"
3 Part of an animated series
4 Send a wire
5 Rectangular court
6 Product on a tub ledge, maybe
7 Mil. medal
8 "Anchors ___"
9 Barry's "Guilty" partner
10 Cloudiness of vision
11 King of tragedy
12 Alien's subj.
13 Start of a Beatles refrain
14 María Luisa, for one
15 Calista Flockhart role
16 Brief plea
17 "Icy Sparks" author Hyman Rubio
22 Precipitous plunge
26 "Meatballs" setting
27 This moment in the next
28 Arthur's onetime court rival
29 Betting odds
31 Grand Marquis, for short
34 '60s antiwar gp.
35 Bumstead canine
37 Rainbows, e.g.
38 Chess regicide
40 Force to work
42 Metroliner parent
43 Walked-on item
45 Like seaweed
47 Utter without restraint
48 Put together
49 Osprey relatives
51 Somme soul
53 Fabulous time
54 1982 Peace Nobelist
55 "Stat!" shouter
56 Term of endearment for a real dish?
57 In very short order
58 Scottie in the White House
62 Squeeze-play essential
63 Q-tip target
65 Ball
66 Swear
67 Pumper's count
69 Outlay
71 Judge Hand
74 Fatted fowl
75 Check
76 Scope verb
77 Hickman who was Dobie Gillis
80 Five-note refrain of puzzles
81 Clark Kent, at birth
83 Praline nut
84 Mexican Mlle.
85 Irish pop-rock family
86 LeAnn Rimes hit
89 Band box
90 Didn't reveal
91 ___-Wan Kenobi
92 TWO UNSERS
93 Wrangler's competition

ACROSS

1 A bit poky
8 Self-admiration
15 Strong wood
18 Double-decker game
19 Censor's concern
20 "Waltz for Eva and ___" ("Evita" tune)
21 Norwegian explorer's other hat?
23 Universal beverage
24 Half of MMMX
25 Special connections
26 Best Actor of 1963
28 Cut off
30 Hot, hurricane-filled month?
35 Part of SASE
39 Robert De ___
40 Grace Adler's husband
41 Joss sticks from an Alabama university?
44 In ___ (testy)
48 GPS heading
49 It can be corny
50 Halsey and Farragut
53 Offer a quick greeting
56 Of interest to 50 Across
60 Dairy query?
61 Unforgettable cowboy?
64 They're often pinched
66 She may remarry
67 Delightful sites
70 Relapsed into sin
72 Trip around a track
74 Scrappy-___
75 Dance lesson bit
76 Like quadraphonic?
82 Computer pioneer Lovelace
85 Scrubbed, in a way
86 Forest-free tracts
87 Young ladies who support and patronize?

92 Rollaway alternative
93 Super Bowl XXVIII host
94 Super Bowl cry
96 No longer edible
99 "Angie" actor
100 Evildoing English poet?
107 Form into a circle
108 Like babka
109 It lacks a charge
110 Words of disagreement
111 Postponed one's decision about
112 She aided Theseus

DOWN

1 Take for a ride
2 Speak highly of
3 Like infomercials
4 Cry from a crib
5 Equal, at first?
6 Grating
7 Chemistry Nobelist Otto
8 Dreyer's ice-cream partner
9 "Is that a fact?!"
10 Scanning gizmo: Abbr.
11 WJM anchor Baxter
12 Ill-suited
13 "Boston Public" setting
14 Bill Clinton memoir
15 Middle of some plays
16 Taffeta quality
17 "Haven't you ___?"
22 That señorita
27 Twin-limbed

28 Green-egg layer
29 "World Cafe" airer
31 Pa's bro
32 Donate, to a Scot
33 Inspiration for Keats
34 McGwire's 1999 rival
35 Lacking, in Limoges
36 Cat-food flavor
37 Suspended state
38 Ancient Greek cyclic festivals
42 Straight, in a round?
43 With one side forward
45 Like Noah's Ark passengers
46 Conduit bend
47 "Bad boy!"
51 Tattoo honoree

52 "Can ___ true?"
54 Teton tribe
55 End of an ailment?
57 Altar commitment
58 Chase Field team, on scoreboards
59 Spearheaded
62 Seminary subj.
63 Hood's honey
64 "Zoboomafoo" network
65 Down a torpedo
68 Nada
69 Applies turf to
71 Cow pie
73 Less uniform
77 Guy on le trône
78 Cabinet dept.
79 E-mail chuckle
80 Early auto inits.
81 Stop being indecisive
83 Capital of Iraq

84 Not just imagined
87 Golden calf crafter
88 In ___ surgery
89 Simple headstones
90 Title lady of a 1933 song
91 U. of ___ Jayewardenepura
95 Black Beauty creator Sewell
96 Frequent flier
97 Buckets
98 Measure of force
101 Cassandra's curse
102 Tiny criticism, slangily
103 "Yang Yang" singer
104 Odense's island
105 On the ___ vive
106 Hagen with three Tonys

168 "EAU, YEAH!" by Arlan and Linda Bushman
23 Across is credited with co-developing the Aqua-Lung.

ACROSS

1 Gung-ho
5 Bouquet
10 Word in a Steinbeck title
14 Tread softly
17 TV cartoon pet
18 Popular fabric
19 Like sandpaper
21 Style popularized by Mucha and Klimt
23 Famed marine explorer
24 Looks over
25 Earthenware crock
27 Hair raiser?
28 Saw point
29 Affirm under oath
31 Whopper
32 Fergie, properly
35 "Walden" author
37 Diamond arbiter
40 Fairies of Mideast folklore
42 Biochemist's concern
43 Not interfere
47 Bud
48 Clarinet wood
49 Mosque figure
51 DDE's opponent
52 Bamboozler
54 Ventricle neighbors
57 Brazilian dances
59 "Puttin' on the ___": Berlin
60 Bride's accumulation
63 Actress Sommer
64 New York lake
66 Baseball great Satchel
67 Groom carefully
68 Org. founded in 1857
69 Govt. watchdog
72 Must, slangily
74 Crescent
75 Take at one's word
77 Tolkien creature
79 Forty-___
80 Role
81 Haute hat?
84 Ointment
86 Last-minute
89 Coach's X's and O's, essentially
91 Carry out
95 Temper
97 Raise upright
98 Jaguar cousin
100 Lighted torch
102 "Time" outpost
104 Dixieland band favorite
105 Up to
106 Subside
107 AL and ME
108 Gray and Candler
109 Flippant
110 German river

DOWN

1 Roll with the punches
2 Small songbird
3 Emcee bit
4 They're good for dunkin'
5 In unison, musically
6 Guns
7 Undivided
8 Woof counterpoint
9 Talisman
10 Cheese partner
11 Nigerian people
12 Original survivor
13 Bridge spot
14 Michelangelo sculpture
15 Prove helpful
16 Tennis call
20 Rodin piece
22 Circular
26 Haley and Bolger cohort
29 Eastern religion
30 Mine runner
33 Merrimack crewman
34 Clamorous
36 Soprano Gluck
37 Straightforward
38 Coleridge protagonist
39 Level off
41 Vermont export
44 Picturesque scene
45 Lab glassware
46 Basic nature
50 Pac-10 mem.
53 Israeli weapon
55 OT book before Jer.
56 ___ of the times
58 Sea, to Henri
60 Prof.'s helpers
61 Self-absorption
62 Leading health insurer
65 Shakespearean verb
67 Nouveau arrivé
70 Kachina maker
71 Floor coverings
73 ___ Aviv
76 Hatch a plot
78 "Peggy Sue Got Married" star
82 German typewriters
83 Planet safe from declassification
85 Admittance
86 Some floaters
87 Switched off
88 Stumbling blocks
90 Hippodrome
92 In the lead
93 Knock off
94 More certain
96 "East of Eden" heroine
98 Trident-shaped letters
99 Skillfully
101 Minor-league designation
103 Lbs. and such

169 CAR TUNES by Fred Piscop
What a great title!

ACROSS

1 Film shorts, for short
4 Mortgage holder, say
12 Beatle hairstyle
18 Mighty Joe Young, e.g.
19 Like a small fire
20 Rodent's stash
21 Sonny Boy Williamson car tune
23 Comment by a dress salesperson
24 Deck out
25 Little green men
26 Reputation ruiner
27 Key contraction
29 Get mellow
30 Slow leaks
34 Paper shut down by Yeltsin
37 Bruce Springsteen car tune
39 Like some excuses
40 Barrel of laughs
42 Is down with
43 Botanist Gray
44 Carrier of 25-A
45 Robt. E. Lee, e.g.
46 Foams at the mouth
48 Gulf capital
49 Barber's need
51 Dagger partner
53 "No sh@#$%t!"
55 Commander Cody car tune
59 Pat on the head, say
62 Derby town
63 Redcap's place
67 "Caroline in the City" restaurateur
68 Totally wreck
71 Twist's request
73 Roy G. Biv gradation
74 "Michael Collins" org.
75 Balaam's beast
76 Not buggy
77 Colossal, for olives
78 Wilson Pickett car tune
83 Big woman
85 In the movies
86 Starting digits under "RHE"
87 Smoke-filled room figure
88 CPR pros
89 Tomlinson's 2006 NFL award
90 Pigeonholes' places
94 Lose fizz
97 Duke Ellington car tune
101 City W of San Antonio
102 Monopoly avenue
103 Hagen who taught McQueen
104 Israeli spy agency
105 French cop
106 Public image, briefly

DOWN

1 "___ Doc" Duvalier
2 Popular MP3 player
3 Prefix with phobia
4 Made up
5 Genetic letters
6 Common Market inits.
7 Apply gently
8 Not on the up-and-up
9 Free of slack
10 Stamp mill materials
11 Condo ad abbr.
12 Sent in
13 Nautilus cousins
14 Kind of scale
15 Take a shot at
16 Noted Dakota resident
17 Nittany Lions' sch.
22 Valuable find
26 Half a Disney duo
28 Recherché
29 Rocky foe
30 Read the UPC of
31 Forest clearing
32 Lets up
33 Barely enough
34 It's a good thing
35 Huck's ride
36 Bow-wielding god
38 Military wear
41 Elevate: Abbr.
45 Ltr. ctrs.
46 Role for Jackie
47 Kosugi in "Enter the Ninja"
48 One of the Brontës
50 Home to Athens
52 "Potemkin" locale
54 Word after "Ye"
56 Dragon parade holiday
57 Diner request
58 "Follow me!"
59 A-1
60 "Seinfeld" showing
61 Stack up
64 Dickens illustrator
65 Anise-flavored liqueur
66 Summer job-seeker
69 They're the latest
70 Org.
72 Haul in
76 Fed the hogs
77 Valentine State capital
79 Antigen attackers
80 "Invincible" fleet of 1588?
81 Took home
82 Hippie protest
84 Interchangeable part
89 "A ___ formality!"
91 Side track
92 Bad check
93 Piece of cake
94 Desk-bottom deposit
95 Ab ___ (from the top)
96 Fourth tones
97 Use a treadmill
98 ___ tizzy
99 Orch. group
100 Wing it, musically

170

ACROSS

1 Woodstock gear
5 Meal for the humble?
9 Beginning of "no idea"
13 Suffix with chick
17 Formerly confederated area
19 Manicurist's secretary?
21 Ristorante salads
22 Pleasing
23 Milk-drinking signs
24 Hoi polloi
25 Two points, in tennis
27 Talk trash
28 Sentence
32 Flabbergasted
34 Pass on the Hill
39 Unwilling
40 Moves nonchalantly
43 Star quality
44 Duty
45 Simpletons
47 Police line
49 Upright
51 Angola neighbor
52 Like mutual funds, generally
53 Woodland heights
55 What busy artists do?
57 "Sister, Sister" actor
58 First name in TV talk
60 Like court testimony
62 Get one's bearings
63 Works the waterfront
65 Slangy suffix
66 Rowlands in "The Notebook"
67 Figures of speech?
69 "Stan the Man" of baseball
71 Dizzy
73 Kline in "The Squid and the Whale"
74 Taco Bell offering
75 New Mexico town
77 That one, in the flesh
80 Losing no time
85 Was high man on the totem pole?
90 Primitive
91 Prove better than
92 Talk trash about commands?
93 Full of zip
94 Coll. entrance exams
95 Irish
96 Antiprohibitionists
97 Spill the beans

DOWN

1 West of Hollywood
2 Cafeteria list
3 Darlings
4 Restaurant bar?
5 Chauffeurs of old
6 "Fools ___" (1997 Hayek comedy)
7 Playful aquatic critter
8 Card game without bidding
9 Trying saying beginning
10 International waters
11 "So soon?"
12 Regards
13 Wistful word
14 They come out
15 Perry's penner
16 Scrapes by
18 Sudden outbursts
20 Discontinue
26 Arafat
28 Racer Yarborough
29 Exhausted
30 "Drop it"
31 Box breakfast?
33 Soft-soap user
35 Most like some minds
36 Assembly areas
37 Decision point
38 Clink
40 Break under strain
41 Sweet liqueur
42 Floating garbage-carrier
46 Shirt label
48 Night birds
50 Young adult
52 Superman's lady
54 Felix Trinidad's nickname
56 Guns, as an engine
57 Frat-party wear
59 Téa of "Fun with Dick and Jane"
61 2004 Emmy Rossum film
63 Was dazed
64 Does a slow burn
68 Comb carrier
70 Lady Liberty's stamp partner
72 Archaic anesthesia
74 Wonderland party pieces
76 Network for "Sopranos" rerun
78 Lost on purpose
79 Paris divider
80 Gets hitched
81 Pelvis parts
82 Student woe
83 Insurance grps.
84 Additional
86 "That'll be the day!"
87 ___ bene
88 Apt anagram for vile
89 King's place

171 BEAT THE CLOCK 53:30 by Harvey Estes
21 Across will always be a jukebox favorite.

ACROSS

1 Hit
7 Nixed
13 Summit goals
18 Sonja Henie's debut film
20 Hells Canyon state
21 Kingston Trio classic
22 Ford flub
23 Pound part
24 Candlemaking ester
25 Like bell-bottoms
26 Fit
27 Classic detective
28 Chi. setting
30 "The Wanderer" singer
31 Show off the bod
32 ___ of relativity
35 Sarouk
36 More bulky
40 This way, or that
41 "Les Misérables" star
43 Nordic alternative
44 Carillon sounds
46 Twisty-horned animals
48 Trials and tribulations
49 Log distances
52 Part of a place setting
53 None of that?
54 Technologists
56 Musician Parsons
57 Pi, e.g.
59 One left of right and right of left
60 Claim-staking word
61 First-born
63 Designing woman
64 Safe to swallow
66 "Giant" heroine
68 Half-brother of Tom Sawyer
69 Blue "Yellow Submarine" villains
70 Coll. major
71 Merging locale
73 Green targets
74 Double
76 T, as in Torah
77 Bran source
78 Not fancy at all
82 Coveted quality
84 Town in a John O'Hara title
87 Feasts
88 Clinton's first Labor Secretary
89 Petrachan verse form
91 Conjure up
92 ABBA hit (with "The")
93 Not bright
94 "Our Man in Havana" author
95 Words of warning

DOWN

1 Kind of buddy
2 When expected
3 Drudges
4 Sales spiel
5 Suffix with refer
6 Long in code
7 Liquor levy, e.g.
8 John on the Mayflower
9 Old movie old flame
10 Christian in fashion
11 "Forget it!"
12 Ad infinitum
13 Place on piles
14 Interjected
15 "I was working in the foundry," e.g.?
16 Former Algonquin Hotel circle
17 "Later"
19 Potato utensil
27 He played God in "Spamalot"
29 Bring to bay
31 Sturgeon steerer
32 Rocky Mountaineer excursion, e.g.
33 Vociferated
34 Pained cry
36 D preceder
37 Fright night
38 Trial separation, e.g.?
39 Wimps
40 Betty Friedan's movement
42 Third Crusade sultan
44 "My Back ___": Dylan
45 Escort an arriving guest
47 Common pentad
50 Large ref. work
51 AARP members
55 Brews
58 Edvard Munch Museum site
62 Windshield feature
65 Russian assents
67 Getting off the tape
69 Like the X-Men
70 Eyed impolitely
72 1975 Belmont winner
73 Wide-mouthed bottle
75 Guitar parts
77 Hunter killed by Artemis
78 Door joint
79 Written record
80 Bristles
81 Makeup maker Lauder
83 Friends pronoun
85 Jerry Herman musical
86 Helm location
87 Procrastinator's opposite
90 HBO alternative

172

BEAT THE CLOCK 52:10   by Harvey Estes
The popemobile would be another example of 83 Across.

ACROSS

1 Bad antenna?
11 It's open to change
19 Where reception is poor
20 "Insomnia" star
21 Queens locale
22 Pirate
23 Rider, e.g.
24 This is one
25 Sweetbread
26 Catechism
27 Ward heelers
28 Pre-euro coin
29 Somewhat, to Solti
30 Rabbit fur
31 Dock
32 Salon requests
33 Andy Warhol's studio
37 "Tarnation!"
38 Corinthian letter
39 In
40 Martin's bill
41 It may be rapid
45 Queen Elizabeth et al.
47 That's French?
48 Bambi's aunt
49 Relate
50 Constitution section
52 River deposits
54 Fraternal Order member
55 Propeller head
57 Cruel tendency
59 Fought on a mat, to some
61 "Sweeney ___"
62 Dupree on "Hope & Gloria"
63 Neb. neighbor
64 Wash out
65 Like brown bread
66 Prison guard
69 Syndicate bigwig
70 USN rank
71 Russian sea
72 Laments loudly
73 Truck compartments
74 High sch. subject
78 Clearance
80 Take the mound
81 Tall and spare
82 Little is a big one
83 Presidential vehicle
85 Changing the handle on
86 Fib without crossing the line?
87 Hyperopic optic?
88 Smooth rocks?

DOWN

1 Key above G
2 Strip away
3 Orange leftovers
4 Bar for teetotallers?
5 Fer opposite
6 "Le Monde" article
7 Height of drama, to Juliet?
8 Without pencil and paper
9 Diner's cards
10 Expressed (a farewell)
11 Volga's outlet
12 Chicago Fire scapegoat
13 Bucky Beaver's toothpaste
14 Antidrug agent
15 Zodiac arachnid
16 Hang in there
17 Like "The Zoo Story"
18 Trunks of photos
27 Skincare subject
28 Read and not post
30 Type of marriage
31 Ringer at Notre Dame
32 "Nothing more to say"
33 Lent observer
34 Hun head
35 Rosy pair, perhaps
36 Just right
37 Govt. branch
38 Short Line et al.
40 Shuttlecock
41 Buffy or Felicity
42 Blue-ribbon
43 Consumer's digest?
44 Put a strain on
46 Like a diamond
47 Dressed
51 Hand over
53 Eye part
56 Poetic period
58 Calls it quits
60 Like the Grim Reaper
61 G.I. lullaby
64 Unilever cosmetics company
65 Prurient periodical
66 "Don't Break My Heart" singer
67 Yalta's peninsula
68 ___ to go (eager)
69 Ant farm
70 Bizet opera
72 "Socrate" composer
73 Papal court
74 "Couldn't get out of it"
75 Peru native
76 Do figure eights
77 Mini Michelin
79 Bar order (with "the")
80 Dutch painter Frans
81 In case
84 TLC specialists

173 BEAT THE CLOCK 51:35 by Harvey Estes
An itch doctor (14-D) is a slang term for dermatologist.

ACROSS
1 Herculean dozen
7 Honey Bun in "Pulp Fiction"
13 Crows
18 Where Horner pulled out a plum
19 Reconciled
20 Attacked
21 Bank percentages
23 Cosmetics name
24 No more, no less
25 Undivided
26 TV listings
27 Racer Yarborough
28 As well
30 Barber's stroke
31 Capp's "Hyena"
32 Sailor's yes
33 Top stories
35 Impressive grouping
39 Type of appeal
41 "The Picture of ___ Gray"
43 Tidy type
45 Lincoln's st.
47 Feared flies
50 No man, to John Donne
51 "It's about time!"
53 Give halftime stats
54 Units of film thickness
55 Munro alias
57 M or G
59 Prepare spuds
60 Putting to work
62 Totaled
64 Gracefully slender
66 Enter quietly
68 Conduit bend
69 More crackers
70 Ameche user
72 Like the hippest software
74 It may be vacant
75 Spheres
77 Shearable she
79 Hindu titles
81 Pairs with drums
82 Plot piece
84 Halfback's pickup
85 Southern school, familiarly
89 Calls it quits
91 Shoplifting deterrents
94 Kind of suspects
95 Where to find acceptable alcohol?
96 Cut up
97 Fake
98 Publication goofs
99 Wound up
100 Moor growths
101 Combed out

DOWN
1 Favors a side
2 Aimée of "La Dolce Vita"
3 Ballet rail
4 Settled on (with "for")
5 Latvian port
6 Medium meeting
7 Gallaudet acronym
8 Donny's sister
9 Clayton of U2
10 Spendable salary
11 Fought it out, in Folkestone
12 Church recesses
13 Suds
14 Itch doctor's diagnosis?
15 Reagan Supreme Court appointee
16 Highland tongue
17 Puts in boiling water
22 Solidarity birthplace
29 Rowers pull them
31 "Coal Miner's Daughter" singer
32 I.W. of USWA fame
34 Stadium level
35 Bad blood
36 Stand fast
37 Took up the cause of
38 How media mail travels?
40 Prompt
42 Palindromic male name
44 Roadblock requests
46 ___ royal
48 Sunday with a parade
49 Earth, e.g.
51 Dossier abbr.
52 "___ 'nuff!"
56 Clearasil target
58 Club for GIs
61 Glitz
63 Additionally
65 TV meteorologist Valerie
67 Rick's old flame
69 Words with notes
71 Get the last bit of suds out
73 Affectionate letter sign-off
75 Applicant's offering
76 Has dinner at home
78 Packed tightly
80 All worked up
83 Chocolate pieces
84 Crystal-lined rock
85 Most-quoted Yankee
86 Met highlights
87 Dull surface
88 Former leader of Syria
90 Eskimo transport
92 Quarterback Flutie
93 Swampy area

BEAT THE CLOCK 54:16   by Harvey Estes
The clue for 10 Down is spot-on.

ACROSS

1 Largest member of the violin family
11 Tolerate Sajak?
19 "You are what you eat," e.g.?
20 Conditionally released
21 Say "Say, Say, Say," say
22 Crockett cap material
23 Door openers
24 Code name
25 Birth announcement beginning
26 Rocks
27 Silent one
28 Nest noise
30 Monogram pt.
31 Like a frisbee
35 "___ Life": Sinatra
36 Long tales
37 Young doctor Kildare?
38 Lines that are several feet long?
39 Electrical unit
40 Longtime Dolphins coach
41 Hunted woman in "The Terminator"
42 Milk containers
46 Lodgin' for Lanford Wilson?
47 "Are you calling me ___?"
48 Mother Goose tumbler
49 Zhao Ziyang's predecessor
50 Like a whacky recluse?
54 Consume
55 Texas Hold'em stake
56 English forest
57 Wanting water
58 Turkish bathwear
60 Creeps
61 Use inelegant language
62 Eight-time Norris Trophy winner
63 West Side Story heroine
64 Worn out
65 Put on
68 "Two Women" Oscar winner
69 Locust cloud
70 Euro forerunners
71 Like crocodile tears
72 Oahu carving material
73 Mellow
74 Word after who or what
75 Julianne in "The Hours"
77 Love child
81 007's martini holder?
83 Undertaking
85 "Don't give up!"
86 Facing
87 Musical movements
88 High-tech radio of 1954

DOWN

1 Neighbor of Mont.
2 Floor piece
3 Count (on)
4 "The Way ___": Bruce Hornsby
5 Turner of a revolution?
6 AMC car that caused a lot of trouble?
7 Side way
8 Oversleeper's need
9 Srs.' worry
10 Engagement?
11 Part of SPCA
12 Some investments
13 Make ___ (blog)
14 Zola work
15 Highest deg. holders
16 Nosing (around)
17 Cher portrayer in "Clueless"
18 Credos
27 Mrs. Dithers of "Blondie"
29 Laundry
30 ". . . walk out, ___ great event": Plath
31 Serve up
32 Not freelance
33 Type of step
34 Violin relative
35 Hebrew scroll
36 Pantry part
38 Satchel of diamonds
39 Wrinkle-resistant textile
41 Narrow cuts
42 Takes the bait
43 Baked eggs
44 Neighbor of Algeria
45 Turns blue
47 Ed of "Studio 60"
48 Region of ancient Palestine
51 One of the little people
52 Senator Hatch
53 Loa preceder
59 Spade, to Bogart
60 Lifeboat pair
61 Caesar's sidekick
63 Interferes with
64 Turns aside
65 James Michener novel
66 Schulz character under a cloud?
67 Fed (on)
68 Canine superstar
69 Veer wildly
71 Lester of bluegrass
72 "___ luck!"
74 Sparkle
76 Estimation words
77 Sea eagles
78 Uproar
79 ___ buco
80 Tea leaves reader
82 4.0, e.g.
84 Hawaiian dish

175 ANIMAL FARM by Jay Sullivan
The NFL Hall-of-Famer at 95-A also played for the Giants and 49ers.

ACROSS

1 Focus of a child study
5 One with a diamond record
12 Head set
17 Novel idea
18 Member of a skeleton crew?
19 Off-course
21 Something about Mary
22 Cervid kiss-off?
24 De-creased
26 Make a pitch for
27 Forest denizens
28 Mudder's fodder
29 It may be burning
30 Additional homework
31 Growing places
32 Belgrade resident
33 Drudge work
36 Having walked?
38 Bridge support
40 Shorebird mating rituals?
43 Gibson guy
44 Bridge over the Grand Canal
45 Geico rival
49 Sunscreen additive
51 Former first lady
52 Power up
55 Stratford stream
56 Bygone ruler
57 Web site?
58 Change for a twenty
59 Touch your toes
61 Last Hawaiian queen
62 "Pygmalion" playwright
63 Halt, in Le Havre
64 Without a leg to stand on
66 Better the cheddar
67 Wilde-beest kingdom?
71 Spam sampler?
72 Bring back
75 In stitches
76 Spellbound
78 This one's ___
79 Some (senoritas)
81 Sock pattern
84 Picnic cooler
85 Sacred Egyptian bull
86 A summer place
89 "The Factory" figure
90 Bunnies on the run?
94 Rhyme scheme
95 Former Colt quarterback
96 Dynamic introduction?
97 "Devil take it!"
98 Anti-inflammatory acronym
99 Horn-swoggles
100 To be, to Satie

DOWN

1 Ladybug's lunch
2 Proclaim loudly
3 Huge swine?
4 More unfeeling
5 Tax write-off
6 It may be after you?
7 Short-billed duck
8 River of Aragon
9 Voodoo amulet
10 Year abroad
11 India's Children's Day honoree
12 Small keyboard instrument
13 Rock group
14 "A-Team" actor
15 Washed-up one
16 Golfing family
20 Assignation
23 "___ is an island"
25 Flub up
30 Razor cut
31 Halves
33 Vessel with three hulls
34 Broadcasting
35 "Survivor" setting
37 Bad Goodyear
38 Leaping antelope
39 Dam site betterer
41 Rub out
42 "Shucks!"
46 Quick buck?
47 Immaturity
48 It's on the tip of your tongue
50 Frankie's "Beach Party" costar
51 VJ's spot
53 "Threepenny Opera" composer
54 Gilbert & Sullivan princess
57 Actor Max Von ___
60 Emperor of LXIX
61 "West Wing" actor Rob
65 Mug
68 Let off steam
69 Results of some wishful thinking?
70 Taps
71 Install a new release
72 Celebrity treatment
73 Cello support
74 Gets the lead out, say
77 Southern constellation
80 One-time Moore costar
82 Pertaining to a lung, perhaps
83 Get high
85 Hun honcho
86 Dog tag
87 Going rate
88 Newspaper section
91 "Give ___ rest"
92 Day-___ colors
93 Middle America?

CITIES THROWN INTO CONFUSION by Fran & Lou Sabin
The site of 28-A's discovery was Virginia City, Nevada.

ACROSS

1 Roe source
5 Symbol of silence
9 Nile reptile
13 Rum cake
17 Teller's workspace
18 Heifer snarer
19 Restaurateur's delight
20 Bully cheers?
21 "Excusez moi!"
22 Pitcher Hershiser
23 Knotted
24 Jazz site
25 Wisconsin regions?
28 Comstock's find
29 Something to plunk
30 Quadruped parent
31 Time-honored
33 Hightail it
37 Congressional vote
38 Heeled over
43 Collapsed suddenly
46 "Too much!"
47 Small orchard
48 Joyce or Oates: Abbr.
49 Iowa elevation?
52 Did a sketch
53 Closes again
55 Bella Coola pole
56 Ancient
57 Aussie bounder
58 Judean king (37–4 BC)
59 Frat letter
60 Sweep
63 Top-notch
64 Character flaws
68 "Isn't It Romantic?" lyricist
69 New York Conservative?
71 Lord's love
72 Maui "Howdy!"
74 Offshore sight
75 Wouldn't hold back
77 Stick-to-itiveness
79 Offensive fellow
81 Rugged ridge
82 NYC music hall
83 Objector's word
84 McBride in "Narc"
86 Auburn feet?
89 Maryland landing site?
97 Way out
98 Outdated Roman coin
99 Wonderland
100 Get by
101 Apart from this
102 Sight site
103 Impending
104 Undo
105 Aase Gynt's son
106 "... five ___ cigar"
107 Piedmont wine city
108 Barber's call

DOWN

1 Grifter's forte
2 Comic's reward
3 Like centenarians
4 Moore in "A Few Good Men"
5 "I am not a ___!": Nixon
6 "SNL" producer Michaels
7 Did likewise
8 Earworm
9 "Sunshine of Your Love" group
10 First name among sitarists
11 Able baker
12 Official naysayer
13 Colorado Rockies hitter, at times?
14 Chorus boy?
15 Necklace unit
16 King Arthur of the courts
26 Waste-disposal pit
27 West who wrote "Sex"
32 Anchor ___
33 Damage
34 Mötley group?
35 Hoe lines
36 Massachusetts pet?
37 Grape drink
38 Checked out
39 Sandler in "Click"
40 "A Doll's House" heroine
41 In any event
42 Like morning grass
44 "Fiesque" composer
45 And mommy makes three?
46 Distiller's vessel
50 Treat badly
51 Comic Amsterdam
54 "Perfect!"
56 "Bali ___"
58 "ASAP!"
59 Mattel sales
60 "Come again?"
61 In great shape
62 "Go" passer
63 Manuscript mark
64 Painter Angelico
65 Put aboard
66 Bowdlerize
67 Highlander's "since"
70 Roulette play
73 Eddie Rickenbacker, e.g.
76 Roman salute
78 Type of type
79 Egg holder
80 Zeus's head child?
83 Orgy
84 Load the dice
85 Painter Matisse
86 Little Bo
87 Machinist's shaft
88 Informed
90 Portentous
91 Ms. Brockovich
92 March time
93 File folder, e.g.
94 Leo or Benedict, e.g.
95 Mountain top
96 Crease

177 MIDDLE AGE   by Maggie Davidson
The paraphrased quip below was spoken from one who lived to see 100.

ACROSS

1 Addition, e.g.
5 Magnate
10 "My bad!"
14 Gaslight
17 Dynamic commencement
18 "___ thee, O Moab!": Jer. 48-46
19 Majority ___
20 Old spy org.
21 **Start of a Bob Hope quip**
23 "Darn!"
24 RR stop
25 The least bit
26 Conservatory grad
28 Deborah in "Black Narcissus"
29 "Dances With Wolves" is one
30 Reno rarity
31 Chinese capital
33 **More of quip**
36 Sch. near Harvard
38 In-flight info
39 Photog's choice
40 Pleasing view
41 ___ Aquarius
44 Choking, on the green
47 Delhi attire
49 Leachman in "High Anxiety"
51 Past due
53 Stops
58 **More of quip**
61 "Told ya!"
62 Ft. Worth's ___ Carter Museum
63 Maryland's state bird
64 Whipped
66 Lose it
68 Poke around
69 Bivouac stop
73 Dolphins' home
75 ___ squared = area of a circle
77 Seat holders
78 **More of quip**
84 "Misty" composer Garner
85 Hair removal brand
86 "10-4" speaker
87 Primer pet
88 ". . . shortly"
90 Negative wish
94 Boating pronoun
95 Spellbound
96 **End of quip**
98 ___ Mae in "Ghost"
99 [sigh]
100 Loose on
101 Morlocks' morsels?
102 Set-___
103 Prank ender
104 Ideal spots
105 Medieval tenant farmer

DOWN

1 BLT option
2 Long time
3 Constant
4 More contrived
5 Double-cross
6 Capital before Des Moines
7 "Miss Pym Disposes" author
8 Ready for takeoff
9 Kind of network
10 First and second
11 Couple's word
12 Missouri feeder
13 Gel
14 Campbell and Conrad
15 Springsteen's band
16 Former Kremlin resident
22 Slangy denial
27 Score curves
28 Yogurt fruit
32 Those giving counsel
33 Did lunch
34 Diurnal
35 Rank
36 Herald Square store
37 Cold weather quarters
42 "Straight" word form
43 Engine-house alarm
45 Sunscreen compound
46 Quarter-note parts
48 Rayban rival
50 "Okey-doke"
52 Carolina college town
54 "Don't rub ___"
55 Odds-on favorite
56 Curved nail
57 Dance components
59 Caddy contract
60 Not suitable
65 Former "YM" subscriber
67 Vocal coach?
69 View
70 Send to the bottom
71 Sky lights
72 Represent graphically
74 Belgian brews
76 Enters Vista anew
79 Escape
80 Popular VW
81 Did art on glass
82 Not an orig.
83 Dunne and Worth
89 Iditarod Trail's end
91 Green or blue shade
92 "___ off?"
93 Weekend-starting cry
95 Battery buys
97 Hot time in Paris

178 INTERNATIONAL LAND DEALS by Elizabeth C. Gorski
52 Down can also be found in the refrain of "Witch Doctor."

ACROSS

1 Angler's complaint?
5 Pianist Ellington
9 Radiance
14 TV spot
17 Peek-___
18 Prime minister Barak
19 Post-lecture session
20 Directly across from: Abbr.
21 CHAD
24 Fleur-de-___
25 Undercover operation
26 Metallica drummer Ulrich
27 Unaccompanied
29 "Duke of ___" (doo-wop classic)
30 Italian capital
31 "The heat ___!"
32 Country singer Travis
35 CHINA
39 NRTA parent
40 Pre-prandial prayer
42 More apt to sob
43 Make joe
45 Destiny
47 Exxon, in Canada
48 Coast unit
49 Wife of Hussein I
51 59 minutes after
52 WALES
57 Beginning of a Dickens title
59 Zaire's Mobutu ___ Seko
60 Hard–rock middle
61 Garage event
62 Accoutered
64 It killed the electric car?
70 Garage floor blotch
72 "Ready ___, here . . ."
73 "This ___ outrage!"
74 PANAMA
77 Hot spots
78 "King Kong" star Faye
79 Coral reefs
80 Loyal
82 African village of huts
84 Asian palm
85 Gateway Arch architect
89 Dogpatch adjective
90 ALTERNATE TITLE
93 Blow-up: Abbr.
94 Pitcher Santana
95 First name of 85 Across
96 Single thing
97 Writer LeShan
98 Flightless critters of Peru
99 Paltrow, to pals
100 Hog holders

DOWN

1 Fan Appreciation Day giveaways
2 Share a border
3 Ellen ___ Barkin
4 Handheld type
5 "Architectural Digest" subject
6 Moving-day rental
7 Conductor Masur
8 Jay's former announcer Hall
9 Trafalgar, for one
10 Enmity
11 Baseball's Slaughter
12 Academic URL suffix
13 "Rocky & Bullwinkle" spy
14 Chopin masterpieces
15 "Wheel of Fortune" turn
16 Sanctuary section
22 Packing ___ (armed)
23 "I Fall To Pieces" singer Patsy
28 Like Baltic Avenue's district
30 With credentials
31 "Oh, now it's clear . . ."
32 Water source
33 Charlotte of crosswords
34 Discount rack abbr.
35 Budgetary excess
36 Hairy Cousin
37 Relaxation go-with
38 Switch suffix
40 Pleased as punch
41 Like white Bengal tigers
44 Wind up in a bandshell?
45 French pâté
46 A father of Dada
50 Goose eggs
51 Port of Algeria
52 Tribe that aided Lewis and Clark
53 Fake fat
54 Advisors to POTUS
55 Spanish step
56 Joseph Conrad's "___ of Six"
57 Beginning with
58 Streamer on a kite
62 Fashion award
63 PO box item
65 Hill denizen
66 "Come on, tell me!"
67 British verb ending
68 Flossie Bobbsey's sister
69 Nav. rank
71 Prayer book
72 "Honestly!"
75 Thorntree
76 Conestogas
77 Communal
80 Linger
81 Affordable silk-like fabric
82 "Diana in the Autumn Wind" artist
83 Orange cover
84 European golf trophy
85 Crockpot filler
86 Bar ___
87 Celtic land
88 They're center court at Wimbledon
91 Brit. monarch's address
92 Photog. master

179 "REAL NUTS!" by Richard Silvestri
Perhaps the title should read: "UNREAL NUTS!"

ACROSS

1 Fundamental
6 Apartheid proponent
12 Found a phrase for
18 San Antonio attraction
19 Touch at the edge of
20 Form concepts
21 Nutty TV host?
23 Sleeve
24 Challenging puzzle
25 Slane Castle locale
26 "Wednesday" singer Amos
27 Gets going fast
29 Nutty boxer?
34 Cat call
37 Cal ___
39 Moon roof's cousin
40 Letters on a street sign
41 Stage direction
43 Stud ploy
45 Canyon area
47 Flush
48 Term of address
50 Cell material
51 Nigerian singer
52 Jaunty
53 Alphabet ender
54 Farewell
56 Capital of Laconia
58 Nutty "Lifestyles" chap?
62 Colgate athlete
66 Wreck beyond repair
67 Spicy cuisine
72 Dermatologist's concern
73 Concert gear for 96-A
76 Flamenco shout
77 Varlet
78 Not in force
79 Tell fish stories
80 Visionary's inspiration
82 Stadium section
83 Assayed stuff
84 Symbol of authority
86 Use a dirk
88 Youth
89 Nutty singer?

94 Ending for young or old
96 The Corrs, e.g.
97 Venice beach
99 Caribbean trip
103 Brute
106 Nutty tycoon?
108 Blackboard adjunct
109 Wilhelm I, for one
110 Shadings
111 Be emphatic
112 Main channel
113 Chip away at

DOWN

1 Matt's brat
2 On the safe side
3 Heroic narrative
4 Plain-living people
5 Come unhinged
6 Heyerdahl transport
7 Up to the task
8 Three-dimensional
9 Say again
10 Superlatively steamed
11 It does a bang-up job
12 Avid golfer's wife
13 The nose knows them
14 Shrine holding
15 Leave it to beavers
16 Sorority letter
17 Trophy room
22 Liberator
26 Not so hot
28 Egyptian amulet
30 Circle dance
31 4-time Wimbledon winner
32 Fend off
33 Gossip
34 Note to the staff
35 Makeup, e.g.

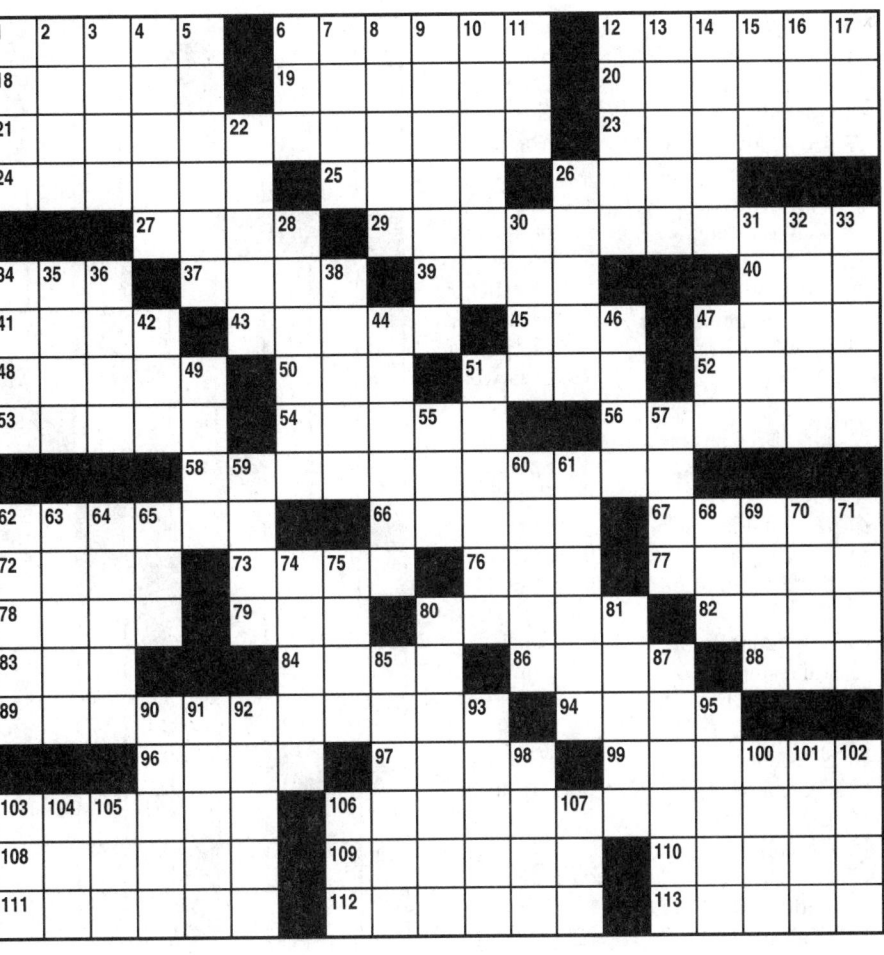

36 Like the Missouri
38 Mysore tongue
42 Make it
44 Peter, Paul and Mary
46 Work well together
47 MPG raters
49 Mule's mom
51 One who woos
55 "Telephone Line" group
57 Settle on
59 Kind of communication
60 The stuff of legends
61 Diamond wear
62 Wouldn't stop
63 Legend maker
64 Narrows
65 Tierra ___ Fuego
68 Colony member
69 Cooler
70 Part of the eye
71 Geeky guy

74 Acted out
75 Crowning point
80 Mark the boundaries of
81 Stick in a box
85 Dickie feature
87 Bawl out
90 Deflate
91 Ale alternative
92 Like krypton
93 Get ___ of one's own medicine
95 Buzz
98 Unmatched item
100 "___ Angel" (Mae West film)
101 Future grass
102 Hebrides dialect
103 Swell place?
104 Start of MGM's motto
105 Anatomical duct
106 Abbr. on a rap sheet
107 Put in a kiln

180 SPOILSPORTS by Fred Piscop

The nickname of 20 Across is "Mr. Hockey."

ACROSS

1 Bob in "Wordplay"
5 Pipe material
8 Fashionable bag
13 Iron-gloved god
17 Carrie Underwood became one
18 Cannon's end
19 Suez Canal sight
20 Hockey's Gordie
21 Prison punishment
23 Bowler's least favorite house style?
25 NASCAR driver's least favorite school offering?
27 Autostrada auto
28 Michael in TV's "The Third Man"
29 Revulsion
33 Yippie Hoffman
37 Take steps
38 Land of Minos
39 Place for a feather
40 Sees the old gang
42 Gave a whipping to
44 Like 13 Across
46 Coworker of Lane
47 Grid prop
49 Caddy's load
50 High-pH stuff
51 Bill Kenny or "Hoppy" Jones
53 Make waves
54 Down the drain
56 Genealogy word
57 Cyclist's least favorite denier of the truth?
60 Euro divs.
63 Sushi need
65 "The Big Easy" hero
66 Like some nighties
68 Witty Mort
70 Reveal, in verse
71 Three min., for a pug
72 ". . . stole ___ and away he run"
73 Rugrat's ride
75 Loath
77 Cloud layers
79 Sushi selection
80 No longer in
82 Cleo's biter
84 Heron or egret
85 Its capital is Malé
87 Camden Yards logo
89 Like many cookies
90 Marathoner's least favorite product holder?
95 Wrestler's least favorite suit pattern?
99 Clearwater's waters
100 Golden Spike locale
101 "Survivor" group
102 Ear: Prefix
103 Baloney
104 Tot's mount
105 Dutch painter Jan
106 Potter pal Weasley
107 "Don't throw bouquets ___ . . ."

DOWN

1 Pog, e.g.
2 Carbon monoxide's lack
3 Kinks classic
4 "Y" sporters
5 Hippie sign-off
6 Turning Stone Casino site
7 Throw in the towel
8 Oater group
9 Like old age?
10 "Snafu" part
11 What Hercules became
12 Oil producer?
13 Sweater letter
14 Car-pool lane
15 Be in the hole
16 Meth. or Luth.
22 Pawnbroker's ball count
24 Grow dark
26 Meter maid of song
29 Had aspirations
30 Pool player's least favorite stationery item?
31 ITAR-___ news agency
32 Light sword
33 Adam of "Chicago Hope"
34 Designer Geoffrey
35 Golfer's least favorite historical site?
36 Blemishes on a QB's record
38 Sundae item
41 It's a wrap
43 Tramp, e.g.
45 Baby docs
48 LAX guesstimate
52 Sgt.'s underling
53 Used the keyhole, in a way
54 It's on the Aire
55 Stamp mill input
58 Valuable finds
59 Buying channel on TV
61 No longer in
62 Cube makeup
64 Sort
67 Mitchell estate
68 Quarter-note part
69 ___ 51 (rumored UFO site)
71 Item in a circuit
74 Bull, of sorts
75 Humbled oneself
76 Mysore garb
78 Weenie
81 Turns away
83 Knish stuffing
86 Full of gossip
87 Merlin of grid fame
88 Slots symbol
90 Nixon pal Rebozo
91 Sunscreen stuff
92 Touch on
93 Sailboater's problem
94 "South Park" kid
95 Little pug
96 Skater Midori
97 Tandoor-baked bread
98 Take-out fare

181 POETIC JUSTICE by Patrick Jordan
The author of the poem reveals himself in the last line.

ACROSS

1 Theatergoer's receipt
5 "Lose it"
9 Kremlin kingpin of yore
13 Treaty-bound nations
17 British composer Thomas
18 Boxcar Willie's persona
19 Yearning feeling
20 Sudden thrill
21 Moviedom's Malden
22 Manta manufacturer
23 Earring variety
24 Wight or Skye
25 **Start of a poem**
29 Trellis climber
30 Unabashed joy
31 Loretta Lockhorn, for one
32 Coeur d'___
34 Immaculate
36 Fewer than many
40 **More of poem**
44 Ouija board answer
45 Flanged supporter
46 Pupil surrounder
47 Pic or tech prefix
48 Places for TSgts.
49 Swab brand
50 Adjective for Seattle
52 Parking attendants
55 Perform a benediction
57 Twitched
58 "Witness" cast
59 Frame of mind
60 Warthog's weapon
61 Mil. unit
62 Beaufort scale category
63 Playback speed, for short
65 Rejuvenation destination
68 **More of poem**
73 Fords introduced in 1927
74 58 Across, for one
75 Utility bill basis
76 ___ Tin Tin
77 Like Sabin's polio vaccine
79 Word on an octagon
80 **End of poem**
88 Wheel rod
89 Last word of the Apostles' Creed
90 Emperor tutored by Seneca
91 Jewish activist Wiesel
92 Legree-like
93 Trio in Matthew
94 Microscope adjuster
95 "But by the ___ token . . ."
96 "Amarantine" album artist
97 Read a bar code
98 They bear farrows
99 Globes

DOWN

1 Munro's pseudonym
2 Coal porter?
3 Falls apart
4 "Norma" composer
5 Excelled
6 "Uh-uh"
7 Dutch explorer Tasman
8 Record label of 1972–98
9 Lake near Squaw Valley
10 Sportscast datum
11 "There'll be ___ time . . ."
12 Spruces up the den, maybe
13 Formed a link between
14 Teeming with vegetation
15 Sonja Henie's hometown
16 Work on a cud
26 Twenty percent
27 Did in, as a dragon
28 "JAG" setting
32 Swimmer Van Dyken
33 Drain cleaner chemical
34 Some bake-sale buys
35 Cable viewing choice
36 Icy sidewalk mishap
37 Cubic conundrum creator
38 Flare-bottomed skirt
39 Harold in "The Freshman"
41 Retreats from shore
42 Partner of starts
43 "A God in Ruins" author Leon
48 DDE defeated him twice
49 Math textbook abbr.
50 Firmly determined
51 Great Flood haven
52 "Barbarella" director Roger
53 Acid in protein
54 Enjoyed oneself fully
55 Gaucho's sling
56 MGM cofounder Marcus
57 Checkers maneuver
59 Large-scale
60 Libel, e.g.
62 Sporty Pontiacs
63 Goes caving
64 Jean-___ Ponty of jazz
65 Shoulder-related
66 Collectible cap
67 Widemouthed emotion
69 Plant with flower spikes
70 1947 Oscar winner Kazan
71 PDQ
72 1962 Paul Anka hit
77 Final part
78 Packed off to the pokey
79 They're no neatniks
80 Unlikely to bite
81 Strong but dumb beasts
82 Oil of ___
83 1998 computer debut
84 Nevada Museum of Art site
85 Figurehead's spot
86 Tree surgeon's removal
87 Fermentation sediment

182 DOWNSIZING by Jay Sullivan

The film director at 33 Down lived on London's Narrow Street for many years.

ACROSS

1 Batista successor
7 Postwar German republic
13 Morsel
18 Pulsating
19 "Twelfth Night" duke
20 "Sun Valley Serenade" skating star
21 Most boring
22 Planning to diet?
24 "How Little We Know" singer
26 For example
27 Western outlaw brothers
28 Con job
30 Polar explorer
31 That's a relief
34 "Cannonball" on sax
36 Regarding
40 Small fly
42 It's quite a stretch
43 "Radio Song" group
45 Be hospitable
46 Great reviews
48 Get behind: Var.
51 Rotterdam's river
52 In groups
54 Certain Ivy Leaguer
55 Former acting president
57 Old times. once upon a time
58 How-to book on modeling?
62 It hangs from the rim
65 Unwilling
67 Piano piece
68 Ancient scrolls
70 Fleece
72 Funny folk
76 Sin city of old
77 Keep to oneself
78 Gunnysack
79 High honor
81 Bay of Fundy attraction
82 Desires
83 Shaky Land O'Lakes practice?
87 According to
88 Degrees of success
91 Ride the waves
93 Bayou canoe: Var.
97 Hit producer
98 1953 Monroe film
102 Leftovers for Jack Sprat?
105 Rift valley
106 Reef denizen
107 In knots
108 Small, dry fruit
109 Seven-year period
110 Top-Flite golf ball
111 Pulls a fast one?

DOWN

1 Men behaving badly
2 Italian bell town
3 It's over a foot
4 Grab the tab
5 Political platforms
6 Stick out
7 Korean currency
8 Eberhard product
9 Six-Day War winner
10 Like a swamp
11 It contains Mayo
12 Clint's "Rawhide" role
13 One who wears little clothing
14 In tatters
15 Pull strings
16 Bearing
17 Growing places
23 Make a dent in
25 "Ditto"
29 Sawbuck
30 Parting words
31 See eye to eye
32 On the whole
33 He lost a lot of pounds on his last film?
35 Goof
36 Flushing stadium eponym
37 Lo-cal party food?
38 Solder or soldier material
39 Half and half
41 Hanoi holiday
44 Get engaged
45 Where the action is
47 Purchaser of Alaska
49 CCI + CCCL
50 Behaves like a pig
53 Chess group
56 Street-smart
59 Queequeg's captain
60 Grand opening?
61 Rigorist
63 Lose ground
64 Kitchen counter?
66 They have pull
69 Ante matter
70 A little short
71 Earth mover
73 Some Apples
74 "That's revolting!"
75 Progeny
80 Navy newbies
84 Zaire neighbor
85 Cheap booze
86 Get ready
88 17th-century diarist
89 Yes, in Yokohama
90 They'll bring tears to your eyes
92 Fine print
93 Dept. store floor
94 Cosmetic additive
95 Run out of gas
96 Gov't. agent
97 Oktoberfest quaff
99 Up to the task
100 Sax object
101 Social workers
103 First-aid item
104 Evian or Vichy

183 "OH, YOU" by Harvey Estes

39 Down has won 14 Grand Slam titles, including two Wimbledon singles.

ACROSS

1 Beams in doorways
6 "Flashdance" hit
12 Specks on a map
18 One score after deuce
19 Potemkin Stairs site
20 John's "Grease" costar
21 Evidence of Miss Muffet sawing wood?
23 Scout's interest
24 Wash. neighbor
25 Golf positions
26 "Madonna of the Rocks" painter
27 "Take a load off"
29 "Hold up!"
32 ___ Cristobal
33 Christmas poem opener
34 Brace some cart wheels?
38 Assistant
41 Tacky
42 TLC specialists
43 Racing paths
44 Sassy kid
45 Finery
49 Hokkaido lake
50 Port-au-Prince place
51 Prejudice
52 Thunder Bay loc.
53 Gore-y film about a shotgun wedding?
57 Quaint quarters
58 Top-drawer
59 Grind your teeth because of Ogden's poems?
60 Queens tennis stadium
61 Cowes Week, for one
63 "ONE" copy
64 Mariana Trench locale
65 I-95, for one
66 Pounds, e.g.
67 Legendary pursuits
68 Cute hare?
72 Supersonic number
73 SEP, e.g.
74 Stairs alternative
75 Ground-level openings
79 Grandiose scheme
83 Hardly the prom queen type
84 Least of the litter
85 Flatt with Scruggs
86 Louse up a Newman role?
90 Where many jokes are set
91 Cost of pitching a product
92 "The Science of Logic" author
93 Aquatic frolickers
94 Like the solar plexus
95 Half of a 45

DOWN

1 Ghost Marley
2 Dig deeply
3 Conventions
4 Treasurer's responsibility
5 D and C, in D.C.
6 Funding
7 Put on
8 Tidings
9 Comedian Kabibble
10 Enzyme ending
11 Coral reef
12 Just a bit
13 Pole, for example
14 Taylor in "Mystic Pizza"
15 Nonetheless
16 Navy destroyer, slangily
17 The Five ___ ('50s group)
22 Bridal path's end
26 Old terr.
28 Blows the minds of
29 Greenpeace target
30 Med. center
31 It turns out lts.
34 Largest Greek island
35 Ring at the door?
36 Uptight feeling
37 U.S. property manager
38 Windbag's output
39 Tennis star Goolagong
40 Ascribing, as blame
41 Leek relative
44 "Care to?"
45 Salon service
46 Unties
47 Because
48 Home of the Georgia Bulldogs
50 Unhappy audience member
51 Boyfriends
54 Like Scar's remarks?
55 Alaska on a map, sometimes
56 Trifecta trio
62 Son of Prince Valiant
63 Long-range projectile, for short
64 Smart comment?
66 Texas Chaparrals' org.
67 Press conference, at times
68 Book lover's prefix
69 Familiarize
70 Pesters
71 Parseghian of football
72 Dadaist Duchamp
75 Bombay-born conductor
76 One of the Mario Brothers
77 Wound up
78 Flair
80 "May ___": Enya
81 Honeybunch
82 Proves to be human?
83 Tenn. neighbor
86 Secret rival
87 Dedicated poem
88 Tony-winning Morse role
89 Doo-wop syllable

FROM THE BEGINNING by Bonnie L. Gentry
The piano concerto at 41 Down was his first.

ACROSS

1 Spruce up, in a way
7 Evidence of a rain
13 Choral group
18 Hardens with experience
19 Away from the mouth
20 One on a pedestal
21 Say "Mm-hmm"
22 Best, on the links
23 How mistakes are marked
24 **Start of a Steven Wright quote**
27 First name at Woodstock
28 Beginning for while
29 "___ tu" (aria for Renato)
30 10th-century Pope
33 Rio and Sportage
34 Aussie jumper
35 Buffalo's pre-Bills NFL team
38 Soccer phenom Freddy
39 Georgia of "Coach"
41 Key of a Prokofiev piano concerto
43 Car with a horse-collar grille
45 When single
46 **More of quote**
51 It may finish second
52 Road Runner's foe
53 Big cat of film
54 Emailed, in a way
57 Nature
60 Letter resembling a trident
61 Checker, of sorts
62 Cousin of "Oy!"
63 "Ya got me"
67 Be a chatterbox
69 **More of quote**
73 Wrestler's rippler
76 "Save Me" singer Mann
77 Disney film set in China
78 Guam capital
80 Rocks in a bucket
81 Statement of confession
85 -osis : -oses :: -y : -___
87 Devoid of emotion
88 Little Dickens girl
90 Frostiness
91 Last Stuart ruler
92 A little of this, a little of that
93 **End of quote**
98 "Wicked Game" singer Chris
100 Pooh's gloomy friend
101 "Elements" writer
102 Tibia connectors
103 Reagan Supreme Court appointee
104 Do a cobble job?
105 Most of the Earth's surface
106 Painfully sensitive
107 Hall-of-Fame QB Bob

DOWN

1 Get up again
2 Send to the Hall
3 Boeing body
4 Gritty
5 Lincoln picture site
6 Feast of Lots book
7 Passes some bad bills
8 Vessel in "The Enemy Below"
9 Out of order
10 Took a straw
11 Sailor's punishment of yore
12 Corrida participant
13 Sarah McLachlan hit
14 Czech court great
15 Lack stamina
16 Native suffix
17 Barrett of Pink Floyd
25 Wear down
26 Max's opposite
31 H.C. Andersen's birthplace
32 Common
35 Metric opening
36 "The ___-Bitsy Spider"
37 Merman's birthplace
40 Abbr. on a copier paper tray
42 Driver's need: Abbr.
44 Hardly Mr. Cool
47 In a hurry
48 Go one better
49 "The Lost Weekend" subject
50 1040–57, for Macbeth
51 Think the world of
54 Nirvana frontman
55 Alternative
56 Some household utensils
58 Canterbury can
59 Frontiersman's first name
64 Lowers, in a way
65 German iPod holder
66 Small punch
68 Aly Khan's father
70 Labrador motto word
71 Puddle-jumper wear?
72 Brief bridge bid
73 Swiss Expressionist
74 Hostile feelings
75 The whole lot
79 Italian dumplings
82 Relative of C4
83 Most outspread
84 Pricing word
86 "Saint Joan" star Jean
89 Capital at 12,000 feet
91 John Denver album
94 Like kissing cousins
95 Cannon in movies
96 Cargo space
97 Violinist who taught Heifetz
98 Ice skater Midori
99 Mil. def. acronym

185 D.B.A. QUESTION by Ernie Lampert
The Wall Street symbol at 14 Across is fitting.

ACROSS

1 Fig
5 It's connected to the ankle bone
10 Apple variety
14 Harley Davidson's NYSE symbol
17 Sir Charles' mate
18 Sixteen oz.
19 Central motif, in music
20 UK honorific
21 **Start of a d.b.a. question**
24 DOD's URL suffix
25 Chilling
26 Drift
27 Alvarado in "The Babe"
29 Ming, for one
31 Unease
33 Prevention measure?
36 A little lower?
38 Prefix meaning "height"
39 Get rid of
40 **More of question**
44 Bum smoke?
46 Quercitron, e.g.
47 "Drums Along the Mohawk" hero
48 Romantic interlude
49 **More of question**
51 Constantine's birthplace
53 Horace's handles
54 Slang for guitar
55 Go at once
57 Songwriter Jones (1894–1956)
62 "Life with Father" author
64 Slideshow instrument?
66 Flawlessly
70 Intimate
72 Rotterdam–Arnhem direction
73 Dogie catchers
74 **More of question**
78 Stooge "Curly-Joe"
79 Highly rated
80 Ko-Ko's blade
81 Doddering
82 2002 Salma Hayek role
84 Redgrave in "Camelot"
89 Share and share ___
91 ___-surface missile
93 "Charlie Chan at the Circus" star
94 "Galloping Ghost" Grange
96 **End of question**
99 Place for a key: Abbr.
100 Neat and tidy
101 Rutger in "Blade Runner"
102 Ethiopian of opera
103 Season
104 Other: Sp.
105 Sound introduction?
106 Anna of "Nana"

DOWN

1 Blown away
2 "Bunk!"
3 Store ashes
4 Adrian in "Rocky Balboa"
5 ___ degree (somewhat)
6 Hot
7 ___ noire
8 Massey in "Love Happy"
9 Nullifies
10 Gomez Addams' cousin
11 Masur's New York predecessor
12 Bose of Bose Corp.
13 Electrolysis particles
14 Man or ape
15 Butterfly tie?
16 Stage-light slide
22 Delineated
23 Conductor Leinsdorf
28 None: Comb. form
30 "___ number please"
32 Neat as a pin
34 Encrusted
35 "James Joyce" biographer
37 NJ base
39 Exotic tangelo
40 It reproduces by spores
41 Turkish honorific
42 "Auld Lang ___": Burns
43 Frisco gridder
44 Dallas-based carrier: Abbr.
45 Browning work?
50 Checkup request
52 "You bet, mister!" in Yucatán
55 Alger of the "Pumpkin Papers"
56 Beat for Solti
58 Union pariah
59 Table d'___
60 Shrink's org.
61 Julio, e.g.
63 Mgr.'s unit, often
64 Somalia's largest city
65 "Coffee ___?"
66 Cry of achievment
67 What "sun" and "moon" have in common
68 Daughter of King Minos
69 Govt. obligation
71 Fiction enthusiast
75 Eroded
76 Water nymph
77 Medium, at times
82 Longest human bone
83 Popular font
85 Maxwell and Martinelli
86 "You ___ here first!"
87 Derogatory
88 Clio contender
90 Ex-Yankees announcer Jim
92 Threaded holder
94 Creek
95 Platypus origin
97 Ike's WW2 arena
98 ___ pro nobis

186 FRUIT PUNCH by Anson Franklin
Steve Jobs should like the clue at 32 Across.

ACROSS

1 See 1 Down
4 Not as hairy
10 El ___
14 Down follower or preceder
17 Pitcher's stat.
18 East Asia
19 Bewildered responses
20 Before, poetically
21 Ref count
22 Boer War battleground
25 Tearjerker
27 Headset set
28 Work at
29 Likelihood
31 Diner dish
32 Mac slogan which targets pupils?
38 Recipe shortening?
41 Guy with a list
42 Egg cell
43 Radius, for one
45 Alaimo of "Deep Space Nine"
46 Assayers' stuff
47 Highest level
49 Fictional governess
50 Scanning ltrs.
51 Outlaw
52 Small fjord
53 Red noisemakers
57 Lively dance
61 Mideast inits.
62 Fishy food
63 Pointed remark
67 Like some families
70 Ruben Studdard in 2003
71 Twistable cookie
72 Unbeatable rival
73 Réunion and others
74 Puts together
75 Gray ode subject
76 Land of gorilla strongholds?
80 Accident investigation grp.
82 Green-eyed monster
83 Latin I verb
84 Sooner
87 Ishmael's spears
92 Cereal endorsed by Mighty Mouse

95 Homeboy
96 Kareem, before
97 Gaetano's "good"
98 Bareback rider
99 Service
100 Urban trains
101 Court advantage
102 Upright
103 Caught, in a way

DOWN

1 Fills 'er up (with 1-A)
2 Bailiwick
3 Take the edge off
4 Quarterback's play
5 Dry gulch
6 Yarn spinner
7 Gainsay
8 Chang's sibling
9 Mapquest rec
10 Put into words
11 Violinist Leopold
12 German ___
13 Easier version, in music scores
14 Chick-fil-A acquisition of 1998
15 Jokester Johnson
16 Ball holders
23 Revenuers
24 Treaty subject
26 Edit, as film
29 Burden of proof
30 Rep. opponent
32 Wile E. Coyote's supplier
33 Talk up?
34 Henry VIII's sixth
35 More than persuasion
36 Infest
37 Bark sharply
39 Bygone blade
40 Hardly coy

44 Hosp. testing techniques
46 Aah's partner
47 Key next to Q
48 Coming
51 "Ciao!"
53 Busy folks in Apr.
54 Tattler
55 Skowron of baseball
56 Novelist Kaufman
57 Not here
58 "For he is cast into ___ . . .": Job 18:8
59 Protection against car-deals that went sour
60 Cause of a drip
63 Error
64 Seed coat
65 Italian artist Guido
66 Large pear
68 Decorated, as with satin strips

69 That Argentine?
70 "Now ___ me down . . ."
73 Short bill
74 Eagerly accepts
77 Spiff up
78 Sothern and Richards
79 Kosher category
81 "Come Back, Little ___"
84 Impolite glance
85 Extinct race in "Forbidden Planet"
86 Certain bond, informally
87 "___ but known . . ."
88 Of the same sort
89 Magnum chaser?
90 Inits. on Mars
91 Copious quantity
93 Kickers' stat
94 Cut off

187 "OH, WOE" by Fran & Lou Sabin
In the old days clues like 1-A and 1-D were strictly taboo.

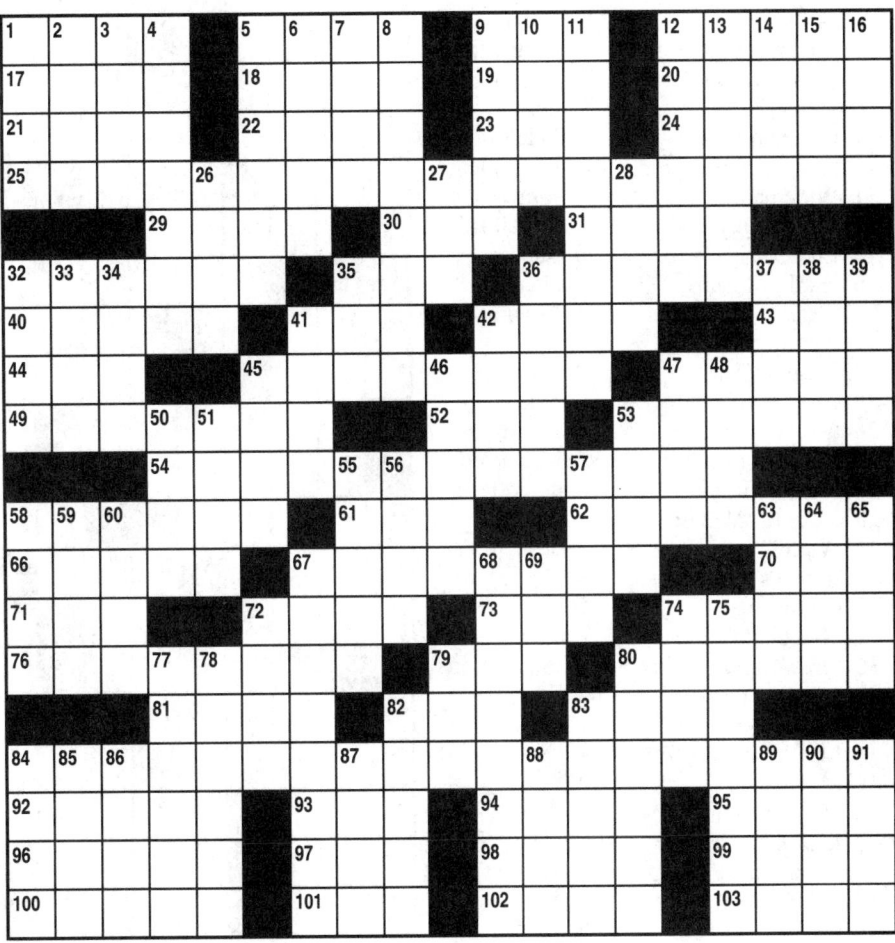

ACROSS

1 Drag-queen wear
5 Bandy words
9 Avenger, for one
12 Religious reading
17 Hick
18 "The Winter's
___": Shak.
19 What Endymion
never did
20 Vaudeville show
21 Jackie Robinson's
alma mater
22 Part of YSL
23 Salary limit
24 It may be grand
25 **Start of a quip**
29 Telepathy,
clairvoyance et al.
30 "Get it?"
31 Furloughs, so to
speak
32 Cop-out
35 Enjoyed foie gras
36 Thin heel
40 Performed a jeté
41 ___, amas, amat
42 Editor's directive
43 Pinna
44 Hilary ___ Swank
45 Down-at-heel
47 "___ bleu!"
49 "King" of jazz
52 Dot follower
53 Ciphers
54 **Middle of quip**
58 Waiting, in a way
61 Cattle call
62 Personal property
66 Winner's take
67 Wondrous events
70 McMansion site
71 Suffering
72 Friable soil
73 Bricklayer's trough
74 Quite serious
76 Livestock feed
79 Jazz job
80 Out of it
81 Tarzan actor
Lincoln
82 Sidekick
83 "___ boy!"
84 **End of quip**
92 Golf's "Army" man
93 ___ Palmas, Spain

94 High ground
95 Royal Saudi
house
96 Haggadah-
reading time
97 Old English
letter
98 First home
of 91 Down
99 Jane Austen
heroine
100 Engine
covers
101 Demure
102 Garden State
five
103 Unwanted
letter

DOWN

1 Fabergé
cologne
2 "That
smarts!"
3 Check over
4 Baby otary
5 Thwart
6 Blacktops
7 Tavern
tipples
8 Off-road
area
9 Hidey-hole
10 Thickening additive
11 Shown again
12 Garden tool
13 Tranquility
14 Say categorically
15 Whey go-with
16 Gunpowder and
hyson
26 Gofer: Abbr.
27 Peg for Furyk
28 Pull out
32 Zest
33 Lawless character
34 Slant
35 Gershwin's "So
___"
36 Zoologic mouth
37 Sort of support
38 Sharp-tongued
39 They lack
refinement
41 Smart guy?
42 Monopoly token

45 Snowboard
46 Neutral vowel
sound
47 Channel-hop
48 "The Night of the
Hunter"
screenwriter
50 Gaffer
51 "___ U": Ashanti
53 Buffoons
55 Jennifer Garner
show
56 Standard
57 "Licorice stick,"
e.g.
58 Kabuki sashes
59 ___ contendere
60 Devout
63 Popular board game
64 Carry
65 Journey kickoff
67 Singular specs
68 Young'uns

69 Kirk's record
72 Jaffe's "Lost
Horizon" role
74 Regarding
75 Many are
dependent
77 Proved otherwise
78 Surgeon General in
1994
79 Sal of song
80 Parthenon's city
82 Self-assertive
83 Black-ink item
84 No decision
85 "Milk's favorite
cookie"
86 Rat on
87 Cussword
88 Helping hand
89 Light source
90 Parliament under
Nicholas II
91 First-family head

188 ICK-Y PUZZLE by Thomas W. Schier

There's nothing distasteful about this theme, although 94-A may be to some!

ACROSS

1 Line from the heart
6 Frosh quarters
10 Downsize unceremoniously
14 Same old, same old
17 Wind danger
18 Ablutionary vessel
19 Like Nash's lama
20 "Sail ___ Ship of State!"
21 Aeroflot's symbol
24 All-out fight
25 Chapter of history
26 "___ Man in Havana" (1960)
27 Rural refusal
28 Mike of "Wayne's World"
30 In one's second childhood
32 "Laughing" doll
36 "New money" girl
38 Shrove Tuesday follower
39 Lunchtime handful
42 Made waves?
43 "Play it again!"
44 Line-score initials
47 Evolutionist's kin
48 "Want to explain that?"
50 Put it to
51 Working class member
52 Describe graphically
54 Shepard in space
57 Silly billies
58 Reaganomics hypothesis
62 Open oysters
63 Where el sol rises
64 Wessex, for one
66 Plumeria garlands
67 Penman?
69 1997 sci-fi film
71 Make a palindromic living?
72 See 65 Down
73 Money guru Dobbs
74 Do a second lube job
76 City SSW of Moscow
77 Condemned contraction
78 Caught in a net
81 Fate's digit?
85 Geological formations
89 Dental filling
90 Supernal altar
91 Routing word
92 Boiling blood
93 House denial
94 Marinated deli offering
100 Get up ___ down
101 "Letters to Father Flye" author
102 Links things
103 Word from on high
104 "Summer of Sam" director
105 "The Mickey Mouse Club" host
106 Water growth
107 Johnny's "Sleep Walk" partner

DOWN

1 Sackcloth and ___
2 Alternative to Midway
3 Bolster the front ___
4 Derby winner Tim ___
5 Cactus bud
6 Sugar substitute?
7 Dominate, in sports lingo
8 Soccer card color
9 Altar ego?
10 ___ point
11 Features of old school desks
12 Fam. reunion attendee
13 Earth, wind, or fire
14 Spur attachment
15 Render weaponless
16 Trunk without a lid
22 "Shoulda, woulda, coulda" thinker
23 Smeared indelibly
29 In the time left
31 NASDAQ debut
32 Gunpowder et al.
33 Tactical advancements
34 Signal an actor
35 Hardly warlike
37 "Wheel" purchase
39 Luck
40 Sobriquet
41 Army boot
44 Command again
45 City north of Springfield
46 50% of Bonn
48 Finn of fiction
49 Home planet in a 1978–82 sitcom
50 Arbor leader
51 Game with a break
53 Muscle spasms
55 Filmmaking area
56 "Very impressive"
57 Lobby plant
59 Velvet ending
60 Freshwater ducks
61 Cry to a plow horse
62 Cautionary sign
65 Baseball's "Little Giant" (with 72-A)
67 Shape of Beldar's head
68 Confronted boldly
70 Place for a stroll
73 Where a frog croaks
74 Kidney-related
75 Humanities subj.
76 Praiseful poem
77 Alias, initially
79 Reagan's Secretary of State
80 Shakes an Etch A Sketch
81 Important exam
82 Sophomoric
83 Aviation pioneer Cessna
84 Ticked off
86 Marketing device
87 Posture-perfect
88 Fistfight
91 MasterCard rival
95 "My turn"
96 H, to Homer
97 Convention rep.
98 Identify, in a way
99 Org. that banned ephedra

189 SUBMISSION OMISSION by Bonnie L. Gentry
. . . also "Twelve" and "Thirteen." (See 39 Across)

ACROSS

1 Musical family name
7 The house of Hernando
13 Women's soccer star Michelle
18 One who gets it on?
19 Studebaker sports car
20 Deep-___ (threw away)
21 Golfer Garcia
22 Put down
23 1992 Nicholson role
24 **Start of a quip**
27 "It's for you," on a ltr.
29 D-day invasion site
30 Stat that's better if it's lower
31 State next to Miss.
32 "Vox populi, vox ___"
33 "Boola Boola" collegian
34 "Cheers" star
37 I, to Einstein
39 Matt in "Ocean's Eleven"
42 "Coming to America" prince
44 Online matchmaker
46 **More of quip**
51 67.5°
52 Offshore driller
53 Prey for a bully
54 SALT signatory
57 Blow the whistle
60 16-year-old's desire
61 Gormé ice-cream?
62 Light red?
63 Car-suspension pieces
67 Memnon's mother
69 **More of quip**
75 More than some
76 Prolonged pain
77 Barbershop item
79 Society newbie
80 Colorful stickers
84 Carrier for people who go Dutch

86 Beehive State athlete
87 Luau chow
89 PC key beside the space bar
90 Pretext
91 Romanov dynasty member
92 **End of quip**
97 Source of morphine
98 Become disenchanted with
99 "You got that right!"
102 Reagan's attorney general
103 Scrutinizing (with "over")
104 Have an address
105 Big Bertha's birthplace
106 Takes potshots
107 Courtesy car

DOWN

1 Stinging remarks?
2 "Told ya!"
3 Like some Canadian provinces
4 "Phantom of the Opera" prop
5 "Doc" Simon
6 Be half asleep
7 Feminine
8 Dispatch boat
9 "Never Be You" singer
10 Archeologist's handle
11 Comedian Wright
12 Helping hands
13 Pasty-faced
14 Plains tribe
15 Flaked off
16 Defiant of authority
17 Mt. Rushmore setting

25 Attorney modifier
26 Great Leap Forward name
27 Say further
28 Cheek glistener
34 Mazar in "GoodFellas"
35 Organic radical
36 Jarrett of Nascar
38 Steers the steers
40 Like the bogey man?
41 "Ladders to Fire" novelist
43 Tokyo, to shoguns
45 Patronizes, in a way
47 Evoking goose bumps
48 Parabolic path
49 Long in "Soul Food"
50 Long-necked wader
54 "¿Como esta ___?"

55 Hats popularized by Lincoln
56 They're important
58 "Desperate Housewives" airer
59 Third of October?
64 Shrinking sea of Asia
65 Board events: Abbr.
66 Start of many Brazilian city names
68 Raised-eyebrow remarks
70 "The Spanish Tragedy" dramatist
71 Vague notions
72 1938 DuPont invention
73 Relies on
74 Theta–kappa go-between
78 For each one

81 Take in takeout
82 Items for those seeking closure?
83 When shadows almost disappear
85 1965 Temptations hit
88 Not available
90 It might be tapped
91 Oral Roberts University site
92 Capitol topper
93 Gathering clouds, say
94 Doctor Zhivago
95 Klutzy entrance
96 Land O'Lakes product
100 Citric quencher
101 "Get ___ Ya-Yas Out": Rolling Stones

190 ALL IN ONE   by Victor Fleming
The phrase at 78-D dates to 1959, but no one seems to know its origin.

ACROSS

1 Needing a wrap
5 Smudge genesis
12 Close tight
18 Skin aid
19 Car manufacturer, often
20 Levels
21 Dear thing?
23 Whispered words
24 Arrested
25 No opposites
26 Rough tools
27 On the surface
29 "Stand" band
31 Not continue
32 Drain
36 Blinker
41 ___ Gonçalo, Brazil
43 1926 "Boy Wonder"
45 "Don't come around here!"
46 Assert
48 On or about
49 Allen or McGraw
50 Western Amerind
51 Serving to punish
53 Some are gold
55 Royal ball
58 Austin and Little Rock attractions
65 Snicker syllable
66 "Lost Horizon" director
67 Pilgrim's destination
68 Firm member's abbr.
71 High-tech appt. book
74 Nigerian currency
76 ___ Flynn Boyle
77 They're not buying it
80 Put a value on
82 Gist
83 Court figure
85 Anesthetist
87 Surgery sites
88 RB's injured knee part, often
90 Short-order spots
93 Kool-Aid parent
96 Dos
100 "Honest"
101 Vent
103 "High" dialect
105 Slow down
106 Like "Vic and Sade," say
107 Mitsubishi models
108 Dark stones
109 Gun point?
110 Vindictive Olympian

DOWN

1 Kind of pants
2 Ersatz fat brand
3 Blackmore book
4 Yen
5 West ender?
6 "Are you kidding me?"
7 ". . . sting like ___"
8 ETS exams
9 Mouth
10 Candy brand
11 Trespass
12 Sautéing sound
13 Forever
14 Santa Anita Racetrack city
15 Metallica drummer Ulrich
16 Lone Star State sch.
17 Dabs
22 Afternoon hour
28 Guinness or Waugh
30 Drink served over cracked ice
31 Bewitch
33 "Where the ___ meet to eat"
34 Marta in "Sirocco"
35 ". . . plus plenty more"
37 VW model
38 Foggy Bottom school
39 It may be cocked
40 Boat rope
41 NFL tackle Warren
42 See 46 Across
44 Russian patron saint of students
47 Elutriate
52 More than a stretch
54 Monitor's demand
56 Hit head-on
57 Jacques of song
59 NY statesman Chauncey and family
60 "Out of the huts of history's shame ___": Angelou
61 Revealed
62 "The feeling's mutual"
63 Light tan
64 Swedish sedan
68 Summer hrs. in CT
69 Frat. counterpart
70 On the ___ vive
72 Juiceless
73 In the Pipeline
75 "It's ___ state of affairs!"
78 Everything (with "whole")
79 Like filet américain
81 Con game
84 Nancy Sinatra's pop in 1967
86 Adequate
89 "Mercy me!"
91 Severity
92 "My strong imagination ___ crown": Shak.
93 Corn-syrup brand
94 Nothing, in Nantes
95 Like Taos
97 "For ___ be Queen o' the May": Tennyson
98 Drill sergeant's command
99 Matching
102 Stats for P. Manning
103 Vest pocket
104 Pocket

191 IT'S AN OLD STORY by Jay Sullivan

The "way" at 23 Across is not recommended in the casinos.

ACROSS

1 Month of VJ Day
4 Barely managing
9 School administration
13 Somewhat
17 Cold call
18 Esteem
19 Singles gp.
20 "Just Like Jesse James" singer
21 Degradation
23 One way to win at blackjack
24 Glazed fabric finish
25 Rapeseed oil
26 Act like
28 Rhetorical understatement
30 During winter?
34 Smart mouths
35 Button decoration
36 X-ray, e.g.
38 Does doilies
41 Social service
42 JFK tenant
43 Leonard ___ (Roy Rogers)
46 Da Gama's gold
47 Becoming fearless?
52 Cinco de Mayo, e.g.
53 Debussy's "___ and Melisande"
55 Washington posts
56 Palette pigment
58 Palm Springs neighbor
59 What manicurists do for a living
60 Bikini, e.g.
61 Cringe in fear
62 Give it your best shot (with "out")
63 Stick out
65 Faulkner's "___ Lay Dying"
66 Liberace's wardrobe?
69 Pierre's, e.g.
70 Matchmaker Dolly
72 Mr. Anderson in "The Matrix"
73 Not done
74 Rx items
75 Price of admission
79 Wipe the slate clean
81 French border region
83 Regular churchgoers?
88 Unpleasant
90 Gulager in "Touched by Love"
91 These days
92 Bummer
93 Hardly ever
95 Social entertainments
98 Perry's progenitor
99 Tom Clancy hero
100 Practical joke
101 Power Spike?
102 Eye, for one
103 Studio gig
104 Maneuvers through muck
105 Beast of burden

DOWN

1 Low-tech calculators
2 Like some legends
3 Steinway model
4 Speed-reading trainer Wood
5 Erotic Indian writing
6 Notre Dame setting
7 "Sound of Music" extra
8 Do so-so on the final
9 Birthplace of Elvis Presley
10 GPS heading
11 Bush supporter
12 Catches something
13 Buttonholes
14 Realtor how-to show?
15 Cliff dwelling
16 Slip cover
22 Takes a bath
27 PAC man
29 Fleming of fiction
31 Crunchy munchies
32 Diamond defect
33 Lacks faith
37 Maxwell Smart foe
38 Of current interest
39 Gritty
40 Recited Chaucer?
44 Gave in
45 Like an elephant seal
47 Conductor Solti
48 "Love Boat" bartender
49 "Jurassic Park" actor
50 California winemaker
51 "Mairzy ___"
54 It's not to be believed
57 NBA position
59 Doze
62 Mottled soil
63 Butler's bride
64 In tears
67 Official, in a way
68 Not kosher
71 Raging
74 Israel Philharmonic director
76 1999 AT&T takeover
77 Tertiary epoch
78 Architectural afterthought
80 Library shelves
81 Long range
82 "Casablanca" actor
84 They're waste-full
85 Gal's date
86 "___ Gold" (Fonda film)
87 Splits (a cell)
89 Celtic New-Age singer
94 Mr. Tinkles, for one
96 WWW destination
97 Santos saint

192 "VEGAN LIFE" INTERVIEW by Richard Silvestri
Solve this one on November 1 (World Vegan Day).

ACROSS

1 Breaks out
8 Splinter groups
13 Professor Higgins' pupil
18 Produce vocal sounds
19 By oneself
20 "Two Women" star
21 Constituent of chalk
22 "The Lady or the ___?": Stockton
23 Spurious
24 **"May I interview you for the local pepper?"**
27 Cobb and Hardin
28 Quick plane trip
29 Tallahassee's county
30 Place for a sock?
33 Hologram creator
36 More than mislead
38 Stereo's predecessor
39 Amnesiac's loss
42 Compadre
43 Storybook elephant
44 **"I yam told you're quitting due to pay issues"**
50 Point at the table
51 Low area
52 Go downhill fast
53 Chewed up
54 Show in the credits
55 Civil-suit subject
56 Nile nipper
59 "Gorgeous George" of baseball
61 Neighbor of Twelve Oaks
62 Objecting to
63 **"Do you carrot all about finding another job?"**
68 End of a Garbo line
69 Get the bronze?
70 Minks' kin
71 Santa makes one
72 Chaff
75 Gives a darn
77 Rug rat
78 Aretha's music
79 Jungle dwelling
80 Like the Beatles
83 **"I have to beet it. Thanks for the interview"**
89 Like a canard
92 More ignoble
93 Slow tempo
94 Send to Siberia
95 Rare air
96 Brandy cocktail
97 Dissuade
98 Slender
99 Adenoids' neighbors

DOWN

1 Orlando attraction
2 Insecure
3 Pension perks
4 Buoy attachment?
5 Well adjunct
6 Equivalent of -ita
7 Get agitated
8 Became attentive
9 Big production
10 Confine
11 High range
12 Sesame, for one
13 Pixyish
14 Citi offering
15 Ruffle feathers
16 The mark of Zorro
17 Clause connector
25 Rocky peak
26 Gumby's pal
30 Fit together
31 Place of worship?
32 Lean and sinewy
33 Nasser, for one
34 It's sold by the yard
35 Subservient
36 Give odds
37 Things to be cured
38 Rembrandt contemporary
39 Mrs. Tom Hanks
40 Radiate
41 Chaplin prop
42 Historic beginning?
43 Better than better
45 "My Eyes Adored You" singer
46 Novelist Glasgow
47 Eight-based
48 Fingerprint feature
49 Museum VIP
54 Orthodontist's concern
56 Mother of George I
57 Cookbook direction
58 Dillies
59 ___ packing (dismissed)
60 Mil. units
61 Sold(i)er material
62 Bachelor's interest?
63 Preserve, in a way
64 Mixed bag
65 Part of MVP
66 Isn't anymore
67 Versatile truck
72 Galas
73 Band material
74 Ointment ingredient
75 Eight fluid ounces
76 Cry of relief
78 Dogie's dad
79 Torment
80 Mold and mildew
81 Russian work collective
82 They make the rounds at Cheers?
83 Tropic locale
84 "Days of Grace" author
85 Requirement
86 Prefix with dermal
87 Point after deuce
88 Serif
89 G-man
90 Firefighting tool
91 Well-matched?

193 DOUBLE ENTENDRES   by Harvey Estes

The comic strip at 35-A was seen in newspapers from 1947 to 1969.

ACROSS

1 Cause trouble
6 "Lady Marmalade" singers
13 Hawkins of Dogpatch
18 Kind of phone?
19 Rampaging
20 Makes level
21 "Believe that life is ___ this optimism with others"
23 "Apocalypto" people
24 A word with you
25 "Boola Boola" collegian
26 What to do?
27 La Scala locale
28 Plain of Sharon locale
30 Capital punishments?
31 Commonly cited auth.
32 Not so great
33 Start for dollar or trash
35 Charles Harris Kuhn comic strip
38 "Contrary to popular belief many Great Danes can ___ actions show it"
43 Coors container
44 "What a relief!"
47 Hurdle for srs.
48 Brings up
49 Subject preceder
50 Zoo creatures
52 Literary pause
54 Puccini character
55 Like pandas
56 With virtue
57 Venetian locale
58 "Guys and Dolls" doll
59 Where to see shorts
60 In the swing
61 Type of history
62 Bridge call, informally
63 Outback hopper
64 Slo-mo replay subjects, often
65 Jacob's fifth son
66 "The prison's top teams got ___ were reserved for them"
70 Stuck it out
72 Dennis the Menace's dog
73 Nothing special
77 Med. choices
78 Call sign at McCarran Int.
81 Bearing
83 Be short with
85 Street blade
86 Traipse (about)
87 VIP in DC
88 Stinging
89 "Pretty women are ___ better in romance"
92 Hombre of the cloth
93 Tailor's bottom edge
94 Crude container
95 Pop singer Leo
96 Magazine store?
97 Wanting

DOWN

1 Have at
2 Soup or salad
3 String adjusters
4 Naval monogram
5 Check word
6 Anderson in "Three on a Date"
7 "What's more . . ."
8 Fortified place
9 Hawke in "Lord of War"
10 Let out and take in?
11 Merry escapades
12 Before, going either way
13 Round table
14 Toyota's flagship sedan
15 "We asked ___ to do a basketball movie"
16 Phrase before instant
17 Canadian pump name
22 Willing to listen
27 Tomei of "Alfie"
29 Hot flick?
30 Brother's title
34 Script ending
35 Singer with the Pacemakers
36 "Splash" creature
37 Discriminating types
39 "A Summer Place" star
40 "You wish!"
41 "Signs" band
42 Lugs
44 Apple-pie order
45 Late finisher
46 "Laurel came in out of the ___ followed"
49 Opening words of "Da Doo Ron Ron"
51 Teen hangout
52 Orders at Ben & Jerry's
53 Site of conflict
56 Hit a bonanza
57 Its player takes a bow
59 Most retiring
60 1941 Lon Chaney role
63 Flag thrower, at times
66 More extensive
67 Carhop employer
68 Heel
69 W-2 info
71 Man in the iron mask?
74 Marked down
75 Do a slow burn
76 Hard to get along with
78 Wedding seater
79 Pillow covers
80 Airplane seat option
82 Build an ell
83 Suckers
84 SEC overseer
86 Highlander
89 Half a dance
90 Some forensic evidence
91 "For shame!"

ACROSS

1 Little nipper
4 Bad memory
8 Kiss
12 "Porgy and Bess" role
17 WW2-era jacket
18 Basso's pitch
19 Blue dye
20 Male seal's domain
21 Dramatis ___
23 Road hog?
24 Perform community service, e.g.
25 Glossy footwear
28 Collation
31 Express distress
32 High-priced spread
33 Bryce Canyon locale
34 Pikachu's pal
36 Rochester's Jane
37 Vegas action
40 Kimmel and O'Brien
45 Ill will
47 Woods rival
48 Germany's Oscar
49 Fail to keep
51 Rose, in a way
52 Ambiance
53 "The Gladiator" set
55 Give way
56 Where to find a million dollar baby?
61 Ship bound for Colchis
62 Kobe cut
63 Vista picture
64 Prove otherwise
66 Clear finish?
67 "Wha hae?" says he
68 Once around the park
71 Lots of dough
73 Impose a long term
76 Roxy Music name
77 Cell: Comb. form
79 "___ Autumn" (1941 tune)
80 Muscat's onetime partner
81 Lt. Kojak's first name
82 Moreover
84 Stats factor
86 Poet laureate under Queen Victoria
92 Protozoa movers
93 Oklahoma city
94 USGA president (1976–77)
98 Familiar Chaplin role
99 "Agreed!"
100 Stick on the table
101 Ground breaker
102 Deciding opinion
103 Air France destination
104 Mr. Untouchable
105 Dominate

DOWN

1 Beaut
2 It's picked in Maui
3 Annum or diem opener
4 Ancient Greek promenades
5 Satisfied
6 Henry Gray's subj.
7 Film holder?
8 De Brunhoff's pachyderm
9 Kwanzaa principle
10 Turbaned Indian
11 Somnolent
12 Takes to task
13 Woodworking tool
14 Buck tag
15 Det. Sheppard of "Homicide"
16 Former Wal-Mart rival
22 Ottoman cavalry corps
26 Reiterate
27 Chophouse order
28 Take charge
29 Bibliography abbr.
30 Eucharist plates
34 Where Shannon Miller found gold
35 ___ Na Na
36 City on the Ruhr
37 Gnat, e.g.
38 Musician's study
39 Use a keyboard
41 Model-kit tube
42 Ring dances
43 Relax
44 Hied
46 Wesleyan College city
50 Leads on
52 Want no part of
54 Gold Cup race of England
56 Banned coolant
57 Nanook's digs
58 Hardly bright
59 Blackjack combo
60 In ___ (entirely)
61 Calvados cleric
65 Nickel-cigar name?
67 Bio, e.g.
68 Trumpmobile
69 Yonder
70 Submarine service sites
72 One-___ jack
74 9:50
75 Marion in "Bewitched"
78 City that lives by the sword?
81 Takes off fat
82 "Boston Legal" procedure
83 "___ enough . . ."
84 Downhill trails
85 Sunday paper sections
86 Book after John
87 Old Calabrian coin
88 Chew out
89 Nonpareil
90 It might read "OPEN"
91 Brown rival
95 Greek P
96 First gear
97 Hankering

SNAP JUDGMENTS by Victor Fleming
Judge Vic thought up this one while in camera.

ACROSS

1 Some count by this
5 River pollutant
8 Booth or Forrest
13 "___ denied" (Supreme Ct. note)
17 Isle of exile
18 Organ with a drum
19 Migratory goose
20 Pulitzer winner James
21 **Start of a Chinese proverb (with "A")**
24 Bradshaw's coach at Pittsburgh
25 Off the table?
26 2005 Prince hit
27 J. Major and T. Blair, e.g.
28 Big name in canned tomatoes
29 SASE part
30 Hardly on a roll
33 Old photos
34 Will in "The Waltons"
35 **Start of a Kafka quote**
37 Kafka novel (with "The")
40 Boston Red or Chicago White
41 Jury leaders
42 Break the bank?
43 Norse "headland"
44 Blitzed
46 Carl Zeiss namesake
47 Tyler in "Stealing Beauty"
48 Bronze finishes?
49 Identify
52 Brazilian macaw
53 **More of Kafka quote**
55 Pale pint
56 Bare peak
57 James Michener book
58 Sub in a tub, e.g.
59 Fashion
60 Ruben in "Disorganized Crime"
61 IRA part
62 Tax type
63 Lucky made man?
66 Pixar collectible
67 Pooh pal
68 **End of Kafka quote**
71 Cookie seen in "Rounders"
72 Island birthplace of Joan Baez
73 Brother-sister dance team
75 Bucks center
78 Shaped like a funnel
79 Butt end
80 Two-piece piece
81 From the top
83 Common links
84 **End of Chinese proverb**
87 Ill-gotten gains
88 Active people
89 ___ Friday's
90 Dressing cheese
91 Grass bristles
92 Wild time
93 Head lines?
94 Huffy

DOWN

1 Fox shelter
2 González of 2000 headlines
3 "Deal or No Deal" airer
4 Stuff to the gills
5 Part of MPG
6 Sid in "Silent Movie"
7 Lively
8 "Charlotte's Web" auth.
9 "Enough!"
10 Sun product
11 Stats for P. Manning
12 High degree
13 Like enclosed cockpits
14 Prima-donna trait
15 Let go of
16 Rats out
22 Wes of the '69 Bullets
23 Tachygraphers
28 Slip
31 Miss-named
32 Turtle type
33 Weather-related absence
34 Pontiac muscle cars
36 "___ more than you'll ever know!"
37 Uncommon major
38 Oldsmobile sedan
39 Source of waves at sea
40 Forbidding
43 Words for a pet pup
44 Key letter
45 Horizontal door piece
47 Kahlil Gibran's homeland
48 New Deal corp.
49 Italian soccer great Rossi
50 Like many statesmen
51 Birds that bear down
53 Like pupils at times
54 "___ for Innocent": Grafton
59 Celebrated clinic
60 Some H.S. lab exams
61 Conditions, in a way
62 Go up and down
63 Milan landmark
64 As of this moment
65 Moët's bubbly partner
66 B.J. Hunnicut's rnk.
67 18th Spanish letter
69 Bacon slice
70 On solid ground
71 Color of Saturn's Titan
74 Itching for a fight
75 Film producer Ponti
76 Bird that bears down
77 Come next
79 On the apex of
82 Oodles
84 Magazine features
85 Kind of tax
86 "___ a Pony": Beatles

196 WRITIN' TO THE CORE by Patrick Jordan
Russell Lynes wrote the "After Hours" column for "Harper's Magazine."

ACROSS

1 Form a scab
5 Amazes
9 Hardly hardy
14 Pegs via DNA, say
17 Harvestable
18 Extinct pigeon relative
19 Monetary gain
20 Complied with
21 **Start of a quip by Russell Lynes**
25 Franciscan friar Junípero
26 Fouled (up)
27 Quick-cooking noodles
28 Lags behind
30 Transmits
31 Horned toad, for one
32 Ate heartily
34 Marked men?
36 Whodunit discovery
39 Brokerage billings
40 They think swill is swell
41 "Scooby-Doo, Where ___ You?"
42 "Way cool!"
43 Rent-strike participant
45 Mike Brady's firstborn
49 Goose egg
50 Eon components
52 Parking valet's venue
53 See 40 Down
54 **Middle of quip**
59 Mournful verse
60 Four-pointer, in bridge
61 Adams in "The Apartment"
62 Mess or press follower
63 Makeover
64 Frisco squad
67 Site of a tryst in "Carmen"
68 Afflicted
69 Altoids alternative
70 ___ erat demonstrandum
72 Bitsy beginner
73 Distance oneself (from)

77 Bivouac shelter
79 Unabashed
80 Metallurgy samples
81 Porky or Stymie, e.g.
85 Cultivation location
86 Outscores
89 Expression of empathy
90 **End of quip**
93 Set ablaze
94 Display conspicuously
95 Quaint expletive
96 In the event that
97 "You called?"
98 Mason's surveying partner
99 Weakening effect
100 Turns blue jeans green

DOWN

1 Cardinal topper
2 Largest human gland
3 Impresario's production
4 Fill with fright
5 Dictionary abbr.
6 Wines and dines
7 School
8 Most contrite
9 Diamond detractions
10 "No peeking," in hide-and-seek
11 Trans-fatty ___
12 Treasury Dept. agcy.
13 Choose to overlook
14 Bo Diddley classic
15 "Lawrence of Arabia" setting
16 Stomachs
22 Nathan Hale's alma mater
23 Potsie, to the Fonz
24 Filminess

29 Tanzania trek
31 Stage legend Alfred
33 Limousine, for instance
34 Envelop in cloth
35 Solder component
36 Marching-band identifier
37 Hanging-nester
38 Examined in detail
40 Rose Red's sister (with 53-A)
42 Hinge (upon)
44 Eddie Munster's pet snake
45 4, on a phone
46 High roller's advice
47 Emulates Amazon
48 How to hold an infant
51 Crude dwelling
53 "___ Irish eyes are smiling . . ."
55 Self-love
56 Crowns a cupcake
57 Dumbbell

58 It may fly up a flue
64 Slender amphibian
65 S&L offering
66 Protested like a piglet
69 Examined eggs the old-fashioned way
71 Steal the scene from
72 "Brrr!"
73 Without harm
74 Mrs. Ed Norton
75 Puts up
76 Whey-faced
77 Make ready
78 Unworldly one
80 A lot
82 Melodious Mariah
83 Achieve prominence
84 Riga residents
86 Trois preceder
87 "Within" prefix
88 Glance over
91 Spartacus' 61
92 Apr. hrs. in Atlanta

197
GOING THROUGH THE MOTIONS by Fran & Lou Sabin

Historians tell us 85-A did not originate that quote — John Soule did.

ACROSS

1 Spice Girls hit
5 Judge's perch
9 Victorian, e.g.
12 On location
17 Shiny fabric
18 Track great Zatopek
19 Took the point
20 One and all
21 Islamic leader
22 Songstress Simone
23 Zoot suit, e.g.
24 Where to get down
25 Alcott teen
26 Stock option?
29 Tar's attention-getter
31 Bronze component
32 Smoke glass
33 Drop by
36 Gumby creator Clokey
37 Noon-to-midnight, say
41 "Stardust" novelist Fannie
42 Resort amenity
43 Indochina, once
44 Mine yield
45 Literary collection
46 Don't roll through this
48 Zaps
50 Tropical hazard
53 ___ Darya (Aral Sea feeder)
54 Salad ingredieent
55 Hesitatation waltzer's query
59 Litmus-test result
62 Ready for delivery
63 Many a John Wayne film
67 High-strung
68 Erupts in applause
71 Quilting session
72 Shelley creation
73 Dash off
74 Realtor's abbr.
75 Kishke
77 Masur and Bernstein
80 Waltz move
81 "Dig in!"
82 Graphite
83 Wrestling victory
84 Painter Chagall
85 Horace Greeley's advice
90 Ryan Seacrest, for one
94 Plumed avian
95 Miss the boat
96 Take in
97 In a bad way
98 Shore ___
99 Wine factor
100 Christening or bar mitzvah
101 Close in
102 Plains home
103 Gypsy bread?
104 Skirt feature
105 Dancer in a cage

DOWN

1 Concrete pouring
2 Break, in a way
3 Drop
4 "Well, maybe"
5 Robby in "One on One"
6 Peaceful relations
7 Barcelona tot
8 Hogwash
9 Puckish
10 Paper purchase, perhaps
11 "New" family member
12 "Scat!"
13 Ducks
14 Turf accountant's ledger item?
15 Blarney talk?
16 Salon specialist
27 Chick ___
28 McCarver and McGraw
30 Long-time runner
33 Phony bit
34 Albacore
35 Doctoral hurdle
36 Cpl.'s address
37 Touch base, in a way
38 Come down in buckets
39 Tuscany river
40 Peeper's digs
42 ER imperative
43 Wedding wheels
46 Aragon affirmative
47 Fills to bursting
48 Falls down
49 Easy pace
51 Middle of a Latin trio
52 Dominate
54 Street ___
56 Superstars
57 Bird food
58 Night people
59 Energy source
60 Castor's mother
61 Tibia neighbor
64 Spain's second largest river
65 Scale notes
66 "That's cool!"
68 Blimp name
69 Painful situations
70 Devilish type
73 Teacher's pest
75 June bug
76 Dürer design
78 Pajama part
79 One caught in the ACT?
80 Cacophony
81 Web-footed seabird
83 Sieved fruit
84 Scottish singer Pellow
85 Moolah
86 Architectural molding
87 Taco or chalupa
88 Wing-ding
89 Spam
91 Jam substitute
92 Smeltery refuse
93 Rookie

198

"IS THAT AWL YOU GOT?" by Tucker Smith
It's tough to punch holes in this tight construction.

ACROSS

1 Potshot
5 Genesis twin
9 TV talk-show pioneer
13 "Check this out!"
17 Buffalo's lake
18 Chem. and bio.
19 Regarding
20 Encumbrance
21 Place in a Redford film
22 San José's land
24 Long and lean
25 Warning about a bad cop?
28 Jeweler's tool
29 Mass. setting
30 Puck slapper
31 Kidman in "The Hours"
34 Shellacking
37 Zeedonk's father
40 Called Hamilton from the deep South?
44 Drops from above
45 "You betcha!"
46 Lea lady
47 Little bit
49 Cards at a reading
50 Neb. neighbor
51 Horse operas
54 Orchestra members
56 Hit the road after closing the bar?
59 Spots
62 Favorite hangouts
63 Flesh and blood
66 Hersey setting
67 Hours in a Saturn day
70 Sault ___ Marie
71 Common mixer
72 Winter woe
73 Eddie cried?
77 Susan Lucci role
79 "Time" 2005 Person of the Year
80 Plummer in "Pulp Fiction"
81 Social class
83 Tenderfoot's org.
86 Elbow-bender
87 Hardly a spread-eagle fowl?

94 It's true
95 Commemo-rating
96 Mask
97 Horse course
98 "So long, Mario!"
99 Boyfriend
100 "Baby Doll" director Kazan
101 Eight bits
102 Jack, once of HUD
103 Succeed at pitching
104 Blended-family prefix

DOWN

1 Grievance
2 Museo holdings
3 Lovely Beatles girl
4 Try harder
5 Richard Kimble, for one
6 Refuse transport
7 Safeway way
8 "¿Como esta ___?"
9 Bad scores for Tiger
10 "Tell me another one!"
11 Not marked up
12 Affront-filled fete
13 Blue-collar job?
14 Sites for quick bites
15 Done for
16 Sound of reproval
23 Elroy's pooch
26 Hang loose
27 Daffy Dean's bro
31 Neighbor of Mont.
32 La Douce of the screen
33 City of NW France
35 Giant outfielder
36 Hagen in "Reversal of Fortune"
38 Profusion

39 Aardvark prey
41 Can't stand
42 ___ 'Pea of "Popeye"
43 "Dead ___": Dick Francis
48 "Touched by an Angel" star
49 Stocking parts
51 "Beetle Bailey" dog
52 A word with you?
53 U.
55 Short order, for short
56 Shore sculpture
57 Talk like Harvey Fierstein
58 Wordsmith: Abbr.
59 "Chantilly ___": Big Bopper
60 Dump emanation
61 Tortie
63 Rhein port

64 Fingered, briefly
65 Zapata "zip"
68 Punk music genre
69 Sister
71 Fabric samples
74 Gotham City hero
75 Blushing
76 Mine, to Maurice
78 Venom source
79 Kippah
82 Take in
84 Persnickety people
85 See eye to eye
87 Deep blue
88 "I'm Your Man" duo
89 Ankh feature
90 Frosty's eyes
91 Bagpiper's wear
92 Uma's "Be Cool" role
93 Tide type
94 Palm (off)

199

PROFESSOR'S LAMENT by Victor Fleming
And to think 61 Across was a high-school dropout.

ACROSS

1 Buffaloed
8 Swell remedy?
14 Mention
18 Designated driver's drink
19 ". . . ___ as a day in June?": Lowell
20 ___ d'oeuvres
21 Not bother
22 **Start of a John Irving quote**
24 Rand McNally blowup
26 Related
27 Source of danger
28 Praiseful poem penner
31 Victor's cry
33 Unigender
34 **More of quote**
37 Kind of headache
38 Yule quaff
39 Horse play?
40 Car loan fig.
41 Old but in
45 Hare with big feet
48 Says suddenly
50 Dashed
51 Greeting-card hugs
52 Victor's cry
53 In ___ (coordinated)
54 **More of quote**
60 May honorees
61 General Motors founder
62 Coastline feature
63 Geologic division
64 Famous fur family
65 Charge for a round
70 Protestant denom.
72 Selling well
73 Country in France
74 Takes too much, briefly
75 Follow advice
77 **More of quote**
80 Hobbyist
83 One-and-only
84 Hurt
85 Like "American Beauty"
86 ___ Lingus
87 Ritchie Valens song
90 **End of quote**
93 ___ point

97 Port near Mascara
98 "Consider the job done"
99 Check marks?
100 Cone makers
101 Place to find a Buddha
102 Does not perpetuate

DOWN

1 Manual lang.
2 Digital feature
3 Oklahoma town
4 Well-appointed
5 Willing to consider
6 Sounds of sorrow
7 SMS Graf
8 ___ "Kinda" suffix
9 Snap, e.g.
10 Stu of early TV
11 Road to Rostock
12 Coach Parseghian
13 Hamburger, e.g.
14 Umbrella inventors
15 Tiny bits
16 Jiffy
17 Robert Devereux's earldom
23 Takes exception
25 Proof of ownership
28 Fesses (up)
29 "Runaround Sue" singer
30 "Let ___!" ("Relax!")
32 Question starter
33 Buster, old-style
35 Supports
36 Likewise
37 Sudden burst
40 In flight
42 "___ Little Tenderness"
43 Heralded

44 Start of "The Raven"
46 Knocks the socks off
47 Bread, at times
48 Benefits
49 Russell in "Spider-Man 3"
52 Circulation director?
53 Ollie's chum
54 Hook hand
55 Cager's target
56 Old Atlanta arena
57 Fleming or Grisham
58 Sing like Crosby
59 You: Ger.
64 Give approval
65 Like some communities
66 Liquor in a shot
67 Chickens and turkeys
68 "What I Am" singer Brickell

69 Like budget amts.
71 Glossy fabrics
73 DC figure
76 Rutabaga, e.g.
77 Passionate
78 Is unable to
79 Break in the action
80 "The ___ the Fugue": Bach
81 Te Reo of New Zealand
82 Fragrance
83 "___ Evil" (Farrow film)
86 Spellbound
88 Caplet shape
89 Epithet
91 Gp. pledged to "do no harm"
92 Rwy. stop
94 Common connection
95 Sporty Volkswagen
96 Medical suffix

200 "TAKE MY (RE)WORD FOR IT!" by Jay Sullivan

The heroine at 34-A is more familiar to solvers than the one at 37-A.

ACROSS

1 Freddy Krueger's street
4 Bulgy battlers
9 Nigerian seaport
14 It may be carved in stone
17 Where Ipanema is
18 Take out lines
19 Skater Sokolova
20 E-mail address ending
21 Post bridge-party chore?
24 Grammy Award category
25 Pointed arch
26 First place
27 "Madama Butterfly" debuted here
29 Tax deduction, perhaps?
33 Beethoven dedicatee
34 "Doctor Zhivago" heroine
35 To be, in Cannes
36 You can sense it
37 "Clan of the Cave Bear" heroine
40 Just open
42 Work like a beaver
44 Much of Mongolia
47 Jupiter and Mars
48 Clancy hero
49 "Three cheers!"
52 It's a pleasure
53 Arab follower?
55 Foreign accent
57 Founder of drama
59 Came down hard
61 Some sitting ducks
63 Basic material
64 Sang like a bard
66 Siphon off
68 Learning centers
69 "Wheel of Fortune" request
70 Took a cruise
72 Has a bawl
74 Palindromic pharaoh
75 Rushed headlong
77 Island ring
78 Pained expression
79 Cobra kin
80 Coop group
82 Joseph's uncle
85 Common rhyme scheme
87 French film award
89 Response to a break in the dike?
94 Obsolete
97 Behave like an ass
98 It takes two
99 Where "Arliss" was first seen
100 "Tidal wave coming!", e.g.?
104 Hang out to dry
105 Melos marketplace
106 It's not free of charge
107 Lincoln center?
108 Born, in bios
109 Out of order
110 Ratted on, perhaps
111 Yellow Monopoly bill

DOWN

1 One way to get to first base
2 Lord of the manor
3 Air base (musically)
4 Australian Open winner Williams
5 Big server
6 Welcome sight
7 Milo in "Ulysses"
8 More dilapidated
9 Horseshoe score
10 Mass apparel
11 Physicist Murray ___-Mann
12 Ground-floor apartment
13 Got smart
14 Sewing job?
15 They're adorable
16 Cocoons' contents
22 Pharynx neighbor
23 Class action?
28 Plumbing problem
30 Sideless cart
31 Indian chief
32 Make over
36 1935 Triple Crown winner
37 Having a knack for
38 "Make up your mind!"
39 End of Prohibition?
41 Pre-med course
43 "The ___ of Survival": Trump
45 Hype
46 Puts one's foot down
48 Goes for a spin
49 Got wind of
50 Boomer Sooner's st.
51 "Jingle Bell Rock" singer
54 Net letters
56 Hand over
58 Go downhill fast
60 Mandel's on-air proposals
62 Spanish ayes
65 Random number generator
67 Without face value
71 Schubert song
73 She played Lilith on "Frasier"
76 "Zounds!"
78 Southern state
79 James ___ Garfield
81 Popular preacher
83 Underground network
84 Razor handle
86 Be there
87 Oscar-winning role for Cagney
88 Tony-winning revue of 1978–79
90 Serengeti laugher
91 Put on
92 Say "yes"
93 Bus fare
95 Buster Brown's pooch
96 They're big in Hollywood
101 Difference between EST and PST
102 Grand Canyon view site
103 Courtroom anonym

201 CENTERPIECE by Harvey Estes
An award-winning challenger by an elite enigmatist.

ACROSS

1 Woodworking tool
5 "I missed the birdie putt, but made ___"
9 Jamaican cultist
14 Rambler maker
18 Switch partner
19 One of the Dixie Chicks
20 Digital dealings
21 "Lo!" on the Po, long ago
22 Wrist bone
23 Spouse of 28 Down
24 Pass out
25 Very revealing photo
26 CENTERPIECE
30 Word to a nag
31 TLC specialists
32 Deducted from gross weight
33 CENTERPIECE
39 Kentucky Derby winner ___ Lee
42 Fruity drinks
43 Corporate department
44 Chewed the scenery
46 Private plane
49 Starts a paragraph
51 Risk taker's challenge
52 Trombonist Winding
53 "Braveheart" group
55 ___ the air (uncertain)
57 Gumshoe
58 Fictional falcon's home
59 Came together
60 Visitor to Siam
61 CENTERPIECE (with 64-Across)
64 See 61-Across
66 Saturn sedans
67 Ten-gallon, for one
68 Figure skater Lutz
69 Cross word
70 On the spot
71 Let out
72 Grille protector
75 Key signature with 4 sharps
77 Mouthy sort
83 Soap, e.g.
85 Pertain
86 Philosopher Diderot
87 The munchies, e.g.
88 Result of a charge
89 CENTERPIECE
95 Base horn
97 Nth deg.
98 Cry out for
99 CENTERPIECE
107 Coventry cleaner
108 American-born Japanese
109 Wooer's dozen
110 Tittle
111 Writer Sarah ___ Jewett
112 It's played at the ballpark
113 What a model strikes
114 Container that sounds nasty?
115 Thigh muscle
116 For ___ (cheap)
117 Whiskey purchase
118 Precollege education

DOWN

1 Verge on
2 "Broken Bridge and the Dream" artist
3 Ointment element
4 Maine, to Monet
5 Explosive containing TNT
6 It's bright red in autumn
7 Der ___ (Adenauer)
8 Reuben ingredient
9 Attach again
10 Rose oil: Var.
11 Told
12 Navy destroyer, slangily
13 Take out, perhaps
14 Like a close neighbor
15 Plot piece
16 Lying lion of film
17 Attention-getting shout
19 ___-Sketch (drawing toy)
27 "How adorable!"
28 Frère de la mère
29 One at court
33 Negative stat for a quarterback
34 It's highly thought of?
35 He loved Lucy
36 Shape of a sink trap
37 IRS info
38 Suffix with sex
40 Tall Sicilian smoker
41 Mocha inhabitant
44 They may be limited
45 Transfer
47 March Madness org.
48 Playing with a full deck
49 All worked up
50 Recap
54 What a rampager goes on
56 Positive thinking proponent
58 British sports cars
60 Biblical transport
61 Roughage
62 Gadded about
63 Take a deep breath
65 Nick's evening?
70 Place to feel a jet stream?
72 Shuttlecock
73 Go ape
74 Yank, for one
76 Talked nonsense
78 Mont. neighbor
79 Making the transition
80 Organic compounds
81 Busy department in December
82 Naval characters
84 Stocking problem
89 Some pens
90 "C'mon!"
91 At the same time (with "in")
92 Double-check
93 Angel portrayer Della
94 Childcare writer LeShan
96 Salami type
99 Finished, in short
100 Mandlikova of tennis
101 Spare
102 Kachina doll maker
103 Not recorded
104 Recipe direction
105 Orrin Hatch's state
106 West African country
107 Chicken, à la française

202 WINNERS by Harvey Estes
"Winners never quit and quitters never win."

ACROSS

1 "Nothing to lose any sleep over"
10 Dramatic dagger-clutcher
17 Country of Ft. Sumter
20 1967 NASA disaster
21 Trading places
22 Solo in space
23 Winner over "The Aviator"
25 Québec comrade
26 Chemical ending
27 "ER" personnel
28 Zadora of "Butterfly"
29 Rugged chains
31 One thing after another
33 Thick-headed fastener
37 Have high hopes
38 Mafia boss
39 Like most TV models
41 Oliver Twist's request
42 Winner over "The Remains of the Day"
47 Tiny bit
48 Cop's contacts
51 Some salon workers
53 Lobe warmers
54 What big eaters do
58 Incentive symbols
61 Was partisan
62 Highway hello
66 Square peg in a round hole
67 "Arabian Nights" name
68 Winner over "Pulp Fiction"
70 St. Pete's state
71 Rainier country
74 Interstate stop
75 Like the Tower of Pisa
77 Sign of a slip
79 Shopper's bag
80 Neil Diamond song
82 Chewed out
85 Hair weavers
86 Civil suffix
88 Winner over "The Green Mile"
93 Lies down on the job?
95 Light work
96 Ex or sub follower
99 El Greco, by birth
102 Cruise's "The ___ Money"
103 Crime jobs
106 Woke up
108 The NCAA Trojans
109 Dean's singing partner
110 Long in code
111 Frost's bite
112 Winner over "The Thin Red Line"
118 ___ Aviv
119 Airport event
120 Got off at the depot
121 U-turn from NNW
122 Bill deadline
123 Praise singers

DOWN

1 Blabs, when doubled
2 Spoke one's mind
3 Matador's jacket
4 Kind of will
5 Move without effort
6 Places for peepholes
7 Many, many moons
8 To boot
9 Conductor Stokowski
10 Mixture
11 Physician's org.
12 Revival technique
13 Go for floating apples
14 Historic spans
15 Legbone
16 Grant's successor
17 Winner over "Reds"
18 O'Hara's "Appointment in ___"
19 Ouzo flavoring
24 Kind of suit
30 Turntable meas.
32 Boot part
33 Lady birds
34 ___ Arann airline
35 Part of MIT
36 Leslie Caron title role
39 Connects with
40 Armed Forces VIP
43 Wrapped up
44 With it
45 Passport feature
46 Hatcher of "Desperate Housewives"
48 Halvah ingredient
49 Customize
50 Winner over "The Elephant Man"
52 B&O and Reading
54 "You Don't Own Me" singer
55 Boom source
56 "___ die for!"
57 Absent from
59 Agriculturist
60 They're blue on Election Day
63 Bear of a Bruin
64 Nasty sort
65 Datebook heading
68 Discussion venue
69 Bay of Bengal port
72 Enzyme ending
73 Bay of Pigs location
75 ___ were
76 Get ready for company
78 Barely manages (with "out")
81 Bardot bathed in it
83 "The Little Mermaid" prince
84 Flintstones' pet
85 Grievance
86 Chants
87 Hangs back
89 Animation unit
90 Not too many
91 Tend with tenderness
92 Rich fabric
94 "Fifth Beatle" Sutcliffe
97 Made over
98 Less yellow
100 Former leader of Syria
101 Kind of jacket
103 Capital near the pyramids
104 Yearly account
105 Throws off
107 Virginia of Roanoke Island
109 Joan of rock
113 Josh around
114 Green spacewalk?
115 Was in session
116 T. follower
117 Abner's adjective

203 LOSERS by Harvey Estes
"Show me a good loser, and I'll show you a loser." — Vince Lombardi

ACROSS

1 Precipitation pellets
5 Woodworking machine
10 Silver screen features
15 God of the Canaanites
19 Money-object bridge
20 Perfectionist's aim
21 Digital dinosaur
22 Hollywood canine
23 Chiang Kai-___
24 Dame predecessor
25 Beatles' drummer
26 Is unlike Peter Pan
27 Loser to "Shakespeare in Love"
31 Western Hemisphere gp.
32 Poet's before
33 Just a bit
34 Greedy people
35 In the dumps
37 Spiff (up)
39 Record spiral
42 Pelts
43 Loser to "A Beautiful Mind"
46 Explosive star
47 Big accounts
50 ___ many words
51 Required readings, at times
55 Teheran dwellers
57 Wild thing
60 Wear down
61 Flip-flop, e.g.
62 Modern TV family member
64 Monkey suit, briefly
65 Couples' org.
66 **What these losers lost**
70 Mag. leafs
71 Courtroom VIPs
72 Hammer and Spade
73 Eradicate
76 Greek P's
78 Fly in the tropics
79 Administers the oath of office to
81 Tap-dancing without taps
83 Face defacer
85 Jaw pairs
86 Pitcher Hideo ___
87 Loser to "Forrest Gump"
92 Caterpillar competitor
94 Adjust for
95 Confirmation, for one
99 "Animal Farm" pen
101 Buck heroine
102 Celt or Highlander
104 FDR program
105 Might
106 Loser to "The Lord of the Rings: The Return of the King"
111 Instant-replay cameras, for short
113 Fast on one's feet
114 Madonna title role
115 Even start
116 Wolfe of fiction
117 Trunk without a lock
118 Mounted
119 Sly stratagem
120 Annoys
121 Barbeque accessories
122 Excalibur, notably
123 Look curiously

DOWN

1 Snake sounds
2 Key by B
3 Words after well
4 Trickster of myth
5 Specialized speeches
6 Make one's own
7 Four-sided figures
8 Mata ___
9 Mountain stat.
10 Ford subcompact
11 One, for one
12 Storytellers
13 Crèche figure
14 "Vamoose!"
15 Ovine entreaty
16 Loser to "Titanic"
17 Base command
18 Burns' misses
28 Mediterranean capital
29 Per
30 Like four Koufax games
36 Fix firmly
38 Kenya neighbor
40 Els, e.g.
41 "Deep Space Nine" character
44 Sturgeon steerer
45 Sandra's "Speed" costar
46 Wallace of "E.T."
47 Liza, to Lorna
48 Oklahoma native
49 Loser to "Chicago"
52 "Son of Frankenstein" role
53 Foundation figure
54 Application question
56 Vatican vestment
57 Malice
58 St. Louis landmark
59 Vintners' vessels
62 Leave in the text
63 Work of art
67 Standard Oil spin-off
68 Kind of cycle
69 Mag. execs
70 Sorrowful sound
71 Highest deg. holders
74 French chef's shout
75 Suffix with lion
77 Mall constituent
78 Howe'er
79 With concealed identity
80 Take home after taxes
82 Test the air
83 Continent of Syr.
84 Op. ___
88 Hardest on the eyes
89 Basic shelters
90 Cool off like a boxer
91 Drogheda locale
92 Part of A.D.
93 Desk drawer item
96 Rarer than rare
97 Rile up
98 Detroit Pistons legend Bob
100 Some studios
101 Cheri of "Park"
103 Millionaire on the Titanic
107 Babe's brunch
108 Rules, for short
109 State positively
110 U. of Maryland athlete
112 "___ yer old man!"

"ARE SO!" by Stella Daily and Bruce Venzke
19-Across gave Harrison Ford bullwhip lessons for his Indiana Jones role.

ACROSS

1 Org. for a TV actor
6 Snazzy Camaro
10 ___-pitch softball
13 Notre Dame won one for him in 1928
19 Lash in "King of the Bullwhip"
20 Romance author Roberts
21 Greetings in the 'hood
22 Brooks Robinson was one
23 Late-morning meal for QB Tom?
26 They spice up tacos
27 "Sweet" girl of song
28 Do this and you'll get burned?
30 It's believing
32 Ned Rorem opus
33 Coup d'___
34 "This massage feels great!"
36 Goes to pot?
39 Manx "thanks"
42 Gaming-table fabric
45 Six-sided state
46 2001 American Airlines purchase
49 "Poppy" star
53 X-ray ___ (binary-star class)
55 Corny exercise motto?
58 Was really offensive?
60 Netman's footwear, familiarly
61 Info near the calorie count
62 NYC's Tappan ___ Bridge
63 Runs, TV-wise
65 Channel owned by SHO
66 Show a preference for
68 Irrigation method: Step 1?
72 Stop a torte action?
74 Of the small intestine
75 Parseghian of coaching fame
76 1977 Indy 500 winner
77 Daytona refueling area
78 Racy diarist
79 They go on and on
81 Tours with a big-name band
86 Bewitching Ben & Jerry's product?
90 65-year-old, often

91 "The Lover in Me" singer Easton
92 "I've got it!"
93 Pulitzer winner for "Picnic"
95 Insulting
96 Short-finned shark
98 Least colorful
100 It may be dropped in squares
101 Part of a farmer's plot
104 Shaquille of the NBA
108 Get better once more
111 Jubilee food request?
116 Spooked steeds
119 Lemmon to Matthau, often
120 Harvest from a secret garden?
122 Tame one's bushy eyebrows
123 Duran Duran album
124 Good way to have it
125 Prince Valiant's kingdom
126 Hawked
127 Pound's preposition
128 Convicted CIA spy of 1994
129 Pumped up in the press

DOWN

1 Claudia ___ Taylor Johnson
2 Saudi king (1982–2005)
3 Ent coverup?
4 Belarus currency
5 Dwelling in the clouds
6 Contract for some servants of old
7 Orbison who sang "Pretty Woman"
8 Eyes, poetically
9 Country-club rental
10 Ecclesiastical lawmakers
11 Sondra in "Sudden Impact"
12 Ice Cube's real first name
13 "Golly gee!"
14 "Dies ___"
15 Thief
16 Suppose to be true
17 One of Jupiter's moons
18 Bowler's button
24 Pianist Fuleihan
25 Author of "Mila 18"
29 Sm. dosage amount
31 "Beat it!"
34 "Chiquitita" group
35 High, in Le Havre
37 Suffix of ethnicity
38 Quantum unit of light
40 Topic for George Noory
41 Oilman's setup
43 Sister to Eva and Magda
44 "And so on and so forth"
46 "The Joy Luck Club" author
47 Chilly and snowy
48 Lively, musically
50 Pre-adult insect stage
51 Wasn't too bad at
52 Rabbit trapper's trap
54 Scratched (out)
56 Hog heaven?
57 Make out like teenagers
59 Museum of Natural History display
64 Upholsterer's sample
66 Suddenly needs smelling salts
67 Joins the cast of
68 Cicero's "It's over!"
69 Tchaikovsky's middle name
70 Tom's "Jerry Maguire" costar
71 ___ avis
72 Herzegovina's partner
73 It's got no point
76 To's opposite
79 Mountaineer's goal
80 Memorable period
82 English muffin topping
83 Request of a tailor to fancify a gown?
84 Big ref. books
85 Rex of film critiques
87 Stuck in place, in a way
88 "Transfer" molecule
89 Photo lab service, for short
94 Teut.
97 Gasp of delight
98 Dip on the ballet stage
99 Pronoun used between Friends
101 "Lost" network
102 Russell in "Cinderella Man"
103 Like oven-ready dough
105 Brain surgeon's prefix
106 Bert's roommate
107 Fire and intensity
109 "Planet of the Apes" planet
110 Cockroach of poetry
112 Steady stare
113 "Street" asset
114 Aretha Franklin's sister
115 Bre-X was one
117 Sparrow, to Carrey
118 Floored it
121 Lines of praise

205 "ER" SERIES by Richard Silvestri
Don't let the title mislead you, there isn't one hospital clue to be found.

ACROSS

1 Rum cake
5 The Green Hornet
9 College World Series site
14 Ponderosa brother
18 Farm team
19 "___ perpetua" (Idaho motto)
20 Harmful gas
21 Radical of the 1920s
22 Aged cheerleader?
24 Goat, in a sketch?
26 Work on pumps
27 Muscovite, for one
29 It flies and floats
30 2006 Olympic mascot
32 Half a sandwich
35 Wee Willie in Cooperstown
36 One of the Windwards
39 In the know about
40 Linen marking
41 Food preservative
42 Apache adder?
45 Confessional confession
49 Make a bust
51 Score
52 Code name
54 Napa Valley vessel
55 More than superficial
57 Venn diagram depiction
58 Song from "Annie"
60 Bonkers
62 Caught one's breath
64 Discourage
66 Tony Rome portrayer
68 Poor house
70 Tighten the laces
72 Smart
73 Like a dunce cap
75 Gets moving
77 Firefly, e.g.
80 White-sale purchase
81 Percussion instrument
83 Spanish diminutive ending
85 Sci-fi character
86 Lime quencher
87 Flip-chart support
89 Young one
91 Yegg's take
92 Versifier
94 Sandwich enumerator?
98 Afore
99 Letters from Greece
101 Pearl setting?
102 Brings together
104 Arthurian paradise
107 Whip-and-chair wielders
109 Staircase part
110 Florida State athlete
112 Do a woodcut
114 Correspondingly
118 Top-notch anesthetic?
121 Communist renter?
123 "The ___ near"
124 Piped up
125 Where Perry triumphed
126 Greek peak
127 Nair alternative
128 Put a spell on
129 Magic stick
130 Tweed's nemesis

DOWN

1 Churlish chap
2 Hot-rod rod
3 A lot of bunk?
4 Whichever person
5 Germane
6 Subj. for immigrants
7 Tabloid twosome
8 Column type
9 Establishes by law
10 Spoil
11 Toothpaste-box abbr.
12 "Why?"
13 Last Stuart queen
14 Like the derby loser
15 Eight-based
16 Part of the act
17 Hurting more
21 Condo caretaker
23 Kate Nelligan film
25 They make a lot of dough
28 Old pal
31 Norse epics
33 Disco ___ on "The Simpsons"
34 Rock opera
36 Where to spend pesewas
37 AMC, airing a Joan Crawford movie?
38 Had the miseries
40 Enclosed
41 Ship slammer
43 Take in or let out
44 Crushes
46 Tusk hauler?
47 Darling dog
48 Pen full of oink?
50 Testify
53 Walking on air
56 Address abusively
58 "Ditto"
59 Seed case
61 Minks' kin
63 Cal. page
65 Bird at the beach
67 Catch red-handed
69 ___ linguae (slip of the tongue)
71 Root of American history
73 Musical finale
74 Property claim
76 Con game
78 Mythomaniacs
79 Sharp surface
80 Bar bill
82 Big name in aluminum
84 Ambry neighbor
88 AA offshoot
89 Appealing place?
90 Complex
93 Set parameters
95 Prosciutto
96 Brightened
97 North Sea feeder
100 Firms the muscles
103 Maryland city
104 Trembly tree
105 "From the Earth to the Moon" author
106 Lidocaine, for one
107 Fiesta Bowl locale
108 Prison guard
111 Opulent
113 Queen of the gods
115 "___ deal!"
116 Famous fed
117 Fieldsian expletive
119 Kind of kite
120 Make do
122 Assault on the ears

UNLIKELY WIVES by Alyssa Brooke
That isn't Martini's wife (unlikely or not) at 113 Across.

ACROSS

1 Midsize auto engine
5 Duke it out
10 South Pacific island
14 Fundamental
19 Davenport site
20 Best Actress winner for "Two Women"
21 Chimp in space
22 Graff of "Mr. Belvedere"
23 Unlikely astronaut's wife?
27 Going ape
28 Point on a metro map
29 Hugh of "Tombstone"
30 Pale gray
31 Russian range
34 For the most part
35 Sleep phenomenon
37 Anakin Skywalker's son
38 Talks a blue streak
39 Recital rebuke
42 Unlikely British politician's wife?
50 Goof off
52 Ovidian outerwear
53 Slangy turn
54 Words before roll
55 Frank, in a diary
56 Citrus drinks
57 Unexpected help
59 Wasn't gentle with
61 1953 Gable/Gardner film
63 Debaters' need
64 Natural light show
65 Unlikely senator's wife?
69 It's a wrap
70 Castle of the ballroom
71 Makes reference
73 What to give it
74 "Cease!" at sea
75 Bound to get there
77 Bristlelike part
78 Southern vacation spot
79 Basilica bench
80 Asian capital
81 "Socrate" composer Satie
82 Unlikely actor's wife?
89 Biol., e.g.
90 Pine for
91 Palindromic time
92 Off. organizer
94 Grover's Street
97 Prepare to flee
101 Foil maker
105 Major depression
106 Lou's "La Bamba" costar
107 Last layers
109 Unlikely songwriter's wife?
113 Martini's partner
114 Calc preceder, perhaps
115 Put in a nutshell
116 On the spot
117 Heels alternative
118 "Bet you can't," e.g.
119 Peewee or Della
120 Ready for press

DOWN

1 Quartet instrument
2 Goes it alone
3 "If only!"
4 Bandleader Cugat
5 Mailbox attachment
6 Greek column style
7 Scacchi in "The Coca-Cola Kid"
8 Former federal dept.
9 It's found in the sticks
10 Dukakis' running mate
11 Green pear
12 Software repetitions
13 Mr. Kabibble
14 Whiny one
15 "Here comes the judge!"
16 Do a butler's job
17 Historic record
18 Comedian Bruce
24 Laura of "ER"
25 Japanese port
26 Island equivalent, to Donne
32 Radius' neighbors
33 Denmates
36 Not set in stone
38 "Disasters of War" painter
39 Bridge triumph
40 Some of a speaker's income
41 Get sloshed
43 "Ditto"
44 Improve, in an oak barrel
45 Former Barbary State
46 For this reason
47 Evoke oohs and aahs
48 Full of zip
49 Zapata "zilch"
51 Spreads
57 Launch, as a campaign
58 Cathedral nook
59 Word by a door handle
60 Rile up
62 Fountain treat
63 Dos follower
64 Gene forms
66 David of "The Pink Panther"
67 Haggard
68 Drink greedily
69 Lacus Solis locale
72 O. Henry contemporary
74 Did an impression of
75 Former hotelier Helmsley
76 Alley in a cave
80 Short snort
83 Crime-lab report
84 Aden residents
85 Tractor handle
86 Vulnerable to fire
87 Kind of boom
88 Talk back, e.g.
93 Dress
94 Eat voraciously
95 Flamboyant Flynn
96 Zesty dip
97 Firma front
98 ___ Force Academy
99 Knocker's announcement
100 Center of power
102 Crusted
103 Cheri of "Scary Movie"
104 Up to the present
108 Vatican resident
110 Flower shop letters
111 Med. land
112 Take to court

WADE IN by Victor Fleming
There are two Wades at 88 Across!

ACROSS

1 "Travelin' Band" band
4 Hudson Bay tribe
8 Pres. or Bapt.
13 Not well conceived
19 Brown quarters
21 "Maria ___" (1963 hit)
22 Dirty
23 Cager whose middle name is Wade
25 Look up to
26 Doily fringe
27 Troyer of Mini-Me fame
28 Ferber novel
30 L.L. or Orson
31 Eventually
33 Home stretch?
35 Trix or Kix
37 ___ the side of caution
39 Rib
41 Uriah of fiction
44 Double reward?
48 Wade Boggs' team (1982–92)
51 Relaxes
52 Wholly absorbed
53 Kind of bomb
54 Does marvelously
55 Do lawn work
56 Greetings
59 Tee privilege
60 One of the Allman Brothers
61 Old French coin
62 Pacific
64 Benjamin Wade's Senate office (1867–69)
71 Much of Siberia
72 Critic's pick?
73 ". . . to fetch ___ . . ."
75 Puts up
80 What that is in Cuba
81 Taijitu representation
82 Ital. volcano
83 "Big deal . . . I was wrong"
85 RAM access time unit
87 Tiger run?
88 Billy Wade and Wade Wilson
91 Go-betweens
92 Program storer
93 Too inquisitive
94 Kramer of "Seinfeld"
95 Evergreen oak
97 Popular side
99 What history repeats
104 Mobile home
107 Name on toy tractors
109 Talk-show tycoon
111 Fan favorite
112 Do a tinker's job
114 Home of Wallace Wade Stadium
117 Killer of Hyacinthus
118 Gold found in Hollywood?
119 Having the most bubbles
120 Hajj maker
121 Like gnats
122 Chess bd. figures
123 Brazilian place-name word

DOWN

1 351, to Brutus and Antony
2 "Little Johnny Jones" composer
3 Undergo chemical change
4 IC more than 1 Down
5 Case words associated with Henry Wade
6 Irish language
7 Biologists' study
8 Free from govt. control, slangily
9 Caribou kin
10 "I Remember Mama" son
11 Forerunner to baseball
12 Noncommittal reply
13 Practice
14 Okay sign
15 Where Virginia Wade beat Stove in 1977
16 "Would ___?"
17 "Will be," to Doris Day
18 Course at St. Andrews
20 Number in Nuremberg
24 Mr. X, for short
29 Grantorto's victim in "The Faerie Queene"
32 Rubeola
34 Mounted on
36 "Billy, Don't Be ___" (1974 hit)
38 Spokesperson
40 Job preceder
42 Gas name in Canada
43 Needy
44 Titleists, at times
45 Slicken the surfboard
46 Felix's apartment mate
47 Dress designer for Pat Nixon
48 Having turned
49 Do some tailoring on
50 Big sizes, for short
52 Orders of drinks
55 Public spectacle
57 Like an O. Henry ending
58 Became widespread
61 University URL ending
62 Place for a massage
63 Snapper trapper
65 "Who's there?" answer
66 Absorbed state
67 Surface-to-air missile
68 Some news essays
69 Sine or cosine, e.g.
70 Unify, in Berlin
74 Filly
75 Title for a legal name
76 Overwhelm
77 Bob in "La Bamba"
78 Wade Miller pitch
79 Blackfoot, e.g.
81 "Absolutely!"
82 Team that drafted Dwyane Wade in 2003
84 Comical Kovacs
86 "The ___ the limit!"
87 Twice, musically
89 Studied in a hurry
90 For the most part
91 Cheap-insurance class
94 "Aye" catcher?
96 Disk of data
98 Like the pun at 94 Down?
100 No-no's opposite?
101 Magnus and McClurg
102 "___ luck!"
103 Jet off for
104 Jam-pack
105 Bank takeback
106 NYSE newcomers
108 Squeaks (out)
110 Stream of literature
113 Seine sight
115 "A rat!"
116 Turning meas.

AT THE DOCTOR'S OFFICE   by Randall J. Hartman

"Never go to a doctor whose office plants have died." — Erma Bombeck

ACROSS

1 Think hard
9 Meeting places
13 Spruce cousin
16 "Addams Family" cousin
19 Narrative by Xenophon
20 Down with, in Caen
21 Plastic Band
22 Gardening aid
23 **The football coach said . . .**
26 MCI Center builder Pollin
27 Put out
28 Blackthorn fruit
29 Las Vegas opening
30 Bear lair
31 Whupped
34 Sharpen
35 Cool ___ cucumber
36 **The marathoner said . . .**
41 Puss
42 Street people, e.g.
44 Customs of a society
45 Leprechaun land
46 Like some side streets
47 Glove material
50 Baseball pioneer Doubleday
51 Salesman, briefly
52 King of the fairies
54 Greta in "Anna Karenina"
56 Roman "Space Odyssey" year
57 T/Gel shampoo ingredient
59 Beachcomber's find
61 Ave. crossers
64 "Ich bin ___ Berliner": JFK
65 **The ticket agent said . . .**
67 "What the Butler ___": Orton
68 Varnish ingredient
69 Cordwood measure
70 Prepares
71 Title bout ending
72 More than dislikes
74 French Socialist Guy ___ (1905–75)
75 Christopher Robin's playmate
76 Bouilla-baisse and gumbo
78 Mountain mint
79 Mental midgets
82 ___ of honor
83 Open wounds
86 Feast of Dedication
88 Pie ___ mode
89 **The mechanic said . . .**
93 "Funeral in Berlin" author Deighton
94 Thailand, once
95 Gibson pearls
96 "___ you kidding?"
97 Start to freeze?
98 Haul around
99 Young herring
104 Realm of Ares
105 **The dawdler said . . .**
110 Off-rd. vehicle
111 ___ Lingus
112 Period of duty
113 Like talk-show calls
114 End of spring?
115 Many mins.
116 Kitzbühel peaks
117 Kalahari quality

DOWN

1 Showed up
2 Intaglio stone
3 Kaplan of "Welcome Back, Kotter"
4 Bridge support
5 Politician's skill
6 Inquire about
7 Summer month in Tehran
8 U-turn from WNW
9 Conquered
10 Elongated
11 Funny lady Martha
12 Louisville Slugger wood
13 Not ___ nor money
14 Drones monotonously
15 Lineup
16 **The rower said . . .**
17 "Absolutely!"
18 Cause of gray hair?
24 Piedmont wine center
25 "Just Like Me" singer
31 Channel marker
32 Fangorn, e.g.
33 Reply to a ques.
36 **The thief said . . .**
37 Kitten cry
38 Genetic inits.
39 Sunday sign-off
40 Cunning critter
42 Cure 81® Ham company
43 Iron-poor blood condition
45 Subside
47 Leave alone
48 Bahrain resident
49 Manolete and others
50 City on the Rhone
52 "Bellefleur" author
53 Hazy image
54 Understand
55 ___ vera
57 Sacred chests
58 German flower?
59 Diminutive
60 Jekyll's alter ego
62 Fanning in "I Am Sam"
63 Nike symbol
66 Place of hero worship?
73 Knock the socks off
74 Opposite of fem.
76 Rascal
77 Put up with
78 Jackson of "Men in Trees"
79 Signs up
80 Demand for payment
81 Skidmore in "Oklahoma!"
83 One taking a cut
84 Pulpit preachers
85 Send money
86 Group of MDs
87 "Atlas Shrugged" novelist Rand
89 Old Testament book
90 RV connection
91 Joins the club
92 Bombed at the Improv
98 Backyard building (with 99-D)
99 See 98 Down
100 Hammer head
101 Actor Auberjonois
102 Senate votes
103 Koppel and Williams
106 Educational org. founded in 1897
107 ". . . ___ friend indeed"
108 IBM competitor
109 Beginning of a cycle

209 STEPPING OUT   by Arlan and Linda Bushman
Let's hope 64 Across is not on the next cruise you take.

ACROSS

1 Symbol of 21 Across
6 Mountaineering hazard
13 Scolds
20 Hold dear
21 Tyre's land
22 Connors rival
23 **Out for a walk, Paul Bunyan . . .**
25 The slightest peep
26 Winter coat
27 Goodman's "Stompin' at the ___"
28 Commotion
30 "Another 48 Hrs." actor Ed
31 Agate relative
33 Gainly
35 Housing choice
36 Winnebago offshoot
37 **Out for a walk, Clayton Moore . . .**
43 Flower parts
46 Relaxed
47 Relay segment
48 Operation launch
49 Ludacris creation
51 Plus
53 Paean
54 D.C. regular
57 **Out for a walk, the Joker . . .**
60 Held
62 Some chits
64 Common stowaway
65 Pour
66 Hands
67 Financially prudent
69 Butter maker
71 Retaliation
74 Pall
75 Coalition
76 Junior
77 Floating clink
78 Western lake
80 **Out for a walk, John Deere . . .**
84 Small amount
85 Schooner fill
86 Indecisive gesture
88 Washington national park
90 Makes an offer
92 Colorful moths
93 Beatles vamp
95 Intertwine
99 **Out for a walk, Cliff Clavin . . .**
103 Cries of approval
104 Vintage cars
105 Just beats out
106 Obvious
109 Combines
111 Not occupied
112 Syrian leader
114 Kingston Trio hit
115 Adjacency
117 **Out for a walk, Charles Goren . . .**
121 Pedigree
122 Earnest
123 Military chaplain
124 Poked one's nose in
125 Takes over
126 Kobe bombs

DOWN

1 Some felines
2 Enlighten
3 Type of trunk
4 Wall St. figure
5 Witherspoon of film
6 Quick-witted
7 Overhaul
8 Popular website
9 Actor Kilmer
10 Theban queen of Greek myth
11 Mention privately
12 Overwhelm
13 Autobahn travelers
14 "Baudolino" novelist
15 Fix storm damage, perhaps
16 Data of "Star Trek"
17 **Out for a walk, George Patton . . .**
18 Long stretches
19 Dates
24 Skate relative
29 Keeps from escaping
32 Scorch
33 Whiskey chaser?
34 Some refrigerators
35 Enclosure
38 In the crow's nest
39 Faux pas
40 Balance
41 Put on board
42 Like Marge Simpson's hair
44 "Well, ___-di-dah!"
45 Rakish
50 Visit
51 Tennis point
52 Whig opponent
54 Sink
55 Sound of delight
56 **Out for a walk, Charles Addams . . .**
58 Respite
59 Canal site
61 TV's Friday
63 Granary
66 Tasty morsel
68 Opposite sides
69 Heavy shoe
70 "And ___!"
71 Auden piece
72 Espionage org.
73 Onetime rival of 72-D
75 Empty talk
76 More reserved
78 Keep ___ on (watch)
79 Settled down
80 Spur
81 Jazz drummer Warren "Baby" ___
82 Arabic letter
83 Racket
87 Gets a move on
89 Thicken
91 Refined rocks
93 Prairie female
94 Pop singer Brun
96 Dessert option
97 Buick or Toyota model
98 Manor settings
100 Kind of code
101 Black Sea port
102 Haunt
107 Tyke
108 Go with the flow
109 Foist (off)
110 Theater award
111 Decamped
112 Sly as ___
113 Turn sharply
116 Span
118 Buffett contraption
119 Quaint interjection
120 Exclude

210 "WHAT'S MY NAME?" by Fran & Lou Sabin
(My name is the real name of 80 Down.)

ACROSS

1 Striplings
5 Depend (on)
9 Young equine
13 Nitpicking profs
18 Vacationing
19 Radio and TV
20 Celebes beast
21 Erno of cube fame
22 "I get no respect" source
25 Toughen up: var.
26 Diner's choice
27 Mrs. David Copperfield
28 Film starring Brando as Napoleon
30 BEVs don't need this
31 Sets of judges
33 Like gossamer wings
34 Walking tempos
38 Focus and Fusion
39 Literary gleanings
43 Nobelist French poet
44 Austrian actor in "Casablanca"
46 Sun or moon
47 Eye impertinently
48 "State Fair" state
49 Passionless
50 Site for 52 Across
51 "Taking Heat" author Fleischer
52 Baby bouncers
54 Hither
55 Wash word
56 Tricky type
58 "Breakout" game maker
60 Least experienced
61 Midas' sin
62 Quaint oaths
63 Ludicrous
64 They're exhausted
66 Western Eire county
67 Katrina, for one
70 Agglomerate
71 House bird
72 Ann "The Oomph Girl"
74 Strong reaction
75 Sticky stuff
76 Leveling stick
77 Part of PAYE
78 Rotter

79 "C'mere, buddy . . ."
80 "Divine Comedy" cantica
84 ___ célèbre
85 Starbuck, to Stubb
87 Fiery horses
88 Williams of talk TV
89 Energy source
90 They get rattled
92 ___ anglais (English horn)
93 ___ d'hotel
96 Norse goddess of fate
97 Scratch-test agent
102 Miho Museum designer
103 James Cagney film classic
106 Doc Adams of "Gunsmoke"
107 One of the Muses
108 1966 Bobby Hebb hit
109 Toiler of yore
110 Gregg writer
111 Building blueprint abbr.
112 "Of ___ I Sing": Gershwin
113 Three-player card game

DOWN

1 "Tomb Raider" heroine
2 Missing from formation
3 The world according to Arp
4 'N ___
5 Stinging colonists
6 Upper hand
7 Fudge the facts
8 Sail support
9 Most even-handed
10 Leader of the Shaq Pack

11 Netscape purchaser
12 Cheryl who was Kris Munroe
13 Auction-house offering
14 ___ Kennedy Shriver
15 Nutmeg State's "Hat City"
16 Wear down
17 ___-Ball (arcade game)
19 Pianist Hess and others
23 Hot to trot
24 Ballet bend
29 Savannah antelope
31 Direct opposite
32 Zen enlightenment
34 "Half ___ is . . ."
35 Pola in "Hi Diddle Diddle"
36 Misplaced modifier
37 NFL kicking aid
38 "Not that many!"
40 White or Blue waterway
41 Lock

42 Red as ___
44 Sank a putt
45 Like "Happy Feet" penguins
48 Lets the car warm up
50 New Zealanders
52 Worrisome conditions
53 Planetary Society cofounder Carl
54 Pluto's place
55 Muslim fasting period
57 Popped up
59 Street coat?
60 Cellist's aid
62 Lacquer base
63 Prefix for stratus
64 Wily women
65 Jakob Ammann's followers
66 Turning points
67 Chance and Koontz
68 Do away with
69 Iconoclast
71 Work up an appetite
73 Some are medicinal

76 Like Joe Miller jokes
78 ___ Remo (Riviera resort)
80 NFL's 1983 Rookie of the Year
81 "Lolita" novelist
82 "___ Jacques"
83 Heartfelt
84 Paint Shop parent
86 Irish moonshine
88 Like Roquefort
91 Warbucks ward
92 Duplicate copy
93 Russian fighters
94 Latin primer word
95 E Indian stableman
97 Top-drawer
98 Roger in "Nicholas Nickleby"
99 Polish seaport
100 Laverne's stepmother
101 Riga rejection
104 Barring none
105 "Got me"

211 FOODIES by Raymond Hamel
None of the foodies below are fattening.

ACROSS

1 Arab of song
5 Vitality
10 They keep their "ears on"
15 River in Serbia
19 "Sanctuary" author Roberts
20 Tournament type
21 Site for sports
22 "Here I am!"
23 Slightly open
24 Kravchuk and Korolev of hockey
25 Sucker for younger ladies?
27 Vaudeville star
29 Crosses the finish line first
30 Atrophy cause
31 Small songbird
32 War of 1812 treaty site
34 IRS Form 1099-___
35 Tooth decay
38 Fundamental belief
39 1960s rival of "Doctor Kildare"
43 Where Socrates shopped
44 Sounds of discomfort
45 Where to ride the Métro
46 Frank Sinatra's ex
47 Straight memorization
48 Half-mask
49 Window maker
50 "Love all, trust ___": Shak.
51 "The Closer" network
52 Hard cache file to delete?
55 Far from lenient
56 Canine
58 Crime in the heat of the moment?
59 Chooses
60 Satyr's love interest
61 Shade of gray
62 Stun
63 Long marches
65 "___ and the Man" (TV oldie)
66 Weight-loss brand
69 "Left Eye" of TLC
70 One who vegetates
72 Tax advisor
73 Big show
74 Ecuador's capital
75 ___ versa
76 Boxing stat
77 Nonexistent
78 Homer Simpson's boss
79 Crash result
81 Where rakes end up?
82 Polar bears ride them
84 "Deep Space Nine" bar owner
85 It may have a subwoofer
86 "I'm game!"
87 Hip-hop artist Rhymes
88 Messrs. partners
89 City in Umbria
92 "Telling ___ in America" (1997)
93 Pushover
98 Leg art
100 Ever
101 Concerning
102 Listen
103 "The Bishop's Wife" star
104 Gem-ring attachment
105 Arabian Sea gulf
106 Has lunch
107 Warty critters
108 Wood-trimming tools
109 Shows fatigue

DOWN

1 Class for future MDs
2 Chain with orange roofs
3 Give ___ (care)
4 It keeps 'em down on the farm
5 Has a view
6 Cathedral instrument
7 Lucky Charms charm
8 What a pilcrow denotes
9 Bounty letters
10 Spot for slots
11 Main thrust
12 Ticker tapes?
13 Genetic messenger letters
14 Pier Angeli's birthplace
15 Mississippi River source
16 Singer Erykah
17 Tacks on
18 Martha in "Monsieur Verdoux"
26 Brake parts
28 Neighborhood
29 Ties the knot
33 Fox's prey
34 Oberon in "Wuthering Heights"
35 ___ blanche
36 Violent struggle
37 Bad Mac?
38 Robitussin target
39 Actress Ina
40 Open-minded crook?
41 Tennis great Chris
42 Signs of boredom
44 River area
45 Sri Lankan tea
48 Curved pieces
49 Hospital area
50 Consumed, Biblically
52 Heavy reading
53 Colorful cat
54 Spinachlike plant
55 Type of replay
57 Universal blood donor
59 Typewriter type
61 Padlocks
62 Singer Roberta
63 Nicolas Gage book
64 Like strychnine
65 New dollars of 2007
66 Cane
67 Fine china
68 Byron's "The Lament of ___"
70 Soaks in a brine
71 Played the ham
74 Part of a formula, maybe
76 Player
78 Respond to a sneeze
79 Mama's boy
80 Turn state's evidence
81 Wineglass part
83 Airplanes or their passengers
84 New York City borough
85 Some T-shirts
87 Eschewed the car
88 Scuffle
89 Joint concern?
90 Kind of butter
91 Candidate's goal
92 Flowing rock
94 Tease
95 Annul
96 Lyricist Ebb
97 Marshy regions
99 AFL partner
100 Appealing org.

ORDINARY PEOPLE   by Theresa Yves
. . . and these ordinary people can be found at 64 Across.

ACROSS

1 "The Burial of Count Orgaz" painter
8 Calico bass
15 Aura, slangily
20 High-tech valley
21 "Don't even think about it!"
22 Unwilling words
23 **One of 64 Across**
25 "Rigoletto" composer
26 Down times
27 Rickey flavoring
28 Commandment pronoun
29 Show disgust
30 Get along
31 ___ QT
34 Vampire chronicler Rice
35 Enemies of Greenpeace
40 **One of 64 Across**
42 Like a melody
43 Apostle Paul, originally
45 Not far apart, as eyes
46 **One of 64 Across**
50 Halves of ems
51 Brazilian map word
52 Lower digit
53 "My Way" lyricist
54 Ont. neighbor
56 Linen letters
57 Ring-shaped
61 Rite receptacle
62 "Ewww!"
64 ORDINARY PEOPLE
69 Put a stop to
71 Egg on
72 Got comfy
76 Ex-frosh
77 Revue segment
78 Hernando de ___
81 Z preceder
82 Henri's here
83 Screen siren West
85 **One of 64 Across**
90 Chip brand
93 "Out of Africa" author Dinesen
94 Like a maid that sleeps over
95 **One of 64 Across**

98 As a rule
100 "Be ___ the tenth Muse": Shak.
101 Security feature
102 Descendent diagram
103 Admiral nicknamed "Bull"
105 Photo finish?
107 Tip
108 Mosque leader
112 ___ fours
113 **One of 64 Across**
117 Paris parents
118 Like a small apartment
119 Acceptances
120 Meredith's "Family Ties" role
121 Really blow it
122 Households

DOWN

1 "SportsCenter" network
2 Old money of Milan
3 Unappetizing fare
4 Eighteen-wheelers
5 Crosswords author?
6 Page sorter
7 Red-hot
8 Foal's father
9 Underground org.
10 Straight up
11 Understand
12 On the same wavelength
13 Cold-weather product prefix
14 Sugar pie
15 Start of a monarchist's cry
16 Glacial chamber
17 Some noble wives
18 Conclude intensely
19 Eyelet creators
24 "Nature" essayist
29 Military probe, briefly
30 Bomb detonator

32 Private eye, slangily
33 Trojan beauty
35 Elbows on the table
36 Betelgeuse setting
37 Tablecloths, e.g.
38 Seat for a Camp Fire Girl
39 Went to the bottom
40 Inventor Whitney
41 Pompous person
44 Overseas article
47 Ask to see ID
48 "Let's get going!"
49 Variety
55 Unknown degree
56 Singer Axton
58 Place for Young men?
59 Part of UCLA
60 Soul on the Seine
61 Send via phone
62 Hurdle for srs.
63 Els
65 "Ew!"

66 Bit of change
67 Mulgrew of "Star Trek: Voyager"
68 Commonly cited auth.
69 She made "No. 5" #1
70 Carried on by letters
73 Sir Freddie of aviation
74 Online sales
75 Feather-soft
76 Stay in
77 South Korean capital
78 Flat consonants?
79 Epps of "Against the Ropes"
80 Break
83 Fallen Russian orbiter
84 In check
86 Madison's st.
87 Prude

88 Get under the skin of
89 Eggs in the lab
91 Musses, as hair
92 Penn., for one
96 Big name in groceries
97 Strike caller
99 Kind of cracker
104 Additional
106 Floating garbage-carrier
107 Street fixture
108 Fancy
109 Flash Gordon's nemesis
110 Initial stake
111 Fail to see
113 Calendar pp.
114 Mandela org.
115 Letters of debt
116 PT boats are in it

213 FIRST GEAR   by James Greene

Follow the advice in 1 Down and you'll soon be out of first gear!

ACROSS

1 Pharaoh in "The Ten Commandments"
8 Spot
14 "La Pucelle d'Orleans"
20 Happening
21 Bad-luck blocker
22 Temper
23 Appliance rating
24 Clenched fist, e.g.
25 Deed authenticator
26 A lot of commuters?
29 Market close
30 Spots on cards
31 Slightly
32 IRS form
35 Day's end?
36 Jetson dog
39 Astra Coupé, for one
43 Short blast
44 DMZ
48 Be in a cast
49 Exams for srs.
50 Reproach
51 "New York Times" section
52 Crew for the Who
54 "The Golden Trashery of ___ Nashery"
55 Place for a computer
57 Poetic dusk
58 Charged
59 More recent
61 Conclusions
63 Carhop's beat
67 Pericles, e.g.
69 Did a blacksmith's job
70 Needing a muffler
73 "The Tell-Tale Heart" author
74 Way off
75 No gleeful giver
77 Where painters profit
79 A place to remember
81 Manufacturer's tag
82 Corp. recruits
83 Gamboling area
84 Cut back
88 Cutlass, for one
89 Campbell's "___ Little Kindness"
90 Sanyo product
91 Compass pt.
92 Lovers' lane event
93 Driver's license datum
95 Rodent exterminators
97 Stick up
98 Robert Atkins' claim to fame
106 Life's work
107 "The Glass Menagerie" mother
108 Stumped
110 Like the titan arum
111 Flaunted (with "over")
112 Demolished
113 Silicon Valley cars
114 Chemical salt
115 Having no point

DOWN

1 Put the pedal to the metal
2 Individually
3 Pfefferberg in "Schindler's List"
4 Springsteen's band
5 Sopping wet
6 Award named after 73 Across
7 No longer secret
8 Nathan Hale, e.g.
9 "Like, no problem, man"
10 Dairy product
11 Swiss painter Paul
12 Browse (through)
13 Songstress James
14 After-hours job, maybe
15 Name on a plane
16 First-aid info
17 Straight up
18 Not (with "a one")
19 Tarzan actor
27 High low grade?
28 "He's a Rebel" singer in 1962
32 Belle of the West
33 Winter warmer
34 Like some plus-sized models?
35 Approaches
36 "I cannot tell ___"
37 Cause a jaw to drop
38 Pro follower
40 For all we know
41 Goofed up
42 City on the Saône
44 Duncan's denial
45 Pilot's affirmative
46 Talks to
47 Nonhuman cyborg parts
49 Replace temporarily
53 Start of a prank, maybe
54 Fess (up to)
55 Worth praising
56 Go public with
60 Berliner's article
61 ___ kwon do
62 Baseball's Slaughter
64 By means of
65 Kind of life
66 Lookout point
67 Separate
68 Chan portrayer
71 Moves using runners
72 Brewer's need
75 Horse hair
76 Scoffing retort
78 Outrageous
80 Have good intentions
81 Archaic attention-getters
82 Smart outfit
85 River to Lake Huron
86 At least once
87 For goods or services only
88 Like a planet's path
92 So far
94 Amtrak express service
95 "Time After Time" singer Lauper
96 Interjected
97 Some used cars
98 Feeble, as an excuse
99 Vein pursuits
100 Hope/Crosby destination
101 Melville classic
102 Fast companion
103 Civil-rights activist Desmond
104 Creator of Perry and Della
105 Woods' pegs
106 AL clock setting
109 Mag execs

214 HAVING A BALL* by Katherine Omak
Asterisked clues tie in with the title.

ACROSS

1 Iraqi or Qatari
5 Ferber novel
10 Novel necessities
15 Sierra Club founder John
19 Risotto ingredient
20 City near Kobe
21 Red Square figure
22 Cartoonist Peter
23 Morning fare*
25 Nonverbal communication of a sort*
27 Cheap accommodations
28 "___ Amore"
30 Holdup man?
31 Carp's kin
32 Come to mind
33 Close at hand
35 River to the Gulf of Mexico
38 Bad drive
39 Chinese dynasty
40 No. 2
44 Smart-___
45 Four-on-the-floor*
47 Commandment word
48 Hero's antithesis
49 1" pencil, say
50 Non-P.C. suffix
51 Anthem word
52 Down East cape
53 Shaman*
57 "Jabberwocky" opener
58 Eleven states, in the 1860s
61 Battery terminal
62 Nancy's rich friend
63 Bygone
64 Pavlova's wardrobe
65 Converted split
67 They're Starr-struck
69 Cock and bull
70 Snipers' perches
73 Ashcroft's predecessor
74 Performance history*
77 "Ulalume" poet
78 Windsor's prov.
79 Skye in "Samantha"
80 Four-stringed instruments
81 Darjeeling duds
82 Put one's foot down?
84 Handy picker-upper*
88 Bochner and Crane
89 Franklin D.'s mother
90 Get mellower
91 Aromatic chemical
92 Once in a blue moon
93 Fox's meat
95 Part of EGBDF
96 "Apotheosis of Homer" artist
97 Bingham of "Baywatch"
100 Wagnerian work
101 Cornerback or free safety
105 One involved in a fling?*
108 Bright red*
110 Role for Ronny
111 Place for a decal
112 Navratilova rival
113 Sermon topic
114 Split apart
115 Galore in "Goldfinger"
116 "Winner" in a 1948 headline
117 Make over

DOWN

1 Electric discharges
2 Haymarket Square event
3 Development unit
4 First name in treason
5 Give comfort to
6 Inedible orange
7 Catch some rays
8 One of the Clantons
9 Like some ulcers
10 Tickles pink
11 MacArthur victory site
12 They're white in Monopoly
13 First X
14 Word with Cone or Cat
15 Madison player
16 Caspian Sea feeder
17 Pizarro victim
18 Goes bad
24 Weenie
26 Slacker at the track
29 Bumpkin
32 Cover story?
33 Treaty signed 12/8/93
34 One ___ (poor odds)
35 Tome-filling tales
36 In bad company, to Bierce
37 Accountant, slangily*
38 Some retired racehorses
39 Blackjack request
41 Himalayan cat*
42 Great buy
43 Middle man?
45 Sirius star
46 Listens to
49 Barrie bad pirate
54 Make airtight
55 Lock opener?
56 "It's ___!" (cry of despair)
57 It's no crime
59 Sailor's saint
60 Shingle letters
62 Churchill's "so few"
64 Be silent, musically
65 More tender
66 Sci-fi vehicles
67 Smeltery waste
68 ___-Car
69 Minister's home
70 "Today" weatherman
71 Lisbon rival
72 Richter scale recording
74 Wave or basin preceder
75 Compact matter
76 Eye-catcher
81 Kennedy press secretary Pierre
83 Really thirsty
85 Soprano Sills
86 Customer
87 Raked, Apache-style
88 Trojan beauty
92 NFL 2-pointer
94 Exxon Valdez spill
95 Blunted blades
96 Model "D" tractor maker
97 Rafter Heyerdahl
98 Ready to pluck
99 Opposed, to a bumpkin
100 Tout's concern
101 Prepared to fire
102 Dumpy bar
103 Geraint's beloved
104 Change cities, in Realtor-speak
106 Sound investment?
107 ___ TURN
109 Secret ending

215 "IT'S A JOB" by Jay Sullivan
12 Down was named after silent-movie star Lillian.

ACROSS

1 Exercise options
5 Turns over
10 De jure
15 L.A. hours
18 Margot Fonteyn's skirt
19 Kind of drab
20 Object of Peeping Tom's peeping
21 One, to Juan
22 Scads
23 Work as a conductor?
25 Propitiatory present
26 Chases
28 Father of Methuselah
29 Group psychology
31 Little people
32 Witchy woman
33 Attractive
34 Fore site
35 In the offing
36 Ostentatious
37 Lays the groundwork
40 Six-Day War battleground
42 Great Plains river
43 It helps a nose make noise?
44 Work as a tailor?
48 Shade tree
51 Rust, say
53 Clueless
54 "Evening Falls . . ." singer
55 Ones who bear down
56 "___ Delight" (1936 Pulitzer winner)
58 Take after
59 Clothes off
61 Dental school exams?
62 Never existed
63 Interest factors
64 Stonehenge priests
66 Tie score
68 Tube trophy
69 Doctor of literature
70 May-day count?
73 Common consent
74 Work as a golf pro?
77 Semantic antic
78 Went for a spin
80 Highways and byways
81 Await action
82 Gets around
83 Lean-cuisine lover
85 This miss
87 Movie makeup
88 Kind of reaction
89 Desertic
93 Approach the midnight hour
94 Dis-tressed
95 Mediator
97 Ring master
98 Work as a hula dancer?
101 It hangs around the house
102 Trash collector
103 Rids of rods
104 Turned back on
105 Beehive State athletes
106 Hang loose
107 Advice that helped Alice grow up?
108 Caddy alternative
109 Big Muddy mud

DOWN

1 Kansas City newspaper
2 Erect
3 When some resume working
4 Day-school closures
5 Counter offer
6 Bring to delight
7 Cuts corners
8 Present opener?
9 Theater scene
10 Loch with "bonnie, bonnie banks"
11 Bring out
12 Smashing Pumpkins album
13 Word form of "bird"
14 Scrape
15 Work as a postman?
16 High-falutin'
17 ___-turvy
20 "Simon Boccanegra" setting
24 Enclosed
27 Blow away
30 One that's held for questioning
32 Plug of tobacco
33 Marketplace
35 Erelong
36 Exodus plague
37 Animal pouch
38 Lennon's love
39 Work as a sales manager?
40 Recipe directive
41 Exchanged words
42 "Hey there!"
44 Composers' closers
45 Previously owned
46 Change sides
47 Plains tribe
49 City on the Rhône
50 Selling point
52 1993 NBA Coach of the Year
54 Ahead of time
56 Notre Dame team
57 Old man
58 Deeds of derring-do
59 Discoverer of heavy hydrogen
60 Personage
61 Boot out
62 Portmanteau ___
64 Gives a head fake
65 Had second thoughts about
66 You might come down with it
67 Sports column
69 They take liberties
70 Dead-on
71 Creature of habit?
72 One whose job is on the line
74 Haitian dance step
75 On the wrong side
76 Horse hue
79 Augsburg article
81 Medusa slayer
82 Supreme Court jurist
83 "My Fair Lady" song
84 Nimoy's "Mission: Impossible" role
85 Sidetracks
86 Scammed
87 Thick slices
88 Incantation
89 Get wind of
90 Bubbling over
91 Valuable viola
92 Lint trap?
94 Ballpark fig.
95 Bar from the kitchen
96 Where the chicks hang out
99 Bambi's aunt
100 Call of the wild

SEARCH IN VEIN by Bonnie Gentry and Victor Fleming

The great-niece of 86 Across has a star on the Hollywood Walk of Fame.

ACROSS

1 Like Road Runner
5 Considerable serving
9 "Crooklyn" actress Woodard
14 Marks on a knee, perhaps
19 Perceive
20 Earth's crust layer
21 Some Surrealist art
22 Kind of checking account
23 Do due diligence
26 Like 43-A, perhaps
27 Harold in FDR's cabinet
28 To be, to Gigi
29 Morals man
31 Not hor.
32 OSS successor
33 Aiming to sire
35 PB&J alternative
36 Unshrouded
38 Fleming of spy novels
39 Tiny part
40 Yucatán years
41 Followed an usher
43 Rathskeller offering
44 ___-Pitch softball
45 Thinker's output
46 Royal band
47 Music industry "first" in 1958
53 Spot markers
54 Ottoman title
57 Lock maker
58 Disdain
60 Like eddies
62 Hymn
65 Cure-all remedies
69 Verse partner
71 Former Chicago slugger
73 Makes part of a city
74 Had delivered
76 Trimmed along the walk
78 Aver
79 Words from East?
80 Pianist Templeton
82 Other Spanish guys
83 Medical suffix
86 "A Free Soul" Oscar winner
91 Singer wearing a Hawaiian shirt
93 Bee's great-nephew
94 Dawn personified
95 Insert
98 H.G. Wells' mad scientist
100 Aspirin is one
101 Smelter's waste
103 Tango quorum
104 "Two mints in one" mints
105 Marijuana intoxicant
106 Social breakdown
108 This girl
109 Disaster-relief org.
110 ___ in the right direction
112 Labs not meant for experiments
113 "Jersey Boys" boy
115 Fall off
117 President who liked to box
120 Phantasmal
121 Soothed
122 Bad attitude, slangily
123 Langston Hughes poem
124 Check for fit
125 Thorny areas
126 Total offense, e.g.
127 Reading areas

DOWN

1 English poet Hemans
2 Hardly gregarious
3 Bing Crosby's boyhood home
4 Trike rider
5 Compass pt.
6 Biography
7 Cherub
8 Popular aftershave
9 Naples school
10 Daisy Mae's groom in 1952
11 Live off charity
12 Cooks one's goose
13 Orr teammate, familiarly
14 ___-Jet (winter vehicle)
15 Service-station adjunct
16 Net
17 Round object, flat at times
18 Michaelmas mo.
24 It's associated with dens: Abbr.
25 Voluminous ref. work
30 "Wham!"
34 Fable
37 November 11 honoree
40 Clamor
42 "One Mic" rapper
44 Dig into
45 Mountaineering tool
47 SOS signaler
48 "The Raven" poet: Inits.
49 Threat ending
50 AOL, e.g.
51 Big sports inits.
52 "___ Fly Now" ("Rocky" theme)
54 Capitol Hill groups
55 First U.S. Open winner
56 White trumpeter
59 Delivers for a price
61 Flat
63 iPod display
64 Zimbabwe president
66 Swimming laps, e.g.: Abbr.
67 Danish island
68 Air France retirees
70 Renaissance artist Guido
72 Lugosi in "Ninotchka"
75 Outback hopper
77 Aachen article
81 A&W product
83 Unmatched
84 Excellent speller?
85 As a reminder (of)
87 Whopper request
88 Byron's "Don Juan" is one
89 Limit
90 Ursine toon
92 Granary grain
95 Jock
96 Not let go of
97 Frito-Lay chips
99 "___ Today"
100 Besides
101 Shots in a bar
102 Formally exit
106 Dig deeply
107 Cain raiser
109 Paws
111 Fr. honorees
114 Rah-rah
116 Still, in verse
118 Bridge expert
119 Social group

217 CELEBRITY VOICES   by Michael Collins
69 Across also played Kato in "The Green Hornet" television series.

ACROSS

1 Goya subject
5 Acts the crybaby
10 Site of Bunning's 1964 perfect game
14 Playground retort
19 Like many thermometers
20 Folder's words
21 Hardy heroine
22 Provo resident
23 Nash priest
24 Kunta of "Roots"
25 Voice of Yar in "Dinosaur"
27 Pop up
29 Earless mammal
31 "Where ___?"
32 A sib
33 They're blind, stereotypically
36 Long. crosser
37 Goes on a winning streak
40 China's Lao-___
41 Balloon material
43 Voice of Princess Bala in "Antz"
46 Tranquil
48 "Slung" fare
49 Bonzo, e.g.
50 Indian tourist mecca
52 Cuts to pieces
54 ___ McAn shoes
56 It's cast
60 Prefix meaning "many"
61 Brown ermines
63 Let out
65 Chalk talk diagram
66 Fix, as a printer
68 Raise a stink?
69 "Enter the Dragon" star
71 ___-cone (cold confection)
72 Voice of Ramón in "Happy Feet"
78 EMTs' destinations
79 Brainiac
81 Island keepsake
82 Nearing the hour
84 Hook up
85 Backwoods rtes., once
87 Gamelan gong
91 Think tank nugget
92 Piece of Bacon?
94 ___ gras
96 Tuscany city
97 Poll answerer: Abbr.
98 Vacation homes, of sorts
100 It's a crock
102 Mallet go-with, for a camper
104 Voice of Hotep in "The Prince of Egypt"
108 Deluxe digs
109 Eerie ability
112 Goes light
113 Wile E. Coyote buy
115 People in Xings
116 Family tree word
117 LA clock setting
118 Unlike a subcompact
122 Kicking back
124 Voice of Chef on "South Park"
127 Richter scale event
130 One-named artist
131 MetLife rival
132 Time to give up?
133 Musical toy
134 Not e'en once
135 Unwelcome forecast
136 D-Day carriers
137 Bock holder
138 Garage figs.

DOWN

1 Maltreat
2 Porthos mate
3 Voice of King Mufasa in "The Lion King"
4 Daminozide, familiarly
5 Shrek in "Shrek"
6 Brit. music label
7 Took the cake
8 Certain Prot.
9 Great buy
10 "Quit it!"
11 Big name in oil
12 In ___ (actually)
13 Crumbly Italian cheese
14 Jersey's chew
15 ___ glance (quickly)
16 Code language in "Windtalkers"
17 Peres of Israel
18 Like some training
26 Makarova of tennis
28 Hockey goalie Worsley
30 Ill-considered
34 Cornrow, e.g.
35 Vanzetti's partner
38 Cooking amts.
39 Treeless tract
42 Win back, as trust
44 "Off the Court" author
45 Equilateral figures
47 "Later!"
50 "Say something funny!"
51 Marine infantry sergeants
53 Pack away
55 Oscar winner Sorvino
57 Voice of Dory in "Finding Nemo"
58 Hamlet's duel opponent
59 Grandma's hand cleaner
62 Circus prop
64 Rum ___ Tugger ("Cats" cat)
67 He pities the fool
70 Chi. hrs.
73 Key contraction
74 Son of Willy Loman
75 Not alfresco
76 Places to graze
77 Puts a cap on
80 Not just diet
83 Word on Irish stamps
86 Dredger's target
88 Prepare to drive
89 Sandy's master
90 Spirit in "Spirit: Stallion of the Cimarron"
93 YSL part
95 Above-the-rest sorts
99 Compress, slangily
101 Cornerstone word
103 Roach, e.g.
104 Some tinted prints
105 Fez feature
106 You can't take it with you
107 Fill with outrage
110 Sonnet ending
111 ___ pence
114 Poachers' prizes
119 Some floor votes
120 Euro fraction
121 Keister
123 Artist Magritte
125 Hydrocarbon suffix
126 Friskies eater
128 Suffix with lion
129 "___ lied!"

CAPITAL IDEA by Jay Sullivan
If you like precise clues, you'll like 43 Across.

ACROSS

1 Tijuana's state, familiarly
5 Romo targets
9 High hat
13 Two-dimensional
19 1957 Stravinsky ballet
20 He put two and two together
21 Fuzzy fruit
22 Wine and dine
23 Philippines resistance fighter?
26 Gathering dust
27 Whopper rival
28 Facial hair
29 Gets smart
31 What was for dinner
33 Fowl language
36 PC key
37 Turkish title
40 Bulgarian mall?
43 ORD Terminal 1 carrier
44 Consider
48 Walk all over
49 Early Rocky foe
51 You can sense it
52 Hang-up
54 Sigma successor
56 "Symphonie Espagnole" composer
57 Well-to-do Frenchwoman?
63 Considering
66 Like a stogie
67 Masters stroke
68 "Not true!"
69 Leaves on the table
71 First name in cosmetics
73 Exceedingly difficult
77 Cheryl on "Charlie's Angels"
79 Common consents
81 Its capital is Hermosillo
83 Leave behind
87 Spanish town won't host Olympics?
89 Coined word
90 Spanish ayes
92 Present, for a Cockney
93 Pat on the buns?
94 Olympus mount
97 Antarctic sea
100 Gives authority to
103 Daycare charge
104 Lebanese car chase?
108 Hwy. caution
109 Whup
110 Prize money
111 Golden-ager
116 Leaps over
119 Ford model
121 Cuts corners
122 Famous last words
124 Musical accompaniment in Venezuela?
128 Batman?
129 Somewhat
130 Belmont border
131 Pitcher Robertson
132 Tiger's tracks
133 Clothing store section
134 "Wizard of the Sea" pirate
135 Acts like

DOWN

1 Stag film?
2 One more time
3 Mah-___
4 Japanese cartoon style
5 One who plays a role
6 Holiday quaff
7 Apply hastily
8 Eastern climbing aide
9 Alpine apparel
10 It's nothing
11 Hogwarts messenger
12 It's not fair
13 Home of Frederick the Great
14 Cornea?
15 Flu symptom
16 Bahamian police?
17 Inn stock
18 Rare color
24 Stock holder
25 "The Man Who Fell to Earth" director
30 ___ Lingus
32 Like Hell
34 Mideast org.
35 It occupies a blind spot
38 California winemaker
39 Far from the madding crowd
41 Arctic resident
42 Net receipts
44 They're just dandy
45 Kitty's doc
46 Jazz pianist Chick
47 Jadzia Dax, for one
50 Miss of Mississippi?
53 Scottish highland
55 Small detail
58 Quench
59 One of Hercules' victims
60 Downs town
61 Former Alaskan capital
62 Golfing family name
64 Left-hand page
65 "The Song ___": Kern/Hammerstein
70 Fails to act
72 Thornfield Hall governess
74 Trailing behind
75 Lofty
76 Rosey of the Rams, formerly
78 Bake eggs
80 Horse fathers
82 Tempests in a teapot
83 Uses one's head, in a way
84 Join the club
85 Presidential prerogative in Ecuador?
86 One who cries foul
88 Take exception
91 Watery course
95 Slower on the uptake
96 They have lots
98 VW predecessors?
99 Oddsmakers estimates
101 Dappled
102 Riverine mammal
105 IRA feature
106 Gyrene's org.
107 Comment
112 Milicevic in "Head Over Heels"
113 Brief summary
114 Get high
115 Sissies, by and large?
117 Chorus girl
118 Money-losing proposition
120 Morales of "NYPD Blue"
122 Goose eggs
123 Tear or Torn
125 Did lunch
126 Behaved cowardly
127 Season opener?

219

ACROSS

1 Bridges in movies
6 "Witness" folks
11 Tasty tubers
15 Boxer's fare
19 A. Lee's creator
20 Coyote customer of Acme
21 Estrada of "CHiPs"
22 Belfry sound
23 Back part
24 Maria's "West Side Story" friend
25 "That's ___ ask!"
26 Hamelin deserters
27 "Easy to say!"*
29 Many a Crosby/Hope flick*
31 Acapulco article
32 Broadband connection
34 Be a windbag
35 Gallic Wars hero
39 Splashy resort
41 Auto extra
44 Satisfy a need*
46 Poacher's foe*
51 Queens tennis stadium
52 Ill will
53 "As I ___ saying . . ."
54 Tasting of wood
55 Whale food
57 Former senator Sam
59 Throws with effort
61 Tijuana title
62 Euphoria
65 Blue-eyed cat
66 "House Party" host*
69 Old Japanese line
73 "I think"
74 Hornets' homes
79 Sue Lyon title role
80 Hobby shop inventory
81 Garfield, for one
83 Dutch explorer Tasman
84 Limbo need
85 Dancers' goofs
87 Give the slip to
88 "Congrats!"*
92 Street smarts*
94 Negatively charged particles
95 Buffalo's summer hrs.
96 "The Devil Wears Prada" star
97 Marlee Matlin's language
101 Org. for court figures
103 Pt. of EEC
104 Slowpoke stroke*
107 Wax nonpoetic*
114 Cartesian conjunction
115 Settled down
116 Parts partner
117 Flexible
118 TV talk pioneer
119 Gambling city
120 Acid type
121 Spoil the surprise
122 Place for a London flat
123 Adam's apple location
124 Wreck completely
125 Flaky falls

DOWN

1 Archaic conjunction
2 Ogden Nash priest
3 Milky stone
4 Egg-salad sandwich ingredient?
5 Biblical femme fatale
6 Gulf War craft
7 Ho Chi ___ City
8 Rival of Bjorn
9 Get specific about the ring
10 Piles
11 Wine list datum
12 Restaurant patron of song
13 Fashionable women
14 Lush place?
15 Ketchup catcher
16 Cut out
17 Place for a grilling
18 "Father Murphy" star
28 Most tender
30 Marge Simpson's mother-in-law
33 Kirk's journal
35 Guys
36 Airline seat choice
37 Hawke of "Training Day"
38 Trial figure
39 Tap type
40 Ante body
42 Plains tribe
43 Fed
45 Newscast part
47 Have itchy feet
48 Humorist Barry
49 Just makes it
50 11 Wall Street org.
56 Frank addition
57 Cooks in a hurry
58 Search engine finds
59 Move thyself quickly
60 Brings home
63 Blast furnace output
64 Hardware item
65 Small porches
67 Genetic info carrier
68 Souvenir shop item
69 Refuse to get rid of
70 Freddie the Freeloader, e.g.
71 Breakfast spread
72 Coat with gold
75 Conger catcher
76 Bakery goody
77 Café cup
78 Like a bluff
80 Moon Mullins' brother
82 Exhausts
84 With streaks or spots
85 2004 Billy Bob Thornton film
86 Heater
89 FDR's pooch
90 How streaking may be done
91 "Monk" network
93 Leisurely walks
97 Able one
98 Tropical eel
99 Samantha in "The Collector"
100 Future fiddlehead
102 A neighbor
103 Flynn who played Robin
105 Occupation
106 Collar kind
108 End note
109 Ellen Barkin in "Mac"
110 Property claim
111 Words after stick
112 AIR
113 Lady birds

220 UNDERCOVER FIGURE by Arlan and Linda Bushman
Wait till the end to uncover the undercover figure at 124 Down.

ACROSS

1 "Lovergirl" singer ___ Marie
6 Video download
13 Germ
20 Defensive cover
21 Hawks home
22 Wakened
23 Michelangelo, at times
25 Boss Tweed's machine
26 Raw, on a menu
27 Asian observance
28 Diminutive
29 Kind of man
30 Make an effort
31 Invest
34 Loose-fitting garments
36 Astringent stuff
38 Visigoth foe
39 Loop
41 Went (for)
45 Albert II's residence
48 Alicia Keys' instrument
49 Where "Lost" is found
52 Object in a counting rhyme
53 Writer LeShan
54 Numbered marker
55 Oil-rich sultanate
57 Hence
59 Drive member
61 Tribute, of a sort
62 Outlandish
64 Hobbit allies
66 Set up tents
68 Legendary fliers
69 Silk Road traveler
72 Café Américan visitor
75 Words of dismay
78 Culbertson and Callaway
79 Flows
82 "Racer's edge" at Indy
84 Early Swedish kings
86 Proceedings
88 Save
89 It can be a big wheel
91 Southwest rival
93 Bitterly cold
95 Hellenic vowel
96 Goldfinger
97 Dissertation, for instance
100 Kirby in "City Slickers"
101 Fictional barbarian
102 Break down
103 Clarinet insert
106 Swimwear label
108 Discuss again
111 Wilbur's friend
113 Passeport datum
116 Pot builder
117 Slipper, for short
118 White pudding
120 Economic sanction
122 Pollster's concern
125 Bolster
126 "The Lion in Winter" queen
127 Mother-of-pearl
128 Women's magazine
129 Official entanglements
130 Elsie's lunch

DOWN

1 Ohio political family
2 Corrections list
3 First name in cooking
4 Patent medicine
5 Medieval chest
6 New Year's Eve wear
7 Hiroshima's river
8 XIX times XXIX
9 ". . . why, oh, why ___?"
10 It helps with snow removal
11 Galley notation
12 Sully
13 Theater offering
14 Qom dweller
15 Gilbert & Sullivan specialty
16 Grog ingredient
17 Anthem start
18 Part of n.b.
19 Ben & Jerry's rival
24 Andean treasure
28 Sweet wine
32 Ticket, slangily
33 One more
34 Bufonidae members
35 Interpretation
37 One with the blues
40 Pamplona shout
42 Tortilla Flat eatery?
43 Author Bagnold
44 Handout
46 Monte Carlo bet
47 Take by surprise
49 This entry, e.g.
50 Verve
51 Incan Empire capital
54 Delt neighbor
56 Wry Rye rhymer
58 Robe for Venus
60 Abel's nephew
63 Webzine
65 Covert surveillance device
67 Architect ___ van der Rohe
70 Long-distance number
71 Fastest-running bird
73 Grime
74 On the main
76 '70s shindig
77 Memphis–Nashville dir.
80 It can be round
81 Pop up again
82 Skin patch
83 Cal. heading
85 Dictator's assistant
87 Ghana's chief city
90 Half of zwei
92 Nabokov novel
94 Top seller
97 Volatile solvent
98 Ready to try a case
99 Workshop
104 Beethoven's Symphony No. 3
105 Designer's results
107 Georgia of "The Mary Tyler Moore Show"
109 Renown
110 Chance
112 Hamlet and Ophelia, e.g.
113 Classic grape soda
114 Sign
115 Corp. fast-trackers
117 Hinny's counterpart
119 Big name in irons
121 Knack
122 Each
123 Hollywood's Balin
124 UNDERCOVER FIGURE

221 BRINGING UP BABY   by Arthur S. Verdesca
The answer to 15 Across is not Yale.

ACROSS

1 Where kip are spent
5 Canary's comment
10 Round of applause
15 What Barnard College is not
19 Voice above tenor
20 Fox hunter's cry
21 Taster
22 Locksmith Linus
23 Tariff
24 Record
25 Like some pads
26 Proper partner
27 Original Mardi Gras home
30 Manner
32 Markey who was Jane
33 Barbarians
34 Regulates
38 Champaign's neighbor
41 Leaf beet
43 Merlot's place
44 High times
45 Full-cellar alternative
47 Right, upstairs
48 Mild reproofs
49 Valentino role
50 Just got by
51 Squat
52 Morticia's cousin
53 Vertically, asea
54 Hingis rival
56 "Holey" bread
58 California river
59 Develops
61 Hay bundlers
62 Grizabella's creator
64 PC key
65 Glacial
66 Change the text
68 Stingray eater
72 Luck
75 Growing out
76 Mrs. Willy Loman
77 Whimpers
78 Dior follower
79 Towel word
80 South American monkey
81 Where Stevenson lived
82 Tizzy
83 Muslim title of honor
85 Old crate
88 Crest
89 Ore refinery
91 Foreign
92 Popular plum
93 Termagants
94 Bric-a-___
95 Kind of pad
96 Complete
97 Cover for a cold, winter's day?
102 Kind of brakes
105 Monotheistic religion
107 Parkinson's drug
108 Storklike bird
110 Smidgen
111 Watts in "I Heart Huckabees"
112 Marco Island bird
113 Cipher
114 Chaps
115 Roast host
116 Rushes
117 Examined

DOWN

1 Tomorrow's man
2 Old grad
3 Composer Luening
4 Sources of protein and oil
5 Muse of comedy
6 Ribbed, like corduroy
7 Napoleon slept here
8 Twelfth Jewish month
9 Long-range cruise missile
10 Leaves in the lurch
11 Poisonous plants
12 Crane in "Psycho"
13 Neck style
14 Predetermined
15 Bayou tree
16 Drink spoon?
17 Inventor Whitney
18 Cousin of dese
28 B&Bs
29 Trunk outgrowth
31 Umbrage
34 Chops
35 Gave a clock a face-lift?
36 More stylish
37 Bewitchments
38 Let loose
39 Way to go
40 Chief cook's other hat?
41 Syllabub ingredient
42 17-syllable verse
43 Stirs
45 Jasper, basically
46 Soccer icon
49 Frighten
53 Like a house ___
54 Latino music
55 Rock follower
56 Quick-pitch infractions
57 Fatima's husband
60 Enrich a roast
61 Kentucky college
63 Place to park
65 Rapid courtly dance
66 Go over and over
67 Poser
68 ___-gritty
69 Element
70 Frugal
71 Mortal
73 Pancho's pal
74 Altar server's holding
76 Kind of poker
80 Forestal crown
81 Purist
82 Wax the car
84 Llama relatives
86 University of Wyoming site
87 Brio
88 Super Bowl XXXIV winners
90 Up to
92 Clarifies broth
94 Hold responsible
95 Sulked
97 Political group
98 2007 Ford crossover
99 Ran full tilt
100 Mind
101 Crosshair
102 Crack
103 Marker
104 Foul place
106 American uncle
109 Put in a lawn

CATCH PHRASES by Fred Piscop
Outfielder's catch phrase? ("I got it!")

ACROSS

1 In the least
6 Went down
10 Pandora's boxful
14 Overexcited, slangily
19 Slayer of Tybalt
20 Trial balloon, e.g.
21 Place to brood
22 Lily variety
23 "The Price Is Right" catch phrase
25 "Friends" catch phrase
27 Skin-diving gear
28 Cornball
30 Embroidery yarn
31 Teed off
32 Poet's preposition
33 Ponzi scheme, e.g.
34 "Poppycock!"
37 "Seinfeld" catch phrase
42 Things to crunch
45 Letter before beth
47 Brandy letters
48 Comprehensive
51 Mary of comics
53 Some summer births
54 "Are you game?"
56 Bireme mover
57 Farrah Fawcett's ex
59 Welsh pooch
60 Largest Finnish company
62 Followed smoothly
63 "The Last of the Mohicans" heroine
64 Silvery fish
65 Indian chief?
67 "Siskel & Ebert" catch phrase
72 "___ Excited": Pointer Sisters
73 Fall away
75 "The Jolly Toper" artist
76 Marzipan flavor
78 Lucy's landlady
79 Miser's stash
81 River craft
84 Reunion bunch
85 "Don't bother!"
87 Sheepish look
88 Iraq's ___ Triangle
89 Five to ten, e.g.
91 "N'est-ce ___?"
92 Cold shoulder
93 Bar stock
94 "Hogan's Heroes" catch phrase
101 Results of ties: Abbr.
102 Goes limp
104 "Michael Collins" org.
105 Synthesizer inventor
107 Jerk
110 One set adrift on April 29, 1789
112 Postcard view
116 "Laugh-In" catch phrase
118 "The Apprentice" catch phrase
120 Give a wide berth to
121 [sigh]
122 Strike out
123 "South Pacific" role
124 Monopoly payments
125 Refuses to
126 Exchange words?
127 Super buys

DOWN

1 Electrical discharges
2 Bugs or Daffy
3 Belt filler
4 Grouchoesque glances
5 Be a spectator
6 Acts crabby?
7 Commotions
8 Like some eBay merchandise
9 "Critique of Pure Reason" author
10 Mariner superstar
11 Riot participant
12 Rob in "The Stand"
13 Wire wearer
14 Legend of the road
15 Mob VIP
16 Farm team's burden
17 Sculptor Nadelman
18 Frontier nickname
24 Seneca tutored him
26 Like telekinesis
29 Two-legged zebra
33 Longtime Chicago maestro
34 Scold (with "out")
35 Lily-family member
36 "Tonight Show" catch phrase
38 Carry too far
39 GI hangouts
40 Terminal abbr.
41 Masculine principle
43 "Hawaii Five-O" catch phrase
44 Slowpokes
46 Md. army base
49 Plasma particles
50 Sister of Urania
52 Witchy woman
53 MGM founder Marcus
54 Early-bird catches
55 Kaffiyeh sporter
58 Stick out
59 Was able to
61 Threatening
63 Easel item
65 Needs a bath badly
66 More chichi
68 Spicy cuisine
69 Language that gave us "Sasquatch"
70 ___ Bator
71 Remittance: Abbr.
74 Ultimatum ender
77 Delivery drs.
79 2006 "American Idol" winner
80 Awaiting customers
81 Where togas may be sported
82 Bolt fastener
83 Close kin
86 Winningest NCAA hoops coach
87 NYC mail center
90 Diagnostic tool
95 Frank Phillips, notably
96 Most ironic
97 Xanthippe, e.g.
98 Turkish inn
99 Zip
100 Pulled a boner
103 Etching supplies
106 Mr. Clean's target
107 Winter Palace bigwig
108 Made a basket
109 Recycle Bin, e.g.
110 Skinny tie
111 Stevenson fiend
112 Hungarian sheepdog
113 Met highlight
114 Cartoonist Lazarus
115 Sidewalk stand buys
117 Observed, à la Tweety
119 Brit. lexicon

223 BRIDGE CROSSINGS   by Raymond Hamel
The only river clue in this puzzle is at 22 Across.

ACROSS

1 Bloodhound features
6 Collect
11 Urban eyesore
15 Former Miss America Myerson
19 Full of frenzied activity
20 Carved-out vessel
21 Soften
22 River through Kazakhstan
23 Chicago's McCormick Place, for one
26 Breathing sound
27 Powder holder
28 "Neither a borrower ___ . . ."
29 Gets rid of, in slang
30 Started the pot
31 Dog created by Jim Davis
32 Eye ID
33 Universals
34 Downtrodden
39 ___ avis
40 Kind of meditation
41 Competitive couplet creation
43 Randolph Scott western (with "The")
45 Greek sandwich
49 An elapid
50 Pitcher's joint?
52 Give a quick once-over
54 Fidgety
58 Overly
60 Outfit, in Oxford
61 They're trying?
62 Kind of hen
64 Theatrical awards
65 "Everybody Loves Raymond" network
66 Lowers the lights
67 Diamond org.
68 Not dozing
71 Lures deceptively
72 Jigsaw parts
76 Restylane alternative
78 ___ es Salaam
79 Holding fast
81 Metro measure
83 Championship
85 Pathet ___
86 Tennis score
87 Speck in the sea
89 Robin Zander's band
93 "A Wizard of Earthsea" hero
95 Olympic swimmer Torres
97 Denounce
98 Baby bed
101 "Perry Mason" investigator
103 Butter substitute
104 Unexciting
105 Point-system writing
107 Teacher's org.
108 Curator's deg.
111 The same, in Latin
112 Claymore, for one
115 Playwright O'Flaherty
116 Measured foot?
117 Lost city discovered by 119 Across
118 Copyrighted
119 Nickname of Dr. Jones
120 Catch a glimpse of
121 Problems
122 Victory shoes?

DOWN

1 Trunk item
2 Wind instrument
3 "2046" director Kar-wai
4 Ullmann or Tyler
5 Thin
6 Ullmann and Tyler
7 Été month
8 "And giving ___, up the chimney . . ."
9 Laker rival, briefly
10 Circle part
11 Brazilian ladies
12 Toss to the side?
13 Employs
14 Mal de ___
15 Dragster doing
16 Lyrist of myth
17 Massachusetts harbor town
18 Polaris products
24 Clamorous
25 Brilliance
30 Camping tool
31 Minor morsel
33 Pontiac SUV
34 Eye-popping designs
35 Unanswerable question
36 Mountain Dew's parent
37 90-degree bends
38 Small amount
42 Putt-putted along
44 First name in Solidarity
46 Elusive mountain creature
47 Like round crosswords
48 Pindar's poems
51 Gets involved in
53 Air Force Academy freshman
55 He sacked his own QB?
56 Maine-based outlet
57 Road curve
59 Concerning dreams
62 Word after bottle or salary
63 Stop for travelers
66 Taj Mahal architect
67 Pitch meas.
68 Courtroom minutes
69 Dictionary entry
70 Jai ___
71 Old autos
73 Salsa legend Cruz
74 Dramatize
75 Stir up the fire
77 Emulate a flying squirrel
79 "Flashdance" heroine
80 Minister's assistant
82 Jeanne Phillips column
84 French beverage
88 Path
90 Moved a gondola
91 Quisling's crime
92 Carnival hot spot
94 Freddy Krueger's street
96 Bootstring ends
98 Cattle drive entree
99 "The Thinker" sculptor
100 Yet to come
102 Gather bit by bit
105 Feathery scarves
106 Pulitzer winner Buchanan
108 Natalie Teeger's boss
109 Footloose
110 Tacks on
112 Bite the dust
113 Musical job
114 Early 20th-c. conflict

The song at 68 Across won an Academy Award.

ACROSS

1 Some read them
5 Jai-alai basket
10 "That's it!"
14 SS Sussex sinker
19 Tennis edge
20 Wing it
21 Novello of old films
22 One of the Corleones
23 Male Dallas cheerleaders? (Welsh corgi mix)
25 Camp Lejeune uniforms? (Weimaraner mix)
27 Move by degrees
28 Antigen attacker
30 Japanese beef city
31 ___ Lingus
32 Charley Weaver's Mt. ___
33 Many-sided problems
37 Full of vigor
40 Get some exposure?
43 Anti-crime act of 1970
46 Do lab work on
47 Pts. and qts.
48 Rotunda stands
49 Stack topper: Var.
50 Dept. of Labor div.
51 Fallen orbiter
52 Pone stacks? (cocker spaniel mix)
55 ___ up (dress finely)
56 Highly rated
57 Deteriorates, in a way
58 "___ my case!"
59 Slopping the hogs, e.g.
61 Aspen wear
63 Liqueur flavoring
64 Like sorted socks
65 Stacks, in a way
66 Item in black
67 Ballet studio need
68 Song from "Nashville"
70 Neatens up
71 Drafted
74 Act like a crab?
75 Take a bite of
76 Post-season goal
77 Scatter's syllable
78 Poet's peeper
79 Son of Meathead? (Boston terrier mix)
82 Baby docs
83 Shakespeare, notably
85 Water carriers
86 Ceremonial staff bearer
87 Swarm member
88 Shirley Temple's ex
89 Gaelic tongue
90 Jimmy Walker was one
91 Diploma word
92 Soprano Scotto
94 Took the cake
95 Help at the diner
96 Have an effect
98 Calyx part
100 "Evil Ways" group
104 Simian triathlete? (Pomeranian mix)
108 Drum major with great footwork? (Rottweiler mix)
110 Moderator's milieu
111 Thomas Friedman's page
112 Henry Ford's son
113 Tabloid topic
114 Oozing with water
115 Soul mate
116 Regards
117 Buffalo Bill

DOWN

1 Garland's 1939 costar
2 Bean sprout?
3 Ancient Brit
4 Arctic vehicles
5 B-baller
6 Cut and paste
7 Camera type, briefly
8 Pinball term
9 X-axis coordinate
10 In a vague manner
11 Cameo shape
12 ___'wester
13 Composer Satie
14 Words on perishables
15 Showed respect for
16 Binary digit
17 Gasteyer of "SNL"
18 Norse war god
24 Muffet's fare
26 Not a chance
29 Old English letter
34 Chinatown gang back in power? (Gordon setter mix)
35 On leave
36 Put on
37 Prayer wheel users
38 Inuit craft
39 High-fiber baby food? (Saint Bernard mix)
40 Record book entries
41 Fast times
42 Gap bridgers
43 Most mellow
44 Maya Angelou's "Still ___"
45 Deadheads, e.g.
48 Bligh's ship
49 Subway ___ (2000 event)
52 Less refined
53 Reunion folks
54 Pimpernel color
60 Bring aboard
62 Campanile sound
63 In the present state
64 Sickly look
66 Gentleman burglar Lupin
67 IHOP mix
68 Weather-map line
69 Cartoon oasis, perhaps
70 A Hilton
71 Pancho's amigo
72 ___ sprawl
73 Elbows, e.g.
75 Way up
76 In-flight convenience
80 1998 Masters winner
81 Gave off
84 Composed
87 Like some ulcers
90 Bushy do
91 "Scarface" star
93 Who opera
94 In need of Roundup
95 Wails
97 TV feature, once
98 Floored it
99 Sourdough's strike
100 Morel morsel
101 Low woman
102 Sine qua non
103 ___ brat
104 Question marks
105 Lobsters-to-be
106 Azurite, e.g.
107 Mil. address
109 Language suffix

225 HIDDEN CASH* by Stella Daily and Bruce Venzke
Coin collectors should appreciate this theme.

ACROSS

1 Pile up
6 Business end of a razor
10 Table
15 "You Shook Me All Night Long" band
19 Father, Biblically
20 Charbroil
21 Slip by
22 Met or Phillie
23 Mideast potentate
24 Domestic
25 Popular salad dressing*
27 Nothing special*
29 Beach toy
30 Stowe character
31 Future lice
32 Madonna hit*
34 Get through arguing
38 Broderick's "The Producers" costar
39 "The Wizard ___"
40 Jewelers' units, for short
41 Spine-tingling
42 Silken wear of India
43 Ancient Dead Sea kingdom
44 From the Bay Area*
48 "The ___ Room" (1962)
54 Tare allowance
55 Getting warm
56 Gift of the Magi
58 Egg's predecessor
59 1983 role for Barbra
61 Tectonic division
63 Like farmland
64 Straggle
67 Radar's quaff*
70 Sack or song preceder
71 Hard up
73 Tape over
74 "___ my case!"
76 Features of fancy hotels
77 Post horse
78 "Say Anything" star Skye
79 Startled exclamation
83 Sunnybrook Farm dweller
85 Szechuan cuisine spice*
89 Farmer's prefix
91 Men on a crew
92 Plastic surgeon's recreations
93 CIA predecessor
96 Arctic sight
97 Princess Fiona, by night
98 Start to see red
100 Related to the nervous system*
103 One and the other
104 "Bravo! Bravo!"
105 Gershwin and Levin
106 Tows away*
110 "Letters From Iwo Jima" et al.*
112 David of "Rhoda"
113 Stand out
115 Middle name in Graceland
116 Goddess of peace
117 "Sweet, dude!"
118 "Symphony in Black" et al.
119 Where a pet door leads to often
120 ___ Moore Beef Stew
121 Superpower of yore
122 Addles

DOWN

1 Presidential nickname
2 Biz communication
3 Ripening chemical
4 Soybean, e.g.
5 First-___ (starter)
6 Dead giveaway?
7 Sweetie pies
8 Like muskox meat
9 Afore
10 Kind of school club
11 "Hollywood Ending" heroine
12 Nuclear reactor tube
13 Academic URL suffix
14 Turns a strip mine into a farm
15 Lay ___ (bomb)
16 Man of the cloth
17 Tucson environs
18 Bass baskets
26 Had in custody
28 Not a thing
29 More than a scare
32 Milky Way creator
33 "You can have my cards!"
34 "Diamond Lil" playwright
35 Aft, aboard
36 "Rule, Britannia!" composer
37 "Peachy-keen!"
38 Wildlife refuge
42 More furfuraceous
43 Mi, musically
45 Subjoin
46 Spend a guilder here: Abbr.
47 Visibly amazed
49 Circle dances
50 Doc Wonmug's assistant
51 Andy Capp's haunts
52 Lois Lane's mother
53 Owner's document
57 Some injuries
60 Punchcard-reading computer
61 What the Devil wears?
62 Vegas or Cruces preceder
63 "Take ___ breath!"
64 Linesman?
65 Pay to play
66 Costume
68 Flamenco dancer José
69 Normandy department
72 Defiant Shakespearean shout
75 Where bad characters are found
77 Myopic Mr.
78 Words on a 2 Down
80 ___ facto
81 Colleague
82 Irish Gaelic
84 Way to avoid your mother-in-law's calls?
86 Hip fitness disciplines
87 Sandwich man
88 Psyched
90 Exercise system
93 Eventually
94 Madame, in Madrid
95 Aid and comfort
96 "The Quiet Man" director
97 "Juno and the Paycock" playwright
98 Pocket-cheeked animal
99 DDE's arena
101 Roly-poly
102 "___, Therefore I Am": Dennis Miller
103 College football QBs, e.g.
106 Where a pupil sits
107 Drag-racing org.
108 Total airhead
109 NY Giants 2004 #2 draft pick
111 He gave Jackie an "O"
112 Bearded beast
114 System starter?

226 "SOUNDS FAKE TO ME!" by Elizabeth C. Gorski
2008 marks the fourth appearance of Sly guy (124 Across).

ACROSS

1 Volunteer's words
5 Beach of California
10 Rescue team members
14 German I pronoun
17 Booted disco figure
19 Begot
21 The chills
22 Perched atop the best ship's planking?
24 "Cornflake Girl" singer Amos
25 Cleaving
26 Skater Babilonia
27 Get A's after getting B's
29 Play segment
30 Rock era?
34 Army division
35 Gardner McKay novel
37 Get Ricki out of the slammer?
41 Never-ending
45 Steakhouse plateful
46 Revolutionary group
47 "Songs of Innocence" poet's prediction?
50 TV screen
52 Bard's "before"
53 Upper hand
54 Royal in "Big Bad Mama"
55 Fill until full
57 U.S. agents
58 Find another chair for
61 English royal house
64 '90s dance craze
66 Mideast tremor?
70 "Heavens!"
73 Baking ___
74 Coca-Cola cel?
78 Self-help guru Wayne
79 Bill Romanowski autobiography
81 ". . . three men in ___"
84 Purple fruit
85 Aachen article
86 Sign of summer
87 Movie trailers for "Anaconda"?
92 Hostile party
94 "Coffee, ___ Me" (1973)
96 Insignificance
97 Confusion during a leaves collection?
99 Gelato holders
100 "Both Sides Now" songwriter Mitchell
101 Titular job?
103 Make-up artist's admission?
108 ___ change (seek reform)
111 "American Gothic" model
112 "Back to original speed": Mus.
113 Sherpa bugaboo
114 Obituary section archives?
119 Creek at the Masters
120 Sub detector
121 Heartened
122 Miss a typo, say
123 Ventura, for one: Abbr.
124 Sly guy?
125 "Calm down . . ."

DOWN

1 Sikorsky and Stravinsky
2 Like a dunce's cap
3 Tequila source
4 ___ situation
5 Gut reaction?
6 Cozy quarters
7 Anat., for one
8 Wise counselor
9 Melodeon
10 Contractor's fig.
11 ISS predecessor
12 It lacks that new-car smell
13 Zaire's Mobuto Sese ___
14 Expression of self-expression
15 Elixir
16 Testament name
18 Set of table and chairs
20 Beta-test
21 Number one Hun
23 Nogales nap
28 Put into play
30 Bishops' council
31 Aquarium favorite
32 NYPD calls
33 Small caves
36 Stumblebum
38 Apricot juice
39 Carpenters' drummer
40 "Maria ___" (1940s hit)
41 "Good buddy"
42 Shoppe descriptive
43 Badgers
44 Swamp buzzer
48 "Watermark" singer
49 Too many spoil the broth
51 News summary
56 MD org.
57 Pancreatic enzyme
59 "Well, lookee here!"
60 Celine Dion song
62 Vintage wheels
63 Famous film producer
65 Blood-typing letters
67 Effortless
68 Designer line?
69 Destiny
70 Less even?
71 Mongoose relative
72 New York Yankees' #2
75 Sailor's direction
76 They run through cornfields
77 "Working Girl" girl
80 "___ me according to thy mercy": Psa. 109:26
82 "The Jungle" novelist
83 Fetch
86 Janet and Loretta
88 Whistle hour
89 "The Da Vinci Code" details
90 Toronto–to–Montreal dir.
91 Schmoozed with
93 Pupil constriction
95 Pearl setting
98 Endowments
99 Robert Altman's art
102 One to meet on Judgment Day
104 Floodplain need
105 "___ bind here!" ("Help!")
106 Blunted swords
107 Frumpish
108 Fiery heap
109 Tail end
110 "We got trouble!"
112 Erma Bombeck's dog
115 Envisioned
116 Like the Wright stuff
117 Big Blue
118 Bean

227 CALLS OF THE WILD   by Norma Steinberg
33 Across debuted as a silent cliffhanger serial in 1914.

ACROSS

1 Gallic god
5 Forehead
9 Opp. of masc.
12 Goober Pyle's cousin
17 Morning-line data
18 Dog in "Top Dog"
19 Father
20 Dry gully
21 Alarming cries from the crow's-nest?
24 Blush
25 Ne'er-do-well
26 "___ Was a Lady"
27 They lit the boonies
28 Tail movement
31 Light source
32 Loses lustre
33 "The ___ of Pauline"
36 Drill sergeant's command
38 Ms. Couric
39 Drivers' org.
40 Takes home after taxes
42 Evening in Milan
43 Uneasy dog star?
45 Itsy-bitsy
46 Oscar winner Thompson
47 Bomb part
48 Enjoys dinner
49 After take or high
50 "The ___ is cast!"
51 Address for a king snake?
55 Cogitated upon
56 Sidekick
58 Flick
59 Fixed responses
60 Tom Jones' birthplace
61 Nudges
62 Pumbaa's pal
63 "Case ___!"
65 ( ), for short
66 Fixes
68 Burly
69 Nobelist who wrote udder nonsense?
72 Pigeon sound
74 Long for
75 Military hooky
76 Jay's class
77 Voting sect
78 "___ Couldn't Say No"
79 Defend one's flock from attack?
83 Fry lightly
84 Bagatelle's adjective
86 Gives the go-ahead
87 Madison Avenue suits
88 "Man of La ___"
89 Make better
91 Dion and Dido
92 Mare's tidbit
93 Barbie's ex
94 Before Sat.
95 To ___ mildly
96 Loosen a knot
98 Ready for company
101 Barking angrily?
106 Mustangs for serpentine roads?
107 Colonist Hutchinson
108 Jai ___
109 Red Skelton's first wife
110 Lopes
111 Page in "Falstaff"
112 Cons out of
113 Fortune teller

DOWN

1 Grumpy leader?
2 Big Daddy's wife
3 Elizabeth I's bro.
4 Former Cold War antagonist
5 Irish accent
6 Encore airing
7 Former
8 Court
9 Longtime Boston Pops conductor
10 "To ___ human . . ."
11 Word known to Daniel
12 Garson in "Random Harvest"
13 Frock
14 Au courant
15 Ogle
16 Senator Wyden
19 Supreme Court justice
20 In ___ (past due)
22 "All That Jazz" subject
23 Lower than
28 Diminished
29 Tiny
30 Kitty's cry for help?
32 "___ in Terris": (John XXIII encyclical)
33 Come-as-you-are ___
34 Brave Meriwether and chicken William?
35 Director Soderbergh
37 ___ single bound
38 Give lip service to?
39 Marble
41 Unkempt
43 Oxidizes
44 Lucie's father and brother
47 Let go
49 Roll-your-own bed?
51 Like Swiss cheese
52 Italian love
53 Extra card
54 Happening
55 Antique office machine
57 Impetuosity
59 VIP cars
61 Paloma's dad
62 More subdued
63 Large hole
64 Dirty old man
65 Story lines
67 Calm down
69 Heeded the alarm
70 Small restaurants
71 Tewkesbury river
73 Indian, for one
75 Tortures
77 Make illegal
80 Loading the trap
81 Counsel
82 Violin maker of note
83 French composer
85 It earns an "A"
88 "Twelfth of Never" singer
90 La Douce, and others
91 One of the Allman Brothers
92 Ready to pour
95 Baby buggy
96 Hard on the eyes
97 Sheepcote matriarchs
98 Behave
99 Rocky outcropping
100 Starz! rival
102 Remind again
103 Keats opus
104 "___ singular sensation . . ."
105 Out there

228 IN A POSSESSIVE MOOD by John Underwood
Don't be thinking vegetable at 71 Across.

ACROSS

1 Hans of "Die Meistersinger"
6 What Libra holds
12 Friday or Sunday person
15 "Not that!"
19 Earmark
20 Part of a Great Lakes address
21 Appreciation class
22 Icky sticky stuff
23 Like ___ in the woods
24 "Born Yesterday" playwright Kanin
25 Means for quick exit?
27 Senator's dog?
30 Not a trace of moisture
31 Je t'___ (I love you)
32 Burlesques
34 Perfect-game pitcher Barker
35 Dress for a party
38 Earth inheritors (with 124-A)
39 Avignon article
41 ___ Park, CO
45 Royal symbol
46 Mexican rebel's residence?
50 Cool
51 Menu item
53 Jim and Tammy's TV network
54 Brilliant success
55 Room opener
56 Mogul governor
58 Fort embankment
62 "Where's Charley?" composer
64 . . . — . . .
66 Broadway restaurateur Vincent
67 Rare Texan
68 OPEC, for one
71 Painter's tater?
74 Blended whiskey
75 Zimbabwe, formerly
77 Japanese noodle dish
78 Flag thrower
80 "Happy Days" catchphrase
81 One above knight
83 Hebrew scroll
87 Munich river
88 French "house"?
90 Habitual, for short
92 French infant
93 Italian Saint Philip
94 Ballroom dancer's palace?
99 Voter, of sorts
100 "Family Ties" member
102 All the same
103 "¿___ que?"
104 Grants use of
106 T-shirt size
108 Marmoset
111 Suzy in "Twister"
112 R. Stroud's Alcatraz nickname
116 Yankee legend's cape?
120 Fort in the Bronx
122 Stop moving around
123 Animal trail
124 See 38 Across
125 Rock's Rose
126 Son of Poseidon
127 Sans ___ (carefree)
128 Avocado, e.g.
129 Kgs. or ozs.
130 White quakers
131 Singers Jones and James

DOWN

1 9-3 auto maker
2 "Dark Angel" star
3 Silent-screen star's curtsy?
4 Frodo, Sam or Merry
5 Mist over
6 Nintendo rival
7 Really vulgar
8 Spa bubble massage facility
9 South Africa surrounds it
10 Adhesive resins
11 More together
12 Palaver
13 Part of UAE
14 Rank above Maj.
15 Poet's classic car?
16 Where the boyz are
17 Koh-i-___ diamond
18 Grand Ole place
26 Kind of jerk
28 Draw up a new plan
29 Surviving species
33 It can be hard or soft
35 Make up
36 A whale of a film
37 ___ 'acte
40 Downhill zigzag
42 Stretching muscle
43 Greasy spoon
44 "A Sentimental Journey" author
47 Felony designation
48 Operatic movement circa 1900
49 Suppliant
52 "Stillmatic" rapper
57 "Dragonheart" knight
59 Bad beginning
60 Adjust in proper relation
61 Campaign slugfest
63 Snowy heron
65 "Penny Serenade" repeated phrase
67 Rogue elephants, e.g.
68 Chemical warfare gas
69 Swindle
70 Community club
72 Supper club
73 Fowl female
76 Philanthropist's nobleman?
79 Trick (with "off")
81 Tiny clucker
82 Four: Comb. form
84 Mystery writer's pub drink?
85 Drive the getaway car
86 Hellespont priestess
89 Depilatory product
91 Trace
95 Asimov's first human emigrants
96 Kind of filter cigarette
97 Short solo piece
98 All together
101 Winged-woman-holding-atom award
105 Shoddy
107 Smits/Hamlin series
109 Jamaican man in slang
110 Astroturf ingredient
112 Bottom apt.
113 Icy decorator?
114 S. Korea's Syngman
115 Immediately following
117 Taste or touch, in Paris
118 Like Ricky Martin's "Vida"
119 Discordia's Greek counterpart
121 Literary monogram

229

AT THE RESTAURANT   by Nancy Nicholson Joline
The MENSA member ordered b r __ __ n s!

ACROSS

1 Metaphorical payee
6 "Aha!"
12 They may be guided
20 Photoshop company
21 Was stuck on
22 Bowl over
23 The golfer ordered a ___
25 The karate black belt favored ___
26 Locales
27 This puzzle has one
29 "Say ___?" ("Huh?")
30 Bank statement abbr.
31 Old Olds
32 Foul-up
36 Plus
38 Hayes or Stern
41 Some are final
45 Film director Kusturica
46 The tipsy patron requested ___
48 Jergens rival
49 "Do ___ say, . . ."
50 Lyon lake
51 Grenoble's river
52 Not more than
53 Disney ant princess
54 "___ by any other name": Shak.
56 Day in Hollywood
58 The fencing master ate ___
60 Tailor's chalk
61 Nosh
62 Canine utterance
63 Reserves
66 Pants parts
69 Rang
73 Last of the Mohicans
76 Down
79 Puccini heroine
80 The complaining patron dined on ___
84 Frasier of "Frasier"
85 "Galveston" composer and family
86 Female lobsters
87 Bring back
89 Hell's Angels member
91 Olé, in Omaha
92 Baba accompaniment
93 Coeur d'___, Idaho
94 The Englishman had a ___
96 One of the Jackson five
98 Brickbats
99 "Playboy" request
100 "Don't ___!"
101 Hustles
103 One of a Dumas trio
105 Dug into
107 It may be tin
109 On the ball, e.g.
110 Worries
115 The minister preferred ___
119 The prosecutor liked ___
121 Inappropriate
122 Make attractive
123 Fontana di ___
124 Bob Gainey's team
125 Takes care of
126 Coupled

DOWN

1 Lobbying gps.
2 Not working
3 Glower
4 Righteous Brothers hit
5 Pine product
6 Kind of war
7 Bettor's concern
8 Winter resort sight
9 Cavilers
10 "Wag the Dog" actress
11 Disciple
12 It's for your own protection
13 Book ending
14 Pack
15 Campus gp.
16 Crackers
17 Lucy in "Charlie's Angels"
18 Austin–to–Houston dir.
19 Scant
24 Capers
28 Saws
31 Olympus products
33 Stradivari's teacher (with 37-D)
34 They're made by hands
35 Dickensian villain
36 Biblical mount
37 See 33 Down
39 Iditarod racers
40 "Rodeo" composer Copland
42 Admits
43 Subatomic particle
44 Petty despot
46 Motorists' woes
47 Stop
52 Suspiciously
53 Burning
55 Cancels an NBC comedy?
57 Luge-run surface
59 Hip-hop Dr.
64 Ltr. abbr.
65 Poe's gold bug, e.g.
67 Camelot knight
68 Dude ranch features
70 Those born on October 5th
71 Make a start
72 Bob in "Don Juan DeMarco"
74 Cub Scout leader
75 Cleave
77 Kind of suit
78 Tea choice
80 Cyber talks
81 Memento
82 "West Side Story" girl
83 "Arabian Nights" voyager
85 Dryly humorous
88 Traces
90 The Black Prince
94 Cliché
95 Title for Maazel
97 Folded fare
102 12-time Emmy winner Morley
104 "Stormy Weather" singer
106 Cross
108 Site of 123 Across
109 Brief affair
110 Louver
111 Racer Palmroth
112 Pursue
113 Gutter's site
114 Lose traction
115 Total
116 "Rising" album artist
117 Nimitz's org.
118 Plug attachment
120 "___ Miz"

230 JAMAICA DATE by Sam Bellotto Jr.
Sam's title says it all.

ACROSS

1 Very, musically
6 Road hazard?
10 Speculative
14 Call to worship
18 Squad-car figure
21 Country singer Evans
22 Shield boss
23 Elmer Fudd's words to Bugs, in Montevideo?
26 Chinese leader?
27 Haunted-house sights
28 Bend
29 URL suffix
30 ___ many words
31 "Nevermind!"
33 Puts on the payroll
35 Smart and Smiley
39 Smith or Jones, often
41 Medium crimson
44 Query of a midday deadline, in Nairobi?
50 Gland atop the kidney
51 "Give ___ break!"
52 Before taker or giver
53 Sticking point
55 Pongids have ten
56 Vault
58 "I've had it ___ here!"
59 Prefix for task
60 Shut up
61 Abbr. on a cornerstone
63 Tugboat operators
64 Order for a Cott soft drink, in Accra?
70 Gourd-shaped rattle
71 Gulf of Aqaba port
72 WCs
73 Veni, to a Latin student
74 Teal genus
75 Exile isle
76 "Oh, ___ in England . . .": Browning
80 Mork's word
81 Walken's "Joe Dirt" role
82 Grain beard
84 Continuously
86 Request to pipe down, in Belmopan?
90 What Au stands for
91 TV-tube gas
92 In ___ (unborn)
93 Body of bees
96 Pooch parasite
97 "The Last of the Mohicans" heroine
100 Yellow vehicle
101 Some are rare
105 Lake effect lake
106 Tomato type
110 Complaint concerning a scam artist, in Cairo?
115 Canine asset
116 City ENE of Moscow
117 Chill factor
118 Bay State motto word
119 Forget about (it)
120 What drums keep
121 "The Gondoliers" girl

DOWN

1 Bird of Paradise
2 Punjab wear
3 Nonlethal phaser setting
4 Jason's ship
5 Letters from a debtor
6 Crew craft
7 Latin-I word
8 Nonessential for a Toyota RAV4 EV
9 Reference bk.
10 St. Lawrence seaway sight
11 Hang down
12 Soleil of "Punky Brewster" fame
13 Oscitation
14 Tied house of London
15 Hot cinder
16 Withstand
17 Aquatic Asian plant
19 Grubby place?
20 Penultimate letters
24 Playground comeback
25 Suffix with walk or talk
30 "For he ___ Englishman": G&S
31 Whereabouts
32 "Voila!"
34 Vaccines
35 Odd-handed card game
36 Word form of "child"
37 As to
38 Takes a gander at
40 Like a dishrag
41 Spaghetti option
42 Saragossa river
43 Aqueous NaOH
45 Principal ore of lead
46 Verdugo in "Little Giant"
47 Org. that once targeted Sen. Sarbanes
48 Warship deck
49 Japanese soybean food
54 Whisk broom
57 Reading room
58 Ogden locale
59 USNA students, for short
60 Velocity
61 Tanguay and Turner
62 Ready-go connection
63 Stately dance
64 "Heaven, ___ heaven . . ."
65 Caged talker
66 Eight-legged horse of myth
67 Hooked
68 Gentle as ___
69 Big cheese
74 Felipe of baseball
75 Car designer Ferrari
76 Bolt attachment
77 Cartoon canine
78 Transvaal settler
79 Core: Comb. form
81 Dancer Lili Saint-___
82 Smart guy
83 One of forty?
85 Pacific hue
87 "The Group" director
88 Take up space
89 Scramble, in a way
93 Shooting-script segment
94 Delivery truck
95 Gulf
96 Onomatopoeic word
98 Beauvais department
99 It's in back
102 Intercom components
103 Smoke
104 "Amber Waves" singer Amos
105 "Terms of Endearment" heroine
106 Bat mitzvah, e.g.
107 Burden of proof
108 J. Torre et al.
109 Under sail
111 16th letter
112 NY wagering parlor
113 Charge
114 Puncheon

231 THAT CHAMPIONSHIP SEASON by Harvey Estes
A salute to eight great NCAA football coaches and their teams.

ACROSS

1 Barbecue entrée
5 Made over
10 Billionaire TV host
15 Excellent, in modern slang
19 Land unit
20 "A Bell For ___"
21 "American Idol" judge Abdul
22 McDonald's arches, e.g.
23 PENN STATE (1986)
25 FLORIDA (2006)
27 Flu fighter
28 Stroll
30 Chin beard
31 Lose one's lap
32 Respond to the doorbell
34 Shea Stadium squad
35 Rules out
37 City of Ohio or Georgia
41 Shapes
45 Vegetable soup bean
46 In the open
47 On ___ with
48 FLORIDA STATE (1999)
51 Not talking
52 Foal's mom
53 Auction stipulation
54 Time off, briefly
55 Macbeth and Duncan, e.g.
57 Sets up
59 Engineer Jones
60 Health clubs
61 Got in the way of
62 Wandered
63 Hitchhiked
66 Part of a U.
67 Calculator symbol
68 Lanky one
69 Face down
71 Emphatic turndown
72 Cotton pod
73 Madame in "The Balcony"
74 Acorn offspring
75 SOUTHERN CAL (2004)

77 Chemical compound
78 Winter wear
81 Anise-flavored liqueur
82 Plait of hair
83 Emperor during WWII
84 Heed
87 Jay of TV
88 Treated with kid gloves
89 Give halftime stats
93 Bad luck blocker
96 Pilgrim John
97 Corsair crew
99 OHIO STATE (2002)
101 ALABAMA (1979)
104 Boxer's fare
105 Up the ante
106 "Three Tall Women" playwright
107 Earthenware material
108 Grate sound
109 Quibbling quarrels
110 Tumbler on a mat?
111 Fashion mag

DOWN

1 Punjabi prince
2 Vista pictures
3 Football great Favre
4 Drawing in brown
5 For adult viewing only
6 Forbidden fruit site
7 Patriotic org.
8 Lodging place
9 End of the world as we know it
10 Works
11 Pear peeler
12 Deep red
13 Menu phrase
14 Useless member
15 Like Punch?

16 Singer/songwriter Axton
17 One-time Met Tommie
18 Rent a tux
24 Moorehead of "Bewitched"
26 Recurring theme
29 Run a tab
32 Cover stories
33 Anesthetizes
34 Mark Antony's mother
36 Brought to an end
37 Like an off track
38 NEBRASKA (1995)
39 Track tipper
40 Octopus's abundance
41 Cass and Phillips
42 Eye-popping paintings
43 MIAMI (2001)
44 Aerosmith's first hit

46 Had title to
48 Bialy relative
49 Daring display
50 Gardens amidst the sands
55 Turned in a tight circle
56 More theatrical
58 Major African artery
59 Shaped like a megaphone
60 Formal will
62 Gets up
63 Be a fink
64 Red Muppet dolls
65 Gives a hand
67 "Live free or die," e.g.
68 Drank a lot
69 Christopher Robin's pal
70 Shankar of sitar
71 Peachy
72 Big bully

75 Lecturers' equipment
76 Baseball accessory
79 Desk style
80 Root in the stands
82 It's human
84 Soup servers
85 "May ___ of service?"
86 "Survivor" units
88 Fortunate, old-style
90 Psychic Edgar
91 In the least
92 Kind of colony
93 Cracked open
94 "___ 18"
95 Diamond figures
96 China setting
97 LBJ or JFK
98 Lid problem
100 Maple fluid
102 Conduit bend
103 Attorney's org.

232 PIE FIGHT* by Michael Collins
Perhaps we should have omitted the asterisk in the clue for 112 Across.

ACROSS

1 Port of Israel
6 Honda's upscale line
11 Water-to-wine site
15 Bowie's wife
19 Belgian painter (1860–1949)
20 Asocial sort
21 They're #2
22 "Beowulf" is one
23 Frank Willard strip*
25 Quilted stove pad*
27 Put in office
28 Grand ___ (Wyoming peak)
30 Like some marshes
31 Have ___ (be connected)
32 "Children of the Albatross" author
33 Rat cheese?
35 Like many cuisines
38 Michael of "Monty Python"
41 Wee-hours broadcast
45 Sphinx, in part
46 Title for Taylor Hicks*
49 "Surfin' ___": Beach Boys
50 Gives a whipping to
52 Fast-shrinking sea
53 Pizazz
54 "Follow me!"
55 High dudgeon
56 Source of patronage jobs*
60 Moscow moola
61 "Gangs of New York" actor
63 Porsche rivals
65 Angler with pots
66 Elite Navy team
67 Violin-playing comedian
69 Blake of ragtime
71 More bummed
73 In a tough spot
75 Pair above the kidneys
78 Beats soundly
79 Way to right a capsized canoe*
82 "Whiffenpoof" syllable
83 Endorses, in a way
84 Hockey's Phil, to fans
86 Z ___ zebra
87 Piped up
89 Alice's sitcom boss
90 Hot breakfast fare*
94 Arabia's Gulf of ___
95 Foretold
97 Like the flu
98 Trailers?
100 Cut close
101 Mal de ___
102 Movie theater
103 Dum ___ spero (SC motto)
106 Buenos ___
108 Short composition
112 Bart Simpson's cry*
115 Dirty fighter?*
117 "Step on it!"
118 Enlarge, in a way
119 Novelist Le Sage
120 New York governor Spitzer
121 Boot fare
122 Adriatic seaport
123 Off the wall
124 Cut out

DOWN

1 Prefix with sphere
2 In a bit
3 Instant-replay cameras, for short
4 Lunt's partner
5 Big name in suits
6 ___ wrench
7 Like vichyssoise
8 Cycle starter
9 Have a flat
10 Poison in mysteries
11 Plumped-up fowl
12 Bell-ringing company
13 MSG hoops tourney
14 Mount Pelée cloud
15 Archipelago units
16 Whipped up
17 Got mellower
18 ___ a soul
24 City on the Mohawk
26 Window style
29 Fey of "SNL" fame
33 Club ___ Bing in "The Sopranos"
34 Like ___ of bricks
35 Heston title role
36 Bejeweled item
37 Rose of song*
38 Job extras
39 Burnoose wearer
40 Oscar winner Kedrova
41 Actress Palmer
42 Modest digs*
43 "___ Mio"
44 Big Poison of baseball
47 Poughkeepsie college
48 Holey-pocketed
51 "Oops! . . . I Did It Again" singer
54 Give info to
57 Hogwarts mail carrier
58 "Amazing" magician
59 Seek a seat
60 Lee's men
62 Vichyssoise veggies
64 Kia minivan
67 Curler's broom
68 Comics shriek
70 E-address
71 Comics colonel
72 Hot shot on the diamond
74 Add cushioning to
75 Mexican Oscar
76 Left Coast hoopster
77 Composer Camille Saint-___
80 Bryn ___
81 Dept. of Labor div.
84 "It follows that …"
85 Slip through the cracks?
88 Recurring Percy Kilbride role
90 St. John's bread
91 In charge of
92 Ax wielder, at times
93 "Know ___ enemy"
96 Fido's fare, maybe
99 "Right away!"
101 2007 Super Bowl site
102 Like "Hee Haw" humor
103 Grifter's game
104 Something to strike
105 "As ___ saying . . ."
106 Ice-cream additive
107 Crewmate of Uhura
108 Houlihan player
109 Pelvic bones
110 Avant-garde sorts
111 Commedia dell'___
113 Populous area
114 PBS supporter
116 "Can't Help Lovin' ___ Man"

233 WATER, WATER EVERYWHERE   by Alyssa Brooke
". . . and not a drop to drink."

ACROSS

1 Clog
8 Vital fluid
13 "Pleasant Valley Sunday" group
20 Fantastik, for one
21 Chophouse selection
22 Used Outlook Express
23 Suquamish chief
24 Checks out rags
25 Mean people
26 Sink your money in a backyard inground?
29 Rutgers residence
30 Jake the Snake's move
31 Opener for two tins?
32 Court great
34 Coalesce
35 Robbery, for short
38 Norse pantheon
41 RSA political party
43 Like some twins
45 Lags
49 Granada greeting
50 Nick's time
51 Former White House daughter
52 Parseghian of football
53 Nada
54 Going full tilt
55 Knickknack holder
57 Bat eyelashes
59 Easily irritated
61 Titanic-seeker's tool
62 Kennedy years ambiance
64 Short-fused
65 Country out of the mainstream?
70 End a union
72 Army-navy stores?
75 Said hello to
76 Flight unit
81 Red Auerbach's team
83 Big name in vermouth
84 Was part of a conspiracy
86 Ruhr valley city
87 Aardvark entree
88 What's happening
93 Cone head?
94 Remarriage prefix
96 Nancy Drew's creator
97 Jason's wife
98 Sixties musical
99 Like Westminster winners
101 David Bowie hit
103 Remote control
107 "Nice!"
110 Movie Superman
111 Emergency burner
115 "Black Cadillac" singer Cash
116 Banana oil, e.g.
117 Tries to form a more perfect union?
118 Spot with drops
119 Brings up
120 Small quakes

DOWN

1 Office dupes, for short
2 Rosie in "Harriet the Spy"
3 Red, white, and brown ice-cream
4 Florida footballer
5 Cover up
6 Emulate Willy Loman
7 Long basket
8 German pastry
9 Thumb-raising critic
10 Leonine protest
11 Sedated
12 Handel oratorio
13 Choice reading
14 Karl's "Patton" role
15 Daytona Beach org.
16 Airborne toys
17 He gave the world a lift
18 Wide size
19 '60s radical org.
27 Not as expected
28 "There's ___ every crowd!"
29 He played a twin in "Twins"
33 Join up
34 Trait bearers
36 Many miles off
37 Driver's license datum
39 Barber's stroke
40 Goofing off
42 Guisewite girl
44 Heirs
46 Hayek in "Once Upon a Time in Mexico"
47 Thorny bush
48 Jumping the gun
49 The poor
56 Capricious
57 "___ chance!"
58 Huge amount
60 Ballet headliners
62 Green center
63 Prefix with heel
66 Turner of records
67 Al Bundy's boy
68 Square O
69 Suffix for Israel
70 "Wuthering Heights" author
71 Ended the defense
73 Maxima maker
74 Like a vista
75 Understanding
76 More willowy
77 Voice-mail prompt
78 Communications co.
79 Couple, to a columnist
80 They party hearty
82 Sleep sound
84 Trim down?
85 Actress Pfeiffer
89 Crimea locale
90 Key in again
91 Price after adjustments
92 More toothsome
95 Tease
98 Bill Clinton's NY office site
100 1814 treaty site
102 "La ___ Vita" (1960)
104 Add-on for Congo
105 Bristlelike part
106 At least once
107 Return addressee
108 Take a bough
109 "For what ___ man, what has he . . ."
112 Turmoil
113 Marseille sight
114 Ends of letters

À LA CARTE   by Norma Steinberg
We recommend the soul-food appetizer at 56 Across.

ACROSS

1 Online junk mail
5 Chaplin role
10 Move quickly
14 Grooming aid
16 Accolades
18 Was under the weather
20 Tex-Mex party?
22 Judaic law
24 Gallivanted
25 Busman's take
26 Egg ___
28 Jedi Master ___ Kloon
29 Little piggy
30 Fathered
31 Foreign Legion hats
32 Merrill Lynch symbol
33 Runs roughshod over
36 Start
37 Renoir's hat
38 In good humor
39 Tantrums
40 Chapati and challah
41 Sacred spots
44 Deep Blue's game
45 Respond
46 Listed, nautically
47 Freeload
48 Sky cop
50 Rudolph II's kingdom
51 Alimentary or Erie
52 Apothecary's wares
53 Kindergartner's break
55 Crossword architect
56 Hors d'oeuvre named after a soul group?
58 Overly
59 SFO info
60 Calms down
61 Poetic justice
62 Pub game
64 Required
66 Construction site sight
67 Disarm
68 On the up-and-up
69 Steve Williams, for one
70 Bad-mouthed

71 "Fur" director Shainberg
73 Colorful eel
74 Prying tool
75 Piercing light
76 Asinine
77 Changed for the better
80 Spoken
81 Hacks
82 Maravich's retired number
83 Bite
85 Play about Capote
86 "___ Now Praise Famous Men"
87 Exhausted
88 Horrible Viking
90 Browbeat
92 Southern love-feast food?
95 Hand-delivers?
96 Fringed vehicle
97 Briny
98 Only
99 Bumps into
100 Jekyll's alter ego

DOWN

1 Tremble
2 Colorless
3 Zealous
4 Belgian sea
5 "___ a small hotel . . ."
6 Lassoed
7 Barbecue buttinskies
8 Hawaiian menu fish
9 Uprisings
10 Clotho and her sisters
11 Half a Jim Carrey title
12 Under the weather
13 Fight at Benihana?
14 Movie-making session
15 Second cups
17 Fires from cover
19 Lost one's edge
20 Pre-LCD monitor
21 "Dreamlover" singer
23 Dunces
27 Cambridge campus
30 Worked for "the Company"
31 Deli item
32 Gray-barked tree
34 Nimble
35 Long pony-tails
36 When to buy a cream puff?
37 Officers
39 Shallow area
40 Uncle Miltie
41 Physique
42 From now on

43 Good ol' marinara and béchamel?
44 Cotton-candy holders
45 Stage a comeback
47 Paired
48 Pooh's creator
49 Chinese philosopher
51 Dromedary
52 Showy flower
54 Said "cheese"
56 Heathen
57 TV bunch
60 Clemson cat
62 Postpone
63 What old MacDonald had
65 What playing fields should be
66 Reiner and Furillo
67 Cornwall's neighbor

69 Raiders' home turf
70 Stands up for
71 Sluggish omnivore
72 Well pitched?
73 Misunderstandings
74 "The Boys From Brazil" author
76 Used the divan
77 Transfers
78 Dynamo
79 Photographer Arbus
81 Concisely worded
82 Hail
84 Snoop
86 Hang around
87 Hell's half-___
88 Consecrated
89 Surrounded by
91 Way of the East
93 "And the finalists ___"
94 "Gotcha!"

SEVENTH HEAVEN* by Harvey Estes
The key to these pearly gates can be found at 114 Across.

ACROSS

1 Sweeping
5 Big hairdo
9 "Air Music" composer
14 Nuclear energy source
19 P's, on the Parthenon
20 Toothy menace
21 Cheri in "Southland Tales"
22 First name in gymnastics
23 Take-home*
25 Doing the Electric Slide*
27 Wise guy
28 Most accessible
30 E-mailed, e.g.
31 "All finished!"
33 On your toes
35 "The Bells of ___" (1945)
38 Pasture grass, perhaps
41 Label letters
46 Small shake
47 Small urban plaza*
50 German auto
51 "Silent" prez
52 Fortune
53 Involved with
54 British flyers
55 Poisons
58 Pencil-game word
60 "The Dukes of Hazzard" lawman
61 Ties up
63 Geologic feature
64 Colman in "Beau Geste"
66 Freelancer's guide*
68 Wave-battling asylum seekers*
72 Permits to pass
73 Ensure, with "up"
74 German mercenary
75 Impudent
78 One of California's Santas
79 Predate
81 Aunt in "Bambi"
82 Lab slide item
84 Simpson trial judge
85 ___ de plume
86 Pony
87 So long ago no one recalls*

91 Distribute, with "out"
93 Phat, for example
94 2006 Winged Foot event
95 "The Miser" playwright
96 Insurance ploy
98 Add as a bonus
101 Sprouting figurine
105 Natural gas alternative
108 Soap Box Derby site
112 Like some old records*
114 Where the first word of clue* answers appear
116 Heavenly messenger
117 Equip anew
118 Secluded spot
119 Wallach and Whitney
120 Edwin of Reagan's Cabinet
121 Code subject
122 Compulsions
123 Becomes Jell-O

DOWN

1 Flying fishers
2 "That was close!"
3 Tiny bit
4 David Caruso series
5 Va. Tech is in it
6 Fern foliage
7 Paris rival
8 Indian, for one
9 Play part
10 Porter miss that was a hit
11 Burt Reynolds police film
12 Before, in the past
13 Around Wednesday
14 Make marginal memos
15 Telling white lies, at times

16 Comics canine
17 Make money
18 Starchy stuff
24 Cardio med
26 JFK info
29 NFL officials
32 Neighbor of Isr.
34 Longley of the NBA
35 Long looks
36 Class cutter
37 Fruit bug
39 Anesthesia of old
40 Some resorts
42 Shorts at resorts
43 Early exile
44 Ponte Vecchio river
45 UPS deliveries
47 Florist's wheels, often
48 Upper classes
49 Broke out
51 Redeem
55 E-mailed a dupe
56 Gentlemanly affirmative

57 Ellipsis element
58 "One ___ customer"
59 Country song?
62 "Twelve Traditions" group
64 Ivanhoe's love
65 Add-on for Congo
67 Hellenic H
68 Track transaction
69 Buchanan's predecessor
70 Piston legend Bob
71 Make possible
73 Saw lumber
75 Dairy slices
76 Silents star Jannings
77 Tomato type
79 Lying over
80 Newspaper div.
83 New York sobriquet
84 1985 Bruce Springsteen hit
86 Corrugation

88 Dog's yellow coat?
89 Anka's "___ Beso"
90 Pt. of IBM
91 "Batman" sound effect
92 "Are you calling me ___?"
95 In a state of fusion
97 Civil War monogram
99 Edible hero
100 Cartridge holder
101 Gooey duck
102 Improve, in a way
103 "Picnic" playwright
104 Many a moon
106 Colleges, to Aussies
107 They're cheaper by the dozen
109 Tick off
110 "Never heard ___"
111 Promontory
113 Ending with law or saw
115 Halves of ems

236 TRIPLE TALENT by Joel Kaplow

82 Across is considered the first muscle car (debuting in 1964).

ACROSS

1 Japanese guard dog
6 TV Batman West
10 Construction component
15 Lend a hand
19 "Girls Lie Too" singer Clark
20 Chanel of No. 5 fame
21 Bad boy Brown of song
22 Peter Fonda's honey of a role
23 Actress-Playwright-Golfer
27 Not pro
28 Jekyll's dark side
29 Information superhighway
30 Everest adjective
31 Do some dental work?
33 Ward in "The Fugitive"
35 Recording or filming effect
36 Ghostly forms
39 Island near Maui
41 Puzzle part
46 Skier-Comic-Hotelier
53 The game may be this
54 D.C. area code, Roman-style
55 Utah mountain bike town
56 Way to go?
57 Like some points
58 Links rental
59 "This ___": Beatles
61 Prepares shrimp
63 Flemish painter Bruegel the Elder
65 Light browns
67 Monterrey money
68 Actor-Singer-Writer
75 Howdy, in Hobart
76 Certain sub
77 Hot whistler
78 "With Six You Get ___" (1968)
82 Pontiac muscle car
83 Decidedly disgusting
85 Danzig denizen
86 La Scala solo
87 Name on every Irish 44 Down
89 King Arthur of the courts
90 Desi's daughter
91 Pitcher-Singer-Theologian
96 Pollution, portmanteau-style
97 Janis Joplin album
98 Miners dig it
99 Sweet citrus swigs
102 Gas for an old Dodge?
104 Points the finger
109 It goes with a nose
113 Euripides play
114 Stratified snack
117 Assemblage of actors
118 Singer-Actor-Hockey Player
122 Feels unfine
123 Light, horse or soap
124 Goldfarb in "Mac"
125 Cough-drop king William H. ___
126 Bear name after Winnipeg
127 Relatively more recent
128 "Preowned" sounds better than this
129 Kegling score

DOWN

1 Up, at Wrigley
2 "Nancy Drew" author
3 Super sore
4 Characteristic
5 Kind of guitar or ball
6 Post-marathon feeling
7 Mamie Eisenhower, née ___
8 Homestead Act units
9 Palindromic parent
10 Douglas in "Grace of My Heart"
11 Word after corn, borscht, or fan
12 Predating, in bardspeak
13 Heart line
14 "I'm culpable!"
15 Fling forcefully
16 Magdeburg river
17 Vintner's "mud"
18 Saucy
24 Heat unit
25 Wedding by-product
26 Hebrew letter
32 "Joy to the World" composer Axton
34 "The Time Machine" race
35 Mutt's moniker
37 Florida resort, for short
38 Hugger-mugger
40 Like an octopus
42 "Bus Stop" playwright
43 Morales of "Vanished"
44 Change component
45 Treebeard types
46 Bay of the Bucs
47 Petrolic
48 Bellowed bovinely
49 "Be Prepared," e.g.
50 Thumb a ride
51 Tired of
52 Health-risk factor
58 Hung up the phone
59 Equus asinus
60 Christiana, after 1924
62 Viva ___ (orally)
64 "Cogito, ___ sum": Descartes
66 Completely swept away
67 Medium
69 Berkeley College student
70 Be
71 Shot
72 Eocene, e.g.
73 "Totally true!"
74 University of Texas animal
78 St. Louis bridge
79 Not so rosy
80 Pyramid of Cheops locale
81 Give a Bronx cheer
82 Autry on Champion
84 Beano cousin
88 Emulates Dr. Dre
89 Woody splinter?
90 Storm preceder or follower
92 Pine pronouncedly
93 "Big Red" of racing
94 Duke's Cameron, for one
95 Troubling toil
100 Mustard with a kick
101 Unite unceremoniously
103 They're verboten
105 Throw a hissy fit
106 "Zoom Zoom Zoom" car
107 It's formed by subglacial streams
108 "People" composer
109 Half-moon tide
110 Pastiche
111 "Saving Private Ryan" town
112 Peter of reggae
113 Pertaining to
115 French jeweler Lalique
116 "Yoicks!"
119 Do a lumberjack's job
120 Ewe homophone
121 Trains seen on "ER"

237 "I SEE!" by Bonnie L. Gentry
Henry Mancini received an Oscar for his work in 122 Across.

ACROSS

1 "The Masters" novelist
7 Guilt-ridden
14 Swell smells
20 Bahamas resort
21 Nursery denizen
22 Burnt shade
23 It may move you
25 Sum component
26 Big name in IRAs
27 Sans rocks, at the bar
28 Spy on the inside
30 More, to a señor
31 Roof adornment
34 Calgary Stampede, e.g.
38 Trelliswork passageway
40 Awkward situation
43 Hedgehog of video games
44 Letter in runes
47 Service closer
48 Hometown-related
49 Vertebral connector
50 Thumbs-down reactions
52 Lifetime Oscar winner Kazan
54 French silk center
56 Religious splinter groups
57 Act curmudgeonly
59 Maj.'s superior
62 Said one's piece
64 V-shaped forts
66 Eighth of a shot
68 Slippers?
71 Chantilly chum
72 Female Indy driver
76 Hound healer
77 Wolverine State
79 Snoopy's former owner
80 More spooky
82 Costly cigars
84 Part of a cassette tape
87 Bangladesh capital, old-style
88 Cleanse totally
90 Some homes are built on it
92 2-D measure
94 RC Cola soda
95 Organic compound suffix
96 Tabriz native
99 Reform targets
101 Dipso
102 Olstead of "Still Standing"
104 Kind of scheme
107 Adjective for Snow White
109 Pope who confronted Attila the Hun
110 Like a pothook
114 West Coast coll.
115 ___-majesté
117 Indiana politician (with 116-D)
119 Symbol of a bright idea
120 Uncle of old TV
122 1982 Blake Edwards film
128 Parisian pupils
129 Conciliate
130 High-priced furs
131 Richard of "L.A. Law"
132 Jots a reminder
133 Shoving match

DOWN

1 They report bear sightings
2 Basketball maneuver
3 Beat, Biblically
4 Bust holders
5 Man. neighbor
6 Xbox rival
7 Youngest Brontë sister
8 Base-6 numeral system
9 Fly-by-nighter
10 Queen's worker
11 Spring time, in Paris
12 King of Siam's abbr.
13 Judge to be
14 It's made at closing time
15 Contract add-ons
16 Multivolume ref. work
17 "Every good boy does fine" et al.
18 Historian
19 Likable losers
24 Amoeba's makeup
29 Go (for)
32 Fund-raising org.
33 Lemon go-with
35 The Divine, to da Vinci
36 O.T. book of teachings
37 Signs off on
39 Expect a Hail Mary
41 Make booties
42 One not big on big weddings
44 Persistence of memory concept
45 Scale starters
46 Wendy Wasserstein play (with "The")
51 Locale with a steam bath
53 "Highway to Hell" band
55 Not yet final, legally
56 Quenched
58 Salad leaf
60 Grad student's grilling
61 Deep-blue gem
63 Old Roman cry
65 Detailed account
67 It was once French Sudan
69 Bounce back again
70 Dardanelles, for one
73 Tandoor-baked breads
74 Where to find baked blackbirds
75 ". . . and here it is!"
78 "Marvelous" Marvin of boxing
81 Served as manager of
83 Some Rockefeller Center murals
85 La Salle of "ER"
86 One of the Blue Brothers
88 Like talcum powder
89 With apprehension
91 Links transport
93 Noted boxing family
97 Valueless
98 Winter craft
100 BYU or NYU
103 More slippery and slimy
104 IMs, Google-style
105 Like the princess with a frog?
106 Meals on a stick
108 "What thou ___, write . . .": Rev. 1:11
111 Reverse stitches
112 Architect Saarinen
113 Early databank software
116 See 117 Across
118 Montand in "Goodbye Again"
121 Flood control proj.
123 Nasdaq news, in brief
124 USAF rank
125 Leaves at 4:00?
126 MN clock setting
127 Sigma's follower

238 FULL OF THE DEVIL by Harvey Estes
"Get an exorcist!"

ACROSS

1 Still
7 Ursa Minor star
14 Pogo, for one
20 Gallic Wars hero
21 Airline ticket class
22 Parthenon figure
23 1946 Mickey Rooney movie
26 Naval characters?
27 Signs of late summer
28 Peter in "Venus"
29 Half a gaffe
30 Waste time
31 Oddly amusing
33 Just what the doctor ordered
36 Union issue
41 Bamako residents
45 Made uniform
46 Enterprise-D defenses
48 Makes spiffy
49 Hayes of "The Mod Squad"
50 Trashy (with "in")
52 Designated driver's drink
53 Like apples during the fall
56 Ends of letters
57 Treated with irreverence
60 Deems necessary
61 Rock on the roof
63 Valletta residents
64 They're black for witches
65 Sling your own hash
66 Locality
67 Move cautiously
70 Fetter
72 Five Nations tribe
76 Battle songs?
77 Oversensitive
79 Prepare for the OR
80 Kind of dive
81 Not taken in by
82 Minute parts, briefly
84 Tijuana time
85 Double-decker checker
86 Throws a hissy fit
90 Vegas line
91 Red Baron's foe
93 Burrowing boars
94 Over
96 Caterwaul
99 Dress up (with "out")
100 Bench item
102 Gallery framings
110 Book before Micah
111 Fanzine focus
112 Go bad
113 Dramatic no-show
115 Elroy's pooch
116 Protein source
117 Einstein's second wife
118 Nick in "Cape Fear"
119 Clipped
120 Velcro alternative
121 Put in stitches
122 Going rate

DOWN

1 Scopes Trial org.
2 New Mexican resort
3 Guns in the garage
4 Tip of the tongue?
5 Get out of the wreckage
6 Brought up the rear
7 Art collector Guggenheim
8 Dos cubed
9 Red-ink amount
10 "Wheel of Fortune" request
11 Magazine section
12 "___ my wit's end!"
13 Where fathers may gather
14 Business end of a missile
15 Moor of Venice
16 Doo-wop syllable
17 Balkan native
18 Edit-menu command
19 Bread spread
24 Google listings
25 Quad quarters
30 Emulates Roberto Herrera
32 Rides, to sailors
33 Sub stations
34 Just like ewe
35 Meaning
36 First baseman of comedy
37 Delta asset
38 Browns up
39 They give
40 '60s radical org.
42 Without dissent
43 Some posers
44 "The Maltese Falcon" sleuth
46 Peyton Manning, to Archie
47 Engine additive
50 Kitties
51 Wit Bombeck
54 Big dos
55 Home page
58 Galley movers
59 Hightails it
61 Bubbles seen at the beach
62 Responds to "Uncle Sam wants you"
67 To-do list entries
68 Novelist Shaw
69 Key location
70 "Subway Series" team
71 At any point
73 Lose ground
74 Cheese food
75 Put to shame
77 Crime lab study
78 Antique coin
81 Coy comment to a beau
83 Hard shot
87 Reckon
88 Oodles
89 Proves wrong
92 Featherless boa
95 Plays 14 Across, for example
97 Formal orders
98 Strung along
100 Part of v.v.
101 Slangy no
102 Victoria Beckham's nickname
103 Grooving on
104 Former KISS drummer Eric
105 Convertible, perhaps
106 Partner of void
107 Cartoon flapper
108 Not in production
109 Haul around
110 Essen assents
114 Guitarist Nugent

239 FUN HOUSE FURNISHINGS by Kelly Clark
96 Across is a good trivia question.

ACROSS

1 Pack down
5 Yule quaffs
9 Macramé, e.g.
14 Memory units
19 Airline to Tel Aviv
20 Andy Taylor's boy
21 Gambler's odds, e.g.
22 Chaucer storyteller
23 "___ girl!"
24 A paramecium has one
25 "Marble Madness" company
26 Like days of yore
27 Enlightening Mother Goose rhyme?
31 Prayers
32 It might be cast
33 Isolates
37 E-mail command: Abbr.
38 To-do list item
39 Memo abbr.
40 Philanthropist Lilly
41 Chesterfield progress report?
45 Municipal lobby seat?
48 Children's refrain
49 Capek play
50 Sandra who played "Gidget"
51 Greek theaters
52 Winged
53 Their sum equals the whole?
55 Census question
56 TV's "Fawlty ___"
58 Retired sound breaker
59 Atlas contents
60 Humorist Bombeck
62 Like Stephen Hawking
63 Wonder-ful clothes cabinet?
66 Some skirts
68 Place for a roast
69 Monk and Carney
70 Vagrant
73 Olfactory stimuli
74 Size above med.
75 Michael's "Multiplicity" costar
77 It's inherited
78 Sons of, in Hebrew
79 Miler Sebastian
80 Every: Rx
81 High-fives
82 Seat made from 85 Down?
86 Broadway shrink's need?
88 Hot time in Paris
89 Long, long time
90 Trottier of hockey
92 Oleo container
93 London's Bow and Bond
95 "The ___ Is Jumpin'": Waller
96 Where Keanu Reeves was born
100 Twin places to take the load off?
103 "And there you have it!"
106 Sexy Beatles girl
107 Broken mirror, to some
108 "___ please the court . . ."
109 Acquired relative
110 Hospital drama setting, literally
111 Prefix for physical
112 Slumgullion
113 Thaws
114 Radiator sound
115 Organic compound
116 Island in a computer game

DOWN

1 Don Juan's "I love you"
2 Place for a sacrifice
3 Motherly prefix
4 Is a good sport
5 "Sorry"
6 Pundit's pieces
7 Arizona river
8 Underestimate
9 Moon depression
10 Baby-shower gifts
11 Whatsoever
12 Passion
13 Eau de ___
14 Hot-tub disinfectant
15 Sharp barks
16 Tycoon Turner
17 Anticipative night
18 D.C. electee
28 "In what way?"
29 Apple bestseller
30 Dealer's demand
34 Plumbiferous
35 Queen of mysteries
36 Marner of Raveloe
38 Heading
39 Suit to ___
41 Huge expanses
42 Some are essential
43 Notable deed
44 Stock charts
46 Tarzan creator's first name
47 Mandel of "Deal or No Deal"
53 Duel measures
54 Wait on
55 Name on a range
56 Musty
57 Bank members
59 Asian starling
61 Bar or bakery order
62 Sleep-inducing
63 Ape
64 "Got it" in radio-speak
65 Lunatic
66 Jazz saxophonist Cobb
67 Body shop vehicle
70 Giver of candy and flowers
71 Saying "man" instead of "person"?
72 Fit together
73 French clerics
74 Hi's better half
76 Away
77 "World culture" policy
79 Is made up of
81 Diver's gear
83 Asinine remarks
84 Part of n.b.
85 Coromandel et al.
86 Harmony
87 Forever and ever
91 "Ghost ___ in the Sky"
94 Conspicuous success
95 Green gemstones
96 Deceive
97 "Keen!"
98 Steinbeck migrants
99 Cereal box fig.
101 Cotton Bowl cries
102 So be it
103 Pep
104 United
105 Not well

ACROSS

1 Private hall?
5 Coke vis-à-vis Pepsi
10 Jeanne of old movies
15 Run words together
19 St. Louis attraction
20 Jung's inner personality
21 Spanish direction
22 Its state flag features a vicuña
23 "See you," in Sorrento
24 Squelched
25 River through Lyons
26 Garfield's friend
27 Simon & Schuster published the first one
30 British mil. decoration
32 Lacquered metalware
33 Hercules fell in love with her
34 Aid for the poor
38 Entrée with a crust
41 Kind of code or colony
43 Casanova
44 It ran through the veins of Venus
45 Film that featured a Simon & Garfunkel song
47 "Little" Stowe girl
48 Lieutenant Kojak, to friends
49 Fuel hunks
50 "Here you go," in Rome
51 Excessively polite and restrained
52 Kind of cookie
54 Chess champ Spassky
56 1776 pamphleteer
57 Govt. financial assistance
58 He played Simon Templar
60 Package
61 Thin soup
63 Cozy stopover
64 A bit, colloquially
65 "Hollywood Madam" Heidi
67 Title setting for a Neil Simon play
71 Org. that's into firing?
74 Greases up
75 Approval power
76 Infiltration
78 Latin trio member
79 Perkins who wrote "Blue Suede Shoes"
80 Four Holy Roman Emperors
81 Soba alternative
82 Verbal zinger
83 Carly Simon hit song
86 Stingless flier
87 Cheerfulness
89 Island from which Icarus escaped
90 Pedestal bases
91 Tendency to sin
92 Start of a whaler's cry
93 [Isn't he dreamy?!]
94 Team leader: Abbr.
95 What "Simon Says" is
100 Like one leg of a triathlon
103 Eastern VIPs
105 Early Russian ruler
106 Languishes
108 River to the Seine
109 Clan symbol
110 Whispered word
111 Mini-nuisance
112 Father of a grand duchess
113 Fencing weapons
114 Oft-reinvented item?
115 "Don't overdo it!"

DOWN

1 iBook, e.g.
2 "Tears in Heaven" singer Clapton
3 Leave a mark on
4 Use a cue
5 Grapple (with), colloquially
6 At a loss for words, maybe
7 Notable role for Marlon
8 Love, in Logroño
9 Airport touchdowns
10 Popular Toyota
11 Prep the soil again
12 "Dilbert" intern
13 BBC rival
14 Couldn't help but
15 Mel Brooks movies, e.g.
16 Paved the way
17 Canton on the Lake of Lucerne
18 Feel regret over
28 Evening abroad
29 Beast hunted by a pigsticker
31 Roy Rogers's birth name
34 WWII women
35 Where Simon Cowell sits in judgment
36 Runoff point
37 Canine covering
38 Actress ZaSu
39 Spanish skating figures
40 Moniker for Simon Bolivar
41 Work (in) gradually
42 Sniggler
43 Desi's daughter
45 Hard to swallow, perhaps
46 Writer Earl __ Biggers
49 Crotchety types
51 Result of hair-splitting?
53 Mr. Perot
54 Reagan's simian costar
55 Charlie's fourth wife
56 KP gadget
59 Farrow and Hamm
60 C-in-C
62 Unburdens (of)
64 Order to attack
65 Light desserts?
66 "Catlow" author Louis
67 Fencing move
68 Country singer Lovett
69 Occupy, as a table
70 Pull strings?
72 TV sports pioneer Arledge
73 Two of Henry's six
75 Impertinent
77 Added fee
79 Not metaphysical
80 Outspend one's account
83 Positive principle
84 Religious splits
85 Like many a thesis defense
86 Rap music's Snoop ___
88 Kvetch
90 Ebert's longtime cohost
92 Lithium's atomic number
93 Less than cordial
95 Summon to court
96 Try to pledge
97 Northern end of I-79
98 First name in the Louvre
99 Brief in-flight announcements
100 Eugene Debs's party: Abbr.
101 Oz musical, with "The"
102 1994 World Cup host
104 Disorderly do
107 Wallowing whereabouts

241 DEAR OLD GUY   by Victor Fleming
Solve this puzzle on the third Sunday in June.

ACROSS

1 Bill ___ & His Comets
6 Drops off
10 Drop
14 Proper companion
18 Down East college town
19 Mowbray in "A Study in Scarlet"
20 Ms. Korbut
21 Old Olds
22 Dad's tastes?
24 Dad from the sticks?
26 Start of many words?
27 Tank buildup
28 "Have a break" candy
29 French article
30 GI-free area
32 Maynard G. of old TV
34 Was
36 What "Big Papi" will do after a balk
41 Shirt end?
42 Diving-board units
43 The Cotton St.
44 Circus Circus game
46 "Touched by an Angel" star
48 Word after fat or alley
49 **Start of a quotation by C.B. Kelland**
54 Deuce taker
56 Original "Dungeons & Dragons" co.
57 Assent by 58 Across
58 Barrie buccaneer
59 Stationary advancers
63 Secs
68 Gaping mouth
69 **Part 2 of quotation**
75 Earlier than
76 Privately
77 James of "Brian's Song"
78 "What a pity!"
80 "Everybody ___ Star"
81 Sign of August
84 "Yeah, right!"
88 **End of quotation**
96 Hockley in "Titanic"
97 Stretched circles
98 Remote settlements
99 In the past
100 . . . than a ___ of monkeys
103 Parisian way
104 Semi-popular place?
106 Saint-___ (Loire's capital)
108 Bacon product
110 He upset TED in 1948
111 Sound booster
112 Shade
114 Eminem's MO birthplace
117 Droid: Comb. form
121 "Dad packages Pepsi"?
123 Dad named for a foot?
125 ". . . on ___ boat to China"
126 Badlands feature
127 Texas-based hotel chain
128 Pollute
129 About 5.88 trillion mi.
130 In the past, in the past
131 Slugger's stats
132 Short timetables

DOWN

1 Kiva builder
2 Presley's middle name
3 Chops (off)
4 Make cryptic
5 "Time" 2006 Person of the Year
6 Pt. of 113 Down
7 Chug-___
8 Pet birds
9 Villain's look
10 Strong lager
11 Plaza Hotel heroine
12 Bust ___
13 Thanks, in Munich
14 Layer
15 Esteem
16 One with pressing work
17 Scooters
21 Chichi to the max
23 Recliner brand
25 IRS agents
31 Fence Mandelbaum (1818–94)
33 Suffix for sermon
35 Dele killers
36 Diplomat's forte
37 Banned orchard chemical
38 Petruchio's wife
39 Word of goodbye from Wolfgang
40 Blind part
45 Prosper
46 Saudi Arabian coin
47 Blissful
50 Check information
51 Austen heroine
52 Gravitate (toward)
53 Dirty
55 Ming of basketball
60 Light lead?
61 Atlas abbr.
62 Mixer
64 Saul's uncle in I Samuel
65 Critic with a handlebar
66 Flood control proj.
67 Salty body
69 "You Can Call ___": Simon
70 Mrs. Al Jolson
71 "The ___ is on!"
72 Endures
73 Apple variety
74 Code carrier
79 Campfire snack
82 Important sign in John 20
83 Kitchen drawer?
85 "Go away!"
86 Parrot in Disney's "Aladdin"
87 Washout
89 "As we speak"
90 Muffin morsel, maybe
91 Dwelled rent-free, in a way
92 Emerald and ruby
93 "Goodbye, Columbus" school
94 Needs scratching
95 Reproaches
100 "C'mon, give me some help"
101 Not more than
102 Undulating
103 Break
105 Birthday suit dash
107 Wonderland cake words
109 Fur capitalist
113 Met or Cub
115 Songwriter Mitchell
116 Mayberry character
118 Mayberry character
119 Municipal offering
120 Acts on a preference
122 NYC div.
124 Part of TGIF

242 INSECT ASIDES   by Marie Langley
Be thinking Saturnia pavonia at 61 Across.

ACROSS

1 "La Vie en Rose" singer
5 Exercise for the abs
10 To-do
14 Washer phase
19 Pac-10 school
20 First name among Latin singers
21 Piece of rodeo gear
22 Vieira's cohost
23 Online manners
25 Arrest at an English school?
27 One way to get a buzz on?
29 Sparkly paperweight
30 Ajax rival
31 "Oh, my . . ."
35 Hedy of "Samson and Delilah"
38 Garment worker
39 Greek cross
40 Part of a whiz kid's report card?
41 Kind of fire
42 Humorous greeting from the Terminix man?
46 Buff up
47 Riding
48 Noncommercial TV network
49 Delicate
50 Despot Amin
51 Rooftop fixture
52 Edginess
56 Earl Hines, familiarly
57 Item served with punch
59 Windbag's output
60 JFK info
61 How the emperor went out in a blaze of glory?
65 Give the ax to
66 Hebron locale
67 Knocks down
70 More off-the-wall
73 Wait on
74 Bottom lines
75 Overpower
76 "M*A*S*H" actor
77 Hail Mary path
78 Commercial snap
79 Kind of van
80 Cry from a swat-team pointer?
86 Rural routes
87 Nice water
88 "___ you serious?"
89 Lord's lodging
90 "Coal ___ Daughter" (1980)
91 Wee wave
93 Failed to
94 Greeted a shepherd
96 What the louse in the toupee was?
102 Best Picture of 1995
105 Reliable union member?
106 Stand for something
107 "Tell me ___ haven't heard!"
108 Put aside
109 All tied up
110 Illicit cab
111 Nair rival
112 Ruhr industrial center
113 Part of DOD

DOWN

1 Ogden Nash forte
2 "Law & Order: SVU" star
3 Choir voices
4 Legitimate target
5 Daze
6 Literate boast?
7 Dime on a dollar
8 Golden Rule word
9 Runs through
10 Emancipated males
11 Mega Millions, e.g.
12 Make ___ (blog)
13 "I Am Sam" star
14 Big shot?
15 Ukrainian city
16 ___-de-sac
17 Grazing land
18 Make a blunder
24 Look into
26 "Snow Falling on ___" (1999)
28 Prayer start
32 Charged
33 One in a book
34 Cushy class
35 "___ Be"
36 Battery part
37 Underling
38 Gas additive
39 Ducky ponds?
42 Totally befuddled
43 Japanese drama
44 "Stiffelio" is one
45 Frightens
47 "Invisible" singer Clay
51 Cape Verde Peninsula capital
52 Dame of South Bend
53 Hawke of "Training Day"
54 Had status
55 Its player takes a bow
56 Doesn't wear well
58 Chicago suburb
59 Party giver
60 Budget alternative
62 Bandleader Miller
63 Galway's instrument
64 Pal of Jerry Seinfeld
68 Dog tag datum
69 Houdini's birth name
70 Job seeker's success
71 Head lama
72 Wither
73 Comedian Johnson
74 Our sun
77 From the beginning
78 New Deal monogram
79 Ordered
81 How some are accused
82 Settler in a foreign land
83 Got down to work
84 Landers and others
85 Sampler's terse critique
86 Lender's rights
90 Gulfstream nonwinner
92 Covers ground, in a way
93 Guitarist Eddy
94 Future plants
95 Twinkle-toed
97 Advertising medium
98 Wraps up on the stage
99 Hoped-for review
100 Lone Star sch.
101 Polite bloke
102 Seek change?
103 2004 Jamie Foxx film
104 Cerastes

243 INDY STOPS by Alan Olschwang

Alan recommends you solve this one on Memorial Day weekend.

ACROSS

1 Where to pitch a tent
5 Leave
11 Tolkien cannibals
15 Lurita Doan's org.
18 Like doves and hawks
20 Glucose, to fructose
21 Entrée choice
22 ___ Angeles
23 Hostess Mesta
24 Layers
25 Arrogance
27 Atonement
29 M. Streep's alma mater
31 In a short time
32 Clerical vestment
33 "The Ghost and Mrs. ___" (1947)
35 Coin tosser's directive
37 ___ on the head
40 Like lotus-eaters
43 Legends of the highway
47 Thinks better of
49 Italian cathedral town
50 Vinyl benzene
51 Traveler's garment bag
53 Maternal aunt, e.g.
55 "Mi casa ___ casa"
56 Juan's leader?
57 Genetic-profile sequence
58 Pts. of speech
61 Irish luck
63 Pocket breads
64 Chatterbox
66 German guns
68 Shade providers
70 Mine, in Milano
71 Inherent baseness
72 Big Daddy's daughter-in-law
73 Romero in "Ocean's Eleven"
76 "Green jacket" golf tourney
77 Stroll
80 A demand for quiet
81 QED part
83 Emancipated
84 Tiverton river
85 Pact of 1948
87 Wm. Morris employees
89 Italian politician Balbo
91 Registration
94 Like Cologne and environs
96 Thus
99 Newborn
100 Smear
101 "Shine, Shine, Shine" singer
103 Gas pumped in 67 Down
104 Enclose
106 Perrier in "Murder by Death"
107 You, in Hamburg
109 1998 DreamWorks film
112 Played a part
114 Empire State governor
119 2005 Drew Barrymore film
121 Magnet alloy
123 1936 Nobelist in medicine
124 Gardner in "Ride, Vaquero!"
125 TLC part
126 Sort of sail
127 Subsequently
128 Crimson
129 Banned substance
130 Capital of ancient Macedonia
131 Elaine Nardo's passenger

DOWN

1 Joe Btfsplk's drawer
2 Declare
3 Joan of art
4 Beats rapidly and strongly
5 Part of D.C.
6 Ballpark figure
7 Permeable
8 Poisonous mushroom
9 Like Dave Cowens' no.
10 Room-service item
11 Egg-like
12 Drive back
13 Yields
14 Disingenuous
15 "For Your Eyes Only" director
16 Mediocre
17 Org.
19 Diamond with platinum
26 One mother
28 From the beginning
30 Flip ___ (decide by chance)
34 Rat race
36 Extremely cold
37 Pothers
38 China Clipper airline
39 Corrida
41 Dame of academia
42 Kind of cooker
44 Breather
45 Vase handles
46 "Bartholomew and the Oobleck" author
48 Sigh
50 Fr. holy women
52 Plant branch
54 Land buy
59 Town near London
60 Mozart's last symphony
62 Flower parts
65 Early ABC show
67 It was first sold in 1957
69 Jeb Stuart, for one
71 Toodle-oo
72 Surrealism pioneer
73 Russian despots
74 Five after three
75 Outlawed pitch
76 Calc and trig
77 Prompt again
78 King of France
79 Brings home the bacon
82 Venture money
86 Western lily
88 Reaction to ragweed
90 1998 World Series star Ricky
92 Bills
93 Recover from a binge
95 Thorpe of freestyle
97 Sweat shop
98 Guantanamo's province
101 Biblical queen
102 WW1 or WW2 side
105 Ghana's capital
108 Cuba, por ejemplo
109 Way off yonder
110 Campbell in "Scream"
111 Spot on the tube
113 Disney chipmunk
115 The fourth Mrs. Chaplin
116 Catherine ___-Jones
117 Still-life subject
118 Laugh, on the Left Bank
120 Indianapolis dome
122 Boy

244 PRE–HIGH SCHOOL EXAM by Fred Piscop
Nathaniel Hawthorne shares his birthday with 62 Down.

ACROSS

1 Coll. drillers
5 Get more life from
10 "Git!"
14 Hotel amenities
19 Fit to serve
20 Classic spokescow
21 Coleridge's sacred river
22 O'Day of jazz
23 Cole Sear's gift
25 Kachina doll maker
26 Pies, to Brits
27 Toothless mammal
28 More bummed
29 ___ up (gets smart)
30 Winnebagos, e.g.
31 A/C stat
33 Arp, notably
35 Cut follower
38 They're squirreled away
41 Ra I, for one
42 Minor-league level
45 Reconsideration
48 Highest degree?
49 ___ Saud (Saudi king)
50 Mexicali Mrs.
51 Like a merino
52 Picnic castoffs
54 Gds.
55 Bagel-shaped
58 SWM's ad
60 Did a croupier's task
61 Univ. figures
63 Whacked-out
64 ___ out (barely making)
65 "GoodFellas" fella
68 Hula-Hoop, e.g.
69 Irish ballerina de Valois
71 Perrier competitor
72 Gestation areas
75 Lecherous sort
76 Puts through a sieve
77 Rustic condition
80 Workbook unit
84 Fill to the gills
85 Second string
86 Verdi's "___ Miller"
88 Soccer star Freddy
89 Biblical suffix
90 Slap-on-the-head cry
91 Stephen Collins series
95 Wine bottle word
96 Chancel cross
98 Render harmless
99 Marina walkways
100 Like a glutton
103 "Plush" group
104 Part of Scand.
105 Florida Keys, e.g.
107 Quick trip
109 Skyscraper, e.g.
114 Sheet-music arcs
115 Celestial bear
116 Britain's "Desert Rats" were part of it
118 ___ plume
119 Wagons-___ (sleeping cars)
120 Man of many words
121 Gen-___ (boomers' kids)
122 Dog tag datum
123 Sat., to Sun.
124 Photo ___
125 "Each Dawn ___" (Cagney film)

DOWN

1 Edwin Drood's fiancée
2 "Come ___!"
3 Mobile message
4 Wait on hand and foot
5 Takes ten
6 General Robt. ___
7 Org. for nonactive sailors
8 Cheer syllable
9 Extra-wide width
10 Satirical Mort
11 It may be seeded
12 Materialize
13 Passing situation
14 Kept company to
15 Diarist Nin
16 Bug-out bag component
17 Cigar's end
18 Talk trash to
24 Safe place
28 Keg stopper
31 Wilderness Road traveler
32 Not so crooked
34 PMs
35 Furtive "Hey!"
36 Prefix with -gram
37 Mark for life
38 Dune buggy, e.g.
39 Casino stack
40 Turin relic
43 Not here
44 Have ___ (hold the advantage)
46 Brainless bunch
47 Add color to
53 "Illmatic" rapper
54 Builders
56 Duller of the senses
57 Dungeon wear
59 ___ mail
60 Taylor of "The Nanny"
62 Neil Simon's birthday
65 Teens' rooms, typically
66 Barnstorm, say
67 The Resistance, to some
68 Set up for a fall
70 God of many fakirs
73 Mardi Gras, e.g.: Abbr.
74 Time-line divisions
75 Passes over
78 Start of a Tony Bennett title
79 Time to crow
81 Closer's success
82 Baltic Sea feeder
83 Order members
85 Knuckle-dragger
87 ___-crab soup
90 Place for shorts
92 Ed Norton wore one
93 Geologic period
94 Provider of short hops
97 Hon
101 Mesa ___ National Park
102 Checks for prints
104 Like mesh
105 "The answer ___!"
106 Ineligible for Mensa
108 Tammany Tiger creator
109 Halloween buy
110 Emu's cousin
111 Teed off
112 Father of Ahab
113 The Big Board, for short
116 Bard's before
117 Showy moths

245 BY REQUEST by Jay Sullivan
The "rara avis" label has definitely left 43 Down.

ACROSS

1 Bogus
5 Blame
9 Up to
14 Protestant denom.
18 Sun screen
20 Columnist Barrett
21 No faster
22 Under sail
23 Base number
24 Request from drug rehab?
27 Kings prophet
29 "Dragnet" org.
30 How the contortionist ended up?
31 Main course
33 It precedes Adar
37 Base directive
38 Request to go to the head?
41 German industrial region
42 Irk
43 Shooter, for one
46 "Pipe down!"
50 It's measured in minutes
53 Finish line
54 Attitude
55 Lyricist Lerner
56 Summer ermine
58 Request from the palmist?
61 Badminton coach's request?
65 Picnic cooler
66 Relatively ridiculous
67 "The Facts of Life" star
68 Dissimilar
72 On the mark
73 Mint inspector's request?
77 Unpretentious restaurant
81 Has it bad
82 No Mr. Nice Guy
83 A relative of mine
84 "Vogue" rival
86 Driver's license datum
87 Pass a bill
88 Frequent flier
89 Takes heed

92 "Wait, there's more!"
95 Touchdown request?
102 Neapolitan tenor
105 Troi of "Star Trek: TNG"
106 Oberon's bride
107 Short poems
109 Band booking
111 Sad songs
112 Request for the cruise orchestra?
117 It's over the fence
118 Chop-shop fodder
119 Skating event
120 Casting choice
121 Fete
122 Ollie's partner
123 Conclude by
124 Sicily's Mongibeddu
125 "Post" game

DOWN

1 Robin Hood's realm
2 Kind of rhododendron
3 Big bear
4 Maroon
5 Sitcom planet
6 Coward of note
7 Not at all casual
8 Greek poetess
9 Excellent!
10 Graceless guy
11 Addams family cousin
12 Classic soft-drink name
13 Site of 1983 U.S. invasion
14 Bad dog
15 Yoga position
16 Cancun cash
17 Altered state?
19 Smog source
25 Greek theater
26 Like some communities
28 Ital. news agency
32 Collegiate letter
34 Class problem
35 Basic material
36 Mobile home
39 Provide an address
40 It's heard from the flock
43 Bird no longer rare
44 Night spot
45 Night spot
46 Why crows are so noisy?
47 Game ending?
48 It's in the NFL
49 At school
51 Take the wrong way
52 "The Purple Rose of ___"
54 Downtown Chicago
56 NYSE odd lot
57 Fish with a net
59 Rosencrantz or Guildenstern
60 Fall guy?
62 Shorts supports
63 French bean
64 Floor models
68 Conversation fillers
69 "Bus Stop" playwright
70 "Show Boat" songwriter
71 Gave the once-over
73 Muddied the waters?
74 Moon of Saturn
75 Threshold
76 Gulf Coast state
77 Short cut
78 The French way?
79 It may be after you
80 Have an off day
85 "Storms in Africa" singer
87 Stupefied
89 Ink-jet alternative
90 Atomic "twin"
91 Atmospheric probe
93 Service call
94 Aforementioned
95 Steamboat man
96 Lacking the knack
97 Squeal on
98 Red Cross founder
99 Auto driver
100 Avoid the limelight
101 They're stunning
102 Closing bars
103 Court standing
104 Oscar de la ___
108 Do a checkout chore
110 Merit pay
113 Rural delivery
114 La-la lead-in
115 Oahu hrs.
116 Some like it hot

SAVOIR-FAIRE   by Bernice Gordon
. . . for the fair sex.

ACROSS

1 Stun
6 Great skiing area
10 Complacent
14 Prods
19 Bridge guru
20 Put down in defeat
21 Smooth sailing
22 Chanteuse Bailey
23 **Start of a quote**
26 Islands north of Tonga
27 Breathed
28 Rich soil
29 Pykrete ingredient
31 What muscle shirts aren't
32 Refusal
34 Exam taker
35 Lunar shuttle
36 Lascivious woodland deity
37 Other than that
39 Have a role
42 A bit batty
43 Plus fours
48 **More of quote**
52 Neckline
53 Captain's account
54 Put off
55 Cookies that unscrew
56 First two-time Nobelist
57 Canned meat
59 "Delta of Venus" author
60 Scotsmen
61 Like some women's shoes
62 Crop-circle makers?
64 **More of quote**
65 Red item
66 Yiddish author Aleichem
69 1989 Tom Hanks comedy (with "The")
70 Share
71 Huck Finn's response
75 One in jail
76 Hit hard
77 Subject of HBO's "61*"
79 "Caught you!"
80 Unresolved
81 **More of quote**
84 Rocket science
86 Bridge biggie
87 "Triple" ice jumps
88 Detergent launched in 1946
89 Twine fiber
91 Across from: Abbr.
92 Island borough of New York
96 ___-day (modern)
98 Like grads at commence-ment's end
102 Of heat
104 Think
105 What the NBA and the NHL have in common?
106 Excessive
107 **End of quote**
110 Give a lift
111 Gem cut in slabs
112 Behind schedule
113 Bristles
114 Sandy's owner
115 Like coq au vin
116 Notable periods
117 Council site of 1545

DOWN

1 Culture mediums
2 Catwalker
3 Get out of bed
4 Led ___
5 Pepped up
6 Dressed to kill?
7 Saddle with
8 Word with up or down
9 Dagger
10 Shanty?
11 ABBA's "___ Mia!"
12 Dos Passos trilogy
13 Roman clan
14 Rising hairdo
15 Examines the books?
16 From A to Z
17 Gnawed away
18 Online news magazine
24 Utah city
25 Panasonic rival
30 Lost
32 "Merrie Melodies" duck
33 Linz art museum
36 Plastic wrap
38 What more can be
39 Saddlery tools
40 Cut of veal
41 Apparel for Brutus
42 Fleur-___
43 Ship spines
44 Sharpness
45 Norse goddess of fate
46 Nuisance
47 Reed for weavers
49 Krait's killer
50 Motorhome bunk?
51 British aliens
56 Male swan
58 Cows
60 "Wild Horses" singer Brooks
61 ___ four (teacake)
63 On account of
64 Red-blooded
65 Pasta flour
66 Willowy
67 Record player
68 Some switches
69 Container for pickles
70 Sinister group
72 Mansard extension
73 Songwriter Silverstein
74 Father of Romulus
76 Calico
77 Strong polyester film
78 Most irate
81 Russian pancakes
82 Put together
83 De Soto or Hudson
85 Repeat
89 Hard and cold
90 "Star" couple
91 Vow
92 Cousteau invention
93 Harpy hook
94 Lincoln–Douglas debate site
95 Trunks
97 Jerry Della Femina, notably
98 Judicial agenda
99 Growing out
100 "The Dragons of Eden" author
101 Winter weather
103 Brag about
105 AARP division
108 Cupola topper
109 Crossette

247 USE THIS AT EVERY TURN   by Harvey Estes
See 27 Across.

ACROSS

1 Curses
9 Fruit of the Loom products
16 Synagogue chests
20 "April Love" singer
21 Romance language
22 Nair rival
23 Not prix fixe
24 Keepsake
25 Sailing the Pacific
26 Where sailors sup
27 Use this at every turn
28 "___ be a pleasure"
29 Sea eagles
30 Fashion mag
31 Emmy nominee
33 "How Does a Poem Mean?" author
37 Spoiled one
38 Legendary lover
40 It goes to pot
41 Bangkok tongue
44 Pilot's OK
46 Race official
47 Folk or fairy follower
48 Streisand title role
50 Four-term Georgian senator
51 Qvack's playmate
52 Ten Commandments word
54 O'Donnell of TV
56 Small particle
58 Greek god of the sea
60 Sirius and Vega
62 Forces forward
68 Tipped off
69 Lose one's lap
70 "No kidding!"
71 Smith's partner in arms
72 Foundation
73 Approach to a turnoff
74 Push, in a way
76 Get the idea
78 Bart's old man
79 Synagogue official
84 Campus mil. group
86 Succotash beans
88 Sound stressed

89 ___ once
90 Figuring everything
92 Belafonte song opener
93 Jason's craft
94 Burned a bit
96 Syllables of triumph
98 O.K. Corral group?
100 Irregular, as fog
101 Where it's at
102 Fingered
104 Capable of
105 Fill with fumes
108 Frozen asset?
113 Hammered obliquely
114 A notch above amateur
115 Interest
116 About, in memos
117 Cutting calories
118 Dreamy state
119 Costner character
120 Ships' bankers
121 Requirements for some licenses

DOWN

1 Front-line chow, once
2 Fabric weave
3 Fraternity letters
4 Early lessons
5 Emulated Simba
6 Sisters' society
7 Dramatist Chekhov
8 Is abundant
9 Cry before a fall
10 Stupendous
11 Linda of "The Terminator"
12 Actress Graff
13 Curling place
14 London gallery
15 Laughs noisily

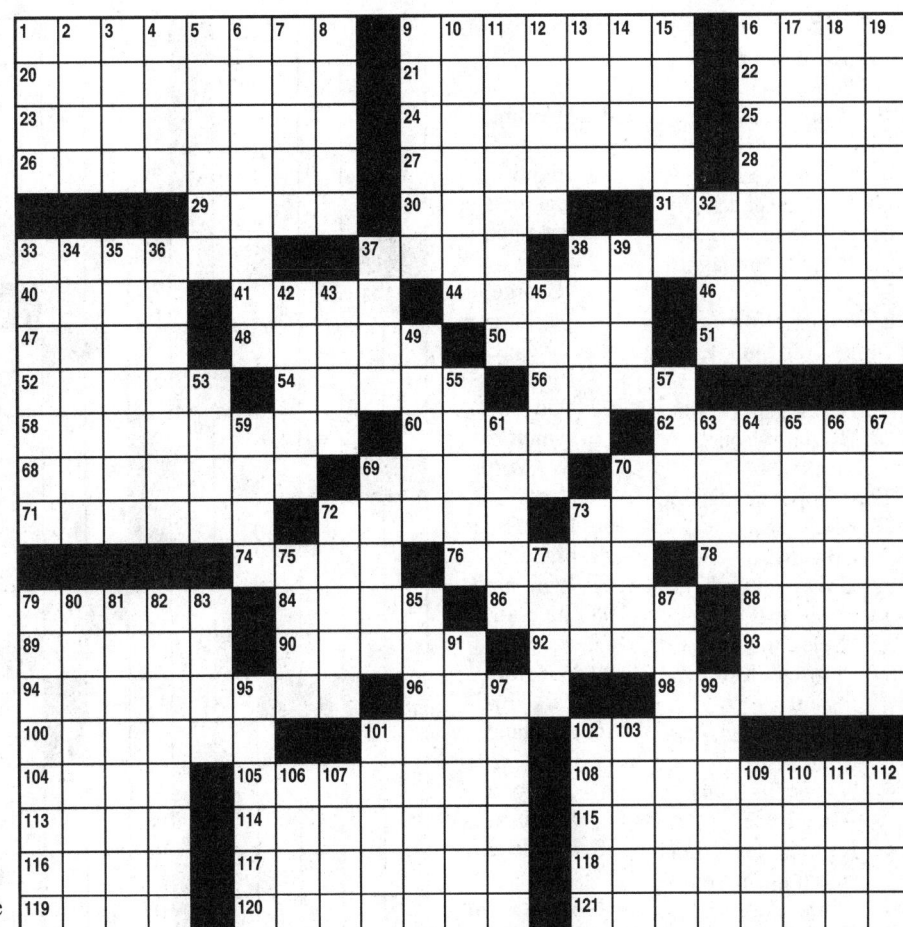

16 "Delta of Venus" author
17 Snooze-alarm setting?
18 Fall in a faint
19 Firm
32 Vintners' vessels
33 U. of New Hampshire logo
34 Having debts
35 They'll show you the way
36 Fishermen, at times
37 Puny pieces
38 Copper coins
39 Pisa's river
42 Christmas story villain
43 Prolific author
45 Watch over
49 Shopping aids
53 Former Yugoslav head

55 Follow Amazon's course
57 "La Bohème" character
59 Game rooms
61 First name in photography
63 Christian denom.
64 Hale telescope site
65 Captivates
66 Family tree
67 Buffet-tray warmers
69 Jack-tars
70 Slangy no
72 Sandy shade
73 Humorist Bombeck
75 Buffalo's lake
77 Verdi opus
79 "Nicholas and Alexandra" role
80 "Public Enemy No. 1" in 1930

81 Ink absorbers
82 Lines in supermarkets?
83 Intense desire
85 Honeybun
87 "I'm telling the truth!"
91 Less callow
95 Mint family herb
97 Bus stops
99 Most peculiar
101 Has trouble on the ice
102 Concerned comment
103 Happy associate?
106 Bill of fare
107 General Bradley
109 Racer Yarborough
110 Bubbly drinks
111 Leave in the text
112 Commuter plane trips

248

K-9 CORPS ARREST? by Harvey Estes
See 103 Across.

ACROSS

1 Vowel sound
6 Papilloma
10 Whit
14 Neighbor of Fiji
19 Scouting group
20 State emphatically
21 Affluent, to Isabella
22 What a rampager goes on
23 Fable fellow
24 Florida State team
26 Vitality
27 Bethlehem product
28 Brigham Young locale
29 Nixon nemesis Sam
30 Made tracks (toward)
32 Brown and others
33 Food stuff
35 "Spare me!"
37 Phrase before instant
38 "Ars Poetica" poet MacLeish
42 Nonfactor at the Astrodome
43 Intimate restaurant
47 Initial group in a product run
48 Hook's ally
51 Like some ski lifts
53 All cozy
54 House-warming party?
57 Wrinkly-skinned dog
58 Snacked
61 Worry
63 Guinness superlative
64 "For ___ know . . ."
65 Raw
66 Preholiday nights
67 Bordello bosses
69 Elbow-bender
70 Had space for
73 River in an Enya song
75 Sunburn victims
77 One way of running?
78 Forwards
79 French I verb
80 "Coal Miner's Daughter" heroine
83 Price displayers
84 "Shane" star Alan
86 Road course
88 Dressing gown
89 Highly regarded
92 Pet a pet, in a way
96 "George Washington ___ here"
97 Bigwigs
102 Had a flu symptom
103 K-9 Corps arrest?
106 Disinfectant brand
107 Work hard
108 Superior body?
109 "Gosford Park" maid
110 Art stand
111 O.K. Corral gunfighter
112 Dollar bills
113 Up the ante
114 Filibuster
115 Biblical you
116 Snug retreat
117 Sing like the birdies sing

DOWN

1 Thief's hoard
2 Minos' home
3 Book between Daniel and Joel
4 Went a-courting
5 Cheddar cheese go-with
6 Winged stinger
7 Indian of Cooperstown
8 Took away
9 Unimportant stuff
10 Rile up
11 Penalty for Tommy Walker
12 Pacific group
13 Hawkeye's 4077 et al.
14 Central Park's ___ on the Green
15 Cheri of "Shrek the Third"
16 Gumption
17 MacLeod of "The Love Boat"
18 Fail to exist
25 Denials
31 Recording studio tasks
34 Footwear in a 1959 Dodie Stevens hit
36 Alexander of the Reagan cabinet
38 Gp. or org.
39 Gambling city
40 Fighting for a cause
41 Where Scots Gaelic is spoken
42 Many a Floridian
43 Motor-mouth of local TV ads
44 They tell you when you're hungry
45 Professional charges
46 Ready for press
48 Frozen fruit purée
49 More substantial
50 Comestible
52 Slice in two
55 Home of some bubbly
56 Flooded
59 St. ___ fire
60 Spoil the hue
62 HI, once
67 More than half
68 Lot measurement
71 Ending for Jean or Ann
72 Like Latin
74 Living within one's means
76 Meager
81 "Hansel and Gretel" prop
82 State of high alarm
85 "Mother of Israel" prophetess
86 Get off at the terminal
87 New shoots
88 "Grease" high school
89 Make one's getaway
90 One-armed bandit
91 Be a tattletale
92 Diamond thefts
93 Ostentatious display
94 Dalai Lama's city
95 Fair kind of playing field
98 Bit of internal governance
99 Davis of "Do the Right Thing"
100 Idaho city
101 Winter driving hazard
104 "Pretty Woman" star
105 End the defense

249 BOOKENDS by Arlan and Linda Bushman
"Bookends" is also the name of a Simon and Garfunkel album and song.

ACROSS

1 Lion's share
5 Fracas
10 Unyielding
15 Bomb
19 Overture follower
20 Tara surname
21 Wetlands denizen
22 Vocation
23 Enrico Caruso, by birth*
25 Bounce*
27 Protective covers
28 Kind of code
30 Emulate
31 "Animal House" animal
32 Escapades
34 Increase
36 Qualifying word
37 Taste and state, e.g.
41 Least complicated
45 Vituperative*
49 Songs like "Orinoco Flow"?*
52 Swiss flower
53 Vixen offspring
54 Brian Wilson's daughter
55 Tyrrhenian island
56 Family moniker
58 San ___, California
60 Fireplace
62 Power source
63 Cooperating
65 Teen talk, often
67 Sporty Spice
69 **Characteristic of clue* answers**
76 Genesis figure
77 First-rate
78 Tough
79 Not chipper
82 Upright
85 Joyous
87 Everest kingdom
88 Intoned
90 House style
92 Vientiane's land
94 Chap
95 "Happy Feet" setting*
97 Frodo Baggins, e.g.?*
99 Chump change
100 Haughty manner
102 "CSI" home
103 Patch again
105 Philippic
110 Catch basket
113 ___ Romana
114 Fizzy concoction
118 Yurt owner
119 Revival cry*
122 Presidential address?*
124 Woody's son
125 Florida citrus city
126 Refinement
127 Key
128 Orderly
129 Out of sorts
130 Rifle feature
131 Proximate

DOWN

1 Tropical ray
2 Milieu of 1 Down
3 Flinch
4 Hedren of "The Birds"
5 Mercury neighbor
6 Links shot
7 Deserve
8 "Man of ___" (1934)
9 Jipijapa hats
10 Dam, for example
11 Bush, notably
12 Fly off the handle
13 Souter attire
14 Rose pt.
15 Reason for a AAA call
16 Filter accumulation
17 Bygone
18 Squint
24 NBA great Robertson
26 Drive, as from bed
29 Character actor Herbert
33 Small cut
35 West Point inits.
36 Unfounded
38 Astringent stuff
39 Not stop at
40 Herd cattle to a fence?
41 Conundrum
42 Some are electric
43 "Jungle Book" actor
44 Federal agt.
45 Katie of sitcoms
46 Eddie LeBec's widow
47 Major range
48 Slackens
50 "Exodus" protagonist
51 Resting spot
54 Use up
57 Caribbean volcano
59 Canal sites
61 Petite
64 Takes away (from)
66 Rubberneck
68 Ebert purview
70 Police concerns
71 Legendary magician
72 Page mission
73 Put in new cushioning
74 Low-lying marshy tract
75 He preceded Polk
79 ___ on a rope
80 "The Temple of Dullness" composer
81 Worf crewmate
83 Dernier ___
84 "Tic ___ Dough"
86 Exercise system
89 Galahad dad
91 Shiny wheels
93 Buttonhole, for instance
96 Belarus currency
97 Rocky's morning gulp
98 Brockovich and Moran
101 Weightlifting unit
103 Jodhpur notables
104 Venerate
106 Spring harbinger
107 Regale
108 Alfalfa's heartthrob
109 Lawn gizmo
110 Pitcher ___ Ho Park
111 Uncommon
112 Hollywood's Raines
113 Fashion hue
115 Dukas ballet (with "La")
116 Unaccompanied
117 Hankering
120 Fate
121 Dobbin munch
123 Thus far

INSIDE 92 ACROSS by Elizabeth C. Gorski
See if you can guess the answer to 92 Across before solving it.

ACROSS

1 Gum balls?
5 Hirt and Hirschfeld
8 Lunch, in London
14 Mar. honoree
19 Succulent houseplant
20 Net income
22 "If only that were true!"
23 Starches, to dieticians
25 Five, in Cancún
26 Eta follower
27 With it
28 Sundae topping
30 A red wine (with 16 Down)
31 Greens keeper?
33 Gumbo pods
36 Not removed
38 Hotel annex?
39 Great Lakes port
40 SACLANT's alliance
41 Rebate document
44 Intelligentsia
48 Blackened fish?
50 Ransacks
51 Dijon denial
52 It's gathered, at times
53 There's something funny about them
55 Thrashed
58 Ladies of Sp.
59 Mosque figures
60 Suggests
62 Wiesbaden, e.g.
63 Tree hugger's plea
69 Fare catch?
71 Crowd favorites
72 "Thanks, Henri!"
75 Sitting on
77 Wesley in "Blade"
78 Tool and die maker, e.g.
82 Eric Clapton classic
84 ___ as dust
85 Yankee who caught Ford
86 Roasting skewer
87 Craziness
89 Hook up with
92 (SEE TITLE)
93 Fairy-tale beginning
94 No. brainer
95 Papas and some mamas?

98 Kind of preview
100 Barnyard babies
105 Chanteuse Edith
106 "Bone" head
108 O'Hare airport code
109 Capri, to an Italian
110 One in a cast
112 "Just wait!"
117 Bring to a near boil
118 Capable of being understood
119 Food stamp
120 Spruce variety
121 "Funny Girl" song
122 Savings-bond series
123 "Boston Public" extra

DOWN

1 Whitman and Whitman Rostow
2 "___ oe" (Hawaii's state song)
3 Carpentry pin
4 Nasal partitions
5 Blood-typing system
6 Womanizers
7 Conn
8 Bon ___
9 UN fiscal agency
10 V-8 Cafe owner in "Cars"
11 "To Your Love" singer Apple
12 Pakistani river
13 Tree house
14 [Not my error]
15 Original name of Hattiesburg, MS
16 See 30 Across
17 PC character set
18 Floribunda feature
21 Pen point
24 Spokes
29 Blind piece
32 Jack Ruby's lawyer

33 Pizarro's favorite colors?
34 Cassis-flavored wine
35 "Shiny Happy People" band
37 Summers, at the Sorbonne
39 Young newts
40 51 past the hour
41 Wusses
42 Coffeehouse come-on
43 "Just kidding!"
44 "That's a ___ malarkey!"
45 Take-off points
46 Where Tiger has a blast?
47 "___ Most Unusual Day"
48 Psi preceder
49 Run smoothly
51 Four-term Georgian senator
54 Invitation request
55 Leonine sounds

56 Adams-___ Treaty (1819)
57 "___ Rosenkavalier"
60 Algonquian speaker
61 Big rig
64 Level ends
65 Take care of
66 Like 74 Down
67 Catch sight of
68 Pick up on
69 Colombian city
70 ___ all-time high
73 CBS drama set in Las Vegas
74 Addams family cousin
76 They're down-to-earth
78 Word Daniel translated
79 Pound sound
80 Largest living reptile
81 Plucked instruments
83 Diarist Frank

85 Reata rancher Benedict
88 "Given that . . ."
89 "Mighty ___ Young" (1998)
90 Man ___ mission
91 San Rafael loc.
95 Bridge call
96 "Addams Family" actress Christina
97 Bother
98 "Alexander" director
99 Not experienced in
100 Diving bird
101 "The jury ___!"
102 From Oslo
103 Fly like an eagle
104 Beelzebub
107 Short cut
108 Mouths, in Latin class
111 Nutritional stat
113 "Right-o!"
114 Texas tea
115 All-purpose truck
116 First-named

251 OPPOSITE NUMBERS by Victor Fleming and Bonnie Gentry
. . . and these opposite numbers are found at 69 Across.

ACROSS

1 "Two By Two" boat
4 The edge of night
8 Deem necessary
14 Ex-Cardinal QB Neil
19 Sugar snap
20 No voter
21 Thin
22 Eleniak of "Baywatch"
23 Taking a position, on Wall Street
25 Designer of the stars
26 Peer Gynt's creator
27 "Bringer" of programs
28 It's circular, in cricket
30 John Reed biopic
31 Big Board newbie
32 No short tale
33 Server's burden
34 Embue with spirit
37 Last pre-AD year
39 "Time" piece
41 Soccer striker's goal?
45 Mrs. Andrew Johnson
48 Elbow
49 Nutrition fig.
50 Toe-stressing activity
53 Slangy refusal
54 Fall time: Abbr.
55 Suit requirement
59 Lie around
60 Singer Brickell
61 1545 council site
62 "But thinking makes ___": Shak.
64 Student's worry
66 Shaw play subject
69 OPPOSITE NUMBERS
72 Thermopylae victor
73 Torpedo or sub
75 Carter in "Ain't Misbehavin' "
76 Equally
78 Turkish bigwig
79 RAF auxiliary of WW2
81 Stand with shelves
83 Moscow loc.
86 Juan or José
87 Benjamins
89 Shirt tag abbr.
90 U.S. coin word
91 Don Imus' network
93 How a geometer looks at a problem?
98 Mowed tracts
101 Florentine sculpture
102 Merman and Mertz
103 Overcome
105 "Sounds good to me!"
108 Bible beginning: Abbr.
109 Market event
110 Shanghai is on it
113 Digestive aid
117 Texas A&M player
118 "Britannicus" dramatist
119 Soma, Mitra or Agni, e.g.
120 L.A. Dodgers, e.g.
121 Angioplasty inserts
122 Performing twosomes
123 Eggs
124 Blasts out
125 In this place, in legalese
126 End at
127 ___ of hope

DOWN

1 Alerts for J. Friday
2 Commit to another hitch
3 Send to the canvas
4 Ballet performer
5 Diabolic
6 Moves a muscle
7 Cousins
8 Biting turtle
9 Stud site
10 Humorist Bombeck
11 Unravels
12 Ancient Greek colony
13 Pang
14 Eric the Red's son
15 Like satellites
16 Economic health gauge
17 Cub Scout leader
18 Cartesian coordinates
24 Bit of progress
29 Rip-roaring time
31 Peruvian ancient
34 "Trader Phil" of hockey
35 Dealer's foe
36 Opening for a tab
37 Working
38 It stands at stands
40 Film locale
42 Steel ingredient
43 Clip joint?
44 Jeff Lynne's group
46 Where Ali beat Foreman
47 Frog removers?
51 Advanced attorney's deg.
52 Alchemic mixture
55 Glom
56 Fame
57 Feast (on)
58 Vogue
60 Vichy verb
61 ___ Bora
63 Season
65 Gridiron feint
66 Burst
67 Colosseum wear
68 1962 Shelley Fabares song
70 Construe
71 Kept quiet
74 Ming of the NBA
77 Look like a creep
80 Justice Dept. division
82 Choreographer Ailey
83 Pulitzer winner for "Picnic"
84 Uninteresting
85 Cathy in "East of Eden"
87 "Proud Mary" group
88 Covering for a bald spot
90 Not yet shaped
92 Alter ego of Barbara Gordon
94 Shade close to plum
95 High place
96 Response to "Who, me?"
97 If nothing else
99 Gillespie's nickname
100 007 foe
103 ". . . ___ other name"
104 Quarter back?
106 Burning up
107 More gracious
109 Kind of nurse
111 "Touched by an Angel" character
112 Hollywood and ___
114 Prince of opera
115 Old Chevy model
116 Mate's cry
119 Ohio Northern's home

252 ENGINEER IN THE CABOOSE   by James Connolly

Before becoming an actor 52-D was a Major League Baseball player for six years.

ACROSS

1 "Give me a single example"
8 Point a finger at
14 Patronize Luxor
20 Containing element 92
21 46th U.S. Vice President
22 Brought up
23 Zen "I'm a Believer" singer?
25 "Garfield" cat
26 Thousands
27 Put up
28 Literary Nobelist Andric
29 Massachusetts cape
30 Skid row figure
31 Pension agcy.
32 Wee
34 WBA stoppages
35 Sir Galahad's mother
38 Wash gently against
42 Hamilton's prov.
43 Go astray
44 Babysitter's whiskers?
46 Out-of-pocket one
48 Tourist ___
49 Witch-hunt
51 BB shooter
54 Barrel-racing venue
57 Prefix with sort or soak
59 Temporary
61 Javits Center architect
62 Explorer Tasman
63 Metallic hut
65 Hydrocarbon suffix
66 Duke's athletic org.
67 OED listing
68 Most immense
69 A truckload
72 "Citizen Kane" studio
73 Vein contents
74 Velvet finish?
75 Was unleashed
77 Walk like a sot
78 Gent, Rasta-style
79 Electric-guitar pioneer
82 Civil War initials
83 Sexologist Hite
84 Pulver's rank
86 Daniel of Nicaragua
88 5K or 10K
90 They get the lead out
92 Carting an Osbourne around?
97 Jan. honoree
98 Way to stand?
99 Xbox fanatic
100 Toughen, in a way
101 Spots for rings
102 Cropped up
104 Taxing mo.
106 Immigrant's course: Abbr.
107 IHOP orders
108 County div.
109 Legalese adverb
113 Satirist Sahl
115 Boastful sort
117 Pollution-filled Western river?
120 Disinclined
121 Richards in "Jurassic Park"
122 Fanfare
123 Be livid
124 Fill out a register
125 Japanese massage

DOWN

1 Well-used pencil
2 Salad green
3 Family head, for one
4 "The NeverEnding Story" author
5 Sounds of awe
6 Rapa ___ (Easter Island)
7 Road twists
8 Wile E.'s supplier
9 Van/___/Straw
10 Euro fraction
11 Broken, as promises
12 Moth-eaten
13 Storm area
14 New hire that gets into the sauce?
15 Flying-related
16 ___ de mer
17 Cleaning up at a Left Bank casino?
18 He wrote "Nowhere Man"
19 Blissful spots
24 Refrain syllables
28 Mae West's "___ Angel"
30 Golfer Hogan
31 Dreamcast maker
33 What Jack took
34 Winter Palace resident
36 Military data, for short
37 "Stoney End" composer
39 2004 Olympics site
40 Stew morsel
41 Raptor's digs
45 Calls into question
46 L.A. hrs.
47 Some street performers
50 Composer Bruckner
52 Bob of "Mr. Belvedere"
53 Richie of "The Simple Life"
54 Radar antenna housing
55 King of the fairies
56 DOD tenant?
58 Small deer
60 Brush up on
63 New York tribe?
64 Biplane part
68 Hagar's wife
70 "Piece ___!" ("Easy!")
71 MASH staffers
76 Prince Valiant's beloved
77 Köln river
80 Lisbon rival
81 MGM motto starter
83 Clinic test
85 Ticks off
87 Pinup's asset
89 Seaweed extract
91 Tombstone name
93 Ticked off
94 Timon in "The Lion King"
95 Nor'___ (gales)
96 Wing of sorts
97 Western desert
99 "Iron Horse" of Cooperstown
101 Frat wear
103 "First ___ see tonight . . ."
105 Annie of "Designing Women"
108 Brit's "Baloney!"
110 "Voice of Israel" author
111 Royal in a sari
112 Popeye Doyle's prototype Richard
113 City bond, for short
114 Hepta- plus one
116 Bulky PC monitor
117 Roadside sign
118 Pep-rally yell
119 ___ de vie (brandy)

253 PIANISSIMO   by Cornelia W. Buss
The festival at 23-A is held each summer in Central Park's Delacorte Theater.

ACROSS

1 Photo finish
6 Rent-___ (security guard)
10 "Put the blame on" her
14 Martin song subject
19 Printers' extras
20 10 C-notes
21 Tissue additive
22 Loudness units
23 NY Shakespeare Festival founder
25 "The Libertine" star
27 New Yorker's neighbor
28 They may have twists
30 Chicago Fire scapegoat
31 Org chart feature
32 Go like the dickens
33 Bake-sale orgs.
34 Places for spankers
36 Grid great Ronnie
37 Malaria symptom
39 The berries
43 Battery units
44 2003 Super Bowl star
46 "Think nothing ___"
47 Skinny
48 Like Groucho
49 Port of old Rome
50 Finder's take
51 Chariot add-on
52 "Sexy" Beatles girl
53 Coat of arms item
54 Chuck-a-luck need
55 Considers, in a way
57 Sporty Pontiacs
58 Pie-eyed
60 "All the King's Men" actress
61 Lou Gehrig replaced him
65 ___ in Victor
66 With suspicion
69 Skye in "River's Edge"
70 Ballroom of Manhattan
74 Blowgun ammo
75 Slip by
78 Charlemagne's father
79 Fork over
80 It lays green eggs
81 Boxing's "Brown Bomber"
82 Thumb one's nose at
83 Movie extra, for short
84 Castel Gandolfo resident
86 Monicagate informant
88 Tartar sauce morsel
89 Lights-out tune
90 Some are fine
91 Brinker of kid lit
92 Seinfeld's "Nazi" sold them
93 Visibly shaken
95 Hard to corner
96 "Cut it out!"
97 Big name in fashion
100 Show again
102 Seasonal farm workers
106 1940 Ronald Reagan role
108 Wildcats coaching legend
110 Send sky-high
111 "Aha!"
112 Mrs. Krank in "Skipping Christmas"
113 Word form of "nine"
114 Windmill part
115 Slate, informally
116 Fast-food order
117 Like a fleabag

DOWN

1 Magic charm
2 Bell-ringing company
3 Crammer's concern
4 Buys for
5 Lotus models
6 Even, at Pinehurst
7 Biggers sleuth
8 "Alley-___" (1960 hit)
9 String-pulling?
10 "Fawlty Towers" resident
11 Oodles
12 Quartz = 7, to him
13 Bard's nightfall
14 Safe havens
15 Home of Gallo Winery
16 Fit to serve
17 Copy of an orig.
18 Catch sight of
24 Hotfoots it
26 Reporters' needs
29 After the whistle
32 Goodie from Linz
33 It grows in the dark
34 Nickel-copper alloy
35 Essen's "Cannon King"
36 J. Lo, e.g.
37 Home of St. Francis
38 Stadium take
40 "Krazy Kat" lawman
41 Rook or knight
42 Knight's mount
43 Is in contention
44 "The Merry ___": Lehár
45 Words of resignation
48 Used to be
52 Did web design?
53 "Gypsy" composer
54 Like some citizenships
56 Part of QED
57 Tongue, anatomically
59 Subway sight
62 Fats, oils, etc.
63 Hosp. preparation areas
64 Easy out at Fenway
66 Crackerjack
67 Mead's milieu
68 Cook up a whopper
71 Watch baby
72 Mane locales
73 Batik worker
76 Tours river
77 Polly, to Tom
78 "The Elder" of Rome
82 Like rose water
83 Dessert wine
85 Cordage grass
87 Like Johnny Damon's mother
88 Whelk look-alikes
92 Inedible cake
94 Something to manage
95 Clad like Dracula
96 1964 Tony Randall role
97 Golden ___ (senior)
98 Move, in Realtor-speak
99 Zoo confinement
100 Actuary's concern
101 Blunted blade
102 Five-time Wimbledon champ
103 Futhark letter
104 Pundit's piece
105 Alter, in a way
107 MRE eaters
109 Scooby-___

254 NAME DROPPERS by Arthur S. Verdesca
Get to know these celebrities on a first-name basis.

ACROSS

1 Cattle driver
5 Funny bone's nerve
10 Bounds
15 Meager
19 Road rig
20 Clavichord's cousin
21 Long green
22 Matting fiber
23 Treats leather
24 Roman ancestral spirits
25 Unapproachable
26 Center of revolution
27 German composer Wilhelm ___
30 Way-off
32 Glass eye
33 Hi's better half
34 Modernizes
38 Across the pond
41 Gambling loss?
43 Bonn expressway
44 Tout
45 Rock musician Howard ___
47 Kingston college
48 Importune
49 Face courageously
50 White vestments
51 Springe
52 Date
53 Permission
54 Sleep disorder
56 Hover
57 Sin
58 Canadian singer Morna ___
60 Yes, he has some bananas
61 Pens
63 Rail support
64 Thicket
65 Singer Cass
67 TV anchor Margaret ___
71 Spoil
74 Competitors
75 Tender spots
76 Bucks
77 Bar org.
78 Oscar's cousin
79 "Lulu" composer
80 Exploiter's knack
81 Hot spot
82 Banns word
83 Hollywood legend Eldred ___
86 Sanction

87 Complex of symptoms
89 "___ la vista, baby!"
90 Olio
91 Bony
92 Kind of movie
93 Eye
94 Word of disgust
95 Film actor Charles ___
100 Monumental
103 Swell smell
105 Ocular activity
106 Muddy the waters
108 Rambler
109 Hang in midair
110 Cross swords
111 Pumice, e.g.
112 Handouts
113 Astringent
114 Charlton Heston role
115 Attack time

DOWN

1 L.A. time
2 Bring up
3 Hawks' old arena
4 Let slip
5 Higher ground
6 They speak with forked tongues
7 Ancient ointment
8 One more time
9 Russell in "Auntie Mame"
10 Destroying angel
11 Espionage figures
12 Lout
13 Labor org.
14 Crisp clothing fabrics
15 Egyptian charm
16 Nova
17 1969 Super Bowl
18 Miniver or Malaprop
28 Warmth
29 Pierce
31 Bath's river
34 Cuban dance
35 French composer Joseph ___
36 Saying
37 Potshot taker

38 Manhandle
39 Auger user
40 Pitching great William ___
41 Urbane
42 Male seal's devotees
43 Lane
45 Gas House Gang brothers
46 Turner in "Latin Lovers"
49 John Brown's eulogist
51 Pinched
53 Nigerian city
54 Al Gore's sign
55 Ready for surgery
56 Entreats
59 Eclectic magazine
60 Brother of 45 Across
62 Ethereal
64 Deadpan
65 Nonetheless
66 Old term for British sailors
67 Catcher Posada

68 It sailed to Colchis
69 Plus
70 Oneida County city
72 Tipping the scales
73 Aromatic herb
75 Looks like
79 Hubbub
80 How salmon run
81 Europe
83 Drink for 66 Down
84 Noisy dispute
85 Bulldog's school
86 Grouse
88 Wild cards, at times
90 Punkies
92 Hot prospect
93 Locale
95 Peregrinate
96 Tenderfoot
97 Fixes a fight
98 Concourse
99 Prima donna
100 Mound stat
101 Ward heeler
102 Doctrine
104 Fabulous flier
107 Wager

BRANDO AND COMPANY   by Raymond Hamel

"An actor is at most a poet and at least an entertainer." — Marlon Brando

ACROSS

1 "___ Trend" magazine
6 Small vial
12 "Scooby dooby" singing
16 Camera type
19 Vapid
20 "Rats!"
21 Paid confidante
22 Chocolate drink (with 34-D)
23 Brando and Frank Sinatra film
25 What an oil lamp provides
27 Revealing swimsuit
28 Smog alert org.
29 "Tales of a Wayside Inn" town
30 Gregg Hughes' radio name
31 Salon jobs
33 Brando and Al Pacino film
37 Radner's "___ Always Something"
40 Make comfortable
41 "Iron Chef America" chef Cat
42 "Let ___": Beatles
43 Brando and Christopher Reeve film
45 Has guests over
47 Elephant ruler
51 Earth's pull, for short
52 Limerick language
54 Brando and George C. Scott film
57 Like ostrich eggs
59 Berger in "The Waltz King"
62 Sea of crosswords
63 Speed-skater Jansen
64 Tone deafness
66 Seeping
68 Tax scare
71 Brando and Lee J. Cobb film
75 Comic verse
78 Pastrami provider
79 Subtle shade
83 "Don't mind ___ do!"
84 Woes
86 Closes up
89 Bangkok residents
90 Brando and Anthony Quinn film
94 Delivered notes?
96 Is broadcast
97 Daughter of William I
98 Form of matter
101 Brando and James Garner film
103 "She Believes ___": Kenny Rogers
106 City near Lake Tahoe
107 Makes a mistake
108 Handyman's cable network
109 Brando and Karl Malden film
113 "Scrooge" director
115 Anne McCaffrey's dragon world
116 Ariz. neighbor
117 Gerundial suffix
119 Unanimously
123 Goes amuck
125 Brando and Shirley Jones film
128 Start of MGM's motto
129 Tilt
130 "The Garden of Cyrus" author
131 "Er . . . um . . ."
132 Like lava
133 "The Four Seasons" director
134 "The Demolished Man" author
135 Put aside

DOWN

1 Russian jets
2 And higher
3 Diggs in "Chicago"
4 Beginning
5 More prepared
6 Introduce
7 Sounded reasonable
8 Stage grip?
9 Open a gate
10 Small, to rappers
11 Wormhole travelers
12 Managed
13 Dante translator John
14 No longer moored
15 President pro ___
16 Slender woman
17 Sarge's superior
18 One of eight
24 Anonymous
26 Pep squad cry
29 Catania's patron saint
32 Royal Russians
34 See 22 Across
35 Whilom
36 E.G., e.g.
37 Bella near Sicily
38 Yellowfin and blackfin
39 Dum spiro ___ ("While I breathe, I hope")
44 Christmas party drink
46 Painting stroke
48 Melville sailor Billy
49 Tien Shan mountains
50 Bombast
53 Ample, to the bard
55 He played Klinger
56 Basketball coach Lute
58 German article
60 Evil "Flushed Away" character
61 Montezuma subject
65 Some hotel lobbies
67 "I can't hear you" reaction
69 "Sometimes you feel like ___ . . ."
70 Arizonian's neighbor
72 "SOS"
73 Joyce and Fitzgerald
74 Chile's president during WW2
75 Edith Piaf, for one
76 "The Wizard ___"
77 Hand to
80 Green nymph
81 Wispy clouds
82 Pope piece
85 Sweetgum resin
87 Karl Benz invention
88 Capture
91 Grays from afar
92 Filled with antics
93 "30 Rock" star Baldwin
95 Rotate, as the hips
99 Tattoo parlor supply
100 Square-dance circles
102 Membrane permeation
104 Like drudge work
105 Oklahoma city
109 Most influential woman
110 Head of surgery?
111 Young's accounting partner
112 Volkswagen model
114 Words on a literary cake
118 Box contents abbr.
120 Champagne name
121 Part of UAE
122 Little "Big Apple"
124 Type of AV input
125 S&P bond rating
126 ". . . Ida, harken ___ I die": Tennyson
127 View from the Riviera

ACROSS

1 In
7 Hunger signal
11 Kett of the comics
15 Forum flier
19 Thicke's sitcom name
20 "___ off?"
21 Losing proposition
22 Knight club
23 Conflicted sage?
26 Draft eligible
27 Ecology org.
28 Govt. branch
29 Desktop symbol
30 Warmongering
32 Sidekick with a headband
34 Smashing
36 Galileo's home
37 HBO alternative
38 The sun, for one
39 "I'm outta here!"
40 Hightails it
41 The other woman
42 Russo-Roman leader?
47 Manages (with "out")
48 Stationary acceleration
51 Bridge declaration
52 Kind of seat
54 Julia's role on "Seinfeld"
55 Starve
57 Big cheese
58 ___ colada
59 James King et al.
60 Ethics teacher
63 TV announcer Hall
64 Royal couch?
68 Cross word
69 "Shampoo" Oscar winner
71 Simoleons
72 Palindromic band
73 Like pocket change
74 Treats unfairly
76 Research centers
78 Elegance
80 Soldier material?
81 High degree
82 Phrase before instant
83 "Fame" singer's parade?
86 Some docs
87 Spine-chilling
89 Lap dog
90 "The Bells ___ Mary's"
94 Not long.
95 Vientiane's land
96 Swindle
99 Safari head
100 Call before the court
102 Page
103 Coleridge work
105 Semi section
106 Having lower digits
107 Headline about Oscar's release?
111 ". . . thrice ___ him off": Shak.
112 Buffalo water hole
113 Asian expanse
114 Soup letter?
115 Is left with
116 Former Russian ruler
117 Pass by
118 "If you're lucky"

DOWN

1 They're sometimes frozen
2 Place for bags
3 1990 Robert Redford film
4 Eggs, scientifically
5 "The Evil That ___" (Bronson film)
6 Art Deco designer
7 Firebird maker
8 Colony resident
9 Sparkle on a diamond mound
10 ___-Roman wrestling
11 Adam's apple location
12 Element #50
13 Helpful group online
14 Military position
15 Out of control
16 Dismissing words for a comic?
17 Greenland feature
18 Upright swimmer
24 Choosing
25 Dandy
31 "___ it something I said?"
33 Matter that doesn't
35 Pork provider?
36 Grade elevator
39 Pedestrian staff
40 School group
43 Coq au ___
44 Anouk in "La Dolce Vita"
45 Cheech and Chong movie
46 Courtroom VIPs
47 Carbon compound
48 Gross out
49 Say "somethin'"
50 Way named for singer Martha's group?
52 Poet Teasdale
53 Israeli statesman Abba
55 Rite receptacle
56 Rambler source
57 Temporary superstar
59 Steward's charge
60 Film thickness units
61 It may get rattled
62 Bangkok natives
64 Old hands
65 Source of diaper discomfort
66 Like some booms
67 Spot, for one
70 Enter or leavin'
72 "Don't delay!"
74 Rollercoaster cry
75 Took flight
76 Church section
77 Olympics chant word
78 Ashtray, vis-à-vis trash
79 Conditionally out
80 Barbra's "A Star Is Born" costar
81 Get there
83 Launderers, at times
84 Do a takeoff on
85 Try to enroll
87 Barney ___ Oldfield
88 Aerie hatchling
91 Pretense
92 Slow movers
93 Gelcap alternative
96 Soft area
97 "Unhand me!"
98 Derby site
99 Donne's "Death ___ Proud"
101 Says further
102 Jethro Bodine portrayer Max
104 "Who's the Boss?" character
108 Routing term
109 Asian waist product?
110 Try for apples

DJ CONVENTION   by Arlan and Linda Bushman
114 Across is also the name of a Marlon Brando film.

ACROSS

1 Formed a parabola
6 New pod members
12 Nutrition letters
15 See 17 Down
19 Sicily neighbor
20 Lively
21 School-spirit builder
23 Ring risk
25 Video game classic
26 Dragnet
27 Davis of "The Brady Bunch"
29 Use a cipher
30 Mission
33 Enthusiasm
36 Rehan and Lovelace
39 Ankara notable
40 Virgil epic
42 Likelihood
45 Bela cohort
46 Tea accompaniment
48 Pear variety
49 Sound off
51 Refer to
52 Still on the shelf
53 Lyrical
56 Negative adverb
57 Queens, for one, informally
59 Certainly
60 Egyptian deity
61 Polity
64 Mix up
66 Courtroom chicanery
68 Jimmy Dean #1 hit of 1961
72 Run (to)
73 Dwindle
74 Sculptor Nadelman
75 Priestly garment
78 Onetime European capital
79 India's smallest state
80 Rappelling objective
82 Sahara dweller
84 Witty saying
88 German city
89 Complainer, perhaps
90 Bell-bottoms, e.g.
93 Kin, for short
94 Collections
95 Sets up
96 Farm prefix
97 Phoenician port
98 CO₂ element
100 "Sorry, that's the way it is"
102 Utterly hopeless
104 Wrangle
107 Earth's lowest point
111 Disregard
114 They're sometimes wild
117 Nielsen-ratings factor
118 Chain links
119 Sharp as ___
120 Eiger home
121 Vintner's term
122 Leaseholder
123 Bingo cousins

DOWN

1 Broadcast designation
2 ___ avis
3 Sept
4 Inscribes
5 Bit of info
6 Cost of hauling
7 Sharapova coup
8 Inc. abroad
9 Singh of the links
10 Author Hunter
11 Basted
12 Tach readout
13 French article
14 Fasten to
15 Masked marauders
16 Mounds' nutty sister
17 Stylish clothes (with 15-A)
18 Holiday song title word
22 Capetown currency
24 Open up
28 Steve Martin prop
31 Empty pretense
32 Nigerian-born singer
34 Amorphous chairs
35 Dream
36 Roberto or Sandy of baseball
37 Scale trio
38 Digital alternative
40 Composer Dvořák
41 Polish
43 Handout
44 Lather
46 Zinnias' spot
47 Ruffle
48 "There was ___ lady . . ."
50 Kingdom near Fiji
52 Suave
54 Like some pools
55 Acadian exile descendant
58 Spherical
62 Burrowed
63 NYC subway line
64 Service pack?
65 Oust
67 Hearth find
68 Gnu feature
69 Chicago Fire name
70 Impede
71 Vex
73 Theater boxes
75 "Waterloo" group
76 Revolutionary Trotsky
77 Summer Olympics event
79 Encircled
81 Puncture sound
83 Hounds
85 Tempos
86 Not quite shut
87 Phone lead-in
90 Datebook abbr.
91 Least humid
92 Having bumps
95 Praises
97 Until now
99 Protest songwriter Phil
100 Refrigerant substance
101 "Wheel of Fortune" wheel
102 Utah ski resort
103 React to a leak
105 Assigned station
106 Chip in
108 Flip through
109 Kitchenware brand
110 Quizzes
112 Rival
113 Antitrust org.
115 Age
116 Inclination

OBJECT LESSON   by Susan Wesley
The answer to 99 Across is in pidgin.

ACROSS

1 Jason in "The Bourne Identity"
5 Rootless type
10 Dundee dude
14 Alexandria's land
19 Connors adversary
20 Having a lot to lose
21 "I did it!"
22 Norse race
23 Groucho's expression
24 Postcard's picture, perhaps
25 Sub-molecule
26 William Bendix TV role
27 Hancock Park attraction that's alive?
31 Fads
32 Works at the Louvre
33 Marin of comedy
37 Anakin's daughter
38 Minor scrape
41 Become payable
42 How boats rock on foamy waves?
45 Suffix with honor
46 Native's suffix
47 "Ew!"
48 Least of the litters
49 AC unit
50 Slightly
51 Apollo part
54 Class of Soviet sub
57 Man of words
59 Poor-box contents
60 Like rich desserts
63 Haughty
64 Result of a good offertory hymn?
68 NBA venue
69 Kind of insurance
70 In vogue
71 Passover dinners
73 Do this with a hand or an ear
74 Must have now, in memos
78 Put up the cash
79 Oft-framed document
81 "What now?!"
83 Season opener
84 Bart Simpson, typically
85 Whiz
86 Hatred of a Hawaiian volcano?
91 Forgo creature comforts
93 Beat up on
94 No-cal bagel part
95 Make certain
96 Sunbather with leathery skin
97 Words of denial
99 "Where did this coin come from?"
106 Coral communities
109 Charlie Chaplin's wife
110 Textile trademark
111 Joker or card
112 Simple plants
113 St. Paul's architect
114 "Sunset Blvd." heroine
115 Cinder ending
116 Team followers
117 Snug retreat
118 Old-time verb
119 Barely gets by

DOWN

1 Teen hangout
2 Whaling, in a sense
3 "Them's ___!" ("Tough luck!")
4 Lay of the land
5 The brightest stars
6 End notes
7 Holey fabric
8 Vino venue
9 Big man on campus
10 Social position
11 College publication
12 Secret targets
13 Pat down
14 Terrestrial
15 Dr. Seuss
16 Haute-couture monogram
17 All-American dessert
18 Give it a go
28 "Yipes!"
29 Central Asian desert
30 Feathered friend of Daedalus
34 Newspaper issue
35 Do the shag?
36 Paid attention to
37 Bats or bonkers
38 Rover's reward
39 Mel of baseball
40 Sounds of surprise
41 Unlikely, as a chance
42 Metal container
43 "Escape From Freedom" author
44 Takes to the station house
49 Mummichog, often
50 Home of the oryx
52 Not just given
53 Like crystal
54 Spoken
55 Lounge about
56 Campus brotherhood
58 Garden pest
60 Intimate restaurant
61 Strong ___ ox
62 Enemy of Antony
64 "Like that'll ever happen!"
65 Father of Antigone
66 Practice origami
67 '70s courtroom drama
68 Go for the gold
72 Relatively nimble
74 Winning coach of Super Bowl XIV
75 No evoker of tears, for some
76 "Alfred" composer
77 Cribbage equipment
80 Like a jalapeño
81 Words with diet or roll
82 "A Man and a Woman" composer
85 "Get real!" and "Get lost!"
86 Iwo Jima flag raisers
87 Not voiced
88 Maritime agcy.
89 Thunderous god
90 Award winner
92 Belly laugh
96 Mind-numbing job
97 Checkout count
98 Note above C
100 Square setting
101 Nirvana, for one
102 Slangy suffix
103 About, in memos
104 Tunnel maker
105 Schedule guesses, briefly
106 Emulate Eminem
107 Conduit bend
108 Id's counterpart

35 Down was written by Stephen King and Stewart O'Nan.

ACROSS

1 Tour de France terminus
6 Used the cuspidor
10 Line crosser, of sorts
14 Divas' deliveries
19 Salt's "Halt!"
20 Big brass
21 Negri of silents
22 Hawaiian governor Lingle
23 Slasher's confinement
25 Like Nancy Lopez's golf swing
27 Pseudo-cultured
28 Helpful contacts
29 Running away
31 "Ditto"
33 Hightails it
34 Expo '98 city
38 Bandmate of the Edge
39 Gerald Ford's cat
40 Surfboard fin
42 Unlock, to a poet
43 Uplifting item
45 Axed Watergate prosecutor
49 Retired fleet
50 Sitarist's tune
52 Irish Spring et al.
53 Mischa in "Destry Rides Again"
54 "I understand now"
55 Sarcastic response
56 George of "CSI"
57 Tuscany city
58 Carol opening
59 Revelatory
61 Beatles' music co.
62 Mideast money
63 Met, as a bet
64 South Lawn parties
65 Not 'neath
66 From Qum
68 Not keyed
70 Prolonged, in obstetrics
75 Coppers
76 BART part
77 Tot's plea
78 "Zip-___-Doo-Dah"
79 Break up, informally
80 Trevi toss-in, once
81 Eunuch's charge
82 Future JD's hurdle
83 Diner on "Alice"
84 Achilles and the tortoise, e.g.
87 Many ER cases
88 It may be inflated
89 Kick back
90 Mixologist's stock
91 Ferocious cat
93 2005 Sprint purchase
95 Up there
97 Shah Pahlavi
98 Pulsar emission
101 "___ 'nuff!"
102 Cut back
106 Where the Civil War ended
109 Former Mexican president
112 Take a powder
113 Take a hit
114 Coupe d'___
115 Mount the soapbox
116 Hen, hopefully
117 North Sea feeder
118 It's $50 for Boardwalk
119 Newbies

DOWN

1 Bearded Smurf
2 Declare as true
3 Go ballistic
4 Parent's words after "because"
5 Cardinal's letters
6 "Funny Girl" composer
7 Dart league locales
8 Blood-typing system
9 Airport queue
10 Burst of growth
11 Gelato holders
12 Zillions
13 Isaac Asimov's Onum
14 Nixon's chief of staff
15 Ugly scenes
16 Colts, on scoreboards
17 Shakespeare title word
18 Instrument inventor Adolphe
24 Indian Ocean arm
26 Fax ancestor
30 Visitor in "Star Trek: DS9"
32 Literary bits
33 Clippers and cutters
35 "Faithful" team
36 Best cases
37 Treehouse builder?
38 Popular New York nosh
39 Lamp cover
40 Postcard feature
41 Imam's book
43 Tube rider
44 Broccoli ___
46 Scuttle load
47 Not of the cloth
48 Matters of honor
49 Communal
51 Magellan launcher
54 Literary no-show
57 Fare under a sneezeguard
60 Checker move?
61 Crazes
64 Enter the draft
66 Blue Jackets, slangily
67 Weasel out
68 City on the Rhône
69 Slangy denial
70 Some jumpers, briefly
71 Having only length
72 Smacker
73 Try for a part
74 Rusty Staub's 1985 team
77 Insertion mark
81 Pollinosis, familiarly
84 Not one of Dobie Gillis' loves
85 BC, e.g.
86 The ___ Affair (1797–98)
89 Tobacco store buy
92 Table linens
94 Valuable find
95 Was aroused
96 Not so rigid
97 He didn't give a damn
99 ___-bitty
100 Siouan Indians
101 Read the UPC
103 Way out there
104 ___-Rooter
105 They're splitsville
106 Every last crumb
107 Thimblerig item
108 Pony up
110 Follower's suffix
111 Rugrat

GYMNOPHOBIAC'S NIGHTMARE?   by Theresa Yves
See 64 Down.

ACROSS

1 Come down with
6 Dharma's guy
10 Point the finger at
15 Palindromic address
19 "Hello" from Ho
20 Anecdotal knowledge
21 William Bendix role
22 Suffix with chick
23 Doris on the stand?
25 Graff of "Mr. Belvedere"
26 Northern Iraqi
27 Take a picture of Puff?
28 Solemn song
29 Novelist Wiesel
30 Hugh Hefner's attire
32 J.R.'s drink?
34 Semiautomatic rifles
38 Greeley's direction
40 Spell of forgetfulness
41 Did business online
42 Main idea
43 Hirohito, e.g.
46 Ivan of the court
47 Mercury capsule inhabitant
49 "Julius Caesar" setting
50 Brakeless sled
51 Florida footballer
53 Garden beauty
55 Gomez Addams portrayer
56 Allow traffic back on a street for kids?
58 Angelic actress?
60 Material for an editor
61 Cellar dweller's position
62 Rowling and Tolkien
68 Buff
74 Appropriate inappropriately
75 Continental coin
76 Offends olfactorily
77 Collar kind
78 Like clown faces
80 Corsair crew
82 Pigs
83 Isolated
85 Grave risk
86 Poe poem of ideal beauty
88 Rash
89 First Olympic site
90 Went on a gamboling spree
91 Record collection?
94 Highlands breads
96 Pieces of a circle
97 Clarinets and flutes
99 Wolverine, for example
104 Ft. or yd., e.g.
105 When prompted
106 Competition for tubers?
107 Round-buyer's words
108 Pure-and-simple
109 Mine, to Maurice
110 Dodge SUV
111 Catches forty winks
112 Exams
113 Rutgers residence
114 City of the Ruhr valley

DOWN

1 Scoundrels
2 Rock pioneer Freed
3 "I Do" singer
4 Bit of chocolate
5 Palmist's fee?
6 Rubbed it in
7 Tiger's aversions
8 Diamond flaw?
9 Spin one's wheels
10 Runner-up
11 Leslie Caron title role
12 On your toes
13 "The Boys From Brazil" doctor
14 "E F P T O Z" events
15 Holds water
16 Add inferior material to
17 Lofty nest
18 Jason's wife
24 Cherry picker
31 Pager summons
33 Be seen by, in a vision
34 Stringed instrument
35 Consumed heartily
36 Where one hears of many firings
37 First State senator
39 ___ Haute, Indiana
42 Scottish singer Sandi
44 Porter's regretful miss
45 Magritte or Russo
47 Watches a late movie, say
48 They're remarkable
51 GM makes
52 Words after easy
54 Remiss
57 Shoulder blades
59 Auction stipulation
62 See red
63 Straight-arrow linkup
64 Gymnophobiac's nightmare
65 Takes a wrong shortcut?
66 Baloney
67 They feel the agony of defeat?
68 Sketchbook
69 Have a hunch
70 More recent
71 Like the Tower of Pisa
72 Gifted person
73 Without a letup
79 Fade gradually
81 Song for Scotto
82 Ute, e.g.
84 Cold War thaw
86 Get ready to shoot
87 Open to view
90 U.S. anti-submarine mine
91 Private Ryan portrayer
92 Contest venue
93 Splinter groups
95 Former governor Mario
98 "Some Velvet Morning" is one
100 "Redemption" author
101 Gym equipment
102 A lot, maybe
103 Sign gas

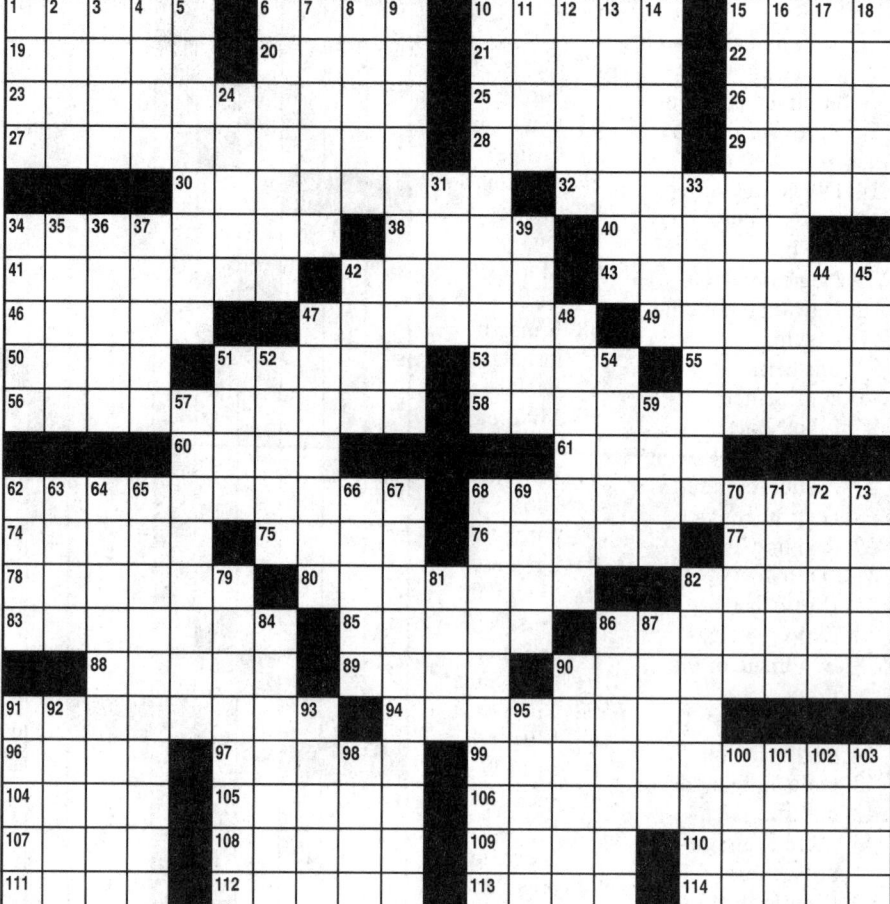

ACROSS

1 The Fuji 50 was one
11 Expo for Angus
21 Guy in the middle
22 Park in N Michigan, oddly
23 Crèche scenes
24 Postpones action
25 Pottery worker, at times
26 English county
27 Speed unit
28 Place on piles
29 Less swift
31 Travolta musical
33 German industrial center
36 Sticks in pits
37 Cleaned some canines
38 It grows eyes
39 "Hooray for yours truly!"
41 Ker finish
42 Beret or beanie
43 Places for fans
44 Castoff sheets
50 Visitor Center freebies
52 Punjab capital
53 Highly unusual
54 Most impudent
55 Ancient warships
57 Kind of bean
58 Church recesses
59 Juicy fruits
60 Tanker
61 Kind of base
62 Casey Jones, e.g.
64 Subtle skill
66 Historic periods
67 "Psycho" psycho
68 Takes care of tykes
69 Treadmill ordeal
71 "I Gotcha" singer
73 Scale notes
74 Brigitte's bear
75 Shakespearean specialty
76 Fully cooked
77 Sense of completeness
81 Monastery dweller
83 First Egyptian king
84 Go lickety-split
85 1956 hit by the Cadillacs
86 Town near Long Beach
88 Anthony's radio partner
89 Toward the future
90 Symbol of absolute rule
94 Critic who's all thumbs?
97 Kenny Baker's "Star Wars" role
99 Nonreciprocal
100 Partake of Bangkok of Panama cuisine?
101 Dakar dweller
102 Poor poets who don't know it

DOWN

1 Hamlet, for one
2 Dreaded tsar
3 Bristlelike part
4 Like some pie-crust edges
5 Collapse
6 Fleet-footed
7 Syllabic arrangement, in poetry
8 Bahrain biggie
9 Charlotte of crosswords
10 T or F, on exams
11 Turn chips to bread?
12 Axis battlers
13 "___ is human . . ."
14 You, to the Amish
15 Child support?
16 Curve shape
17 Keeps the fire burning
18 "Splash" star Daryl
19 Indolent
20 Hosed
26 TV commercial
29 Arp's movement
30 Elevator pioneer Elisha
31 Grabs at
32 Kentucky arena name
33 Adventures
34 Repair shop item
35 Celeb
36 Coal holders
37 Trumpet sound
39 Some S&L accounts
40 Part of DOD
41 Senior dances
43 "Daniel Boone" actor Ed
44 Snorkel, to Beetle Bailey
45 Shout of encouragement
46 Adversaries in "Risk"
47 "You Can Call Me Al" singer
48 Lily's "one ringy-dingy" lady
49 Goes back
51 Military position
52 Bedding
55 Cuts away
56 Charged
59 Fairy tale tyrants
60 Ornamental chalcedony
62 Protect
63 Dame predecessor
64 Destiny
65 "That'll be the day!"
68 Nota ___
70 Motown music
71 Steinbeck hero
72 Not taken in by
75 Eskimo transport
76 Least able to hear
77 Singing group
78 Singer/actress Patti
79 Starting point
80 Essayist Sir Richard
81 Milieus of spear carriers
82 Pete Best was one
83 Sergio of easy listening
85 Author Hite
86 Brunhilda's transport
87 Arledge of crosswords
89 Cain's sibling
90 ___-bitty
91 Start of a Spillane title
92 Rise above it all
93 Shavers
95 Upbeat tune
96 JFK info
97 Ireland's ___ Lingus
98 Root word

262 "ZOUNDS!" by Arlan and Linda Bushman
"Egad, get thee to a punnery!"

ACROSS

1 Fan noise
5 Planted
9 Key
13 Rice grounds
19 Dies ___
20 Employee reward
22 Father of Orpheus
23 Show delight
24 Car-rental ad slogan?
25 Disperse
26 CSA general dubbed "Old Reliable"
28 Final
29 Kingpin
31 Kind of hat
33 Criticize
35 Thole insert
36 ___-garde
37 Stunning time?
44 Long ___ (13)
46 Southern sky formation
48 Jason Lee TV role
49 Underhanded
50 Sovereign title
51 Vogue
53 ___ bono
55 "Un Regalo Que ___ La Vida": Il Divo
56 Long spell
57 Golden Gate, for one?
61 Effort
62 Frisbee, to Fido
64 "Lion King" hero
65 Zorro's alter ego
67 He served both Nixon and Reagan
69 Fancy headband
71 Nearly hopeless
72 Dry red wine
76 Simper
78 Bistro figure
82 Culture medium
83 Browse through a medical subject?
86 Rush
87 Call on
89 That, to Juanita
90 Cleveland's "The Q"
91 DC figures

92 1963 AL MVP Howard
94 Diamond of Queens
97 Flight stat
98 Sides with
99 Fight tooth . . . and nail?
102 Word of regret
104 Deuce
105 Trajectory
106 Flashes
109 Break-through
115 Jilt
117 Carey of pop music
118 Busy
119 Worm in a tequila bottle?
122 Hammett pooch
123 Mustachioed detective
124 Ersatz
125 Powerful appointed official
126 Admission
127 Guru
128 Assigned time
129 Disk extension

DOWN

1 "Exactly!"
2 Panoply
3 Like a Monk's tonsure?
4 Provide, as a temp
5 Malice
6 Treasure of Sierra Madre
7 Like textiles
8 Colo. neighbor
9 Make an inventory
10 General address
11 Mississippi statesman
12 Automaker Ferrari
13 Walled citadels of N Africa
14 Clear
15 Eve's counterpart
16 Supplication

17 ___ Bator
18 Pop
21 "From the Terrace" author
27 Panache
30 Ante body
32 "Pong" parent
34 It can be a snap
37 Phrase of annoyance
38 Frodo pursuers
39 Highly changeable
40 More in need of hoeing
41 "___ Was a Lady" (1945 film)
42 Scratching (out)
43 Former capital of Japan
44 Exploit
45 South Seas tale
47 Film about John Reed
51 Vexatious
52 End

54 Hilfiger rival
57 Tusker
58 Prairie State statesman
59 Cooked cereal
60 Conundrum
63 Astaire put it on, in song
66 Oxen pull
68 "Chicago" actor
70 Turkish peak
72 Speleologist's concerns
73 Gainly
74 Low men at the Met
75 Café container
77 Name in mail-order records
79 Scrutinize a Hungarian composer?
80 Greeting from a pen pal
81 Stack part
84 Anchor Paula

85 Coming up
88 In direct opposition
91 Clambake contest
93 Innocence
95 Greek letter
96 When a show is to be shown
98 Silent films vamp
100 Tweedle who wasn't Dum
101 "Thunderball" gear
103 Elegy
106 Coddle
107 Really bother
108 Allotment
109 Chowderhead
110 Work (out)
111 Flap
112 "It Must Be Him" singer
113 DH's stats
114 Arizona city
116 Witty remarks
120 Booking
121 Chaotic situation

263 1 + 1 = 1 by Nancy Nicholson Joline
Wit + Originality = A puzzler named Nancy

ACROSS

1 Many a comedian
6 One of a '60s folk trio
10 It may be vaulted
14 Age
19 In agreement
20 Deborah in "The King and I"
21 Where to find Shiraz
22 Hardly milquetoastian
23 **Rich + Chris = a state capital**
25 **Larry + Eddie = a bird**
27 "Great Expectations" girl
28 Map part
30 Web-footed ones
31 Bean
33 She played Golda on film
35 Buffalo's county
36 Without
39 ___ space
41 Caught
43 **Joaquin + Peter = an NHLer**
47 Set
48 Speakers' no-nos
51 Pres. candidate of 1952
52 Horatian creation
53 Badlands rise
54 Asmara is its capital
56 ___ d'hotel
58 Signs in
61 B-boy connection
62 Tense
63 General Motors subsidiary
65 **Donald + Andrew = a clincher**
68 Seance sound
70 Remove, tactfully
71 **James + Phoebe = a floatable bar**
74 ___ Floyd
75 Charitable sporting event
78 "Naw"
79 Kind of plate
81 "Bon ___!": Child
83 Jockey with three Kentucky Derby wins
86 Whizzes
88 Application form abbr.
89 U.N. org.
90 Golfer Alcott
91 Stephen King's Christine, e.g.
92 **Patty + David = a Durham athlete**
95 Fancy do

97 "What's in ___?": Shak.
98 Start of a child's rhyme
99 Boggs of Cooperstown
102 Flying object
104 Talking head
107 Use one's head
109 Cleared (of)
111 Courtroom statements, often
115 **Donna + Steve = temporary employment**
117 **Patti + Ted = a riveting book**
119 Gantry of fiction
120 Olympic event
121 "Got it!"
122 Rhubarb
123 Apt anagram of NOTES
124 Legendary marksman
125 Anka's "___ a Lady"
126 Spellchecks

DOWN

1 Like barbershop quartets
2 "How sweet ___!": Gleason
3 First American "feminist"
4 Strong
5 Straddled instrument
6 Wise fool et al.
7 What an opera opens with
8 Little Eva's rescuer
9 Superior, e.g.
10 "Touch" singer Clay
11 Aileen of silent films
12 Comedienne Bernhard
13 One of the Bunker twins
14 Release
15 Belted
16 Earth tone
17 Oteri in "Scary Movie"
18 Mule's mom
24 "Mr. Blue Sky" group
26 Cow chow
29 Luminous opal: Var.
32 Robitaille of hockey
34 Sweet young thing

36 E-plague
37 Forward
38 Base denial
40 Sneaker aperture
42 ___ Lilly and Company
44 1994 Olympics host
45 Phishing catches: Abbr.
46 Epithet
48 Bear aloft
49 Name in a will
50 Kind of flea
55 Tic-___
57 Well pitched?
59 NBA coach Van Gundy
60 City on the Ural
63 Oklahoma native
64 Man who would be queen
66 Tot
67 Magenta
69 Neighbor of France
70 "Wonderful Town" sister
71 Speaker of Quechua
72 Va-va follower
73 Grand Ole ___
74 HP cofounder

76 Grisham's "___ To Kill"
77 Italian fashion hub
80 T, as in Thebes
81 Ticketed ones, often
82 Jamie Lee's dad
84 System starter
85 Fund-
87 Hardly painstaking
92 Sound measure
93 Aussie creature
94 Hit the hay
95 Shellbacks
96 2006 Ryder Cup winners
99 ___ up (gets with it)
100 Film category
101 "Silence of the Lambs" director
103 Henry Ford's son
105 P.D. rank
106 Occupied
108 Indy driver Palmroth
110 Christian denom.
112 Prefix with body
113 One of a Baltic people
114 Signs of success
116 Li in "Kiss of the Dragon"
118 "Shucks!"

264 THESE EYES by Bonnie Gentry and Victor Fleming
The team at 34 Across became part of the NBA in 1976.

ACROSS

1 Long cigar
10 Is contemptuous toward
16 Papers, briefly
20 Sexually stimulating
21 Banderillero's target
22 Caplet shape
23 What got the Evian smugglers off?
25 Miles of film
26 Ode preposition
27 Spanish muralist
28 Got well
30 At hand
34 Julius Erving's ABA team
36 Ho Chi Minh trail locale
37 Inspire respect
38 This, in Latin
39 Wall St. deals
41 Berkshire brews
43 Marshal Kane's time
45 Fibs
50 Chatter idly
53 "Stay ___!" (coach's cry)
54 Get away without delay
55 Louis of the FBI
57 NFL guard Faneca
58 Water-soluble vitamin
61 Pal, in Perth
64 Robert ___
65 Small fry
66 Balder, Bragi and Loki
69 Fridge section
71 Musical perception
74 Pare eider to fit pillows?
77 That, in Tijuana
78 Swell
80 Lemony Snicket et al.
82 Call's partner
83 Like a sloe
86 Smudge
87 1960 "Camelot" star
91 Rugby competitor
92 Creepy one?
94 Meal source
96 Rich source
97 Bo of "10"
99 Old Nick dressed as St. Nick?
104 Like some passes
106 Opera conductor Daniel
107 Boot attachment
108 Cartoon Chihuahua
109 Race abbr.
111 Stag parties
114 No longer on active duty: Abbr.
116 Majestic
118 Woody Hayes Athletic Center site
121 Chief Big Bear, for one
123 1996 Olympic host
124 Tabloids
125 The Bund shocker?
131 Workplace safety org.
132 Mack or Sellecca
133 Unfurl
134 Famed loch
135 Hulk and Ben
136 Wet

DOWN

1 Bench with a back
2 Neighbor of Scorpius
3 "Waste ___ . . ."
4 James and Tommie
5 Motown singer Tammi
6 1976 raid site
7 Napoleonic law?
8 Hauls
9 Far from florid
10 "Frasier" setting
11 Tie indicator
12 The cooler
13 "Longitude" author Dava
14 Novelist Jong
15 "Already?"
16 Peace symbol
17 Examine too carefully
18 Angel who wore #29
19 Senator Gorton
24 Take care of
29 Brandy bottle abbr.
30 Celtic Woman woman
31 Suet sources
32 Mendelssohn's "Opus 20" is one
33 Cry of pain
35 ___-help
40 Dishonored
42 Produce
44 Captivate a crowd, perhaps
46 Catchers of tax cheats
47 Adult insect
48 Lamprey
49 Deem necessary
51 Bits of filming
52 Diciembre follower
56 Saul Bellow book
59 Kind of candy
60 Vinegar vessels
62 Word with ghost or boom
63 Ferber and Mode
67 Leave high and dry
68 Houston pro, slangily
70 Saarinen of Finland
71 Fell away
72 Mountain pass
73 Triple-platinum sales?
75 Stars with a belt
76 Menu section
79 Take ___ (rest on the sideline)
81 Enterprise helmsman
84 Scottish Arctic explorer
85 "Time shifting" recorder
88 Orleans river
89 1959 Corsair
90 Small
93 Penn Sta. line
95 Inclines
98 They're often tapped out
100 Bloodsuckers
101 IV part
102 Stitches in a clinic
103 Try to get some straws?
105 Coup d'état, perhaps
109 Fool
110 Part of growing up
112 "Hurray!"
113 Arnold in "Ghost Dad"
115 Voltaire's belief
117 Cuban afternoon
119 Cuban she-bears
120 Sicilian resort
122 Hockey great Phil, for short
126 Kind of mill
127 William Tell's canton
128 It might react negatively
129 Go after, in a way
130 Online order info: Abbr.

265 CHARACTER STUDY* by Robert Zimmerman
... and there's a man of mystery linked to this character study.

ACROSS

1 Resort
4 Portuguese explorer
10 Youth org. since 1910
13 Whatsoever
18 Lana of Smallville
20 Greek marketplaces
21 Expressions of surprise
22 Green Goblin actor
23 Northern Japanese
24 19th-century murdered Parisian entertainer*
26 Inner self
27 Anna Nicole Smith was one
29 Gullible person
30 German spa
32 Mardi ___
33 Venetian VIP
34 Site of a 1971 prison riot
36 Begrudge
38 Sperm cells
41 NYC's "Garden"
42 Director Peckinpah
43 Overhead
44 His house needs repairs, big time*
50 Ripped
51 Omit
54 Beluga delicacy
55 He's speechless
56 Made a bad buy
58 Explosive laugh
62 Capital of Bulgaria
63 Gilda Radner role
64 Unique fellow
65 Clara Bow's sobriquet
66 MAN OF MYSTERY LINKED TO CLUE* ANSWERS
70 Free-for-all
74 Fighting
75 Archaeologist's find
80 Father of Rachel and Leah
81 Assignations
83 Grand place for happy hour?
84 At any time
85 ___ Miguel
86 Beliefs
87 Took a trishaw
88 He was haunted by a doppel-gänger*
94 Moves slightly
95 20-year sleeper
96 Conceal
97 Medicine containers
99 Rough
103 Land and buildings
104 Intend
105 ___ avis
106 Rail support
108 The word?
109 ABBA hit
113 With a cold demeanor
115 She lived in a kingdom by the sea*
118 Field protection
119 Made a crescent
120 "Golly!"
121 Light amplifiers
122 Molding
123 Prepares a frozen dinner
124 UK lexicon
125 Born first
126 Kind of tax

DOWN

1 Sharp rebuke
2 Sandbox toy
3 King Mongkut's governess
4 Claims adjuster's concern
5 Prized marbles
6 Carnage
7 "Exodus" hero
8 Muti, e.g.
9 Holed some golf greens
10 Water pepper's home
11 Old Arab kingdom
12 Travel industry org.
13 Oklahoma city
14 Sharp flavors
15 Oxidizing rapidly
16 Salesman played by Hoffman
17 Slightest
19 Faithless lover of Lenore*
25 Venture a view
28 Speck
31 S.F. Bay discoverer
34 NRTA parent
35 Hybrid, perhaps
37 Kiwi's cousin
38 Everglades native
39 From the start
40 Social attitudes
42 Barge
45 Investment inits.
46 Something in the air
47 45 player
48 Gulf potentate
49 Bona fide
51 Smoothes wood
52 "Lisey's Story" author
53 Lightbulb, to Humphry Davy
57 Hymn of praise
58 Barnyard butters
59 In the dark
60 Fabrics for padding
61 ___ Angelico
62 Friend of Alice B. Toklas
65 Small bits
67 "Cry" singer
68 Carpet features
69 Dainty
70 Glided
71 Saxophonist Coltrane
72 Genesis shepherd
73 Olympian Lewis
76 His thirst for wine cost him dearly*
77 Roiling
78 Corps core
79 Lock of hair
81 Pack down
82 Spat
85 Superdome gridder
86 Really dark
89 Choler
90 Cube of hip-hop
91 Alpaca's cousin
92 Easily dissolved
93 Breakfast choice
94 Bridge
97 Muslim princes
98 Barely at all
99 Hypocrite Heep
100 Mother-of-pearl
101 "An Unmarried Woman" heroine
102 Jeeves, for one
103 Zellweger in "Cinderella Man"
107 Shakespeare heavy
109 Run away
110 Equine losers
111 Half of sechs
112 Big tournament
114 Gridiron meas.
116 Nancy Drew's boyfriend
117 Illegal drug

266 SHELL GAME   by Fred Piscop
41 Down closely relates to the title.

ACROSS

1 Braddock's 1935 opponent
5 Performed satisfactorily
10 ___ metabolism
15 Beelzebub's doings
19 Suffix for the well-to-do
20 Cybermemo
21 1936 Olympics star
22 "Eh"
23 They have shells
25 They have shells
27 Not all the same
28 Pool setting
30 Lets up
31 Within earshot
32 They were burned in the '60s
33 Biplane part
36 Some sheets
39 Model "A" tractor maker
40 Skier's lift
44 Half-witted
45 They have shells
48 Kramden laugh syllable
49 Triangle sound
50 Much of Mongolia
51 Razor-billed birds
52 Islands carving
53 Do some grilling
54 They have shells
58 Ike's better half
59 ___ U.S. Pat. Off.
60 On the DL
61 Mideast VIPs
62 Bronx ___ (Yankee)
63 Kwanzaa principle
65 Anthem ender
66 Chart support
67 Course endings
69 "Age of Reason" author
70 Shoppe sign word
71 Some TV drama settings
74 Sandy's mistress
75 They have shells
77 Legendary flier
78 Field of honor event
79 They may be bent
80 "Mississippi Masala" director
81 Dog tag
82 Pull a boner
83 They have shells
87 Niamey's country
88 Can't stomach
90 J.E.B. Stuart's superior
91 Kermit's creator
92 Byrd chronicle
94 Epps of "House"
95 Led Zeppelin guitarist
96 Buffalo wing
99 Meet again
101 Sri Lanka, in ancient times
105 They have shells
108 They have shells
110 King Harald's capital
111 River to the Oise
112 Sam in "The Piano"
113 Barflies
114 Just right
115 Hangs out
116 Like some Pamplona runners
117 See 81 Across

DOWN

1 Cake with a kick
2 Snooty put-on
3 Bullpen stats
4 Changing residential to business, say
5 They're found in big mouths
6 ___ Hebrides
7 Maiden name of 58 Across
8 "Little Giant" Mel
9 Sparrow hawk
10 Literary twins' name
11 Base truant
12 Classic battle sides
13 Queen's worker
14 Baton Rouge sch.
15 Waugh's Brideshead, e.g.
16 Peyton Manning's NCAA team
17 Words of understanding
18 Item in red
24 Sherlock's Miss Adler
26 Stays on
29 Bern's waters
32 Dahomey, today
34 Tour de France bikes
35 Does galley work
36 George Harrison played one
37 Ouzo flavoring
38 They have shells
39 Kind of card
41 They have shells
42 Double-take master Jack
43 More ironic
45 Long in the tooth
46 Inner circle
47 "Demon" drinks
50 Overstuffs
52 Unlikely to bite
54 Lover's ending
55 Be worthy of
56 Big name in heating
57 Big name in skin care
58 Great Grandma
62 Ruth ___ Ginsburg
64 Do perfectly
65 Met heavies?
66 Literary Bell
67 Like some new jeans
68 Habituate
69 Bob ___ (Mr. Incredible)
70 Orange of crosswords
72 Barrel race event
73 Treat like a pariah
75 Communion plate
76 Stevens of '60s TV
79 Gas brand in Canada
81 It's measured in karats
83 Suez Canal sight
84 Interferes with
85 300C engine
86 Sending, in a way
87 Beersheba's locale
89 Polly
91 Politico Stassen
93 IRA-establishing law
95 "Wind Quintet No. 4" composer
96 Nicol Williamson, for one
97 17 Down, facetiously
98 Banjo virtuoso Fleck
100 Counting-out word
101 Mix together
102 Stop attending
103 Stick ___ (treat unfairly)
104 Furtive call
106 ___ in yo-yo
107 Indy 500 locale
109 Mr. Anderson's new name

267 CANADIAN CLUB by Lou Kirkley
We counted nine members in this talented, high-proof club.

ACROSS

1 Name in a mild oath
8 "Common Sense," e.g.
13 The U.S., to Mexicans
20 Pupil surrounders
21 Monsieur Matisse
22 With more foliage
23 Canadian border river
24 Dog on "Frasier"
25 Brake part
26 "The Blues Brothers" star
28 "Cuts Like a Knife" singer
30 W-2 info
31 Emphatic turndown
33 Wolfe of fiction
34 Host Gibbons
36 Cain's sibling
38 Canada/USA/Mexico pact
43 "The Number 23" star
47 Royal Canadians bandleader
50 Conceives
51 Pack animal
52 With wetter eyes
53 Type of ton
54 Accts. of interest
56 Do an impression of
58 Pager sounds
59 Give thumbs up
60 Serious trouble
63 Increase, as the pot
64 "You're Still the One" singer
67 Terse denial
72 Distributor's reminder
73 Understanding
79 Like otologists' tests
80 Superlative suffix
81 AARP members
82 Liturgical hymn
83 He has a twinkle in his eye?
85 "Unforgettable" Cole
87 Proteus and Nereus
88 "Deal or No Deal" host
91 "Uncle Buck" star
93 Plants
94 Gutter locale
95 Take the soapbox
96 Talc target
98 Worked with rattan
100 Bill provider
103 Celeb impersonator
109 "My Heart Will Go On" singer
113 Haifa inhabitant
114 Lands in water
116 Chip away at
117 Take the cake
118 Heaps
119 Freeloads
120 Basket made with both hands
121 Parts of floats
122 How one may approach an IRS audit

DOWN

1 Take the edge off
2 Sills selections
3 Stands for
4 Wrestling Hulk
5 Part of a Faulkner title
6 Frolic
7 Successful students
8 Aphorism addendum
9 ___-wip topping
10 Partners' go-between
11 Bed with bars
12 "Laura" star Gene
13 Dana of "The Sting"
14 Bill Withers classic
15 Feisty Disney female
16 "The Wizard ___"
17 Philbin cohort
18 Be abundant
19 Proves to be human?
27 Seep slowly
29 Raise a ruckus
32 Tattered attire
34 Kind of quarter
35 Puts up
37 Clear dishes
39 Quintain rhyme scheme
40 Got along
41 Heard a case
42 Able one
43 Iwo ___
44 Big date
45 New York nine
46 Be concerned
48 Cheri in "The Ant Bully"
49 Give or take
51 Moving
54 Bedlam
55 Coffee go-with
56 Engaged in hostilities
57 Ding-dongs, e.g.
61 Dough roll
62 Bikini blowout
65 Carrion carnivore
66 Rocker Ted
67 Singer Graham
68 Words before sight and mind
69 Dragnet
70 Puzo or Cuomo
71 Big name in bonding
74 Standing
75 Gaius' garb
76 Rock-'n'-roll middle name
77 Scottish pirate
78 "Whoa, boy!"
84 Texas Panhandle city
85 Neighbor of Cal.
86 Stout Guinness
87 Least trustworthy
89 Hawk's home
90 Showy bloomers
91 Peer-pressure group?
92 City W of Yelets
97 Leaning a bit
99 Amtrak speedster
100 Tennis scores after deuce
101 Hint of color
102 Stop on the road
103 Barbecue entrée
104 Words of comprehension
105 Bureau attachment?
106 Bean toppers
107 Levi's mother
108 1964 teammate of Hull
110 Puppy pickup point
111 Thames college
112 Meddling
115 Pot top

268

"SAY IT AGAIN, SAM" by Harvey Estes
Close your eyes when you think of the answer to 23 Across.

ACROSS

1 Paper package
6 Low-heeled shoes
13 Donned in the dressing room
20 Crude carrier
21 Down here
22 Rope with rungs
23 **Movie quote of 1939**
26 Pencil-game word
27 Heart exam
28 Cup material
29 Lazybones, perhaps
30 Pontiac was one
32 Stay flat
34 Norm's wife on "Cheers"
35 Has a bug
37 Flip comment?
39 Breakfast bread, often
44 **Movie quote of 1954**
51 Long in code
52 By-the-book
53 Getting carried away
54 Enemy of the Moor
55 Series terminal
57 Said, "Not me!" e.g.
60 Elton John song
62 "Beat it!"
64 "Musée des Beaux Arts" poet
66 Upset (with "up")
67 **Movie quote of 1967**
76 Last of a drink
77 Tally mark
78 Exhaust, as supplies
79 Parking-lot worker
85 Special Forces headgear
88 Kett of the comics
89 Water-to-wine site
90 Scout group
92 Readies for release
94 Alf and others
95 **Movie quote of 1995**
100 Makeup maker Lauder
101 "Eat up!"
102 Punch
103 TV angel Downey

107 Potok's "My Name is Asher ___"
108 Hot symbol
112 Cause to blush
117 Catch forty winks
119 Seashell seller
120 Feel sorrow about
121 **Movie quote of 1992**
125 Went wild
126 Stunned
127 Capital of Ghana
128 Arrangement between nations
129 In demand
130 California cager

DOWN

1 Under, in Umbria
2 Part of a drum kit
3 Vote to office
4 Atmosphere (prefix)
5 Discretion to choose
6 B.D. of "Law & Order"
7 Rocker Brian
8 Org. division
9 Ancient Roman province
10 Persian, now
11 Yadda-yadda-yadda . . .
12 "A Boy Named Sue" writer Silverstein
13 Lacking freshness
14 Gardener, at times
15 Stress, in a way
16 Pertaining to most students
17 Durango deity
18 Round-buyer's words
19 At no time, poetically

24 Burnt with water
25 Little john?
31 Nonprofessional sports gp.
33 Red rind contents
36 Brush head?
37 Dirigible contents
38 Lout of "The Lion King"
40 Taking care of business
41 Man with no childhood memories
42 Video game name
43 Accelerator suffix
44 Relative of exempli gratia
45 Hidden problem
46 Busy hub airport
47 Humdrum
48 "Double Fantasy" artist
49 Area of expertise
50 Volunteer
56 Set down

58 She played a dreamy Jeannie
59 Discharge from the RAF
61 Senate accusation
63 Big name in shoes
65 Nick's time
68 Build on
69 Get the idea
70 Review applicants
71 ___ Bara
72 Expert finish
73 "South Pacific" nut
74 Steep hill
75 Sudden outburst
79 Dull discomfort
80 New Mexico town
81 Hardware item
82 Cushiness
83 Impatient demand
84 Having lower digits
86 Helpful hints
87 Opening section, in Greek poetry
91 Marlo's hubby
93 Like some norms

96 Ground
97 Axes to grind
98 "The Four Seasons" composer
99 Lib. inventory
104 Phrase from Ripley
105 Lusterless finish
106 Havana hanging
109 Pickup, e.g.
110 Beyond the fringe
111 Operettist Franz
112 Fictional governess
113 Lamentation
114 It may be a sacrifice
115 Plot piece
116 Spoke
118 Nectar-bearing fruit
119 Throw off
122 U-turn from SSW
123 Chinese philosopher Mo-___
124 Company with a dog of a logo

"SAY IT AGAIN, SAM—AGAIN" by Harvey Estes
Raise a glass when you come to 27 Across.

ACROSS

1 Soft ball material
5 Gads about
10 Rooftop fixture
14 Put down
19 Often-dunked item
20 Quick on the uptake
21 Hannibal, to Hopkins
22 Catches some rays
23 Symbol before 69
24 In need of a backrub
25 Out of the office
26 Snow White and the dwarfs, e.g.
27 **Movie quote of 1942**
31 Vacation in Aspen
32 Underling
33 Holds title to
34 Gets
38 Ancient fiddler
39 Dead-end street
43 **Movie quote of 1996**
46 Holy, to José
47 Lao-tse's "way"
48 Jack of "Barney Miller"
49 Reserved
52 Rising row
53 Spat spot
56 Tom of "The Dukes of Hazzard"
60 Old foes of the Spanish
62 Pizza style
63 William Tell's canton
65 Contract provision
67 Darkening
69 **Movie quote of 1927**
74 Harem guards
75 With disapproval
76 Aardvark entree
77 Long-green dispenser
78 Miser's stash
80 Shooting type
82 Incriminating evidence (with "the")
86 Hit flies
88 Elders and alders
90 Outrageous
92 Architect I.M.
93 ___ over (assisted)
95 **Movie quote of 1939**
101 Tablet used in a pool
104 Silents vamp Theda
105 Kind of shot
106 CSA member
107 Lab fluids
109 Twitch
110 **Movie quote of 1977**
117 Gibson costar in "Ransom"
118 Schlep
119 Fair attractions
120 Snaky swimmers
121 Furrier John Jacob
122 Shacks
123 Motionless
124 Stuffing herb
125 Menial laborers
126 Oodles
127 Yawn inducers
128 Food fish

DOWN

1 Have some chips, say
2 Art deco illustrator
3 Like Hitchcock's window
4 Predicted
5 Ropes on board
6 Breakfast spread
7 Maliciousness
8 "Tobacco Road" writer Caldwell
9 Feminist and former Playboy Bunny
10 Cavalry unit
11 Hoover, for one
12 Wooden piece
13 Verbal tap on the shoulder
14 Teems
15 Inferior position
16 Home of some bubbly
17 TV listings
18 NY hrs.
28 Barely read
29 Robert De ___
30 Night flyer
34 Hollywood canine
35 Instead of
36 Left the ground, with "off"
37 Put in the overhead rack
39 Printer's blue
40 Short-tempered
41 Base command
42 One of a "Music Man" 110
44 Spirits, slangily
45 Designer Aigner
50 Rap singer-actor
51 Black Sea villa
54 Outdoor party
55 "Love Story" novelist Segal
57 Asked on bended knee
58 Battery buys
59 Ankara residents
61 Cast carrier
64 Water front?
66 Pierre's home (abbr.)
68 Grooving on
69 Brewers' needs
70 Steal a march on
71 Like a messy bed
72 Former Russian ruler
73 "Scary Movie" Cheri
79 Tim of "Sister, Sister"
81 Kipling's "Rikki-tikki-___"
83 Iridescent stone
84 Ashton's tasse size?
85 Ireland's ___ Fein
87 "Idylls of the King" poet
89 Least loaded
91 Enamel workers
94 Treats
96 Bust maker
97 Bone attached to the sternum
98 New York crime family
99 ___ were
100 Women's school in Durham?
102 "Fiddlesticks!"
103 Motown's Franklin
107 Under, in Umbria
108 Passover dinner
110 Erato or Clio
111 Regarding
112 Cager's offense
113 "What ___ you thinking?!"
114 Okey-dokey
115 Russian gymnast Korbut
116 Like hand-me-downs
117 Dre genre

270 TEN RBIS by Stella Daily and Bruce Venzke
. . . and none of these RBIs are on the scoreboard.

ACROSS

1 In medias ___
4 Duly follower
9 Broker's offerings, for short
13 Special delivery?
18 Ken of "thirtysomething"
20 Student of French
21 Sushi wrapper, often
22 Lexus competitor
23 Dish list
24 Puts the whammy on
25 Yves Saint Laurent's birthplace
26 Computer geek, often
27 Famed Schubert song
29 Orchard blade
32 Rutgers locale
34 No prom king
35 Square one
36 Pilot's guess: Abbr.
37 Wii disc
42 Downward slide
46 "That was something!"
47 Knocked the socks off
48 "The Jungle" novelist
51 Grouchy
54 National Guard rel.
55 Bane of planes
58 Heavy drinker
59 Sounds of disapproval
60 Increased, as a tab
62 Failed to lose?
64 Runner's goal
66 Nirvana's music
69 Dazed
74 Sparkling wine of Spain
75 Seeking a moray
77 Loser to Dwight in 1952
78 "Bear of very little brain"
81 Self-confident person's trait
83 Tough
86 Obi-Wan's portrayer
87 Annapolis' county
90 Facewear in a Dumas title
92 Sycophant's quality, slangily
93 It comes after the band?

94 Cotton ___ ("Show Boat" boat)
96 Thin-skinned
99 It's due a doctor
100 "Concentration" puzzle
104 Command to Rover
105 Old-time luggage
109 Weekly menu special?
114 With no time to fuss
115 "Le Grand Orange" of baseball
116 Icicle's place
117 Clarifying phrase
119 Sweet'___ (sugar sub)
120 "Finding Nemo" pelican
121 Former "Time" film critic
122 Place for an event
123 Fabulous event
124 As a fox would act
125 Go at breakneck speed
126 Sinuous characters
127 ___ one's trade

DOWN

1 Pasta cheese
2 Luis Aparicio's number
3 Tough tissues
4 Popular jacket style, once
5 Fat component
6 Where the San Jacinto flows
7 Anticipatory night
8 Even though
9 Aimée in "La Dolce Vita"
10 Internet problem
11 Grapefruit-league drills, etc.
12 Fell from grace
13 Chicken out
14 Religious image

15 Gernreich of monokini fame
16 Like bacon and ham
17 Tortoise's running mate
19 CPAs
28 Communist co-op
30 Big name in radio, once
31 Test for adv. study
33 Jazzdom's Montgomery
37 ___ deferens
38 "The Ring Cycle" opera
39 They can be boring
40 Mouselike
41 Pedagogues' degs.
43 Trail
44 What to inhale
45 Rival of 68 Down
46 A quarry is an open one
48 OR figure: Abbr.
49 Bavarian river
50 Half an Orkan farewell

51 Noisy clatter
52 Campus cadet org.
53 Home of the Jazz
56 Defense against muggers
57 Made a comparison (to)
61 Part of golf's Grand Slam
63 Frank Herbert classic
65 Sidekick, e.g.
67 "Did you ___?!"
68 Rival of 45 Down
70 Marsh of detective novels
71 Bridal designer ___-Maija
72 Caledonian denials
73 Start off the football game
76 AOL "ha-ha!"
78 Get rid of the football
79 "Take ___" (a-ha hit)
80 One of Judah's sons
82 As a rule
84 31-Down takers

85 Rocky's greetings
88 How some divorces are done
89 Peter out
91 Irangate name
94 Super-high hairdo
95 Gamboling mecca
97 Pomeranian or Pekingese
98 "Whew! Time for a nap!"
99 Anti-monopoly org.
101 Potato-sack material
102 Get the futon ready
103 Urban footbridge
105 Villain's look
106 Looks
107 Occur next
108 Emulates Ebert
109 Data often entered in forms
110 Elec., for one
111 Ladislav of the NHL
112 It might follow a slap
113 It's between the sclera and the retina
118 ___ Plaines

271 CELEBRITY TREATMENT by James Arthur
69 Across was his real one; two more are Martin Dexter and Peter Dawson.

ACROSS

1 Major tennis tournaments
6 Not al fresco
12 Made a bad impression on
19 A pencil game (with 87-D)
21 Deep Throat, for one
22 In a perfect world
23 Heifer named Sue?
25 Wright-Patterson, e.g.
26 Low note
27 Trib's town
28 "Unforgettable" Cole
30 Joined together
31 "Mi casa ___ casa"
33 Super duper?
35 Fireplace fixture
37 Songwriter's kid?
44 Gambling mecca of China
47 Painful reminder
48 A few laughs
49 ___ about (circa)
50 Jazz man on a roll?
54 Falstaff title
55 Queen of Spain
56 "Lassie, Come Home" author Knight
57 Part of VC
58 Night spot
59 Heating unit
60 Truffaut's field
61 Meteor tail
62 Old West fiction writing?
66 LAX info.
67 Twilled fabric
68 Poetic praise
69 Frederick Schiller Faust?
74 Hacker's headache
75 Portend
79 Relief pitcher?
80 Part of the JFK taxi squad?
81 Schlep
82 Uzbekistan lake
83 Mont Blanc cover
84 E-mail tag
85 Safe place for a film star?
88 Pelvic bones
89 No visible means of support
90 Surfing buddy
91 Behaves like a pig
92 Singer's anniversary bash?
98 Enraged
99 Indonesian vessel
100 Give a hand to
104 English Renaissance composer
108 Circus catch need
109 "___ Believer": Monkees
110 Back in time
111 "Big Brother" ruled it
113 Comedian at bat?
119 Schubert specialty
120 Not so colorful?
121 "Apparently"
122 Cleanse
123 Bar necessities
124 Becomes boring

DOWN

1 "From Memphis to ___"
2 Service club
3 Is more than sore
4 K2, e.g.
5 Pedro or Pablo
6 Major prophet of the Bible
7 Discouraging words
8 Stupid reply
9 Tolkien beast
10 "All in the Family" star
11 Rolls in a ball again
12 Cinco de Mayo, e.g.
13 "Money" changers
14 Playwright Molnar
15 Rhyme scheme
16 Quiet type
17 Otherwise
18 Changed locks?
20 Recurring pattern
24 Ante matter
29 Religious obligation
32 Employment
34 Iranian provincial capital
35 "___ lot of good that'll do!"
36 Back end
38 Got back?
39 Barracks VIP
40 Commotion
41 Read between the lines
42 Orleans river
43 Play fare
44 Very short time
45 Puzzling bell town
46 "Double Indemnity" author
51 Lloyd Webber title character
52 Moon of Saturn
53 Wye follower
54 Dirk
55 Eye sore
58 "A Loss of Roses" playwright
62 Ardor
63 Shot spot
64 Way to go
65 Outer limits
66 Perry's progenitor
67 Hitch or glitch
69 "Our ___ Havana": Greene
70 "Die Fledermaus" soubrette
71 Prohibition amendment
72 Scarface, to some
73 Heartwood
74 Final act of "Hamlet"?
75 They wear little clothing
76 Albert Camus' birthplace
77 Unpleasantly humid
78 Service club
81 Prepare to drive
84 Toward the mouth
85 Newscaster Roger
86 Dictionary abbr.
87 See 19 Across
89 Prejudicial activity
90 Task for an M.E.
93 Key of Beethoven's Ninth
94 Some sorority sisters
95 Shrubby thickets
96 Part of a meter
97 Waikiki wing-dings
101 Stock holder
102 Feverish
103 Peter and Paul
104 Fairy-tale prince, perhaps
105 It's a plot
106 Riga resident
107 Perform light surgery
112 Get on
114 "Well, well, well!"
115 Copa locale
116 Hair raiser
117 Big bird
118 It's nothing

ACROSS

1 Brake part
5 Bop pioneer Young
9 Sketches
14 Sierra Club conc.
18 Flight of fancy
19 Sponge or Spiker, to James
20 Circle of color
22 "It Ain't Gonna Rain ___ "
23 Catcall at Coors Field?
25 Long-term project?
27 Moonshine maker
28 Enjoy a lollipop
30 Entertaining lavishly
31 Word of woe
33 "M*A*S*H" protocol
36 A sister of Clio
37 Admission
41 Some time ago
42 Fictional rafter
43 Casting mold
44 Attila the junk collector?
47 Small salamanders
51 "Need You Tonight" band
53 One of the Dixie Chicks
54 Chutney ingredient
56 S&L offering
57 Desert wanderer
59 Sch. affiliate
60 Anchorage for yachts
62 Long tresses
64 Weak
66 Christmas tree topper
68 Gets payback for
70 Synopsize
72 Evans and Earnhardt
74 Considerable
75 Round up
78 Come up again
80 Camper's fuel
83 Little swamp
84 Eye opener?
86 Dallas NBAer
88 Adrien of cosmetics
89 Put out, in a way
90 California's Point ___

92 Sine or cosine
94 Orange-red gem
95 Crude cartel
97 Bread offering to the gods?
101 Correct ending?
102 Indy circuits
104 Phillips U. site
105 Servant
107 With wisdom
110 Sayings
112 Criticize severely
113 From Zagreb
115 River to the Caspian
117 Amtrak bullet train
120 Carl Lewis, for one?
123 Evergreen forest?
126 Busy as ___
127 John Travolta movie
128 Give off
129 Incriminating information
130 Young salmon
131 Fugard's "A Lesson From ___ "
132 Lee side?
133 Field

DOWN

1 Attended to
2 Mid-March date
3 E-mailed
4 Expensive spread
5 Speech
6 Summon a genie
7 Son of Seth
8 Black-and-tan ingredient
9 Deficient
10 High dudgeon
11 What boys will be
12 Dame of South Bend
13 Turn on a pivot
14 Board at Newark
15 Golfer Montgomerie
16 Yemeni's neighbor
17 "Late" vowel sound
21 Forensic activity
24 Greece, to the Greeks
26 Skein component
29 Old pal
32 Rascal
34 Star of the rotation
35 Bugs
37 Twin Cities suburb
38 Curtain material
39 Cowboy communication?
40 1980 Tony winner
42 Bottling aid
45 Kudu kin
46 Rapunzel's ladder
48 Hangnail?
49 House site
50 Get fresh with
52 Inventor Colt

55 Why Fat Tony won't talk?
58 Switch control
60 Brazilian port
61 Smart guy?
63 Burns up
65 Hoyt Wilhelm, in 1970
67 "Young Frankenstein" actress
69 Anatomical duct
71 Desert drainage areas
73 Poison ___
75 Concerning
76 Kind of meet
77 Engr.'s specialty
79 Standard and Poor's employee
81 Chutzpah
82 Of earlier vintage
85 Comparable to a beet
87 Aura

91 Sighting
92 Bill addition
93 Survives
96 Windex, for one
98 Pig–poke link
99 Numerical symbols
100 Springarn Medal org.
103 Height, in combinations
106 Mrs. Marcos
107 Get rid of
108 Caribbean resort
109 Dead duck
110 Photographer Adams
111 "60 Minutes" man
114 City on the Jumna
116 Margarita garnish
118 Hideaway
119 4,840 square yards
121 Confucian truth
122 Enzyme suffix
124 Poke fun at
125 Greek letter

273 RAH-RAH AVIS by Alyssa Brooke
A no-nonsense theme with a few puns (3 Down, notably).

ACROSS

1 Part of an unwelcome phrase
6 End a relationship with
10 Remains of the tray
15 "Cool it!"
19 Turn color, maybe
20 Morales in movies
21 Like cut-rate bread
22 Mannheim man
23 Raised
24 Frond-bearing plant
25 Model asset
26 Marine flyer
27 MLB team
30 Parseghian et al.
31 Haunting
32 Rob's dad
33 Skedaddles
35 Polyester brand
37 "Chicago Hope" actress Christine
39 Commercial snap
41 Fair grade
42 Prepare, as incoming students
43 NFL team
46 Portrayer of Fred, the junkman
47 Ax
48 Islamic ruler
49 Philosopher Weininger
50 Ending for opal
51 Classic toothpaste
53 Drops in
55 ___ impasse
56 Shoots (for)
58 Ant architecture
59 Out loud
60 NFL team
65 Clark's interest
67 Homer hit
68 Italian seaport
72 Superior to a bo's'n
73 Waiting room handouts
75 Cups and saucers
77 Driveway blotch
78 Back a baddie
79 Interruption starter
80 Loaf, with "off"
81 Helped with a line
82 NBA team
86 Golf lesson topic
88 All alternative
89 Shrill barks
90 Very much
91 Encumber
92 Fullback, at times
94 Hairy copiers
95 Dramatic no-show
96 Suffix with refer
97 NFL team
104 Noted Christian
105 "Inferno" division
106 Stirred
107 Bender at the bar
108 Pulled apart
109 Wears down
110 Garfield's sidekick
111 Taco topping
112 Change for a fin
113 Toast serving
114 Hit the runway
115 Cheer for 27 Across?

DOWN

1 Oater eats
2 Cohort of Philbin
3 Press release?
4 Looked about to topple
5 Fireplace stand
6 He wrote about Friday
7 Exploiter
8 Stable female
9 40-point meld
10 Heart protector
11 Where a barfly alights
12 Flag down
13 Other than this
14 Is an astronomer?
15 Wind danger
16 Brownish-orange
17 Like some shrubs
18 Perseveres
28 Moneymaking venture
29 Pro follower
34 Rank of H. Sanders
35 Day of some old movies
36 "Looks ___ everything"
37 Been abed
38 Blade brand
39 Starve
40 Words after what
44 "Signs" band
45 Gauche
47 Lent activity
51 Currier's companion
52 Black eye locale
53 Travel papers
54 "___ Three Lives"
57 Digs
58 Survivor, sometimes
59 Abbreviated Broadway musical?
61 Go-getters
62 Andean animal
63 "Tell me another one!"
64 Lacking color
65 Seeker of benefits
66 Music for "Aida," e.g.
69 Place for knightly meals?
70 She may cry "Uncle"
71 Longer in the tooth
72 Waited on
73 Waterfalls
74 Stack acronym
75 Mrs. Dithers of "Blondie"
76 Med. center
80 Deserts, perhaps
81 Vatican dogma
83 Comic Louis
84 Infant Indian
85 Following that
86 Did blacksmith work
87 Shipshape to the max
93 Toast opener
94 Montezuma, for one
95 Midas undoing
98 Fence part
99 Religious inscription
100 Musical finale
101 Similar in nature
102 Leave in the dust
103 Kind of team

LEGAL JARGON   by Arlan and Linda Bushman
The ferocious feline at 31 Across is found only on the island of Madagascar.

ACROSS

1 Cagney's final film
8 Monopoly pieces
14 Vistula River city
20 Going on and on
21 Talisman
22 Dutch royal house
23 Lawyer's special promotion?
25 Dispatch
26 Police weapon
27 Westminster sound
28 Mope
30 Curved-bill bird
31 Madagascar cat
34 Hendrix of rock
35 Seraglio nook
36 Sonoma neighbor
39 Fully customized filing?
44 Org. concerned with pins
47 Food thickener
48 Size up
49 Blini cousins
51 Computer image
53 Hagar's pooch
54 Maids and such
56 Corrida call
57 Rural home
59 Cobbler's stock
61 Singer ___ P. Morgan
62 Judge's cold-weather need?
66 Attila, notably
67 Election staples
68 Cry of warning
69 Gallery bane
71 Scope
74 Flattens
75 Bailiff prone to silliness?
79 Gallivant
80 One in a NY cap
82 Whammy
83 "Fields of Gold" singer Cassidy
84 Future American Beauties?
86 More fishy
89 Went through all stages
91 Welcomes, in a way
92 Seeker of the Golden Fleece
94 Bus starter
95 Catch on
96 Well-mannered attorney's forte?
99 Brussels group
100 JVC products
102 Auto pioneer
103 Theatrical no-show
105 Bygone
107 Alto partner
108 First-in-space Gagarin
111 Noted nuclear physicist
115 Rough-sounding
117 Perusal of a law document?
121 Bouillabaisse tidbit
122 "Strut" vocalist
123 Spartan
124 React to an allergen
125 Keyboard user
126 Sack and shift

DOWN

1 Deprived
2 Razor name
3 Opposite of haws
4 Business with a timber line
5 Words preceding an act
6 Spoil
7 Son of Archie Manning
8 Circular band
9 Melville tale
10 Rock of volcanic residue
11 Pointy-eared one
12 Starboard, when wind is off the port
13 Plays a banjo
14 Figure (out)
15 100 square meters
16 Fleet
17 Motion for a haughty client?
18 Culture lead-in
19 Dry opponents
24 Stands by for
29 Lucy of "Kill Bill"
32 Instructions segment
33 Nordic carrier
34 VW model
35 Juanita's other
36 Big wheel
37 Limber
38 Church plate
40 Memorial designer Maya
41 Folded dish
42 Less common
43 Pastry specialist
45 Emerald, for one
46 Some hoofed mammals
50 Relishes
52 ___ in the dark
54 Grasshopper's trill
55 Perimeter, for one
58 Jabbered
60 Grand
63 Regions
64 Heritage
65 Disarrange
67 College head, slangily
69 Mad about
70 Booted out
71 Wall adornment
72 LOOM member
73 Litigation about some wickerwork?
75 Mooch
76 Hopkins of "Gimme a Break"
77 Occurrence
78 Art Bell's medium
80 Paul in "Juarez"
81 First Family of 1976
85 Pen choices
87 Compass pt.
88 Greeted the New Year
90 List of books
92 "We're No Angels" actor
93 GI entertainers
97 Intl. broadcaster
98 Skeptic's retort
101 Quatrain
104 Helpful
105 Resistance units
106 Subject, usually
107 Soccer's "Black Pearl"
108 Legendary being
109 Strange sightings
110 "Over the Moon" musical
112 Ways, in brief
113 Trifling
114 Aggravates
116 "Oh yeah? ___ who?"
118 EarthLink, e.g.
119 Heel
120 Group's possessive

275 DOUBLE-EDGED   by Jordan P. Conway
28 Across is doubly double-edged.

ACROSS

1 One to hang with
4 Teacher's deg.
8 Rocker Matthews
12 Docket items
17 Morris in "Ruthless People"
20 Gassy prefix
21 Blue-pencil
22 Minute Maid Park player
23 LILI St. Cyr's specialty
25 Bird feeder stuff
26 Calf catcher
27 Bit of 1773 Boston Harbor jetsam
28 BABA WAWA player
30 Absorbed by
31 Ox's burden
32 Forum cry
33 Stench
37 Teed off
38 Bull Run, to the Rebs
43 I.W. of labor
44 BEBE Rebozo's high-profile friend
47 It's needed for a break
48 High ground
49 Depend
50 "User-friendly" feature
51 Galileo's hometown
52 Fiji is part of it
56 Farm team?
57 June player in "Walk the Line"
58 Where not to be caught?
59 River to the Wash
61 Speed skater Blair
62 "The Simpsons" bartender
64 Grid great, and ex of JOJO Starbuck
68 Rolodex no.
69 Stir up
71 Overly suave
72 Former Cabbage Patch Kids maker
74 On the unsavory side
75 Like naturists
77 Acts like an angel
80 Cone makers
81 Links heads-up
82 A Marx
84 It's not even close
85 Bachelor's last words
86 KOKO the gorilla is adept at this
90 Indian tourist town
91 Hybrid citruses
93 Ferrante & Teicher number
94 Races with checkpoints
96 Willard's Ben
97 One may spill them
98 Downsize
99 TOTO's traveling companion
104 Sunday server
109 Make fit
110 Nursery cry
111 KIKI Cuyler is in it
113 Turn away
114 Suffix with pluto
115 Otherwise
116 Gym team
117 Sports headline subject
118 Up to it
119 Abandoned lot sight
120 Dickens tot

DOWN

1 It could be checkered
2 Hold'em payment
3 Trevi toss-in, once
4 Baton wielders
5 Bygone pact
6 Peep pursuers
7 Fawning one?
8 In demand
9 He's no kid
10 Went head-to-head
11 Kett of old comics
12 Dodge minivan
13 Parenthetical lines
14 Asian nation suffix
15 De Tirtoff's alias
16 Get high?
18 Little jerk
19 Ladybug's prey
24 Ronan Tynan, e.g.
28 Cartoonist Trudeau
29 Yakked, yakked, yakked . . .
31 Saar resource
33 Country teacher
34 Anne Nichols hero
35 GIGI portrayer
36 Ersatz fat brand
37 Mets' Polo Grounds successor
38 Timid ones
39 Neural transmitter
40 MIMI Rogers introduced Tom Cruise to it
41 Queenslander
42 Conger, for one
45 Old source of news
46 Put the kibosh on
51 Its tip may be felt
53 Decked out
54 Gen. Robt. ___
55 Topham Hatt's title
56 Key's opener
57 One in a galley
59 "Sister Act" won one
60 Dot-com's address
61 Putz's boo-boo
62 One of the out crowd
63 Turning Stone Casino tribe
65 Peak call?
66 Met's Italian counterpart
67 Snookums
70 Real-time AOL exchanges
73 Pinkish hue
75 NASA scrub
76 Caterer's containers
77 Drier than sec
78 Carrot, on occasion
79 Embarkation pts.
81 Crud
82 Coach Rockne
83 Who-knows-how-long
86 Grunge rock hub
87 Put on a pedestal
88 Gave the third degree to
89 Have an ___ the ground
92 Searched blindly
95 Browses
97 Egypt's Nasser
98 Flip-a-coin test answer
99 Old Dodge
100 River of Silesia
101 ___ Nui (Easter Island)
102 Gym site, for short
103 Attire
105 The Nats' home
106 2000 Jamie Foxx film
107 Bygone sci-fi mag
108 Polite rural assent
111 Cut down
112 Publican's stock

ACROSS

1 Box-office disaster
5 "Lost Horizon" director Frank
10 Send
14 Prefix meaning one billion
18 Green light
19 Edmonton skater
20 Most merited
22 Where Vida nests?
24 Marie of France
25 "Three Tall Women" playwright
26 Kiddie racers
28 Alcohol found in plants
29 "Of course!"
32 Lift with great effort
35 ___ of the above
36 The Feds
38 Stretching muscle
40 Wahine's welcome
43 Sportscaster Hershiser
44 Luxurious
45 "Hello Mary Lou" singer
50 Some hairsprays
52 Bygone ruler
54 They'll give you the slip
55 Something of little value
56 Mooring posts
57 Conducive to peace
58 Santa Clara chip company
59 Draw forth
61 Egyptian god of the universe
63 Day of rest: Abbr.
64 Where Jack nests?
67 Lateral lead-in
70 Directionless
73 Anoint with sacred oil
74 Movie-chain name
76 Bye-bye birdies
78 Cocoon spinner
80 Crunchy snack for Mr. Ed
81 "The Kiss" sculptor Rodin
83 "What ___ be done?"
84 Where Barry nests?
86 Outgoing
88 Deadly Asian snake
90 Entr'___
91 Rhone River city
92 One accused of discrimination
94 Iowa State locale
95 In the Red
98 Pub order
100 Flu season arrival
102 Balanced states
105 Be a bad loser
107 Basketry twig
110 Go blog hopping
113 PUZZLE SUBTITLE
117 Willie Stark and Jack Sparrow
118 Come up
119 Name on a jet
120 Aircraft designer Sikorsky
121 Pepper and Bilko, e.g.
122 Type of bolt
123 Certain IRAs

DOWN

1 Barker on daytime TV
2 Sooner state, briefly
3 Handle without care
4 Everly Brothers hit
5 Grapples (with)
6 Cause of inflation?
7 Perfect introduction?
8 Guesses
9 Part of WATS
10 Smart set
11 Space-bar neighbor
12 Worldwide workers' agcy.
13 Floral loops
14 Where Seth nests?
15 Opening statement
16 Board
17 Designer Simpson
20 Amphibious rodent
21 Flicker food
23 "As ___ on TV"
27 Letter after pi
30 "___ cost you!"
31 God, in Latin class
33 Short holiday?
34 Sommer in "Jenny's War"
36 Elope to ___ Green
37 Scout's honor?
39 Comedian's gimmick
41 Open to inspection
42 "Sweeney Todd" actor George
43 Desert stop
44 Spanish preposition
46 Agcy. with agents
47 Hill competition?
48 ". . . ___ quit!"
49 Pres. advisory group
51 Seasoning of 64 Down
53 "Young Turks" singer
56 Tampa Bay NFLer
59 Seasonal helper
60 Not dis
61 Every little bit
62 Skier Tommy
64 Paris eatery
65 Put forward
66 Rustic setting
68 Perches
69 ___ good old days
71 Where Haig nests?
72 Express anew
74 Scone grain
75 2006 Beyoncé Knowles film
76 Nobelist Hammarskjöld
77 Hemingway's "In ___ Time"
78 Lucy in "Lucky Number Slevin"
79 Wartime attacks
80 Op. ___
82 Half of zwei
84 Laundry basket contents
85 Korean beer
87 East of Germany
89 John and Tex
93 Pontiac model
94 Down Under: Abbr.
95 Allegro ___ (briskly)
96 Scammed
97 Turn a deaf ___
99 S-shapes
101 "Cosby" actress Lisa
103 Archaic verb ending
104 Spike Lee's "___ Gotta Have It"
106 Latin I verb
108 Bigfoot's shoe size?
109 Harvest
111 Ten-millionth of a joule
112 Word in eight Commandments
114 Zip
115 Prefix meaning "uniform"
116 AARP members

277 SHAKESPEAREAN PUNS by Sam Bellotto Jr.
"The play's the thing . . ." — Hamlet

ACROSS

1 Beeswax product
7 Baltic native
11 Maladies
15 Jim Kirk's brother
18 Chef Lagasse
19 Mideast prince
20 Year in the Middle Ages
21 Lhasa ___
22 Abdul Qadir Bajamal, for one
23 W.S. play that'll make you quiver with laughter?
26 Turndowns
27 Korean War pres.
29 Develop gradually
30 Emmy-winning TV host
31 Arctic bird
33 Cocoon sites
34 Turn to Jell-O?
36 Cremona crowd
37 "Tiny Alice" playwright
40 XX Olympic Winter Games site
42 Ideologies of the Informbiro period
44 W.S. play about some NBA team-mates?
47 Gametes
48 Butcherbird
49 "Bulldog" Hershiser
50 Somme summers
53 "5 Branded Women" director
55 Suffixes for aster
56 City on the Tanaro
58 English logician (1815–64)
59 Beginning to end
61 Eighth part of a circle
63 Swamp bird
64 W.S. play about a dog of "the Child King"?
70 Broadway's "___ Time"
71 Gable window
72 English essayist
73 Pub sign
74 Marina structure
75 Guinea pig kin
77 Gelato ingredient
81 In a dilemma
82 Strings heard at La Scala
84 Prepare haddock
86 Avril Lavigne's "Sk8er ___"
87 W.S. play that will leave you gushing?
92 Contract language
94 In a derby
95 Odessa resident
96 Short coming?
97 Adidas founder Dassler
98 Choreographer Alvin
99 Fehr of "Presidio Med"
101 Mr. Universe's pride
103 Lineage: Abbr.
105 Hindu address
106 Tanqueray, for one
109 W.S. play about a calf-roping Capulet?
112 Warp-knit fabric
115 "Waiting for the Robert ___"
116 Jean in "The Da Vinci Code"
117 Betting money
118 Emmenthaler, e.g.
119 Gore and more
120 Spark
121 Sew together
122 Eli Roth horror film of 2006

DOWN

1 "Penguin" of baseball
2 Paula Cole hit
3 Winsor McCay character
4 Wardrobe assistant
5 Vietnam Memorial designer
6 Social reformer Burritt
7 Word form of 77-A
8 Punk music genre
9 Like watch watchers?
10 1968 U.S. Open winner
11 Pastoral poems
12 Ukrainian city
13 Modeled on a 1:1 ratio
14 "Breathe Me" singer
15 News about the Chicago Fire, e.g.
16 Buzzing
17 Dances in a pit
21 Contemporary of Modigliani
24 "A ___ Flanders": Ouida
25 Palindromic armature
28 Ridiculed in a sense
32 Grammy winner Alicia
33 Long hauls
35 Inclusive abbr.
37 He aims for the heart
38 Golda's predecessor
39 Eric Cartman, for one
41 Roman versifier
42 Taking its toll
43 Chinese character
45 Word before "de-doo"
46 Brunhilde's father
51 Mountain meas.
52 ET-seeking org.
54 Devil's island
56 Sharon in "Point Blank"
57 Pokey
58 Bolivian river
60 Corvette roof
61 "Spoke scandy ___ . . .": Shak.
62 "Three Days of ___" (1975)
64 Yard/3
65 ___ uncertain terms
66 Moves backward
67 Bring down the house
68 Cantilevered window
69 Taurotragus oryx
75 Piddling
76 What Ali stung like
78 Eurasian goat
79 "Kinky Boots" cabaret singer
80 Brick-baking oven
82 Bowled over
83 He took the job and shoved it
84 NBC news show
85 Renaissance patron
88 Colombian plain
89 S. Vietnam's Nguyen Van ___
90 100 equal a rial
91 Pulled pranks?
92 Tar pits in "Volcano"
93 He played "Misty"
98 Green pear
100 Clinton's ___ (Erie Canal)
102 Like the Indian in the cupboard
104 "Hairspray" heroine
105 Cherry throwaway
107 "Turn This Mutha Out" rapper
108 Kind of dive
110 Wall Street whiz
111 Grand Central abbr.
113 Fraternity letter
114 Part of AT&T

278 ROYAL FLUSH by Harvey Estes
This is one hand that can't be beat!

ACROSS

1 Central point
7 Petition
14 Watergate judge
20 Quintuplets born in 1934
21 Lively, in scores
22 Key of all white notes
23 Mexican ma'am
24 "Sense and Sensibility" star
25 Seaport of Italia
26 Rules for Iowa's conference?
29 Research rooms
32 First follower
33 Place for mail
34 Nationality ending
35 Menu phrase
36 Sault ___ Marie
37 Gradually disappear
41 La Douce of film
44 Rebuke to Peter Cottontail?
51 Resort lake
52 Don't quit
53 Expressing anguish
55 "Now the recollection is clear!"
58 Final, for one
60 It may be icy
61 Chemical compound
62 Auction stipulation
65 Remote letters
67 FDR program
68 Benediction for Helmsley?
75 Detroit org.
76 That, to Juan
77 Armchair athlete's channel
78 Tyne of "Judging Amy"
79 Impressive mount
82 Goes downhill fast
84 REO Speedwagon's genre
89 Delayed
91 Put a border around
94 Bobettes hit of 1957
95 Horror novelist in Congress?
99 Nair rival
100 Nicholas or Peter
101 Small batteries
102 Garfield's doc
103 "Gotcha!"
106 What you can take from me
109 Calc. display
110 Fly traps
111 Roger Federer seeing red?
119 Daiquiri flavoring
120 "Told ya!"
121 Spock, for one
125 Paperback publisher
126 Commercial activity?
127 Corrida figure
128 Lucy, to Ethel
129 Become involved with
130 Reddish brown

DOWN

1 Stats for P. Manning
2 Hasten (thyself)
3 Long stretch
4 They're exclusive
5 Crucifix letters
6 Channel to the ocean
7 Worked in a lumber mill
8 Words coming after "come"
9 Omar's "Mod Squad" role
10 "___ Tired": Beatles
11 Collected
12 Twos in the news
13 All of the above
14 Where a duffer has a blast?
15 Mosque leader
16 Ready for pickers
17 Combined
18 Super Bowl XLI winners
19 Come to mind
27 Bleacher feature
28 Roulette bet
29 "Chicago Hope" Emmy winner
30 "Doubt truth to be ___": Shak.
31 Come clean
36 "Queen of the Jungle"
37 Fawcett in "Extremities"
38 Last of a drink
39 CD players
40 Goes light
42 Corp. recruits
43 Somewhat
45 Voluminous volumes
46 Expose, in verse
47 Courteney of "Dirt"
48 Rogue
49 Totally ridiculous
50 Earth, in sci-fi
54 Official with a list
56 Checkers turn
57 Respond to a sneeze
59 Renoir's world
63 Deems appropriate
64 Mensa data
66 Type of shark
68 Talk effusively
69 Hall partner
70 Didst reside
71 Minimal, as resistance
72 Captivate
73 Red-hot NHL team?
74 Incense resin
80 "I Dream of Jeannie" star
81 Take in
83 Calligrapher's need
85 One in stripes
86 Kind of drab
87 Big shot
88 Ancient Brits: Var.
90 Game bird
92 IV givers
93 Turkish title
96 Place in a Redford movie
97 RPM dial
98 Invited for dinner, say
103 Trip to the plate
104 Pitch
105 Peace Nobelist Kofi
107 Danish topper
108 Black tea
109 Discharge
110 Shoemaker's strips
112 Disney lioness
113 Party to
114 Part of MIT
115 Old fruit drink
116 Leia, to Luke
117 Suggestion
118 Lollapalooza
122 Comedian Bill, briefly
123 Art, these days
124 End of Ripley's slogan

279 "WHAT'S YOUR SIGN?" by Arlan and Linda Bushman

The sign at 24 Across is outside the magazine shop.

ACROSS

1 Blockbuster
6 Hold out
11 Wisecrack
15 Lading site
19 Conversation starter
20 Eucalyptus muncher
21 One of a '70s R&B group
22 Mideast sultanate
23 Over
24 Sign in a barren bus-station terminal?
27 Car mechanism
29 Tabloid favorites
30 Scope
31 The Nittany Lions: abbr.
32 Taking one's cuts
33 Salt's ref.
35 Light source
36 Sign at a nudist camp?
42 Ceiling
44 Level
45 Charge
46 Tough
51 Drinking mug
52 Upset
53 Mata Hari portrayer
55 Part
56 From scratch
57 Sign in a school library?
60 Handful
61 Lucille Ball, famously
63 Give a hand to
64 Benefactor
65 Suffolk neighbor
67 W. Ferrell alma mater
68 1998 Nobelist in medicine Gertrude
71 Greek Orthodox treasures
74 Trendy decoration
77 Scorpio's brightest
81 Tie
82 Sign at a park concert?
85 Fontanne partner
86 Overgrown
87 Hastings hauler
88 Fanfare syllables
89 Many a trucker
90 Outside
92 Caribou milieu
94 Cohan's "Over ___"
95 Bronze component
96 Sign in a prenuptial counselor's office?
100 Iota
103 Woods org.
105 Oafs
106 Aggravate
107 Certain brick
109 Givens
111 Their "La Bamba" reached #1 in 1987
116 Sign backstage at an amateur talent show?
119 Accustom
120 Spare
121 Dusty
122 "Uncle Vanya" character
123 Ancient Mexican
124 Additional
125 Zoom by
126 Lure
127 Errata, often

DOWN

1 Dance or carpet
2 Hertz add-on
3 Melodramatic cry
4 Sign in a cutlery shop?
5 Lincoln trait
6 Pod vegetable
7 Thwart
8 Whim
9 Orestes' sister
10 Melted cheese dish
11 Williams of "The Big Chill"
12 Silhouettes hit "Get ___"
13 Analyze
14 Pupil setting
15 Qatar capital
16 Harbingers
17 Freight
18 Pay homage
25 Smelting waste
26 Misgiving
28 Brace
32 Epic Latin poem
34 Seafood choice
36 Rigel or Spica, for example
37 Expiate
38 Like most choirs
39 Transistor forerunner
40 Shipwreck
41 Ornate chair
43 Sign in a cereal café?
47 ___ Simbel
48 Midday
49 Ticklish name in toys
50 Some browsers
52 Biochemist's concerns
53 Rapid pace
54 Frazier rival
58 "___ Rides Again" (1939)
59 Late-night visitor
62 Pothook shape
64 Tiny mark
66 Nissan SUV
69 Four-wheeled carriage
70 "Benson" actress Swenson
71 Unfounded
72 Essential point
73 Brewery object
75 ___ Lingus
76 Fiber ___
78 "American Idol" winner Studdard
79 Diciembre follower
80 Disperse
82 Scottish dance
83 Pooh cohort
84 Bard villain
91 Not as green
92 Mocked
93 Gallery event
94 "April is the cruellest month" poet
97 Name in insurance
98 Jobs for a wrecker
99 Hwy. travelers
100 Yarn
101 Flawless
102 Ball attire
104 "Ran" director Kurosawa
108 Swelter
110 Mark Harmon series
111 Stand-up guy
112 Anthem start
113 Displace
114 Cruciverbalist's cookie?
115 Jiffs
117 "Raven" monogram
118 Room to relax

280 INTERSTATE by Fred Piscop
All-star clues with an All-American theme.

ACROSS

1 Nikita's successor
7 Some soccer shots
14 Pokes around
20 Chant
21 Come apart
22 Hairlines do it
23 Inborn hairdo?
25 Achieve
26 The Monkees' "___ Believer"
27 Actor Stoltz
28 Publican's offering
29 Eastern bigwig
31 Nov. 11 honoree
32 "___ as good a time . . ."
34 Shelley queen
36 Sentence shortener
38 Rock-hard fruit?
44 ___ generis
45 Nest eggs, briefly
48 Air Force ___
49 Oater brawl site
51 Napoleon, for one
53 All thumbs
57 Part of TNT
58 Impenetrable, in a way
59 Brittany city
60 Loop transports
62 Mule of song
63 Horned Frogs' sch.
64 Ballpark figure?
65 Politico Evan
66 Hoover's org.
67 Bishop's seat
70 Lhasa ___
71 "___ you loud and clear"
74 Nine: Comb. form
75 "Boola Boola" collegians
78 Attack verbally
80 Starbucks sight
81 In ___ (where found)
82 Prefix with friendly
84 Ltr. addenda
85 Source of iron
87 Initials on 60 Across
88 Riverbank romper
89 Easter wear
91 Scrooge McDuck, e.g.
93 Kneeler's words
95 Wine may do it
97 Parlor piece
99 Antique auto
100 Appear to be
101 Leave speechless
103 Demand for a sneak preview?
108 Was catty?
110 It starts in Mar.
111 Flat formation
112 Chucklehead
114 Cajun cook's vegetable
115 Trig fig.
118 Knotted attire
121 Guinness suffix
122 Freddie who played Chico
124 Moon-shiner's corn patch?
128 Grinch player
129 Along the way
130 Cartwright player
131 Chilling out
132 Caterers' cans
133 More blue

DOWN

1 Jacket part
2 Win the heart of
3 Senators' home
4 ___ TURN
5 Concerning, on a memo
6 Salutation starter
7 Car collectibles?
8 Suffix with butyl
9 Gazetteer datum
10 Willy Wonka's creator
11 '60s singer Sands
12 Flock leader, familiarly
13 Obeys the hypnotist
14 Result of a midwestern monsoon?
15 In, again
16 Reggie Jackson's mo.
17 Dam builders' civil rights issue?
18 Carmela player
19 Posted, say
24 Mojito ingredient
30 Whittier's "___ Muller"
33 Arctic wear
35 Trivial amount, slangily
37 Sister of Bart
39 ___ the finish
40 Painter Gerard ___ Borch
41 Pugilist Laila
42 Shelter array
43 Newsman Greeley
46 Calla lily's family
47 Aerobic bit
50 Ryan in the Hall
52 Carb source, slangily
53 "Mamma Mia!" group
54 Cylindrical sandwich
55 Land governed by comedy cops?
56 Explosion remains
61 Creditor's claim
63 Aries
66 Donald Sutherland, in "MASH"?
68 Bolt holder
69 Where to go?
72 They form bonds
73 Flat-bottomed boats
76 Tabloid twosome
77 "No problemo"
79 In ___ (sulking)
82 Falls back
83 Reactor part
86 Baltic resident
87 Shell teams
88 Cookie since 1912
90 Point a finger at
92 Ike's arena: Abbr.
94 ___ gratia artis
96 Basin adjunct
98 Returned bottles
102 Mingo, on "Daniel Boone"
104 Moran of "Happy Days"
105 Had to have
106 Dead Sea ascetic
107 "Prison Break" producer
109 Moves like sludge
112 Humane org.
113 Trapped like ___
115 Medical researcher's goal
116 ___ about (near)
117 Send reeling
119 Poacher's meal?
120 "Blacklist" author Paretsky
123 Piece-keeping org.
125 3 Down's prov.
126 ___ Z (everything)
127 Deficit shade

281 PHYSICAL EXAM by E. G. Harris
64 Down was a comic-strip character that debuted on June 19, 1923.

ACROSS

1 Captain America's weapon
7 "Judgment at Nuremberg" Oscar winner
13 Plastic with a PIN
20 Whoop it up
21 Rug not for a floor
22 Movie promo
23 Pep paucity
24 Joined by treaty
25 Rudolph's night light
26 Football coach's shout at the goosepile?
28 Ovine entreaty
29 Sprouting "pet"
30 Deuce toppers
31 Give a chiromancer reading material?
33 Plane surface for planes
38 Pool wear
40 Workplace newbie
41 Unarmed, to a cop
43 Just over two pounds
48 Sounds an alarm
49 Space to maneuver
52 2001 Peace Nobelist
53 Oklahoma Indians
55 Antidiscrimination letters
56 Respectful Hindu title
57 Publisher Adolph
58 Mystic Johannes
60 "I Like Birds" group
62 Perceptive
63 Wisenheimers
66 Language of India
68 Strays
69 ACC's Virginia ___
72 "Got it?"
74 Schoolyard retort
75 To boot
76 "The Sopranos" channel
77 Meredith of "The Today Show"
81 Aerial show showoff
83 Plead poverty
86 Obi material
87 Lawn-tennis tourney rankers?
89 Inclined to be bungling
90 Erté forte
92 Got the idea
94 Some newspaper employees
95 "Hurry up!"
99 Sumptuous supper
101 Film composer Schifrin
102 Dollar divs.
103 Place for a shawl?
110 Rank higher than
112 Diet lunches
113 Bird on a baseball cap
114 Pittsburgh pro
115 ". . . black-birds, baked ___"
116 Canine superstar
117 Ushers in
118 Tree trimming
119 Scheduled

DOWN

1 Carpet type
2 Improve, in a way
3 Landlord's self-description?
4 "Men in Trees" setting
5 Mariner Ericson
6 Non-volunteer
7 Stuck it out
8 Mild cheese
9 Luau dances
10 "Iliad," for one
11 Vichyssoise veggie
12 Ran first
13 Willy-nilly
14 Trample
15 Burned up
16 Sure thing
17 "Hello" from Ho
18 Pine sap
19 Hate the thought of
27 Hit for the Bobbettes
28 Busy one
31 Maiden in "The Raven"
32 No longer in port
33 Welk's second beat
34 Roth offerings
35 Avis adjective
36 Poi, for one
37 Raid targets
38 Use the Singer
39 Break down
41 Speaker on the road
42 Ill-gotten gains
44 Be at odds with
45 Acquire, as debt
46 Actress Christine
47 Advent
50 Charge for using
51 Driveway eyesore
54 Kind of boot
59 Upset (with "up")
61 Kind of enc.
62 Basketball stat
63 Makes a switch
64 "Moon Mullins" cook
65 Usher's walkway
67 Ariz. neighbor
70 Making dove sounds
71 "Stormy Weather" singer
72 Blender option
73 Go to the edge of
78 Part of a checklist
79 Pilaf ingredient
80 Commonly cited auth.
82 Beginning for photo
83 Devotional literature
84 Size abbr.
85 Unduly severe
88 Wasn't passive
91 Updates, as machinery
93 Legal matter
94 Bunch
95 Shore sound
96 ___ couture
97 Shorten, maybe
98 Divided nation
99 Ruckuses
100 "Frasier" dog
103 Pleading child's words
104 "The Good Earth" heroine
105 Russian river
106 Bart Simpson's sis
107 Biblical verb
108 Novelist Wiesel
109 Clarinet part
111 Best effort
112 Pose for a picture

282 ADDING WITH EASE by John Underwood
. . . with the accent on EASE!

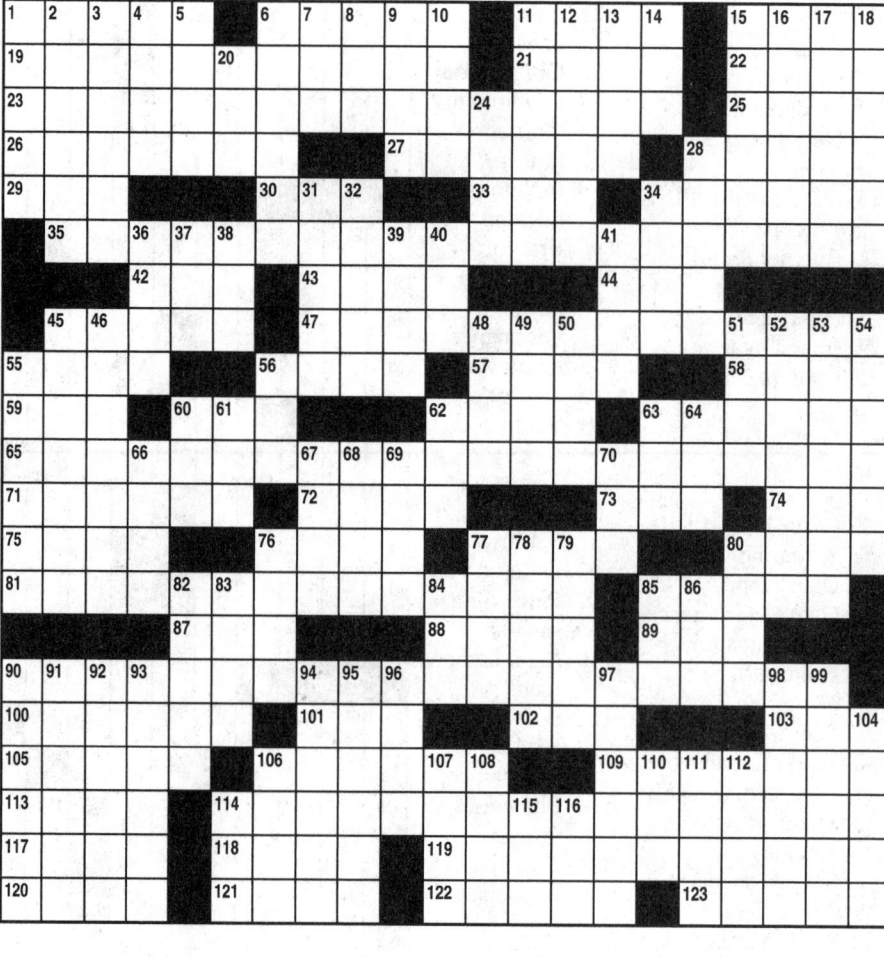

ACROSS

1 Trod the boards
6 Castles
11 "Yo!"
15 Aerial bombs
19 Like Shiatsu
21 Luxuriant
22 You're looking at one now
23 Crosby caroused?
25 Nonclerical
26 The Merchant of Venice
27 Bachelor-at-arms, e.g.
28 Table item
29 Wed preceder
30 It taxes your resources
33 Rapper's article
34 Tempted
35 Why hacks can't hack it?
42 Pilots' org.
43 Game named after Egyptian rulers
44 Composer Ornstein
45 Pastoral
47 Criticism by a crazy critic?
55 Chico, for one
56 Clucks
57 CBS eye, e.g.
58 Cow-headed goddess
59 Here, over there
60 Gardner in "The Sentinel"
62 Weak
63 Least freaked out
65 Summary of TV police show?
71 "___ and Mrs. Miller" (1971)
72 De Gaulle alternative
73 Kabuki ancestor
74 Divot-prone area
75 Part of ANTA
76 Synthesizer inventor
77 Alien incubators?
80 Grisham novel (with 14 Down)
81 Restaurant special for Big Al?
85 French fuzz
87 Beta-carotene source
88 First of a breakfast trio
89 Twenty-vol. reference
90 Odilon did some refurbishing?

100 Slipped by
101 "That hurts!"
102 AAA info
103 She in Lisbon
105 Bellwether
106 Deep-blue snake
109 Kegling target
113 Rocker Lofgren
114 Masters hopeful scored high?
117 Hydrocarbon suffixes
118 A sprinkling of
119 Principal principles
120 Milk for the lactose intolerant
121 Partner for ever
122 Le ___ (Channel port)
123 One sort of bigot

DOWN

1 Chasing a slider
2 Gym lift
3 Cloth-stretching framework
4 Cogito sum connector
5 Aurora
6 "Girl with a Watering Can" artist
7 Passé
8 Sioux speaker
9 Hose woe
10 Channel surf
11 Tight spot
12 Tropical headgear
13 USAF rank above senior airman
14 See 80 Across
15 Finger-shaped pastry
16 "My pleasure!"
17 "The wiles and ___ that women work": Shak.
18 Leave the group
20 Architect I.M.
24 Take the bait
28 Preface to luxury
31 Melodic jazz phrases
32 Follow your star?
34 With "La" it's the pits
36 Cameo stone
37 "Platoon" character
38 ___-Mart
39 The Mauve Decade et al.
40 Korean novelist ___ Geo-il
41 Cookie Monster's pal
45 Former Chrysler star
46 Water-catching window molding
48 Washout
49 Joeys
50 Grimm creature
51 Type of type
52 Germfree
53 Smackers?
54 Go gaga over, with style
55 Eastern Canadian Indian
56 Topcoat color
60 Wright-Pat, for one
61 Wrestle
62 Uncap
63 ___-Cat
64 Wiesbaden wail
66 Sea of Japan island
67 Room access
68 Caiman's cousin
69 Anton Chekhov's wife
70 Court scores
76 Gallery near St. Pat's
77 Tadpole's home
78 "SNL" sign
79 Armory
80 Lincoln's dog
82 It merged into Verizon
83 King of Saudi Arabia
84 Nittany Lions school
85 Venom, to Spider-Man
86 Held a baton
90 Catherine and Marie de Médicis
91 Meteorological "boy"
92 He played Arthur twice
93 Potemkin mutiny site
94 Live wire
95 Like Crawford in "Rain"?
96 Christmas-bulb site
97 Sharpen repeatedly
98 Language spoken in Katmandu
99 Says less
104 "___ of robins in her hair": Kilmer
106 Fe
107 Theo van ___
108 Orozco's other
110 Byrnes of "77 Sunset Strip"
111 Royal Mughal city
112 Coke, e.g.
114 Youth org. founded 1912
115 URL ending for 30 Across
116 Possessive for two

283 OLLA PODRIDA by Harvey Estes
The answer to 113 Across is not upper abdomen.

ACROSS

1 End of a dash
5 Libertine's opposite
9 Flight part
14 Second-stringer
19 Enclosed in
20 Minibar site
21 Throng of people
22 Brunch serving
23 Basis of an unfair hiring practice
26 Like a hard-liner
27 Sorbet maker
28 Off the mark
29 List of players
30 Fax function
31 "Holy cow!"
33 Sale sign
36 Collectively
39 Deadly sins, e.g.
42 Itinerant
46 Maintained
48 Humorist Bombeck
50 C&W's McEntire
51 City south of Moscow
52 Porto ___, Benin
53 "Take it easy!"
55 Time periods
56 Spoiled one
57 2006 Sony animated film
59 Quiznos fixtures
60 Soda bottle units
62 Rents out again
63 Like circus elephants
65 Menu choice
66 Book-smart
68 Caught some rays
71 Civic-minded company?
73 Radiant
74 Maestro Toscanini
75 Tip over
77 Parenthesis
80 Khomeini's land
81 Hot under the collar
82 Dances with dips
83 Dollar-store sale sticker?
84 ___ buco
85 Some den leaders
86 Press for
87 Bikini, for one
88 Demonstrate disdain
89 One of the first bloomers
91 Specter of government
94 Leave in the text
96 Oliver Twist's half-brother
98 Home-coming guest
100 Commences
105 Psychoanalysis biggie
107 Connoisseur qualities
112 "Singing Cowboy" Gene
113 Liver's location?
114 "One of ___ days . . ."
115 Corned-beef solution
116 Blockhead
117 Step up the ladder
118 Goofed up
119 Turns state's evidence
120 Hook's ally
121 Lid problem

DOWN

1 Snooty animal
2 Shell alternative
3 Mounds
4 Official decree
5 Grasping tool
6 Costa ___
7 Moslem cleric
8 Attacks Baltusrol
9 Lusters
10 City in Spain or Ohio
11 N. Mex. neighbor
12 Nice notion
13 Prepare beans in a way
14 Scuffle
15 McGruff's bailiwick
16 Mildred Ratched, for one
17 "Breaking ___ Hard to Do"
18 Take them lying down
24 Tire pattern
25 Scratch
32 Part of Caesar's boast
34 Bugs Bunny's boast?
35 Grave
37 Some kiosks
38 Rubik of cube fame
40 Abba not in the music biz
41 ITAR's news partner
42 Highborn
43 Senator Hatch
44 Stick it in some turkey
45 Tack
47 John Reid's epithet
49 Alpine sight
52 Snooped (about)
53 Pokes fun at
54 More like a horse opera?
58 Mr. Bill's nemesis
59 "In Too Deep" actor Epps
61 Rip to bits
64 "___ told by an idiot . . .": Shak.
67 Quick responses
69 Degauss a tape
70 Blood bank depositor
72 Many miles away
75 Letters at Camp Lejeune
76 Really lame
78 Swenson of sitcoms
79 Opening words of "Da Doo Ron Ron"
82 Elephant tooth
87 Become accustomed (to)
88 Lift, in a way
90 Like traditional Aran sweaters
92 Adding kick to
93 Shakes off
95 Heir's concern
97 Nikola Tesla et al.
99 Does some darning
101 Old Russian despots
102 Ambulate with attitude
103 Word with bopper
104 Native Kansan
105 The inevitable
106 German industrial locale
108 Gilpin of "Frasier"
109 "The doctor ___"
110 Bit to split
111 Major African artery

284 BEER BLAST   by Bruce Key
You'll be at lager heads over some of these heady puns!

ACROSS

1 Genesis creator
5 "Peg Woffington" author
10 Birthplace of Pythagoras
15 Photon's lack
19 Touch on
20 Cruel dudes
21 Deal maker
22 Samoa's capital
23 The ___ got stoned
25 The ___ got stewed
27 Insignia spots
28 Ali portrayer
30 Surfer girl
31 Needle-shaped
32 Comment to a dentist
33 Eastern shrines
34 The ___ got crocked
40 Winter coat
44 Hot Stove League news
45 Is an opposite?
51 Finish off
53 Touched down
54 Gelato holder
56 Be of service
57 Seine feeder
58 Fact-check
59 One having a blast at a beer blast
60 Needing sterilization
61 Whips up
63 Red-tag event
64 Lobbyist for seniors
65 PBS supporter
66 The ___ got lit
70 Upper-left key
73 Rioter's take
76 Bird or birdbrain
77 Take hold of
80 Chip, to a Brit
82 In pieces
84 ___ generis
85 Chipped in
86 Target path
87 Like some excuses
88 Lukas of "Witness"
89 Puréeing utensil
90 Subway drivers
92 Katzenberg's boss at Disney
94 IMAX dinosaur film

95 The ___ got oiled
99 Concert headliner, usually
104 Terok of "Deep Space Nine"
105 Screw up
110 Last syllable
111 "Get cold feet" is one
113 1992 campaign slogan word
114 The ___ got tanked
116 The ___ got wasted
119 Puff, to a hippie
120 Swiftly, to the Bard
121 Mark down, perhaps
122 Prefix with byte
123 Coal-rich German state
124 Oliver Twist's half-brother
125 Public to-do
126 "Come ___!"

DOWN

1 "Beowulf" et al.
2 "Movie Home Companion" author
3 Like mucilage
4 Lagoon perimeter
5 Ent's bane?
6 Shirred items
7 Jackie's O
8 Montreal's Place ___ Arts
9 Ballpark figs.
10 "Green Eggs and Ham" character
11 Contemporary of Erle
12 Fit well together
13 Windsor's prov.
14 "Maggie May" singer
15 Like Rambo
16 Rose pest
17 Tuscany city

18 Hotel amenities
24 Act impulsively
26 Gossip source
29 "Say Hey Kid" of baseball
33 Pan handle?
35 Go places
36 "Honor Thy Father" author
37 Cut and paste
38 Emeritus: Abbr.
39 Hearst-like character
40 Spock is half this
41 Inedible orange
42 The ___ got looped
43 Pipsqueak
46 Music to Mysore ears
47 State firmly
48 The ___ got plastered
49 Cratchit lad
50 Full of guile
52 Thimblerig item

54 Condi's secretary of state predecessor
55 Crude org.
59 Divination deck
62 Hué holiday
63 Chain unit
64 Santa ___ winds
67 Mercenaria mercenaria
68 Galápagos lizard
69 Out of the sack
71 Cooperstown's Carlton
72 Scriptures volume
74 Nobel Peace Center city
75 Phone letters
78 Hitting stats
79 "Don't bet ___!"
80 Pushrod pusher
81 Las Vegas casino
82 Rat Island native
83 Respire, dog-style
84 Pageant attire
88 Sound from 59 Across

91 Runway makeup
92 Eliel Saarinen's son
93 Chest protector?
96 Up next
97 Wavy fabrics
98 Snake target
99 Yearnings
100 Reynolds Wrap maker
101 Luftwaffe bomber
102 Rome's river
103 "I ___ man whom Fortune . . .": Shak.
106 "___ a customer"
107 Mount Holyoke collegians
108 Japanese porcelain
109 Irish tenor Ronan
111 Director Reitman
112 Dept. bosses
113 "Voice of Israel" author
115 Wall St. launch
117 NRC forerunner
118 MapQuest offering: Abbr.

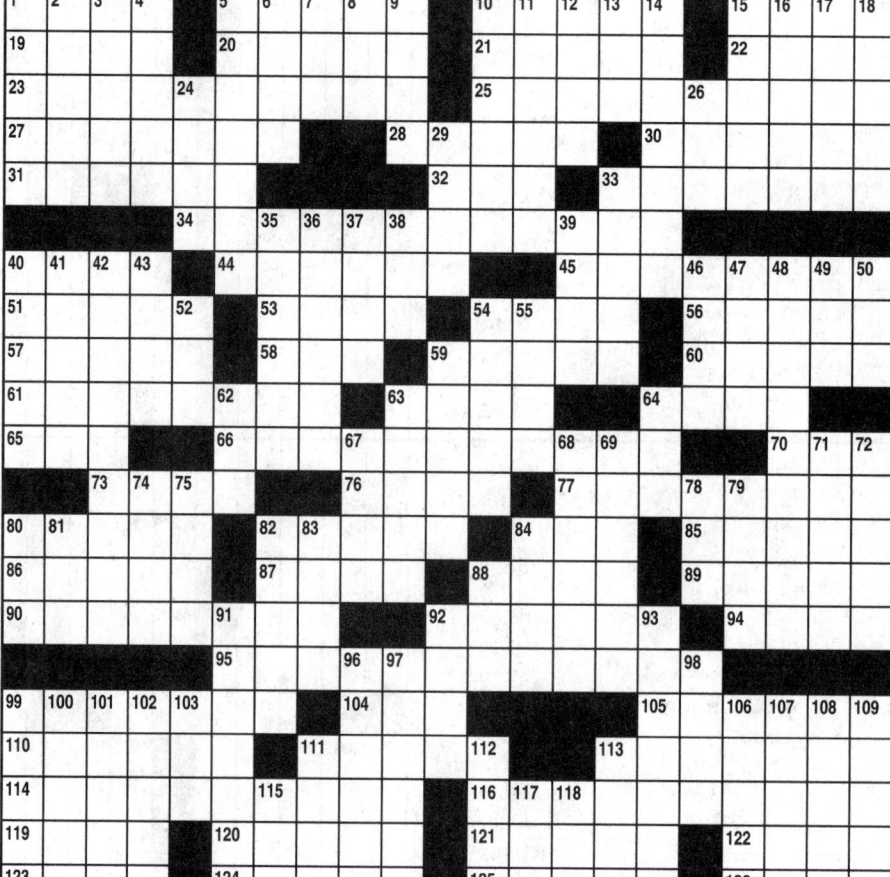

Papa's not going to like the review at 23 Across.

ACROSS

1 Musical arrangers
9 Eliminates, on "The Sopranos"
13 Merida
19 Mason's fee
20 Gags
22 World Heritage Site manager
23 Surprise review of Haydn's "Surprise Symphony"?
25 Gulf War army
26 Biblical stringed instrument
27 Mountaineer's spikes
28 Get by
29 Injure
32 Azerbaijan's capital
34 Headache drug combo
35 Go to court
37 Pompous fool
38 Swiss chalet housekeeping?
41 Wood parer
44 Mrs. Gorbachev
45 Stone slab
47 Gangsta rap trio
48 Cat call
50 Carrier letters
51 It has some ER members
54 Foul remark?
56 "It's coooold!"
58 It may be on the house: Abbr.
60 Folded snack
61 Data, e.g.
63 Talk type
66 Nixon and Bush, once
68 Charlemagne's realm
70 Nissan competitor
71 Post-its, often
73 Preserves railroad ties
75 And others
76 "Quiet."
78 "Thanks, Pierre."
79 Draft grp.
80 Stephen, in Sèvres
82 "Alas!"
84 Assns.
86 Mideast currency
87 Neologism
89 Composer Delibes
90 Pop genre
93 Fort Worth school
94 "___ tu" (Verdi aria)
95 "Das Boot" vessel
98 It's a small cell
100 One who gets the word out
103 Stuff of hundreds?
106 "One for My Baby" setting
108 Ethnic ending
109 Hyundai models
111 Year in the reign of Caesar Augustus
112 Doubloon metal
113 Anchor position
115 Tug on
117 Lilt
119 Corrupts
121 1944 field hospital?
126 Peaceful
127 Alley button
128 ___ comforts
129 Cherry brandy
130 Passe pol. units
131 Reportedly

DOWN

1 S.A. republic
2 RFK's party
3 Loss leader
4 Cat's sleepwear?
5 Pedro's uncles
6 Drape
7 Make a new sketch
8 Delhi title
9 City near Santa Barbara
10 Roman holiday
11 Camera with a time-exposure setting?
12 Stink
13 ___ generis
14 Unwind a roll of film
15 Patricia in "Hud"
16 Drafting tool's origin?
17 HCl and HF
18 Pries
21 SAT takers
24 Gush
29 Luke Skywalker's wife
30 Distant
31 Blue, in Paris Hilton's eyes
33 Some WBA endings
35 Grooves
36 Reversal toward a slippery road?
39 Proper address
40 Kal-El's Earth family
42 Call ___ day
43 Early growth stages
46 Mauna ___
49 Pens
52 Video Music Awards parties?
53 Ex-Met Tommie
55 "May the ___ be with you!"
57 Food-label abbrs.
59 Ballad endings
62 Coiffures
63 First NBAer to score 20,000 points
64 BlackBerry, for one?
65 Amasses
67 "Aw, gee!"
69 Messes up
71 Fish hangout
72 Diarist Anaïs
74 Env. science
77 Timer for an invasion launch?
78 Gironde wine-growing region
81 Strange
83 Character in "Pamela"
85 Irish Spring, e.g.
88 Guru
90 Defaulter's loss
91 Walter in "Kiss and Tell"
92 Western buddy
96 "Ring My Bell" singer Ward
97 "Mazel ___!"
99 Fuchsia
101 Digestive
102 Oozes
104 Spuds
105 Draws out
106 Cloth-dyeing method
107 "Space Invaders" company
110 More foxy
114 Places to stay
115 Doctor's drug bk.
116 Bible book
118 "Cool!"
120 Univ.
122 Elvis Presley's label
123 Mild reproof
124 Prior's prior
125 Ant color

286 12:15 by Harvey Estes
A themeless challenge with twelve 15-letter grid answers.

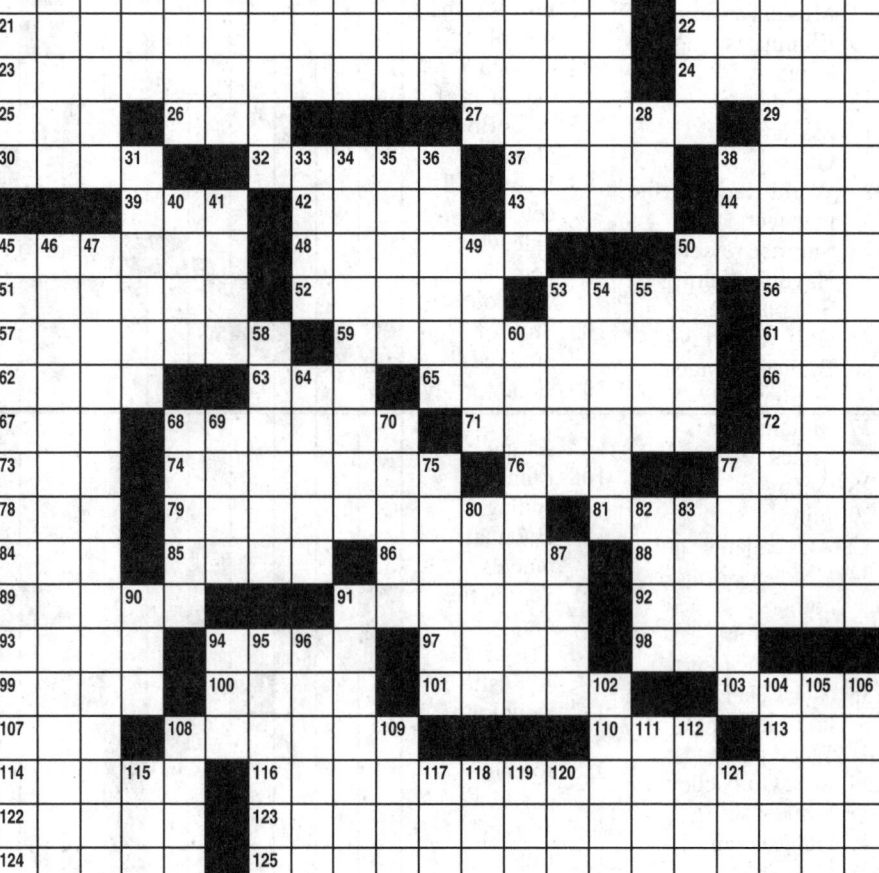

ACROSS

1 Antiglare wear
16 Beginnings
21 Lex talionis part or canine swap?
22 "___ an arrow . . .": Longfellow
23 Gross businessman?
24 Director Kurosawa
25 DDE opponent
26 Scale tone
27 Mae-un tang eater
29 Orch. section
30 Rocker Fure
32 Wash against
37 Prof. Jones, familiarly
38 Olympians: Abbr.
39 Bottom line?
42 "America, the Beautiful" pronoun
43 Cong. period
44 Bother for a boxer
45 Like batting pitchers, usually
48 Big man on campus
50 Back on the briny
51 Sports artist LeRoy
52 Parsley-family member
53 Durango engine
56 Boxing div.
57 "If I Ran the Zoo" author
59 Maureen of Tarzan films
61 Sibling, in brief
62 Body-shop figs.
63 Helmet add-on for TV
65 Level off
66 Actor with a Mohawk
67 Shad delicacy
68 Basket maker, e.g.
71 Attacks vigorously
72 Donne's "done"
73 Spike TV, formerly
74 Barrio residents
76 Funny pair?
77 Hun king
78 Laugh-track sounds
79 "Christmas comes but ___ . . ."
81 British fellow
84 Tolkien creature
85 Political pundit Mort
86 Shaw of swing
88 Epoch in which mammals arose
89 Rushing sound: Var.
91 Swank
92 Squash and pumpkin
93 Professor 'iggins
94 Herr's her
97 Use a keyhole
98 Yearbook gp.
99 Like cheddar
100 Animal shelter
101 Women's group
103 Biblical word endings
107 Sung syllable
108 Apron, of a sort
110 Travel org.
113 Louis XIV, for one
114 Speeders make it
116 Contract provision for a high-rise project?
122 Some collars
123 County or parish?
124 Philippics
125 Lyrical lead-in to "goodbye"

DOWN

1 Grab for clumsily
2 Multiple-choice answer
3 Like some cannons
4 One path to the WWW
5 Short itineraries
6 Gershwin's "___ Nice"
7 "___ else fails . . ."
8 U.S. bill
9 Test for college srs.
10 Chap
11 Bolted down
12 Take to the cleaners
13 Concerto performer
14 Perpetual, in verse
15 Reduces to confetti
16 "Gorillas in the Mist" author Fossey
17 Set a price of
18 She raised a thickhead?
19 One of the four Home Nations
20 Beach Boys' last album
28 Positive votes
31 North Sea feeder
33 Razor handle?
34 They're extraordinary
35 Sponsorship
36 Gets ready to swing
38 Back on the briny
40 Jacob's hairy brother
41 Orology study: Abbr.
45 A walk in the rain may lead you there?
46 Unwelcome
47 Monitors a cover story?
49 Memorable Manhattan nightclub
50 Hole in the head
53 Try to pick up
54 Extremely
55 Webb address?
58 Rob Roy need
60 One up at the crack of noon
64 Disney mermaid
68 Shore sound
69 Water-to-wine town
70 Adjective for purple
75 Angel of Isaiah 6
77 Point a finger at
80 Bewildered
82 Piano quartet?
83 "In" place
87 Brontë woman
90 "Providence" character
91 Orange liqueur
94 Neighbor of Ala.
95 Least seen
96 Intends
102 Tennis star Safin
104 Test answers
105 Egypt's Mubarak
106 Seven, in Seville
108 Hardy soul?
109 Suffragist Carrie
111 Kind of phobia
112 Part in an ensemble
115 Explosive monogram
117 Null service
118 Rhubarb
119 Auto racer Fabi
120 Elect (to)
121 Montreal transit org.

287 PATRIOT NAMES   by James Arthur
Sources of the quotations below are patriot names.

ACROSS

1 1994 Peace Nobelist
6 Copy cats?
10 Spot of tea
15 Not exactly wide open
19 Afghan neighbor
20 Rival rival
21 That Dern actress
22 Pop, to baby?
23 Von Trapp, for one
24 Israeli prime minister (1969–74)
25 Balloon material
26 Harbinger
27 **"Beware of the young doctor and the old barber."**
31 REO part
32 Bad spell
33 Didn't just sit there
34 Year in Yucatan
35 Bindi Irwin, for one
37 Gran finale?
38 WW2 arena
39 Gaucho's gear
41 Quiet type
42 Shade tree
43 **"There, I guess King George will be able to read that."**
46 Suit top
47 Alfalfa and Buckwheat
49 Lt. factory
50 "Angela's Ashes" sequel
52 Cheese choice
55 Lucky strike
56 Thickness
57 Parishioners
59 Sundial figure
60 Irene in "Zorba the Greek"
63 Make an effort
64 Klein of fashion
65 May I have your attention?
66 Like ancient history
67 **"These are the times that try men's souls."**
69 Part
70 Trading places
71 Diner's dinner
72 NYC sports arena
73 Chow palace
74 More than oft
75 In unison
76 Ring highlight
77 Whisper sweet nothings
78 Berth place
80 "Sure thing!"
81 "Awesome, dude!"
82 South African rebellion (1899–1902)
86 Newsroom newcomer
88 **"Mankind are governed more by their feelings than by reason."**
92 It makes Cher cheer?
93 Opera by Delibes
95 "___ luck!"
96 Expert finish?
97 Hood's heat
98 Unusual key
100 AAA recommendation
101 Actor Davis
103 Howdy-dos
104 Farm female
105 **"A government is like fire, a handy servant, but a dangerous master."**
110 Fine-tune
112 Pepe Le Pew's quest
113 Couple of cpls.
114 It's from the heart
116 Goes astray
117 Get down, in a way
118 Marine abbr.
119 Gave a shot
120 Algerian governors, formerly
121 Mama's boy
122 Music and dance
123 Downhill racers

DOWN

1 Poke fun at
2 Strauss title character
3 Legal hurdles
4 Privy to
5 Japanese mercenary of old
6 Ice Age pachyderms
7 Kyrie ___
8 Sound off
9 Enterprise officer
10 Record holder
11 Reject
12 Mope about
13 Central Asian sea
14 Tony's "West Side Story" love
15 Rumpus
16 **"All men having power ought to be mistrusted."**
17 Antarctic penguin
18 Washington peak
28 Iris part
29 "Casablanca" cop
30 Insensitive
32 Clod buster
36 "Your highness!"
39 Off-color
40 Civil disobedience, e.g.
43 Has an impact
44 1988 Eddie Murphy film
45 Bank fraud
48 Glowing embers
51 Last word of a New Year's favorite
53 I'll homophone
54 High hat
56 It's brought to the table
57 Racing circuit
58 Oakland's county
60 Peter and Paul
61 "The Tempest" pixie
62 **"Give me liberty or give me death."**
63 Luther's 95
64 Chi. time
65 Rap sheet item
67 Self-serving need
68 Peer Gynt's mother
73 Carries out
76 Big bash
77 Radio operator's request
79 Mountain lion
81 Do the seam thing all over again
82 String section
83 Overdone musical number
84 Consecrated ceremoniously
85 Burgundy and claret
87 It goes with the floe
89 Newspaper reference rooms
90 Through and through
91 Dispense
93 Cracked the whip
94 Taking liberty
99 Natural highs
101 Green Muppet
102 Old expletive
106 Former Atlanta arena
107 Shad delicacies
108 Visitor to Siam
109 Gimlet or screwdriver
111 Slalom maneuver
115 Classified info

288

"O SAY CAN YOU SEE . . ." by Fred Piscop
There's no need to stand when you solve this one.

ACROSS

1 It moves by foot
6 Indy letters
9 Mini-albums
12 "Who's Who" entry
19 "___ Paris"
20 Director Teshigahara
22 Barhopping
23 Actor Sal's GPS?
25 Printer's primary color
26 Côte d' ___
27 "Where's your homework?" response
28 Opera's Lily
29 Polo Grounds hero
30 Nymph pursuers
32 Went to the polls
34 Tom Swiftie wd.
36 Send sky-high
40 In accord
41 Director Sergio
44 Devotion to Marlon's films?
49 Blotto
51 San ___ (Riviera resort)
52 House makeup?
53 Peep show crowd
55 Baseball card fig.
56 Wall St. debuts
57 "The Addams Family" star
58 Large molding
59 Palindromist Jon
60 Attacked violently
62 Salt a cloud
64 Super fielding play
65 Follow-the-leader sorts
66 Jackie's designer
68 TiVo button
70 Dubai dignitary
72 Pure, to a pusher
75 Churchill's "so few"
78 Cooperstown charter member
81 Numskulls
85 Knight fight
86 Mailroom stamp
88 Bigwigs
90 Olympian's path
91 Prefix with skeleton
92 ___-Prussian War of 1866
93 Betray, in a way
94 Philbin cohort
95 Prepares to play again
97 Ray's break from filming?
100 Milo in "Barbarella"
101 Past plump
103 Lawn figure
104 "Thimble Theatre" name
105 More tender
106 Cast-of-thousands group
111 ___ and Fox
113 Hirsute Tibetans
115 Cruet filler
120 ___ Hashanah
121 Romanian oil center
123 Janet partners with a fat cat?
125 Expansion card
126 Pacific wreckage
127 Make tough
128 Record collection?
129 Kasparov's horses: Abbr.
130 Saucer contents?
131 Indiana's state flower

DOWN

1 Arizona Indians
2 'Enry's pupil
3 Spare tire
4 Hi-fi pioneer Fisher
5 Bloom in "The Producers"
6 Writer Silverstein
7 Bandleader Puente
8 C. in C.
9 Of summer
10 Copy of yore
11 Attenborough's title
12 Pitcher Hideo's alias?
13 Son of Judah
14 Pre-move events
15 Took tiffin
16 Irish singer's world tour?
17 2000 Senate majority whip
18 Coup d'___
21 Reggie Jackson's mo.
24 Knock out of kilter
28 Big house
31 Blushing
33 Shih Tzu, e.g.
35 Twister Joey
37 [sigh]
38 One-L's course
39 Steve's singing partner
42 "When pigs fly!"
43 Cube's twelve
44 Bubble eater
45 Defaulter's loss
46 Love personified
47 Just beat
48 "Roots" Emmy winner
50 "___ a deal!"
54 Script addition?
59 Based on hypothesis
61 Cruising fig.
63 Boxing Day mo.
65 SOS response
67 Ex-NYSE chairman's hula attire?
69 Mongoose's foe
71 "Mule" for "donkey" et al.
72 In ___ (not yet born)
73 Puts the kibosh on
74 Fate's winter attire?
76 Court fig.
77 "Cyrano de Bergerac" star
79 Took along, to a hillbilly
80 Track handoff
82 "Metamorphoses" author
83 Spanish bite
84 Do in
86 Invoice word
87 "My Day" columnist
89 Artsy Big Apple area
92 Market gurus
96 One-eighty
98 Spanish sheep
99 Big Apple ave.
102 Fenway team, on scoreboards
107 Moth-eaten
108 Tybalt's slayer
109 Forest quaker
110 In an "aw-shucks" way
111 Surveyor's nail
112 Pierce of "M*A*S*H"
114 Suit to ___
116 "___ to worry!"
117 The life of Riley
118 Swarm member
119 USN bigwigs
122 Ecol. watchdog
123 1960s atty. gen.
124 Dosage amt.

289 LIGHT MOTIF by Tucker Smith
"When to go bowling?" (See 41 Down)

ACROSS

1 Ananias, for one
5 Brown relative
9 Going on
14 Entree fowl
19 Best of the theater
20 Stock remarks?
21 "Taxi" character Elaine
22 Save wedding bills
23 Pit area
26 Frasier's brother
27 Delhi?
28 Circus prop
29 Rod of reels
30 Blood line
31 Tiger's final stroke
32 "Think we'll have a white Christmas?"?
35 Exceptional
39 Where a pupil sits
43 Service receivers
44 Like a large garage
45 Tree candy
46 Armchair athlete's channel
47 Stadium strata
49 Lang of Smallville
50 Brewmaster Coors
52 Inscribe indelibly
55 Mine, to Maurice
56 Oater actor Jack
57 Unlike 96 Down
60 Tolled
62 Like some cold sprays
64 Crane, e.g.
65 Toy instrument
66 Implore
69 Arrow shaft
70 "That'll be the day!"
71 The Vice President is president here
72 Like some nouns in Ger.
74 Send out
76 "Fudge!"
78 Kind of a bore
79 Food on the floor
80 Metal fastener
82 "Háry János" heroine
85 Jodie role
86 Ruth, to Gehrig
88 "Pulp Fiction" designation
91 Leaden
92 Home wreckers
93 Bubble makers
95 Emerald isle
96 Lawn application
97 Just after the hour
102 Evita portrayer Lupone
104 Hold nothing back from
108 Clubby
109 Long-lasting soap
110 Blabs, when doubled
111 Magritte and Lalique
112 Shed
113 Paper maker
114 Sound from a nest
115 Meredith's "Family Ties" role
116 Often-dunked item
117 Scores on serve

DOWN

1 Track star Carl
2 Words of denial
3 Battery part
4 They go to the center
5 High rank
6 Is in command of
7 Harassed
8 Country in a Beatles song
9 Like the Sphinx
10 Most like Arbuckle?
11 Betelgeuse setting
12 Nose activator
13 Obie relative
14 Chew out
15 Pope's "dang'rous thing"
16 Party person
17 Autobahn auto
18 Snug retreat
24 Practical jokers
25 Nixon nemesis Sam
31 Cat and carpet?
33 Rain check
34 Gave temporarily
35 Flower supporter
36 High chairs
37 Zola work
38 Light weight
39 Boast beginning
40 Trooper's device
41 When to go bowling?
42 Choosy group?
48 Villainous "Othello" fellow
51 Doom
53 Grumble
54 Pestered pledges
58 Swallow
59 Solitary soul
61 ___ bene
63 Leave in the text
65 Box with a tail
67 Dickens title opener
68 Brit's boob tube
71 Rayless
72 Homer's creator
73 Nautical adverb
75 Folk singer Burl
77 Romance writer's award
81 They're learning the ropes
83 Board blemish
84 Goes along with
87 Most mucky
89 Deep regret
90 NBA venue
94 Break under strain
96 Vegetarian shark in "Shark Tale"
98 Kind of ballerina
99 Top floor
100 Like cut-rate bread
101 Crossing charges
102 Cooped (up)
103 What there oughta be
104 Very nasty sort
105 Strip
106 Salt's saint
107 Restaurateur Toots

290 LANGUAGE OF MATH by Arlan and Linda Bushman
Mathematician Tao (Terence) has a name custom-made for crosswords.

ACROSS

1 Save
7 John Steinbeck novel
15 "Alas . . ."
20 Within reach
21 Bombast
22 Parting word
23 Stray from Euclid's theme?
25 Sweetheart
26 Facial contortion
27 Grays, to George Noory
28 Pact of 1948
29 Ruins visitor
31 Dropping-off spots?
33 EPA concern
34 Made cents
35 Film-preservation org.
38 No wiggle room for Fourier?
41 Big bird
44 Doorway headers
46 Opry regular Acuff
47 "Three Sisters" sister
48 Ersatz
49 Lament
50 Krypton, for one
51 Shorthand chuckle
52 Shelter
54 Cherbourg she
55 When the stars shine on Euler's set?
58 Pantry
59 Zip
60 Richmond of "Van Wilder"
61 Gives off
63 Room to relax
64 Name
66 West of rap
68 Sweetly charming
72 "Grey's Anatomy" extras
73 Housing choice
75 Spurs curs
76 Cambodia's Lon
___
77 Zeno's followers
80 Declaration of loyalty from Archimedes?
83 Here, in Veracruz
84 Put the ___ on (squelch)
85 Cote denizen
86 Bellini's "Giovanni ___"
87 David of "CSI: Miami"
89 Tennis champ Lendl
90 Erma Bombeck's dog
92 Preserve
93 Most gossamer
94 Mickey Cohen's group
95 Ironclad confirmation for Fermat?
98 Legal thing
99 Least industrious
101 Unlock, in verse
102 "Chicago Sun-Times" critic
104 The blahs
106 Pharaonic symbol
107 Network
108 Relay race prop
112 Layoff phase
113 Newton, to his acolytes?
117 Ryder with the Detroit Wheels
118 Like biopics, hopefully
119 Amends maker
120 So far
121 Dürer, notably
122 Go-getter

DOWN

1 Crusader Rabbit's pal
2 Harrow rival
3 Clog
4 Latte spots
5 Thawed out
6 Shogun capital
7 "Really?"
8 Porkpies
9 Piece of the past
10 Splendid array
11 Undertake
12 Man has seven
13 Kennel area
14 Easing (up)
15 Toast
16 Relish
17 Descartes' battle plan?
18 Dregs
19 Mongolian tent
24 Almost equals
30 Available if summoned
32 Highlighter
33 Dr. Seuss' Thidwick
34 Polo stick
35 American auto of 1910–1914
36 Inducement
37 Most likely, per Pascal?
39 Ore hauler
40 Grace, to Will
42 Remote button
43 107 Down, in old Rome
45 Hitch
48 Charges
50 Tonic companion
51 Alkaline, as soil
53 Gains
56 OCS relative
57 Mortise fit
60 Tape alternatives
62 Reel
65 Edible bulb
66 Have insight about
67 Together, in music
69 Glacial chamber
70 Creamy dessert
71 Ness and Spitzer
74 Spotted wildcat
75 ___-Cone
77 Riffle through
78 Digital recorder
79 Wall Street block parties
81 Annoy
82 Book of Mormon book
83 The D'backs, on scoreboards
88 Sharpness
91 Pinkish
92 "Lost in Translation" director
93 Former Cheney aide Scooter
95 Dilemma
96 More fashionable
97 Wobble
100 Twyla Tharp forte
103 Append
104 "Papa Loved ___": Garth Brooks
105 Alliance
106 Give ___ (pull on)
107 One of a household pair
109 Skipjack cousin
110 Provo neighbor
111 Pupil of Seneca
114 Spigoted item
115 Randall's "6 Rms ___ Vu"
116 Rage

291 COLLEGE FOOD by Fred Piscop
Fred says he lived on pizza while a student at Cornell.

ACROSS

1 "Zounds!"
6 Act the lookout, say
10 Rapper ___ Rhymes
15 Stand at a wake
19 Naive sorts
20 Boffo review
21 Mortify
22 Sheba's creator
23 COLLEGE FOOD
25 No-goodniks
26 Encircled
27 Conceive a picture of
28 COLLEGE FOOD
31 Belmonts leader
32 Agriculturist Jethro
34 Playwright Chayefsky
35 Full of vigor
36 Isle of Man man, e.g.
38 Coin-___ (candy machines, e.g.)
40 Do some woolgathering?
42 Slot machine symbol
45 COLLEGE FOOD
49 D.C. player
52 Dislike, plus
54 Ballot abbr.
55 Prez before Jack
56 Frat-pin wearer
58 Cabinet officer
61 They've got it coming
63 Glass eel
64 Salad green
65 Trill's need
66 "The French Revolution" author
68 G.W. Bush's degree
70 COLLEGE FOOD
73 ___-relief
74 Roll-on alternative
77 Gazillions
78 Plaza imp
81 Parkinson's treatment
82 Armadillo feature
84 Obliquely
87 White-sale items
89 Caesar's end?
90 Do terrific on
91 "___ impressed"
92 Record label inits.
93 COLLEGE FOOD
98 Milk source
99 Not so rigid
100 Man in blue
101 Speakeasy risk
103 Jeanne of "State Fair"
106 Nerdy sorts
109 LAX guesstimates
111 "Gotcha!"
115 COLLEGE FOOD
118 Like a raw recruit
120 Kicking back
121 Give a lift to
122 COLLEGE FOOD
124 Org. chart feature
125 Take hold
126 New or golden follower
127 Rent anew
128 PlayStation name
129 ABC's "Men in ___"
130 ___ Parker
131 Tech-support callers

DOWN

1 Went down
2 "With parsley"
3 From square one
4 Moistening, in a way
5 1040 IDs
6 Salad green
7 Ring bread
8 Lovelace in "Morning Glory"
9 Time served
10 Sod grass
11 Knock for a loop
12 Good base-stealer
13 Fox hunter's cry
14 "Not to mention . . ."
15 Kerouac classic
16 ". . . and everything ___ place": Beeton
17 Plume source
18 Take another stab at
24 Beyond full
29 Lhasa ___
30 Ghetto ___
33 Crackers
37 Used a scope
39 Shipping letters
41 Some MIT grads
42 Logan Airport code
43 Cannon attachment
44 COLLEGE FOOD
46 He may take you on
47 Is connected
48 Muscular dog
49 COLLEGE FOOD
50 ___ Rogers St. Johns
51 Rolls radials
53 Joe holder
57 Wing of sorts
59 Popular DVR
60 St. Teresa's city
61 Make good on
62 '50s actress Gia
65 Go deep
67 Pharaoh's deity
68 "Pretty Baby" director
69 Make obscure
71 Egypt's Nasser
72 Troy name
75 Unveil, in poetry
76 "Smooth" band
79 Reply to "Who's there?"
80 Personal ad abbr.
83 No-goodnik
84 Suffix with moon
85 "___-hoo!"
86 Barnyard home
88 ID information
90 Sling's contents
94 Yenta
95 Give the boot to
96 Wheat holder
97 Bridge seats
99 Servant's garb
102 Dispenses gossip
103 IOUs
104 FDR's "fireside chats" medium
105 "Stormy Weather" composer
107 Make more secure
108 Loudly laments
110 Monkey suits
112 Place for a coin slot
113 Angler with pots
114 Cuts and pastes
116 Take ten
117 Marvel's Lee
119 Neutral tone
123 It may be inflated

292 INNER PEACE by Alyssa Brooke

Another popular recording of 61 Across was by the Flamingos in 1959.

ACROSS

1 Naturally bright
7 "Ditto!"
14 Tomei in "Alfie"
20 "Becket" actor
21 Parked one
22 Bosses over other suits?
23 Jack Nicholson classic
25 Brown area?
26 Mobile location
27 Chiang Kai-___
28 "China Beach" setting, for short
29 It gets picked out
30 His, to Henri
31 Natural
34 "Just wondering"
36 Halves of ems
38 Bahrain biggie
39 Hairy wave
40 Promethium, for one
45 Rep with a cut
46 Formal ceremony
47 Cross or star, often
48 Small low island
51 Staff positions?
52 Borders
54 Shaq's game
55 Like cut-rate bread
57 Camels' cousins
59 By itself
60 Brat
61 1975 Art Garfunkel hit
65 Near miss, for a high-honors student
66 Try to deceive
67 Left over, perhaps
69 Coyote of "Looney Tunes"
70 Stands behind
71 John who played Gomez
73 Nice beach season?
74 Mil. ranks
75 Somewhat, slangily
76 Cave effect
77 Beatrice's adorer
79 One who keeps reinventing the wheel?
83 Sail at the America's Cup
86 Like Sun Ming Ming
87 Agency under FDR
88 Ordered
89 Result of an infraction
91 Crossword-solving moment
94 Above-ground trains
95 California's Big ___
96 Shows on TV
97 Helping
100 James Michener novel
102 Trying to make something from nothing?
105 Avis patron
106 Series opener
107 Three in one
108 Main squeeze
109 Lack
110 More popular

DOWN

1 Remote spots?
2 Handy
3 Stellar events
4 "Stay" singer Lisa
5 Lower alimentary canal sections
6 1992 Olympic hoop champs
7 Old pronoun
8 Dance in socks
9 Radiating
10 "Look, you!"
11 Followed a curved path
12 Hardly demanding
13 Mag. execs
14 Where Elijah defeated the prophets of Baal
15 Syriac
16 Coke companion
17 Make obligatory
18 Incite
19 Give the nod
24 Honshu honorific
28 Like Joe Average
32 Beginning for four
33 Misses
34 Fir coat
35 Aardvark snack
36 Article in "Der Spiegel"
37 "No idea"
39 "Aw, c'mon!"
40 Avis adjective
41 Bar barrier
42 Sacks
43 Puppy love
44 Early stage
48 Beta follower
49 French folk song
50 "___ durn tootin'!"
53 Acknowledges the moon
54 Red veggies
55 Sri Lanka, in Arabic
56 "___ Little Tenderness"
58 Mrs. Shakespeare
59 Get a glimpse of
60 Collette in "Little Miss Sunshine"
62 Apprehensive
63 McLaglen in "The Informer"
64 Sleep on it
65 Leather sticker
68 Literary adverb
70 Washington of education
71 Amtrak's bullet train
72 Shuck oysters
75 Bronze area in the Met
76 City on Lake Michigan
78 Start for log or gram
79 In addition
80 Not invited
81 Say again
82 Blythe Danner's daughter
83 Dirty attacks
84 Mattress of straw
85 Crackers
89 Where ships come in
90 Reason to keep playing
91 One score after deuce
92 Lena in "The Wiz"
93 In search of
96 Show horse
98 Popular '60s hairstyle
99 "___ ain't broke . . ."
101 RR terminus
102 Apr. 15 advisor
103 Business mag
104 Peace sign (in 5 answers)

293 ICE-CREAM OUTTAKES by James Connolly
24 Across was first seen on "Seasame Street" in 1993.

ACROSS

1 Plays table soccer
7 Make available
13 Ceremonial staff carriers
19 Make small repairs to
20 Ivanhoe's love
21 Of a battery terminal
22 Ice-cream flavor for lepidopterists?
24 Hispanic Muppet
25 Sporty auto, for short
26 Shoebox letters
27 Recipe word
29 Oscar's makeup, mostly
30 Pitcher plant's meal
34 Flavor for inconsiderate drivers?
39 Noisy snake
41 Cambodia's Lon ___
42 Durante's "___ Dinka Doo"
43 Ideal ending?
44 ___ Bator, Mongolia
46 Of a heart chamber
48 Meat in a can
52 Flavor for pyrotechnicians?
57 Suffix with scram
58 Toast opener
59 Emmy winner Arthur
60 ___ Zeppelin
61 Like a live ball
63 In ___ (actually)
64 Arlo sang of her
66 Spanish sherry
67 Flavor for Bowery bums?
73 Forcedly attractive
76 Barker's accomplice
77 Act of faith?
81 Bells and whistles, e.g.
82 Hwy. sign no.
85 Susie B. denomination
86 "___ a stinker?": Bugs Bunny
87 "Newhart" setting
88 Flavor for rodents?
93 Track has-beens
95 Dolphin legend Dan
96 VCR supplanter
97 Curly poker
98 Celestial bruin
101 Minded junior
102 Set right
104 Flavor for souses?
109 Landlord
110 Hayes in "Flags of Our Fathers"
111 Alaska, once: Abbr.
112 Gold of "Entourage"
114 Man Ray's genre
117 Having limits
119 Flavor for WW1 GIs?
126 Not so skewed
127 Develop gradually
128 "Letters to My Daughters" author
129 Dig fragments
130 Done for
131 City on the Weser

DOWN

1 Grounds for a penalty kick
2 Uniform suppliers
3 45-degree sector
4 "Round and round ___ goes . . ."
5 San Marino loc.
6 Tanning-lotion letters
7 Channing of the NBA
8 Name in polls
9 Yeanling's parent
10 Common Market inits.
11 Merkel in "The Bank Dick"
12 Violet variety
13 Francis "the Swamp Fox"
14 Arctic outerwear
15 Hearty lettuce
16 Head of costume design
17 Percentage
18 Like "dis"
19 Schedule abbr.
23 Court do-over
28 Sing like a bird
31 Some un-PC remarks
32 Hard to handle
33 Fiddler on the reef
35 "As seen ___!"
36 Pinkish hue
37 Kevin in "A Prairie Home Companion"
38 Courtroom figs.
39 Nouveau ___
40 Phoenix's origin
45 Barnes partner
46 Early adders
47 Bail out
49 Game you can't play left-handed
50 "A pity!"
51 It's held in diners
53 Doobie
54 A woman called Golda
55 "Blazing Saddles" heroine
56 Bartlett's abbr.
62 Undercard match
64 Show wear
65 Mini-albums
66 Barn denizen
68 "Semper Fi" org.
69 Act the gossip
70 Kind of ID
71 Area of expertise
72 Send to the Hill
73 A TV Superman
74 Carpus neighbor
75 Astronaut's ade
78 Like a census population, ideally
79 7 for N, 8 for O, etc.
80 Infantry weapons of old
82 Nipper's co.
83 Some sculptures
84 Walter ___ Disney
86 Footless creatures
89 Astrologer Sydney
90 Opposed to
91 Bring on board
92 Name in printmaking
94 Don the feedbag
99 Went bad
100 Takes the joystick
103 Chelsea's Uncle Hugh
104 Jazzman's licks
105 Bathsheba's husband
106 Beatle follower?
107 Rainbow-shaped
108 Born yesterday
109 Something to flip
113 Marsh plant
115 Blow away
116 Novelist Rand
118 Like many vbs.
120 Ab ___ (from the top)
121 Reset reading
122 Royal Dutch carrier
123 Govt. fiscal agcy.
124 Old Mideast inits.
125 Co. that merged into Verizon

ACROSS

1 Ava and Lana's ex
6 1935 Triple Crown winner
11 Sanka alternative
15 Despicable
19 Not fair
20 Former Mauritian avifauna
21 Picture part
22 Paradise lost
23 "Medical Center" star
25 Call out
26 Picture part
27 Like the White Rabbit
28 Autumn pears
30 Spring awards
32 They're taken for granted
35 "Mr. Television"
36 You can sense it
37 Uranium ore
38 Spokes, essentially
39 Like some lenses
43 Tehran tender
44 Phyllis George, in 1971
46 Where a Cockney 'angs 'is 'at
47 1832 erupter
48 It means well in Milano
49 Excessively
50 Furrow
52 Santos saint
53 Porcelain ware
58 Sheridan and Sothern
59 In the shape of a cross
61 Brightest asteroid
62 ". . . And God Created Woman" star
64 Late start?
65 Berth place
66 Cow catcher
67 Keep in
69 Not so
70 Wait patiently
73 Vitality
74 Feast of Christmas
77 Sun. delivery
78 Birdie's better
80 Deut. predecessor
81 Not e'en once
82 Blackjack option
83 One-time link
84 "Carousel" heroine
89 Dispositions
90 "Manon" composer
92 Work around
93 Improvise
94 Evening hour, in Essen
95 Alpha's antithesis
96 "Pinocchio" cat
97 Humbert Humbert's passion
100 Snake charmee?
101 Kodaly's "___ Janos"
102 In the thick of
103 Average guy?
105 Southern Illinois, familiarly
111 Cellmates
112 Kick start?
113 Persona
114 Cliff dwelling
115 The Lord High Executioner
116 Expression of disgust
117 Flakes off
118 Put back

DOWN

1 Semicircle, for one
2 Sporting chant
3 ___ Maria
4 Written with two sharps
5 Places for laces
6 "The Country Girl" playwright
7 "A Man for All Seasons"
8 Gator tail?
9 Trouble spots
10 Columbia River town
11 Utah canyon
12 Forest denizens
13 Prepared introduction?
14 Tuneful
15 Fastening tape
16 Brainstorm
17 King of tragedy
18 Good hands people
24 Turbine blade
29 Be a loser
31 Coin collectors?
32 Kithara kin
33 Motorist's plaint
34 TV handyman
35 Stationed
36 Pleiades pursuer
37 Louder, in mus.
38 Dentist's directive
39 Parisian crowd?
40 Der Wienerschnitzel order
41 Essential acid
42 Extreme amount
44 Intersects
45 Former number
48 1971 Peace Nobelist
51 They carry a lot of weight
53 Zoologist Fossey
54 School for Raoul
55 Full of gossip
56 Balboa's rival
57 One who stems the tide
60 Elvis' "Don't Be ___"
63 Stargazer's sci.
65 Opera by Delibes
66 Fourth-anniversary gift
67 Crest competitor
68 Cow catcher
69 It grows on trees
70 Slammin' Sam
71 One way to park
72 Romantic rendezvous
75 Vacant
76 "I Am Not My Hair" singer Arie
79 Remote possibility?
82 Loudness unit
85 Inept
86 Doorway part
87 Impinge on
88 Hair restorer
89 Major test
91 Averred
93 Electrical conductor
95 Extra effort
96 Big dos
97 Cry out for
98 Tale of the South Pacific
99 It's on the cuff
100 Gator kin
101 WWW language
104 Vein component
106 Haberdashery item
107 Do the right thing?
108 Jr. and Sr.
109 "National Velvet" horse
110 Asian occasion

ACROSS

1 Stops up
5 Memphis river
9 Work ___
14 Put away
19 Comics canine
20 Heavy load
21 Old pal
22 Leghorn's land
23 Mr. Fixit's mixed drink?
25 Poet Doolittle
26 Obliging spirit
27 Visits to the shrink
28 What Mr. Fixit shares with other repairmen?
30 Basilica area
31 "Mission: Impossible" actress
32 Mex. miss
33 "The Sopranos" restaurateur
36 Hollywood Bowl event
39 Morgan Stanley Dean ___
43 Not nerdy
44 Crockett cap critter
46 9-5 carmaker
48 Intro to surgery?
49 Piece of Duroc?
50 Mr. Fixit's brazen ad-libbed ad?
54 Water from the Seine
55 Soap-___-rope
56 Assume to be
57 Look through a keyhole
58 Ferrara family
59 Port of old Rome
61 Telling card
63 Lay atop
65 Writer of lofty lyrics
68 Criminal subduer
70 Alfalfa's love
71 Interior design crew
74 Turkish currency
76 To date
79 NASA walks
80 Places for pins
82 Annie and Oliver
85 Wright sense of humor
86 Profs' aides

87 Mr. Fixit's quit-smoking method?
89 Like a Pfc.
90 Competitor of Coco
92 Killebrew was one
93 Letters near 0
94 Ballet bend
95 Get more intense
97 Puzzle solver's action
100 Pesach feast
101 "How sweet ___!"
103 Go one better
104 Roe source
106 Mr. Fixit's recorder type?
111 Papa Doc and Baby Doc, e.g.
115 Obie contender
116 Not straight
117 Mr. Fixit's opener?
118 Desert dearth
119 W., at the U.
120 "Picnic" playwright
121 Indian tourist spot
122 Put the whammy on
123 Blockage reliever
124 Irate (with "off")
125 Timely blessing

DOWN

1 Diana in "Dance Hall"
2 Together, musically
3 Get wrong
4 Shove off
5 They're verboten
6 Harebrained
7 Aparicio in Cooperstown
8 Subj. for immigrants
9 Imitative
10 Result of diet and exercise
11 Oscar winner Celeste
12 ___-European languages
13 Blue shades
14 In the ring
15 "Say it again, Sam"
16 Colleague of Kent
17 Essayist's alias
18 Like batik
24 "Holy Toledo!"
28 Give the boot to
29 Credit-report co.
31 Candlemaking ingredient
33 Cold sound
34 Colorful horses
35 Mr. Fixit's pizza sauce ingredient?
36 Haley bandmate
37 Talk like Froggy
38 Come to a point
40 Mr. Fixit's favorite actress?
41 Sister of Clio

42 Where Joan of Arc was tried
44 Dance step?
45 Cork source
47 Apply leeches to
50 Flight segment
51 Pertaining to folk knowledge
52 Beach problem
53 Celestial creature
58 Jellied delicacies
60 Fateful date
62 ___ Haute
64 Totally ruin
66 Rest area sight
67 Revival handout
69 Fellow feeling
71 "For ___ sake!"
72 Call to a swabby
73 Topsy's creator
75 Something to get into
77 Journalist Pyle
78 Big Whig
81 The big house
83 Packed away

84 ATM maker
87 Spayed
88 "The Comancheros" actress
91 One of a series
94 Velotaxi
96 Casino area
98 Grumpy group, say?
99 Bring into play
100 Pre-coll. exams
102 Doesn't fold
104 Boot camp biggie
105 Followed a trail
106 Payment means
107 Have a yen
108 Brand of Lay's potato chips
109 Coup d'___
110 Bathroom square
111 Fine-tune
112 Medea sailed on it
113 Rex's detective
114 Certain trumpeter
117 Op. ___

CRIES OF DISGUST   by Harvey Estes

"Tirlin' at the window, cryin' at the lock" is a line from 40 Across.

ACROSS

1 Spoke pigeon English?
6 Plum-pudding ingredient
10 Toward shelter
14 Taking a cut, maybe
19 Spiritual
20 One-named singer
21 Framework piece
22 Stage
23 Young lycanthrope
26 Break down
27 Teamwork deterrent
28 "Where ___?"
29 Telescope part
30 Basketball Hall-of-Famer Bob
31 Spilled the beans
33 Prison stormed on July 14, 1789
36 A way to stand
37 Prefix in a kids' clothing line
38 Just right
40 Nursery rhyme originally written in Scots
43 Manhattan buyer
45 Vacation souvenirs
46 Musically slow
47 Right, in a way
48 NFL gains
49 Room with a vue
51 Be "it"
55 Home of soccer's United
57 Cold War threat
59 It may split heirs
61 Brown bread
64 Middle name in California politics
66 Impressive grouping
67 Graffiti?
72 "Presto!"
73 Donnybrook
74 Engaging parts
75 Intrude upon
77 In the least bit
79 Not set in stone
84 Slightest sound
85 Pie fight sound
87 Donne's "done"
90 Lack of color
91 Mar. honoree
93 "Once and Again" actress Ward

94 Like Neptune's spear
95 Film that ends with: ". . . tomorrow is another day."
101 "TV Guide" info
102 Ocean State sch.
103 Pump spec
104 Flip out
106 Chimp in space
108 Took a little drink
110 Title role for Kevin Kline
111 Ball thrower
113 Go out ___ limb
114 Pale yellow
115 Aaron Burr's birthplace
119 Without equal
120 Shooting star, maybe
121 Prefix with dollar
122 Lascivious looks
123 Lets off steam
124 Counter offer
125 "Freeze!"
126 It's catching

DOWN

1 References
2 Universal donor's blood type
3 Two-person meetings
4 Night of poetry
5 Oater challenge
6 Show uncertainty
7 In an ill-considered way
8 Potato peeper?
9 Prefix with heel
10 In addition
11 Toy train maker
12 Elbows under the sink
13 Keebler's Zack, e.g.
14 Word after bon
15 What this isn't
16 Hungarian composer
17 Umbrian town
18 What babies do
24 Chew the fat
25 Word on a New York harbor map
30 Plains tribe
32 Very thin
34 Angry (with "off")
35 "If only!"
36 Sunburn result
39 Penny pincher
41 Unsuccessful guesser's phrase
42 Cosa ___
43 Gaping chasm
44 "___ coffee?"
49 Stag
50 In the midst of
52 Banjoist Scruggs
53 Series terminal
54 Bit of Florida
56 Injure seriously
58 Cream cheese go-with
60 Reacted to a blow, in a way
62 Bomber type
63 ___-Whirl
65 Quack
67 Dialing need
68 Bee flat?
69 Pass
70 Straight up
71 Blow one's top
72 BMOC, e.g.
76 Saw
78 "Camelot" composer
80 Much the same
81 Puritanical persons
82 Bloomsbury residents
83 Long beginning
86 Crown without jewels
88 Lamb pen name
89 Dogie catcher
92 Is plucky?
93 Cut off
95 Composer Mahler
96 Firebird
97 Japan, to the Japanese
98 Running again
99 Where the Maine sank
100 '50s music style
105 Financial daily, initially
107 Authority
109 Cool off like a boxer
110 Test-drive car
112 Unconventional apple-splitter
115 ATM input
116 Lien's "Star Trek: Voyager" role
117 Loony tune
118 Stephen in "Breakfast on Pluto"

SILENT GEORGE by Katherine Omak
The alternate clue for 3 Down was: "Emulate Rachel Carson?"

ACROSS

1 Does galley work
5 NYSE newcomers
9 Astrologer Dixon
14 Spar, say
19 Trevi toss-in, now
20 Concordes once broke it
21 Call Domino's, e.g.
22 Sonata finale, often
23 Slaving away
24 Dyan's "Deathtrap" role
25 Most feared employee at the poultry farm?
27 "Hmmm . . ."
29 Decorative metalwork
31 Drooling comic canine
32 Busch in "Foolish Wives"
33 FEMA food
34 Place to moor
35 It may fall into a gap
38 "19th Nervous Breakdown" group
40 Fill beyond full
41 ___ Lanka
42 Code-cracking org.
43 Clerks, at times
45 Annex land without firing a shot?
50 Furtive "Hey!"
51 ___-Aryan language group
53 Walk like a tosspot
54 Get an eyeful
55 Gds.
56 Autumn gem
57 Much of suburbia
61 Rebels
63 "Tuna Fishing" artist
65 "Don't fall for that!"
68 Rapa ___ (Easter Island)
69 Took notes in class?
72 It's inflatable
73 Castel ___ (papal summer home)
75 Niger neighbor
76 Refuses to
78 Prefix with -plasty
79 "Follow me!"
81 Cheat, in a way
83 Low-lying isles
84 St. Francis, e.g.
87 "___ From Muskogee"
88 "Oxford Blues" heroine
89 Like comic Steven's fans?
93 One on your side
95 Polly's nephew
96 Sought a seat
97 Angular lead-in
99 Schindler player
102 Hollywood pursuit
105 Public uproar
107 NL East city
108 Something to break
109 Hoe victim
110 Understood by few
111 Museum displays
113 Christmas Eve happening?
116 Came down
118 Strike out
119 Impresario Sol
120 "___ by Me": Ben E. King
121 Supergirl's Krypton name
122 Autobahn auto
123 Looks out for, say
124 Mountain lakes
125 Author Silverstein
126 Spare in a boot

DOWN

1 Spheres
2 Defeat, à la Takeru Kobayashi
3 What budding poets do in late March?
4 They're wasted
5 Dunk
6 Check casher
7 Text scanner: Abbr.
8 Mutt Lange's wife
9 Loupe user
10 Country singer Steve
11 Not straight
12 Composer Rota
13 Famous Siamese twin
14 Bit of sports news
15 Former women's magazine
16 Wave catcher
17 Suffix with chlor-
18 Alesund loc.
26 Working on 57 Across
28 Got a whiff of
30 Bisected
35 Sine language?
36 Upper-left key
37 Canada explorer John
39 Some 1940s internees
40 Payroll IDs
41 He exiled Trotsky
44 Frees from
46 Discovery
47 Rwy. stop
48 Mammal's coat
49 QED middle
50 New Guinea native
52 "___ Dinah": Avalon
54 Din of fiction
55 Saunders of jazz
56 Ersatz fat brand
58 Cartoon show featuring a bird and a cat?
59 Honshu port
60 Ladybug features
62 Sportswear logo
64 Praline ingredient
66 Less of a mess
67 Hoity-toity one
70 Warning signal
71 Ilsa's love
74 Like a bishop's move: Abbr.
77 Teacart goodie
80 Checker, e.g.
82 Falling-out
85 Took steps
86 Shia leader
87 Theater name
88 Walks like a tosspot
89 Kg. and mg.
90 Raise a stink?
91 "You don't have to tell me"
92 Gofer tasks
94 All together
98 Halloween sounds
100 More smarmy
101 Crunch maker
103 Transplant
104 Some Chippendales
105 Frock wearer
106 Huskies' sch.
107 Full of ardor
110 Charles family member
112 Sweep's schmutz
113 "Huh!?"
114 Hamlet's sticking point
115 Former member of the jet set
117 "Well, ___-di-dah"

298 IT'S THE REGAL THING by Harvey Estes
In 1985 they ruled! (See 103 Across).

ACROSS

1 "M*A*S*H" extra
6 "Alfie" star Michael
11 Homeland
15 Teen fave
19 Playground retort
20 Woodwind section
21 Señora's home
22 Proscribed act
23 Regal insect?
26 Alabama and Auburn, e.g.
27 Ruckus
28 Smoking and nonsmoking
29 Sly stratagem
30 Brings on
31 Fixed design
33 Slip up
35 Color threads
36 Beloved ones
37 Regal Golding novel?
41 Fixed, as pumps
43 Lived
44 Give a do to
47 Mark of omission
48 Work gangs
50 Regal Bogart film?
53 Shoots
58 European air hub
59 Unknown degree
60 Java vessels
61 Early computer
62 Easter flowers
64 Half a state name
66 Blake of "Gunsmoke"
67 It happens
68 Bog material
69 Retired speedster
71 Dark greenish blue
72 Twill fabric
73 Regal Disney classic?
77 Goes up and down
78 Prefix with dollar
79 Bunnies
80 Biting
84 "Grease" actress
86 Regal Carolina college?
89 Pizarro victims
92 Arctic inhabitants
93 December ditty
94 Kind of fiction
96 Money drawers
97 Pops
99 Bygone communication
101 Keystone figure
102 Place-kickers' props
103 Regal baseball team?
107 Northern metropolis
108 "___, Brute?"
109 "Giant" of wrestling
110 "Taxi" character Elaine
111 Tommy's gun
112 Trickle through
113 Snide expression
114 Muscle problem

DOWN

1 "Last of the Red Hot ___"
2 Undercut
3 Stand for
4 O.T. book
5 Sea garden
6 "Suzanne" songwriter Leonard
7 Palindromic pop quartet
8 Debtor's slips
9 Lets touch this
10 "Dulce et decorum ___": Horace
11 Neck region
12 Ungraceful group
13 Wight, for one
14 Set down
15 Mound setting
16 All-out
17 Like the jack of hearts
18 Standings column
24 Matt Dillon film of 2005
25 Slangy ending
30 Sound system, briefly
32 Using successfully
33 Kermit's color
34 Off the wall
35 Della's angel
37 Sucker at the lake
38 Earthenware jar
39 Kilmer poem
40 Chopped down
42 Clean up a rag
44 Some scarves
45 Blossom
46 Disney classic "Old ___"
48 Bit for Miss Muffet
49 Actor Auberjonois
51 TLC specialists
52 Target amount
53 Foreign-language dict. label
54 Absorbed
55 One-dimensional
56 Curie's title
57 Head covers
63 Summer, to Chirac
64 Take from square one
65 Makes bales on the farm
66 Fueled up
68 It has a set price?
69 Runaway cat
70 Restaurateur Toots
73 Howard's "WKRP" costar
74 "On the Beach" author Shute
75 Air for two
76 Checkers masters
77 Compulsions
80 Least significant
81 Island strings
82 Sandy of 1972 Olympics fame
83 Bravery
84 Vane dir.
85 Sous-chef, at times
86 Says "That goes for me too"
87 Ultimately becomes
88 Parks of Birmingham
90 Mideast capital
91 Dresses down
94 More devious
95 Derby site
97 Take out
98 Initial stake
99 Ocean motion
100 "To be" to Henri
103 Jennifer Lien's "Star Trek: Voyager" role
104 Swedish flier
105 FNC rival
106 High-pitched woof

299 AFTER WORDS   by Arlan and Linda Bushman
"Words follow words, sense seems to follow sense." — Wordsworth

ACROSS

1 Rain protection
7 Carson seer
13 Let loose a salvo
20 Drives out
21 Silky-haired goat
22 South Pacific island group
23 WHISTLING LA-LA BRASS?
25 Piled
26 Yemen port
27 Wide sash
28 Tends the garden
30 Mork's people
31 Climber's platform
33 Acad.
36 Leaves holder
38 SUNNY MOON CLEARANCE?
42 Cloverleaf segment
46 Joyful laugh
50 Met moment
51 Balladeer
53 Captured again
54 Woods display
57 Because of
58 Really enjoy
59 Mooches
60 Chat room abbr.
61 Continued ahead
62 Harrow rival
63 Overburden
64 CHINESE FARM CHILI?
66 Willy Wonka creator
68 Miscreant's dodge
70 Odds and ends: abbr.
71 SPARE BIG NOSE?
75 Routine
76 Jalopy
80 Ancient malls
81 Chivvy
82 She played Glinda in "The Wiz"
84 Not interfere
85 Aromatic herb
86 Overbearing
88 Parish head
89 Office gizmo
91 It's a certainty
92 Discombobulate
93 Assay
94 DOUBLE FANCY WORK?
98 Snapshots
100 ___ de Matteo of "Joey"
101 Spring harbinger
106 Old World palms
109 Phuket dweller
112 Ring stat
114 Pupil of Seneca
115 Van Loon's "The Story of ___"
117 BLUE BREAKFAST CHEESE?
121 Cold storage
122 Cockapoo parent
123 Bisects
124 Consummate skill
125 Get ready to preside
126 Fleet-footed

DOWN

1 Cycle
2 Zinc ___ (zinc white)
3 Vetoed
4 Hold fast
5 Start of a bray
6 Kon-Tiki Museum locale
7 Incisor neighbor
8 Further
9 Primary-colors trigram
10 First name in lexicography
11 Pisa river
12 West Pointers
13 Diddley and Derek
14 United Nations Day month
15 Stiller partner
16 HORSE CAMP SPOT?
17 "Lonely Boy" singer
18 Naught, in Nantes
19 Pops
24 Put up with
29 Multitude
32 Prohibit legally
34 Bee team
35 Kauai crop
37 Tigers won it in 2006: Abbr.
39 Stripe
40 Effrontery
41 Coffee liqueur
43 "Should ___ arise . . ."
44 "Ditto"
45 Pitchfork part
46 Hudson Bay tribe
47 Florida team
48 Camp Swampy canine
49 BONUS FIELD LOTTERY?
52 Secret targets?
54 Red-carpet wear
55 Solar wind particles
56 Bugling creature
59 Emollient
61 Canter, for one
63 "___ Boy's Life" (1993)
64 Sloop sail
65 Wedding reception song
67 Whatsoever
68 Cracked
69 End an online session
71 "Blue Ribbon" beer
72 Small print
73 Bonheur and Parks
74 Stumble
75 Colony member
77 Disk extension
78 Omar's dad
79 Criminal, slangily
82 Intertwined
83 Put down
84 Bounded
86 Cut ___ (dance)
87 Long-jawed fish
88 Pi follower
90 Santa portrayer in "Elf"
92 Military dress hat
95 Lunar New Year
96 Dowsing-rod form
97 Nonnegotiable charge
99 Corn's alter ego
102 Word of capitulation
103 Furlough
104 Ruffled
105 Versifier's art
106 Radio designation
107 ___ avis
108 Chemical suffixes
110 By and by
111 Horror film hunchback
113 Cries of delight
116 Uninteresting
118 Shogun capital
119 Court deg.
120 Skip stones

300

"... THAT'S ALL FFOLKS!" by Raymond Hamel
"If you want to know the end, look at the beginning." — African proverb

ACROSS

1 Aquatic rodent
7 Chancel user
13 Fog-machine fuel
19 Will of "Arrested Development"
20 Call from the hayloft
21 Like the Lhasa Apso
22 Inability to tell C from G
23 His assassination was WW1's casus belli
25 Spiny-leafed plant
27 Old game show "Answer Yes ___"
28 Role in "Black Narcissus"
29 Your, to Yvonne
30 Don McLean classic
34 Kitt who was Catwoman
37 Predecessor of Juan Carlos
39 Scandalous
43 Dublin hrs.
44 Protein sources
45 "Good Will Hunting" school
46 Imaginary
47 Silk stockings
49 1958 Mideast alliance
50 Region
52 Where Catalan is spoken
53 Dumbfounded
55 1982 Jessica Lange role
57 "___ I can help it!"
58 Covenant
59 Ho ___ Minh City
60 Braving the waves
61 1976 "Charlie's Angels" star
67 Creole stew
71 Unit of resistance
72 "Dies ___"
73 Chair designer Charles
78 Baseball MVP of 1931
82 Heartfelt
84 Maritime cargo measure
85 Companion of aahs
86 Chimp genus
87 "Not ___ many words"
88 Type of snowmobile race
89 Mr. Sun
90 Blood carrier

92 Swede in Britten's "Paul Bunyan"
93 Writer Zora ___ Hurston
94 "La Strada" director
98 Dismissive looks
100 Neat and tidy
101 Pitchfork-shaped letter
104 Brain scan
105 Train in the ring
106 Mount Holyoke founder Mary
107 She played Dobie Gillis' mom
112 "Grosse ___ Blank" (1997)
116 Charleston college
117 Glacial grooves
118 Involve
119 Remain longer
120 The "Mother of Miami"
121 "Will you marry me?" follow-up

DOWN

1 Mellow-voiced Cole
2 Canton divided by the Reuss
3 "AP" of India
4 Gain back
5 Slanted type
6 Heinous
7 Sta-___ fabric softener
8 Timely
9 "Dr. Zhivago" star
10 Fin
11 Soup pasta
12 Official whistleblower
13 Jimmy Webb's "___ We"
14 What you get for driving someone home
15 Nikkei currency
16 "Let's just leave ___ that!"

17 Sugar source
18 Some are offensive
21 Town on Cape Cod
24 Pass into law
26 Tough teachers don't give them out
30 Knit blanket
31 Fictional Interpol agent
32 Causes distress to
33 CSA member
34 Pioneer computer
35 Pilot maker
36 Disney's "Sleeping Beauty" princess
38 Service closer
40 Contractual conditions
41 Peep show
42 Jupiter moon
46 Not suitable
48 Philip Roth's "fanatic"
50 Crafty
51 Chimaera
52 Old court name

54 Switch position
55 Govt. transportation watchdog
56 "___ homo"
58 Univ. title
62 Isuzu SUV
63 President exiled to Hawaii in 1960
64 Story lines
65 Nursery cry
66 Dutch artist Gerard ___ Borch
67 Most times
68 Danish currency
69 "Dance With Me" director Haines
70 Cancels
74 Singer DiFranco
75 Standing stone
76 Ancient library keeper
77 Like Mr. Spock
79 Actress Valentine
80 Crosses
81 Hercules' captive
82 A lot to listen to

83 Earlier versions
86 Spot for a slide
89 Calligraphy flourish
90 Increase
91 Pennsylvania coal city
94 Wild
95 "The Fog" director Wainwright
96 Before too long
97 Opposite of harshness
99 German seaport
101 USMC newbies
102 Narrow opening
103 Tiny particle
105 In ___ (undisturbed)
108 New Orleans mayor Nagin
109 Testimony lead-in
110 They come before U
111 Witness
113 Not so
114 0–0, for one
115 Ernie of the PGA

ANSWERS

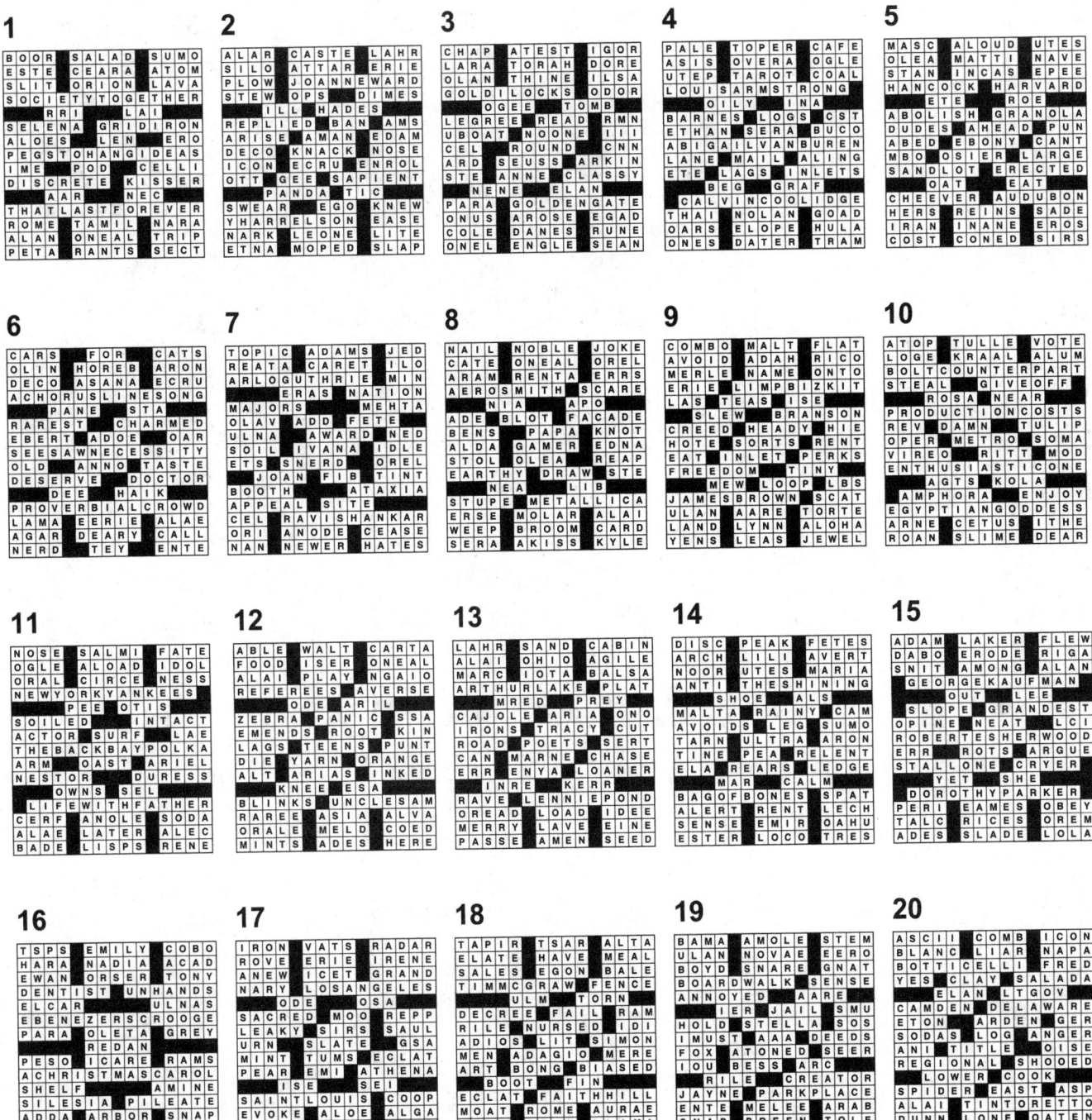

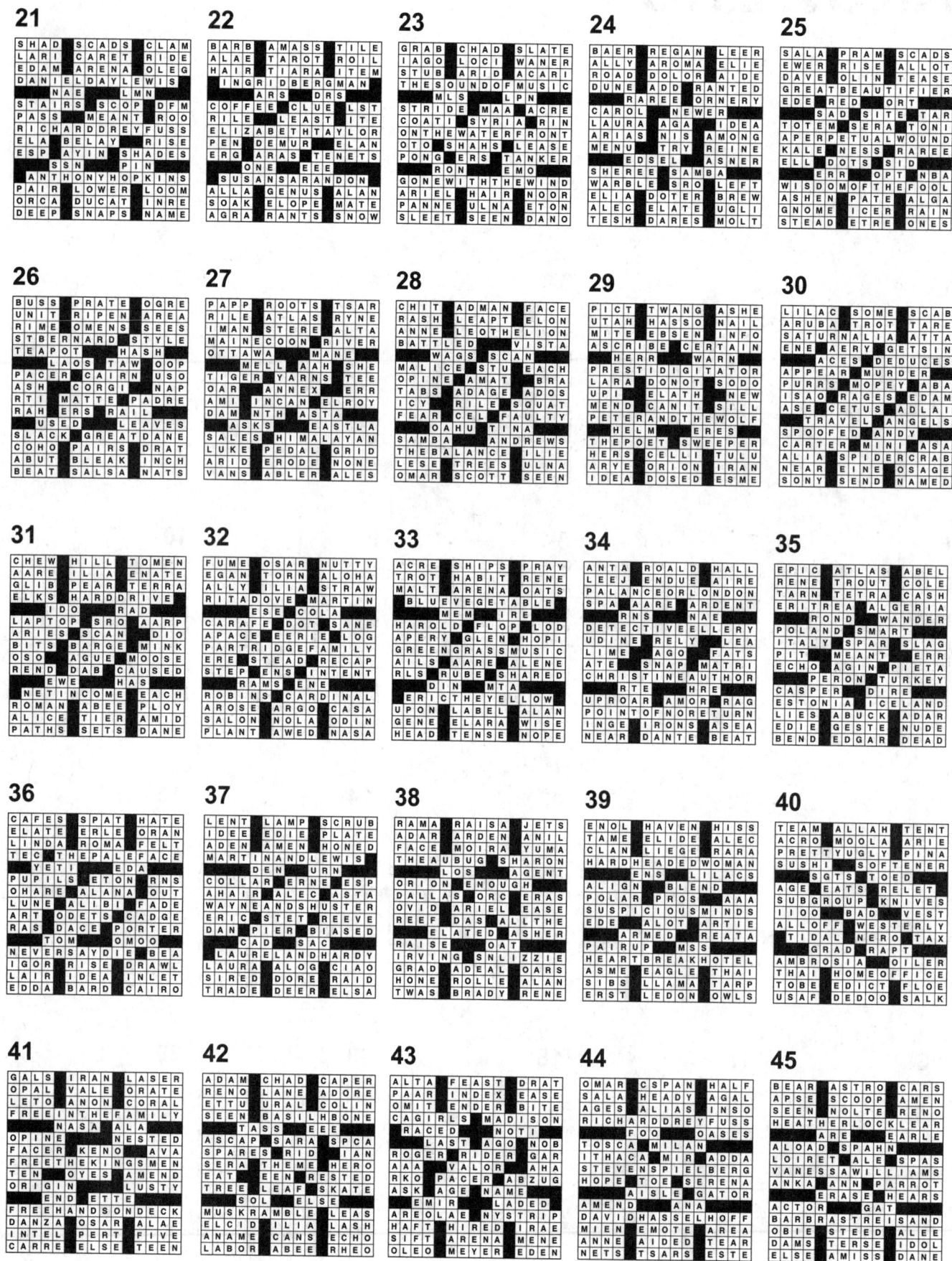

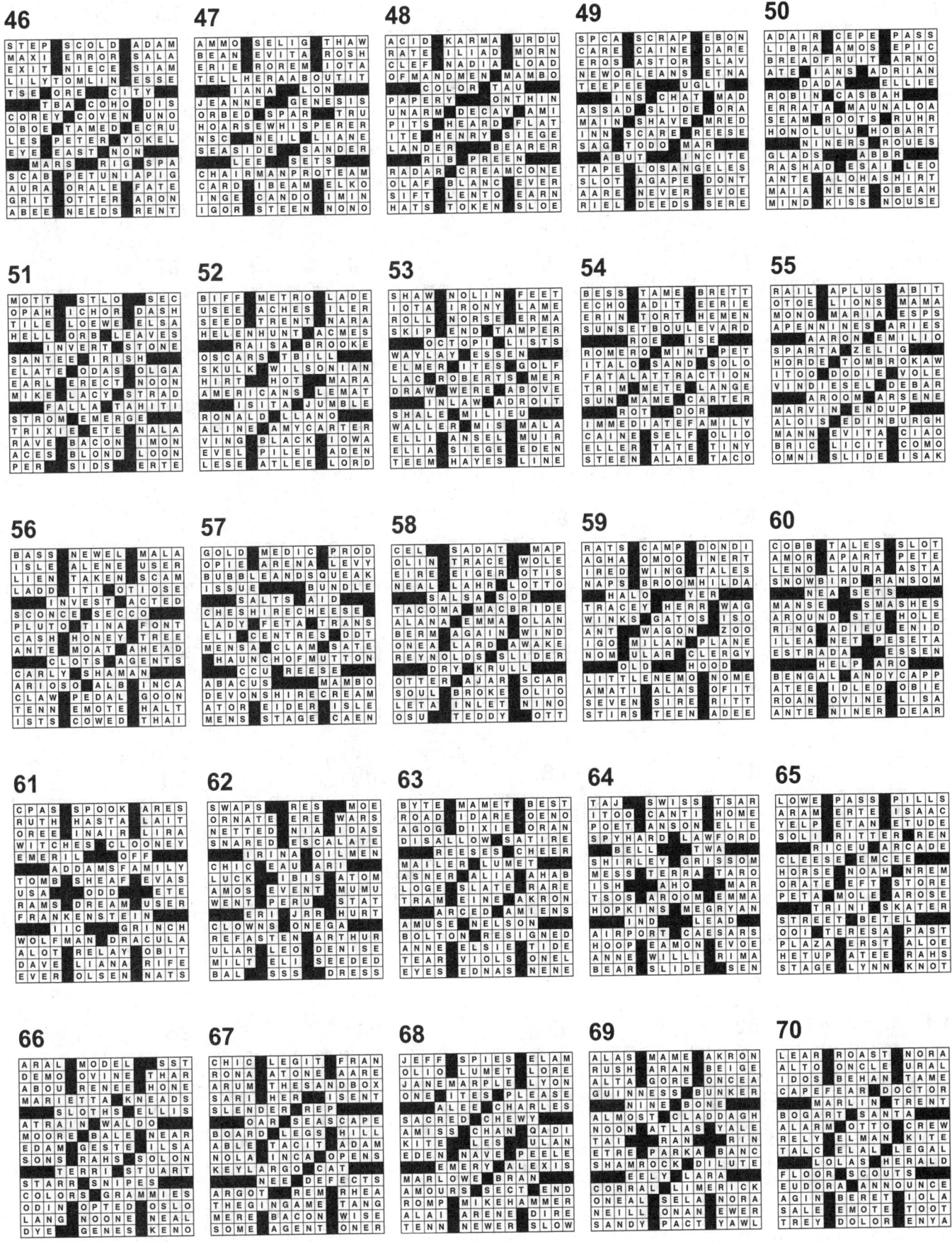

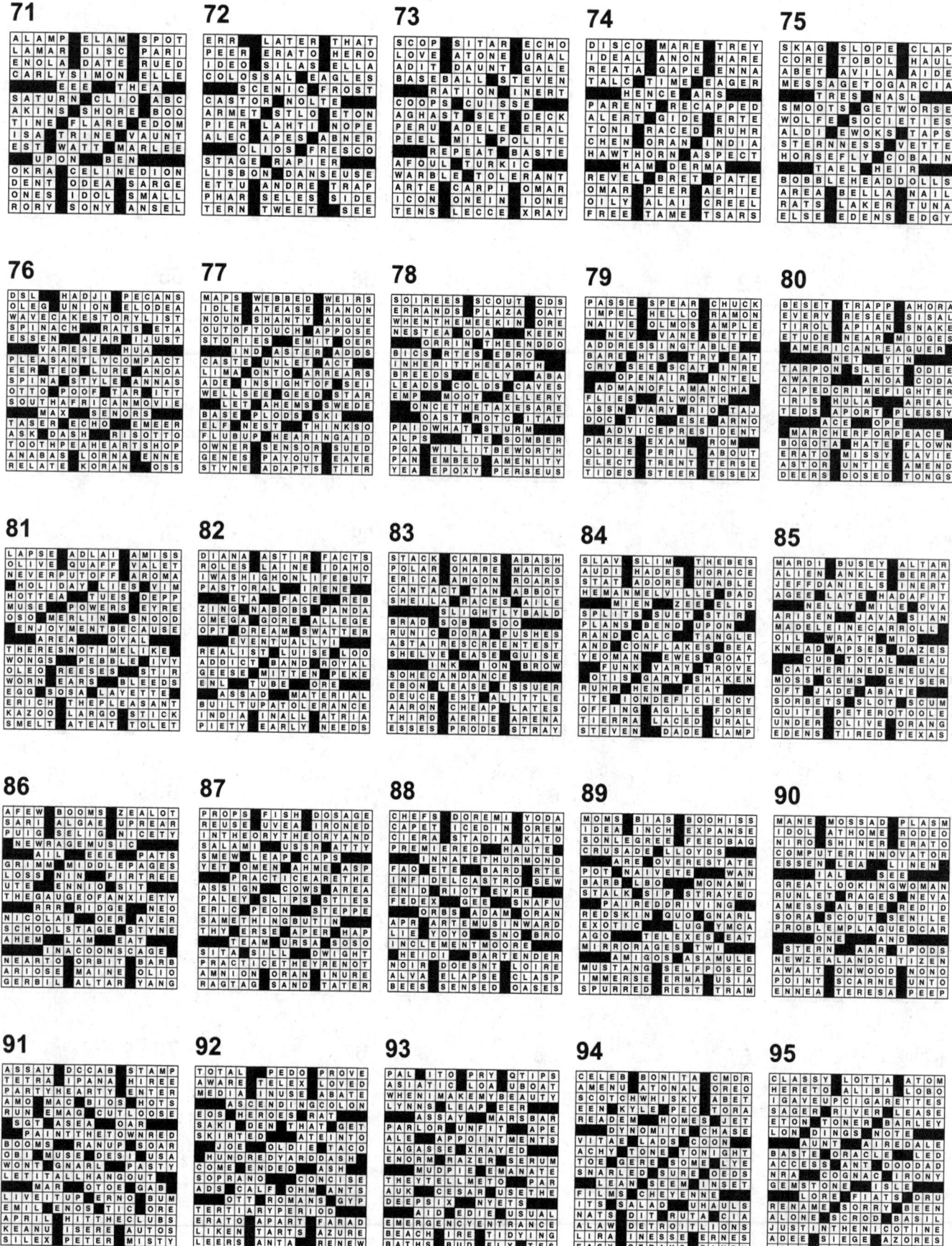

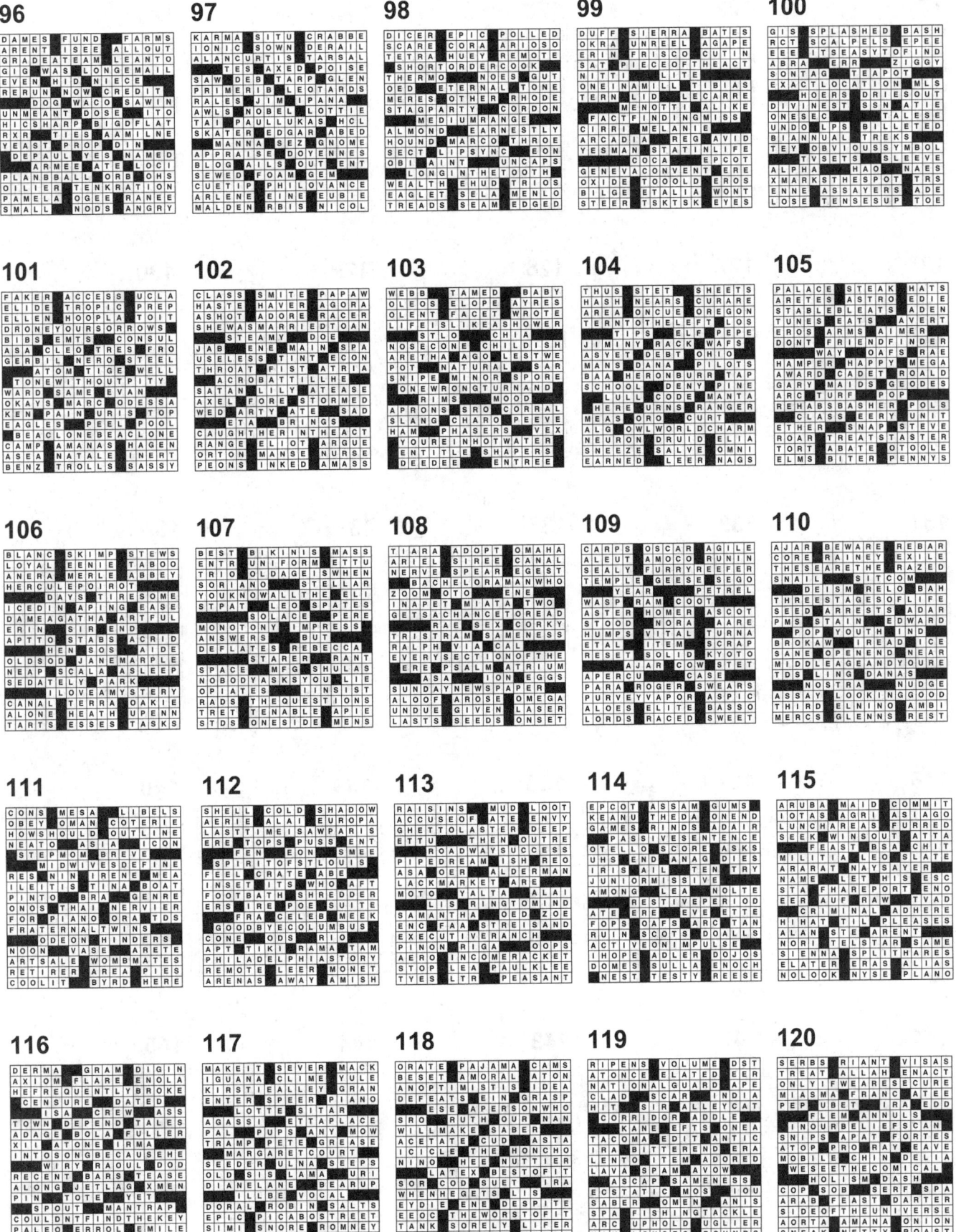

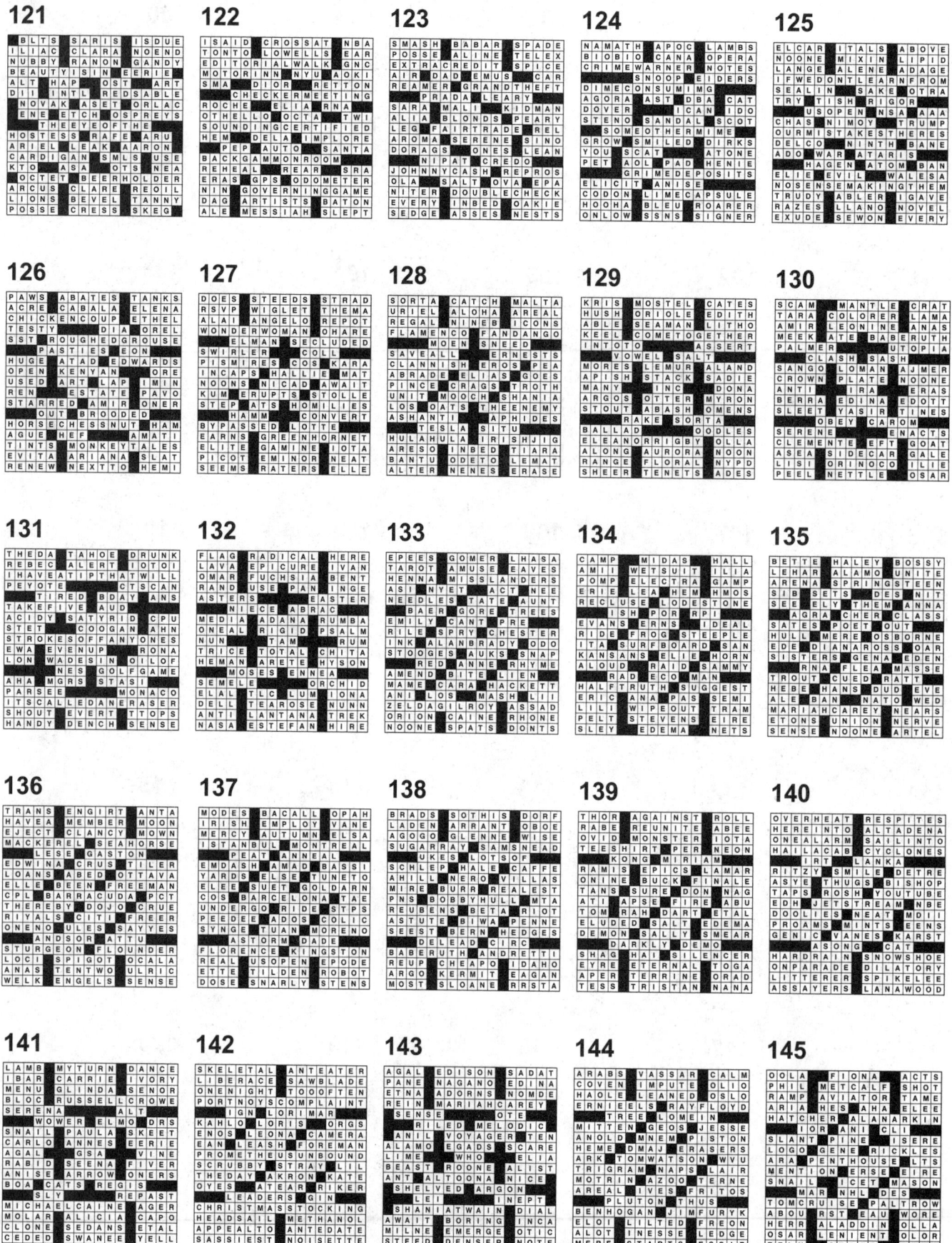

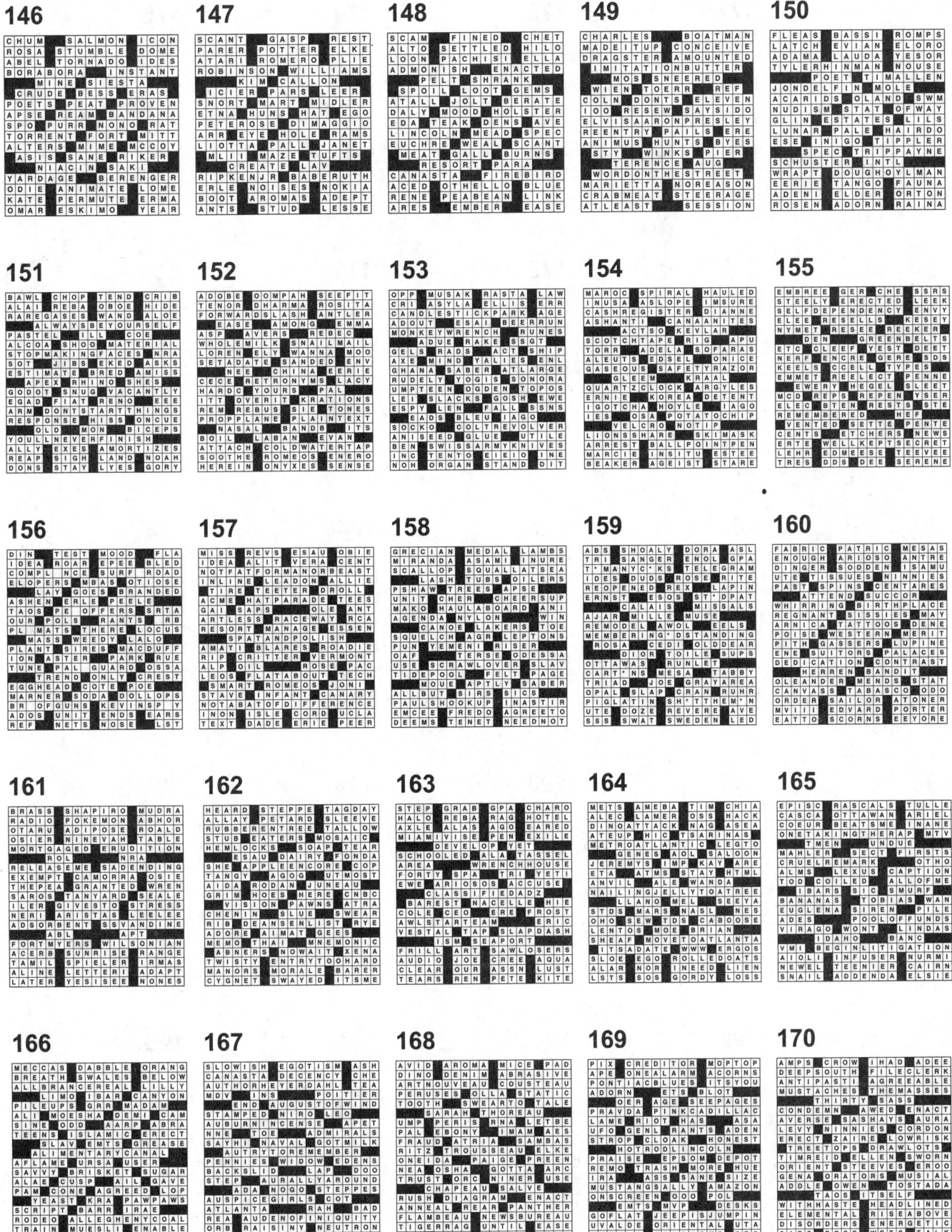

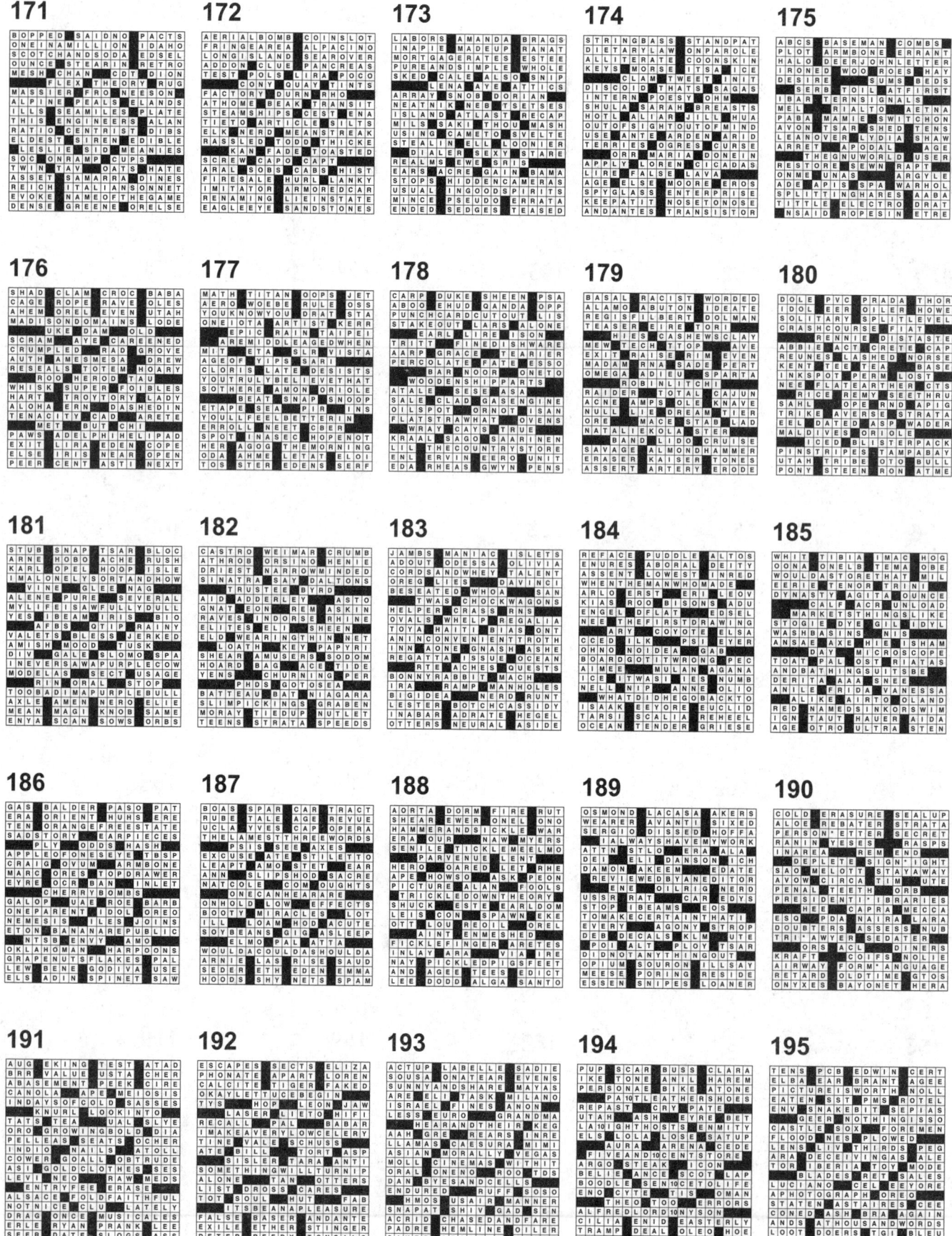

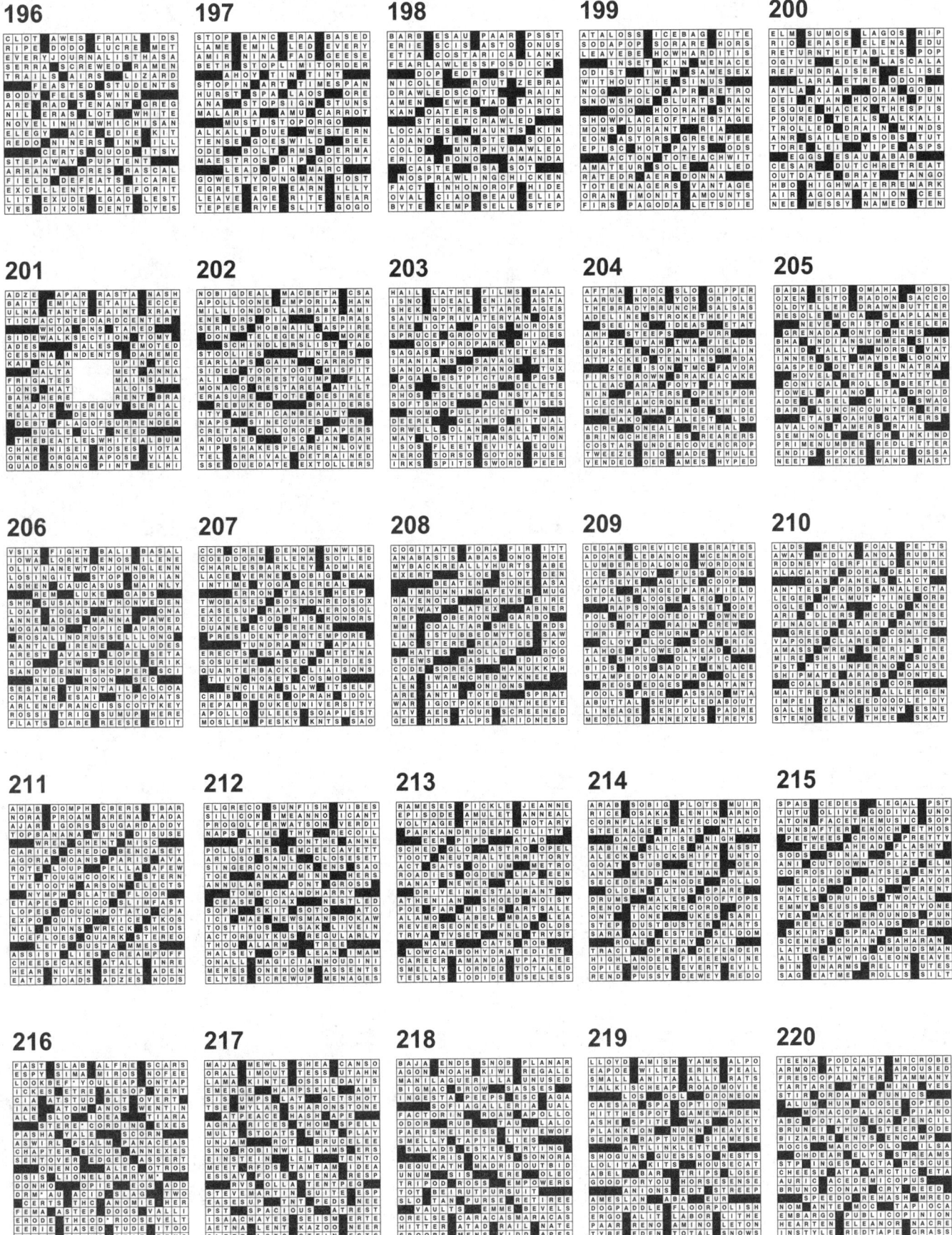

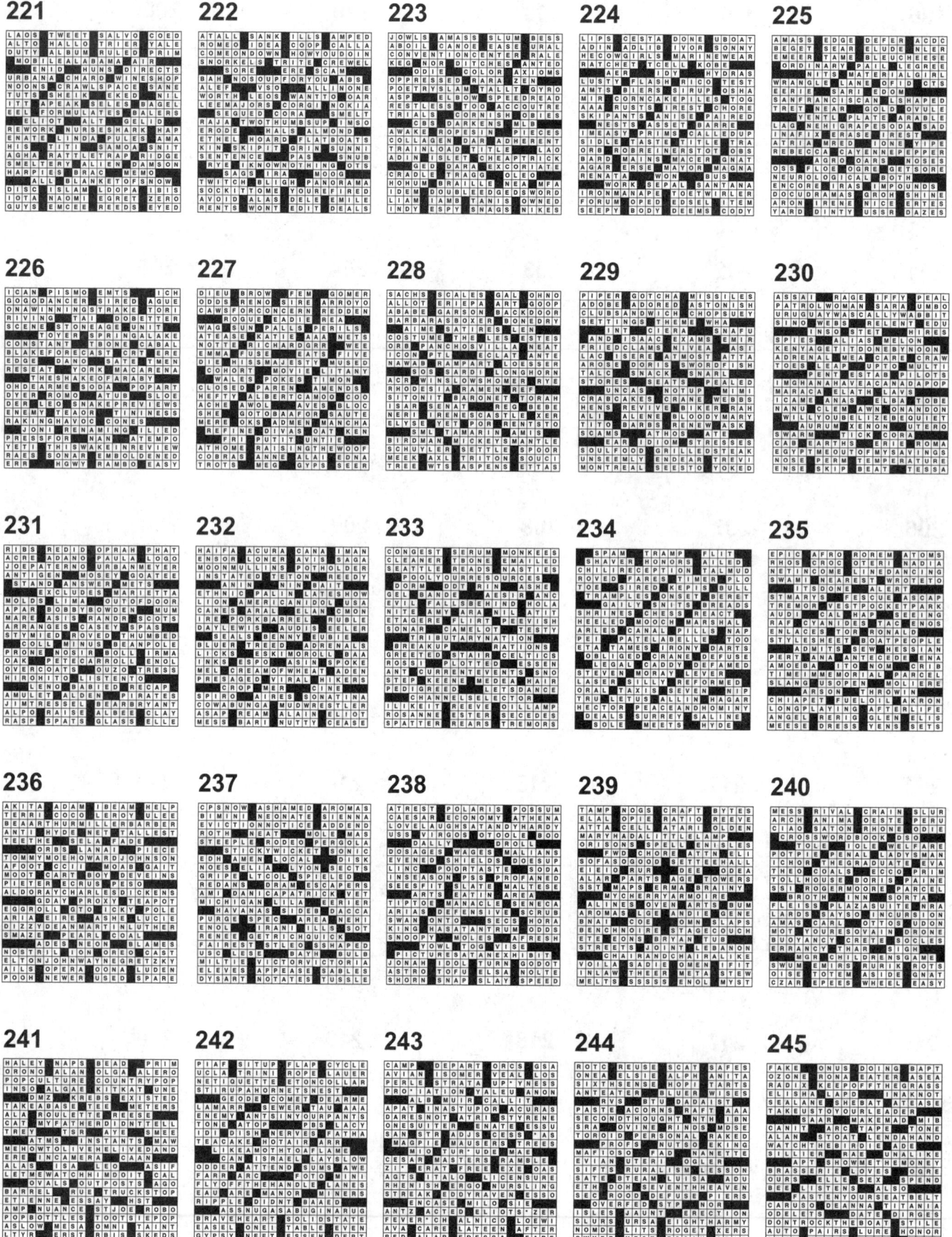

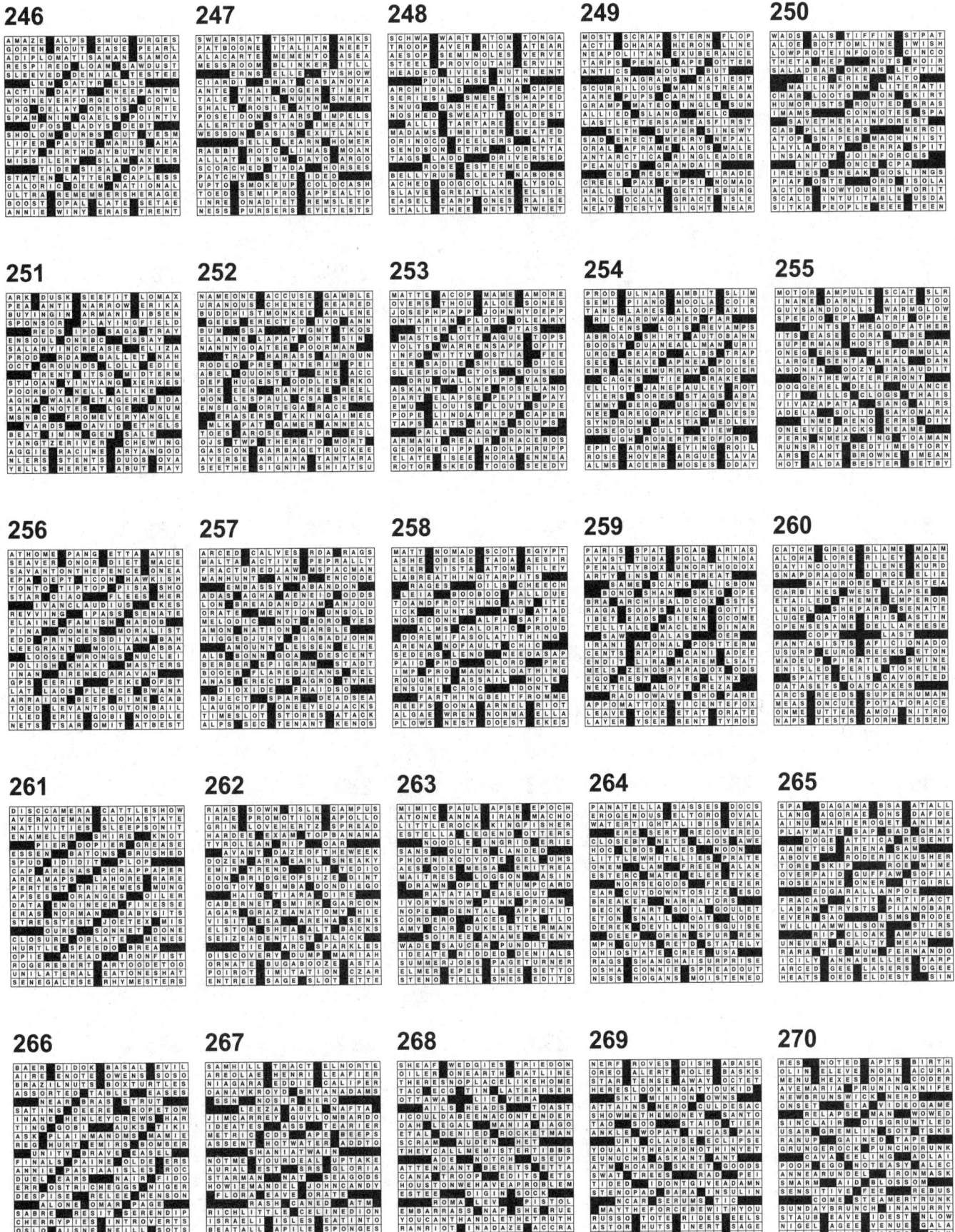

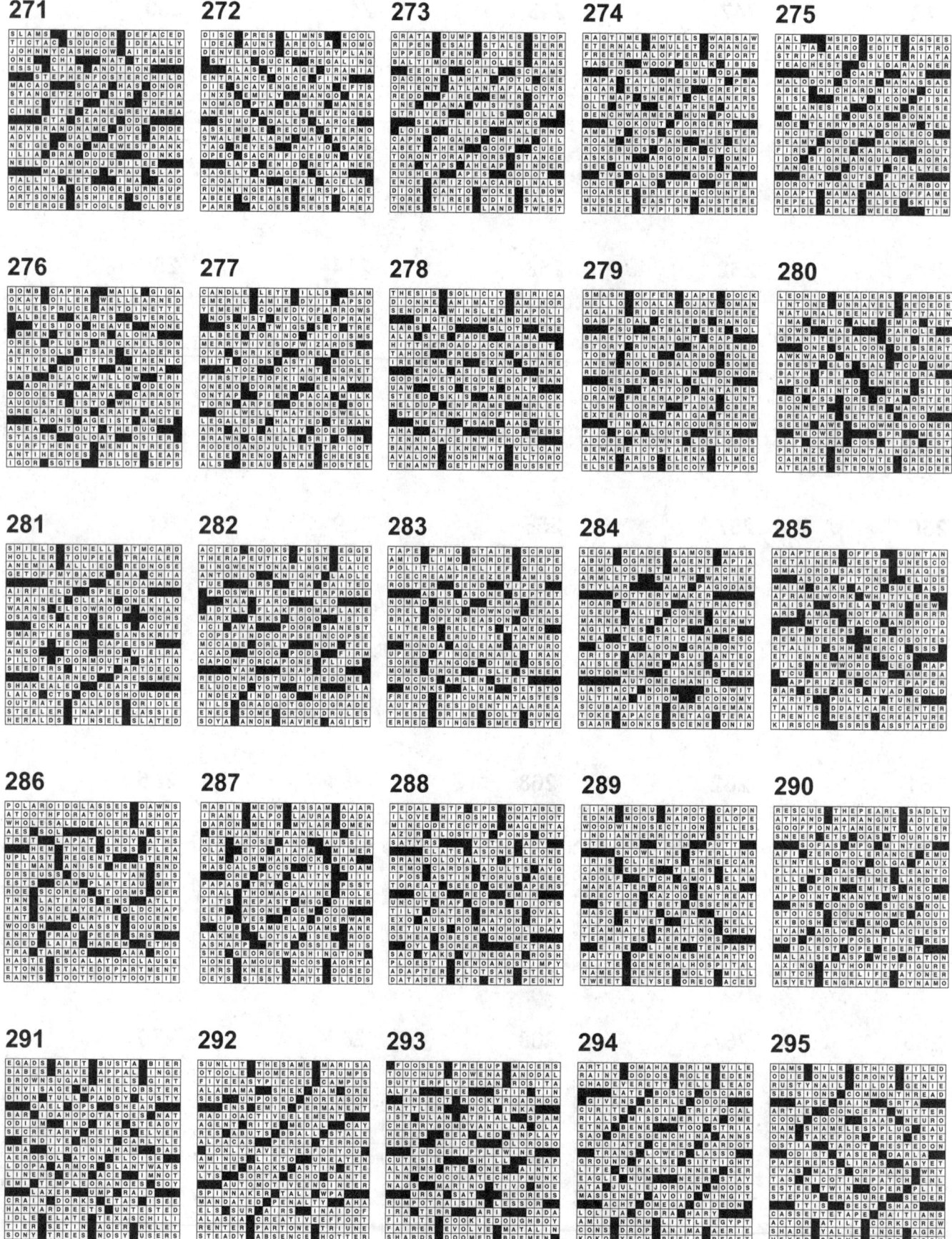

296

```
COOED SUET ALEE ATBAT
INNER ENYA SILL PHASE
TEENAGEWEREWOLF PARSE
EGO WASI LENS PETTIT
SANG BASTILLE PAT OSH
TOAT WEEWILLIEWINKIE
MINUIT LEIS LENTO
AVENGE YDS SALLE SEEK
WESTHAM HBOMB ESTATE
TOAST ALOIS ARRAY
THEWRITINGONTHEWALL
VOILA MELEE GEARS
INVADE ATALL MUTABLE
PEEP SPLAT DER PALLOR
STPAT SELA TRIUNE
GONEWITHTHEWIND SKED
URI EEE HAVEACOW ENOS
SIPPED DAVE HOST ONA
TOPAZ NEWARKNEWJERSEY
ALONE OMEN EURO LEERS
VENTS SODA STOP LASSO
```

297

```
ROWS IPOS JEANE TRAIN
EURO MACH EATIN RONDO
ATIT MYRA WRINGMASTER
LETSSEE NIELLO ODIE
MAE MRE INLET TWEENER
STONES SATE SHI NSA
FILERS WRESTINPEACE
PSST INDO STAGGER
GAPE MDSE OPAL LAWNS
UPRISES DALI ITSATRAP
NUI WROTELEARNING EGO
GANDOLFO MALI DOESNOT
ANGIO CMON CRIB CAYS
ASSISAN OKIE RONA
WRIGHTMINDED FRIEND
TOM RAN RECT NEESON
STARDOM FUROR ATL TIE
WEED ARCANE FOSSILS
WRAPSESSION ALIT OMIT
HUROK STAND KARA OPEL
ABETS TARNS SHEL TYRE
```

298

```
MEDIC CAINE SOIL IDOL
ARESO OBOES CASA NONO
MONARCHBUTTERFLY FOES
ADO AREAS RUSE HIRES
SETPLAN GOOF TIEDYE
DEARS LORDOFTHEFLIES
REHEELED RESIDED
STYLE DELE CREWS
THEAFRICANQUEEN FILMS
ORLY NTH URNS ENIAC
LILIES RHODE AMANDA
EVENT PEAT SST TEAL
SERGE LADYANDTHETRAMP
YOYOS EURO HARES
PUNGENT EVEARDEN
DUKEUNIVERSITY INCAS
INUITS NOEL SCIENCE
TILLS DADS TELEX KOP
TEES KANSASCITYROYALS
OSLO ETTU ANDRE NARDO
STEN SEEP SNEER SPASM
```

299

```
PONCHO CARNAC BOMBARD
EXILES ANGORA OCEANIA
DIXIELANDBAND STACKED
ADEN OBI HOES ORKANS
LEDGE INST TEABAG
SIDEWALKSALE RAMP
CHORTLE ARIA CROONER
RETOOK TROPHIES DUETO
EATUP BUMS LOL GONEON
ETON TAX JUNKYARDDOG
DAHL ALIAS MISC
PARTTIMEJOB ACT HEAP
AGORAS RAG LENA LETBE
BASIL ARROGANT RECTOR
STAPLER FACT SHAKEUP
TEST DUTYFREESHOP
IMAGES DREA TULIP
ARECAS THAI TKO NERO
MANKIND ANGELFOODCAKE
FREEZER POODLE HALVES
MASTERY ENROBE SPEEDY
```

300

```
NUTRIA PASTOR DRYICE
ARNETT UPHERE TIBETAN
TINEAR FRANZFERDINAND
ALOE ORNO NUN TES
AMERICANPIE EARTHA
FRANCISCOFRANCO OUTRE
GMT SOYAS MIT UNREAL
HOSE UAR AREA ANDORRA
ATALOSS FRANCESFARMER
NOTIF PACT CHI ASEA
FARRAHFAWCETT
OKRA MHO IRAE EAMES
FRANKIEFRISCH EARNEST
TONNAGE OOHS PAN INSO
ENDURO SOL AORTA HEL
NEALE FEDERICOFELLINI
SNEERS UNCLUTTERED
PSI MRI SPAR LYON
FLORIDAFRIEBUS POINTE
CITADEL STRIAE ENTAIL
STAYON TUTTLE SAYYES
```

ANSWER KEYS

#190   *=ALL

#216   *=ORE

#243   *=PIT

INTRODUCING THE NEW MEGA SERIES,
continuing the grand crossword tradition begun by Simon & Schuster in 1924.

Simon & Schuster Mega Crossword Puzzle Books

978-1-4165-5700-5   978-1-4165-5906-1   978-1-4165-5909-2   978-1-4165-8781-1

And complete your collection with these classic titles:

Simon & Schuster Super Crossword Books

0-671-79232-6	#7	Nov. 92	Maleska	$10.00
0-671-89709-8	#8	Nov. 94	Maleska	$10.00
0-684-82964-9	#9	Nov. 96	Maleska	$10.00
0-684-84365-x	#10	Oct. 98	Samson	$10.00
0-684-87186-6	#11	May 01	Samson	$10.00
0-7432-5538-0	#12	Nov. 04	Samson/Maleska	$10.00
0-7432-9321-5	#13	Nov. 06	Samson	$10.00

The <u>Original</u> Crossword Puzzle Series

0-7432-0537-5	#223	Dec. 01	Samson	$9.95
0-7432-5096-6	#236	Feb. 04	Samson	$9.95
0-7432-5112-1	#238	June 04	Samson	$9.95
0-7432-5122-9	#240	Oct. 04	Samson	$9.95
0-7432-5125-3	#243	Apr. 05	Samson	$9.95
0-7432-5128-8	#246	Oct. 05	Samson	$9.95
0-7432-5129-6	#247	Dec. 05	Samson	$9.95
0-7432-8313-9	#248	Jan. 06	Samson	$9.95
0-7432-8314-7	#249	Apr. 06	Samson	$9.95
0-7432-8318-x	#253	Dec. 06	Samson	$9.95
0-7432-8319-8	#254	Feb. 07	Samson	$9.95
0-7432-8320-1	#255	Apr. 07	Samson	$9.95
0-7432-8321-x	#256	June 07	Samson	$9.95
0-7432-8322-8	#257	Aug. 07	Samson	$9.95
0-7432-8323-6	#258	Oct. 07	Samson	$9.95

ORDER YOURS TODAY!

SEND ORDERS TO:
Simon & Schuster Inc.
Order Processing
Department
100 Front Street
Riverside, NJ 08075
Customer Service:
1-800-223-2336
Fax: 1-800-943-9831

Total Cost of All Books Ordered _____

Add Applicable State Sales Tax _____

Check or Money Order Enclosed for _____

Please Charge VISA _____ MASTERCARD _____ AMEX _____

Card # _____ Exp. Date _____

Signature _____

Ship to:

Name _____

Address _____

City _____ State _____ Zip Code_____

PLEASE NOTE:
Prices subject to change without prior notice. If any part of your order is out of stock when we receive it, we will ship available titles and will send a refund for the portion we cannot fill.

FIRESIDE
A Division of Simon & Schuster
A CBS COMPANY